CRIMINAL PROCEDURE: INVESTIGATION

ASPEN PUBLISHERS

CRIMINAL PROCEDURE: INVESTIGATION

Erwin Chemerinsky

Dean
University of California at Irvinc, School of Law

Laurie L. Levenson

Professor of Law, William M. Rains Fellow,
and Director, Center for Ethical Advocacy,
Loyola Law School

 Wolters Kluwer
Law & Business

AUSTIN   BOSTON   CHICAGO   NEW YORK   THE NETHERLANDS

http://lawschool.aspenpublishers.com
No part of this publication may be reproduced or transmitted in any form or by any means, electronic or mechanical, including photocopy, recording, or any information storage and retrieval system, without permission in writing from the publisher. Requests for permission to make copies of any part of this publication should be mailed to:

>   Aspen Publishers
>   Attn: Permissions Department
>   76 Ninth Avenue, 7th Floor
>   New York, NY 10011-5201

To contact Customer Care, e-mail customer.care@aspenpublishers.com, call 1-800-234-1660, fax 1-800-901-9075, or mail correspondence to:

>   Aspen Publishers
>   Attn: Order Department
>   PO Box 990
>   Frederick, MD 21705

Printed in the United States of America.

3 4 5 6 7 8 9 0

ISBN 978-0-7355-7786-2

Library of Congress Cataloging-in-Publication Data

Chemerinsky, Erwin.
    Criminal procedure: investigation / Erwin Chemerinsky, Laurie L. Levenson.
        p. cm.
    Includes index.
    ISBN 978-0-7355-7786-2 (alk. paper)
    1. Criminal investigation — United States. 2. Criminal procedure — United States. 3. Due process of law — United States. 4. Criminal procedure — United States — Cases. 5. Criminal investigation — United States — Cases. I. Levenson, Laurie L., 1956- II. Title.

KF9619.C483 2008
345.73'05 — dc22

                                                                  2008025575

About Wolters Kluwer Law & Business

Wolters Kluwer Law & Business is a leading provider of research information and workflow solutions in key specialty areas. The strengths of the individual brands of Aspen Publishers, CCH, Kluwer Law International and Loislaw are aligned within Wolters Kluwer Law & Business to provide comprehensive, in-depth solutions and expert-authored content for the legal, professional and education markets.

CCH was founded in 1913 and has served more than four generations of business professionals and their clients. The CCH products in the Wolters Kluwer Law & Business group are highly regarded electronic and print resources for legal, securities, antitrust and trade regulation, government contracting, banking, pension, payroll, employment and labor, and healthcare reimbursement and compliance professionals.

Aspen Publishers is a leading information provider for attorneys, business professionals and law students. Written by preeminent authorities, Aspen products offer analytical and practical information in a range of specialty practice areas from securities law and intellectual property to mergers and acquisitions and pension/ benefits. Aspen's trusted legal education resources provide professors and students with high-quality, up-to-date and effective resources for successful instruction and study in all areas of the law.

Kluwer Law International supplies the global business community with comprehensive English-language international legal information. Legal practitioners, corporate counsel and business executives around the world rely on the Kluwer Law International journals, loose-leafs, books and electronic products for authoritative information in many areas of international legal practice.

Loislaw is a premier provider of digitized legal content to small law firm practitioners of various specializations. Loislaw provides attorneys with the ability to quickly and efficiently find the necessary legal information they need, when and where they need it, by facilitating access to primary law as well as state-specific law, records, forms and treatises.

Wolters Kluwer Law & Business, a unit of Wolters Kluwer, is headquartered in New York and Riverwoods, Illinois. Wolters Kluwer is a leading multinational publisher and information services company.

For our families and for our students

SUMMARY OF CONTENTS

Contents		xi
Preface		xix
Acknowledgments		xxi
The Constitution of the United States		xxiii
Chapter 1.	Introduction to Criminal Procedure	1
Chapter 2.	Searches and Seizures	29
Chapter 3.	The Exclusionary Rule	291
Chapter 4.	Police Interrogation and the Privilege Against Self-Incrimination	357
Chapter 5.	Identification Procedures	515
Chapter 6.	Right to Counsel	553
Table of Cases		585
Index		589

CONTENTS

Preface   xix
Acknowledgments   xxi
The Constitution of the United States   xxiii

CHAPTER 1

INTRODUCTION TO CRIMINAL PROCEDURE   1

A. The Participants in the Criminal Justice System   1
   1. Defendants   2
   2. Defense Counsel   2
   3. Prosecutors   2
   4. Victims   3
   5. Police and Other Law Enforcement Officers   3
   6. Magistrates and Judges   3
   7. Jurors   4
   8. Corrections Officials   4
   9. Public   4
   10. Media   4
B. Stages of the Criminal Justice Process   5
   Step 1: Pre-Arrest Investigation   5
   Step 2: Arrest   5
   Step 3: Filing the Complaint   6
   Step 4: *Gerstein* Review   6
   Step 5: First Appearance/Arraignment on Complaint   7
   Step 6: Grand Jury or Preliminary Hearing   7
   Step 7: Arraignment on Indictment or Information   8
   Step 8: Discovery   8
   Step 9: Pretrial Motions   8
   Step 10: Plea Bargaining and Guilty Pleas   8
   Step 11: Trial   9
   Step 12: Sentencing   10
   Step 13: Appeals and Habeas Corpus   10
C. The Purpose of Procedural Rules   11
           Powell v. Alabama   11
           Patterson, Plaintiff v. Former Chicago
           Police Lt. Jon Burge   14
D. Key Provisions of the Bill of Rights   17

E. The Application of the Bill of Rights to the States   18
    1. The Provisions of the Bill of Rights and the Idea of
        "Incorporation"   18
    2. The Debate over Incorporation   19
    3. The Current Law as to What's Incorporated   21
            Duncan v. Louisiana   *21*
    4. The Content of Incorporated Rights   24
F. Retroactivity   26

CHAPTER 2

SEARCHES AND SEIZURES   29

A. Introduction   29
B. What Is a Search?   30
            Katz v. United States   *30*
    1. Open Fields   36
            Oliver v. United States   *36*
            United States v. Dunn   *42*
    2. Aerial Searches   45
            California v. Ciraolo   *46*
            Florida v. Riley   *49*
    3. Thermal Imaging of Homes   55
            Kyllo v. United States   *55*
    4. Searches of Trash   61
            California v. Greenwood   *61*
    5. Observation and Monitoring of Public Behavior   65
            United States v. Knotts   *65*
            United States v. Karo   *68*
            Smith v. Maryland   *74*
    6. Use of Dogs to Sniff for Contraband   78
            Illinois v. Caballes   *79*
C. The Requirement for Probable Cause   82
    1. What Is Sufficient Belief to Meet the Standard for
        Probable Cause?   82
            Illinois v. Gates   *83*
            Maryland v. Pringle   *90*
    2. Is It an Objective or a Subjective Standard?   92
            Whren v. United States   *92*
D. The Warrant Requirement   96
    1. What Information Must Be Included in the Application
        for a Warrant?   97
    2. What Form Must the Warrant Take?   98
            Andresen v. Maryland   *98*
            Groh v. Ramirez   *101*
    3. What Are the Requirements in Executing Warrants?   106
        a. How May Police Treat Those Who Are Present
            When a Warrant Is Being Executed?   107
                Muehler v. Mena   *107*

b. Do Police Have to Knock and Announce
    Before Searching a Dwelling?   110
        Wilson v. Arkansas   *110*
        Richards v. Wisconsin   *112*
c. What If There Are Unforeseen Circumstances
    or Mistakes While Executing a Warrant?   116
        Maryland v. Garrison   *116*
        Los Angeles County, California v. Rettele   *119*

E. Exceptions to the Warrant Requirement   122
    1. Searches Incident to Arrest   122
            Chimel v. California   *122*
            Knowles v. Iowa   *126*
    2. Searches Made in Hot Pursuit   127
            Warden, Md. Penitentiary v. Hayden   *127*
            Payton v. New York   *128*
    3. Plain View   131
            Coolidge v. New Hampshire   *131*
            Horton v. California   *133*
            Minnesota v. Dickerson   *136*
    4. The Automobile Exception   138
        a. The Exception and Its Rationale   138
                California v. Carney   *139*
        b. Searches of Containers in Automobiles   142
                California v. Acevedo   *142*
        c. Searches Incident to Arrest   147
                New York v. Belton   *147*
                Thornton v. United States   *150*
    5. Inventory Searches   153
                South Dakota v. Opperman   *153*
                Illinois v. Lafayette   *157*
    6. Border Crossing and Checkpoints   159
                United States v. Flores-Montano   *159*
                United States v. Ramsey   *162*
                United States v. Montoya-Hernandez   *164*
    7. Checkpoints   169
                Michigan Dept. of State Police v. Sitz   *169*
                City of Indianapolis v. Edmond   *171*
    8. Consent   176
                Schneckloth v. Bustamonte   *176*
                Georgia v. Randolph   *182*
    9. Searches of Those on Probation and Parole   186
                United States v. Knights   *186*
                Samson v. California   *188*
    10. Searches When There Are "Special Needs"   191
        a. Administrative Searches   191
                *Camara v. Municipal Court of City and County
                    of San Francisco*   *191*
                New York v. Burger   *196*
        b. Drug Testing   199
                Vernonia School Dist. 47J v. Acton   *201*

Board of Education of Independent School District
No. 92 of Pottawatomie County v. Earls   208
Ferguson v. City of Charleston   215
11. Exigent Circumstances   219
Welsh v. Wisconsin   220
Brigham City, Utah v. Stuart   222
F. Seizures and Arrests   224
1. Is a Warrant Needed for Arrests?   224
United States v. Watson   224
2. When Is a Person Seized?   229
United States v. Mendenhall   229
California v. Hodari D.   235
3. For What Crimes May a Person Be Arrested?   239
Atwater v. City of Lago Vista   239
G. Stop and Frisk   246
1. The Authority for Police to Stop and Frisk   246
Terry v. Ohio   247
2. The Distinction Between Stops and Arrests   255
3. What May Police Do When They Stop
an Individual?   256
Hiibel v. Sixth Judicial Dist. Court of Nevada   257
4. What Is Sufficient for Reasonable Suspicion? 260
a. Reasonable Suspicion for Stopping Cars   260
United States v. Arvizu   260
b. Reasonable Suspicion Based on Informants' Tips 263
Alabama v. White   264
Florida v. J.L.   266
c. Reasonable Suspicion on a Person's Trying to
Avoid a Police Officer   268
Illinois v. Wardlow   269
d. Reasonable Suspicions Based on Profiles   273
United States v. Sokolow   273
H. Electronic Surveillance   277
1. Is Electronic Eavesdropping a Search?   278
2. Statutory Requirements   280
3. Warrantless Eavesdropping   282
United States v. United States District Court for 283
the Eastern District of Michigan

CHAPTER 3

THE EXCLUSIONARY RULE   291

A. Is the Exclusionary Rule a Desirable Remedy for Unconstitutional
Police Behavior?   291
Hudson v. Michigan   292
B. The Origins of the Exclusionary Rule   296
Weeks v. United States   296
Mapp v. Ohio   299

C. Who Can Object to the Introduction of Evidence and Raise
    the Exclusionary Rule?   304
            Rakas v. Illinois   *304*
            Minnesota v. Carter   *311*
            Brendlin v. California   *314*
D. Exceptions to the Exclusionary Rule   317
    1.   Independent Source   318
            Murray v. United States   *318*
    2.   Inevitable Discovery   323
            Nix v. Williams   *323*
    3.   Inadequate Causal Connection — Attenuation of the Taint   329
            Brown v. Illinois   *330*
    4.   The Good Faith Exception to the Exclusionary Rule   336
            United States v. Leon   *336*
    5.   The Exception for Violations of the Requirement for
         "Knocking and Announcing"   353
E. Suppression Hearings   355

CHAPTER 4

POLICE INTERROGATION AND THE PRIVILEGE
AGAINST SELF-INCRIMINATION   357

A. Due Process and the Requirement for Voluntariness   358
    1.   The Requirement for Voluntariness   358
            Brown v. Mississippi   *359*
    2.   Determining Whether a Confession Is Voluntary   361
            The Length of the Interrogation and Whether the
            Defendant Was Deprived of Basic Bodily Functions   361
            The Use of Force and Threats of Force   361
            Arizona v. Fulminante   *361*
            Psychological Pressure Tactics   364
            Spano v. New York   *364*
            Deception   367
            The Age, Level of Education, and Mental
            Condition of a Suspect   368
            Colorado v. Connelly   *368*
    3.   Is the Voluntariness Test Desirable?   373
    4.   Coercive Questioning, Torture, and the War
         on Terrorism   373
B. Fifth Amendment Limits on In-Custodial Interrogation:
    Miranda v. Arizona   374
    1.   Miranda v. Arizona and Its Affirmation by the Supreme Court   374
            Miranda v. Arizona   *374*
            Dickerson v. United States   *389*
    2.   Is *Miranda* Desirable?   393
    3.   What Are the Requirements for *Miranda* to Apply?   395
            a.   When Is a Person "In Custody"?   395

			Oregon v. Mathiason	396
			Yarborough v. Alvarado	398
			Berkemer v. McCarty	403
		b.	What Is an "Interrogation"?	407
			Rhode Island v. Innis	407
			Illinois v. Perkins	413
		c.	What Is Required of the Police?	417
			California v. Prysock	417
			Duckworth v. Eagan	420
	4.		What Are the Consequences of a Violation of *Miranda*?	423
			Oregon v. Elstad	424
			Missouri v. Seibert	430
			United States v. Patane	436
	5.		What Are the Exceptions to *Miranda*?	439
		a.	Impeachment	439
			Harris v. New York	440
		b.	Emergencies	442
			New York v. Quarles	442
		c.	Booking Exception	449
		d.	Waiver	450
			What Is Sufficient to Constitute a Waiver?	450
			North Carolina v. Butler	450
			How Is a Waiver After the Assertion of Rights Treated?	452
			Michigan v. Mosley	452
			Edwards v. Arizona	455
			Minnick v. Mississippi	458
			Davis v. United States	462
C.	The Sixth Amendment Right to Counsel and Police Interrogations			466
	1.		The Sixth Amendment Right to Counsel During Interrogations	467
			Massiah v. United States	467
			Brewer v. Williams	471
	2.		The Sixth Amendment Right to Counsel Is Offense Specific	477
			Texas v. Cobb	477
	3.		Waivers	481
			Michigan v. Jackson	481
	4.		What Is Impermissible Police Eliciting of Statements?	486
			United States v. Henry	486
			Kuhlmann v. Wilson	490
D.	The Privilege Against Self-Incrimination in Other Contexts			493
	1.		What Are the Requirements for the Privilege Against Self-Incrimination to Apply?	494
		a.	Only Individuals May Invoke the Privilege	494
		b.	The Privilege Applies Only to That Which Is Testimonial	494
			Schmerber v. California	494
		c.	There Must Be Compulsion	497
		d.	There Must Be the Possibility of Incrimination	498

2. When May the Government Require the Production
    of Documents and Other Things?   501
        Fisher v. United States   *501*
3. May the Government Require Testimony If It Provides
    Immunity?   506
        Kastigar v. United States   *506*
        United States v. Hubbell   *510*

CHAPTER 5

IDENTIFICATION PROCEDURES   515

A. The Right to Counsel   516
    1. The Right to Counsel in Lineups   516
        United States v. Wade   *516*
    2. Limits on the Right to Counsel in Identification Procedures   526
        Illinois v. Kirby   *526*
        United States v. Ash   *530*
B. Due Process Protection for Identification Procedures   536
    1. Unnecessarily Suggestive Identification Procedures
        Violate Due Process   536
        Foster v. California   *538*
    2. Limits on the Ability of Courts to Find That Identification
        Procedures Violate Due Process   540
        Simmons v. United States   *541*
        Neil v. Biggers   *543*
        Manson v. Brathwaite   *546*

CHAPTER 6

RIGHT TO COUNSEL   553

A. Introduction   553
B. When the Right to Counsel Applies   554
        Argersinger v. Hamlin   *555*
C. Appointment of Counsel   557
        Gideon v. Wainwright   *558*
D. Standard for "Effective Assistance" of Counsel   560
        Strickland v. Washington   *560*
        Florida v. Nixon   *571*
E. Right of Self-Representation   576
        Faretta v. California   *576*
F. Right of Counsel for Enemy Combatants   584

Table of Cases   585
Index   589

PREFACE

Our goal is to write the most student-friendly book we can to help teach students about the fascinating area of criminal procedure. Between us, we have almost 50 years of experience of teaching in law schools. We have used many different casebooks in teaching criminal procedure and other subjects. We have consistently seen that students strongly prefer a casebook that presents the material in a clear and well organized fashion and that does not hide the law. That is our goal for this book.

In aspiring to provide such a book, we have made several choices. First, the book focuses on the key cases regarding each issue of criminal procedure. To help students in understanding these cases and provide a context for understanding them, we provide brief comments before and after the cases. We recognize that professors have different ways in which they like to discuss these cases. Therefore, rather than providing lengthy notes and questions after each case, we provide suggested discussion questions in our teacher's manual. This approach has the benefit of not limiting professors in how they approach the discussion. Also, our experience is that students often find notes filled with rhetorical questions frustrating and only occasionally do they reflect the questions that the instructor wants to raise.

Second, there are no long passages excerpting the scholarly literature. There is a rich scholarly literature concerning almost every aspect of criminal procedure. At many places, we provide brief essays that describe and cite to this literature. But we have eschewed providing long bloc quotes of this material and make no pretense of being comprehensive in summarizing the literature. Our goal is to provide a casebook, not a reference tool.

Third, we decided to include "practical" materials in a supplement rather than the casebook. For example, we think it is useful for students in studying the Fourth Amendment to see a search warrant or in learning about the Fifth Amendment to see an indictment. We considered including these in the casebook, but decided for reasons of length to place them in a separate supplement. We recognize that instructors vary as to how they wish to use this material and having the materials in a supplement was the best solution. We also will provide material using other media, such as PowerPoint slides, for professors who wish to use them.

Fourth, the major cases are presented in slightly longer form, with a bit less editing than in many other books. Criminal procedure, of course, is an area of constitutional law and the law is very much the product of the Supreme Court's decisions. Lawyers practicing criminal law base their arguments on these decisions and thus we believe that it is desirable to expose students to the cases in their fuller form. Space constraints required more editing than we would have liked, but we have done our best to present the cases in as accurate and full a form as possible.

We do not indicate deletions of material in the cases by ellipses. Our experience is that the necessary frequent use of ellipses is distracting and does not provide useful information to the students. On the other hand, any addition, however small, is indicated by brackets.

Because we know that aspects of Criminal Procedure are often taught in shorter, more focused courses, we decided to also provide professors and students with two shorter volumes, Criminal Procedure: Investigation and Criminal Procedure: Adjudication, in addition to the primary volume, Criminal Procedure. These separate volumes are a "repackaging" of chapters from the primary volume. This volume, Investigation, comprises Chapters 1-5 and 11 of Criminal Procedure and deals comprehensively with investigating a criminal case, from search and seizure to the defendant's right to counsel. As in the primary volume, each chapter is independent so that professors can cover the material in any order. Occasionally we cross reference to the other short volume, citing simply to Criminal Procedure: Adjudication.

Criminal procedure, of course, is an area where there are constantly new developments. We plan to provide an annual supplement and write new editions of these books about every four years. We welcome comments and suggestions from faculty and students who use it. Our goal is to provide the best possible teaching tool for criminal procedure and we very much would appreciate any ideas for how to better accomplish this objective.

Erwin Chemerinsky
Laurie L. Levenson
August 2008

ACKNOWLEDGMENTS

This book is the product of our having taught this material for many years. We are very grateful to our students, who have constantly challenged us to think about this material in new ways. It is to them that we dedicate this book. We also dedicate this book to our families, whose patience, support, and love made this book — and everything else we do — possible.

THE CONSTITUTION OF THE UNITED STATES

We the People of the United States, in Order to form a more perfect Union, establish Justice, insure domestic Tranquility, provide for the common defense, promote the general Welfare, and secure the Blessings of Liberty to ourselves and our Posterity, do ordain and establish this Constitution for the United States of America.

ARTICLE I

Section 1. All legislative Powers herein granted shall be vested in a Congress of the United States, which shall consist of a Senate and House of Representatives.

Section 2. [1] The House of Representatives shall be composed of Members chosen every second Year by the People of the several States, and the Electors in each State shall have the Qualifications requisite for Electors of the most numerous Branch of the State Legislature.

[2] No Person shall be a Representative who shall not have attained to the Age of twenty five Years, and been seven Years a Citizen of the United States, and who shall not, when elected, be an Inhabitant of that State in which he shall be chosen.

[3] Representatives and direct Taxes shall be apportioned among the several States which may be included within this Union, according to their respective Numbers, which shall be determined by adding to the whole Number of free Persons, including those bound to Service for a Term of Years, and excluding Indians not taxed, three fifths of all other Persons. The actual Enumeration shall be made within three Years after the first Meeting of the Congress of the United States, and within every subsequent Term of ten Years, in such Manner as they shall by Law direct. The Number of Representatives shall not exceed one for every thirty Thousand, but each State shall have at Least one Representative; and until such enumeration shall be made, the State of New Hampshire shall be entitled to chuse three, Massachusetts eight, Rhode Island and Providence Plantations one, Connecticut five, New York six, New Jersey four, Pennsylvania eight, Delaware one, Maryland six, Virginia ten, North Carolina five, South Carolina five, and Georgia three.

[4] When vacancies happen in the Representation from any State, the Executive Authority thereof shall issue Writs of Election to fill such Vacancies.

[5] The House of Representatives shall chuse their Speaker and other Officers; and shall have the sole Power of Impeachment.

Section 3. [1] The Senate of the United States shall be composed of two Senators from each State, chosen by the Legislature thereof, for six Years; and each Senator shall have one Vote.

[2] Immediately after they shall be assembled in Consequence of the first Election, they shall be divided as equally as may be into three Classes. The Seats of the Senators of the first Class shall be vacated at the Expiration of the second Year, of the second Class at the Expiration of the fourth Year, and of the third Class at the Expiration of the sixth Year, so that one third may be chosen every second Year; and if Vacancies happen by Resignation, or otherwise, during the Recess of the Legislature of any State, the Executive thereof may make temporary Appointments until the next Meeting of the Legislature, which shall then fill such Vacancies.

[3] No Person shall be a Senator who shall not have attained to the Age of thirty Years, and been nine Years a Citizen of the United States, and who shall not, when elected, be an Inhabitant of that State for which he shall be chosen.

[4] The Vice President of the United States shall be President of the Senate, but shall have no Vote, unless they be equally divided.

[5] The Senate shall chuse their other Officers, and also a President pro tempore, in the absence of the Vice President, or when he shall exercise the Office of President of the United States.

[6] The Senate shall have the sole Power to try all Impeachments. When sitting for that Purpose, they shall be on Oath or Affirmation. When the President of the United States is tried, the Chief Justice shall preside: And no Person shall be convicted without the Concurrence of two thirds of the Members present.

[7] Judgment in Cases of Impeachment shall not extend further than to removal from Office, and disqualification to hold and enjoy any Office of honor, Trust or Profit under the United States: but the Party convicted shall nevertheless be liable and subject to Indictment, Trial, Judgment and Punishment, according to Law.

Section 4. [1] The Times, Places and Manner of holding Elections for Senators and Representatives, shall be prescribed in each State by the Legislature thereof; but the Congress may at any time by Law make or alter such Regulations, except as to the Places of chusing Senators.

[2] The Congress shall assemble at least once in every Year, and such Meeting shall be on the first Monday in December, unless they shall by Law appoint a different Day.

Section 5. [1] Each House shall be the Judge of the Elections, Returns and Qualifications of its own Members, and a Majority of each shall constitute a Quorum to do Business; but a smaller Number may adjourn from day to day, and may be authorized to compel the Attendance of absent Members, in such Manner, and under such Penalties as each House may provide.

[2] Each House may determine the Rules of its Proceedings, punish its Members for disorderly Behaviour, and, with the Concurrence of two thirds, expel a Member.

[3] Each House shall keep a Journal of its Proceedings, and from time to time publish the same, excepting such Parts as may in their Judgment require Secrecy; and the Yeas and Nays of the Members of either House on any question shall, at the Desire of one fifth of those Present, be entered on the Journal.

[4] Neither House, during the Session of Congress, shall, without the Consent of the other, adjourn for more than three days, nor to any other Place than that in which the two Houses shall be sitting.

Section 6. [1] The Senators and Representatives shall receive a Compensation for their Services, to be ascertained by Law, and paid out of the Treasury of the United States. They shall in all Cases, except Treason, Felony and Breach of the Peace, be privileged from Arrest during their Attendance at the Session of their respective Houses, and in going to and returning from the same; and for any Speech or Debate in either House, they shall not be questioned in any other Place.

[2] No Senator or Representative shall, during the Time for which he was elected, be appointed to any civil Office under the Authority of the United States, which shall have been created, or the Emoluments whereof shall have been increased during such time; and no Person holding any Office under the United States, shall be a Member of either House during his Continuance in Office.

Section 7. [1] All Bills for raising Revenue shall originate in the House of Representatives; but the Senate may propose or concur with Amendments as on other Bills.

[2] Every Bill which shall have passed the House of Representatives and the Senate, shall, before it become a Law, be presented to the President of the United States; If he approve he shall sign it, but if not he shall return it, with his Objections to that House in which it shall have originated, who shall enter the Objections at large on their Journal, and proceed to reconsider it. If after such Reconsideration two thirds of that House shall agree to pass the Bill, it shall be sent, together with the Objections, to the other House, by which it shall likewise be reconsidered, and if approved by two thirds of that House, it shall become a Law. But in all such Cases the Votes of both Houses shall be determined by Yeas and Nays, and the Names of the Persons voting for and against the Bill shall be entered on the Journal of each House respectively. If any Bill shall not be returned by the President within ten Days (Sundays excepted) after it shall have been presented to him, the Same shall be a Law, in like Manner as if he had signed it, unless the Congress by their Adjournment prevent its Return, in which Case it shall not be a Law.

[3] Every Order, Resolution, or Vote to which the Concurrence of the Senate and House of Representatives may be necessary (except on a question of Adjournment) shall be presented to the President of the United States; and before the Same shall take Effect, shall be approved by him, or being disapproved by him, shall be repassed by two thirds of the Senate and House of Representatives, according to the Rules and Limitations prescribed in the Case of a Bill.

Section 8. [1] The Congress shall have Power To lay and collect Taxes, Duties, Imposts and Excises, to pay the Debts and provide for the common Defence and general Welfare of the United States; but all Duties, Imposts and Excises shall be uniform throughout the United States;

[2] To borrow money on the credit of the United States;

[3] To regulate Commerce with foreign Nations, and among the several States, and with the Indian Tribes;

[4] To establish an uniform Rule of Naturalization, and uniform Laws on the subject of Bankruptcies throughout the United States;

[5] To coin Money, regulate the Value thereof, and of foreign Coin, and fix the Standard of Weights and Measures;

[6] To provide for the Punishment of counterfeiting the Securities and current Coin of the United States;

[7] To establish Post Offices and post Roads;

[8] To promote the Progress of Science and useful Arts, by securing for limited Times to Authors and Inventors the exclusive Right to their respective Writings and Discoveries;

[9] To constitute Tribunals inferior to the supreme Court;

[10] To define and punish Piracies and Felonies committed on the high Seas, and Offences against the Law of Nations;

[11] To declare War, grant Letters of Marque and Reprisal, and make Rules concerning Captures on Land and Water;

[12] To raise and support Armies, but no Appropriation of Money to that Use shall be for a longer Term than two Years;

[13] To provide and maintain a Navy;

[14] To make Rules for the Government and Regulation of the land and naval Forces;

[15] To provide for calling forth the Militia to execute the Laws of the Union, suppress Insurrections and repel Invasions;

[16] To provide for organizing, arming, and disciplining, the Militia, and for governing such Part of them as may be employed in the Service of the United States, reserving to the States respectively, the Appointment of the Officers, and the Authority of training the Militia according to the discipline prescribed by Congress;

[17] To exercise exclusive Legislation in all Cases whatsoever, over such District (not exceeding ten Miles square) as may, by Cession of particular States, and the Acceptance of Congress, become the Seat of the Government of the United States, and to exercise like Authority over all Places purchased by the Consent of the Legislature of the State in which the Same shall be, for the Erection of Forts, Magazines, Arsenals, dock-Yards, and other needful Buildings; — And

[18] To make all Laws which shall be necessary and proper for carrying into Execution the foregoing Powers, and all other Powers vested by this Constitution in the Government of the United States, or in any Department or Officer thereof.

Section 9. [1] The Migration or Importation of such Persons as any of the States now existing shall think proper to admit, shall not be prohibited by the Congress prior to the Year one thousand eight hundred and eight, but a Tax or duty may be imposed on such Importation, not exceeding ten dollars for each Person.

[2] The Privilege of the Writ of Habeas Corpus shall not be suspended, unless when in Cases of Rebellion or Invasion the public Safety may require it.

[3] No Bill of Attainder or ex post facto Law shall be passed.

[4] No Capitation, or other direct, Tax shall be laid, unless in Proportion to the Census or Enumeration herein before directed to be taken.

[5] No Tax or Duty shall be laid on Articles exported from any State.

[6] No Preference shall be given by any Regulation of Commerce or Revenue to the Ports of one State over those of another: nor shall Vessels bound to, or from, one State, be obliged to enter, clear, or pay Duties in another.

[7] No Money shall be drawn from the Treasury, but in Consequence of Appropriations made by Law; and a regular Statement and Account of the Receipts and Expenditures of all public Money shall be published from time to time.

[8] No Title of Nobility shall be granted by the United States: And no Person holding any Office of Profit or Trust under them, shall, without the Consent of the Congress, accept of any present, Emolument, Office, or Title, of any kind whatever, from any King, Prince, or foreign State.

Section 10. [1] No State shall enter into any Treaty, Alliance, or Confederation; grant Letters of Marque and Reprisal; coin Money; emit Bills of Credit; make any Thing but gold and silver Coin a Tender in Payment of Debts; pass any Bill of Attainder, ex post facto Law, or Law impairing the Obligation of Contracts, or grant any Title of Nobility.

[2] No State shall, without the Consent of the Congress, lay any Imposts or Duties on Imports or Exports, except what may be absolutely necessary for executing its inspection Laws: and the net Produce of all Duties and Imposts, laid by any State on Imports or Exports, shall be for the Use of the Treasury of the United States; and all such Laws shall be subject to the Revision and Controul of the Congress.

[3] No State shall, without the Consent of Congress, lay any Duty of Tonnage, keep Troops, or Ships of War in time of Peace, enter into any Agreement or Compact with another State, or with a foreign Power, or engage in War, unless actually invaded, or in such imminent Danger as will not admit of delay.

ARTICLE II

Section 1. [1] The executive Power shall be vested in a President of the United States of America. He shall hold his Office during the Term of four Years, and, together with the Vice President, chosen for the same Term, be elected, as follows:

[2] Each State shall appoint, in such Manner as the Legislature thereof may direct, a Number of Electors, equal to the whole Number of Senators and Representatives to which the State may be entitled in the Congress: but no Senator or Representative, or Person holding an Office of Trust or Profit under the United States, shall be appointed an Elector.

[3] The Electors shall meet in their respective States, and vote by Ballot for two Persons, of whom one at least shall not be an Inhabitant of the same State with themselves. And they shall make a List of all the Persons voted for, and of the Number of Votes for each; which List they shall sign and certify, and transmit sealed to the Seat of the Government of the United States, directed to the President of the Senate. The President of the Senate shall, in the Presence of the Senate and House of Representatives, open all the Certificates, and the Votes shall then be counted. The Person having the greatest Number of Votes shall be the President, if such Number be a Majority of the whole Number of Electors appointed; and if there be more than one who have such Majority, and have an equal Number of Votes, then the House of Representatives shall immediately chuse by Ballot one of them for President; and if no Person have a Majority, then from the five highest on the List the said House shall in like Manner chuse the President. But in chusing the President, the Votes shall be taken by States, the Representation from each State having one Vote; a quorum for this Purpose shall consist of a Member or Members from two thirds of the States, and a Majority of all the States shall be necessary to a Choice. In every Case, after the Choice of the President, the Person having the greatest Number of Votes of the Electors shall be

the Vice President. But if there should remain two or more who have equal Votes, the Senate shall chuse from them by Ballot the Vice President.

[4] The Congress may determine the Time of chusing the Electors, and the Day on which they shall give their Votes; which Day shall be the same throughout the United States.

[5] No Person except a natural born Citizen, or a Citizen of the United States, at the time of the Adoption of this Constitution, shall be eligible to the Office of President; neither shall any Person be eligible to that Office who shall not have attained to the Age of thirty five Years, and been fourteen Years a Resident within the United States.

[6] In Case of the Removal of the President from Office, or of his Death, Resignation, or Inability to discharge the Powers and Duties of the said Office, the Same shall devolve on the Vice President, and the Congress may by Law provide for the Case of Removal, Death, Resignation or Inability, both of the President and Vice President, declaring what Officer shall then act as President, and such Officer shall act accordingly, until the Disability be removed, or a President shall be elected.

[7] The President shall, at stated Times, receive for his Services, a Compensation, which shall neither be increased nor diminished during the Period for which he shall have been elected, and he shall not receive within that Period any other Emolument from the United States, or any of them.

[8] Before he enter on the Execution of his Office, he shall take the following Oath or Affirmation: "I do solemnly swear (or affirm) that I will faithfully execute the Office of President of the United States, and will to the best of my Ability, preserve, protect and defend the Constitution of the United States."

Section 2. [1] The President shall be Commander in Chief of the Army and Navy of the United States, and of the Militia of the several States, when called into the actual Service of the United States; he may require the Opinion, in writing, of the principal Officer in each of the executive Departments, upon any subject relating to the Duties of their respective Offices, and he shall have Power to grant Reprieves and Pardons for Offences against the United States, except in Cases of Impeachment.

[2] He shall have Power, by and with the Advice and Consent of the Senate, to make Treaties, provided two thirds of the Senators present concur; and he shall nominate, and by and with the Advice and Consent of the Senate, shall appoint Ambassadors, other public Ministers and Consuls, Judges of the supreme Court, and all other Officers of the United States, whose Appointments are not herein otherwise provided for, and which shall be established by Law: but the Congress may by Law vest the Appointment of such inferior Officers, as they think proper, in the President alone, in the Courts of Law, or in the Heads of Departments.

[3] The President shall have Power to fill up all Vacancies that may happen during the Recess of the Senate, by granting Commissions which shall expire at the End of their next Session.

Section 3. He shall from time to time give to the Congress Information of the State of the Union, and recommend to their Consideration such Measures as he shall judge necessary and expedient; he may, on extraordinary Occasions, convene both Houses, or either of them, and in Case of Disagreement between them, with Respect to the Time of Adjournment, he may adjourn them to such Time as he shall think proper; he shall receive Ambassadors and other public Ministers; he shall take Care that the Laws be faithfully executed, and shall Commission all the Officers of the United States.

Section 4. The President, Vice President and all civil Officers of the United States, shall be removed from Office on Impeachment for, and Conviction of, Treason, Bribery, or other high Crimes and Misdemeanors.

ARTICLE III

Section 1. The judicial Power of the United States shall be vested in one supreme Court, and in such inferior Courts as the Congress may from time to time ordain and establish. The Judges, both of the supreme and inferior Courts, shall hold their Offices during good Behaviour, and shall, at stated Times, receive for their Services a Compensation, which shall not be diminished during their Continuance in Office.

Section 2. [1] The Judicial Power shall extend to all Cases, in Law and Equity, arising under this Constitution, the Laws of the United States, and Treaties made, or which shall be made, under their Authority; — to all Cases affecting Ambassadors, other public Ministers and Consuls; — to all Cases of admiralty and maritime Jurisdiction; — to Controversies to which the United States shall be a Party; — to Controversies between two or more States; — between a State and Citizens of another State; — between Citizens of different States; — between Citizens of the same State claiming Lands under Grants of different States, and between a State, or the Citizens thereof, and foreign States, Citizens or Subjects.

[2] In all Cases affecting Ambassadors, other public Ministers and Consuls, and those in which a State shall be Party, the supreme Court shall have original Jurisdiction. In all the other Cases before mentioned, the supreme Court shall have appellate Jurisdiction, both as to Law and Fact, with such Exceptions, and under such Regulations as the Congress shall make.

[3] The Trial of all Crimes, except in Cases of Impeachment, shall be by Jury; and such Trial shall be held in the State where the said Crimes shall have been committed; but when not committed within any State, the Trial shall be at such Place or Places as the Congress may by Law have directed.

Section 3. [1] Treason against the United States, shall consist only in levying War against them, or in adhering to their Enemies, giving them Aid and Comfort. No Person shall be convicted of Treason unless on the Testimony of two Witnesses to the same overt Act, or on Confession in open Court.

[2] The Congress shall have Power to declare the Punishment of Treason, but no Attainder of Treason shall work Corruption of Blood, or Forfeiture except during the Life of the Person attainted.

ARTICLE IV

Section 1. Full Faith and Credit shall be given in each State to the public Acts, Records, and judicial Proceedings of every other State. And the Congress may by general Laws prescribe the Manner in which such Acts, Records and Proceedings shall be proved, and the Effect thereof.

Section 2. [1] The Citizens of each State shall be entitled to all Privileges and Immunities of Citizens in the several States.

[2] A Person charged in any State with Treason, Felony, or other Crime, who shall flee from Justice, and be found in another State, shall on demand of the executive Authority of the State from which he fled, be delivered up, to be removed to the State having Jurisdiction of the Crime.

[3] No Person held to Service or Labour in one State, under the Laws thereof, escaping into another, shall, in Consequence of any Law or Regulation therein, be discharged from such Service or Labour, but shall be delivered up on Claim of the Party to whom such Service or Labour may be due.

Section 3. [1] New States may be admitted by the Congress into this Union; but no new State shall be formed or erected within the Jurisdiction of any other State; nor any State be formed by the Junction of two or more States, or Parts of States, without the Consent of the Legislatures of the States concerned as well as of the Congress.

[2] The Congress shall have Power to dispose of and make all needful Rules and Regulations respecting the Territory or other Property belonging to the United States; and nothing in this Constitution shall be so construed as to Prejudice any Claims of the United States, or of any particular State.

Section 4. The United States shall guarantee to every State in this Union a Republican Form of Government, and shall protect each of them against Invasion; and on Application of the Legislature, or of the Executive (when the Legislature cannot be convened) against domestic Violence.

ARTICLE V

The Congress, whenever two thirds of both Houses shall deem it necessary, shall propose Amendments to this Constitution, or, on the Application of the Legislatures of two thirds of the several States, shall call a Convention for proposing Amendments, which, in either Case, shall be valid to all Intents and Purposes, as Part of this Constitution, when ratified by the Legislatures of three fourths of the several States, or by Conventions in three fourths thereof, as the one or the other Mode of Ratification may be proposed by the Congress; Provided that no Amendment which may be made prior to the Year One thousand eight hundred and eight shall in any Manner affect the first and fourth Clauses in the Ninth Section of the first Article; and that no State, without its Consent, shall be deprived of its equal Suffrage in the Senate.

ARTICLE VI

[1] All Debts contracted and Engagements entered into, before the Adoption of this Constitution, shall be as valid against the United States under this Constitution, as under the Confederation.

[2] This Constitution, and the Laws of the United States which shall be made in Pursuance thereof; and all Treaties made, or which shall be made, under the

Authority of the United States, shall be the supreme Law of the Land; and the Judges in every State shall be bound thereby, any Thing in the Constitution or Laws of any State to the Contrary notwithstanding.

[3] The Senators and Representatives before mentioned, and the Members of the several State Legislatures, and all executive and judicial Officers, both of the United States and of the several States, shall be bound by Oath or Affirmation, to support this Constitution; but no religious Test shall ever be required as a Qualification to any Office or public Trust under the United States.

ARTICLE VII

The Ratification of the Conventions of nine States, shall be sufficient for the Establishment of this Constitution between the States so ratifying the Same.

Done in Convention by the Unanimous Consent of the States present the Seventeenth Day of September in the Year of our Lord one thousand seven hundred and Eighty seven and of the Independence of the United States of America the Twelfth.

ARTICLES IN ADDITION TO, AND AMENDMENT OF THE CONSTITU-TION OF THE UNITED STATES OF AMERICA, PROPOSED BY CONGRESS, AND RATIFIED BY THE LEGISLATURES OF THE SEVERAL STATES, PUR-SUANT TO THE FIFTH ARTICLE OF THE ORIGINAL CONSTITUTION.

AMENDMENT I [1791]

Congress shall make no law respecting an establishment of religion, or prohibiting the free exercise thereof; or abridging the freedom of speech, or of the press; or the right of the people peaceably to assemble, and to petition the Government for a redress of grievances.

AMENDMENT II [1791]

A well regulated Militia, being necessary to the security of a free State, the right of the people to keep and bear Arms, shall not be infringed.

AMENDMENT III [1791]

No Soldier shall, in time of peace be quartered in any house, without the consent of the Owner, nor in time of war, but in a manner to be prescribed by law.

AMENDMENT IV [1791]

The right of the people to be secure in their persons, houses, papers, and effects, against unreasonable searches and seizures, shall not be violated, and no Warrants shall issue, but upon probable cause, supported by Oath or affirmation, and particularly describing the place to be searched, and the persons or things to be seized.

AMENDMENT V [1791]

No person shall be held to answer for a capital, or otherwise infamous crime, unless on a presentment or indictment of a Grand Jury, except in cases arising in the land or naval forces, or in the Militia, when in actual service in time of War or public danger; nor shall any person be subject for the same offence to be twice put in jeopardy of life or limb; nor shall be compelled in any criminal case to be a witness against himself, nor be deprived of life, liberty, or property, without due process of law; nor shall private property be taken for public use, without just compensation.

AMENDMENT VI [1791]

In all criminal prosecutions, the accused shall enjoy the right to a speedy and public trial, by an impartial jury of the State and district wherein the crime shall have been committed, which district shall have been previously ascertained by law, and to be informed of the nature and cause of the accusation; to be confronted with the witnesses against him; to have compulsory process for obtaining witnesses in his favor, and to have the Assistance of Counsel for his defence.

AMENDMENT VII [1791]

In Suits at common law, where the value in controversy shall exceed twenty dollars, the right of trial by jury shall be preserved, and no fact tried by a jury, shall be otherwise reexamined in any Court of the United States, than according to the rules of the common law.

AMENDMENT VIII [1791]

Excessive bail shall not be required, nor excessive fines imposed, nor cruel and unusual punishments inflicted.

AMENDMENT IX [1791]

The enumeration in the Constitution, of certain rights, shall not be construed to deny or disparage others retained by the people.

AMENDMENT X [1791]

The powers not delegated to the United States by the Constitution, nor prohibited by it to the States, are reserved to the States respectively, or to the people.

AMENDMENT XI [1798]

The Judicial power of the United States shall not be construed to extend to any suit in law or equity, commenced or prosecuted against one of the United States by Citizens of another State, or by Citizens or Subjects of any Foreign State.

AMENDMENT XII [1804]

The Electors shall meet in their respective states and vote by ballot for President and Vice-President, one of whom, at least, shall not be an inhabitant of the same state with themselves; they shall name in their ballots the person voted for as President, and in distinct ballots the person voted for as Vice-President, and they shall make distinct lists of all persons voted for as President, and of all persons voted for as Vice-President, and of the number of votes for each, which lists they shall sign and certify, and transmit sealed to the seat of the government of the United States, directed to the President of the Senate; — The President of the Senate shall, in the presence of the Senate and House of Representatives, open all the certificates and the votes shall then be counted; — The person having the greatest number of votes for President, shall be the President, if such number be a majority of the whole number of Electors appointed; and if no person have such majority, then from the persons having the highest numbers not exceeding three on the list of those voted for as President, the House of Representatives shall choose immediately, by ballot, the President. But in choosing the President, the votes shall be taken by states, the representation from each state having one vote; a quorum for this purpose shall consist of a member or members from two-thirds of the states, and a majority of all the states shall be necessary to a choice. And if the House of Representatives shall not choose a President whenever the right of choice shall devolve upon them, before the fourth day of March next following, then the Vice-President shall act as President, as in case of the death or other constitutional disability of the President. — The person having the greatest number of votes as Vice-President, shall be the Vice-President, if such number be a majority of the whole number of Electors appointed, and if no person have a majority, then from the two highest numbers on the list, the Senate shall choose the Vice-President; a quorum for the purpose shall consist of two-thirds of the whole number of Senators, and a majority of the whole number shall be necessary to a choice. But no person constitutionally ineligible to the office of President shall be eligible to that of Vice-President of the United States.

AMENDMENT XIII [1865]

Section 1. Neither slavery nor involuntary servitude, except as a punishment for crime whereof the party shall have been duly convicted, shall exist within the United States, or any place subject to their jurisdiction.

Section 2. Congress shall have power to enforce this article by appropriate legislation.

AMENDMENT XIV [1868]

Section 1. All persons born or naturalized in the United States, and subject to the jurisdiction thereof, are citizens of the United States and of the State wherein they reside. No State shall make or enforce any law which shall abridge the privileges or immunities of citizens of the United States; nor shall any State deprive any person of life, liberty, or property, without due process of law; nor deny to any person within its jurisdiction the equal protection of the laws.

Section 2. Representatives shall be apportioned among the several States according to their respective numbers, counting the whole number of persons in each State, excluding Indians not taxed. But when the right to vote at any election for the choice of electors for President and Vice-President of the United States, Representatives in Congress, the Executive and Judicial officers of a State, or the members of the Legislature thereof, is denied to any of the male inhabitants of such State, being twenty-one years of age, and citizens of the United States, or in any way abridged, except for participation in rebellion, or other crime, the basis of representation therein shall be reduced in the proportion which the number of such male citizens shall bear to the whole number of male citizens twenty-one years of age in such State.

Section 3. No person shall be a Senator or Representative in Congress, or elector of President and Vice-President, or hold any office, civil or military, under the United States, or under any State, who, having previously taken an oath, as a member of Congress, or as an officer of the United States, or as a member of any State legislature, or as an executive or judicial officer of any State, to support the Constitution of the United States, shall have engaged in insurrection or rebellion against the same, or given aid or comfort to the enemies thereof. But Congress may by a vote of two-thirds of each House, remove such disability.

Section 4. The validity of the public debt of the United States, authorized by law, including debts incurred for payment of pensions and bounties for services in suppressing insurrection or rebellion, shall not be questioned. But neither the United States nor any State shall assume or pay any debt or obligation incurred in aid of insurrection or rebellion against the United States, or any claim for the loss or emancipation of any slave; but all such debts, obligations and claims shall be held illegal and void.

Section 5. The Congress shall have the power to enforce, by appropriate legislation, the provisions of this article.

AMENDMENT XV [1870]

Section 1. The right of citizens of the United States to vote shall not be denied or abridged by the United States or by any State on account of race, color, or previous condition of servitude.

Section 2. The Congress shall have the power to enforce this article by appropriate legislation.

AMENDMENT XVI [1913]

The Congress shall have power to lay and collect taxes on incomes, from whatever source derived, without apportionment among the several States, and without regard to any census or enumeration.

AMENDMENT XVII [1913]

[1] The Senate of the United States shall be composed of two Senators from each State, elected by the people thereof, for six years; and each Senator shall have one vote. The electors in each State shall have the qualifications requisite for electors of the most numerous branch of the State legislatures.

[2] When vacancies happen in the representation of any State in the Senate, the executive authority of such State shall issue writs of election to fill such vacancies: *Provided,* That the legislature of any State may empower the executive thereof to make temporary appointments until the people fill the vacancies by election as the legislature may direct.

[3] This amendment shall not be so construed as to affect the election or term of any Senator chosen before it becomes valid as part of the Constitution.

AMENDMENT XVIII [1919]

Section 1. After one year from the ratification of this article the manufacture, sale, or transportation of intoxicating liquors within, the importation thereof into, or the exportation thereof from the United States and all territory subject to the jurisdiction thereof for beverage purposes is hereby prohibited.

Section 2. The Congress and the several States shall have concurrent power to enforce this article by appropriate legislation.

Section 3. This article shall be inoperative unless it shall have been ratified as an amendment to the Constitution by the legislatures of the several States, as provided in the Constitution, within seven years from the date of the submission hereof to the States by the Congress.

AMENDMENT XIX [1920]

[1] The right of citizens of the United States to vote shall not be denied or abridged by the United States or by any State on account of sex.

[2] Congress shall have power to enforce this article by appropriate legislation.

AMENDMENT XX [1933]

Section 1. The terms of the President and the Vice President shall end at noon on the 20th day of January, and the terms of Senators and Representatives at noon on the 3d day of January, of the years in which such terms would have ended if this article had not been ratified; and the terms of their successors shall then begin.

Section 2. The Congress shall assemble at least once in every year, and such meeting shall begin at noon on the 3d day of January, unless they shall by law appoint a different day.

Section 3. If, at the time fixed for the beginning of the term of the President, the President elect shall have died, the Vice President elect shall become President. If a President shall not have been chosen before the time fixed for the beginning of his term, or if the President elect shall have failed to qualify, then the Vice President elect shall act as President until a President shall have qualified; and the Congress may by law provide for the case wherein neither a President elect nor a Vice President shall have qualified, declaring who shall then act as President, or the manner in which one who is to act shall be selected, and such person shall act accordingly until a President or Vice President shall have qualified.

Section 4. The Congress may by law provide for the case of the death of any of the persons from whom the House of Representatives may chuse a President whenever the right of choice shall have devolved upon them, and for the case of the death of any of the persons from whom the Senate may choose a Vice President whenever the right of choice shall have devolved upon them.

Section 5. Sections 1 and 2 shall take effect on the 15th day of October following the ratification of this article.

Section 6. This article shall be inoperative unless it shall have been ratified as an amendment to the Constitution by the legislatures of three-fourths of the several States within seven years from the date of its submission.

AMENDMENT XXI [1933]

Section 1. The eighteenth article of amendment to the Constitution of the United States is hereby repealed.

Section 2. The transportation or importation into any State, Territory, or Possession of the United States for delivery or use therein of intoxicating liquors, in violation of the laws thereof, is hereby prohibited.

Section 3. This article shall be inoperative unless it shall have been ratified as an amendment to the Constitution by conventions in the several States, as provided in the Constitution, within seven years from the date of the submission hereof to the States by the Congress.

AMENDMENT XXII [1951]

Section 1. No person shall be elected to the office of the President more than twice, and no person who has held the office of President, or acted as President, for more than two years of a term to which some other person was elected President shall be elected to the office of President more than once. But this Article shall not apply to any person holding the office of President when this Article was proposed by Congress, and shall not prevent any person who may be holding the office of President, or acting as President, during the term within which this Article becomes operative from holding the office of President or acting as President during the remainder of such term.

Section 2. This article shall be inoperative unless it shall have been ratified as an amendment to the Constitution by the legislatures of three-fourths of the several States within seven years from the date of its submission to the States by the Congress.

AMENDMENT XXIII [1961]

Section 1. The District constituting the seat of Government of the United States shall appoint in such manner as Congress may direct: A number of electors of

President and Vice President equal to the whole number of Senators and Representatives in Congress to which the District would be entitled if it were a State, but in no event more than the least populous State; they shall be in addition to those appointed by the States, but they shall be considered, for the purposes of the election of President and Vice President, to be electors appointed by a State; and they shall meet in the District and perform such duties as provided by the twelfth article of amendment.

Section 2. The Congress shall have power to enforce this article by appropriate legislation.

AMENDMENT XXIV [1964]

Section 1. The right of citizens of the United States to vote in any primary or other election for President or Vice President, for electors for President or Vice President, or for Senator or Representative in Congress, shall not be denied or abridged by the United States or any State by reason of failure to pay poll tax or other tax.

Section 2. The Congress shall have power to enforce this article by appropriate legislation.

AMENDMENT XXV [1967]

Section 1. In case of the removal of the President from office or of his death or resignation, the Vice President shall become President.

Section 2. Whenever there is a vacancy in the office of the Vice President, the President shall nominate a Vice President who shall take office upon confirmation by a majority vote of both Houses of Congress.

Section 3. Whenever the President transmits to the President pro tempore of the Senate and the Speaker of the House of Representatives his written declaration that he is unable to discharge the powers and duties of his office, and until he transmits to them a written declaration to the contrary, such powers and duties shall be discharged by the Vice President as Acting President.

Section 4. Whenever the Vice President and a majority of either the principal officers of the executive departments or of such other body as Congress may by law provide, transmit to the President pro tempore of the Senate and the Speaker of the House of Representatives their written declaration that the President is unable to discharge the powers and duties of his office, the Vice President shall immediately assume the powers and duties of the office as Acting President.

Thereafter, when the President transmits to the President pro tempore of the Senate and the Speaker of the House of Representatives his written declaration that no inability exists, he shall resume the powers and duties of his office unless the Vice President and a majority of either the principal officers of the executive department or of such other body as Congress may by law provide, transmit within four days to the President pro tempore of the Senate and the Speaker of the House of Representatives their written declaration that the President is unable to discharge the powers and duties of his office. Thereupon Congress shall decide the issue, assembling within forty-eight hours for that purpose if not in session. If the Congress, within twenty-one days after receipt of the latter written declaration, or, if Congress is not in session, within twenty-one days after Congress is required to assemble, determines by two-thirds vote of both Houses that the President is unable to discharge the powers and duties of his office, the Vice President shall continue to discharge the same as Acting President; otherwise, the President shall resume the powers and duties of his office.

AMENDMENT XXVI [1971]

Section 1. The right of citizens of the United States, who are eighteen years of age or older, to vote shall not be denied or abridged by the United States or by any State on account of age.

  Section 2. The Congress shall have power to enforce this article by appropriate legislation.

AMENDMENT XXVII [1992]

No law, varying the compensation for the services of the Senators and Representatives, shall take effect, until an election of representatives shall have intervened.

CRIMINAL PROCEDURE: INVESTIGATION

CHAPTER

1

INTRODUCTION TO CRIMINAL PROCEDURE

Criminal procedure covers the rules and practices that govern the investigation and prosecution of criminal cases. "Investigatory criminal procedure" generally refers to the rules governing police conduct in investigating a case. These rules derive from the Fourth, Fifth, and Sixth Amendments to the United States Constitution. "Accusatory criminal procedure" generally refers to the rights of a defendant as a case proceeds through the criminal justice system. The rules governing this stage of the criminal process generally derive from the Fifth and Fourteenth Amendment rights to due process, the Sixth Amendment right to counsel and a speedy and public trial, the Eighth Amendment prohibition on excessive bail and double jeopardy, and the rules of procedure enacted by Congress or the states. Although federal constitutional rules govern these areas of criminal procedure, there are other laws that may control, including federal statutory laws, state constitutions, state laws, court rules of procedure, and ethical codes.

Section A of this introduction reviews the roles of the various participants in the criminal justice process. Section B provides an overview of how a case progresses through the criminal justice system. Section C then discusses why procedural rules are important, and Section D sets forth the governing constitutional principles. Finally, Section E discusses the applicability of constitutional rights to the states through the Incorporation Doctrine, with Section F addressing the test for determining when new procedural rules are to be applied retroactively.

A. THE PARTICIPANTS IN THE CRIMINAL JUSTICE SYSTEM

Many types of individuals play a role in the criminal justice system. The rules of procedure constantly attempt to address the needs of each of these participants while also respecting the rights and interests of the others.

1. Defendants

All defendants have an interest in ensuring that their constitutional rights are respected, and that they have an opportunity to zealously contest the charges brought against them. To ensure that they receive fair trials, defendants will ordinarily be represented by defense counsel — either retained or appointed by the court (see Chapter 6). Moreover, although some refer to the adversarial system as a "search for the truth," criminal defendants' main interest and goal is to avoid conviction.

2. Defense Counsel

Defense counsel represent defendants in criminal actions. Unlike prosecutors, who must serve the "interests of justice" regardless of whether doing so entails convicting or acquitting a defendant, "[t]he basic duty defense counsel owe[] to the administration of justice and as . . . officer[s] of the court is to serve as [defendants'] counselor[s] and advocate[s] with courage and devotion and to render effective, quality representation." ABA Standards Relating to the Administration of Criminal Justice, Defense Standard 4-1.2(b).

Many defendants cannot afford a lawyer, yet a lawyer is critical to having a fair adversarial process. Accordingly, the Supreme Court has recognized a right to the assistance of counsel in all cases in which the defendant faces incarceration. The right to counsel and the standards for effective assistance of counsel are discussed in Chapters 5 and 6.

3. Prosecutors

Currently, prosecutors file over ten million criminal cases annually in the United States.[1] Prosecutors represent the community in criminal actions. Federal prosecutors represent the United States and are assigned either by the local U.S. Attorney's Office or the Department of Justice. City attorneys, district attorneys, and county prosecutors represent local jurisdictions; the state attorney general represents the state at large. Unlike U.S. Attorneys, most states' prosecutors are elected officials.

The prosecutor has a unique role in the criminal justice system. "The prosecutor is an administrator of justice, an advocate, and an officer of the court. . . . The duty of the prosecutor is to seek justice, not merely to convict." ABA Standards Relating to the Administration of Criminal Justice, Prosecution Standard 3-1.2(b)–(c).

Prosecutors enjoy great discretion in the exercise of their duties. Prosecuters can decide which cases and defendants to charge, what charges to bring, and how serious a sentence to seek.

---

1. For more information regarding criminal caseloads in state courts, *see* National Center for State Courts, Examining the Work of State Courts, 2005: A National Perspective from the Court Statistics Project, http://www.ncsconline.org/d_research/csp/2005_files/0-EWWhole%20Document_final_1.pdf.

If a case goes to trial, the prosecutor has a duty to represent the government in those prosecutions. Moreover, during the investigative phase of trial, a prosecutor may also be responsible for supervising the work of police and investigators. This may require the prosecutor to prepare search warrants, issue subpoenas, and supervise grand jury proceedings.

4. Victims

Victims' interests are represented in criminal cases by the prosecutor. Prosecutors, not victims, decide which cases to charge, whether to plea bargain, trial strategies, and even sentencing recommendations. Criminal victims' roles are circumscribed. Some states have recently passed laws that provide victims a limited right to observe criminal proceedings, see, e.g., Ariz. Const. art. II, § 2.1(3), and to speak at sentencing, see, e.g., N.Y. Crim. Proc. Law § 380.50(2) (McKinney 2007). However, because a crime is considered to be an offense against the entire community and not just individual victims, victims do not control the handling of criminal cases.

5. Police and Other Law Enforcement Officers

Police officers are on the front line of the criminal justice system. They serve several purposes, from ensuring the public's safety to investigating allegations of crimes to apprehending individuals responsible for those crimes. Police officers, like prosecutors, wield an enormous amount of discretion. They make the initial decision of whether to investigate a case, and whether to arrest and charge an individual with an offense. Police officers make these decisions even though they are not ordinarily lawyers.

The focus of police officers is on the safety of the community. Although they may be aware of defendants' constitutional rights, the pressure on police officers to ensure community safety and their eagerness to secure convictions may lead to violation of these rights.

Investigative criminal procedure focuses on what procedures police may use when apprehending and investigating defendants. Specifically, it addresses the rules for searches, seizures, and interrogations of defendants.

There are many different types of law enforcement officers in the United States. Each jurisdiction is likely to have its own police force. Currently, there are over 18,000 law enforcement agencies in the United States, with over 15,000 of them consisting of municipal police departments. The primary federal law enforcement agencies include the Federal Bureau of Investigation (FBI), the Secret Service, the Drug Enforcement Administration (DEA), the Bureau of Alcohol, Tobacco and Firearms (ATF), the Bureau of Customs and Borders Prosecution (CBP), Immigration and Customs Enforcement (ICE), and the Securities and Exchange Commission (SEC).

6. Magistrates and Judges

Magistrates and judges are the neutral decision makers in the criminal justice system. One crucial aspect of their role is to ensure that defendants' constitutional rights are respected. Thus, magistrates determine whether search or arrest warrants should issue, whether there is sufficient evidence to hold an arrested defendant, and even whether bail should be granted. Both magistrates and judges may review police conduct to determine if evidence should be suppressed because of constitutional violations. Judges have the additional responsibility of supervising criminal trials. Magistrates and judges must perform their responsibilities both efficiently and fairly, and are often faced with huge dockets of cases to process through their courts.

7. Jurors

There are two types of jurors in the criminal justice system: grand jurors and trial jurors (see Criminal Procedure: Adjudication). Grand jurors oversee investigations of cases and decide whether to return indictments against individuals for specific crimes. Trial jurors, by contrast, are the fact-finders in most criminal trials. After listening to all of the evidence, they decide whether there is sufficient evidence to convict a defendant. To make this decision, trial jurors ordinarily have to make key credibility decisions in the case by deciding which side's witnesses to believe.

8. Corrections Officials

Once defendants are convicted, corrections officials have the responsibility of supervising defendants' incarceration or release on parole or probation. Like police officers and prosecutors, corrections officials often have huge caseloads. For instance, in 2004, the federal system alone had over 109,000 offenders under active supervision.[2]

9. Public

The general public also has an interest in the criminal justice system. Indeed, one of the primary concerns for members of the public is their safety.[3] The public also has a financial interest in ensuring that cases are efficiently processed, and that government officials respect the constitutional rights of citizens. In a criminal prosecution, the prosecutor has the responsibility of representing the interests of the public. However, the legislature also represents the public by enacting the laws that, to a large extent, govern the prosecutor's and judge's authority.

10. Media

Finally, the media has an interest in covering criminal cases and serving as a check on government powers. However, the First Amendment rights and

2. United States Department of Justice, Bureau of Justice Statistics, Compendium of Federal Justice Statistics, 2004, at 91, http://www.ojp.usdoj.gov/bjs/pub/pdf/cfjs0407.pdf.
3. See, e.g., Lydia Saad, Worry About Crime Remains at Last Year's Elevated Levels, http://www.gallup.com/poll/25078/Worry-About-Crime-Remains-Last-Years-Elevated-Levels.aspx

interests of the media easily come into conflict with a defendant's Sixth Amendment right to a fair trial. As discussed in Chapter 6, judges must ensure, to the greatest extent possible, that both the media's and defendants' constitutional rights are respected.

B.   STAGES OF THE CRIMINAL JUSTICE PROCESS

Before embarking upon a detailed discussion of the rules governing criminal procedure, it is helpful to understand how a case proceeds through the criminal justice system. Although there may be slight variations in the process depending upon the nature of a particular case and the jurisdiction in which it is adjudicated,[4] the typical route for criminal cases is as follows:

Step 1: Pre-Arrest Investigation[5]

If a crime occurs, the police may have little time to investigate the case. When time is of the essence, police officers may have to make their own observations, or use the accounts of others at the scene, to gather the minimal amount of information necessary to execute an arrest. For these on-the-scene arrests, the majority of the investigation will occur after the suspect is already in custody. Such investigations may include witness and victim interviews, interrogations of the suspect, identification procedures, undercover follow-up investigations, searches, and issuance of evidence subpoenas. Close to 50 percent of all criminal cases are handled in this manner. Thus, police officers will often have only a few minutes to decide whether to arrest a suspect, and their ability to conduct a pre-arrest investigation will be greatly limited.

In the remainder of cases, however, a lengthy investigation will typically occur before a suspect is arrested. Police will use their investigative tools, such as search warrants, interviews, informants, and evidence collection, to seek formal charges against the suspect before they execute an arrest. A magistrate may then issue an arrest warrant, together with a formal complaint filed by the prosecution, or the prosecution will obtain an arrest warrant in conjunction with a grand jury indictment. When there has been a grand jury indictment, months or years of pre-arrest investigation may have occurred, including witnesses testifying before the grand jury.

Step 2: Arrest[6]

Police have enormous discretion to decide whether to arrest a suspect. When an arrest occurs, it may be with or without a warrant. Once a suspect is taken into

---

4. There are 52 different jurisdictions (each State, the District of Columbia, and federal prosecutions), each having its own rules of procedure.

5. For a detailed discussion of the rules governing pretrial investigations, see Chapters 2 through 5.

6. See Chapter 3.

custody, he begins his journey through the criminal justice process. If the police did not use an arrest warrant, they must file an affidavit with the court setting forth the probable cause for the arrest and getting a complaint to hold the defendant for further proceedings. Even if the police did use an arrest warrant, the defendant has the right to appear before a judge, be informed of his constitutional rights, be advised of the charges against him, and be assigned counsel.

For some minor offenses, a suspect may merely receive a citation and will not be formally arrested. A citation or summons requires that the suspect appear at a later date to answer the charges against him. Likewise, if a suspect is not a flight risk, an indictment may be issued along with a summons for the suspect to appear instead of an authorization for an arrest warrant.

If a suspect is arrested, he is taken to the police station for booking. Once his picture and background information is taken, the suspect is placed into a holding facility. Depending on the offense, the suspect may be able to post bail based upon an approved bail schedule. If the suspect posts bail, he will be ordered to appear in court on a specific date for further proceedings. If the suspect does not post bail, he will be held in jail until he is released by the court.

Step 3: Filing the Complaint [7]

In order for police to be able to hold a suspect after arrest, the prosecution must file charges. Once the prosecution does so, it takes over the decision-making process from the police, and has discretion as to which charges to file. If the suspect has not been indicted, the prosecutor will use a complaint to file initial charges against the suspect. The complaint must be supported by a showing of probable cause based upon a sworn affidavit by law enforcement officers.

Step 4: Gerstein Review [8]

The magistrate judge must review the prosecution's complaint and supporting affidavit to determine whether there is probable cause supporting the initial charges against the defendant. This review is called a "*Gerstein* review" because it was first prescribed by the Supreme Court in Gerstein v. Pugh, 420 U.S. 103 (1975). The magistrate's review for probable cause is done ex parte and is based upon the filings alone — no evidentiary hearing is required. Often, the court will conduct a *Gerstein* review at the time of the defendant's first appearance, so long as that first appearance occurs within 48 hours of the defendant's arrest, as required by the Supreme Court in County of Riverside v. McLaughlin, 500 U.S. 44 (1991).

---

7. See Criminal Procedure: Adjudication.
8. See Chapter 3.

Step 5: First Appearance / Arraignment on Complaint[9]

Once the prosecution files a complaint, the defendant is also entitled to appear before the court to be advised of the charges against him, have an opportunity to seek bail, and be advised of his right to retain counsel or to have counsel assigned. For example, Rule 5 of the Federal Rules of Criminal Procedure requires that arresting officers bring the accused before a magistrate judge "without unnecessary delay." Ordinarily, the first appearance, sometimes called an "initial arraignment" or "preliminary arraignment," depending on the jurisdiction, will occur within 48 hours of the defendant's arrest. This proceeding is usually a brief one, and is merely a minimal check to ensure that a basis for the defendant's arrest exists.

Step 6: Grand Jury or Preliminary Hearing[10]

Before a defendant is required to stand trial, there must be another screening of the cases that establishes the charges the defendant will face at trial. The Fifth Amendment promises that for all federal felonies, a defendant is entitled to grand jury indictment. With ancient roots in British common law, the grand jury serves as a screening process to formalize charges for trial. It serves as a minimum check on the prosecutor's decision to bring charges.

A grand jury consists of 23 members of the community who listen to evidence presented by the prosecution and decide whether there is probable cause to prosecute the defendant. There is no judge in the grand jury, nor is the defendant or defense counsel entitled to be present.

The prosecutor generally directs the grand jury operations. If there is probable cause, the grand jury issues an indictment, or "true bill." The indictment sets forth the charges the defendant will face at trial. If the grand jury does not want to indict, it issues a "no bill." Grand juries also have the power to investigate cases by calling witnesses or issuing subpoenas.

Although some states choose to use grand juries in felony prosecutions, they are not bound to do so by the Fifth Amendment. In addition, they need not use the same procedures as federal grand juries. Thus, unlike federal grand juries, some states may limit the type of evidence that grand juries may hear, or give the defense a greater opportunity to present evidence to the grand jury. See Criminal Procedure: Adjudication for a detailed analysis of grand jury proceedings.

Another mechanism to screen cases before trial is the preliminary hearing. The Constitution does not require preliminary hearings, but a majority of jurisdictions use them to decide whether there is enough evidence to hold a defendant for trial, and to settle on which charges the prosecution will bring. A preliminary hearing is very different from a grand jury proceeding. No jury is present during a preliminary hearing. The judge presiding over the hearing decides whether there is probable cause to "bind the case over" for trial. Although procedures can differ by jurisdiction, both sides are generally given an opportunity to present evidence during the preliminary hearing. In some jurisdictions, hearsay evidence can be used to establish probable cause. As an adversarial process, both sides have an

---

9. See Chapter 3.
10. See Criminal Procedure: Adjudication.

opportunity to cross-examine witnesses. The preliminary hearing gives the defendant a preview of the prosecution's case. If the prosecution does not establish probable cause for a particular charge, the court can reject that charge. If all charges are rejected, the court may order the case dismissed. If the defendant is bound over for trial, however, the court will replace the complaint with a formal information charging the defendant with the offenses he will face at trial. Preliminary hearings are also discussed in Criminal Procedure: Adjudication.

Step 7: Arraignment on Indictment or Information

Once an indictment or information is filed, the defendant will appear for arraignment on those charges. At the arraignment, the defendant will typically be asked to enter a plea of guilty or not guilty, be advised of the charges against him, and be assigned counsel if counsel has not yet been assigned. The court will then assign a trial date. The trial date must comply with constitutional standards for a speedy trial and any applicable Speedy Trial Acts.

Step 8: Discovery[11]

To prepare for trial, the parties will engage in discovery. Discovery is the process by which the parties seek to examine the evidence that the other party is likely to use at trial. Statutes and procedural rules often govern discovery. However, defendants also have a due process right to exculpatory evidence and evidence that may impeach the prosecution's witnesses.

In the federal system, discovery of witness statements is covered by separate statutes. In state courts, comprehensive discovery statutes often cover both inculpatory and exculpatory evidence, including witness statements.

Step 9: Pretrial Motions

Frequently, the parties will file pretrial motions regarding a variety of issues. The defense will seek to suppress evidence illegally obtained by the prosecution, move to change venue, and seek dismissal for speedy trial violations or problems with the charges. The prosecution will also have an opportunity to file pretrial motions. For example, the prosecution may file pretrial motions *in limine* to get pretrial rulings on key evidentiary issues in the case. Pretrial motions help the parties define the scope of their own cases, and to assess the relative strength of the other side's case.

Step 10: Plea Bargaining and Guilty Pleas[12]

More than 90 percent of all criminal cases never go to trial. Rather, the vast majority of cases end with a guilty or *nolo contendere* (no contest) plea. During the

11. See Criminal Procedure: Adjudication.
12. See Criminal Procedure: Adjudication.

plea bargaining process, prosecutors may choose to reduce the charges or sentence exposure for a defendant in exchange for the defendant's guilty plea, and oftentimes, the defendant's cooperation. Anticipating that plea bargaining will occur, it is not unusual for prosecutors to load up charges against the defendant so that there is room to compromise during plea bargaining.

If a defendant decides to plead guilty, a formal hearing is held for the defendant to enter his plea. A guilty plea is both an admission that the defendant committed the crime, and a waiver of all of the rights the defendant would have had if he proceeded to trial. Thus, at a guilty plea hearing, the defendant will be advised of his right to counsel, right to confront witnesses, right to present evidence, right to a jury, and privilege against self-incrimination. If the defendant waives these rights, the court will ask for a factual basis for the plea. Either the prosecutor or the defense may provide the recitation necessary to establish that there is a basis for the plea. The court will also determine whether the plea is voluntary, and the nature of any inducements for the plea. Finally, the court will advise the defendant of the consequences of pleading guilty. If the defendant's guilty plea is knowing and voluntary, the court will accept the plea. The guilty plea obviates the need for a trial.

A defendant may also enter a *nolo contendere* plea. A *nolo contendere* plea has the same effect in the criminal case as a guilty plea. The defendant can receive the same criminal punishment as a defendant who enters a guilty plea. However, unlike a guilty plea, which serves as an admission for a civil case that the defendant is responsible, a *nolo contendere* plea has no impact on any companion civil case.

Step 11: Trial[13]

If a defendant does not plead guilty, the case proceeds to trial. A trial may be a court ("bench") trial or jury trial. If the case is going to be decided by a judge alone, both sides must agree to waive the right to jury trial. The judge will then hear the evidence adduced at trial, and decide whether there is proof beyond reasonable doubt for each of the charges.

The right to jury trial is guaranteed by the Sixth Amendment for all serious offenses, which the Supreme Court has defined as offenses that carry a possible sentence of more than six months in custody. Although there is a popular notion that 12 persons must sit on a jury, the Supreme Court has held to the contrary. States may choose to have juries as small as six persons for non-capital felony cases. Moreover, there is no constitutional requirement that the jurors' verdict be unanimous. Depending on the size of the jury, a non-unanimous jury may be sufficient.

The jury selection process begins with a panel of jurors (called the "venire") being summoned for jury selection. Potential jurors are questioned in a process called "voir dire" to reveal their backgrounds, attitudes, and any possible biases they may hold. The parties can excuse jurors from the jury by using challenges for cause, or by exercising peremptory challenges. Challenges for cause are allegations that specific jurors cannot be fair. Each side has an unlimited

---

13. See Chapter 6.

number of challenges for cause. By contrast, each party will have a limited number of peremptory challenges. Peremptory challenges need not be supported by a showing of actual bias by the juror. Each side has wide discretion in exercising peremptory challenges, although it is improper to use them in a discriminatory manner. Once jurors are finally chosen to sit on a case, they are referred to as the "petit" jury.

It is the jury's job to listen to all of the evidence, consider the court's jury instructions, and decide whether the defendant is guilty beyond a reasonable doubt. If the jury is not able to reach a decision, it constitutes a hung jury, and the court will declare a mistrial. In general, the prosecution can retry a defendant following a hung jury.

Step 12: Sentencing[14]

If the defendant is convicted, he will be sentenced by the court, ordinarily at a separate sentencing hearing. Before deciding on a sentence, the court will receive reports by the probation officer and input from the parties. At the sentencing hearing, the defendant has an opportunity to address the court. Sentencing systems vary greatly in the United States. In some jurisdictions, judges have broad discretion in imposing a sentence. In other jurisdictions, sentencing guidelines and mandatory sentences control a judge's sentence. If the judge's sentence must be based upon specific factual findings other than a defendant's prior criminal record, the trier of fact must find the existence of those facts beyond a reasonable doubt if they will increase the defendant's sentence beyond the presumptive sentence for that crime.

Step 13: Appeals and Habeas Corpus[15]

Finally, a defendant is entitled to challenge his conviction on direct appeal or through collateral proceedings known as habeas corpus proceedings. On direct appeal, the defendant may challenge errors by the court or prosecution at trial. A defendant has the right to an initial appeal to an intermediate court. Unless otherwise provided by statute, a defendant does not have the right to review by the state's high court. On appeal, the burden shifts to the defendant to demonstrate why he did not receive a fair trial, or that there was insufficient evidence to support the jury's verdict.

A defendant also may challenge constitutional violations in his case through a habeas corpus petition. Habeas corpus petitions are suits that allege that the defendant is being held unconstitutionally. Both state and federal courts hear habeas petitions. One of the primary grounds for habeas corpus petitions is ineffective assistance of counsel. Fourth Amendment search and seizure issues are not sufficient bases for habeas corpus challenges. In a habeas corpus petition, the court may hold an evidentiary hearing to determine whether there has been a constitutional violation. However, most habeas petitions are decided without a hearing. Because habeas corpus petitions are considered civil

14. See Criminal Procedure: Adjudication.
15. See Criminal Procedure: Adjudication.

proceedings, defendants are not constitutionally entitled to the assistance of counsel.

If a defendant succeeds on appeal or with a habeas corpus petition, the ordinary remedy is a retrial. However, if the appellate court finds that there was insufficient evidence to support the verdict, the defendant may not be retried because of double jeopardy principles.

C.   THE PURPOSE OF PROCEDURAL RULES

To understand why procedural rules are important, it is helpful to consider situations in which fair procedures are not afforded to defendants. In the infamous "Scottsboro trial," nine young black men were accused of raping two white women on a train from Chattanooga to Memphis, Tennessee. The train was intercepted as it traveled through Alabama, and the boys were captured and nearly lynched. There, they faced trial. Newspapers decried them as guilty, and all of the ugly traits of racism in the South in 1931 took hold. The defendants were brought to trial six days after they were indicted. The newspapers proclaimed them guilty of their "atrocious crime" even before the trial began. The judge perfunctorily appointed the entire local bar to represent the boys, although none of them investigated the case or assumed the role of zealous representatives of the defendants. The defendants were convicted and sentenced to death after a one-day trial before an all-white jury. During the trial, the credibility of the alleged victims was seriously impeached. Even though the victims, Victoria Price and Ruby Bates, were known prostitutes and transients, and Bates later recanted her testimony, it took years before the defendants' sentences were finally vacated.

As you read the Supreme Court's decision in their appeal, consider the importance of the rights to a fair trial, effective counsel, discovery, and due process. Consider also the role that race and economic status play in the criminal justice system.

POWELL v. ALABAMA
287 U.S. 45 (1932)

Justice SUTHERLAND delivered the opinion of the Court.

The petitioners, hereinafter referred to as defendants, are negroes charged with the crime of rape, committed upon the persons of two white girls. The crime is said to have been committed on March 25, 1931. The indictment was returned in a state court of first instance on March 31, and the record recites that on the same day the defendants were arraigned and entered pleas of not guilty. There is a further recital to the effect that upon the arraignment they were represented by counsel. But no counsel had been employed, and aside from a statement made by the trial judge several days later during a colloquy immediately preceding the trial, the record does not disclose when, or under what circumstances, an appointment of counsel was made, or who was appointed.

Each of the three trials was completed within a single day. Under the Alabama statute the punishment for rape is to be fixed by the jury, and in its discretion may be from ten years imprisonment to death. The juries found defendants guilty and imposed the death penalty upon all.

In this court the judgments are assailed upon the grounds that the defendants, and each of them, were denied due process of law and the equal protection of the laws, in contravention of the Fourteenth Amendment, specifically as follows: (1) they were not given a fair, impartial and deliberate trial; (2) they were denied the right of counsel, with the accustomed incidents of consultation and opportunity of preparation for trial; and (3) they were tried before juries from which qualified members of their own race were systematically excluded.

The only one of the assignments which we shall consider is the second, in respect of the denial of counsel; and it becomes unnecessary to discuss the facts of the case or the circumstances surrounding the prosecution except in so far as they reflect light upon that question.

The record shows that on the day when the offense is said to have been committed, these defendants, together with a number of other negroes, were upon a freight train on its way through Alabama. On the same train were seven white boys and the two white girls. A fight took place between the negroes and the white boys, in the course of which the white boys, with the exception of one named Gilley, were thrown off the train. A message was sent ahead, reporting the fight and asking that every negro be gotten off the train. The participants in the fight, and the two girls, were in an open gondola car. The two girls testified that each of them was assaulted by six different negroes in turn, and they identified the seven defendants as having been among the number. None of the white boys was called to testify, with the exception of Gilley, who was called in rebuttal.

Before the train reached Scottsboro, Alabama, a sheriff's posse seized the defendants and two other negroes. Both girls and the negroes then were taken to Scottsboro, the county seat. Word of their coming and of the alleged assault had preceded them, and they were met at Scottsboro by a large crowd. The sheriff thought it necessary to call for the militia to assist in safeguarding the prisoners. It is perfectly apparent that the proceedings, from beginning to end, took place in an atmosphere of tense, hostile and excited public sentiment. [T]he record clearly indicates that most, if not all, of them were youthful, and they are constantly referred to as "the boys." They were ignorant and illiterate. All of them were residents of other states, where alone members of their families or friends resided.

However guilty defendants, upon due inquiry, might prove to have been, they were, until convicted, presumed to be innocent. It was the duty of the court having their cases in charge to see that they were denied no necessary incident of a fair trial. With any error of the state court involving alleged contravention of the state statutes or constitution we, of course, have nothing to do. The sole inquiry which we are permitted to make is whether the federal Constitution was contravened and as to that, we confine ourselves, as already suggested, to the inquiry whether the defendants were in substance denied the right of counsel, and if so, whether such denial infringes the due process clause of the Fourteenth Amendment.

First. The record shows that immediately upon the return of the indictment defendants were arraigned and pleaded not guilty. Apparently they were not asked whether they had, or were able to employ, counsel, or wished to have counsel appointed; or whether they had friends or relatives who might assist in that regard if communicated with. "They were nonresidents," he said, "and had little time or opportunity to get in touch with their families and friends who were scattered throughout two other states, and time has demonstrated that they could or would have been represented by able counsel had a better opportunity been given by a reasonable delay in the trial of the cases. . . ."

April 6, six days after indictment, the trials began. When the first case was called, the court inquired whether the parties were ready for trial. The state's attorney replied that he was ready to proceed. No one answered for the defendants or appeared to represent or defend them. Mr. Roddy, a Tennessee lawyer not a member of the local bar, addressed the court, saying that he had not been employed, but that people who were interested had spoken to him about the case. He was asked by the court whether he intended to appear for the defendants, and answered that he would like to appear along with counsel that the court might appoint. The record then proceeds:

"Mr. Roddy: Your Honor has appointed counsel, is that correct?

"The Court: I appointed all the members of the bar for the purpose of arraigning the defendants and then of course I anticipated them to continue to help them if no counsel appears.

"Mr. Roddy: Then I don't appear then as counsel but I do want to stay in and not be ruled out in this case.

* * *

"Mr. Roddy: I merely came down here as a friend of the people who are interested and not as paid counsel I am merely here at the solicitation of people who have become interested in this case without any payment of fee and without any preparation for trial and I think the boys would be better off if I step entirely out of the case according to my way of looking at it and according to my lack of preparation of it and not being familiar with the procedure in Alabama, . . ."

"The Court: All right."

It thus will be seen that until the very morning of the trial no lawyer had been named or definitely designated to represent the defendants. Prior to that time, the trial judge had "appointed all the members of the bar" for the limited "purpose of arraigning the defendants."

That this action of the trial judge in respect of appointment of counsel was little more than an expansive gesture, imposing no substantial or definite obligation upon any one, is borne out by the fact that prior to the calling of the case for trial on April 6, a leading member of the local bar accepted employment on the side of the prosecution and actively participated in the trial. [T]he circumstance lends emphasis to the conclusion that during perhaps the most critical period of the proceedings against these defendants, that is to say, from the time of their arraignment until the beginning of their trial, when consultation, thoroughgoing investigation and preparation were vitally important, the defendants did not have the aid of counsel in any real sense. . . .

Under the circumstances disclosed, we hold that defendants were not accorded the right of counsel in any substantial sense. To decide otherwise, would simply be to ignore actualities.

In the light of the facts outlined in the forepart of this opinion — the ignorance and illiteracy of the defendants, their youth, the circumstances of public hostility, the imprisonment and the close surveillance of the defendants by the military forces, the fact that their friends and families were all in other states and communication with them necessarily difficult, and above all that they stood in deadly peril of their lives — we think the failure of the trial court to give them reasonable time and opportunity to secure counsel was a clear denial of due process.

Judgments reversed.

Why are procedures so important? As *Powell* demonstrates, without fair procedures and respect for constitutional rights, there is a strong likelihood that the defendants will not be treated fairly, and that persons will be held accountable for crimes they did not commit. Procedural rules thus play a crucial role in ensuring the fair and efficient processing of cases, as well as the perception of the public and defendants that the criminal justice system has acted in a reliable and fair manner.

Even today, there are numerous obstacles to the fair handling of criminal investigations and prosecutions. Many defendants are poor and do not receive effective representation in asserting their rights. A large percentage of defendants are uneducated, unemployed, and have a substance abuse problem. Law enforcement officials are often overworked and undertrained. Racial stereotypes permeate society, including the criminal justice system. There can also be political pressure on prosecutors to secure convictions. All of these factors may impact how effectively our laws are implemented.

Moreover, it is not just the courts who must abide by fair procedures. Much of criminal procedure is devoted to ensuring that law enforcement officers respect the rights of defendants during the investigative phase of cases. Consider how police conduct affects the likelihood of reaching a correct and fair result in a case.

PATTERSON, PLAINTIFF v. FORMER CHICAGO POLICE LT. JON BURGE

328 F. Supp. 2d 878 (N.D. Ill. 2004)

Opinion by Joan B. GOTTSCHALL:

After being convicted for the 1986 murders of Rafaela and Vincent Sanchez and spending 13 years on death row, plaintiff Aaron Patterson was pardoned by Illinois Governor George Ryan on January 10, 2003. Patterson filed this civil action in June of 2003, asserting that defendants, individually and in conspiracy, violated his rights under the United States Constitution when they knowingly filed false charges and framed him for the Sanchez murders, tortured and beat him at Chicago Police Department's Area 2 headquarters, fabricated his "confession" and falsified inculpatory evidence, coerced witnesses to testify against him, gave perjured testimony, published defamatory statements regarding his guilt, and obstructed justice and suppressed exculpatory evidence throughout his suppression hearing, trial, and post-conviction proceedings.

I. BACKGROUND

On April 19, 1986, Chicago Police Department officers discovered the dead bodies of Rafaela and Vincent Sanchez in their apartment at 8849 South Burley. Officers and defendants Lt. Jon Burge, Sgt. John Byrne, Detectives James Pienta,

William Marley, Daniel McWeeny, Joseph Danzl (collectively, "Area 2 defendants"), and other Area 2 detectives were assigned to investigate the Sanchez murders. On April 21, Danzl allegedly coerced and intimidated 16 year-old Marva Hall, whose uncle was a suspect in the murders, into falsely implicating Patterson. On April 22, Burge and another Area 2 detective took a different suspect, Michael Arbuckle, into custody at Area 2 headquarters. Burge allegedly told Arbuckle that they "really wanted to get Aaron Patterson" and wanted Arbuckle to say that Patterson was involved in the murders. When Arbuckle refused to implicate Patterson and asked for his lawyer, Burge threatened him with electrocution and lethal injection and told him that they would get Arbuckle to "cooperate one way or another." Still, Arbuckle denied his and Patterson's involvement.

On or about April 23, McWeeny, Byrne, and other Area 2 detectives on the case were informed by several persons that Willie Washington and his brother killed Rafaela and Vincent Sanchez. Nevertheless, for the next week, Byrne, McWeeny, and other Area 2 detectives searched unsuccessfully for Patterson. On April 30, Patterson was arrested on an outstanding warrant by Chicago Police Department officers from the Fourth District. Defendants Pienta, Marley, and Pedersen were called to transport Patterson from the Fourth District police station to Area 2. During the ride, Pienta allegedly told Patterson that if he had arrested him, he would have killed him.

At Area 2 Patterson was placed in an interview room, handcuffed to the wall, and questioned by Area 2 detectives about the Sanchez murders for about an hour. Patterson denied any involvement. He was then taken to 11th and State before being returned to the interview room at Area 2. After brief questioning, Pienta told Patterson that he was "tired of this bullshit," left the room, and came back with a grey typewriter cover. When Patterson refused to implicate himself in the murders, the Area 2 defendants, including Pienta, Marley, and Pedersen, handcuffed him behind his back, turned out the lights, and repeatedly beat him in the chest and suffocated him by holding the typewriter cover over his face and ears for at least a minute. Pienta continued to urge Patterson to "cooperate," and when he refused, the Area 2 defendants again turned out the lights and suffocated Patterson with the plastic cover. The second time, the "bagging" and beating lasted for over two minutes. Patterson found the abuse unbearable and told the detectives he would "say anything you say" if they would stop the suffocation and beating.

After Patterson agreed to cooperate, the Area 2 defendants left the room to get a state's attorney from the felony review division to take his statement. While alone in the room, Patterson used a paper clip to scratch into the interview room bench that he was "suffocated with plastic" and that his statement to the police was false. Defendant Burge returned with an Assistant State's Attorney ("ASA") who said that Burge told him Patterson wanted to make a statement. After Burge left the room at Patterson's request, Patterson told the ASA that he had nothing to say. The ASA left and told Burge that Patterson refused to confess. Burge then returned to the room, told Patterson "you're fucking up," placed his handgun on the table in front of Patterson, and said "we told you if you don't do what we tell you to, you're going to get something worse than before — it will have been a snap compared to what you will get." He also told Patterson that if he revealed the torture, "it's your word against ours and who are they going to believe, you or us." Burge then told Patterson that they could do anything they wanted to him.

Next, defendant Peter Troy, an ASA with the State's Attorney's Office ("SAO"), entered the interview room with Area 2 defendant Madigan. Initially,

Patterson agreed to make a statement in exchange for phone privileges, but he refused to sign the statement Troy had written out after the Area 2 defendants terminated his calls. In an attempt to make Patterson sign the statement, Troy and Madigan physically attacked Patterson. McWeeny entered the room at this time, professing not to be involved in the prior beatings and suffocation, and urged Patterson to cooperate because the other defendants "could do something serious to him if he didn't." As a result of this coercion and under threat of continued torture, Patterson said he would agree with whatever the Area 2 defendants and Troy said had happened.

Around the same time, defendant Pienta arrested Eric Caine, Patterson's co-defendant in the Sanchez murder prosecution. Caine was interrogated and beaten and told that if he did not make a statement he would get the same treatment as Patterson. Caine initially gave a statement, but when he tried to repudiate it Madigan hit Caine with his open hand over his ear and cheekbone, causing a loud pop and rupturing his ear drum. Caine screamed in pain; he later gave and signed a court-reported statement prepared by the Area 2 defendants which falsely implicated Patterson in the murders.

The Area 2 defendants, together with SAO defendants Troy and William Lacy, allegedly fabricated oral admissions and reduced these "admissions" to false reports implicating Patterson and Caine in the Sanchez murders. Defendants communicated these false reports to the prosecuting attorneys, who used them at Patterson's suppression hearing and at trial. Defendants also testified falsely about the fabricated admissions and the torture and abuse which produced them throughout Patterson's prosecution. No physical evidence linking Patterson to the murders was ever discovered, though a bloody fingerprint that was not Patterson's was found at the scene and not introduced at trial. Patterson was convicted for the Sanchez murders on the basis of his false confession and the testimony of Marva Hall and defendants. Patterson was sentenced to death, and after his conviction was affirmed on appeal, spent over 13 years incarcerated on death row until his pardon in January of 2003.

In a televised interview in December of 1999 defendant Byrne made defamatory statements concerning Patterson's protestations of his innocence and claims of torture at Area 2, including that Patterson was "without a doubt" "guilty of the [Sanchez] murders" and that "the detectives who worked with him would not" and did not torture suspects. On January 10, 2003, then Governor of Illinois George Ryan granted Patterson and three other death row victims allegedly tortured by Burge and other Area 2 detectives pardons on the basis of innocence. In granting the pardons Governor Ryan announced that "the category of horrors was hard to believe," and the evidence showed that the four men — Patterson, Madison Hobley, Leroy Orange, and Stanley Howard — had been "beaten and tortured and convicted on the basis of confessions they allegedly provided." In response, State's Attorney Devine publicly condemned the pardons of the four men, whom he referred to as "evil" and "convicted murderers," as "outrageous" and "unconscionable."

As *Patterson* illustrates, constitutional rights are not just formalities. They are critical to ensuring that police respect people's rights and that the right people are held responsible for criminal actions.

D.   KEY PROVISIONS OF THE BILL OF RIGHTS

The Bill of Rights protect individuals against the power of the State. Fundamental rights ensured by a number of the first ten Amendments have been made applicable to the states under the Fourteenth Amendment's Due Process Clause. The key constitutional provisions that will be covered in this book include:

UNITED STATES CONSTITUTION

AMENDMENT IV

The right of the people to be secure in their persons, houses, papers, and effects, against unreasonable searches and seizures, shall not be violated, and no Warrants shall issue but upon probable cause, supported by Oath or affirmation, and particularly describing the place to be searched, and the persons or things to be seized.

The Fourth Amendment is the key constitutional provision governing police conduct during searches and arrest. As discussed in Chapter 2, the Amendment has been interpreted as generally requiring a warrant based upon probable cause for a search or arrest. However, there are numerous exceptions that allow for warrantless searches and stops so long as they are "reasonable."

AMENDMENT V

No person shall be held to answer for a capital, or otherwise infamous crime, unless on a presentment or indictment of a Grand Jury . . . ; nor shall any person be subject for the same offense to be twice put in jeopardy of life or limb; nor shall be compelled in any criminal case to be a witness against himself, nor be deprived of life, liberty, or property, without due process of law.

There are several aspects to the Fifth Amendment. It sets forth the right in federal cases to indictment by a grand jury. It also provides for the right against double jeopardy, the privilege against self-incrimination (Chapter 4), and the general right of due process in criminal cases.

AMENDMENT VI

In all criminal prosecutions, the accused shall enjoy the right to a speedy and public trial, by an impartial jury of the State and district wherein the crime shall have been committed, which district shall have been previously ascertained by law; and to be informed of the nature and cause of the accusation; to be confronted with the witnesses against him; to have compulsory process for obtaining witnesses in his favor, and to have the Assistance of Counsel for his defense.

The Sixth Amendment guarantees a defendant the right to a speedy and public jury trial. It also requires that the defendant be given an opportunity to confront the witnesses against him and to call his own witnesses. However, the most important right that the defendant enjoys under the Sixth Amendment is the right to assistance of counsel. (See Chapter 6.) Through counsel's diligent efforts, a defendant can preserve his other rights.

AMENDMENT VIII

Excessive bail shall not be required, nor excessive fines imposed, nor cruel and unusual punishment inflicted.

The Eighth Amendment prohibits cruel and unusual punishment. The standard for "cruel and unusual punishment" evolves. Generally, the term "cruel and unusual punishment" relates to the proportionality of the sentence, not just the manner in which the sentence is imposed.

E.   THE APPLICATION OF THE BILL OF RIGHTS TO THE STATES

1.   The Provisions of the Bill of Rights and the Idea of "Incorporation"

There are a few criminal procedure protections in the first seven articles of the Constitution, such as the prohibition on Congress suspending the writ of habeas corpus found in Article I, section 9, and the assurance of trial by jury in Article III. But the key protections of criminal procedure examined through this book are found in the Fourth, Fifth, Sixth, and Eighth Amendments.

In understanding the material in this book, it is important to know that these provisions of the Bill of Rights did not apply to state governments until the twentieth century and generally not until the second half of the twentieth century. Initially, it was thought that the Bill of Rights was meant just to limit the federal government; state constitutions were deemed adequate to protect people from abuses by state and local governments.

In Barron v. Mayor & City of Baltimore, 32 U.S. (7 Pet.) 243 (1833), the Supreme Court held that the Bill of Rights did not apply to the states. The specific issue was whether the states had to comply with the Fifth Amendment's prohibition of the taking of private property without just compensation. The Court, in an opinion by Chief Justice John Marshall, declared: "The question thus presented is, we think, of great importance, but not of much difficulty. The constitution was ordained and established by the people of the United States for themselves, for their own government, and not for the government of the individual states." The Court held that the Bill of Rights simply did not apply to the States: "If these propositions be correct, the fifth amendment must be understood as restraining the power of the general government, not as applicable to the states. In their several constitutions, they have imposed such restrictions on their respective governments, as their own wisdom suggested; such as they deemed most proper for themselves."

In the late nineteenth century, the Supreme Court suggested an alternate approach: finding that at least some of the Bill of the Rights provisions are part of the liberty protected from state interference by the Due Process Clause of the Fourteenth Amendment. In other words, the Court indicated that the Due Process Clause of the Fourteenth Amendment, which applies to state and local governments, incorporates and protects at least some of the Bill of Rights.

In 1897, in Chicago, Burlington & Quincy Railroad Co. v. City of Chicago, 166 U.S. 226 (1897), the Supreme Court ruled that the Due Process Clause of the Fourteenth Amendment prevents states from taking property without just compensation. Although the Court did not speak explicitly of the Fourteenth Amendment incorporating the Takings Clause, that was the practical effect of the decision.

In Twining v. New Jersey, 211 U.S. 78 (1908), the Supreme Court first expressly discussed applying the Bill of Rights to the states through the process of incorporation. The specific issue was whether a jury in state court could draw an adverse inference against a criminal defendant for failing to testify. Although the Court held that this does not apply to the states (a conclusion that the Court later would reverse in Griffin v. California, 380 U.S. 609 (1965)), it stated: "[I]t is possible that some of the personal rights safeguarded by the first eight Amendments against national action may also be safeguarded against state action, because a denial of them would be a denial of due process of law. If this is so, it is not because those rights are enumerated in the first eight Amendments, but because they are of such a nature that they are included in the conception of due process of law."

Twining expressly opened the door to the Supreme Court applying provisions of the Bill of Rights to the states by finding them to be included — incorporated — into the Due Process Clause of the Fourteenth Amendment. Soon the Court began to use this door. In Gitlow v. New York, 268 U.S. 652 (1925), the Court for the first time said that the First Amendment's protection of freedom of speech applies to the states through its incorporation into the Due Process Clause of the Fourteenth Amendment. The Court declared: "For present purposes we may and do assume that freedom of speech and of the press — which are protected by the First Amendment from abridgment by Congress — are among the fundamental personal rights and liberties protected by the due process clause of the Fourteenth Amendment from impairment by the States." In *Gitlow*, the Court actually rejected the constitutional challenge to a state law that made it a crime to advocate the violent overthrow of government by force or violence. Two years later, in Fiske v. Kansas, 274 U.S. 380 (1927), the Court for the first time found that a state law regulating speech violated the Due Process Clause of the Fourteenth Amendment.

In 1933, in Powell v. Alabama, 287 U.S. 45 (1932), which is presented above, the Court found that a state's denial of counsel in a capital case denied due process, thereby in essence applying the Sixth Amendment to the states in capital cases. The infamous Scottsboro trial involved two African-American men who were convicted of rape without the assistance of an attorney at trial and with a jury from which all blacks had been excluded. The Supreme Court concluded that the Due Process Clause of the Fourteenth Amendment protects fundamental rights from state interference and that this can include Bill of Rights provisions. But the Court said that "[i]f this is so, it is not because those rights are enumerated in the first eight Amendments, but because they are of such a nature that they are included in the 'conception of due process of law.'" The Court held that in a capital case, "it [is] clear that the right to the aid of counsel is of this fundamental character."

2.   *The Debate over Incorporation*

Once the Court found that the Due Process Clause of the Fourteenth Amendment protected fundamental rights from state infringement, there was a major debate over which liberties are safeguarded. For many years, this debate raged among Justices and commentators. On the one side, there were the total incorporationists who believed that all of the Bill of Rights should be deemed to be included in the Due Process Clause of the Fourteenth Amendment. Justices Black and Douglas were the foremost advocates of this position.[16]

On the other side, there were the selective incorporationists who believed that only some of the Bill of Rights were sufficiently fundamental to apply to state and local governments. Justice Cardozo, for example, wrote that "[t]he process of absorption . . . [applied to rights where] neither liberty nor justice would exist if they were sacrificed."[17] Justice Cardozo said that the Due Process Clause included "principles of justice so rooted in the tradition and conscience of our people as to be ranked as fundamental" and that were therefore "implicit in the concept of ordered liberty."[18] Justice Frankfurter said that due process precludes those practices that "offend those canons of decency and fairness which express the notions of justice of English-speaking peoples."[19]

The debate between total and selective incorporation was extremely important because it determined the reach of the Bill of Rights and the extent to which individuals could turn to the federal courts for protection from state and local governments.

For example, in Palko v. Connecticut, 302 U.S. 319 (1937), the Court held the prohibition of double jeopardy, which keeps states from appealing acquittals in criminal cases, does not apply to the states. Justice Cardozo, writing for the Court, stated: "Is [allowing the State to appeal the] kind of double jeopardy to which the statute has subjected him a hardship so acute and shocking that our policy will not endure it? Does it violate those 'fundamental principles of liberty and justice which lie at the base of all our civil and political institutions'? The answer surely must be 'no.' There is here no seismic innovation. The edifice of justice stands."

Similarly, in Adamson v. California, 332 U.S. 46 (1947), the Court held that states were not obligated to follow the Fifth Amendment's prohibition on a prosecutor's commenting on a criminal defendant's failure to take the witness stand. Justice Black wrote a famous dissent. He declared:

> The first 10 amendments were proposed and adopted largely because of fear that Government might unduly interfere with prized individual liberties. . . . My study of the historical events that culminated in the Fourteenth Amendment, and the expressions of those who sponsored and favored, as well as those who opposed its submission and passage, persuades me that one of the chief objects that the provisions of the Amendment's first section, separately, and as a whole, were intended to accomplish was to make the Bill of Rights applicable to the states. With full knowledge of the import of the *Barron* decision, the framers and backers of the Fourteenth Amendment proclaimed its purpose to be to overturn the constitutional rule that case had announced. This historical purpose has never received full consideration or exposition in any opinion of this Court interpreting the Amendment."[20]

---

16. *See, e.g.*, Adamson v. California, 332 U.S. 46, 71-72 (1947) (Black, J., dissenting).
17. 302 U.S. 319, 326 (1937).
18. *Id.* at 325.
19. Adamson v. California, 332 U.S. 46, 67 (1947) (Frankfurter, J., concurring).
20. In Griffin v. California, 380 U.S. 609 (1965), the Supreme Court overruled *Adamson* and held that the Due Process Clause of the Fourteenth Amendment was violated by a prosecutor's comments on a defendant's silence.

The debate over incorporation primarily was centered on three issues.[21] First, the debate was over history and whether the framers of the Fourteenth Amendment intended for it to apply the Bill of Rights to the states. Both sides of the debate claimed that history supported their view.

Second, the incorporation debate was over federalism. Applying the Bill of Rights to the states imposes a substantial set of restrictions on state and local governments. Not surprisingly, opponents of total incorporation argued based on federalism: the desirability of preserving state and local governing autonomy by freeing them from the application of the Bill of Rights. Defenders of total incorporation responded that federalism is not a sufficient reason for tolerating violations of fundamental liberties.

Third, the debate was over the appropriate judicial role. Advocates of total incorporation, such as Justice Black, claimed that allowing the Court to pick and choose which rights to incorporate left too much to the subjective preference of the Justices. In contrast, advocates of selective incorporation denied this and maintained that total incorporation would mean more judicial oversight of state and local actions and thus less room for democracy to operate.

3. The Current Law as to What's Incorporated

The selective incorporationists prevailed in this debate in that the Supreme Court never has accepted the total incorporationist approach. However, from a practical perspective, the total incorporationists largely succeeded in their objective because, one by one, the Supreme Court found almost all of the provisions to be incorporated. This is reflected in the following case, Duncan v. Louisiana, which summarizes the many decisions, particularly of the Warren Court during the 1950s and 1960s, finding almost all of the Bill of Rights to be incorporated.

DUNCAN v. LOUISIANA
391 U.S. 145 (1968)

Justice WHITE delivered the opinion of the Court.

Appellant, Gary Duncan, was convicted of simple battery in the Twenty-fifth Judicial District Court of Louisiana. Under Louisiana law simple battery is a misdemeanor, punishable by a maximum of two years' imprisonment and a $300 fine. Appellant sought trial by jury, but because the Louisiana Constitution grants jury trials only in cases in which capital punishment or imprisonment at hard labor may be imposed, the trial judge denied the request. Appellant was convicted and sentenced to serve 60 days in the parish prison and pay a fine of $150.

The Fourteenth Amendment denies the States the power to "deprive any person of life, liberty, or property, without due process of law." In resolving conflicting claims concerning the meaning of this spacious language, the

---

21. For a detailed description of the debate and the issues, see Jerold Israel, *Selective Incorporation Revisited*, 71 Geo. L.J. 253, 336-338 (1982).

Court has looked increasingly to the Bill of Rights for guidance; many of the rights guaranteed by the first eight Amendments to the Constitution have been held to be protected against state action by the Due Process Clause of the Fourteenth Amendment. That clause now protects the right to compensation for property taken by the State, Chicago, B. & Q.R. Co. v. City of Chicago (1897); the rights of speech, press, and religion covered by the First Amendment, see, e.g., Fiske v. State of Kansas (1927); the Fourth Amendment rights to be free from unreasonable searches and seizures and to have excluded from criminal trials any evidence illegally seized, Mapp v. State of Ohio (1961); the right guaranteed by the Fifth Amendment to be free of compelled self-incrimination, Malloy v. Hogan (1964); and the Sixth Amendment rights to counsel, Gideon v. Wainwright (1963); to a speedy, Klopfer v. State of North Carolina (1967) and public trial, In re Oliver (1948); to confrontation of opposing witnesses, Pointer v. State of Texas (1965); and to compulsory process for obtaining witnesses, Washington v. State of Texas (1967).

The test for determining whether a right extended by the Fifth and Sixth Amendments with respect to federal criminal proceedings is also protected against state action by the Fourteenth Amendment has been phrased in a variety of ways in the opinions of this Court. The question has been asked whether a right is among those "fundamental principles of liberty and justice which lie at the base of all our civil and political institutions," Powell v. State of Alabama, (1932); whether it is "basic in our system of jurisprudence," In re Oliver (1948); and whether it is "a fundamental right, essential to a fair trial," Gideon v. Wainwright (1963).

The claim before us is that the right to trial by jury guaranteed by the Sixth Amendment meets these tests. The position of Louisiana, on the other hand, is that the Constitution imposes upon the States no duty to give a jury trial in any criminal case, regardless of the seriousness of the crime or the size of the punishment which may be imposed. Because we believe that trial by jury in criminal cases is fundamental to the American scheme of justice, we hold that the Fourteenth Amendment guarantees a right of jury trial in all criminal cases which — were they to be tried in a federal court — would come within the Sixth Amendment's guarantee.

The guarantees of jury trial in the Federal and State Constitutions reflect a profound judgment about the way in which law should be enforced and justice administered. A right to jury trial is granted to criminal defendants in order to prevent oppression by the Government. Those who wrote our constitutions knew from history and experience that it was necessary to protect against unfounded criminal charges brought to eliminate enemies and against judges too responsive to the voice of higher authority. The framers of the constitutions strove to create an independent judiciary but insisted upon further protection against arbitrary action. Providing an accused with the right to be tried by a jury of his peers gave him an inestimable safeguard against the corrupt or overzealous prosecutor and against the compliant, biased, or eccentric judge. If the defendant preferred the common-sense judgment of a jury to the more tutored but perhaps less sympathetic reaction of the single judge, he was to have it. Beyond this, the jury trial provisions in the Federal and State Constitutions reflect a fundamental decision about the exercise of official power — a reluctance to entrust plenary powers over the life and liberty of the citizen to one judge or to a group of judges. Fear of unchecked power, so typical of our State and Federal Governments in other respects, found expression in the criminal law in this insistence upon community participation in the determination of guilt or innocence. The deep commitment of the Nation to the right of jury trial in serious criminal cases as a defense against arbitrary law enforcement qualifies for protection under the Due Process Clause of the Fourteenth Amendment, and must therefore be respected by the States.

Justice BLACK, with whom Justice DOUGLAS joins, concurring.

The Court today holds that the right to trial by jury guaranteed defendants in criminal cases in federal courts by Art. III of the United States Constitution and by the Sixth Amendment is also guaranteed by the Fourteenth Amendment to defendants tried in state courts. With this holding I agree for reasons given by the Court.

I am very happy to support this selective process through which our Court has since the *Adamson* case held most of the specific Bill of Rights' protections applicable to the States to the same extent they are applicable to the Federal Government. All of these holdings making Bill of Rights' provisions applicable as such to the States mark, of course, a departure from the *Twining* doctrine holding that none of those provisions were enforceable as such against the States.

My view has been and is that the Fourteenth Amendment, as a whole, makes the Bill of Rights applicable to the States. This would certainly include the language of the Privileges and Immunities Clause, as well as the Due Process Clause. I can say only that the words "No State shall make or enforce any law which shall abridge the privileges or immunities of citizens of the United States" seem to me an eminently reasonable way of expressing the idea that henceforth the Bill of Rights shall apply to the States. What more precious "privilege" of American citizenship could there be than that privilege to claim the protections of our great Bill of Rights? I suggest that any reading of "privileges or immunities of citizens of the United States" which excludes the Bill of Rights' safeguards renders the words of this section of the Fourteenth Amendment meaningless. Senator Howard, who introduced the Fourteenth Amendment for passage in the Senate, certainly read the words this way.

Finally I want to add that I am not bothered by the argument that applying the Bill of Rights to the States "according to the same standards that protect those personal rights against federal encroachment," interferes with our concept of federalism in that it may prevent States from trying novel social and economic experiments. I have never believed that under the guise of federalism the States should be able to experiment with the protections afforded our citizens through the Bill of Rights.

In closing I want to emphasize that I believe as strongly as ever that the Fourteenth Amendment was intended to make the Bill of Rights applicable to the States. I have been willing to support the selective incorporation doctrine, however, as an alternative, although perhaps less historically supportable than complete incorporation. The selective incorporation process, if used properly, does limit the Supreme Court in the Fourteenth Amendment field to specific Bill of Rights' protections only and keeps judges from roaming at will in their own notions of what policies outside the Bill of Rights are desirable and what are not. And, most importantly for me, the selective incorporation process has the virtue of having already worked to make most of the Bill of Rights' protections applicable to the States.

There are still five provisions of the Bill of Rights that never have been incorporated and do not apply to state and local governments. First, the Supreme Court has ruled that Second Amendment "right to bear arms" is not incorporated.[22] Therefore, courts repeatedly have upheld state and local gun control laws because the Second Amendment does not apply.[23]

Second, the Third Amendment right to not have soldiers quartered in a person's home never has been deemed incorporated. The reason almost certainly is that a Third Amendment case presenting the incorporation question never has reached the Supreme Court. If ever such a case would arise, the Supreme Court surely would find this provision applies to the states.[24]

Third, the Court has held that the Fifth Amendment's right to a grand jury indictment in criminal cases is not incorporated.[25] Thus, states need not use grand juries and can chose alternatives such as preliminary hearings and prosecutorial informations.

Fourth, the Court has ruled that the Seventh Amendment right to jury trial in civil cases is not incorporated.[26] States therefore can eliminate juries in some or even all civil suits without violating the United States Constitution.

Finally, the Court never has ruled as to whether the prohibition of excessive fines in the Eighth Amendment is incorporated.[27]

All of the rest of the Bill of Rights, as detailed above, have been deemed incorporated. Technically, the Bill of Rights still applies directly only to the federal government; Barron v. Mayor & City Council of Baltimore never has been expressly overruled. Therefore, whenever a case involves a state or local violation of a Bill of Rights provision, to be precise, it involves that provision as applied to the states through the Due Process Clause of the Fourteenth Amendment.

4. The Content of Incorporated Rights

If a provision of the Bill of Rights applies to the states, is its content identical as to when it is applied to the federal government? Or as it is sometimes phrased, does the Bill of Rights provision apply "jot for jot"?[28]

---

22. Presser v. Illinois, 116 U.S. 252 (1886) (refusing to incorporate the Second Amendment).

23. Love v. Pepersack, 47 F.3d 120 (4th Cir. 1995); Fresno Rifle & Pistol Club, Inc. v. Van de Kamp, 965 F.2d 723 (9th Cir. 1992); Quilici v. Village of Morton Grove, 695 F.2d 261 (7th Cir. 1982), *cert. denied,* 464 U.S. 863 (1983); Citizens for a Safer Community v. City of Rochester, 627 N.Y.S.2d 193 (1994); Arnold v. Cleveland, 616 N.E.3d 163 (Ohio 1993); New Hampshire v. Sanne, 364 A.2d 630 (N.H. 1976).

24. *See* Engblom v. Carey, 677 F.2d 957 (2d Cir. 1982) (finding that the Third Amendment is incorporated).

25. Hutardo v. California, 110 U.S. 516 (1884).

26. Minneapolis & St. Louis Railroad Co. v. Bombolis, 241 U.S. 211 (1916).

27. Browning-Ferris Industries of Vt., Inc. v. Kelco Disposal, Inc., 492 U.S. 257, 262, 276 n.2 (1989).

28. *See* Duncan v. Louisiana, 391 U.S. at 181 (Harlan, J., dissenting) (using the "jot-for-jot" language).

The Supreme Court has not consistently answered these questions. In some cases, the Court has expressly stated that the Bill of Rights provision applied in exactly the same manner whether it is a federal or a state government action. For example, the Supreme Court has declared that it is "firmly embedded in our constitutional jurisprudence . . . that the several States have no greater power to restrain the individual freedoms protected by the First Amendment than does the Congress of the United States."[29] Similarly, the Court has said that "the guarantees of the First Amendment, the prohibition of unreasonable searches and seizures of the Fourth Amendment, and the right to counsel guaranteed by the Sixth Amendment, are all to be enforced against the States under the Fourteenth Amendment according to the same standards that protect those personal rights against federal encroachment."[30] The Court said that it "rejected the notion that the Fourteenth Amendment applies to the states only a watered-down, subjective version of the individual guarantees of the Bill of Rights."[31]

However, in other instances, the Court has ruled that some Bill of Rights provisions apply differently to the states than to the federal government. In *Williams v. Florida*, 399 U.S. 78 (1970), the Supreme Court held that states need not use 12-person juries in criminal cases, even though that is required by the Sixth Amendment for federal trials. The Court upheld the constitutionality of six-person juries in state criminal trials and explained that the jury of 12 was "a historical accident, unnecessary to effect the purposes of the jury system."

In *Apodaca v. Oregon*, 406 U.S. 404 (1972), and *Johnson v. Louisiana*, 406 U.S. 356 (1972), the Supreme Court held that states may allow non-unanimous jury verdicts in criminal cases. Although the Sixth Amendment has been interpreted to require unanimous juries in federal criminal trials, the Supreme Court ruled that states may allow convictions based on 11-1 or 10-2 jury votes. However, the Court has ruled that conviction by a non-unanimous six-person jury violates due process.[32]

From a practical perspective, except for the requirements of a 12-person jury and a unanimous verdict, the Bill of Rights provisions that have been incorporated apply to the states exactly as they apply to the federal government. This might be criticized on federalism grounds as unduly limiting the states. But rights such as freedom of speech are fundamental liberties and there is no reason why their content should vary depending on the level of government.

Of course, apart from the Bill of Rights, there are many differences between criminal procedure in federal and state courts. The Federal Rules of Criminal Procedure, mentioned at many points throughout this book, are sometimes different than the rules followed in many states. Also, the Supreme Court often articulates requirements as part of its supervisory role over federal courts in areas where states are free to follow their own procedures. For example, the contempt powers of a federal court, as defined by the Supreme Court, may be different than those in a state court.

Although the debate over incorporation raged among Justices and scholars during the 1940s, 1950s, and 1960s, now the issue seems settled. Except for the few provisions mentioned above, the Bill of Rights do apply to state and local

29. Wallace v. Jaffree, 472 U.S. 38, 48-49 (1985).
30. Malloy v. Hogan, 378 U.S. at 10.
31. *Id.* at 10-11 (citations omitted).
32. Burch v. Louisiana, 441 U.S. 130 (1979).

governments and, in almost all instances, with the same content regardless of whether it is a challenge to federal, state, or local actions.

F.   RETROACTIVITY

In reading the cases throughout this book, it is important to keep in mind that generally criminal procedure decisions apply only in that case and in future ones; they do not apply retroactively to already decided cases. Actually, to be more precise, a Supreme Court decision recognizing a right of criminal procedure generally applies to that case, to any cases pending at the time (in a trial court or on appeal, but not to those pending on habeas corpus), and to future cases. Generally, Supreme Court criminal procedure rulings do not apply retroactively to cases where the appeals have already been completed.

It is easy to understand the reason for this. If Supreme Court decisions recognizing new criminal procedure rights applied retroactively, hundreds or thousands of convicted criminals would seek to reopen their cases to take advantage of the new right. The burden on the courts, depending on the new right, would be enormous. In many instances, the government simply could not retry the person because witnesses would no longer be available. But there is a serious cost to not applying Supreme Court decisions retroactively: People remain in prison, or even are executed, in violation of the Constitution. An accident of timing is determinative; those whose appeals are pending get the benefit of the new right, which could lead to the reversal of their conviction, but those whose appeal is over are out of luck in taking advantage of the new right.

Occasionally, though rarely, the Supreme Court will apply a criminal procedure protection retroactively. The Court has identified two situations in which this will occur. One situation is where a Supreme Court decision places a matter beyond the reach of the criminal law; that is, the Court holds that certain behavior cannot be criminally punished. For instance, in Lawrence v. Texas, 539 U.S. 558 (2003), the Court held that states may not punish private consensual homosexual activity between adults. This obviously puts such conduct beyond the reach of the criminal law and thus the decision would apply retroactively.

Second, the Supreme Court has said that a "watershed" rule of criminal procedure would apply retroactively. Rarely, though, has the Supreme Court found any decision to constitute a watershed rule of criminal procedure.

In a recent case, Whorton v. Bocking, 127 S. Ct. 1173 (2007), the Supreme Court elaborated that it must be a " 'watershed rul[e] of criminal procedure' implicating the fundamental fairness and accuracy of the criminal proceeding."[33] The Court said that "[t]his exception is 'extremely narrow.' " Justice Alito, writing for a unanimous Court, stated: "In order to qualify as watershed, a new rule must meet two requirements. First, the rule must be necessary to

33. Whorton v. Bocking involved whether a major Supreme Court decision concerning the Confrontation Clause of the Sixth Amendment applies retroactively. Crawford v. Washington, 541 U.S. 36 (2004), held that a prosecutor could not use "testimonial" statements against a criminal defendant that had been made by a witness who was unavailable at trial on the grounds that they were reliable. In *Whorton*, the Court unanimously held that *Crawford* does not apply retroactively to those whose convictions were final before it was decided.

prevent an 'impermissibly large risk' of an inaccurate conviction. Second, the rule must 'alter our understanding of the bedrock procedural elements essential to the fairness of a proceeding.' "

In theory, it is possible that a criminal procedure decision would apply retroactively. Gideon v. Wainwright, 372 U.S. 335 (1963), which held that criminal defendants have a right to counsel at trial in any case where the sentence potentially includes imprisonment, is often mentioned as the classic example of a decision that would apply retroactively. Without counsel there is an impermissibly large risk of a wrongful conviction and *Gideon* altered the basic understanding "of the bedrock procedural elements essential to the fairness of a proceeding." But this is the exception; in reality, almost always, criminal procedure rulings, such as those in this book, apply only prospectively.

CHAPTER
2

SEARCHES AND SEIZURES

A. INTRODUCTION

The Fourth Amendment states:

> The right of the people to be secure in their persons, houses, papers, and effects against unreasonable searches and seizures, shall not be violated, and no warrants shall issue, but upon probable cause, supported by oath or affirmation, and particularly describing the place to be searched and the persons or things to be seized.

No technique of law enforcement is more important than the ability of the police to search for evidence and the ability of the police to seize what they find and to arrest individuals suspected of criminal activity. No aspect of criminal procedure has produced more Supreme Court decisions or arises more frequently in the lower courts.

In England and in the American colonies, general warrants were issued where entire neighborhoods could be searched. The Fourth Amendment was a reaction to such practices and embodies a requirement for individualized suspicion: Generally, a person can be searched only if there is reason to believe that person committed a crime or has evidence of one.

There are many interrelated aspects of the Fourth Amendment. There is the prohibition of "unreasonable searches and seizures." The Supreme Court often has emphasized that "its 'central requirement' is one of reasonableness." Illinois v. McArthur, 531 U.S. 326 (2001). Of course, the key is deciding what is reasonable. The Amendment also says that warrants must be based upon probable cause. But when is a warrant required? What is sufficient for probable cause?

All of this is the focus of this chapter. The next chapter considers the remedies for violation of the Fourth Amendment, especially the exclusionary rule. This chapter, in considering the requirements of the Fourth Amendment, considers a number of key issues. Section B looks at what a "search" is. Section C focuses on the requirement for "probable cause." The warrant requirement and the execution of search warrants is discussed in Section D. Next, Section E looks at the many exceptions to the warrant requirement. Section F examines seizures and arrests. Section G looks at "stop and frisk." Finally, Section H considers electronic eavesdropping.

A consistent theme throughout this material is how to balance the privacy interests protected by the Fourth Amendment with the government's need for effective law enforcement techniques. In reading the many cases below, it is important to consider whether the Court has struck the right balance between these competing interests.

In reading this material it is important to remember that the Fourth Amendment applies to actions by government officials (or those acting in concert with the government), but that like all of the Bill of Rights it does not apply to purely private conduct. Also, it is important to note that the Supreme Court has said that the initial words of the Fourth Amendment — "The right of the people to be secure" — means that it applies only within the United States. In United States v. Verdugo-Urquidez, 494 U.S. 259 (1990), the Court held that the Fourth Amendment did not apply to a search by United States law enforcement officials in Mexico. The Court said that the emphasis in the Amendment on protecting "the people" means that it does not apply even to actions of United States law enforcement personnel when operating in a foreign country.

B. WHAT IS A SEARCH?

In Olmstead v. United States, 277 U.S. 438 (1928), the Supreme Court held that electronic eavesdropping without a physical trespass was not a search within the meaning of the Fourth Amendment. This very limited view of a "search" was overruled and rejected in the landmark case of Katz v. United States.

KATZ v. UNITED STATES
389 U.S. 347 (1967)

Justice STEWART delivered the opinion of the Court.

The petitioner was convicted in the District Court for the Southern District of California under an eight-count indictment charging him with transmitting wagering information by telephone from Los Angeles to Miami and Boston in violation of a federal statute. At trial the Government was permitted, over the petitioner's objection, to introduce evidence of the petitioner's end of telephone conversations, overheard by FBI agents who had attached an electronic listening and recording device to the outside of the public telephone booth from which he had placed his calls. In affirming his conviction, the Court of Appeals rejected the contention that the recordings had been obtained in violation of the Fourth Amendment, because "[t]here was no physical entrance into the area occupied by, [the petitioner]."

We decline to adopt this formulation of the issues. In the first place the correct solution of Fourth Amendment problems is not necessarily promoted by incantation of the phrase "constitutionally protected area." Secondly, the Fourth Amendment cannot be translated into a general constitutional "right to privacy." That Amendment protects individual privacy against certain kinds of governmental intrusion, but its protections go further, and often have nothing to do with privacy at all. Other provisions of the Constitution protect personal privacy from other forms of governmental invasion. But the protection of a person's general right to privacy — his right to be let alone by other people — is, like the protection of his property and of his very life, left largely to the law of the individual States.

Because of the misleading way the issues have been formulated, the parties have attached great significance to the characterization of the telephone booth from which the petitioner placed his calls. The petitioner has strenuously argued that the booth was a "constitutionally protected area." The Government has maintained with equal vigor that it was not. But this effort to decide whether or not a given "area," viewed in the abstract, is "constitutionally protected" deflects attention from the problem presented by this case. For the Fourth Amendment protects people, not places. What a person knowingly exposes to the public, even in his own home or office, is not a subject of Fourth Amendment protection. But what he seeks to preserve as private, even in an area accessible to the public, may be constitutionally protected.

The Government stresses the fact that the telephone booth from which the petitioner made his calls was constructed partly of glass, so that he was as visible after he entered it as he would have been if he had remained outside. But what he sought to exclude when he entered the booth was not the intruding eye — it was the uninvited ear. He did not shed his right to do so simply because he made his calls from a place where he might be seen. No less than an individual in a business office, in a friend's apartment, or in a taxicab, a person in a telephone booth may rely upon the protection of the Fourth Amendment. One who occupies it, shuts the door behind him, and pays the toll that permits him to place a call is surely entitled to assume that the words he utters into the mouthpiece will not be broadcast to the world. To read the Constitution more narrowly is to ignore the vital role that the public telephone has come to play in private communication.

The Government contends, however, that the activities of its agents in this case should not be tested by Fourth Amendment requirements, for the surveillance technique they employed involved no physical penetration of the telephone booth from which the petitioner placed his calls. It is true that the absence of such penetration was at one time thought to foreclose further Fourth Amendment inquiry, Olmstead v. United States, fix for that Amendment was thought to limit only searches and seizures of tangible property. But "[t]he premise that property interests control the right of the Government to search and seize has been discredited." Thus, although a closely divided Court supposed in *Olmstead* that surveillance without any trespass and without the seizure of any material object fell outside the ambit of the Constitution, we have since departed from the narrow view on which that decision rested. Indeed, we have expressly held that the Fourth Amendment governs not only the seizure of tangible items, but extends as well to the recording of oral statements overheard without any "technical trespass under local property law." Once this much is acknowledged, and once it is recognized that the Fourth Amendment protects people — and not simply "areas" — against unreasonable searches and seizures it becomes clear that the reach of that Amendment cannot turn upon the presence or absence of a physical intrusion into any given enclosure.

We conclude that the underpinnings of *Olmstead* have been so eroded by our subsequent decisions that the "trespass" doctrine there enunciated can no longer be regarded as controlling. The Government's activities in electronically listening to and recording the petitioner's words violated the privacy upon which he justifiably relied while using the telephone booth and thus constituted a "search and seizure" within the meaning of the Fourth Amendment. The fact that the electronic device employed to achieve that end did not happen to penetrate the wall of the booth can have no constitutional significance.

The question remaining for decision, then, is whether the search and seizure conducted in this case complied with constitutional standards. In that regard, the Government's position is that its agents acted in an entirely defensible manner: They did not begin their electronic surveillance until investigation of the petitioner's activities had established a strong probability that he was using the telephone in question to transmit gambling information to persons in other States, in violation of federal law. Moreover, the surveillance was limited, both in scope and in duration, to the specific purpose of establishing the contents of the petitioner's unlawful telephonic communications. The agents confined their surveillance to the brief periods during which he used the telephone booth, and they took great care to overhear only the conversations of the petitioner himself.

Accepting this account of the Government's actions as acccurate, it is clear that this surveillance was so narrowly circumscribed that a duly authorized magistrate, properly notified of the need for such investigation, specifically informed of the basis on which it was to proceed, and clearly apprised of the precise intrusion it would entail, could constitutionally have authorized, with appropriate safeguards, the very limited search and seizure that the Government asserts in fact took place. Here, too, a similar judicial order could have accommodated "the legitimate needs of law enforcement" by authorizing the carefully limited use of electronic surveillance.

The Government urges that, because its agents relied upon the decision in *Olmstead* and [other cases], and because they did no more here than they might properly have done with prior judicial sanction, we should retroactively validate their conduct. That we cannot do. It is apparent that the agents in this case acted with restraint. Yet the inescapable fact is that this restraint was imposed by the agents themselves, not by a judicial officer. They were not required, before commencing the search, to present their estimate of probable cause for detached scrutiny by a neutral magistrate. They were not compelled, during the conduct of the search itself, to observe precise limits established in advance by a specific court order. Nor were they directed, after the search had been completed, to notify the authorizing magistrate in detail of all that had been seized. In the absence of such safeguards, this Court has never sustained a search upon the sole ground that officers reasonably expected to find evidence of a particular crime and voluntarily confined their activities to the least intrusive means consistent with that end. Searches conducted without warrants have been held unlawful "notwithstanding facts unquestionably showing probable cause," for the Constitution requires "that the deliberate, impartial judgment of a judicial officer . . . be interposed between the citizen and the police." Over and again this Court has emphasized that the mandate of the [Fourth] Amendment requires adherence to judicial processes, and that searches conducted outside the judicial process, without prior approval by judge or magistrate, are per se unreasonable under the Fourth Amendment—subject only to a few specifically established and well-delineated exceptions.

It is difficult to imagine how any of those exceptions could ever apply to the sort of search and seizure involved in this case. Even electronic surveillance substantially contemporaneous with an individual's arrest could hardly be deemed an "incident" of that arrest. Nor could the use of electronic surveillance without prior autorization be justified on grounds of "hot pursuit." And, of course, the very nature of electronic surveillance precludes its use pursuant to the suspect's consent.

These considerations do not vanish when the search in question is transferred from the setting of a home, an office, or a hotel room to that of a telephone booth. Wherever a man may be, he is entitled to know that he will remain free from unreasonable searches and seizures. The government agents here ignored "the procedure of antecedent justification . . . that is central to the Fourth Amendment," a procedure that we hold to be a constitutional precondition of the kind of electronic surveillance involved in this case. Because the surveillance here failed to meet that condition, and because it led to the petitioner's conviction, the judgment must be reversed.

Justice Douglas, with whom Justice Brennan joins, concurring.

While I join the opinion of the Court, I feel compelled to reply to the separate concurring opinion of my Brother White, which I view as a wholly unwarranted green light for the Executive Branch to resort to electronic eavesdropping without a warrant in cases which the Executive Branch itself labels "national security" matters.

Neither the President nor the Attorney General is a magistrate. In matters where they believe national security may be involved they are not detached, disinterested, and neutral as a court or magistrate must be. Under the separation of powers created by the Constitution, the Executive Branch is not supposed to be neutral and disinterested. Rather it should vigorously investigate and prevent breaches of national security and prosecute those who violate the pertinent federal laws. The President and Attorney General are properly interested parties, cast in the role of adversary, in national security cases. They may even be the intended victims of subversive action. Since spies and saboteurs are as entitled to the protection of the Fourth Amendment as suspected gamblers like petitioner, I cannot agree that where spies and saboteurs are involved adequate protection of Fourth Amendment rights is assured when the President and Attorney General assume both the position of adversary-and-prosecutor and disinterested, neutral magistrate.

Justice Harlan, concurring.

I join the opinion of the Court, which I read to hold only (a) that an enclosed telephone booth is an area where, like a home, and unlike a field, a person has a constitutionally protected reasonable expectation of privacy; (b) that electronic as well as physical intrusion into a place that is in this sense private may constitute a violation of the Fourth Amendment; and (c) that the invasion of a constitutionally protected area by federal authorities is, as the Court has long held, presumptively unreasonable in the absence of a search warrant.

As the Court's opinion states, "the Fourth Amendment protects people, not places." The question, however, is what protection it affords to those people. Generally, as here, the answer to that question requires reference to a "place." My understanding of the rule that has emerged from prior decisions is that there is a twofold requirement, first that a person have exhibited an actual (subjective) expectation of privacy and, second, that the expectation be one that society is prepared to recognize as "reasonable." Thus a man's home is, for most purposes, a place where he expects privacy, but objects, activities, or statements that he exposes to the "plain view" of outsiders are not "protected" because no intention to keep them to himself has been exhibited. On the other hand, conversations in the open would not be protected against being overheard, for the expectation of privacy under the circumstances would be unreasonable.

The critical fact in this case is that "[o]ne who occupies it [a telephone booth], shuts the door behind him, and pays the toll that permits him to place a call is surely entitled to assume" that his conversation is not being intercepted. The point is not that the booth is "accessible to the public" at other times, but that it is a temporarily private place whose momentary occupants' expectations of freedom from intrusion are recognized as reasonable.

Finally, I do not read the Court's opinion to declare that no interception of a conversation one-half of which occurs in a public telephone booth can be reasonable in the absence of a warrant. As elsewhere under the Fourth Amendment, warrants are the general rule, to which the legitimate needs of law enforcement may demand specific exceptions. It will be time enough to consider any such exceptions when an appropriate occasion presents itself, and I agree with the Court that this is not one.

Justice WHITE, concurring.

I agree that the official surveillance of petitioner's telephone conversations in a public booth must be subjected to the test of reasonableness under the Fourth Amendment and that on the record now before us the particular surveillance undertaken was unreasonable absent a warrant properly authorizing it. This application of the Fourth Amendment need not interfere with legitimate needs of law enforcement.

In joining the Court's opinion, I note the Court's acknowledgment that there are circumstance in which it is reasonable to search without a warrant. Wiretapping to protect the security of the Nation has been authorized by successive Presidents. The present Administration would apparently save national security cases from restrictions against wiretapping. We should not require the warrant procedure and the magistrate's judgment if the President of the United States or his chief legal officer, the Attorney General, has considered the requirements of national security and authorized electronic surveillance as reasonable.

Justice BLACK, dissenting.

If I could agree with the Court that eavesdropping carried on by electronic means (equivalent to wiretapping) constitutes a "search" or "seizure," I would be happy to join the Court's opinion.

My basic objection is twofold: (1) I do not believe that the words of the Amendment will bear the meaning given them by today's decision, and (2) I do not believe that it is the proper role of this Court to rewrite the Amendment in order "to bring it into harmony with the times" and thus reach a result that many people believe to be desirable.

While I realize that an argument based on the meaning of words lacks the scope, and no doubt the appeal, of broad policy discussions and philosophical discourses on such nebulous subjects as privacy, for me the language of the

Amendment is the crucial place to look in construing a written document such as our Constitution.

The first clause protects "persons, houses, papers, and effects, against unreasonable searches and seizures." These words connote the idea of tangible things with size, form, and weight, things capable of being searched, seized, or both. The second clause of the Amendment still further establishes its Framers' purpose to limit its protection to tangible things by providing that no warrants shall issue but those "particularly describing the place to be searched, and the persons or things to be seized." A conversation overheard by eavesdropping, whether by plain snooping or wiretapping, is not tangible and, under the normally accepted meanings of the words, can neither be searched nor seized. In addition the language of the second clause indicates that the Amendment refers not only to something tangible so it can be seized but to something already in existence so it can be described. Yet the Court's interpretation would have the Amendment apply to overhearing future conversations which by their very nature are nonexistent until they take place. How can one "describe" a future conversation, and, if one cannot, how can a magistrate issue a warrant to eavesdrop one in the future?

Tapping telephone wires, of course, was an unknown possibility at the time the Fourth Amendment was adopted. But eavesdropping (and wiretapping is nothing more than eavesdropping by telephone) was "an ancient practice which at common law was condemned as a nuisance." There can be no doubt that the Framers were aware of this practice, and if they had desired to outlaw or restrict the use of evidence obtained by eavesdropping, I believe that they would have used the appropriate language to do so in the Fourth Amendment. They certainly would not have left such a task to the ingenuity of language-stretching judges.

The crucial question after *Katz* is in defining when a person has a "reasonable expectation of privacy." On the one hand, the test has the advantage that, as the Court says, it focuses on persons and not property; it puts a central aspect of the Fourth Amendment, protecting privacy, at the core of analysis as to whether there has been a search. On other hand, "reasonable expectation of privacy" is inherently vague and there is the concern that the government could undermine it just by making clear that people should not expect privacy in certain circumstances.

The Court has considered the application of this test in a number of specific contexts. For example, the Court has considered whether the following violate a reasonable expectation of privacy: searches in open fields; aerial searches; use of thermal imaging devices directed at homes; searches of a person's trash; observation and monitoring of public behavior; and use of dogs to sniff for contraband. Each is discussed below. These are important areas where the Court has applied the "reasonable expectation of privacy" standard, but these are by no means the only areas where the issue arises. In considering these cases, it is important to consider whether they follow a sensible approach to determining what is a search and to effectuating the Fourth Amendment, or whether they are an inconsistent body of decisions that shows the problems with a vague standard like "reasonable expectation of privacy."

1. Open Fields

A half century before *Katz*, in Hester v. United States, 265 U.S. 57 (1924), the Supreme Court held that "[t]he special protection accorded by the Fourth Amendment to the person in their 'persons, houses, papers, and effects' is not extended to the open fields. The distinction between the latter and the house is as old as the common law." A distinction thus developed between police actions in open fields, where the Fourth Amendment does not apply, and searches of a person's home and the areas immediately adjacent to it (the "curtilage"), where the Fourth Amendment applies. Oliver v. United States is an important case, decided after *Katz*, which reaffirms the "open fields" doctrine.

OLIVER v. UNITED STATES
466 U.S. 170 (1984)

Justice POWELL delivered the opinion of the Court.

The "open fields" doctrine, first enunciated by this Court in Hester v. United States (1924), permits police officers to enter and search a field without a warrant. We granted certiorari in these cases to clarify confusion that has arisen as to the continued vitality of the doctrine.

I

Acting on reports that marihuana was being raised on the farm of petitioner Oliver, two narcotics agents of the Kentucky State Police went to the farm to investigate.[1] Arriving at the farm, they drove past petitioner's house to a locked gate with a "No Trespassing" sign. A footpath led around one side of the gate. The agents walked around the gate and along the road for several hundred yards, passing a barn and a parked camper. At that point, someone standing in front of the camper shouted: "No hunting is allowed, come back up here." The officers shouted back that they were Kentucky State Police officers, but found no one when they returned to the camper. The officers resumed their investigation of the farm and found a field of marihuana over a mile from petitioner's home.

Petitioner was arrested and indicted for "manufactur[ing]" a "controlled substance." After a pretrial hearing, the District Court suppressed evidence of the discovery of the marihuana field. Applying Katz v. United States (1967), the court found that petitioner had a reasonable expectation that the field would remain private because petitioner "had done all that could be expected of him to assert his privacy in the area of farm that was searched." He had posted "No Trespassing" signs at regular intervals and had locked the gate at the entrance to the center of the farm. Further, the court noted that the field itself is highly secluded: it is bounded on all sides by woods, fences, and embankments and

---

1. It is conceded that the police did not have a warrant authorizing the search, that there was no probable cause for the search, and that no exception to the warrant requirement is applicable. [Footnote by the Court.]

cannot be seen from any point of public access. The court concluded that this was not an "open" field that invited casual intrusion.

The Court of Appeals for the Sixth Circuit, sitting en banc, reversed the District Court. The court concluded that *Katz*, upon which the District Court relied, had not impaired the vitality of the open fields doctrine of *Hester*.

II

The rule announced in Hester v. United States was founded upon the explicit language of the Fourth Amendment. That Amendment indicates with some precision the places and things encompassed by its protections. As Justice Holmes explained for the Court in his characteristically laconic style: "[T]he special protection accorded by the Fourth Amendment to the people in their 'persons, houses, papers, and effects,' is not extended to the open fields."

Nor are the open fields "effects" within the meaning of the Fourth Amendment. In this respect, it is suggestive that James Madison's proposed draft of what became the Fourth Amendment preserves "[t]he rights of the people to be secured in their persons, their houses, their papers, and their other property, from all unreasonable searches and seizures. . . ." Although Congress' revisions of Madison's proposal broadened the scope of the Amendment in some respects, the term "effects" is less inclusive than "property" and cannot be said to encompass open fields. We conclude, as did the Court in deciding Hester v. United States, that the government's intrusion upon the open fields is not one of those "unreasonable searches" proscribed by the text of the Fourth Amendment.

III

This interpretation of the Fourth Amendment's language is consistent with the understanding of the right to privacy expressed in our Fourth Amendment jurisprudence. Since Katz v. United States (1967), the touchstone of Amendment analysis has been the question whether a person has a "constitutionally protected reasonable expectation of privacy." The Amendment does not protect the merely subjective expectation of privacy, but only those "expectation[s] that society is prepared to recognize as 'reasonable.'"

No single factor determines whether an individual legitimately may claim under the Fourth Amendment that a place should be free of government intrusion not authorized by warrant. In assessing the degree to which a search infringes upon individual privacy, the Court has given weight to such factors as the intention of the Framers of the Fourth Amendment, the uses to which the individual has put a location, and our societal understanding that certain areas deserve the most scrupulous protection from government invasion. These factors are equally relevant to determining whether the government's intrusion upon open fields without a warrant or probable cause violates reasonable expectations of privacy and is therefore a search proscribed by the Amendment.

In this light, the rule of Hester v. United States that we reaffirm today, may be understood as providing that an individual may not legitimately demand privacy for activities conducted out of doors in fields, except in the area immediately surrounding the home. This rule is true to the conception of the right to privacy embodied in the Fourth Amendment. The Amendment reflects the recognition of the Framers that certain enclaves should be free from arbitrary government interference. For example, the Court since the enactment of the Fourth Amendment has stressed "the overriding respect for the sanctity of the home that has been embedded in our traditions since the origins of the Republic."

In contrast, open fields do not provide the setting for those intimate activities that the Amendment is intended to shelter from government interference or surveillance. There is no societal interest in protecting the privacy of those activities, such as the cultivation of crops, that occur in open fields. Moreover, as a practical matter these lands usually are accessible to the public and the police in ways that a home, an office, or commercial structure would not be. It is not generally true that fences or "No Trespassing" signs effectively bar the public from viewing open fields in rural areas. [P]etitioner Oliver concede[s] that the public and police lawfully may survey lands from the air. For these reasons, the asserted expectation of privacy in open fields is not an expectation that "society recognizes as reasonable."

Nor is the government's intrusion upon an open field a "search" in the constitutional sense because that intrusion is a trespass at common law. The existence of a property right is but one element in determining whether expectations of privacy are legitimate. "The premise that property interests control the right of the Government to search and seize has been discredited." "[E]ven a property interest in premises may not be sufficient to establish a legitimate expectation of privacy with respect to particular items located on the premises or activity conducted thereon."

The common law may guide consideration of what areas are protected by the Fourth Amendment by defining areas whose invasion by others is wrongful. The law of trespass, however, forbids intrusions upon land that the Fourth Amendment would not proscribe. For trespass law extends to instances where the exercise of the right to exclude vindicates no legitimate privacy interest. Thus, in the case of open fields, the general rights of property protected by the common law of trespass have little or no relevance to the applicability of the Fourth Amendment.

Justice MARSHALL, with whom Justice BRENNAN and Justice STEVENS join, dissenting.

[P]olice officers, ignoring clearly visible "No Trespassing" signs, entered upon private land in search of evidence of a crime. At a spot that could not be seen from any vantage point accessible to the public, the police discovered contraband, which was subsequently used to incriminate the owner of the land. In neither case did the police have a warrant authorizing their activities.

The Court holds that police conduct of this sort does not constitute an "unreasonable search" within the meaning of the Fourth Amendment. The Court reaches that startling conclusion by two independent analytical routes. First, the Court argues that, because the Fourth Amendment by its terms renders people secure in their "persons, houses, papers, and effects," it is inapplicable to trespasses upon land not lying within the curtilage of a dwelling. Second, the Court contends that "an individual may not legitimately demand privacy for activities conducted out of doors in fields, except in the area immediately surrounding the home." Because I cannot agree with either of these propositions, I dissent.

I

The first ground on which the Court rests its decision is that the Fourth Amendment "indicates with some precision the places and things encompassed by its protections," and that real property is not included in the list of protected spaces and possessions. This line of argument has several flaws. Most obviously, it is inconsistent with the results of many of our previous decisions, none of which the Court purports to overrule. For example, neither a public telephone booth nor a conversation conducted therein can fairly be described as a person, house, paper, or effect; yet we have held that the Fourth Amendment forbids the police without a warrant to eavesdrop on such a conversation. Nor can it plausibly be argued that an office or commercial establishment is covered by the plain language of the Amendment; yet we have held that such premises are entitled to constitutional protection if they are marked in a fashion that alerts the public to the fact that they are private.

Indeed, the Court's reading of the plain language of the Fourth Amendment is incapable of explaining even its own holding in this case. The Court rules that the curtilage, a zone of real property surrounding a dwelling, is entitled to constitutional protection. We are not told, however, whether the curtilage is a "house" or an "effect" — or why, if the curtilage can be incorporated into the list of things and spaces shielded by the Amendment, a field cannot.

The Court's inability to reconcile its parsimonious reading of the phrase "persons, houses, papers, and effects" with our prior decisions or even its own holding is a symptom of a more fundamental infirmity in the Court's reasoning. The Fourth Amendment, like the other central provisions of the Bill of Rights that loom large in our modern jurisprudence, was designed, not to prescribe with "precision" permissible and impermissible activities, but to identify a fundamental human liberty that should be shielded forever from government intrusion. The liberty shielded by the Fourth Amendment, as we have often acknowledged, is freedom "from unreasonable government intrusions into . . . legitimate expectations of privacy." That freedom would be incompletely protected if only government conduct that impinged upon a person, house, paper, or effect were subject to constitutional scrutiny. Accordingly, we have repudiated the proposition that the Fourth Amendment applies only to a limited set of locales or kinds of property.

II

The second ground for the Court's decision is its contention that any interest a landowner might have in the privacy of his woods and fields is not one that "society is prepared to recognize as 'reasonable.'" But the Court's conclusion cannot withstand scrutiny.

As the Court acknowledges, we have traditionally looked to a variety of factors in determining whether an expectation of privacy asserted in a physical space is "reasonable." Though those factors do not lend themselves to precise taxonomy, they may be roughly grouped into three categories. First, we consider whether the expectation at issue is rooted in entitlements defined by positive law. Second, we consider the nature of the uses to which spaces of the sort in question can be put. Third, we consider whether the person claiming a privacy interest manifested that interest to the public in a way that most people would understand and respect. When the expectations of privacy asserted by petitioner Oliver [is] examined through these lenses, it becomes clear that those expectations are entitled to constitutional protection.

We have frequently acknowledged that privacy interests are not coterminous with property rights. However, because "property rights reflect society's explicit recognition of a person's authority to act as he wishes in certain areas, [they] should be considered in determining whether an individual's expectations of privacy are reasonable." Indeed, the Court has suggested that, insofar as "[o]ne of the main rights attaching to property is the right to exclude others, . . . one who owns or lawfully possesses or controls property will in all likelihood have a legitimate expectation of privacy by virtue of this right to exclude."

It is undisputed that Oliver owned the land into which the police intruded. That fact alone provides considerable support for their assertion of legitimate privacy interests in their woods and fields. But even more telling is the nature of the sanctions that Oliver could invoke, under local law, for violation of [his] property rights. In Kentucky, a knowing entry upon fenced or otherwise enclosed land, or upon unenclosed land conspicuously posted with signs excluding the public, constitutes criminal trespass. Thus, positive law not only recognizes the legitimacy of Oliver's fix insistence that strangers keep off [his] land, but subjects those who refuse to respect their wishes to the most severe of penalties — criminal liability. Under these circumstances, it is hard to credit the Court's assertion that Oliver's expectations of privacy were not of a sort that society is prepared to recognize as reasonable.

The uses to which a place is put are highly relevant to the assessment of a privacy interest asserted therein. If, in light of our shared sensibilities, those activities are of a kind in which people should be able to engage without fear of intrusion by private persons or government officials, we extend the protection of the Fourth Amendment to the space in question, even in the absence of any entitlement derived from positive law.

Privately owned woods and fields that are not exposed to public view regularly are employed in a variety of ways that society acknowledges deserve privacy. Many landowners like to take solitary walks on their property, confident that they will not be confronted in their rambles by strangers or policemen. Others conduct agricultural businesses on their property. Some landowners use their secluded spaces to meet lovers, others to gather together with fellow worshippers, still others to engage in sustained creative endeavor. Private land is sometimes used as a refuge for wildlife, where flora and fauna are protected from human intervention of any kind. Our respect for the freedom of landowners to use their posted "open fields" in ways such as these partially explains the seriousness with which the positive law regards deliberate invasions of such spaces, and substantially reinforces the landowners' contention that their expectations of privacy are "reasonable."

Whether a person "took normal precautions to maintain his privacy" in a given space affects whether his interest is one protected by the Fourth Amendment. The reason why such precautions are relevant is that we do not insist that a person who has a right to exclude others exercise that right. A claim to privacy is therefore strengthened by the fact that the claimant somehow manifested to other people his desire that they keep their distance.

Certain spaces are so presumptively private that signals of this sort are unnecessary; a homeowner need not post a "Do Not Enter" sign on his door in order to deny entrance to uninvited guests. Privacy interests in other spaces are more ambiguous, and the taking of precautions is consequently more important; placing a lock on one's footlocker strengthens one's claim that an examination of its contents is impermissible. Still other spaces are, by positive law and social convention, presumed accessible to members of the public unless the owner manifests his intention to exclude them.

Undeveloped land falls into the last-mentioned category. If a person has not marked the boundaries of his fields or woods in a way that informs passersby that they are not welcome, he cannot object if members of the public enter onto the property. There is no reason why he should have any greater rights as against government officials. Accordingly, we have held that an official may, without a warrant, enter private land from which the public is not excluded and make observations from that vantage point.

A very different case is presented when the owner of undeveloped land has taken precautions to exclude the public. As indicated above, a deliberate entry by a private citizen onto private property marked with "No Trespassing" signs will expose him to criminal liability. I see no reason why a government official should not be obliged to respect such unequivocal and universally understood manifestations of a landowner's desire for privacy.

In sum, examination of the three principal criteria we have traditionally used for assessing the reasonableness of a person's expectation that a given space would remain private indicates that interests of the sort asserted by Oliver are entitled to constitutional protection. An owner's right to insist that others stay off his posted land is firmly grounded in positive law. Many of the uses to which such land may be put deserve privacy. And, by marking the boundaries of the land with warnings that the public should not intrude, the owner has dispelled any ambiguity as to his desires.

III

A clear, easily administrable rule emerges from the analysis set forth above: Private land marked in a fashion sufficient to render entry thereon a criminal trespass under the law of the State in which the land lies is protected by the Fourth Amendment's proscription of unreasonable searches and seizures. One of the advantages of the foregoing rule is that it draws upon a doctrine already familiar to both citizens and government officials.

By contrast, the doctrine announced by the Court today is incapable of determinate application. Police officers, making warrantless entries upon private land, will be obliged in the future to make on-the-spot judgments as to how far the curtilage extends, and to stay outside that zone. In addition, we may expect to see a spate of litigation over the question of how much improvement is necessary to remove private land from the category of "unoccupied or undeveloped area" to which the "open fields exception" is now deemed applicable.

The Court's holding not only ill serves the need to make constitutional doctrine "workable for application by rank-and-file, trained police officers," it withdraws the shield of the Fourth Amendment from privacy interests that clearly deserve protection. By exempting from the coverage of the Amendment large areas of private land, the Court opens the way to investigative activities we would all find repugnant.

The Fourth Amendment, properly construed, embodies and gives effect to our collective sense of the degree to which men and women, in civilized society, are entitled "to be let alone" by their governments. The Court's opinion bespeaks and will help to promote an impoverished vision of that fundamental right.

The Court in *Oliver* says that the Fourth Amendment applies if police search a person's home or the "curtilage" immediately adjacent to the home, but not if the police are searching in an open field. The distinction between curtilage and open fields is thus crucial in determining whether the Fourth Amendment applies at all. In United States v. Dunn, the Court attempted to clarify this distinction.

UNITED STATES v. DUNN
480 U.S. 294 (1987)

Justice WHITE delivered the opinion of the Court.

We granted the Government's petition for certiorari to decide whether the area near a barn, located approximately 50 yards from a fence surrounding a ranch house, is, for Fourth Amendment purposes, within the curtilage of the house. We conclude that the barn and the area around it lay outside the curtilage of the house.

I

Respondent Ronald Dale Dunn and a codefendant, Robert Lyle Carpenter, were convicted by a jury of conspiring to manufacture phenylacetone and amphetamine, and to possess amphetamine with intent to distribute, in violation of 21 U.S.C. § 846. Respondent was also convicted of manufacturing these two controlled substances and possessing amphetamine with intent to distribute. The events giving rise to respondent's apprehension and conviction began in 1980 when agents from the Drug Enforcement Administration (DEA) discovered that Carpenter had purchased large quantities of chemicals and equipment used in the manufacture of amphetamine and phenylacetone. DEA agents obtained warrants from a Texas state judge authorizing installation of miniature electronic transmitter tracking devices, or "beepers," in an electric hot plate stirrer, a drum of acetic anhydride, and a container holding phenylacetic acid, a precursor to phenylacetone. All of these items had been ordered by Carpenter. On September 3, 1980, Carpenter took possession of the electric hot plate stirrer, but the agents lost the signal from the "beeper" a few days later. The agents were able to track the "beeper" in the container of chemicals, however, from October 27, 1980, until November 5, 1980, on which date Carpenter's pickup truck, which was carrying the container, arrived at respondent's ranch. Aerial photographs of the ranch property showed Carpenter's truck backed up to a barn behind the ranch house. The agents also began receiving transmission signals from the "beeper" in the hot plate stirrer that they had lost in early September and determined that the stirrer was on respondent's ranch property.

Respondent's ranch comprised approximately 198 acres and was completely encircled by a perimeter fence. The property also contained several interior fences, constructed mainly of posts and multiple strands of barbed wire. The ranch residence was situated 1/2 mile from a public road. A fence encircled the residence and a nearby small greenhouse. Two barns were located approximately 50 yards from this fence. The front of the larger of the two barns was enclosed by a wooden fence and had an open overhang. Locked, waist-high gates barred entry into the barn proper, and netting material stretched from the ceiling to the top of the wooden gates.

On the evening of November 5, 1980, law enforcement officials made a warrantless entry onto respondent's ranch property. A DEA agent accompanied by an officer from the Houston Police Department crossed over the perimeter fence and one interior fence. Standing approximately midway between the residence and the barns, the DEA agent smelled what he believed to be phenylacetic acid, the odor coming from the direction of the barns. The officers approached the smaller of the barns — crossing over a barbed wire fence — and, looking into the barn, observed only empty boxes. The officers then proceeded to the larger barn, crossing another barbed wire fence as well as a wooden fence that enclosed the front portion of the barn. The officers walked under the barn's overhang to the locked wooden gates and, shining a flashlight through the netting on top of the gates, peered into the barn. They observed what the DEA agent thought to be a phenylacetone laboratory. The officers did not enter the barn. At this point the officers departed from respondent's property, but entered it twice more on November 6 to confirm the presence of the phenylacetone laboratory.

On November 6, 1980, at 8:30 P.M., a Federal Magistrate issued a warrant authorizing a search of respondent's ranch. DEA agents and state law enforcement officials executed the warrant on November 8, 1980. The officers arrested respondent and seized chemicals and equipment, as well as bags of amphetamines they discovered in a closet in the ranch house.

II

The curtilage concept originated at common law to extend to the area immediately surrounding a dwelling house the same protection under the law of burglary as was afforded the house itself. The concept plays a part, however, in interpreting the reach of the Fourth Amendment. Hester v. United States (1924), held that the Fourth Amendment's protection accorded "persons, houses, papers, and effects" did not extend to the open fields, the Court observing that the distinction between a person's house and open fields "is as old as the common law."

[W]e believe that curtilage questions should be resolved with particular reference to four factors: the proximity of the area claimed to be curtilage to the home, whether the area is included within an enclosure surrounding the home, the nature of the uses to which the area is put, and the steps taken by the resident to protect the area from observation by people passing by. We do not suggest that combining these factors produces a finely tuned formula that, when mechanically applied, yields a "correct" answer to all extent-of-curtilage questions. Rather, these factors are useful analytical tools only to the degree that, in any given case, they bear upon the centrally relevant consideration — whether the area in question is so intimately tied to the home itself that it should be placed under the home's "umbrella" of Fourth Amendment protection. Applying these factors to respondent's barn and to the area immediately surrounding it, we have little difficulty in concluding that this area lay outside the curtilage of the ranch house.

First. The record discloses that the barn was located 50 yards from the fence surrounding the house and 60 yards from the house itself. Standing in isolation, this substantial distance supports no inference that the barn should be treated as an adjunct of the house.

Second. It is also significant that respondent's barn did not lie within the area surrounding the house that was enclosed by a fence. Viewing the physical layout of respondent's ranch in its entirety, it is plain that the fence surrounding the residence serves to demark a specific area of land immediately adjacent to the house that is readily identifiable as part and parcel of the house. Conversely, the barn — the front portion itself enclosed by a fence — and the area immediately surrounding it, stands out as a distinct portion of respondent's ranch, quite separate from the residence.

Third. It is especially significant that the law enforcement officials possessed objective data indicating that the barn was not being used for intimate activities of the home.

Fourth. Respondent did little to protect the barn area from observation by those standing in the open fields. Nothing in the record suggests that the various interior fences on respondent's property had any function other than that of the typical ranch fence; the fences were designed and constructed to corral livestock, not to prevent persons from observing what lay inside the enclosed areas.

Justice BRENNAN, with whom Justice MARSHALL joins, dissenting.

The Government agents' intrusions upon Ronald Dunn's privacy and property violated the Fourth Amendment for two reasons. First, the barnyard invaded by the agents lay within the protected curtilage of Dunn's farmhouse. Second, the agents infringed upon Dunn's reasonable expectation of privacy in the barn and its contents. Our society is not so exclusively urban that it is unable to perceive or unwilling to preserve the expectation of farmers and ranchers that barns and their contents are protected from (literally) unwarranted government intrusion.

Thus, case law demonstrates that a barn is an integral part of a farm home and therefore lies within the curtilage. The Court's opinion provides no justification for its indifference to the weight of state and federal precedent.

First, the distance between the house and the barn does not militate against the barn or barnyard's presence in the curtilage. Many of the cases cited involve a barn separated from a residence by a distance in excess of 60 yards. Second, the cases make evident that the configuration of fences is not determinative of the status of an outbuilding. Here, where the barn was connected to the house by a "well walked" and a "well driven" and was clustered with the farmhouse and other outbuildings in a clearing surrounded by woods, the presence of intervening fences fades into irrelevance.

The third factor in the test — the nature of the uses to which the area is put — has been badly misunderstood and misapplied by the Court. The Court reasons that, because the barn and barnyard were not actually in domestic use, they were not within the curtilage. This reveals a misunderstanding of the level of generality at which the constitutional inquiry must proceed and is flatly inconsistent with the Court's analysis in *Oliver*.

Finally, neither the smell of the chemicals nor the sound of the motor running would remove the protection of the Fourth Amendment from an otherwise protected structure. A barn, like a home, may simultaneously be put to domestic and nondomestic uses, even the manufacture of drugs. Dual use does not strip a home or any building within the curtilage of Fourth Amendment protection. What the evidence cited by the Court might suggest is that the DEA agents had probable cause to enter the barn or barnyard before they made any unconstitutional intrusion. If so — and I do not concede it — they should have obtained a warrant.

With regard to the fourth factor of the curtilage test, I find astounding the Court's conclusion that "[r]espondent did little to protect the barn area from observation by those standing in the open fields." Initially, I note that the fenced area immediately adjacent to the barn in this case is not part of the open fields, but is instead part of the curtilage and an area in which Dunn had a reasonable expectation of privacy. Second, Dunn, in fact, took elaborate measures to ensure his privacy. He locked his driveway, fenced in his barn, and covered its open end with a locked gate and fishnetting. The Fourth Amendment does not require the posting of a 24-hour guard to preserve an expectation of privacy.

Even if Dunn's barn were not within the curtilage of his farmhouse, his reasonable expectation of privacy in the barnyard would bring the Fourth Amendment into play. It is well established that the Fourth Amendment protects a privacy interest in commercial premises.

The Fourth Amendment prohibits police activity which, if left unrestricted, would jeopardize individuals' sense of security or would too heavily burden those who wished to guard their privacy. In this case, in order to look inside respondent's barn, the DEA agents traveled a one-half mile off a public road over respondent's fenced-in property, crossed over three additional wooden and barbed wire fences, stepped under the eaves of the barn, and then used a flashlight to peer through otherwise opaque fishnetting. For the police habitually to engage in such surveillance — without a warrant — is constitutionally intolerable. Because I believe that farmers' and ranchers' expectations of privacy in their barns and other outbuildings are expectations society would regard as reasonable, and because I believe that sanctioning the police behavior at issue here does violence to the purpose and promise of the Fourth Amendment, I dissent.

2. Aerial Searches

What if the police observe behavior in a person's home and curtilage by use of low flying airplanes? Does this violate a person's reasonable expectation of privacy? The Court has found that such police conduct is not a search within the meaning of the Fourth Amendment and thus need not comply with the Fourth Amendment's requirements.

CALIFORNIA v. CIRAOLO
476 U.S. 207 (1986)

Chief Justice BURGER delivered the opinion of the Court.

We granted certiorari to determine whether the Fourth Amendment is violated by aerial observation without a warrant from an altitude of 1,000 feet of a fenced-in backyard within the curtilage of a home.

I

On September 2, 1982, Santa Clara Police received an anonymous telephone tip that marijuana was growing in respondent's backyard. Police were unable to observe the contents of respondent's yard from ground level because of a 6-foot outer fence and a 10-foot inner fence completely enclosing the yard. Later that day, Officer Shutz, who was assigned to investigate, secured a private plane and flew over respondent's house at an altitude of 1,000 feet, within navigable airspace; he was accompanied by Officer Rodriguez. Both officers were trained in marijuana identification. From the overflight, the officers readily identified marijuana plants 8 feet to 10 feet in height growing in a 15- by 25-foot plot in respondent's yard; they photographed the area with a standard 35mm camera.

On September 8, 1982, Officer Shutz obtained a search warrant on the basis of an affidavit describing the anonymous tip and their observations; a photograph depicting respondent's house, the backyard, and neighboring homes was attached to the affidavit as an exhibit. The warrant was executed the next day and 73 plants were seized; it is not disputed that these were marijuana.

II

The touchstone of Fourth Amendment analysis is whether a person has a "constitutionally protected reasonable expectation of privacy." Katz v. United States (1967). *Katz* posits a two-part inquiry: first, has the individual manifested a subjective expectation of privacy in the object of the challenged search? Second, is society willing to recognize that expectation as reasonable?

Clearly — and understandably — respondent has met the test of manifesting his own subjective intent and desire to maintain privacy as to his unlawful agricultural pursuits. However, we need not address that issue, for the State has not challenged the finding of the California Court of Appeal that respondent had such an expectation. It can reasonably be assumed that the 10-foot fence was placed to conceal the marijuana crop from at least street-level views. So far as the normal sidewalk traffic was concerned, this fence served that purpose, because respondent "took normal precautions to maintain his privacy."

Yet a 10-foot fence might not shield these plants from the eyes of a citizen or a policeman perched on the top of a truck or a two-level bus. Whether respondent therefore manifested a subjective expectation of privacy from all observations of his backyard, or whether instead he manifested merely a hope that no one would observe his unlawful gardening pursuits, is not entirely clear in these circumstances. Respondent appears to challenge the authority of government to observe his activity from any vantage point or place if the viewing is motivated by a law enforcement purpose, and not the result of a casual, accidental observation.

We turn, therefore, to the second inquiry under *Katz*, i.e., whether that expectation is reasonable. In pursuing this inquiry, we must keep in mind that "[t]he test of legitimacy is not whether the individual chooses to conceal assertedly 'private' activity," but instead "whether the government's intrusion infringes upon the personal and societal values protected by the Fourth Amendment." Respondent argues that because his yard was in the curtilage of his home, no governmental aerial observation is permissible under the Fourth Amendment without a warrant.

The history and genesis of the curtilage doctrine are instructive. "At common law, the curtilage is the area to which extends the intimate activity associated with the 'sanctity of a man's home and the privacies of life.'" The protection afforded the curtilage is essentially a protection of families and personal privacy in an area intimately linked to the home, both physically and psychologically, where privacy expectations are most heightened. The claimed area here was immediately adjacent to a suburban home, surrounded by high double fences. This close nexus to the home would appear to encompass this small area within the curtilage. Accepting, as the State does, that this yard and its crop fall within the curtilage, the question remains whether naked-eye observation of the curtilage by police from an aircraft lawfully operating at an altitude of 1,000 feet violates an expectation of privacy that is reasonable.

That the area is within the curtilage does not itself bar all police observation. The Fourth Amendment protection of the home has never been extended to require law enforcement officers to shield their eyes when passing by a home on public thoroughfares. Nor does the mere fact that an individual has taken measures to restrict some views of his activities preclude an officer's observations from a public vantage point where he has a right to be and which renders the activities clearly visible. "What a person knowingly exposes to the public, even in his own home or office, is not a subject of Fourth Amendment protection."

The observations by Officers Shutz and Rodriguez in this case took place within public navigable airspace, see 49 U.S.C. App. § 1304, in a physically non-intrusive manner; from this point they were able to observe plants readily discernible to the naked eye as marijuana. That the observation from aircraft was directed at identifying the plants and the officers were trained to recognize marijuana is irrelevant. Such observation is precisely what a judicial officer needs to provide a basis for a warrant. Any member of the public flying in this airspace who glanced down could have seen everything that these officers observed. On this record, we readily conclude that respondent's expectation that his garden was protected from such observation is unreasonable and is not an expectation that society is prepared to honor.

Justice POWELL, with whom Justice BRENNAN, Justice MARSHALL, and Justice BLACKMUN join, dissenting.

Concurring in Katz v. United States (1967), Justice Harlan warned that any decision to construe the Fourth Amendment as proscribing only physical intrusions by police onto private property "is, in the present day, bad physics as well as bad law, for reasonable expectations of privacy may be defeated by electronic as well as physical invasion." Because the Court today ignores that warning in an opinion that departs significantly from the standard developed in *Katz* for deciding when a Fourth Amendment violation has occurred, I dissent.

The Fourth Amendment protects "[t]he right of the people to be secure in their persons, houses, papers, and effects, against unreasonable searches and seizures." While the familiar history of the Amendment need not be recounted here, we should remember that it reflects a choice that our society should be one in which citizens "dwell in reasonable security and freedom from surveillance."

This case involves surveillance of a home, for as we stated in Oliver v. United States, the curtilage "has been considered part of the home itself for Fourth Amendment purposes."

The Court begins its analysis of the Fourth Amendment issue posed here by deciding that respondent had an expectation of privacy in his backyard. I agree with that conclusion because of the close proximity of the yard to the house, the nature of some of the activities respondent conducted there, and because he had taken steps to shield those activities from the view of passersby.

The Court concludes, nevertheless, that Shutz could use an airplane — a product of modern technology — to intrude visually into respondent's yard. The Court argues that respondent had no reasonable expectation of privacy from aerial observation. It then relies on the fact that the surveillance was not accompanied by a physical invasion of the curtilage. Reliance on the manner of surveillance is directly contrary to the standard of *Katz*, which identifies a constitutionally protected privacy right by focusing on the interests of the individual and of a free society. Since *Katz*, we have consistently held that the presence or absence of physical trespass by police is constitutionally irrelevant to the question whether society is prepared to recognize an asserted privacy interest as reasonable.

The Court's holding, therefore, must rest solely on the fact that members of the public fly in planes and may look down at homes as they fly over them. The Court does not explain why it finds this fact to be significant. One may assume that the Court believes that citizens bear the risk that air travelers will observe activities occurring within backyards that are open to the sun and air. This risk, the Court appears to hold, nullifies expectations of privacy in those yards even as to purposeful police surveillance from the air.

This line of reasoning is flawed. First, the actual risk to privacy from commercial or pleasure aircraft is virtually nonexistent. Travelers on commercial flights, as well as private planes used for business or personal reasons, normally obtain at most a fleeting, anonymous, and nondiscriminating glimpse of the landscape and buildings over which they pass. The risk that a passenger on such a plane might observe private activities, and might connect those activities with particular people, is simply too trivial to protect against. It is no accident that, as a matter of common experience, many people build fences around their residential areas, but few build roofs over their backyards. Therefore, contrary to the Court's suggestion, people do not "knowingly expos[e]" their residential yards "to the public" merely by failing to build barriers that prevent aerial surveillance.

Comings and goings on public streets are public matters, and the Constitution does not disable police from observing what every member of the public can see. The activity in this case, by contrast, took place within the private area immediately adjacent to a home. Yet the Court approves purposeful police surveillance of that activity and area similar to that approved with respect to public activities and areas. The only possible basis for this holding is a judgment that the risk to privacy posed by the remote possibility that a private airplane passenger will notice outdoor activities is equivalent to the risk of official aerial surveillance. But the Court fails to acknowledge the qualitative difference between police surveillance and other uses made of the airspace.

Since respondent had a reasonable expectation of privacy in his yard, aerial surveillance undertaken by the police for the purpose of discovering evidence of crime constituted a "search" within the meaning of the Fourth Amendment.

In *Ciraolo*, the Court stressed that the plane was flying lawfully at a level of 1,000 feet. In another case, decided the same day, Dow Chemical v. United States, 476 U.S. 227 (1986), the Court considered whether aerial surveillance and photography of an industrial plant was a search. Although the factory had implemented elaborate security precautions to scrutiny its activities from view, the Court concluded that "the taking of aerial photographs of an industrial plant complex from navigable airspace is not a search prohibited by the Fourth Amendment."

Florida v. Riley, below, involved aerial surveillance from a helicopter at 400 feet. In reading the case, it is important to note that there was no majority opinion and the distinctly different approaches taken by Justice White's plurality opinion, Justice O'Connor's opinion concurring in the judgment, and the dissents of Justice Brennan and Justice Blackmun. These differing approaches would lead to very different results as to many other questions of what is a search.

FLORIDA v. RILEY
488 U.S. 445 (1989)

Justice WHITE announced the judgment of the Court and delivered an opinion, in which THE CHIEF JUSTICE, Justice SCALIA, and Justice KENNEDY join.

On certification to it by a lower state court, the Florida Supreme Court addressed the following question: "Whether surveillance of the interior of a partially covered greenhouse in a residential backyard from the vantage point of a helicopter located 400 feet above the greenhouse constitutes a 'search' for which a warrant is required under the Fourth Amendment and Article I, § 12 of the Florida Constitution." The court answered the question in the affirmative.

Respondent Riley lived in a mobile home located on five acres of rural property. A greenhouse was located 10 to 20 feet behind the mobile home. Two sides of the greenhouse were enclosed. The other two sides were not enclosed but the contents of the greenhouse were obscured from view from surrounding property by trees, shrubs, and the mobile home. The greenhouse was covered by corrugated roofing panels, some translucent and some opaque. At the time relevant to this case, two of the panels, amounting to approximately 10% of the roof area, were missing. A wire fence surrounded the mobile home and the greenhouse, and the property was posted with a "DO NOT ENTER" sign.

This case originated with an anonymous tip to the Pasco County Sheriff's office that marijuana was being grown on respondent's property. When an investigating officer discovered that he could not see the contents of the greenhouse from the road, he circled twice over respondent's property in a helicopter at the height of 400 feet. With his naked eye, he was able to see through the openings in the roof and one or more of the open sides of the greenhouse and to identify what he thought was marijuana growing in the structure. A warrant was obtained based on these observations, and the ensuing search revealed marijuana growing in the greenhouse. Respondent was charged with possession of marijuana under Florida law.

We agree with the State's submission that our decision in California v. Ciraolo (1986), controls this case.

We arrive at the same conclusion in the present case. In this case, as in *Ciraolo*, the property surveyed was within the curtilage of respondent's home. Riley no doubt intended and expected that his greenhouse would not be open to public inspection, and the precautions he took protected against ground-level observation. Because the sides and roof of his greenhouse were left partially open, however, what was growing in the greenhouse was subject to viewing from the air. Under the holding in *Ciraolo*, Riley could not reasonably have expected the contents of his greenhouse to be immune from examination by an officer seated in a fixed-wing aircraft flying in navigable airspace at an altitude of 1,000 feet or, as the Florida Supreme Court seemed to recognize, at an altitude of 500 feet, the lower limit of the navigable airspace for such an aircraft. Here, the inspection was made from a helicopter, but as is the case with fixed-wing planes, "private and commercial flight [by helicopter] in the public airways is routine" in this country, and there is no indication that such flights are unheard of in Pasco County, Florida. Riley could not reasonably have expected that his greenhouse was protected from public or official observation from a helicopter had it been flying within the navigable airspace for fixed-wing aircraft.

Nor on the facts before us, does it make a difference for Fourth Amendment purposes that the helicopter was flying at 400 feet when the officer saw what was growing in the greenhouse through the partially open roof and sides of the structure. We would have a different case if flying at that altitude had been contrary to law or regulation. But helicopters are not bound by the lower limits of the navigable airspace allowed to other aircraft. Any member of the public could legally have been flying over Riley's property in a helicopter at the altitude of 400 feet and could have observed Riley's greenhouse. The police officer did no more. This is not to say that an inspection of the curtilage of a house from an aircraft will always pass muster under the Fourth Amendment simply because the plane is within the navigable airspace specified by law. But it is of obvious importance that the helicopter in this case was not violating the law, and there is nothing in the record or before us to suggest that helicopters flying at 400 feet are sufficiently rare in this country to lend substance to respondent's claim that he reasonably anticipated that his greenhouse would not be subject to observation from that altitude. Neither is there any intimation here that the helicopter interfered with respondent's normal use of the greenhouse or of other parts of the curtilage. As far as this record reveals, no intimate details connected with the use of the home or curtilage were observed, and there was no undue noise, and no wind, dust, or threat of injury. In these circumstances, there was no violation of the Fourth Amendment.

Justice O'CONNOR, concurring in the judgment.

I concur in the judgment reversing the Supreme Court of Florida because I agree that police observation of the greenhouse in Riley's curtilage from a helicopter passing at an altitude of 400 feet did not violate an expectation of privacy "that society is prepared to recognize as 'reasonable.'" I write separately, however, to clarify the standard I believe follows from California v. Ciraolo (1986). In my view, the plurality's approach rests the scope of Fourth Amendment protection too heavily on compliance with FAA regulations whose purpose is to promote air safety, not to protect "[t]he right of the people to be secure in their persons, houses, papers, and effects, against unreasonable searches and seizures."

Observations of curtilage from helicopters at very low altitudes are not perfectly analogous to ground-level observations from public roads or sidewalks. While in both cases the police may have a legal right to occupy the physical space from which their observations are made, the two situations are not necessarily comparable in terms of whether expectations of privacy from such vantage points should be considered reasonable. Public roads, even those less traveled by, are clearly demarked public thoroughfares. Individuals who seek privacy can take precautions, tailored to the location of the road, to avoid disclosing private activities to those who pass by. They can build a tall fence, for example, and thus ensure private enjoyment of the curtilage without risking public observation from the road or sidewalk. If they do not take such precautions, they cannot reasonably expect privacy from public observation. In contrast, even individuals who have taken effective precautions to ensure against ground-level observations cannot block off all conceivable aerial views of their outdoor patios and yards without entirely giving up their enjoyment of those areas. To require individuals to completely cover and enclose their curtilage is to demand more than the "precautions customarily taken by those seeking privacy." The fact that a helicopter could conceivably observe the curtilage at virtually any altitude or angle, without violating FAA regulations, does not in itself mean that an individual has no reasonable expectation of privacy from such observation.

In determining whether Riley had a reasonable expectation of privacy from aerial observation, the relevant inquiry after Ciraolo is not whether the helicopter was where it had a right to be under FAA regulations. Rather, consistent with Katz, we must ask whether the helicopter was in the public airways at an altitude at which members of the public travel with sufficient regularity that Riley's expectation of privacy from aerial observation was not "one that society is prepared to recognize as 'reasonable.'" Thus, in determining "whether the government's intrusion infringes upon the personal and societal values protected by the Fourth Amendment," it is not conclusive to observe, as the plurality does, that "[a]ny member of the public could legally have been flying over Riley's property in a helicopter at the altitude of 400 feet and could have observed Riley's greenhouse." Nor is it conclusive that police helicopters may often fly at 400 feet. If the public rarely, if ever, travels overhead at such altitudes, the observation cannot be said to be from a vantage point generally used by the public and Riley cannot be said to have "knowingly expose[d]" his greenhouse to public view. However, if the public can generally be expected to travel over residential backyards at an altitude of 400 feet, Riley cannot reasonably expect his curtilage to be free from such aerial observation.

In my view, the defendant must bear the burden of proving that his expectation of privacy was a reasonable one, and thus that a "search" within the meaning of the Fourth Amendment even took place. Because there is reason to believe that there is considerable public use of airspace at altitudes of 400 feet and above, and because Riley introduced no evidence to the contrary before the Florida courts, I conclude that Riley's expectation that his curtilage was protected from naked-eye aerial observation from that altitude was not a reasonable one. However, public use of altitudes lower than that — particularly public observations from helicopters circling over the curtilage of a home — may be sufficiently rare that police surveillance from such altitudes would violate reasonable expectations of privacy, despite compliance with FAA air safety regulations.

Justice BRENNAN, with whom Justice MARSHALL, and Justice STEVENS, join, dissenting.

The Court holds today that police officers need not obtain a warrant based on probable cause before circling in a helicopter 400 feet above a home in order to investigate what is taking place behind the walls of the curtilage. I cannot agree that the Fourth Amendment to the Constitution tolerates such an intrusion on privacy and personal security.

The opinion for a plurality of the Court reads almost as if Katz v. United States (1967) had never been decided. Notwithstanding the disclaimers of its final paragraph, the opinion relies almost exclusively on the fact that the police officer conducted his surveillance from a vantage point where, under applicable Federal Aviation Administration regulations, he had a legal right to be. *Katz* teaches, however, that the relevant inquiry is whether the police surveillance "violated the privacy upon which [the defendant] justifiably relied," — or, as Justice Harlan put it, whether the police violated an "expectation of privacy . . . that society is prepared to recognize as 'reasonable.'"

The plurality undertakes no inquiry into whether low-level helicopter surveillance by the police of activities in an enclosed backyard is consistent with the "aims of a free and open society." Instead, it summarily concludes that Riley's expectation of privacy was unreasonable because "[a]ny member of the public could legally have been flying over Riley's property in a helicopter at the altitude of 400 feet and could have observed Riley's greenhouse." This observation is, in turn, based solely on the fact that the police helicopter was within the airspace within which such craft are allowed by federal safety regulations to fly.

I agree, of course, that "[w]hat a person knowingly exposes to the public . . . is not a subject of Fourth Amendment protection." But I cannot agree that one "knowingly exposes [an area] to the public" solely because a helicopter may legally fly above it. Under the plurality's exceedingly grudging Fourth Amendment theory, the expectation of privacy is defeated if a single member of the public could conceivably position herself to see into the area in question without doing anything illegal. It is defeated whatever the difficulty a person would have in so positioning herself, and however infrequently anyone would in fact do so. In taking this view the plurality ignores the very essence of *Katz*. The reason why there is no reasonable expectation of privacy in an area that is exposed to the public is that little diminution in "the amount of privacy and freedom remaining to citizens" will result from police surveillance of something that any passerby readily sees. To pretend, as the plurality opinion does, that the same is true when the police use a helicopter to peer over high fences is, at best, disingenuous. Notwithstanding the plurality's statistics about the number of helicopters registered in this country, can it seriously be questioned that Riley enjoyed virtually complete privacy in his backyard greenhouse, and that that privacy was invaded solely by police helicopter surveillance? Is the theoretical possibility that any member of the public (with sufficient means) could also have hired a helicopter and looked over Riley's fence of any relevance at all in determining whether Riley suffered a serious loss of privacy and personal security through the police action?

The police officer positioned 400 feet above Riley's backyard was not, however, standing on a public road. The vantage point he enjoyed was not one any citizen could readily share. His ability to see over Riley's fence depended on his use of a very expensive and sophisticated piece of machinery to which few ordinary citizens have access. In such circumstances it makes no more sense to rely on the legality of the officer's position in the skies than it would to judge the constitutionality of the wiretap in *Katz* by the legality of the officer's position outside the telephone booth. The simple inquiry whether the police officer had the legal right to be in the position from which he made his observations cannot suffice, for we cannot assume that Riley's curtilage was so open to the observations of passersby in the skies that he retained little privacy or personal security to be lost to police surveillance. The question before us must be not whether the police were where they had a right to be, but whether public observation of Riley's curtilage was so commonplace that Riley's expectation of privacy in his backyard could not be considered reasonable. To say that an invasion of Riley's privacy from the skies was not impossible is most emphatically not the same as saying that his expectation of privacy within his enclosed curtilage was not "one that society is prepared to recognize as 'reasonable.'"

Equally disconcerting is the lack of any meaningful limit to the plurality's holding. It is worth reiterating that the FAA regulations the plurality relies on as establishing that the officer was where he had a right to be set no minimum flight altitude for helicopters. It is difficult, therefore, to see what, if any, helicopter surveillance would run afoul of the plurality's rule that there exists no reasonable expectation of privacy as long as the helicopter is where it has a right to be.

If indeed the purpose of the restraints imposed by the Fourth Amendment is to "safeguard the privacy and security of individuals," then it is puzzling why it should be the helicopter's noise, wind, and dust that provides the measure of whether this constitutional safeguard has been infringed. Imagine a helicopter capable of hovering just above an enclosed courtyard or patio without generating any noise, wind, or dust at all — and, for good measure, without posing any threat of injury. Suppose the police employed this miraculous tool to discover not only what crops people were growing in their greenhouses, but also what books they were reading and who their dinner guests were. Suppose, finally, that the FAA regulations remained unchanged, so that the police were undeniably "where they had a right to be." Would today's plurality continue to assert that "[t]he right of the people to be secure in their persons, houses, papers, and effects, against unreasonable searches and seizures" was not infringed by such surveillance? Yet that is the logical consequence of the plurality's rule that, so long as the police are where they have a right to be under air traffic regulations, the Fourth Amendment is offended only if the aerial surveillance interferes with the use of the backyard as a garden spot. Nor is there anything in the plurality's opinion to suggest that any different rule would apply were the police looking from their helicopter, not into the open curtilage, but through an open window into a room viewable only from the air.

Perhaps the most remarkable passage in the plurality opinion is its suggestion that the case might be a different one had any "intimate details connected with the use of the home or curtilage [been] observed." What, one wonders, is meant by "intimate details"? If the police had observed Riley embracing his wife in the backyard greenhouse, would we then say that his reasonable expectation of privacy had been infringed? Where in the Fourth Amendment or in our cases is there any warrant for imposing a requirement that the activity observed must be "intimate" in order to be protected by the Constitution?

It is difficult to avoid the conclusion that the plurality has allowed its analysis of Riley's expectation of privacy to be colored by its distaste for the activity in which he was engaged. It is indeed easy to forget, especially in view of current concern over drug trafficking, that the scope of the Fourth Amendment's protection does not turn on whether the activity disclosed by a search is illegal or innocuous. But we dismiss this as a "drug case" only at the peril of our own liberties. Justice Frankfurter once noted that "[i]t is a fair summary of history to say that the safeguards of liberty have frequently been forged in controversies involving not very nice people," and nowhere is this observation more apt than in the area of the Fourth Amendment, whose words have necessarily been given meaning largely through decisions suppressing evidence of criminal activity. The principle enunciated in this case determines what limits the Fourth Amendment imposes on aerial surveillance of any person, for any reason. If the Constitution does not protect Riley's marijuana garden against such surveillance, it is hard to see how it will prohibit the government from aerial spying on the activities of a law-abiding citizen on her fully enclosed outdoor patio. As Professor Amsterdam has eloquently written: "The question is not whether you or I must draw the blinds before we commit a crime. It is whether you and I must discipline ourselves to draw the blinds every time we enter a room, under pain of surveillance if we do not."

Justice BLACKMUN, dissenting.

The question before the Court is whether the helicopter surveillance over Riley's property constituted a "search" within the meaning of the Fourth Amendment. I believe that answering this question depends upon whether Riley has a "reasonable expectation of privacy" that no such surveillance would occur, and does not depend upon the fact that the helicopter was flying at a lawful altitude under FAA regulations. A majority of this Court thus agrees to at least this much.

Thus, because I believe that private helicopters rarely fly over curtilages at an altitude of 400 feet, I would impose upon the prosecution the burden of proving contrary facts necessary to show that Riley lacked a reasonable expectation of privacy. Indeed, I would establish this burden of proof for any helicopter surveillance case in which the flight occurred below 1,000 feet — in other words, for any aerial surveillance case not governed by the Court's decision in California v. Ciraolo (1986).

In this case, the prosecution did not meet this burden of proof. This failure should compel a finding that a Fourth Amendment search occurred. But because our prior cases gave the parties little guidance on the burden of proof issue, I would remand this case to allow the prosecution an opportunity to meet this burden.

3.   *Thermal Imaging of Homes*

Justice Brennan's dissent in Florida v. Riley raises many hypotheticals as to what types of government surveillance might be allowed. In Kyllo v. United States, the Court considered whether police use of a device to take a "thermal image" of a home is a search. In examining the Court's opinion and its conclusion that there is a search, it is important to consider whether there is a meaningful difference between surveillance from a low-flying helicopter and via a thermal imaging device. The Court says that the former is not a search, but the latter is and must comply with the Fourth Amendment. *Kyllo* is based, in part, on the special place of homes in the Fourth Amendment, though the aerial surveillance cases above also involved people's homes. The Court in *Kyllo* also stressed that the technology is "not in general public use." It is worth considering whether this should matter and whether it distinguishes aerial surveillance.

KYLLO v. UNITED STATES
533 U.S. 27 (2001)

Justice SCALIA delivered the opinion of the Court.

This case presents the question whether the use of a thermal-imaging device aimed at a private home from a public street to detect relative amounts of heat within the home constitutes a "search" within the meaning of the Fourth Amendment.

I

In 1991 Agent William Elliott of the United States Department of the Interior came to suspect that marijuana was being grown in the home belonging to petitioner Danny Kyllo, part of a triplex on Rhododendron Drive in Florence, Oregon. Indoor marijuana growth typically requires high-intensity lamps. In order to determine whether an amount of heat was emanating from petitioner's home consistent with the use of such lamps, at 3:20 A.M. on January 16, 1992, Agent Elliott and Dan Haas used an Agema Thermovision 210 thermal imager to scan the triplex. Thermal imagers detect infrared radiation, which virtually all objects emit but which is not visible to the naked eye. The imager converts radiation into images based on relative warmth—black is cool, white is hot, shades of gray connote relative differences; in that respect, it operates somewhat like a video camera showing heat images. The scan of Kyllo's home took only a few minutes and was performed from the passenger seat of Agent Elliott's vehicle across the street from the front of the house and also from the street in back of the house. The scan showed that the roof over the garage and a side wall of petitioner's home were relatively hot compared to the rest of the home and substantially warmer than neighboring homes in the triplex. Agent Elliott concluded that petitioner was using halide lights to grow marijuana in his house, which indeed he was. Based on tips from informants, utility bills, and the thermal imaging, a Federal Magistrate Judge issued a warrant authorizing a search of petitioner's home, and the agents found an indoor growing operation involving more than 100 plants. Petitioner was indicted on one count of manufacturing marijuana, in violation of 21 U.S.C. § 841(a)(1). He unsuccessfully moved to suppress the evidence seized from his home and then entered a conditional guilty plea.

II

At the very core of the Fourth Amendment stands the right of a man to retreat into his own home and there be free from unreasonable governmental intrusion. With few exceptions, the question whether a warrantless search of a home is reasonable and hence constitutional must be answered no.

On the other hand, the antecedent question whether or not a Fourth Amendment "search" has occurred is not so simple under our precedent. The permissibility of ordinary visual surveillance of a home used to be clear because, well into the 20th century, our Fourth Amendment jurisprudence was tied to common-law trespass. Visual surveillance was unquestionably lawful because "'the eye cannot by the laws of England be guilty of a trespass.'" We have since decoupled violation of a person's Fourth Amendment rights from trespassory violation of his property, but the lawfulness of warrantless visual surveillance of a home has still been preserved. As we observed in California v. Ciraolo (1986), "[t]he Fourth Amendment protection of the home has never been extended to require law enforcement officers to shield their eyes when passing by a home on public thoroughfares."

One might think that the new validating rationale would be that examining the portion of a house that is in plain public view, while it is a "search" despite the absence of trespass, is not an "unreasonable" one under the Fourth Amendment. But in fact we have held that visual observation is no "search" at all — perhaps in order to preserve somewhat more intact our doctrine that warrantless searches are presumptively unconstitutional. In assessing when a search is not a search, we have applied somewhat in reverse the principle first enunciated in Katz v. United States (1967). As Justice Harlan's oft-quoted concurrence described it, a Fourth Amendment search occurs when the government violates a subjective expectation of privacy that society recognizes as reasonable.

The present case involves officers on a public street engaged in more than naked-eye surveillance of a home. We have previously reserved judgment as to how much technological enhancement of ordinary perception from such a vantage point, if any, is too much.

III

It would be foolish to contend that the degree of privacy secured to citizens by the Fourth Amendment has been entirely unaffected by the advance of technology. The question we confront today is what limits there are upon this power of technology to shrink the realm of guaranteed privacy.

The Katz test — whether the individual has an expectation of privacy that society is prepared to recognize as reasonable — has often been criticized as circular, and hence subjective and unpredictable. While it may be difficult to refine Katz when the search of areas such as telephone booths, automobiles, or even the curtilage and uncovered portions of residences is at issue, in the case of the search of the interior of homes — the prototypical and hence most commonly litigated area of protected privacy — there is a ready criterion, with roots deep in the common law, of the minimal expectation of privacy that exists, and that is acknowledged to be reasonable. To withdraw protection of this minimum expectation would be to permit police technology to erode the privacy guaranteed by the Fourth Amendment. We think that obtaining by sense-enhancing technology any information regarding the interior of the home that could not otherwise have been obtained without physical "intrusion into a constitutionally protected area," constitutes a search — at least where (as here) the technology in question is not in general public use. This assures preservation of that degree of privacy against government that existed when the Fourth Amendment was adopted. On the basis of this criterion, the information obtained by the thermal imager in this case was the product of a search.[2]

The Government maintains, however, that the thermal imaging must be upheld because it detected "only heat radiating from the external surface of the house." The dissent makes this its leading point, contending that there is a fundamental difference between what it calls "off-the-wall" observations and "through-the-wall" surveillance." But just as a thermal imager captures only heat emanating from a house, so also a powerful directional microphone picks up only sound emanating from a house — and a satellite capable of scanning from many miles away would pick up only visible light emanating from a house. We rejected such a mechanical interpretation of the Fourth Amendment in *Katz*, where the eavesdropping device picked up only sound waves that reached the exterior of the phone booth. Reversing that approach would leave the homeowner at the mercy of advancing technology — including imaging technology that could discern all human activity in the home. While the technology used in the present case was relatively crude, the rule we adopt must take account of more sophisticated systems that are already in use or in development. The dissent's reliance on the distinction between "off-the-wall" and "through-the-wall" observation is entirely incompatible with the dissent's belief, which we discuss below, that thermal-imaging observations of the intimate details of a home are impermissible. The most sophisticated thermal-imaging devices continue to measure heat "off-the-wall" rather than "through-the-wall"; the dissent's disapproval of those more sophisticated thermal-imaging devices, is an acknowledgement that there is no substance to this distinction. As for the dissent's extraordinary assertion that anything learned through "an inference" cannot be a search, that would validate even the "through-the-wall" technologies that the dissent purports to disapprove. Surely the dissent does not believe that the

[handwritten margin note: Gov. argument]

2. The dissent's repeated assertion that the thermal imaging did not obtain information regarding the interior of the home, is simply inaccurate. A thermal imager reveals the relative heat of various rooms in the home. The dissent may not find that information particularly private or important, but there is no basis for saying it is not information regarding the interior of the home. The dissent's comparison of the thermal imaging to various circumstances in which outside observers might be able to perceive, without technology, the heat of the home — for example, by observing snowmelt on the roof, is quite irrelevant. The fact that equivalent information could sometimes be obtained by other means does not make lawful the use of means that violate the Fourth Amendment. The police might, for example, learn how many people are in a particular house by setting up year-round surveillance; but that does not make breaking and entering to find out the same information lawful. In any event, on the night of January 16, 1992, no outside observer could have discerned the relative heat of Kyllo's home without thermal imaging. [Footnote by the Court.]

through-the-wall radar or ultrasound technology produces an 8-by-10 Kodak glossy that needs no analysis (i.e., the making of inferences).

The Government also contends that the thermal imaging was constitutional because it did not "detect private activities occurring in private areas." The Fourth Amendment's protection of the home has never been tied to measurement of the quality or quantity of information obtained. In the home, our cases show, all details are intimate details, because the entire area is held safe from prying government eyes. Limiting the prohibition of thermal imaging to "intimate details" would not only be wrong in principle; it would be impractical in application. To begin with, there is no necessary connection between the sophistication of the surveillance equipment and the "intimacy" of the details that it observes — which means that one cannot say (and the police cannot be assured) that use of the relatively crude equipment at issue here will always be lawful. The Agema Thermovision 210 might disclose, for example, at what hour each night the lady of the house takes her daily sauna and bath — a detail that many would consider "intimate"; and a much more sophisticated system might detect nothing more intimate than the fact that someone left a closet light on. We could not, in other words, develop a rule approving only that through-the-wall surveillance which identifies objects no smaller than 36 by 36 inches, but would have to develop a jurisprudence specifying which home activities are "intimate" and which are not. And even when (if ever) that jurisprudence were fully developed, no police officer would be able to know in advance whether his through-the-wall surveillance picks up "intimate" details — and thus would be unable to know in advance whether it is constitutional.

We have said that the Fourth Amendment draws "a firm line at the entrance to the house." That line, we think, must be not only firm but also bright — which requires clear specification of those methods of surveillance that require a warrant. While it is certainly possible to conclude from the videotape of the thermal imaging that occurred in this case that no "significant" compromise of the homeowner's privacy has occurred, we must take the long view, from the original meaning of the Fourth Amendment forward.

Where, as here, the Government uses a device that is not in general public use, to explore details of the home that would previously have been unknowable without physical intrusion, the surveillance is a "search" and is presumptively unreasonable without a warrant.

Since we hold the Thermovision imaging to have been an unlawful search, it will remain for the District Court to determine whether, without the evidence it provided, the search warrant issued in this case was supported by probable cause — and if not, whether there is any other basis for supporting admission of the evidence that the search pursuant to the warrant produced.

Justice STEVENS, with whom THE CHIEF JUSTICE, Justice O'CONNOR, and Justice KENNEDY join, dissenting.

There is, in my judgment, a distinction of constitutional magnitude between "through-the-wall surveillance" that gives the observer or listener direct access to information in a private area, on the one hand, and the thought processes used to draw inferences from information in the public domain, on the other hand. The Court has crafted a rule that purports to deal with direct observations of the inside of the home, but the case before us merely involves indirect deductions from "off-the-wall" surveillance, that is, observations of the exterior of the home. Those observations were made with a fairly primitive thermal imager that gathered data exposed on the outside of petitioner's home but did not invade any constitutionally protected interest in privacy. Moreover, I believe that the supposedly "bright-line" rule the Court has created in response to its concerns about future technological developments is unnecessary, unwise, and inconsistent with the Fourth Amendment.

I

There is no need for the Court to craft a new rule to decide this case, as it is controlled by established principles from our Fourth Amendment jurisprudence. One of those core principles, of course, is that "searches and seizures inside a home without a warrant are presumptively unreasonable." But it is equally well settled that searches and seizures of property in plain view are presumptively reasonable. Whether that property is residential or commercial, the basic principle is the same: "'What a person knowingly exposes to the public, even in his own home or office, is not a subject of Fourth Amendment protection.'" That is the principle implicated here.

While the Court "take[s] the long view" and decides this case based largely on the potential of yet-to-be-developed technology that might allow "through-the-wall surveillance," this case involves nothing more than off-the-wall surveillance by law enforcement officers to gather information exposed to the general public from the outside of petitioner's home. All that the infrared camera did in this case was passively measure heat emitted from the exterior surfaces of petitioner's home; all that those measurements showed were relative differences in emission levels, vaguely indicating that some areas of the roof and outside walls were warmer than others. As still images from the infrared scans show, no details regarding the interior of petitioner's home were revealed. Unlike an x-ray scan, or other possible "through-the-wall" techniques, the detection of infrared radiation emanating from the home did not accomplish "an unauthorized physical penetration into the premises," nor did it "obtain information that it could not have obtained by observation from outside the curtilage of the house."

Indeed, the ordinary use of the senses might enable a neighbor or passerby to notice the heat emanating from a building, particularly if it is vented, as was the case here. Additionally, any member of the public might notice that one part of a house is warmer than another part or a nearby building if, for example, rainwater evaporates or snow melts at different rates across its surfaces. Such use of the senses would not convert into an unreasonable search if, instead, an adjoining neighbor allowed an officer onto her property to verify her perceptions with a sensitive thermometer. Nor, in my view, does such observation become an unreasonable search if made from a distance with the aid of a device that merely discloses that the exterior of one house, or one area of the house, is much warmer than another. Nothing more occurred in this case.

Thus, the notion that heat emissions from the outside of a dwelling are a private matter implicating the protections of the Fourth Amendment is not only unprecedented but also quite difficult to take seriously. Heat waves, like aromas that are generated in a kitchen, or in a laboratory or opium den, enter the public domain if and when they leave a building. A subjective expectation that they would remain private is not only implausible but also surely not "one that society is prepared to recognize as 'reasonable.'"

To be sure, the homeowner has a reasonable expectation of privacy concerning what takes place within the home, and the Fourth Amendment's protection against physical invasions of the home should apply to their functional equivalent. But the equipment in this case did not penetrate the walls of petitioner's home, and while it did pick up "details of the home" that were exposed to the public, it did not obtain "any information regarding the interior of the home." In the Court's own words, based on what the thermal imager "showed" regarding the outside of petitioner's home, the officers "concluded" that petitioner was engaging in illegal activity inside the home. It would be quite absurd to characterize their thought processes as "searches," regardless of whether they inferred (rightly) that petitioner was growing marijuana in his house, or (wrongly) that "the lady of the house [was taking] her daily sauna and bath." For the first time in its history, the Court assumes that an inference can amount to a Fourth Amendment violation.

Notwithstanding the implications of today's decision, there is a strong public interest in avoiding constitutional litigation over the monitoring of emissions from homes, and over the inferences drawn from such monitoring. Just as "the police cannot reasonably be expected to avert their eyes from evidence of criminal activity that could have been observed by any member of the public," so too public officials should not have to avert their senses or their equipment from detecting emissions in the public domain such as excessive heat, traces of smoke, suspicious odors, odorless gases, airborne particulates, or radioactive emissions, any of which could identify hazards to the community. In my judgment, monitoring such emissions with "sense-enhancing technology," and drawing useful conclusions from such monitoring, is an entirely reasonable public service.

On the other hand, the countervailing privacy interest is at best trivial. After all, homes generally are insulated to keep heat in, rather than to prevent the detection of heat going out, and it does not seem to me that society will suffer from a rule requiring the rare homeowner who both intends to engage in uncommon activities that produce extraordinary amounts of heat, and wishes to conceal that production from outsiders, to make sure that the surrounding area is well insulated. The interest in concealing the heat escaping from one's house pales in significance to "the chief evil against which the wording of the Fourth Amendment is directed," the "physical entry of the home," and it is hard to believe that it is an interest the Framers sought to protect in our Constitution.

Since what was involved in this case was nothing more than drawing inferences from off-the-wall surveillance, rather than any "through-the-wall" surveillance, the officers' conduct did not amount to a search and was perfectly reasonable.

II

Instead of trying to answer the question whether the use of the thermal imager in this case was even arguably unreasonable, the Court has fashioned a rule that is intended to provide essential guidance for the day when "more sophisticated systems" gain the "ability to 'see' through walls and other opaque barriers." The newly minted rule encompasses "obtaining [1] by sense-enhancing technology [2] any information regarding the interior of the home [3] that could not otherwise have been obtained without physical intrusion into a constitutionally protected area . . . [4] at least where (as here) the technology in question is not in general public use." In my judgment, the Court's new rule is at once too broad and too narrow, and is not justified by the Court's explanation for its adoption. As I have suggested, I would not erect a constitutional impediment to the use of sense-enhancing technology unless it provides its user with the functional equivalent of actual presence in the area being searched.

Despite the Court's attempt to draw a line that is "not only firm but also bright," the contours of its new rule are uncertain because its protection apparently dissipates as soon as the relevant technology is "in general public use." Yet how much use is general public use is not even hinted at by the Court's opinion, which makes the somewhat doubtful assumption that the thermal imager used in this case does not satisfy that criterion. In any event, putting aside its lack of clarity, this criterion is somewhat perverse because it seems likely that the threat to privacy will grow, rather than recede, as the use of intrusive equipment becomes more readily available.

III

Although the Court is properly and commendably concerned about the threats to privacy that may flow from advances in the technology available to the law enforcement profession, it has unfortunately failed to heed the tried and true counsel of judicial restraint. Instead of concentrating on the rather mundane issue that is actually presented by the case before it, the Court has endeavored to craft an all-encompassing rule for the future. It would be far wiser to give legislators an unimpeded opportunity to grapple with these emerging issues rather than to shackle them with prematurely devised constitutional constraints.

4. Searches of Trash

Does a person have a reasonable expectation of privacy in his trash? If police go through a person's garbage, do the officers need to follow the Fourth Amendment's requirements? In California v. Greenwood, the Court considered this and found no reasonable expectation of privacy in what a person chooses to discard.

CALIFORNIA v. GREENWOOD
486 U.S. 35 (1988)

Justice WHITE delivered the opinion of the Court.

The issue here is whether the Fourth Amendment prohibits the warrantless search and seizure of garbage left for collection outside the curtilage of a home. We conclude, in accordance with the vast majority of lower courts that have addressed the issue, that it does not.

I

In early 1984, Investigator Jenny Stracner of the Laguna Beach Police Depart-ment received information indicating that respondent Greenwood might be engaged in narcotics trafficking. Stracner learned that a criminal suspect had informed a federal drug enforcement agent in February 1984 that a truck filled with illegal drugs was en route to the Laguna Beach address at which Greenwood resided. In addition, a neighbor complained of heavy vehicular traffic late at night in front of Greenwood's single-family home. The neighbor reported that the vehicles remained at Greenwood's house for only a few minutes.

Stracner sought to investigate this information by conducting a surveillance of Greenwood's home. She observed several vehicles make brief stops at the house during the late-night and early morning hours, and she followed a truck from the house to a residence that had previously been under investigation as a narcotics-trafficking location.

On April 6, 1984, Stracner asked the neighborhood's regular trash collector to pick up the plastic garbage bags that Greenwood had left on the curb in front of his house and to turn the bags over to her without mixing their contents with garbage from other houses. The trash collector cleaned his truck bin of other refuse, collected the garbage bags from the street in front of Greenwood's house, and turned the bags over to Stracner. The officer searched through the rubbish and found items indicative of narcotics use. She recited the infor-mation that she had gleaned from the trash search in an affidavit in support of a warrant to search Greenwood's home.

Police officers encountered both respondents at the house later that day when they arrived to execute the warrant. The police discovered quantities of cocaine and hashish during their search of the house. Respondents were arrested on felony narcotics charges. They subsequently posted bail.

The police continued to receive reports of many late-night visitors to the Greenwood house. On May 4, Investigator Robert Rahaeuser obtained Green-wood's garbage from the regular trash collector in the same manner as had Stracner. The garbage again contained evidence of narcotics use.

Rahaeuser secured another search warrant for Greenwood's home based on the information from the second trash search. The police found more narcotics and evidence of narcotics trafficking when they executed the warrant. Green-wood was again arrested.

II

The warrantless search and seizure of the garbage bags left at the curb outside the Greenwood house would violate the Fourth Amendment only if respon-dents manifested a subjective expectation of privacy in their garbage that society accepts as objectively reasonable. Respondents do not disagree with this standard.

They assert, however, that they had, and exhibited, an expectation of privacy with respect to the trash that was searched by the police: The trash, which was placed on the street for collection at a fixed time, was contained in opaque plastic bags, which the garbage collector was expected to pick up, mingle with the trash of others, and deposit at the garbage dump. The trash was only temporarily on the street, and there was little likelihood that it would be inspected by anyone.

It may well be that respondents did not expect that the contents of their garbage bags would become known to the police or other members of the public. An expectation of privacy does not give rise to Fourth Amendment protection, however, unless society is prepared to accept that expectation as objectively reasonable.

Here, we conclude that respondents exposed their garbage to the public sufficiently to defeat their claim to Fourth Amendment protection. It is common knowledge that plastic garbage bags left on or at the side of a public street are readily accessible to animals, children, scavengers, snoops, and other members of the public. Moreover, respondents placed their refuse at the curb for the express purpose of conveying it to a third party, the trash collector, who might himself have sorted through respondents' trash or permitted others, such as the police, to do so. Accordingly, having deposited their garbage "in an area particularly suited for public inspection and, in a manner of speaking, public consumption, for the express purpose of having strangers take it," respondents could have had no reasonable expectation of privacy in the inculpatory items that they discarded.

Furthermore, as we have held, the police cannot reasonably be expected to avert their eyes from evidence of criminal activity that could have been observed by any member of the public.

Justice BRENNAN, with whom Justice MARSHALL joins, dissenting.

Every week for two months, and at least once more a month later, the Laguna Beach police clawed through the trash that respondent Greenwood left in opaque, sealed bags on the curb outside his home. Complete strangers minutely scrutinized their bounty, undoubtedly dredging up intimate details of Greenwood's private life and habits. The intrusions proceeded without a warrant, and no court before or since has concluded that the police acted on probable cause to believe Greenwood was engaged in any criminal activity.

Scrutiny of another's trash is contrary to commonly accepted notions of civilized behavior. I suspect, therefore, that members of our society will be shocked to learn that the Court, the ultimate guarantor of liberty, deems unreasonable our expectation that the aspects of our private lives that are concealed safely in a trash bag will not become public.

"A container which can support a reasonable expectation of privacy may not be searched, even on probable cause, without a warrant." United States v. Jacobsen (1984). Thus, as the Court observes, if Greenwood had a reasonable expectation that the contents of the bags that he placed on the curb would remain private, the warrantless search of those bags violated the Fourth Amendment.

Respondents deserve no less protection just because Greenwood used the bags to discard rather than to transport his personal effects. Their contents are not inherently any less private, and Greenwood's decision to discard them, at least in the manner in which he did, does not diminish his expectation of privacy.

A trash bag, like any of the above-mentioned containers, "is a common repository for one's personal effects" and, even more than many of them, is "therefore . . . inevitably associated with the expectation of privacy." A single bag of trash testifies eloquently to the eating, reading, and recreational habits of the person who produced it. A search of trash, like a search of the bedroom, can relate intimate details about sexual practices, health, and personal hygiene. Like rifling through desk drawers or intercepting phone calls, rummaging through trash can divulge the target's financial and professional status, political affiliations and inclinations, private thoughts, personal relationships, and romantic interests. It cannot be doubted that a sealed trash bag harbors telling evidence of the "intimate activity associated with the 'sanctity of a man's home and the privacies of life,'" which the Fourth Amendment is designed to protect.

Had Greenwood flaunted his intimate activity by strewing his trash all over the curb for all to see, or had some nongovernmental intruder invaded his privacy and done the same, I could accept the Court's conclusion that an expectation of privacy would have been unreasonable. Similarly, had police searching the city dump run across incriminating evidence that, despite commingling with the trash of others, still retained its identity as Greenwood's, we would have a different case. But all that Greenwood "exposed . . . to the public," were the exteriors of several opaque, sealed containers. Until the bags were opened by police, they hid their contents from the public's view every bit as much as did Chadwick's double-locked footlocker and Robbins' green, plastic wrapping. Faithful application of the warrant requirement does not require police to "avert their eyes from evidence of criminal activity that could have been observed by any member of the public." Rather, it only requires them to adhere to norms of privacy that members of the public plainly acknowledge.

The mere possibility that unwelcome meddlers might open and rummage through the containers does not negate the expectation of privacy in their contents any more than the possibility of a burglary negates an expectation of privacy in the home; or the possibility of a private intrusion negates an expectation of privacy in an unopened package; or the possibility that an operator will listen in on a telephone conversation negates an expectation of privacy in the words spoken on the telephone. "What a person . . . seeks to preserve as private, even in an area accessible to the public, may be constitutionally protected."

Nor is it dispositive that "respondents placed their refuse at the curb for the express purpose of conveying it to a third party, . . . who might himself have sorted through respondents' trash or permitted others, such as the police, to do so." In the first place, Greenwood can hardly be faulted for leaving trash on his curb when a county ordinance commanded him to do so. Unlike in other circumstances where privacy is compromised, Greenwood could not "avoid exposing personal belongings . . . by simply leaving them at home." More importantly, even the voluntary relinquishment of possession or control over an effect does not necessarily amount to a relinquishment of a privacy expectation in it. Were it otherwise, a letter or package would lose all Fourth Amendment protection when placed in a mailbox or other depository with the "express purpose" of entrusting it to the postal officer or a private carrier; those bailees are just as likely as trash collectors (and certainly have greater incentive) to "sor[t] through" the personal effects entrusted to them, "or permi[t] others, such as police to do so." Yet, it has been clear for at least 110 years that the possibility of such an intrusion does not justify a warrantless search by police in the first instance.

In holding that the warrantless search of Greenwood's trash was consistent with the Fourth Amendment, the Court paints a grim picture of our society. It depicts a society in which local authorities may command their citizens to dispose of their personal effects in the manner least protective of the "sanctity of [the] home and the privacies of life," and then monitor them arbitrarily and without judicial oversight—a society that is not prepared to recognize as reasonable an individual's expectation of privacy in the most private of personal effects sealed in an opaque container and disposed of in a manner designed to commingle it imminently and inextricably with the trash of others. The American society with which I am familiar "chooses to dwell in reasonable security and freedom from surveillance," and is more dedicated to individual liberty and more sensitive to intrusions on the sanctity of the home than the Court is willing to acknowledge.

5. Observation and Monitoring of Public Behavior

As indicated above, the Supreme Court frequently has stated: "'What a person knowingly exposes to the public, even in his own home or office, is not a subject of Fourth Amendment protection.'" California v. Ciraolo (1986) (quoting Katz v. United States (1967)). But what is considered public behavior? The Court has considered this in a number of contexts. For instance, in United States v. Knotts, the Court considered whether the police putting a radio-transmitter in a container is a search.

UNITED STATES v. KNOTTS
460 U.S. 276 (1983)

Justice REHNQUIST announced the opinion of the Court.

A beeper is a radio transmitter, usually battery operated, which emits periodic signals that can be picked up by a radio receiver. In this case, a beeper was placed in a five gallon drum containing chloroform purchased by one of respondent's codefendants. By monitoring the progress of a car carrying the chloroform Minnesota law enforcement agents were able to trace the can of chloroform from its place of purchase in Minneapolis, Minnesota to respondent's secluded cabin near Shell Lake, Wisconsin. The issue presented by the case is whether such use of a beeper violated respondent's rights secured by the Fourth Amendment to the United States Constitution.

Respondent and two codefendants were charged in the United States District Court for the District of Minnesota with conspiracy to manufacture controlled substances, including but not limited to methamphetamine, in violation of 21 U.S.C. § 846 (1976). One of the codefendants, Darryl Petschen, was tried jointly with respondent; the other codefendant, Tristan Armstrong, pleaded guilty and testified for the government at trial.

Suspicion attached to this trio when the 3M Company, which manufactures chemicals in St. Paul, notified a narcotics investigator for the Minnesota Bureau of Criminal Apprehension that Armstrong, a former 3M employee, had been stealing chemicals which could be used in manufacturing illicit drugs. Visual surveillance of Armstrong revealed that after leaving the employ of 3M Company, he had been purchasing similar chemicals from the Hawkins Chemical Company in Minneapolis. The Minnesota narcotics officers observed that after Armstrong had made a purchase, he would deliver the chemicals to codefendant Petschen.

With the consent of the Hawkins Chemical Company, officers installed a beeper inside a five gallon container of chloroform, one of the so-called "precursor" chemicals used to manufacture illicit drugs. Hawkins agreed that when Armstrong next purchased chloroform, the chloroform would be placed in this particular container. When Armstrong made the purchase, officers followed the car in which the chloroform had been placed, maintaining contact by using both visual surveillance and a monitor which received the signals sent from the beeper.

Armstrong proceeded to Petschen's house, where the container was transferred to Petschen's automobile. Officers then followed that vehicle eastward towards the state line, across the St. Croix River, and into Wisconsin. During the latter part of this journey, Petschen began making evasive maneuvers, and the pursuing agents ended their visual surveillance. At about the same time officers lost the signal from the beeper, but with the assistance of a monitoring device located in a helicopter the approximate location of the signal was picked up again about one hour later. The signal now was stationary and the location identified was a cabin occupied by respondent near Shell Lake, Wisconsin. The record before us does not reveal that the beeper was used after the location in the area of the cabin had been initially determined.

Relying on the location of the chloroform derived through the use of the beeper and additional information obtained during three days of intermittent visual surveillance of respondent's cabin, officers secured a search warrant. During execution of the warrant, officers discovered a fully operable, clandestine drug laboratory in the cabin. In the laboratory area officers found formulas for amphetamine and methamphetamine, over $10,000 worth of laboratory equipment, and chemicals in quantities sufficient to produce 14 pounds of pure amphetamine. Under a barrel outside the cabin, officers located the five gallon container of chloroform.

After his motion to suppress evidence based on the warrantless monitoring of the beeper was denied, respondent was convicted for conspiring to manufacture controlled substances in violation of 21 U.S.C. § 846 (1976). He was sentenced to five years imprisonment.

II

The governmental surveillance conducted by means of the beeper in this case amounted principally to the following of an automobile on public streets and highways. We have commented more than once on the diminished expectation of privacy in an automobile: "One has a lesser expectation of privacy in a motor vehicle because its function is transportation and it seldom serves as one's residence or as the repository of personal effects. A car has little capacity for escaping public scrutiny. It travels public thoroughfares where both its occupants and its contents are in plain view." Cardwell v. Lewis (1974).

A person travelling in an automobile on public thoroughfares has no reasonable expectation of privacy in his movements from one place to another. When Petschen travelled over the public streets he voluntarily conveyed to anyone who wanted to look the fact that he was travelling over particular roads in a particular direction, the fact of whatever stops he made, and the fact of his final destination when he exited from public roads onto private property.

Respondent Knotts, as the owner of the cabin and surrounding premises to which Petschen drove, undoubtedly had the traditional expectation of privacy within a dwelling place insofar as the cabin was concerned. But no such expectation of privacy extended to the visual observation of Petschen's automobile arriving on his premises after leaving a public highway, nor to movements of objects such as the drum of chloroform outside the cabin in the "open fields." Visual surveillance from public places along Petschen's route or adjoining Knotts' premises would have sufficed to reveal all of these facts to the police. The fact that the officers in this case relied not only on visual surveillance, but on the use of the beeper to signal the presence of Petschen's automobile to the police receiver, does not alter the situation. Nothing in the Fourth Amendment prohibited the police from augmenting the sensory faculties bestowed upon them at birth with such enhancement as science and technology afforded them in this case.

We thus return to the question posed at the beginning of our inquiry: did monitoring the beeper signals complained of by respondent invade any legitimate expectation of privacy on his part? For the reasons previously stated, we hold they did not. Since they did not, there was neither a "search" nor a "seizure" within the contemplation of the Fourth Amendment.

Justice STEVENS, with whom Justice BRENNAN and Justice MARSHALL join, concurring in the judgment.

Since the respondent in this case has never questioned the installation of the radio transmitter in the chloroform drum, I agree that it was entirely reasonable for the police officers to make use of the information received over the airwaves when they were trying to ascertain the ultimate destination of the chloroform. I do not join the Court's opinion, however, because it contains two unnecessarily broad dicta: One distorts the record in this case, and both may prove confusing to courts that must apply this decision in the future.

First, the Court implies that the chloroform drum was parading in "open fields" outside of the cabin, in a manner tantamount to its public display on the highways. The record does not support that implication. [T]his case does not pose any "open fields" issue.

Second, the Court suggests that the Fourth Amendment does not inhibit "the police from augmenting the sensory facilities bestowed upon them at birth with such enhancement as science and technology afforded them." But the Court held to the contrary in Katz v. United States (1967). Although the augmentation in this case was unobjectionable, it by no means follows that the use of electronic detection techniques does not implicate especially sensitive concerns.

Interestingly, in United States v. Karo, the Court found that the placement of a beeper in a container was a search. In reading the case, it is worth considering whether there is a meaningful distinction with *Knotts* and what is the rule that emerges as to when police can plant tracking devices or beepers.

UNITED STATES v. KARO

468 U.S. 705 (1984)

Justice WHITE delivered the opinion of the Court.

In United States v. Knotts (1983), we held that the warrantless monitoring of an electronic tracking device ("beeper") inside a container of chemicals did not violate the Fourth Amendment when it revealed no information that could not have been obtained through visual surveillance. In this case, we are called upon to address two questions left unresolved in *Knotts:* (1) whether installation of a beeper in a container of chemicals with the consent of the original owner constitutes a search or seizure within the meaning of the Fourth Amendment when the container is delivered to a buyer having no knowledge of the presence of the beeper, and (2) whether monitoring of a beeper falls within the ambit of the Fourth Amendment when it reveals information that could not have been obtained through visual surveillance.[3]

I

In August 1980 Agent Rottinger of the Drug Enforcement Administration (DEA) learned that respondents James Karo, Richard Horton, and William Harley had ordered 50 gallons of ether from Government informant Carl Muehlenweg of Graphic Photo Design in Albuquerque, N.M. Muehlenweg told Rottinger that the ether was to be used to extract cocaine from clothing that had been imported into the United States. The Government obtained a court order authorizing the installation and monitoring of a beeper in one of the cans of ether. With Muehlenweg's consent, agents substituted their own can containing a beeper for one of the cans in the shipment and then had all 10 cans painted to give them a uniform appearance.

On September 20, 1980, agents saw Karo pick up the ether from Muehlenweg. They then followed Karo to his house using visual and beeper surveillance. At one point later that day, agents determined by using the beeper that the ether was still inside the house, but they later determined that it had been moved undetected to Horton's house, where they located it using the beeper. Agent Rottinger could smell the ether from the public sidewalk near Horton's residence. Two days later, agents discovered that the ether had once again been moved, and, using the beeper, they located it at the residence of Horton's father. The next day, the beeper was no longer transmitting from Horton's father's house, and agents traced the beeper to a commercial storage facility.

Because the beeper equipment was not sensitive enough to allow agents to learn precisely which locker the ether was in, agents obtained a subpoena for the records of the storage company and learned that locker 143 had been rented by Horton. Using the beeper, agents confirmed that the ether was indeed in one of the lockers in the row containing locker 143, and using their noses they detected the odor of ether emanating from locker 143. On October 8 agents obtained an order authorizing installation of an entry tone alarm into the door jamb of the

---

3. A beeper is a radio transmitter, usually battery operated, which emits periodic signals that can be picked up by a radio receiver. [Footnote by the Court.]

locker so they would be able to tell when the door was opened. While installing the alarm, agents observed that the cans containing ether were still inside. Agents ceased visual and beeper surveillance, relying instead on the entry tone alarm. However, on October 16 Horton retrieved the contents from the locker without sounding the alarm. Agents did not learn of the entry until the manager of the storage facility notified them that Horton had been there.

Using the beeper, agents traced the beeper can to another self-storage facility three days later. Agents detected the smell of ether coming from locker 15 and learned from the manager that Horton and Harley had rented that locker using an alias the same day that the ether had been removed from the first storage facility. The agents obtained an order authorizing the installation of an entry tone alarm in locker 15, but instead of installing that alarm, they obtained consent from the manager of the facility to install a closed-circuit video camera in a locker that had a view of locker 15. On February 6, 1981, agents observed, by means of the video camera, Gene Rhodes and an unidentified woman removing the cans from the locker and loading them onto the rear bed of Horton's pickup truck. Using both visual and beeper surveillance agents tracked the truck to Rhodes' residence where it was parked in the driveway. Agents then observed Rhodes and a woman bringing boxes and other items from inside the house and loading the items into the trunk of an automobile. Agents did not see any cans being transferred from the pickup.

At about 6 P.M. on February 6, the car and the pickup left the driveway and traveled along public highways to Taos. During the trip, the two vehicles were under both physical and electronic surveillance. When the vehicles arrived at a house in Taos rented by Horton, Harley, and Michael Steele, the agents did not maintain tight surveillance for fear of detection. When the vehicles left the Taos residence, agents determined, using the beeper monitor, that the beeper can was still inside the house. Again on February 7, the beeper revealed that the ether can was still on the premises. At one point, agents noticed that the windows of the house were wide open on a cold windy day, leading them to suspect that the ether was being used. On February 8, the agents applied for and obtained a warrant to search the Taos residence based in part on information derived through use of the beeper. The warrant was executed on February 10, 1981, and Horton, Harley, Steele, and Evan Roth were arrested, and cocaine and laboratory equipment were seized.

II

Because the judgment below in favor of Karo rested in major part on the conclusion that the installation violated his Fourth Amendment rights and that any information obtained from monitoring the beeper was tainted by the initial illegality, we must deal with the legality of the warrantless installation. It is clear that the actual placement of the beeper into the can violated no one's Fourth Amendment rights. The can into which the beeper was placed belonged at the time to the DEA, and by no stretch of the imagination could it be said that respondents then had any legitimate expectation of privacy in it. The ether and the original 10 cans, on the other hand, belonged to, and were in the possession of, Muehlenweg, who had given his consent to any invasion of those items that occurred. Thus, even if there had been no substitution of cans and the agents had placed the beeper into one of the original 10 cans, Muehlenweg's consent was sufficient to validate the placement of the beeper in the can.

We conclude that no Fourth Amendment interest of Karo or of any other respondent was infringed by the installation of the beeper. Rather, any impairment of their privacy interests that may have occurred was occasioned by the monitoring of the beeper.[4]

III

Here, there is no gainsaying that the beeper was used to locate the ether in a specific house in Taos, N.M., and that that information was in turn used to secure a warrant for the search of the house. This case thus presents the question whether the monitoring of a beeper in a private residence, a location not open to visual surveillance, violates the Fourth Amendment rights of those who have a justifiable interest in the privacy of the residence. Contrary to the submission of the United States, we think that it does.

At the risk of belaboring the obvious, private residences are places in which the individual normally expects privacy free of governmental intrusion not authorized by a warrant, and that expectation is plainly one that society is prepared to recognize as justifiable. Our cases have not deviated from this basic Fourth Amendment principle. Searches and seizures inside a home without a warrant are presumptively unreasonable absent exigent circumstances. In this case, had a DEA agent thought it useful to enter the Taos residence to verify that the ether was actually in the house and had he done so surreptitiously and without a warrant, there is little doubt that he would have engaged in an unreasonable search within the meaning of the Fourth Amendment. For purposes of the Amendment, the result is the same where, without a warrant, the Government surreptitiously employs an electronic device to obtain information that it could not have obtained by observation from outside the curtilage of the house. The beeper tells the agent that a particular article is actually located at a particular time in the private residence and is in the possession of the person or persons whose residence is being watched. Even if visual surveillance has revealed that the article to which the beeper is attached has entered the house, the later monitoring not only verifies the officers' observations but also establishes that the article remains on the premises. Here, for example, the beeper was monitored for a significant period after the arrival of the ether in Taos and before the application for a warrant to search.

The monitoring of an electronic device such as a beeper is, of course, less intrusive than a full-scale search, but it does reveal a critical fact about the interior of the premises that the Government is extremely interested in knowing and that it could not have otherwise obtained without a warrant. The case is thus not like *Knotts*, for there the beeper told the authorities nothing about the interior of Knotts' cabin. The information obtained in *Knotts* was "voluntarily conveyed to anyone who wanted to look . . ."; here, as we have said, the

---

4. Despite this holding, warrants for the installation and monitoring of a beeper will obviously be desirable since it may be useful, even critical, to monitor the beeper to determine that it is actually located in a place not open to visual surveillance. As will be evident below, such monitoring without a warrant may violate the Fourth Amendment. [Footnote by the Court.]

monitoring indicated that the beeper was inside the house, a fact that could not have been visually verified.

We also reject the Government's contention that it should be able to monitor beepers in private residences without a warrant if there is the requisite justification in the facts for believing that a crime is being or will be committed and that monitoring the beeper wherever it goes is likely to produce evidence of criminal activity. Warrantless searches are presumptively unreasonable, though the Court has recognized a few limited exceptions to this general rule. The Government's contention that warrantless beeper searches should be deemed reasonable is based upon its deprecation of the benefits and exaggeration of the difficulties associated with procurement of a warrant. The Government argues that the traditional justifications for the warrant requirement are inapplicable in beeper cases, but to a large extent that argument is based upon the contention, rejected above, that the beeper constitutes only a minuscule intrusion on protected privacy interests. The primary reason for the warrant requirement is to interpose a "neutral and detached magistrate" between the citizen and "the officer engaged in the often competitive enterprise of ferreting out crime." Those suspected of drug offenses are no less entitled to that protection than those suspected of nondrug offenses. Requiring a warrant will have the salutary effect of ensuring that use of beepers is not abused, by imposing upon agents the requirement that they demonstrate in advance their justification for the desired search. This is not to say that there are no exceptions to the warrant rule, because if truly exigent circumstances exist no warrant is required under general Fourth Amendment principles.

We are also unpersuaded by the argument that a warrant should not be required because of the difficulty in satisfying the particularity requirement of the Fourth Amendment. The Government contends that it would be impossible to describe the "place" to be searched, because the location of the place is precisely what is sought to be discovered through the search. However true that may be, it will still be possible to describe the object into which the beeper is to be placed, the circumstances that led agents to wish to install the beeper, and the length of time for which beeper surveillance is requested. In our view, this information will suffice to permit issuance of a warrant authorizing beeper installation and surveillance.

In sum, we discern no reason for deviating from the general rule that a search of a house should be conducted pursuant to a warrant.

Justice O'CONNOR, with whom Justice REHNQUIST joins, concurring in part and concurring in the judgment.

I agree with the Court that the installation of a beeper in a container with the consent of the container's present owner implicates no Fourth Amendment concerns. The subsequent transfer of the container, with the unactivated beeper, to one who is unaware of the beeper's presence is also unobjectionable. It is when the beeper is activated to track the movements of the container that privacy interests are implicated.

In my view, however, these privacy interests are unusually narrow — narrower than is suggested by the Court. If the container is moved on the public highways, or in other places where the container's owner has no reasonable expectation that its movements will not be tracked without his consent, activation of the beeper infringes on no reasonable expectation of privacy. In this situation the location of the container defeats any expectation that its movements will not be tracked.

In addition, one who lacks ownership of the container itself or the power to move the container at will, can have no reasonable expectation that the movements of the container will not be tracked by a beeper within the container, regardless of where the container is moved. In this situation the absence of an appropriate interest in the container itself defeats any expectation of privacy in the movements of the container, even when the container is brought into places where others may have a privacy interest.

I would use a different and generally narrower test than the one proposed by the Court for determining when an activated beeper in a closed container violates the privacy of a homeowner into whose home the container is moved. I would use as the touchstone the defendant's interest in the container in which the beeper is placed. When a closed container is moved by permission into a home, the homeowner and others with an expectation of privacy in the home itself surrender any expectation of privacy they might otherwise retain in the movements of the container — unless it is their container or under their dominion and control. A privacy interest in a home itself need not be coextensive with a privacy interest in the contents or movements of everything situated inside the home.

The beeper in this case, however, transmitted information about the location, not the contents, of the container. Conceivably, location in a home is an attribute partly of the home and partly of the container itself. But the primary privacy interest is not the homeowner's. By giving consent to another to move a closed container into and out of the home the homeowner has effectively surrendered his privacy insofar as the location of the container may be concerned, or so we should assume absent evidence to the contrary. In other words, one who lacks dominion and control over the object's location has no privacy interest invaded when that information is disclosed. It is simply not his secret that the beeper is disclosing, just as it is not his privacy that would be invaded by a search of the container whose contents he did not control.

In sum, a privacy interest in the location of a closed container that enters a home with the homeowner's permission cannot be inferred mechanically by reference to the more general privacy interests in the home itself. The homeowner's privacy interests are often narrower than those of the owner of the container. A defendant should be allowed to challenge evidence obtained by monitoring a beeper installed in a closed container only if (1) the beeper was monitored when visual tracking of the container was not possible, so that the defendant had a reasonable expectation that the container's movements would remain private, and (2) the defendant had an interest in the container itself sufficient to empower him to give effective consent to a search of the container. A person's right not to have a container tracked by means of a beeper depends both on his power to prevent visual observation of the container and on his power to control its location, a power that can usually be inferred from a privacy interest in the container itself. One who lacks either power has no legitimate expectation of privacy in the movements of the container.

Justice STEVENS, with whom Justice BRENNAN and Justice MARSHALL join, concurring in part and dissenting in part.

The beeper is a species of radio transmitter. Mounted inside a container, it has much in common with a microphone mounted on a person. It reveals the location of the item to which it is attached — the functional equivalent of a radio transmission saying "Now I am at _____."

The threshold question in this case is whether the beeper invaded any interest protected by the Fourth Amendment. In my opinion the surreptitious use of a radio transmitter — whether it contains a microphone or merely a signalling device — on an individual's personal property is both a seizure and a search within the meaning of the Fourth Amendment. Part III of the opinion of the Court correctly concludes that when beeper surveillance reveals the location of property that has been concealed from public view, it constitutes a "search" within the meaning of the Fourth Amendment. I join Part III on that understanding. However, I find it necessary to write separately because I believe the Fourth Amendment's reach is somewhat broader than that which is explicitly acknowledged by the Court, and in particular because my understanding of the Fourth Amendment, as well as my understanding of the issues that have been framed for us by the parties to this case, leads me to a different result than that reached by the Court.

The attachment of the beeper, in my judgment, constituted a "seizure." The owner of property, of course, has a right to exclude from it all the world, including the Government, and a concomitant right to use it exclusively for his own purposes. When the Government attaches an electronic monitoring device to that property, it infringes that exclusionary right; in a fundamental sense it has converted the property to its own use. Surely such an invasion is an "interference" with possessory rights; the right to exclude, which attached as soon as the can respondents purchased was delivered, had been infringed. That interference is also "meaningful"; the character of the property is profoundly different when infected with an electronic bug than when it is entirely germ free.

The impact of beeper surveillance upon interests protected by the Fourth Amendment leads me to what I regard as the perfectly sensible conclusion that absent exigent circumstances Government agents have a constitutional duty to obtain a warrant before they install an electronic device on a private citizen's property.

The issue of what is sufficiently "public behavior" arises in other contexts as well. For example, in United States v. White, 401 U.S. 745 (1971), the Court considered whether there was a search when a government informer carrying a radio transmitter engaged in a conversation with a suspect. The Court held that the listening to this conversation by another agent, in possession of a radio receiver, was not a search. Justice White wrote for a plurality of four and concluded that the suspect had no reasonable expectation of privacy in the conversation. He wrote:

> Concededly a police agent who conceals his police connections may write down for official use his conversations with a defendant and testify concerning them, without a warrant authorizing his encounters with the defendant and without otherwise violating the latter's Fourth Amendment rights. For constitutional purposes, no different result is required if the agent instead of immediately reporting and transcribing his conversations with defendant, either (1) simultaneously records them with electronic equipment which he is carrying on his person;

(2) or carries radio equipment which simultaneously transmits the conversations either to recording equipment located elsewhere or to other agents monitoring the transmitting frequency. If the conduct and revelations of an agent operating without electronic equipment do not invade the defendant's constitutionally justifiable expectations of privacy, neither does a simultaneous recording of the same conversations made by the agent or by others from transmissions received from the agent to whom the defendant is talking and whose trustworthiness the defendant necessarily risks.

The Court has similarly found that inspection of bank records are not searches under the Fourth Amendment because banks are parties to any transactions and thus have knowledge of them. California Bankers Assn. v. Schultz, 416 U.S. 21 (1974). The case involved a federal law, the Bank Secrecy Act of 1970, which required that banks file reports with the federal government of certain types of transactions. A Fourth Amendment challenge was rejected by the Court on the grounds that people have no reasonable expectation of privacy as to this information because it is known by others, the banks that process the transactions. In other words, because some others in the government will see the bank records, the Court concluded that there is no privacy expectation in them.

The Court has gone even further and found that people have no reasonable expectation of privacy in the phone numbers they dial or receives calls from. The specific issue was whether police use of "pen registers" — sometimes called "trap" and "trace" equipment — to monitor calls is a search.

SMITH v. MARYLAND

442 U.S. 735 (1979)

Justice BLACKMUN delivered the opinion of the Court.

This case presents the question whether the installation and use of a pen register constitutes a "search" within the meaning of the Fourth Amendment.[5] A pen register is "usually installed at a central telephone facility [and] records on a paper tape all numbers dialed from [the] line" to which it is attached.

I

On March 5, 1976, in Baltimore, Md., Patricia McDonough was robbed. She gave the police a description of the robber and of a 1975 Monte Carlo automobile she had observed near the scene of the crime. After the robbery, McDonough began receiving threatening and obscene phone calls from a man identifying himself as the robber. On one occasion, the caller asked that she step out on her front porch; she did so, and saw the 1975 Monte Carlo she had earlier described to police moving slowly past her home. On March 16, police spotted a man who met McDonough's description driving a 1975 Monte Carlo in her neighborhood.

---

5. A pen register is a mechanical device that records the numbers dialed on a telephone by monitoring the electrical impulses caused when the dial on the telephone is released. It does not overhear oral communications and does not indicate whether calls are actually completed. [Footnote by the Court.]

By tracing the license plate number, police learned that the car was registered in the name of petitioner, Michael Lee Smith.

The next day, the telephone company, at police request, installed a pen register at its central offices to record the numbers dialed from the telephone at petitioner's home. The police did not get a warrant or court order before having the pen register installed. The register revealed that on March 17 a call was placed from petitioner's home to McDonough's phone. On the basis of this and other evidence, the police obtained a warrant to search petitioner's residence. The search revealed that a page in petitioner's phone book was turned down to the name and number of Patricia McDonough; the phone book was seized. Petitioner was arrested, and a six-man lineup was held on March 19. McDonough identified petitioner as the man who had robbed her.

II

In determining whether a particular form of government-initiated electronic surveillance is a "search" within the meaning of the Fourth Amendment, our lodestar is Katz v. United States (1967). Consistently with *Katz*, this Court uniformly has held that the application of the Fourth Amendment depends on whether the person invoking its protection can claim a "justifiable," a "reasonable," or a "legitimate expectation of privacy" that has been invaded by government action. This inquiry, as Justice Harlan aptly noted in his *Katz* concurrence, normally embraces two discrete questions. The first is whether the individual, by his conduct, has "exhibited an actual (subjective) expectation of privacy," — whether, in the words of the *Katz* majority, the individual has shown that "he seeks to preserve [something] as private." The second question is whether the individual's subjective expectation of privacy is "one that society is prepared to recognize as 'reasonable,'" — whether, in the words of the *Katz* majority, the individual's expectation, viewed objectively, is "justifiable" under the circumstances.

In applying the *Katz* analysis to this case, it is important to begin by specifying precisely the nature of the state activity that is challenged. The activity here took the form of installing and using a pen register. Since the pen register was installed on telephone company property at the telephone company's central offices, petitioner obviously cannot claim that his "property" was invaded or that police intruded into a "constitutionally protected area." Petitioner's claim, rather, is that, notwithstanding the absence of a trespass, the State, as did the Government in *Katz*, infringed a "legitimate expectation of privacy" that petitioner held. Yet a pen register differs significantly from the listening device employed in *Katz*, for pen registers do not acquire the contents of communications.

Given a pen register's limited capabilities, therefore, petitioner's argument that its installation and use constituted a "search" necessarily rests upon a claim that he had a "legitimate expectation of privacy" regarding the numbers he dialed on his phone.

This claim must be rejected. First, we doubt that people in general entertain any actual expectation of privacy in the numbers they dial. All telephone users realize that they must "convey" phone numbers to the telephone company, since it is through telephone company switching equipment that their calls are completed. All subscribers realize, moreover, that the phone company has facilities for making permanent records of the numbers they dial, for they see a list of their long-distance (toll) calls on their monthly bills. In fact, pen registers and similar devices are routinely used by telephone companies "for the purposes of checking billing operations, detecting fraud and preventing violations of law." Electronic equipment is used not only to keep billing records of toll calls, but also "to keep a record of all calls dialed from a telephone which is subject to a special rate structure." Pen registers are regularly employed "to determine whether a home phone is being used to conduct a business, to check for a defective dial, or to check for overbilling." Although most people may be oblivious to a pen register's esoteric functions, they presumably have some awareness of one common use: to aid in the identification of persons making annoying or obscene calls. Telephone users, in sum, typically know that they must convey numerical information to the phone company; that the phone company has facilities for recording this information; and that the phone company does in fact record this information for a variety of legitimate business purposes. Although subjective expectations cannot be scientifically gauged, it is too much to believe that telephone subscribers, under these circumstances, harbor any general expectation that the numbers they dial will remain secret.

Petitioner argues, however, that, whatever the expectations of telephone users in general, he demonstrated an expectation of privacy by his own conduct here, since he "us[ed] the telephone in his house to the exclusion of all others." But the site of the call is immaterial for purposes of analysis in this case. Although petitioner's conduct may have been calculated to keep the contents of his conversation private, his conduct was not and could not have been calculated to preserve the privacy of the number he dialed. Regardless of his location, petitioner had to convey that number to the telephone company in precisely the same way if he wished to complete his call. The fact that he dialed the number on his home phone rather than on some other phone could make no conceivable difference, nor could any subscriber rationally think that it would.

Second, even if petitioner did harbor some subjective expectation that the phone numbers he dialed would remain private, this expectation is not "one that society is prepared to recognize as 'reasonable.'" This Court consistently has held that a person has no legitimate expectation of privacy in information he voluntarily turns over to third parties.

This analysis dictates that petitioner can claim no legitimate expectation of privacy here. When he used his phone, petitioner voluntarily conveyed numerical information to the telephone company and "exposed" that information to its equipment in the ordinary course of business. In so doing, petitioner assumed the risk that the company would reveal to police the numbers he dialed. The switching equipment that processed those numbers is merely the modern counterpart of the operator who, in an earlier day, personally completed calls for the subscriber.

Justice STEWART, with whom Justice BRENNAN joins, dissenting.

I am not persuaded that the numbers dialed from a private telephone fall outside the constitutional protection of the Fourth and Fourteenth Amendments. In Katz v. United States, the Court acknowledged the "vital role that the public telephone has come to play in private communication[s]." The role played by a private telephone is even more vital, and since *Katz* it has been abundantly clear that telephone conversations carried on by people in their homes or offices are fully protected by the Fourth and Fourteenth Amendments.

Nevertheless, the Court today says that those safeguards do not extend to the numbers dialed from a private telephone, apparently because when a caller dials a number the digits may be recorded by the telephone company for billing purposes. But that observation no more than describes the basic nature of telephone calls. A telephone call simply cannot be made without the use of telephone company property and without payment to the company for the service. The telephone conversation itself must be electronically transmitted by telephone company equipment, and may be recorded or overheard by the use of other company equipment. Yet we have squarely held that the user of even a public telephone is entitled "to assume that the words he utters into the mouthpiece will not be broadcast to the world."

The central question in this case is whether a person who makes telephone calls from his home is entitled to make a similar assumption about the numbers he dials. What the telephone company does or might do with those numbers is no more relevant to this inquiry than it would be in a case involving the conversation itself. It is simply not enough to say, after *Katz*, that there is no legitimate expectation of privacy in the numbers dialed because the caller assumes the risk that the telephone company will disclose them to the police.

I think that the numbers dialed from a private telephone — like the conversations that occur during a call — are within the constitutional protection recognized in *Katz*. It seems clear to me that information obtained by pen register surveillance of a private telephone is information in which the telephone subscriber has a legitimate expectation of privacy. The information captured by such surveillance emanates from private conduct within a person's home or office — locations that without question are entitled to Fourth and Fourteenth Amendment protection. Further, that information is an integral part of the telephonic communication that under *Katz* is entitled to constitutional protection, whether or not it is captured by a trespass into such an area.

The numbers dialed from a private telephone — although certainly more prosaic than the conversation itself — are not without "content." Most private telephone subscribers may have their own numbers listed in a publicly distributed directory, but I doubt there are any who would be happy to have broadcast to the world a list of the local or long distance numbers they have called. This is not because such a list might in some sense be incriminating, but because it easily could reveal the identities of the persons and the places called, and thus reveal the most intimate details of a person's life.

In 1986, Congress enacted a statute that prohibits the installation or use of pen registers, except relating to the "operation, maintenance, and testing of a wire or electronic communication service or to the protection of the rights or property of such a provider" without a court order. 18 U.S.C. § 2131. A federal court may issue such an order for a 60-day period upon application of a United States Attorney or a state law enforcement officer, if the federal or state attorney "has certified to the court that the relevant information is likely to be obtained by such installation and [its] use is relevant to an ongoing criminal investigation." 18 U.S.C. § 3132(a)(1) and (2). The law also provides that a pen register may be installed without a court order for a period of 48 hours if there is an emergency involving "immediate death or serious bodily injury."

The USA Patriot Act allows the Attorney General to obtain authority for a pen register from the Foreign Intelligence Surveillance Court "for any investigation to obtain foreign intelligence information not concerning a United States person or to protect against international terrorism or clandestine intelligence activities, provided that such investigation of a United States person is not conducted solely upon the basis of activities protected by the First Amendment to the Constitution." 50 U.S.C. § 1842(a)(1).

6. *Use of Dogs to Sniff for Contraband*

Is it a search if the police use drug-sniffing dogs? There is no overall answer to this question yet from the Supreme Court. But the Supreme Court has found the use of such dogs is not a search in a couple of contexts. In United States v. Place, 462 U.S. 696 (1983), the Court held that a canine sniff of closed luggage is not a search. Place aroused police suspicions when he was flying out of the Miami Airport to LaGuardia. Police were waiting for Place there. Justice O'Connor, who wrote the Court's opinion, stated the facts:

> The agents then took the bags to Kennedy Airport, where they subjected the bags to a "sniff test" by a trained narcotics detection dog. The dog reacted positively to the smaller of the two bags but ambiguously to the larger bag. Approximately 90 minutes had elapsed since the seizure of respondent's luggage. Because it was late on a Friday afternoon, the agents retained the luggage until Monday morning, when they secured a search warrant from a magistrate for the smaller bag. Upon opening that bag, the agents discovered 1,125 grams of cocaine.

The Court held that the dog sniff was not a search within the meaning of the Fourth Amendment:

> The purpose for which respondent's luggage was seized, of course, was to arrange its exposure to a narcotics detection dog. Obviously, if this investigative procedure is itself a search requiring probable cause, the initial seizure of respondent's luggage for the purpose of subjecting it to the sniff test — no matter how brief — could not be justified on less than probable cause.
>
> The Fourth Amendment "protects people from unreasonable government intrusions into their legitimate expectations of privacy." We have affirmed that a person possesses a privacy interest in the contents of personal luggage that is protected by the Fourth Amendment. A "canine sniff" by a well-trained narcotics detection dog, however, does not require opening the luggage. It does not expose noncontraband items that otherwise would remain hidden from public view, as does, for example, an officer's rummaging through the contents of the luggage. Thus, the manner in which information is obtained through this investigative technique is much less intrusive than a typical search. Moreover, the sniff discloses only the presence or absence of narcotics, a contraband item. Thus, despite the fact that the sniff tells the authorities something about the contents of the luggage, the information obtained is limited. This limited disclosure also ensures that the owner of the property is not subjected to the embarrassment and inconvenience entailed in less discriminate and more intrusive investigative methods.

In these respects, the canine sniff is sui generis. We are aware of no other investigative procedure that is so limited both in the manner in which the information is obtained and in the content of the information revealed by the procedure. Therefore, we conclude that the particular course of investigation that the agents intended to pursue here — exposure of respondent's luggage, which was located in a public place, to a trained canine — did not constitute a "search" within the meaning of the Fourth Amendment.

In its more recent decision, Illinois v. Caballes, the Court considered dog sniffs in another context: a traffic stop. Again, the Court found that there was not a search. In light of *Place* and *Caballes*, it is worth thinking of other situations where dogs might be used and whether these uses should be regarded as searches.

ILLINOIS v. CABALLES

543 U.S. 405 (2005)

Justice STEVENS delivered the opinion of the Court.

Illinois State Trooper Daniel Gillette stopped respondent for speeding on an interstate highway. When Gillette radioed the police dispatcher to report the stop, a second trooper, Craig Graham, a member of the Illinois State Police Drug Interdiction Team, overheard the transmission and immediately headed for the scene with his narcotics-detection dog. When they arrived, respondent's car was on the shoulder of the road and respondent was in Gillette's vehicle. While Gillette was in the process of writing a warning ticket, Graham walked his dog around respondent's car. The dog alerted at the trunk. Based on that alert, the officers searched the trunk, found marijuana, and arrested respondent. The entire incident lasted less than 10 minutes.

Respondent was convicted of a narcotics offense and sentenced to 12 years' imprisonment and a $256,136 fine. The trial judge denied his motion to suppress the seized evidence and to quash his arrest. He held that the officers had not unnecessarily prolonged the stop and that the dog alert was sufficiently reliable to provide probable cause to conduct the search. Although the Appellate Court affirmed, the Illinois Supreme Court reversed, concluding that because the canine sniff was performed without any "specific and articulable facts" to suggest drug activity, the use of the dog "unjustifiably enlarg[ed] the scope of a routine traffic stop into a drug investigation."

The question on which we granted certiorari is narrow: "Whether the Fourth Amendment requires reasonable, articulable suspicion to justify using a drug-detection dog to sniff a vehicle during a legitimate traffic stop." Thus, we proceed on the assumption that the officer conducting the dog sniff had no information about respondent except that he had been stopped for speeding; accordingly, we have omitted any reference to facts about respondent that might have triggered a modicum of suspicion.

Here, the initial seizure of respondent when he was stopped on the highway was based on probable cause and was concededly lawful. It is nevertheless clear that a seizure that is lawful at its inception can violate the Fourth Amendment if its manner of execution unreasonably infringes interests protected by the Constitution. A seizure that is justified solely by the interest in issuing a warning

#2

ticket to the driver can become unlawful if it is prolonged beyond the time reasonably required to complete that mission.

Official conduct that does not "compromise any legitimate interest in privacy" is not a search subject to the Fourth Amendment. We have held that any interest in possessing contraband cannot be deemed "legitimate," and thus, governmental conduct that only reveals the possession of contraband "compromises no legitimate privacy interest." This is because the expectation "that certain facts will not come to the attention of the authorities" is not the same as an interest in "privacy that society is prepared to consider reasonable." In United States v. Place, we treated a canine sniff by a well-trained narcotics-detection dog as "sui generis" because it "discloses only the presence or absence of narcotics, a contraband item." Respondent likewise concedes that "drug sniffs are designed, and if properly conducted are generally likely, to reveal only the presence of contraband." Although respondent argues that the error rates, particularly the existence of false positives, call into question the premise that drug-detection dogs alert only to contraband, the record contains no evidence or findings that support his argument. Moreover, respondent does not suggest that an erroneous alert, in and of itself, reveals any legitimate private information, and, in this case, the trial judge found that the dog sniff was sufficiently reliable to establish probable cause to conduct a full-blown search of the trunk.

Rule
#3

Accordingly, the use of a well-trained narcotics-detection dog—one that "does not expose noncontraband items that otherwise would remain hidden from public view,"—during a lawful traffic stop, generally does not implicate legitimate privacy interests. In this case, the dog sniff was performed on the exterior of respondent's car while he was lawfully seized for a traffic violation. Any intrusion on respondent's privacy expectations does not rise to the level of a constitutionally cognizable infringement.

This conclusion is entirely consistent with our recent decision that the use of a thermal-imaging device to detect the growth of marijuana in a home constituted an unlawful search. Kyllo v. United States (2001). Critical to that decision was the fact that the device was capable of detecting lawful activity—in that case, intimate details in a home, such as "at what hour each night the lady of the house takes her daily sauna and bath." The legitimate expectation that information about perfectly lawful activity will remain private is categorically distinguishable from respondent's hopes or expectations concerning the non-detection of contraband in the trunk of his car. A dog sniff conducted during a concededly lawful traffic stop that reveals no information other than the location of a substance that no individual has any right to possess does not violate the Fourth Amendment.

Justice SOUTER, dissenting.

I would hold that using the dog for the purposes of determining the presence of marijuana in the car's trunk was a search unauthorized as an incident of the speeding stop and unjustified on any other ground.

In United States v. Place (1983), we categorized the sniff of the narcotics-seeking dog as "sui generis" under the Fourth Amendment and held it was not a search. The classification rests not only upon the limited nature of the intrusion, but on a further premise that experience has shown to be untenable, the assumption that trained sniffing dogs do not err. What we have learned about the fallibility of dogs in the years since *Place* was decided would itself be reason to call for reconsidering *Place*'s decision against treating the intentional use of a trained dog as a search. The portent of this very case, however, adds insistence to the call, for an uncritical adherence to *Place* would render the Fourth Amendment indifferent to suspicionless and indiscriminate sweeps of cars in parking garages and pedestrians on sidewalks; if a sniff is not preceded by a seizure subject to Fourth Amendment notice, it escapes Fourth Amendment review entirely unless it is treated as a search. We should not wait for these developments to occur before rethinking *Place*'s analysis, which invites such untoward consequences.

At the heart both of *Place* and the Court's opinion today is the proposition that sniffs by a trained dog are sui generis because a reaction by the dog in going alert is a response to nothing but the presence of contraband. Hence, the argument goes, because the sniff can only reveal the presence of items devoid of any legal use, the sniff "does not implicate legitimate privacy interests" and is not to be treated as a search.

The infallible dog, however, is a creature of legal fiction. Although the Supreme Court of Illinois did not get into the sniffing averages of drug dogs, their supposed infallibility is belied by judicial opinions describing well-trained animals sniffing and alerting with less than perfect accuracy, whether owing to errors by their handlers, the limitations of the dogs themselves, or even the pervasive contamination of currency by cocaine. Indeed, a study cited by Illinois in this case for the proposition that dog sniffs are "generally reliable" shows that dogs in artificial testing situations return false positives anywhere from 12.5% to 60% of the time, depending on the length of the search. In practical terms, the evidence is clear that the dog that alerts hundreds of times will be wrong dozens of times.

Once the dog's fallibility is recognized, however, that ends the justification claimed in *Place* for treating the sniff as sui generis under the Fourth Amendment: The sniff alert does not necessarily signal hidden contraband, and opening the container or enclosed space whose emanations the dog has sensed will not necessarily reveal contraband or any other evidence of crime.

It makes sense, then, to treat a sniff as the search that it amounts to in practice, and to rely on the body of our Fourth Amendment cases, including *Kyllo*, in deciding whether such a search is reasonable. As a general proposition, using a dog to sniff for drugs is subject to the rule that the object of enforcing criminal laws does not, without more, justify suspicionless Fourth Amendment intrusions.

Justice GINSBURG, with whom Justice SOUTER joins, dissenting.

Illinois State Police Trooper Daniel Gillette stopped Roy Caballes for driving 71 miles per hour in a zone with a posted speed limit of 65 miles per hour. Trooper Craig Graham of the Drug Interdiction Team heard on the radio that Trooper Gillette was making a traffic stop. Although Gillette requested no aid, Graham decided to come to the scene to conduct a dog sniff.

It is hardly dispositive that the dog sniff in this case may not have lengthened the duration of the stop. *Terry*, it merits repetition, instructs that any investigation must be "reasonably related in scope to the circumstances which justified the interference in the first place." The unwarranted and nonconsensual expansion of the seizure here from a routine traffic stop to a drug investigation broadened the scope of the investigation in a manner that, in my judgment, runs afoul of the Fourth Amendment.

C. THE REQUIREMENT FOR PROBABLE CAUSE

A core requirement of the Fourth Amendment is the requirement for probable cause. Generally, a judge may issue a search or arrest warrant only if there is probable cause. If it is a circumstance where a warrant is not required (and these are discussed below in Section E), a police officer generally can search or arrest only if there is probable cause. There are exceptions. For example, in some situations searches are allowed with less than probable cause. As discussed below, in schools, searches of students' purses requires only the lesser standard of "reasonable suspicion," not the usual requirement of probable cause. New Jersey v. T.L.O., 469 U.S. 325 (1986). Sometimes searches are even allowed without any individualized suspicion, such as when the Court has approved random drug testing (also discussed below). *See, e.g.,* Vernonia School Dist. 47J v. Acton, 515 U.S. 646 (1995) (upholding random drug testing for student athletes).

But the Supreme Court has been clear that probable cause is the "traditional standard" of the Fourth Amendment. Arizona v. Hicks, 480 U.S. 321 (1987). There is no precise definition of probable cause. The classic definition of probable cause, often cited by the Supreme Court, was articulated in Carroll v. United States, 267 U.S. 132 (1878). The Supreme Court said that the question is whether "the facts and circumstances before the officer are such to warrant a man of prudence and caution in believing that the offense had been committed."

Two questions are particularly important in understanding probable cause. First, what is sufficient belief to meet the standard for probable cause? Second, is it an objective or a subjective standard?

1. *What Is Sufficient Belief to Meet the Standard for Probable Cause?*

The Supreme Court has said that "in dealing with probable cause . . . we deal with probabilities." Brinegar v. United States, 338 U.S. 160 (1949). But the Court did not attempt to define what probabilities are sufficient. The Court simply said that "more than bare suspicion," but "less than evidence which would justify conviction."

The Supreme Court has confronted this question of what is sufficient for probable cause in determining whether information from informants was sufficient to constitute probable cause. Initially, the Court addressed this in two cases in the 1960s: Aguilar v. Texas, 378 U.S. 108 (1964), and Spinelli v. United States, 393 U.S. 410 (1969). These cases gave rise to the *Aguilar-Spinelli* two-part test. First, was the informant credible — was it likely that he or she was telling the truth? Second, was the informant reliable — was it likely that the informant had knowledge? If an informant did not meet these requirements, there was not probable cause and the fruits of the search had to be excluded.

In Illinois v. Gates, below, the Court departed from the *Aguilar-Spinelli* approach and emphasized the need to consider the "totality of the circumstances." This is the general approach used in determining whether there is probable cause, even beyond the issue of determining whether an informant is reliable.

ILLINOIS v. GATES

462 U.S. 213 (1983)

Justice REHNQUIST delivered the opinion of the Court.

Respondents Lance and Susan Gates were indicted for violation of state drug laws after police officers, executing a search warrant, discovered marijuana and other contraband in their automobile and home. Prior to trial the Gateses moved to suppress evidence seized during this search. The Illinois Supreme Court affirmed the decisions of lower state courts, granting the motion. It held that the affidavit submitted in support of the State's application for a warrant to search the Gateses' property was inadequate under this Court's decisions in Aguilar v. Texas (1964) and Spinelli v. United States (1969).

[I]

We turn to the question presented in the State's original petition for certiorari, which requires us to decide whether respondents' rights under the Fourth and Fourteenth Amendments were violated by the search of their car and house. A chronological statement of events usefully introduces the issues at stake. Bloomingdale, Ill., is a suburb of Chicago located in DuPage County. On May 3, 1978, the Bloomingdale Police Department received by mail an anonymous handwritten letter which read as follows:

> This letter is to inform you that you have a couple in your town who strictly make their living on selling drugs. They are Sue and Lance Gates, they live on Greenway, off Bloomingdale Rd. in the condominiums. Most of their buys are done in Florida. Sue his wife drives their car to Florida, where she leaves it to be loaded up with drugs, then Lance flys down and drives it back. Sue flys back after she drops the car off in Florida. May 3 she is driving down there again and Lance will be flying down in a few days to drive it back. At the time Lance drives the car back he has the trunk loaded with over $100,000.00 in drugs. Presently they have over $100,000.00 worth of drugs in their basement.
>
> They brag about the fact they never have to work, and make their entire living on pushers.
>
> I guarantee if you watch them carefully you will make a big catch. They are friends with some big drug dealers, who visit their house often.

The letter was referred by the Chief of Police of the Bloomingdale Police Department to Detective Mader, who decided to pursue the tip. Mader learned, from the office of the Illinois Secretary of State, that an Illinois driver's license had been issued to one Lance Gates, residing at a stated address in Bloomingdale. He contacted a confidential informant, whose examination of certain financial records revealed a more recent address for the Gateses, and he also learned from a police officer assigned to O'Hare Airport that "L. Gates" had made a reservation on Eastern Airlines flight 245 to West Palm Beach, Fla., scheduled to depart from Chicago on May 5 at 4:15 P.M.

Mader then made arrangements with an agent of the Drug Enforcement Administration for surveillance of the May 5 Eastern Airlines flight. The agent later reported to Mader that Gates had boarded the flight, and that federal agents in Florida had observed him arrive in West Palm Beach and take a taxi to the nearby Holiday Inn. They also reported that Gates went to a room registered to one Susan Gates and that, at 7:00 A.M. the next morning, Gates and an unidentified woman left the motel in a Mercury bearing Illinois license plates and drove northbound on an interstate frequently used by travelers to the Chicago area. In addition, the DEA agent informed Mader that the license plate number on the Mercury registered to a Hornet station wagon owned by Gates. The agent also advised Mader that the driving time between West Palm Beach and Bloomingdale was approximately 22 to 24 hours.

Mader signed an affidavit setting forth the foregoing facts, and submitted it to a judge of the Circuit Court of DuPage County, together with a copy of the anonymous letter. The judge of that court thereupon issued a search warrant for the Gateses' residence and for their automobile. The judge, in deciding to issue the warrant, could have determined that the modus operandi of the Gateses had been substantially corroborated. As the anonymous letter predicted, Lance Gates had flown from Chicago to West Palm Beach late in the afternoon of May 5th, had checked into a hotel room registered in the name of his wife, and, at 7:00 A.M. the following morning, had headed north, accompanied by an unidentified woman, out of West Palm Beach on an interstate highway used by travelers from South Florida to Chicago in an automobile bearing a license plate issued to him.

At 5:15 A.M. on March 7th, only 36 hours after he had flown out of Chicago, Lance Gates, and his wife, returned to their home in Bloomingdale, driving the car in which they had left West Palm Beach some 22 hours earlier. The Bloomingdale police were awaiting them, searched the trunk of the Mercury, and uncovered approximately 350 pounds of marijuana. A search of the Gateses' home revealed marijuana, weapons, and other contraband. The Illinois Circuit Court ordered suppression of all these items, on the ground that the affidavit submitted to the Circuit Judge failed to support the necessary determination of probable cause to believe that the Gateses' automobile and home contained the contraband in question. This decision was affirmed in turn by the Illinois Appellate Court and by a divided vote of the Supreme Court of Illinois.

The Illinois Supreme Court concluded — and we are inclined to agree — that, standing alone, the anonymous letter sent to the Bloomingdale Police Department would not provide the basis for a magistrate's determination that there was probable cause to believe contraband would be found in the Gateses' car and home. The letter provides virtually nothing from which one might conclude that its author is either honest or his information reliable; likewise, the letter gives absolutely no indication of the basis for the writer's predictions regarding the Gateses' criminal activities. Something more was required, then, before a magistrate could conclude that there was probable cause to believe that contraband would be found in the Gateses' home and car.

The Illinois Supreme Court also properly recognized that Detective Mader's affidavit might be capable of supplementing the anonymous letter with information sufficient to permit a determination of probable cause. In holding that the affidavit in fact did not contain sufficient additional information to sustain a determination of probable cause, the Illinois court applied a "two-pronged test," derived from our decision in Spinelli v. United States (1969).

We agree with the Illinois Supreme Court that an informant's "veracity," "reliability" and "basis of knowledge" are all highly relevant in determining the value of his report. We do not agree, however, that these elements should be understood as entirely separate and independent requirements to be rigidly exacted in every case, which the opinion of the Supreme Court of Illinois would imply. Rather, as detailed below, they should be understood simply as closely intertwined issues that may usefully illuminate the common-sense, practical question whether there is "probable cause" to believe that contraband or evidence is located in a particular place.

[II]

This totality-of-the-circumstances approach is far more consistent with our prior treatment of probable cause than is any rigid demand that specific "tests" be satisfied by every informant's tip. Perhaps the central teaching of our decisions bearing on the probable cause standard is that it is a "practical, nontechnical conception." "In dealing with probable cause, . . . as the very name implies, we deal with probabilities. These are not technical; they are the factual and practical considerations of everyday life on which reasonable and prudent men, not legal technicians, act."

As our language indicates, we intended neither a rigid compartmentalization of the inquiries into an informant's "veracity," "reliability" and "basis of knowledge," nor that these inquiries be elaborate exegeses of an informant's tip. Rather, we required only that some facts bearing on two particular issues be provided to the magistrate.

The process does not deal with hard certainties, but with probabilities. Long before the law of probabilities was articulated as such, practical people formulated certain common-sense conclusions about human behavior; jurors as fact-finders are permitted to do the same — and so are law enforcement officers. Finally, the evidence thus collected must be seen and weighed not in terms of library analysis by scholars, but as understood by those versed in the field of law enforcement.

As these comments illustrate, probable cause is a fluid concept — turning on the assessment of probabilities in particular factual contexts — not readily, or even usefully, reduced to a neat set of legal rules. Informants' tips doubtless come in many shapes and sizes from many different types of persons.

Moreover, the "two-pronged test" directs analysis into two largely independent channels — the informant's "veracity" or "reliability" and his "basis of knowledge." There are persuasive arguments against according these two elements such independent status. Instead, they are better understood as relevant considerations in the totality-of-the-circumstances analysis that traditionally has guided probable cause determinations: a deficiency in one may be compensated for, in determining the overall reliability of a tip, by a strong showing as to the other, or by some other indicia of reliability.

If, for example, a particular informant is known for the unusual reliability of his predictions of certain types of criminal activities in a locality, his failure, in a particular case, to thoroughly set forth the basis of his knowledge surely should not serve as an absolute bar to a finding of probable cause based on his tip. Likewise, if an unquestionably honest citizen comes forward with a report of criminal activity — which if fabricated would subject him to criminal liability — we have found rigorous scrutiny of the basis of his knowledge unnecessary. Conversely, even if we entertain some doubt as to an informant's motives, his explicit and detailed description of alleged wrongdoing, along with a statement that the event was observed first-hand, entitles his tip to greater weight than might otherwise be the case. Unlike a totality-of-the-circumstances analysis, which permits a balanced assessment of the relative weights of all the various indicia of reliability (and unreliability) attending an informant's tip, the "two-pronged test" has encouraged an excessively technical dissection of informants' tips, with undue attention being focused on isolated issues that cannot sensibly be divorced from the other facts presented to the magistrate.

Finally, the direction taken by decisions following *Spinelli* poorly serves "the most basic function of any government": "to provide for the security of the individual and of his property." The strictures that inevitably accompany the "two-pronged test" cannot avoid seriously impeding the task of law enforcement. If, as the Illinois Supreme Court apparently thought, that test must be rigorously applied in every case, anonymous tips seldom would be of greatly diminished value in police work. Ordinary citizens, like ordinary witnesses, generally do not provide extensive recitations of the basis of their everyday observations. Likewise, as the Illinois Supreme Court observed in this case, the veracity of persons supplying anonymous tips is by hypothesis largely unknown, and unknowable. As a result, anonymous tips seldom could survive a rigorous application of either of the *Spinelli* prongs. Yet, such tips, particularly when supplemented by independent police investigation, frequently contribute to the solution of otherwise "perfect crimes." While a conscientious assessment of the basis for crediting such tips is required by the Fourth Amendment, a standard that leaves virtually no place for anonymous citizen informants is not.

For all these reasons, we conclude that it is wiser to abandon the "two-pronged test" established by our decisions in *Aguilar* and *Spinelli*. In its place we reaffirm the totality-of-the-circumstances analysis that traditionally has informed probable cause determinations. The task of the issuing magistrate is simply to make a practical, common-sense decision whether, given all the circumstances set forth in the affidavit before him, including the "veracity" and "basis of knowledge" of persons supplying hearsay information, there is a fair probability that contraband or evidence of a crime will be found in a particular place. And the duty of a reviewing court is simply to ensure that the magistrate had a "substantial basis for . . . conclud[ing]" that probable cause existed. We are convinced that this flexible, easily applied standard will better achieve the accommodation of public and private interests that the Fourth Amendment requires than does the approach that has developed from *Aguilar* and *Spinelli*.

Our earlier cases illustrate the limits beyond which a magistrate may not venture in issuing a warrant. A sworn statement of an affiant that "he has cause to suspect and does believe that" liquor illegally brought into the United States is located on certain premises will not do. An affidavit must provide the magistrate with a substantial basis for determining the existence of probable cause, and [a] wholly conclusory statement fail[s] to meet this requirement. An officer's statement that "affiants have received reliable information from a credible person and believe" that heroin is stored in a home, is likewise inadequate. [T]his is a mere conclusory statement that gives the magistrate virtually no basis at all for making a judgment regarding probable cause. Sufficient information must be presented to the magistrate to allow that official to determine probable cause; his action cannot be a mere ratification of the bare conclusions of others. In order to ensure that such an abdication of the magistrate's duty does not occur, courts must continue to conscientiously review the sufficiency of affidavits on which warrants are issued. But when we move beyond the "bare bones" affidavits, this area simply does not lend itself to a prescribed set of rules. Instead, the flexible, common-sense standard articulated better serves the purposes of the Fourth Amendment's probable cause requirement.

[III]

Our decisions applying the totality-of-the-circumstances analysis outlined above have consistently recognized the value of corroboration of details of an informant's tip by independent police work. Likewise, we recognized the probative value of corroborative efforts of police officials.

In addition, the magistrate could rely on the anonymous letter, which had been corroborated in major part by Mader's efforts. The corroboration of the letter's predictions that the Gateses' car would be in Florida, that Lance Gates would fly to Florida in the next day or so, and that he would drive the car north toward Bloomingdale all indicated, albeit not with certainty, that the informant's other assertions also were true. "Because an informant is right about some things, he is more probably right about other facts," including the claim regarding the Gateses' illegal activity. This may well not be the type of "reliability" or "veracity" necessary to satisfy some views of the "veracity prong" of *Spinelli*, but we think it suffices for the practical, common-sense judgment called for in making a probable cause determination. It is enough, for purposes of assessing probable cause, that "corroboration through other sources of information reduced the chances of a reckless or prevaricating tale," thus providing "a substantial basis for crediting the hearsay."

This is perfectly reasonable. As discussed previously, probable cause requires only a probability or substantial chance of criminal activity, not an actual showing of such activity. By hypothesis, therefore, innocent behavior frequently will provide the basis for a showing of probable cause; to require otherwise would be to sub silentio impose a drastically more rigorous definition of probable cause than the security of our citizens demands. We think the Illinois court attempted a too rigid classification of the types of conduct that may be relied upon in seeking to demonstrate probable cause. In making a determination of probable cause the relevant inquiry is not whether particular conduct is "innocent" or "guilty," but the degree of suspicion that attaches to particular types of non-criminal acts.

Finally, the anonymous letter contained a range of details relating not just to easily obtained facts and conditions existing at the time of the tip, but to future actions of third parties ordinarily not easily predicted. The letter writer's accurate information as to the travel plans of each of the Gateses was of a character likely obtained only from the Gateses themselves, or from someone familiar with their not entirely ordinary travel plans. If the informant had access to accurate information of this type a magistrate could properly conclude that it was not unlikely that he also had access to reliable information of the Gateses' alleged illegal activities. Of course, the Gateses' travel plans might have been learned from a talkative neighbor or travel agent; under the "two-pronged test" developed from *Spinelli*, the character of the details in the anonymous letter might well not permit a sufficiently clear inference regarding the letter writer's "basis of knowledge." But, as discussed previously, probable cause does not demand the certainty we associate with formal trials. It is enough that there was a fair probability that the writer of the anonymous letter had obtained his entire story either from the Gates or someone they trusted. And corroboration of major portions of the letter's predictions provides just this probability. It is apparent, therefore, that the judge issuing the warrant had a "substantial basis for . . . conclud[ing]" that probable cause to search the Gateses' home and car existed.

Justice BRENNAN, with whom Justice MARSHALL joins, dissenting.

Although I join Justice Stevens' dissenting opinion and agree with him that the warrant is invalid even under the Court's newly announced "totality of the circumstances" test, I write separately to dissent from the Court's unjustified and ill-advised rejection of the two-prong test for evaluating the validity of a warrant based on hearsay announced in Aguilar v. Texas (1964), and refined in Spinelli v. United States (1969).

I

In recognition of the judiciary's role as the only effective guardian of Fourth Amendment rights, this Court has developed over the last half century a set of coherent rules governing a magistrate's consideration of a warrant application and the showings that are necessary to support a finding of probable cause. We start with the proposition that a neutral and detached magistrate, and not the police, should determine whether there is probable cause to support the issuance of a warrant. In order to emphasize the magistrate's role as an independent arbiter of probable cause and to insure that searches or seizures are not effected on less than probable cause, the Court has insisted that police officers provide magistrates with the underlying facts and circumstances that support the officers' conclusions. The Court stated that "[u]nder the Fourth Amendment, an officer may not properly issue a warrant to search a private dwelling unless he can find probable cause therefor from facts or circumstances presented to him under oath or affirmation. Mere affirmance of belief or suspicion is not enough."

The Aguilar standard was refined in Spinelli v. United States (1969). In Spinelli, the Court reviewed a search warrant based on an affidavit that was "more ample," than the one in Aguilar. The affidavit in Spinelli contained not only a tip from an informant, but also a report of an independent police investigation that allegedly corroborated the informant's tip. Under these circumstances, the Court stated that it was "required to delineate the manner in which Aguilar's two-pronged test should be applied. . . ."

The Court held that the Aguilar test should be applied to the tip, and approved two additional ways of satisfying that test. First, the Court suggested that if the tip contained sufficient detail describing the accused's criminal activity it might satisfy Aguilar's basis of knowledge prong. Such detail might assure the magistrate that he is "relying on something more substantial than a casual rumor circulating in the underworld or an accusation based merely on an individual's general reputation." "A magistrate, when confronted with such detail, could reasonably infer that the informant had gained his information in a reliable way."

Second, the Court stated that police corroboration of the details of a tip could provide a basis for satisfying *Aguilar*.

I find this reasoning persuasive. Properly understood, therefore, *Spinelli* stands for the proposition that corroboration of certain details in a tip may be sufficient to satisfy the veracity, but not the basis of knowledge, prong of *Aguilar*. As noted, *Spinelli* also suggests that in some limited circumstances considerable detail in an informant's tip may be adequate to satisfy the basis of knowledge prong of *Aguilar*.

Although the rules drawn from the cases discussed above are cast in procedural terms, they advance an important underlying substantive value: Findings of probable cause, and attendant intrusions, should not be authorized unless there is some assurance that the information on which they are based has been obtained in a reliable way by an honest or credible person. As applied to police officers, the rules focus on the way in which the information was acquired. As applied to informants, the rules focus both on the honesty or credibility of the informant and on the reliability of the way in which the information was acquired. Insofar as it is more complicated, an evaluation of affidavits based on hearsay involves a more difficult inquiry. This suggests a need to structure the inquiry in an effort to insure greater accuracy. The standards announced in *Aguilar*, as refined by *Spinelli*, fulfill that need. The standards inform the police of what information they have to provide and magistrates of what information they should demand. The standards also inform magistrates of the subsidiary findings they must make in order to arrive at an ultimate finding of probable cause. *Spinelli*, properly understood, directs the magistrate's attention to the possibility that the presence of self-verifying detail might satisfy *Aguilar*'s basis of knowledge prong and that corroboration of the details of a tip might satisfy *Aguilar*'s veracity prong. By requiring police to provide certain crucial information to magistrates and by structuring magistrates' probable cause inquiries, *Aguilar* and *Spinelli* assure the magistrate's role as an independent arbiter of probable cause, insure greater accuracy in probable cause determinations, and advance the substantive value identified above.

In light of the important purposes served by *Aguilar* and *Spinelli*, I would not reject the standards they establish. If anything, I simply would make more clear that *Spinelli*, properly understood, does not depart in any fundamental way from the test established by *Aguilar*. For reasons I shall next state, I do not find persuasive the Court's justifications for rejecting the test established by *Aguilar* and refined by *Spinelli*.

II

In rejecting the *Aguilar-Spinelli* standards, the Court suggests that a "totality-of-the-circumstances approach is far more consistent with our prior treatment of probable cause than is any rigid demand that specific 'tests' be satisfied by every informant's tip."

The Court also insists that the *Aguilar-Spinelli* standards must be abandoned because they are inconsistent with the fact that non-lawyers frequently serve as magistrates. To the contrary, the standards help to structure probable cause inquiries and, properly interpreted, may actually help a non-lawyer magistrate in making a probable cause determination. Moreover, the *Aguilar* and *Spinelli* tests are not inconsistent with deference to magistrates' determinations of probable cause. *Aguilar* expressly acknowledged that reviewing courts "will pay substantial deference to judicial determinations of probable cause. . . ."

At the heart of the Court's decision to abandon *Aguilar* and *Spinelli* appears to be its belief that "the direction taken by decisions following *Spinelli* poorly serves 'the most basic function of any government: to provide for the security of the individual and of his property.'" This conclusion rests on the judgment that *Aguilar* and *Spinelli* "seriously imped[e] the task of law enforcement," and render anonymous tips valueless in police work. Surely, the Court overstates its case. But of particular concern to all Americans must be that the Court gives virtually no consideration to the value of insuring that findings of probable cause are based on information that a magistrate can reasonably say has been obtained in a reliable way by an honest or credible person.

Gates remains one of the Supreme Court's most important decisions concerning the standard for probable cause. Yet, there is an inherent uncertainty as to what is enough. Probable cause is more than the lesser standard of "reasonable suspicion," and it is thought to be less than preponderance of the evidence. A recent case that raised this question was Maryland v. Pringle. If a police officer knows that someone within the car is responsible for contraband, is there probable cause to arrest all of those within the car?

MARYLAND v. PRINGLE
540 U.S. 366 (2003)

Chief Justice REHNQUIST delivered the opinion of the Court.

In the early morning hours a passenger car occupied by three men was stopped for speeding by a police officer. The officer, upon searching the car, seized $763 of rolled-up cash from the glove compartment and five glassine baggies of cocaine from between the back-seat armrest and the back seat. After all three men denied ownership of the cocaine and money, the officer arrested each of them. We hold that the officer had probable cause to arrest Pringle — one of the three men.

At 3:16 A.M. on August 7, 1999, a Baltimore County Police officer stopped a Nissan Maxima for speeding. There were three occupants in the car: Donte Partlow, the driver and owner, respondent Pringle, the front-seat passenger, and Otis Smith, the back-seat passenger. The officer asked Partlow for his license and registration. When Partlow opened the glove compartment to retrieve the vehicle registration, the officer observed a large amount of rolled-up money in the glove compartment. The officer returned to his patrol car with Partlow's license and registration to check the computer system for outstanding violations. The computer check did not reveal any violations. The officer returned to the stopped car, had Partlow get out, and issued him an oral warning.

After a second patrol car arrived, the officer asked Partlow if he had any weapons or narcotics in the vehicle. Partlow indicated that he did not. Partlow then consented to a search of the vehicle. The search yielded $763 from the glove compartment and five plastic glassine baggies containing cocaine from behind the back-seat armrest. When the officer began the search the armrest was in the upright position flat against the rear seat. The officer pulled down the armrest and found the drugs, which had been placed between the armrest and the back seat of the car.

The officer questioned all three men about the ownership of the drugs and money, and told them that if no one admitted to ownership of the drugs he was going to arrest them all. The men offered no information regarding the ownership of the drugs or money. All three were placed under arrest and transported to the police station.

Later that morning, Pringle waived his rights under Miranda v. Arizona (1966), and gave an oral and written confession in which he acknowledged that the cocaine belonged to him, that he and his friends were going to a party, and that he intended to sell the cocaine or "[u]se it for sex." Pringle maintained that the other occupants of the car did not know about the drugs, and they were released.

The trial court denied Pringle's motion to suppress his confession as the fruit of an illegal arrest, holding that the officer had probable cause to arrest Pringle. A jury convicted Pringle of possession with intent to distribute cocaine and possession of cocaine. He was sentenced to 10 years' incarceration without the possibility of parole. The Court of Special Appeals of Maryland affirmed. The Court of Appeals of Maryland, by divided vote, reversed, holding that, absent specific facts tending to show Pringle's knowledge and dominion or control over the drugs, "the mere finding of cocaine in the back armrest when [Pringle] was a front seat passenger in a car being driven by its owner is insufficient to establish probable cause for an arrest for possession."

It is uncontested in the present case that the officer, upon recovering the five plastic glassine baggies containing suspected cocaine, had probable cause to believe a felony had been committed. The sole question is whether the officer had probable cause to believe that Pringle committed that crime.

The long-prevailing standard of probable cause protects "citizens from rash and unreasonable interferences with privacy and from unfounded charges of crime," while giving "fair leeway for enforcing the law in the community's protection."

The probable-cause standard is incapable of precise definition or quantification into percentages because it deals with probabilities and depends on the totality of the circumstances. We have stated, however, that "[t]he substance of all the definitions of probable cause is a reasonable ground for belief of guilt," and that the belief of guilt must be particularized with respect to the person to be searched or seized.

To determine whether an officer had probable cause to arrest an individual, we examine the events leading up to the arrest, and then decide "whether these historical facts, viewed from the standpoint of an objectively reasonable police officer, amount to" probable cause. In this case, Pringle was one of three men riding in a Nissan Maxima at 3:16 A.M. There was $763 of rolled-up cash in the glove compartment directly in front of Pringle. Five plastic glassine baggies of cocaine were behind the back-seat armrest and accessible to all three men. Upon questioning, the three men failed to offer any information with respect to the ownership of the cocaine or the money.

We think it an entirely reasonable inference from these facts that any or all three of the occupants had knowledge of, and exercised dominion and control over, the cocaine. Thus, a reasonable officer could conclude that there was probable cause to believe Pringle committed the crime of possession of cocaine, either solely or jointly.

"[A] person's mere propinquity to others independently suspected of criminal activity does not, without more, give rise to probable cause to search that person. Where the standard is probable cause, a search or seizure of a person must be supported by probable cause particularized with respect to that person. This requirement cannot be undercut or avoided by simply pointing to the fact that coincidentally there exists probable cause to search or seize another or to search the premises where the person may happen to be."

We hold that the officer had probable cause to believe that Pringle had committed the crime of possession of a controlled substance. Pringle's arrest therefore did not contravene the Fourth and Fourteenth Amendments.

2.   Is It an Objective or a Subjective Standard?

Often, a crucial question is whether probable cause focuses on the subjective knowledge and intent of the particular officer, or whether it is an objective standard focusing on what the reasonable officer in the circumstances would do. A subjective standard provides a basis for challenging officers who act in bad faith or for impermissible purposes. But the problem is that subjective standards are far harder to administer because of the difficulty of ever knowing the officers' subjective intention. The objective standard focuses on what the reasonable officer could have done in the circumstances.

In the last decade, the Court has expressly held that the test for probable cause is an objective one. Whren v. United States is a key case adopting and elaborating the subjective standard.

WHREN v. UNITED STATES
517 U.S. 806 (1996)

Justice SCALIA delivered the opinion of the Court.

In this case we decide whether the temporary detention of a motorist who the police have probable cause to believe has committed a civil traffic violation is inconsistent with the Fourth Amendment's prohibition against unreasonable seizures unless a reasonable officer would have been motivated to stop the car by a desire to enforce the traffic laws.

I

On the evening of June 10, 1993, plainclothes vice-squad officers of the District of Columbia Metropolitan Police Department were patrolling a "high drug area" of the city in an unmarked car. Their suspicions were aroused when they passed a dark Pathfinder truck with temporary license plates and youthful occupants waiting at a stop sign, the driver looking down into the lap of the passenger at his right. The truck remained stopped at the intersection for what seemed an unusually long time — more than 20 seconds. When the police car executed a U-turn in order to head back toward the truck, the Pathfinder turned suddenly to its right, without signaling, and sped off at an "unreasonable" speed. The policemen followed, and in a short while overtook the Pathfinder when it stopped behind other traffic at a red light. They pulled up alongside, and Officer Ephraim Soto stepped out and approached the driver's door, identifying himself as a police officer and directing the driver, petitioner Brown, to put the vehicle in park. When Soto drew up to the driver's window, he immediately observed two large plastic bags of what appeared to be crack cocaine in petitioner Whren's hands. Petitioners were arrested, and quantities of several types of illegal drugs were retrieved from the vehicle.

Petitioners were charged in a four-count indictment with violating various federal drug laws, including 21 U.S.C. §§ 844(a) and 860(a). At a pretrial suppression hearing, they challenged the legality of the stop and the resulting seizure of the drugs. They argued that the stop had not been justified by probable cause to believe, or even reasonable suspicion, that petitioners were engaged in illegal drug-dealing activity; and that Officer Soto's asserted ground for approaching the vehicle — to give the driver a warning concerning traffic violations — was pretextual. The District Court denied the suppression motion, concluding that "the facts of the stop were not controverted," and "[t]here was nothing to really demonstrate that the actions of the officers were contrary to a normal traffic stop."

Petitioners were convicted of the counts at issue here. The Court of Appeals affirmed the convictions, holding with respect to the suppression issue that, "regardless of whether a police officer subjectively believes that the occupants of an automobile may be engaging in some other illegal behavior, a traffic stop is permissible as long as a reasonable officer in the same circumstances could have stopped the car for the suspected traffic violation."

II

Temporary detention of individuals during the stop of an automobile by the police, even if only for a brief period and for a limited purpose, constitutes a "seizure" of "persons" within the meaning of this provision. An automobile stop is thus subject to the constitutional imperative that it not be "unreasonable" under the circumstances. As a general matter, the decision to stop an automobile is reasonable where the police have probable cause to believe that a traffic violation has occurred.

Petitioners accept that Officer Soto had probable cause to believe that various provisions of the District of Columbia traffic code had been violated. They argue, however, that "in the unique context of civil traffic regulations" probable cause is not enough. Since, they contend, the use of automobiles is so heavily and minutely regulated that total compliance with traffic and safety rules is nearly impossible, a police officer will almost invariably be able to catch any given motorist in a technical violation. This creates the temptation to use traffic stops as a means of investigating other law violations, as to which no probable cause or even articulable suspicion exists. Petitioners, who are both black, further contend that police officers might decide which motorists to stop based on decidedly impermissible factors, such as the race of the car's occupants. To avoid this danger, they say, the Fourth Amendment test for traffic stops should be, not the normal one (applied by the Court of Appeals) of whether probable cause existed to justify the stop; but rather, whether a police officer, acting reasonably, would have made the stop for the reason given.

A

Petitioners contend that the standard they propose is consistent with our past cases' disapproval of police attempts to use valid bases of action against citizens as pretexts for pursuing other investigatory agendas.

We think [our earlier] cases foreclose any argument that the constitutional reasonableness of traffic stops depends on the actual motivations of the individual officers involved. We of course agree with petitioners that the Constitution prohibits selective enforcement of the law based on considerations such as race. But the constitutional basis for objecting to intentionally discriminatory application of laws is the Equal Protection Clause, not the Fourth Amendment. Subjective intentions play no role in ordinary, probable-cause Fourth Amendment analysis.

B

Recognizing that we have been unwilling to entertain Fourth Amendment challenges based on the actual motivations of individual officers, petitioners disavow any intention to make the individual officer's subjective good faith the touchstone of "reasonableness." They insist that the standard they have put forward — whether the officer's conduct deviated materially from usual police practices, so that a reasonable officer in the same circumstances would not have made the stop for the reasons given — is an "objective" one.

But although framed in empirical terms, this approach is plainly and indisputably driven by subjective considerations. Its whole purpose is to prevent the police from doing under the guise of enforcing the traffic code what they would like to do for different reasons. Petitioners' proposed standard may not use the word "pretext," but it is designed to combat nothing other than the perceived "danger" of the pretextual stop, albeit only indirectly and over the run of cases. Instead of asking whether the individual officer had the proper state of mind, the petitioners would have us ask, in effect, whether (based on general police practices) it is plausible to believe that the officer had the proper state of mind.

Why one would frame a test designed to combat pretext in such fashion that the court cannot take into account actual and admitted pretext is a curiosity that can only be explained by the fact that our cases have foreclosed the more sensible option. If those cases were based only upon the evidentiary difficulty of establishing subjective intent, petitioners' attempt to root out subjective vices through objective means might make sense. But they were not based only upon that, or indeed even principally upon that. Their principal basis — which applies equally to attempts to reach subjective intent through ostensibly objective means — is simply that the Fourth Amendment's concern with "reasonableness" allows certain actions to be taken in certain circumstances, whatever the subjective intent. But even if our concern had been only an evidentiary one, petitioners' proposal would by no means assuage it. Indeed, it seems to us somewhat easier to figure out the intent of an individual officer than to plumb the collective consciousness of law enforcement in order to determine whether a "reasonable officer" would have been moved to act upon the traffic violation. While police manuals and standard procedures may sometimes provide objective assistance, ordinarily one would be reduced to speculating about the hypothetical reaction of a hypothetical constable—an exercise that might be called virtual subjectivity.

Moreover, police enforcement practices, even if they could be practicably assessed by a judge, vary from place to place and from time to time. We cannot accept that the search and seizure protections of the Fourth Amendment are so variable, and can be made to turn upon such trivialities. The difficulty is illustrated by petitioners' arguments in this case. Their claim that a reasonable officer would not have made this stop is based largely on District of Columbia police regulations which permit plainclothes officers in unmarked vehicles to enforce traffic laws "only in the case of a violation that is so grave as to pose an immediate threat to the safety of others." This basis of invalidation would not apply in jurisdictions that had a different practice. And it would not have applied even in the District of Columbia, if Officer Soto had been wearing a uniform or patrolling in a marked police cruiser.

III

In what would appear to be an elaboration on the "reasonable officer" test, petitioners argue that the balancing inherent in any Fourth Amendment inquiry requires us to weigh the governmental and individual interests implicated in a traffic stop such as we have here.

It is of course true that in principle every Fourth Amendment case, since it turns upon a "reasonableness" determination, involves a balancing of all relevant factors. With rare exceptions not applicable here, however, the result of that balancing is not in doubt where the search or seizure is based upon probable cause.

Where probable cause has existed, the only cases in which we have found it necessary actually to perform the "balancing" analysis involved searches or seizures conducted in an extraordinary manner, unusually harmful to an individual's privacy or even physical interests—such as, for example, seizure by means of deadly force, unannounced entry into a home, entry into a home without a warrant, or physical penetration of the body. The making of a traffic stop out of uniform does not remotely qualify as such an extreme practice, and so is governed by the usual rule that probable cause to believe the law has been broken "outbalances" private interest in avoiding police contact.

For the run-of-the-mine case, which this surely is, we think there is no realistic alternative to the traditional common-law rule that probable cause justifies a search and seizure.

On many occasions since *Whren*, the Supreme Court has reaffirmed that the test for probable cause is objective and focuses on whether the reasonable officer could have found probable cause under the circumstances; the subjective intent of that officer does not matter. For example, in Devenpeck v. Alford, 543 U.S. 146 (2004), Jerome Alford was arrested for recording without permission a conversation with the police officer who stopped him for allegedly impersonating a police officer. The arresting officer believed, wrongly it turned out, that it violated the State of Washington's privacy law to record a conversation without permission of both parties.

Alford sued the officer, Devenpeck, for violating his Fourth Amendment rights. The Supreme Court ruled against Alford and made clear that the test for probable cause is objective, not subjective. Justice Scalia, writing for the Court, declared:

> Our cases make clear that an arresting officer's state of mind (except for the facts that he knows) is irrelevant to the existence of probable cause. That is to say, his subjective reason for making the arrest need not be the criminal offense as to which the known facts provide probable cause. As we have repeatedly explained, the fact that the officer does not have the state of mind which is hypothecated by the reasons which provide the legal justification for the officer's action does not invalidate the action taken as long as the circumstances, viewed objectively, justify that action.

The Court held that the arrest did not violate the Fourth Amendment because there was probable cause that Alford violated other state laws (such as the prohibition of impersonating an officer), even though the grounds given for the arrest were wrong. The Court stated: "Subjective intent of the arresting officer, however it is determined (and of course subjective intent is always determined by objective means), is simply no basis for invalidating an arrest. Those are lawfully arrested whom the facts known to the arresting officers give probable cause to arrest."

D. THE WARRANT REQUIREMENT

The Fourth Amendment states that "no Warrants shall issue, but upon probable cause, supported by oath or affirmation, and particularly describing the place to be searched, and the persons or things to be seized." There is no doubt that the warrant requirement is a crucial aspect of the Fourth Amendment. It functions as a check on the police; a search or arrest must be approved by a neutral judge. Also, the warrant limits the police conduct by restricting the scope of the search or the seizure; that which is to be searched or seized must be described with specificity in the warrant.

Yet, there is even dispute among the Justices, and some inconsistency in the Court's opinion, as to whether there actually is a warrant requirement, or whether the Fourth Amendment only requires that searches and seizures be reasonable and a warrant is part of that analysis. Justice Thomas, in a recent dissenting opinion, summarized this when he stated:

> The precise relationship between the Amendment's Warrant Clause and Unreasonableness Clause is unclear. But neither Clause explicitly requires a warrant. While it is of course textually possible to consider [a warrant requirement] implicit within the requirement of reasonableness, the text of the Fourth Amendment certainly does not mandate this result. Nor does the Amendment's history, which is clear as to the Amendment's principal target (general warrants), but not as clear with respect to when warrants were required, if ever. Indeed, because

of the very different nature and scope of federal authority and ability to conduct searches and arrests at the founding, it is possible that neither the history of the Fourth Amendment nor the common law provides much guidance.

As a result, the Court has vacillated between imposing a categorical warrant requirement and applying a general reasonableness standard. The Court has most frequently held that warrantless searches are presumptively unreasonable, but has also found a plethora of exceptions to presumptive unreasonableness. That is, our cases stand for the illuminating proposition that warrantless searches are per se unreasonable, except, of course, when they are not.

Groh v. Ramirez, 540 U.S. 551 (2004) (Thomas, J., dissenting). To say that the search is presumptively reasonable means that the defendant has the burden of challenging the legality of the search, whereas if conduct is presumptively unreasonable the burden is on the government to demonstrate its legality.

There are four important issues to be considered with regard to the warrant. First, what must be included in the application for a warrant? Second, what form must the warrant take in order to be valid? Third, what are the requirements police must follow in executing the warrant? These questions are discussed in subsections 1-3 below.

Fourth and finally, when is a warrant required? A warrant is often required, but not always. The Supreme Court has created many exceptions to the warrant requirement and, at times, has declared that a search or seizure is allowed so long as it is "reasonable." The exceptions to the warrant requirement, and thus the issue of when a warrant is needed, is discussed in the following section, Section F., below.

1.   What Information Must Be Included in the Application for a Warrant?

Warrants are used both for searches and for arrests. For example, the Federal Rules of Criminal Procedure provide that a warrant may be sought for: evidence of a crime; contraband, fruits of a crime, or other items illegally possessed; property designed for use, intended for use, or used in committing a crime; or a person to be arrested or a person who is unlawfully restrained. Federal Rule of Criminal Procedure 41.

The Fourth Amendment requires that the warrant be based on probable cause and "supported by oath or affirmation, and particularly describing the place to be searched, and the persons or things to be seized." The affidavit supporting the request for a warrant must include the information that provides a basis for concluding that there is probable cause. The affidavit may be based on hearsay. Federal Rule of Criminal Procedure 41. Often prosecutors and police present their request for warrants in person to the court, but the rules also allow for requesting a warrant by telephone. Federal Rule of Criminal Procedure 41.

The warrant will specify the time period for its execution. For instance, Rule 41 of the Federal Rules of Criminal Procedure provides that the warrant shall command the officer to "execute the warrant within a specified time not longer than 10 days." It also provides that a warrant for a "tracking device" must "specify a reasonable length of time that the device may be used. This time must not exceed 45 days from the date the warrant was issued."

The Supreme Court has held that the warrant must be issued by a "neutral and detached magistrate." Coolidge v. New Hampshire, 403 U.S. 443 (1971). In

Coolidge, the Court ruled that allowing the state attorney general to issue warrants violated the Fourth Amendment. The key, the Court has said, is that the magistrate be "neutral and detached" and "capable of determining whether probable cause exists." Shadwick v. City of Tampa, 407 U.S. 345 (1972) (holding that a clerk of court could issue warrants consistent with the Fourth Amendment). For example, in Lo-Ji Sales, Inc. v. New York, 442 U.S. 319 (1979), the Court held that the requirement for a neutral and detached magistrate was violated when the judge who issued the warrant essentially became the "leader of the search party which was essentially a police operation."

2. What Form Must the Warrant Take?

The warrant must detail with specificity that which is to be searched or seized. Andresen v. Maryland addresses this requirement.

ANDRESEN v. MARYLAND

427 U.S. 463 (1976)

Justice BLACKMUN delivered the opinion of the Court.

We must determine whether the particular searches and seizures here were "unreasonable" and thus violated the prohibition of the Fourth Amendment.

I

In early 1972, a Bi-County Fraud Unit, acting under the joint auspices of the State's Attorneys' Offices of Montgomery and Prince George's Counties, Md., began an investigation of real estate settlement activities in the Washington, D.C., area. At the time, petitioner Andresen was an attorney who, as a sole practitioner, specialized in real estate settlements in Montgomery County. During the Fraud Unit's investigation, his activities came under scrutiny, particularly in connection with a transaction involving Lot 13T in the Potomac Woods subdivision of Montgomery County. The investigation, which included interviews with the purchaser, the mortgage holder, and other lienholders of Lot 13T, as well as an examination of county land records, disclosed that petitioner, acting as settlement attorney, had defrauded Standard-Young Associates, the purchaser of Lot 13T. Petitioner had represented that the property was free of liens and that, accordingly, no title insurance was necessary, when in fact, he knew that there were two outstanding liens on the property. In addition, investigators learned that the lienholders, by threatening to foreclose their liens, had forced a halt to the purchaser's construction on the property. When Standard-Young had confronted petitioner with this information, he responded by issuing, as an agent of a title insurance company, a title policy guaranteeing clear title to the property. By this action, petitioner also defrauded that insurance company by requiring it to pay the outstanding liens.

The investigators, concluding that there was probable cause to believe that petitioner had committed the state crime of false pretenses against Standard-Young, applied for warrants to search petitioner's law office and the separate office of Mount Vernon Development Corporation, of which petitioner was incorporator, sole shareholder, resident agent, and director. The application sought permission to search for specified documents pertaining to the sale and conveyance of Lot 13T. A judge of the Sixth Judicial Circuit of Montgomery County concluded that there was probable cause and issued the warrants.

The searches of the two offices were conducted simultaneously during daylight hours on October 31, 1972. Petitioner was present during the search of his law office and was free to move about. Counsel for him was present during the latter half of the search. Between 2% and 3% of the files in the office were seized. A single investigator, in the presence of a police officer, conducted the search of Mount Vernon Development Corporation. This search, taking about four hours, resulted in the seizure of less than 5% of the corporation's files.

Petitioner eventually was charged with the crime of false pretenses, based on his misrepresentation to Standard-Young concerning Lot 13T, and with fraudulent misappropriation by a fiduciary, based on similar false claims made to three home purchasers. Before trial began, petitioner moved to suppress the seized documents.

At trial, the State proved its case primarily by public land records and by records provided by the complaining purchasers, lienholders, and the title insurance company. It did introduce into evidence, however, a number of the seized items. Three documents from the "Potomac Woods General" file, seized during the search of petitioner's corporation, were admitted. These were notes in the handwriting of an employee who used them to prepare abstracts in the course of his duties as a title searcher and law clerk. The notes concerned deeds of trust affecting the Potomac Woods subdivision and related to the transaction involving Lot 13T. Five items seized from petitioner's law office were also admitted. One contained information relating to the transactions with one of the defrauded home buyers. The second was a file partially devoted to the Lot 13T transaction; among the documents were settlement statements, the deed conveying the property to Standard-Young Associates, and the original and a copy of a notice to the buyer about releases of liens. The third item was a file devoted exclusively to Lot 13T. The fourth item consisted of a copy of a deed of trust, dated March 27, 1972, from the seller of certain lots in the Potomac Woods subdivision to a lienholder. The fifth item contained drafts of documents and memoranda written in petitioner's handwriting.

After a trial by jury, petitioner was found guilty upon five counts of false pretenses and three counts of fraudulent misappropriation by a fiduciary. He was sentenced to eight concurrent two-year prison terms.

We turn to petitioner's contention that rights guaranteed him by the Fourth Amendment were violated because the descriptive terms of the search warrants were so broad as to make them impermissible "general" warrants.

The specificity of the search warrants. Although petitioner concedes that the warrants for the most part were models of particularity, he contends that they were rendered fatally "general" by the addition, in each warrant, to the exhaustive list of particularly described documents, of the phrase "together with other fruits, instrumentalities and evidence of crime at this (time) unknown." The quoted language, it is argued, must be read in isolation and without reference to the rest of the long sentence at the end of which it appears. When read "properly," petitioner contends, it permits the search for and seizure of any evidence of any crime.

General warrants of course, are prohibited by the Fourth Amendment. "[T]he problem (posed by the general warrant) is not that of intrusion Per se, but of a general, exploratory rummaging in a person's belongings. . . . [The Fourth Amendment addresses the problem] by requiring a 'particular description' of the things to be seized." This requirement "makes general searches . . . impossible and prevents the seizure of one thing under a warrant describing another. As to what is to be taken, nothing is left to the discretion of the officer executing the warrant."

In this case we agree with the determination of the Court of Special Appeals of Maryland that the challenged phrase must be read as authorizing only the search for and seizure of evidence relating to "the crime of false pretenses with respect to Lot 13T." The challenged phrase is not a separate sentence. Instead, it appears in each warrant at the end of a sentence containing a lengthy list of specified and particular items to be seized, all pertaining to Lot 13T. We think it clear from the context that the term "crime" in the warrants refers only to the crime of false pretenses with respect to the sale of Lot 13T. The "other fruits" clause is one of a series that follows the colon after the word "Maryland." All clauses in the series are limited by what precedes that colon, namely, "items pertaining to . . . lot 13, block T." The warrants, accordingly, did not authorize the executing officers to conduct a search for evidence of other crimes but only to search for and seize evidence relevant to the crime of false pretenses and Lot 13T.

Petitioner also suggests that the specific list of the documents to be seized constitutes a "general" warrant. We disagree. Under investigation was a complex real estate scheme whose existence could be proved only by piecing together many bits of evidence. Like a jigsaw puzzle, the whole "picture" of petitioner's false-pretense scheme with respect to Lot 13T could be shown only by placing in the proper place the many pieces of evidence that, taken singly, would show comparatively little. The complexity of an illegal scheme may not be used as a shield to avoid detection when the State has demonstrated probable cause to believe that a crime has been committed and probable cause to believe that evidence of this crime is in the suspect's possession.

We recognize that there are grave dangers inherent in executing a warrant authorizing a search and seizure of a person's papers that are not necessarily present in executing a warrant to search for physical objects whose relevance is more easily ascertainable. In searches for papers, it is certain that some innocuous documents will be examined, at least cursorily, in order to determine whether they are, in fact, among those papers authorized to be seized. Similar dangers, of course, are present in executing a warrant for the "seizure" of telephone conversations. In both kinds of searches, responsible officials, including judicial officials, must take care to assure that they are conducted in a manner that minimizes unwarranted intrusions upon privacy.

Justice BRENNAN, dissenting.

I believe that the warrants under which petitioner's papers were seized were impermissibly general. I therefore dissent.

General warrants are specially prohibited by the Fourth Amendment. The problem to be avoided is "not that of intrusion Per se, but of a general, exploratory rummaging in a person's belongings." Thus the requirement plainly appearing on the face of the Fourth Amendment that a warrant specify with particularity the place to be searched and the things to be seized is imposed to the end that "unauthorized invasions of 'the sanctity of a man's home and the privacies of life'" be prevented. "As to what is to be taken, nothing is left to the discretion of the officer executing the warrant."

The Court recites these requirements, but their application in this case renders their limitation on unlawful governmental conduct an empty promise. After a lengthy and admittedly detailed listing of items to be seized, the warrants in this case further authorized the seizure of "other fruits, instrumentalities and evidence of crime at this (time) unknown." The Court construes this sweeping authorization to be limited to evidence pertaining to the crime of false pretenses with respect to the sale of Lot 13T. However, neither this Court's construction of the warrants nor the similar construction by the Court of Special Appeals of Maryland was available to the investigators at the time they executed the warrants. The question is not how those warrants are to be viewed in hindsight, but how they were in fact viewed by those executing them. The overwhelming quantity of seized material that was either suppressed or returned to petitioner is irrefutable testimony to the unlawful generality of the warrants. The Court's attempt to cure this defect by Post hoc judicial construction evades principles settled in this Court's Fourth Amendment decisions. "The scheme of the Fourth Amendment becomes meaningful only when it is assured that at some point the conduct of those charged with enforcing the laws can be subjected to the more detached, neutral scrutiny of a judge . . . ." Terry v. Ohio (1968). It is not the function of a detached and neutral review to give effect to warrants whose terms unassailably authorize the far-reaching search and seizure of a person's papers especially where that has in fact been the result of executing those warrants.

The Supreme Court recently considered the requirement for particularity in the warrant in the context of a situation where the affidavit in support of the warrant contained the necessary particularity, but the warrant itself did not list specifically what was to be searched for or seized. The Court found that this warrant violated the Fourth Amendment. In reading the case, it is important to note the different ways that the majority and the dissent interpret the Fourth Amendment's warrant clause. Justice Stevens' majority opinion sees it as an independent requirement and the failure to comply makes the search illegal. By contrast, Justice Thomas' dissent argues that even if the warrant is defective, there is no Fourth Amendment violation so long as the search is reasonable.

GROH v. RAMIREZ
540 U.S. 551 (2004)

Justice STEVENS delivered the opinion of the Court.

Petitioner conducted a search of respondents' home pursuant to a warrant that failed to describe the "persons or things to be seized." The question presented [is] whether the search violated the Fourth Amendment.[6]

---

6. There also was an issue of whether the officers could be held civilly liable for relying on such a warrant. The specific question was whether they violated clearly established law that the reasonable officer should know. This issue is omitted from the opinion. [Footnote by casebook authors.]

I

Respondents, Joseph Ramirez and members of his family, live on a large ranch in Butte-Silver Bow County, Montana. Petitioner, Jeff Groh, has been a Special Agent for the Bureau of Alcohol, Tobacco and Firearms (ATF) since 1989. In February 1997, a concerned citizen informed petitioner that on a number of visits to respondents' ranch the visitor had seen a large stock of weaponry, including an automatic rifle, grenades, a grenade launcher, and a rocket launcher. Based on that information, petitioner prepared and signed an application for a warrant to search the ranch. The application stated that the search was for "any automatic firearms or parts to automatic weapons, destructive devices to include but not limited to grenades, grenade launchers, rocket launchers, and any and all receipts pertaining to the purchase or manufacture of automatic weapons or explosive devices or launchers." Petitioner supported the application with a detailed affidavit, which he also prepared and executed, that set forth the basis for his belief that the listed items were concealed on the ranch. Petitioner then presented these documents to a Magistrate, along with a warrant form that petitioner also had completed. The Magistrate signed the warrant form.

Although the application particularly described the place to be searched and the contraband petitioner expected to find, the warrant itself was less specific; it failed to identify any of the items that petitioner intended to seize. In the portion of the form that called for a description of the "person or property" to be seized, petitioner typed a description of respondents' two-story blue house rather than the alleged stockpile of firearms. The warrant did not incorporate by reference the itemized list contained in the application. It did, however, recite that the Magistrate was satisfied the affidavit established probable cause to believe that contraband was concealed on the premises, and that sufficient grounds existed for the warrant's issuance.

Respondents sued petitioner and the other officers. The District Court entered summary judgment for all defendants. The court found no Fourth Amendment violation.

II

The warrant was plainly invalid. The Fourth Amendment states unambiguously that "no Warrants shall issue, but upon probable cause, supported by Oath or affirmation, and particularly describing the place to be searched, and the persons or things to be seized." The warrant in this case complied with the first three of these requirements: It was based on probable cause and supported by a sworn affidavit, and it described particularly the place of the search. On the fourth requirement, however, the warrant failed altogether. Indeed, petitioner concedes that "the warrant . . . was deficient in particularity because it provided no description of the type of evidence sought."

The fact that the application adequately described the "things to be seized" does not save the warrant from its facial invalidity. The Fourth Amendment by its terms requires particularity in the warrant, not in the supporting documents. And for good reason: "The presence of a search warrant serves a high function," and that high function is not necessarily vindicated when some other document, somewhere, says something about the objects of the search, but the contents of that document are neither known to the person whose home is being searched nor available for her inspection. We do not say that the Fourth Amendment prohibits a warrant from cross-referencing other documents. Indeed, most Courts of Appeals have held that a court may construe a warrant with reference to a supporting application or affidavit if the warrant uses appropriate words of incorporation, and if the supporting document accompanies the warrant. But in this case the warrant did not incorporate other documents by reference, nor did either the affidavit or the application (which had been placed under seal) accompany the warrant. Hence, we need not further explore the matter of incorporation.

Petitioner argues that even though the warrant was invalid, the search nevertheless was "reasonable" within the meaning of the Fourth Amendment. He notes that a Magistrate authorized the search on the basis of adequate evidence of probable cause, that petitioner orally described to respondents the items to be seized, and that the search did not exceed the limits intended by the Magistrate and described by petitioner. Thus, petitioner maintains, his search of respondents' ranch was functionally equivalent to a search authorized by a valid warrant.

We disagree. This warrant did not simply omit a few items from a list of many to be seized, or misdescribe a few of several items. Nor did it make what fairly could be characterized as a mere technical mistake or typographical error. Rather, in the space set aside for a description of the items to be seized, the warrant stated that the items consisted of a "single dwelling residence . . . blue in color." In other words, the warrant did not describe the items to be seized at all. In this respect the warrant was so obviously deficient that we must regard the search as "warrantless" within the meaning of our case law. "We are not dealing with formalities." Because "'the right of a man to retreat into his own home and there be free from unreasonable governmental intrusion'" stands "'[a]t the very core' of the Fourth Amendment," our cases have firmly established the "'basic principle of Fourth Amendment law' that searches and seizures inside a home without a warrant are presumptively unreasonable."

We have clearly stated that the presumptive rule against warrantless searches applies with equal force to searches whose only defect is a lack of particularity in the warrant. Petitioner asks us to hold that a search conducted pursuant to a warrant lacking particularity should be exempt from the presumption of unreasonableness if the goals served by the particularity requirement are otherwise satisfied. He maintains that the search in this case satisfied those goals — which he says are "to prevent general searches, to prevent the seizure of one thing under a warrant describing another, and to prevent warrants from being issued on vague or dubious information," — because the scope of the search did not exceed the limits set forth in the application. But unless the particular items described in the affidavit are also set forth in the warrant itself (or at least incorporated by reference, and the affidavit present at the search), there can be no written assurance that the Magistrate actually found probable cause to search for, and to seize, every item mentioned in the affidavit. In this case, for example, it is at least theoretically possible that the Magistrate was satisfied that the search for weapons and explosives was justified by the showing in the affidavit, but not convinced that any evidentiary basis existed for rummaging through respondents' files and papers for receipts pertaining to the purchase or manufacture of such items. Or, conceivably, the Magistrate might have believed that some of the weapons mentioned in the affidavit could have been lawfully possessed and therefore should not be seized. The mere fact that the Magistrate issued a warrant does not necessarily establish that he agreed that the scope of the search should be as broad as the affiant's request. Even though petitioner acted with restraint in conducting the search, "the inescapable fact is that this restraint was imposed by the agents themselves, not by a judicial officer."

We have long held, moreover, that the purpose of the particularity requirement is not limited to the prevention of general searches. A particular warrant also "assures the individual whose property is searched or seized of the lawful authority of the executing officer, his need to search, and the limits of his power to search."

It is incumbent on the officer executing a search warrant to ensure the search is lawfully authorized and lawfully conducted. Because petitioner did not have in his possession a warrant particularly describing the things he intended to seize, proceeding with the search was clearly "unreasonable" under the Fourth Amendment. The Court of Appeals correctly held that the search was unconstitutional.

Justice THOMAS, with whom Justice SCALIA joins, dissenting.

Today the Court holds that the warrant in this case was "so obviously deficient" that the ensuing search must be regarded as a warrantless search and thus presumptively unreasonable. However, the text of the Fourth Amendment, its history, and the sheer number of exceptions to the Court's categorical warrant requirement seriously undermine the bases upon which the Court today rests its holding. Instead of adding to this confusing jurisprudence, as the Court has done, I would turn to first principles in order to determine the relationship between the Warrant Clause and the Unreasonableness Clause. But even within the Court's current framework, a search conducted pursuant to a defective warrant is constitutionally different from a "warrantless search." Consequently, despite the defective warrant, I would still ask whether this search was unreasonable and would conclude that it was not. For these reasons, I respectfully dissent.

"[A]ny Fourth Amendment case may present two separate questions: whether the search was conducted pursuant to a warrant issued in accordance with the second Clause, and, if not, whether it was nevertheless 'reasonable' within the meaning of the first." By categorizing the search here to be a "warrantless" one, the Court declines to perform a reasonableness inquiry and ignores the fact that this search is quite different from searches that the Court has considered to be "warrantless" in the past. Our cases involving "warrantless" searches do not generally involve situations in which an officer has obtained a warrant that is later determined to be facially defective, but rather involve situations in which the officers neither sought nor obtained a warrant. By simply treating this case as if no warrant had even been sought or issued, the Court glosses over what should be the key inquiry: whether it is always appropriate to treat a search made pursuant to a warrant that fails to describe particularly the things to be seized as presumptively unreasonable.

The Court also rejects the argument that the details of the warrant application and affidavit save the warrant, because "[t]he presence of a search warrant serves a high function." But it is not only the physical existence of the warrant and its typewritten contents that serve this high function. The Warrant Clause's principal protection lies in the fact that the "'Fourth Amendment has interposed a magistrate between the citizen and the police . . . so that an objective mind might weigh the need to invade [the searchee's] privacy in order to enforce the law.'"

But the actual contents of the warrant are simply manifestations of this protection. Hence, in contrast to the case of a truly warrantless search, where a warrant (due to a mistake) does not specify on its face the particular items to be seized but the warrant application passed on by the magistrate judge contains such details, a searchee still has the benefit of a determination by a neutral magistrate that there is probable cause to search a particular place and to seize particular items. In such a circumstance, the principal justification for applying a rule of presumptive unreasonableness falls away.

In the instant case, the items to be seized were clearly specified in the warrant application and set forth in the affidavit, both of which were given to the Judge (Magistrate). The Magistrate reviewed all of the documents and signed the warrant application and made no adjustment or correction to this application. It is clear that respondents here received the protection of the Warrant Clause. I would not hold that any ensuing search constitutes a presumptively unreasonable warrantless search. Instead, I would determine whether, despite the invalid warrant, the resulting search was reasonable and hence constitutional.

Because the search was not unreasonable, I would conclude that it was constitutional. Prior to execution of the warrant, petitioner briefed the search team and provided a copy of the search warrant application, the supporting affidavit, and the warrant for the officers to review. Petitioner orally reviewed the terms of the warrant with the officers, including the specific items for which the officers were authorized to search. Petitioner and his search team then conducted the search entirely within the scope of the warrant application and warrant; that is, within the scope of what the Magistrate had authorized. Finding no illegal weapons or explosives, the search team seized nothing. When petitioner left, he gave respondents a copy of the search warrant. Upon request the next day, petitioner faxed respondents a copy of the more detailed warrant application. Indeed, putting aside the technical defect in the warrant, it is hard to imagine how the actual search could have been carried out any more reasonably.

An interesting issue that recently arose concerning the content of warrants is whether anticipatory warrants are allowed. An anticipatory warrant is where the affidavit for a search warrant states that the search will occur only if certain events take place. In United States v. Grubbs, 547 U.S. 90 (2006), "[f]ederal law enforcement officers obtained a search warrant for respondent's house on the basis of an affidavit explaining that the warrant would be executed only after a controlled delivery of contraband to that location."

The Court held that anticipatory warrants are permissible. Justice Scalia, writing for the Court, explained:

> Anticipatory warrants are, therefore, no different in principle from ordinary warrants. They require the magistrate to determine (1) that it is now probable

that (2) contraband, evidence of a crime, or a fugitive will be on the described premises (3) when the warrant is executed. It should be noted, however, that where the anticipatory warrant places a condition (other than the mere passage of time) upon its execution, the first of these determinations goes not merely to what will probably be found if the condition is met. (If that were the extent of the probability determination, an anticipatory warrant could be issued for every house in the country, authorizing search and seizure if contraband should be delivered — though for any single location there is no likelihood that contraband will be delivered.) Rather, the probability determination for a conditioned anticipatory warrant looks also to the likelihood that the condition will occur, and thus that a proper object of seizure will be on the described premises. In other words, for a conditioned anticipatory warrant to comply with the Fourth Amendment's requirement of probable cause, two prerequisites of probability must be satisfied. It must be true not only that if the triggering condition occurs "there is a fair probability that contraband or evidence of a crime will be found in a particular place," but also that there is probable cause to believe the triggering condition will occur. The supporting affidavit must provide the magistrate with sufficient information to evaluate both aspects of the probable-cause determination.

3. What Are the Requirements in Executing Warrants?

Rule 41 of the Federal Rules of Criminal Procedure provides that the warrant must command the officer to "execute the warrant during the daytime, unless the judge for good cause expressly authorizes execution at another time." The Rule defines daytime to be the hours from 6:00 A.M. to 10:00 P.M. (Rule 41(a)(2)(B).) However, there is a federal statute that provides that there does not have to be a special showing of need for searches of narcotics. (21 U.S.C. § 879.)

There also is a federal statute limiting searches of newsrooms. In Zurcher v. Stanford Daily, 436 U.S. 547 (1978), the Supreme Court rejected any special protections for newsrooms. The police had obtained a warrant to search the newsroom of a college newspaper, the Stanford Daily, for negatives of photographs that had been taken of demonstrators attacking police officers. The Court upheld the search and said: "Under existing law, valid warrants may be issued to search *any* property, whether or not occupied by a third party, at which there is probable cause to believe that fruits, instrumentalities, or evidence of a crime will be found." The Court expressly rejected any special First Amendment protection for newsrooms.

However, Congress reacted by adopting the Privacy Protection Act of 1990, 42 U.S.C. § 2000a, to protect the press from searches of newsrooms. The law prohibits law enforcement from searches of those reasonably believed to be engaged in disseminating information to the public unless there is probable cause to believe that the person committed a crime or that giving notice by subpoena likely would result in the loss of evidence.

Several issues have arisen concerning the requirements when executing a warrant. First, how may police treat those who are present when the warrant is being executed; may they be searched or detained? Second, do the police have to knock and announce their presence before executing a warrant to search a dwelling? Third, what happens if there are unforeseen circumstances or if mistakes are made in executing a warrant?

a.   How May Police Treat Those Who Are Present When a Warrant Is Being Executed?

The Supreme Court has held that a person who happens to be present in premises that are subject to a search cannot be searched just by virtue of being there. Ybarra v. Illinois, 444 U.S. 85 (1979). The Court explained that a search "must be supported by probable cause particularized with respect to that person."

However, in Michigan v. Summers, 452 U.S. 692 (1981), the Supreme Court has held that when there is a search of a residence, those present at the time of the search may be detained. The Court explained that allowing such detentions serves many purposes: preventing flight by the individual in case incriminating evidence is found; minimizing the risk of harm to the police; and helping the police complete the search in the event that questions arise. The Court applied this in the recent case of Muehler v. Mena.

MUEHLER v. MENA
541 U.S. 93 (2005)

Chief Justice Rehnquist delivered the opinion of the Court.

Respondent Iris Mena was detained in handcuffs during a search of the premises that she and several others occupied. Petitioners were lead members of a police detachment executing a search warrant of these premises. She sued the officers under 42 U.S.C. § 1983, and the District Court found in her favor. The Court of Appeals affirmed the judgment, holding that the use of handcuffs to detain Mena during the search violated the Fourth Amendment and that the officers' questioning of Mena about her immigration status during the detention constituted an independent Fourth Amendment violation. We hold that Mena's detention in handcuffs for the length of the search was consistent with our opinion in Michigan v. Summers (1981), and that the officers' questioning during that detention did not violate her Fourth Amendment rights.

Based on information gleaned from the investigation of a gang-related, driveby shooting, petitioners Muehler and Brill had reason to believe at least one member of a gang — the West Side Locos — lived at 1363 Patricia Avenue. They also suspected that the individual was armed and dangerous, since he had recently been involved in the driveby shooting. As a result, Muehler obtained a search warrant for 1363 Patricia Avenue that authorized a broad search of the house and premises for, among other things, deadly weapons and evidence of gang membership. In light of the high degree of risk involved in searching a house suspected of housing at least one, and perhaps multiple, armed gang members, a Special Weapons and Tactics (SWAT) team was used to secure the residence and grounds before the search.

At 7 A.M. on February 3, 1998, petitioners, along with the SWAT team and other officers, executed the warrant. Mena was asleep in her bed when the SWAT team, clad in helmets and black vests adorned with badges and the word "POLICE," entered her bedroom and placed her in handcuffs at gunpoint. The SWAT team also handcuffed three other individuals found on the property. The SWAT team then took those individuals and Mena into a converted garage, which contained several beds and some other bedroom furniture. While the search proceeded, one or two officers guarded the four detainees, who were allowed to move around the garage but remained in handcuffs.

Aware that the West Side Locos gang was composed primarily of illegal immigrants, the officers had notified the Immigration and Naturalization Service (INS) that they would be conducting the search, and an INS officer accompanied the officers executing the warrant. During their detention in the garage, an officer asked for each detainee's name, date of birth, place of birth, and immigration status. The INS officer later asked the detainees for their immigration documentation. Mena's status as a permanent resident was confirmed by her papers.

The search of the premises yielded a .22 caliber handgun with .22 caliber ammunition, a box of .25 caliber ammunition, several baseball bats with gang writing, various additional gang paraphernalia, and a bag of marijuana. Before the officers left the area, Mena was released.

In her § 1983 suit against the officers she alleged that she was detained "for an unreasonable time and in an unreasonable manner" in violation of the Fourth Amendment. In addition, she claimed that the warrant and its execution were overbroad, that the officers failed to comply with the "knock and announce" rule, and that the officers had needlessly destroyed property during the search. After a trial, a jury, pursuant to a special verdict form, found that Officers Muehler and Brill violated Mena's Fourth Amendment right to be free from unreasonable seizures by detaining her both with force greater than that which was reasonable and for a longer period than that which was reasonable. The jury awarded Mena $10,000 in actual damages and $20,000 in punitive damages against each petitioner for a total of $60,000.

The Court of Appeals affirmed the judgment on two grounds. [I]t first held that the officers' detention of Mena violated the Fourth Amendment because it was objectively unreasonable to confine her in the converted garage and keep her in handcuffs during the search. In the Court of Appeals' view, the officers should have released Mena as soon as it became clear that she posed no immediate threat. The court additionally held that the questioning of Mena about her immigration status constituted an independent Fourth Amendment violation. *Id.*, at 1264-1266.

In Michigan v. Summers (1981), we held that officers executing a search warrant for contraband have the authority "to detain the occupants of the premises while a proper search is conducted." Such detentions are appropriate, we explained, because the character of the additional intrusion caused by detention is slight and because the justifications for detention are substantial. We made clear that the detention of an occupant is "surely less intrusive than the search itself," and the presence of a warrant assures that a neutral magistrate has determined that probable cause exists to search the home. Against this incremental intrusion, we posited three legitimate law enforcement interests that provide substantial justification for detaining an occupant: "preventing flight in the event that incriminating evidence is found"; "minimizing the risk of harm to the officers"; and facilitating "the orderly completion of the search," as detainees' "self-interest may induce them to open locked doors or locked containers to avoid the use of force."

Mena's detention was, under *Summers,* plainly permissible. An officer's authority to detain incident to a search is categorical; it does not depend on the "quantum of proof justifying detention or the extent of the intrusion to be imposed by the seizure." Thus, Mena's detention for the duration of the search was reasonable under *Summers* because a warrant existed to search 1363 Patricia Avenue and she was an occupant of that address at the time of the search.

Inherent in *Summers'* authorization to detain an occupant of the place to be searched is the authority to use reasonable force to effectuate the detention. Indeed, *Summers* itself stressed that the risk of harm to officers and occupants is minimized "if the officers routinely exercise unquestioned command of the situation."

The officers' use of force in the form of handcuffs to effectuate Mena's detention in the garage, as well as the detention of the three other occupants, was reasonable because the governmental interests outweigh the marginal intrusion. The imposition of correctly applied handcuffs on Mena, who was already being lawfully detained during a search of the house, was undoubtedly a separate intrusion in addition to detention in the converted garage. The detention was thus more intrusive than that which we upheld in *Summers*.

But this was no ordinary search. The governmental interests in not only detaining, but using handcuffs, are at their maximum when, as here, a warrant authorizes a search for weapons and a wanted gang member resides on the premises. In such inherently dangerous situations, the use of handcuffs minimizes the risk of harm to both officers and occupants. Though this safety risk inherent in executing a search warrant for weapons was sufficient to justify the use of handcuffs, the need to detain multiple occupants made the use of handcuffs all the more reasonable.

Mena argues that, even if the use of handcuffs to detain her in the garage was reasonable as an initial matter, the duration of the use of handcuffs made the detention unreasonable. The duration of a detention can, of course, affect the balance of interests. However, the 2- to 3-hour detention in handcuffs in this case does not outweigh the government's continuing safety interests. As we have noted, this case involved the detention of four detainees by two officers during a search of a gang house for dangerous weapons. We conclude that the detention of Mena in handcuffs during the search was reasonable.

The Court of Appeals also determined that the officers violated Mena's Fourth Amendment rights by questioning her about her immigration status during the detention. This holding, it appears, was premised on the assumption that the officers were required to have independent reasonable suspicion in order to question Mena concerning her immigration status because the questioning constituted a discrete Fourth Amendment event. But the premise is faulty. We have "held repeatedly that mere police questioning does not constitute a seizure." "[E]ven when officers have no basis for suspecting a particular individual, they may generally ask questions of that individual; ask to examine the individual's identification; and request consent to search his or her luggage." As the Court of Appeals did not hold that the detention was prolonged by the questioning, there was no additional seizure within the meaning of the Fourth Amendment. Hence, the officers did not need reasonable suspicion to ask Mena for her name, date and place of birth, or immigration status.

In summary, the officers' detention of Mena in handcuffs during the execution of the search warrant was reasonable and did not violate the Fourth Amendment. Additionally, the officers' questioning of Mena did not constitute an independent Fourth Amendment violation. Mena has advanced in this Court, as she did before the Court of Appeals, an alternative argument for affirming the judgment below. She asserts that her detention extended beyond the time the police completed the tasks incident to the search. Because the Court of Appeals did not address this contention, we too decline to address it.

b.   Do Police Have to Knock and Announce Before Searching a Dwelling?

The Supreme Court has held that absent exigent circumstances, the police must knock and announce their presence before entering a residence to execute a search warrant. This was initially articulated as a requirement in Wilson v. Arkansas.

WILSON v. ARKANSAS
514 U.S. 927 (1995)

Justice THOMAS delivered the opinion of the Court.

At the time of the framing, the common law of search and seizure recognized a law enforcement officer's authority to break open the doors of a dwelling, but generally indicated that he first ought to announce his presence and authority. In this case, we hold that this common-law "knock and announce" principle forms a part of the reasonableness inquiry under the Fourth Amendment.

I

During November and December 1992, petitioner Sharlene Wilson made a series of narcotics sales to an informant acting at the direction of the Arkansas State Police. In late November, the informant purchased marijuana and methamphetamine at the home that petitioner shared with Bryson Jacobs. On December 30, the informant telephoned petitioner at her home and arranged to meet her at a local store to buy some marijuana. According to testimony presented below, petitioner produced a semiautomatic pistol at this meeting and waved it in the informant's face, threatening to kill her if she turned out to be working for the police. Petitioner then sold the informant a bag of marijuana.

The next day, police officers applied for and obtained warrants to search petitioner's home and to arrest both petitioner and Jacobs. Affidavits filed in support of the warrants set forth the details of the narcotics transactions and stated that Jacobs had previously been convicted of arson and firebombing. The search was conducted later that afternoon. Police officers found the main door to petitioner's home open. While opening an unlocked screen door and entering the residence, they identified themselves as police officers and stated that they had a warrant. Once inside the home, the officers seized marijuana, methamphetamine, valium, narcotics paraphernalia, a gun, and ammunition. They also found petitioner in the bathroom, flushing marijuana down the toilet. Petitioner and Jacobs were arrested and charged with delivery of marijuana, delivery of methamphetamine, possession of drug paraphernalia, and possession of marijuana.

Before trial, petitioner filed a motion to suppress the evidence seized during the search. Petitioner asserted that the search was invalid on various grounds, including that the officers had failed to "knock and announce" before entering her home. The trial court summarily denied the suppression motion. After a jury trial, petitioner was convicted of all charges and sentenced to 32 years in prison. The Arkansas Supreme Court affirmed petitioner's conviction on appeal.

We granted certiorari to resolve the conflict among the lower courts as to whether the common-law knock and announce principle forms a part of the Fourth Amendment reasonableness inquiry. We hold that it does, and accordingly reverse and remand.

II

The Fourth Amendment to the Constitution protects "[t]he right of the people to be secure in their persons, houses, papers, and effects, against unreasonable searches and seizures." In evaluating the scope of this right, we have looked to the traditional protections against unreasonable searches and seizures afforded by the common law at the time of the framing. "Although the underlying command of the Fourth Amendment is always that searches and seizures be reasonable," our effort to give content to this term may be guided by the meaning ascribed to it by the Framers of the Amendment. An examination of the common law of search and seizure leaves no doubt that the reasonableness of a search of a dwelling may depend in part on whether law enforcement officers announced their presence and authority prior to entering.

Although the common law generally protected a man's house as "his castle of defense and asylum," 3 W. Blackstone, Commentaries, common-law courts long have held that "when the King is party, the sheriff (if the doors be not open) may break the party's house, either to arrest him, or to do other execution of the K[ing]'s process, if otherwise he cannot enter." *Semayne's Case* (K.B.1603). To this rule, however, common-law courts appended an important qualification: "But before he breaks it, he ought to signify the cause of his coming, and to make request to open doors . . . , for the law without a default in the owner abhors the destruction or breaking of any house (which is for the habitation and safety of man) by which great damage and inconvenience might ensue to the party, when no default is in him; for perhaps he did not know of the process, of which, if he had notice, it is to be presumed that he would obey it. . . ."

Several prominent founding-era commentators agreed on this basic principle. According to Sir Matthew Hale, the "constant practice" at common law was that "the officer may break open the door, if he be sure the offender is there, if after acquainting them of the business, and demanding the prisoner, he refuses to open the door." Sir William Blackstone stated simply that the sheriff may "justify breaking open doors, if the possession be not quietly delivered."

The common-law knock and announce principle was woven quickly into the fabric of early American law. Most of the States that ratified the Fourth Amendment had enacted constitutional provisions or statutes generally incorporating English common law.

Our own cases have acknowledged that the common-law principle of announcement is "embedded in Anglo-American law," but we have never squarely held that this principle is an element of the reasonableness inquiry under the Fourth Amendment. We now so hold. Given the long-standing common-law endorsement of the practice of announcement, we have little doubt that the Framers of the Fourth Amendment thought that the method of an officer's entry into a dwelling was among the factors to be considered in assessing the reasonableness of a search or seizure. Contrary to the decision below, we hold that in some circumstances an officer's unannounced entry into a home might be unreasonable under the Fourth Amendment.

This is not to say, of course, that every entry must be preceded by an announcement. The Fourth Amendment's flexible requirement of reasonableness should not be read to mandate a rigid rule of announcement that ignores countervailing law enforcement interests. As even petitioner concedes, the common-law principle of announcement was never stated as an inflexible rule requiring announcement under all circumstances.

Indeed, at the time of the framing, the common-law admonition that an officer "ought to signify the cause of his coming," had not been extended conclusively to the context of felony arrests. Thus, because the common-law rule was justified in part by the belief that announcement generally would avoid "the destruction or breaking of any house . . . by which great damage and inconvenience might ensue," courts acknowledged that the presumption in favor of announcement would yield under circumstances presenting a threat of physical violence. Similarly, courts held that an officer may dispense with announcement in cases where a prisoner escapes from him and retreats to his dwelling. Proof of "demand and refusal" was deemed unnecessary in such cases because it would be a "senseless ceremony" to require an officer in pursuit of a recently escaped arrestee to make an announcement prior to breaking the door to retake him. Finally, courts have indicated that unannounced entry may be justified where police officers have reason to believe that evidence would likely be destroyed if advance notice were given.

We need not attempt a comprehensive catalog of the relevant countervailing factors here. For now, we leave to the lower courts the task of determining the circumstances under which an unannounced entry is reasonable under the Fourth Amendment. We simply hold that although a search or seizure of a dwelling might be constitutionally defective if police officers enter without prior announcement, law enforcement interests may also establish the reasonableness of an unannounced entry.

Soon after Wilson v. Arkansas, the Supreme Court faced the question of whether there are inherently exigent circumstances in drug cases that justify a categorical exception to the knock and announce requirement.

RICHARDS v. WISCONSIN
520 U.S. 385 (1997)

Justice STEVENS delivered the opinion of the Court.

In Wilson v. Arkansas (1995), we held that the Fourth Amendment incorporates the common law requirement that police officers entering a dwelling must knock on the door and announce their identity and purpose before attempting forcible entry. At the same time, we recognized that the "flexible requirement of reasonableness should not be read to mandate a rigid rule of announcement that ignores countervailing law enforcement interests," and left "to the lower courts the task of determining the circumstances under which an unannounced entry is reasonable under the Fourth Amendment."

In this case, the Wisconsin Supreme Court concluded that police officers are never required to knock and announce their presence when executing a search warrant in a felony drug investigation. We disagree with the court's conclusion that the Fourth Amendment permits a blanket exception to the knock-and-announce requirement for this entire category of criminal activity. But because the evidence presented to support the officers' actions in this case establishes that the decision not to knock and announce was a reasonable one under the circumstances, we affirm the judgment of the Wisconsin court.

I

On December 31, 1991, police officers in Madison, Wisconsin, obtained a warrant to search Steiney Richards' motel room for drugs and related paraphernalia. The search warrant was the culmination of an investigation that had uncovered substantial evidence that Richards was one of several individuals dealing drugs out of motel rooms in Madison. The police requested a warrant that would have given advance authorization for a "no-knock" entry into the motel room, but the Magistrate explicitly deleted those portions of the warrant.

The officers arrived at the motel room at 3:40 A.M. Officer Pharo, dressed as a maintenance man, led the team. With him were several plainclothes officers and at least one man in uniform. Officer Pharo knocked on Richards' door and, responding to the query from inside the room, stated that he was a maintenance man. With the chain still on the door, Richards cracked it open. Although there is some dispute as to what occurred next, Richards acknowledges that when he opened the door he saw the man in uniform standing behind Officer Pharo. He quickly slammed the door closed and, after waiting two or three seconds, the officers began kicking and ramming the door to gain entry to the locked room. At trial, the officers testified that they identified themselves as police while they were kicking the door in. When they finally did break into the room, the officers caught Richards trying to escape through the window. They also found cash and cocaine hidden in plastic bags above the bathroom ceiling tiles.

Richards sought to have the evidence from his motel room suppressed on the ground that the officers had failed to knock and announce their presence prior to forcing entry into the room. The trial court denied the motion, concluding that the officers could gather from Richards' strange behavior when they first sought entry that he knew they were police officers and that he might try to destroy evidence or to escape. The judge emphasized that the easily disposable nature of the drugs the police were searching for further justified their decision to identify themselves as they crossed the threshold instead of announcing their presence before seeking entry. Richards appealed the decision to the Wisconsin Supreme Court and that court affirmed.

II

We recognized in *Wilson* that the knock-and-announce requirement could give way "under circumstances presenting a threat of physical violence," or "where police officers have reason to believe that evidence would likely be destroyed if advance notice were given." It is indisputable that felony drug investigations may frequently involve both of these circumstances. The question we must resolve is whether this fact justifies dispensing with case-by-case evaluation of the manner in which a search was executed.

The Wisconsin court explained its blanket exception as necessitated by the special circumstances of today's drug culture, and the State asserted at oral argument that the blanket exception was reasonable in "felony drug cases because of the convergence in a violent and dangerous form of commerce of weapons and the destruction of drugs." But creating exceptions to the knock-and-announce rule based on the "culture" surrounding a general category of criminal behavior presents at least two serious concerns.

First, the exception contains considerable overgeneralization. For example, while drug investigation frequently does pose special risks to officer safety and the preservation of evidence, not every drug investigation will pose these risks to a substantial degree. For example, a search could be conducted at a time when the only individuals present in a residence have no connection with the drug activity and thus will be unlikely to threaten officers or destroy evidence. Or the police could know that the drugs being searched for were of a type or in a location that made them impossible to destroy quickly. In those situations, the asserted governmental interests in preserving evidence and maintaining safety may not outweigh the individual privacy interests intruded upon by a no-knock entry. Wisconsin's blanket rule impermissibly insulates these cases from judicial review.

Additionally, when police enter a residence without announcing their presence, the residents are not given any opportunity to prepare themselves for such an entry. The State pointed out at oral argument that, in Wisconsin, most search warrants are executed during the late night and early morning hours. The brief interlude between announcement and entry with a warrant may be the opportunity that an individual has to pull on clothes or get out of bed.

A second difficulty with permitting a criminal-category exception to the knock-and-announce requirement is that the reasons for creating an exception in one category can, relatively easily, be applied to others. Armed bank robbers, for example, are, by definition, likely to have weapons, and the fruits of their crime may be destroyed without too much difficulty. If a per se exception were allowed for each category of criminal investigation that included a considerable — albeit hypothetical — risk of danger to officers or destruction of evidence, the knock-and-announce element of the Fourth Amendment's reasonableness requirement would be meaningless.

Thus, the fact that felony drug investigations may frequently present circumstances warranting a no-knock entry cannot remove from the neutral scrutiny of a reviewing court the reasonableness of the police decision not to knock and announce in a particular case. Instead, in each case, it is the duty of a court confronted with the question to determine whether the facts and circumstances of the particular entry justified dispensing with the knock-and-announce requirement.

In order to justify a "no-knock" entry, the police must have a reasonable suspicion that knocking and announcing their presence, under the particular circumstances, would be dangerous or futile, or that it would inhibit the effective investigation of the crime by, for example, allowing the destruction of evidence. This standard — as opposed to a probable-cause requirement — strikes the appropriate balance between the legitimate law enforcement concerns at issue in the execution of search warrants and the individual privacy interests affected by no-knock entries. This showing is not high, but the police should be required to make it whenever the reasonableness of a no-knock entry is challenged.

III

Although we reject the Wisconsin court's blanket exception to the knock-and-announce requirement, we conclude that the officers' no-knock entry into Richards' motel room did not violate the Fourth Amendment. We agree with the trial court that the circumstances in this case show that the officers had a reasonable suspicion that Richards might destroy evidence if given further opportunity to do so.

In arguing that the officers' entry was unreasonable, Richards places great emphasis on the fact that the Magistrate who signed the search warrant for his motel room deleted the portions of the proposed warrant that would have given the officers permission to execute a no-knock entry. But this fact does not alter the reasonableness of the officers' decision, which must be evaluated as of the time they entered the motel room. At the time the officers obtained the warrant, they did not have evidence sufficient, in the judgment of the Magistrate, to justify a no-knock warrant. Of course, the Magistrate could not have anticipated in every particular the circumstances that would confront the officers when they arrived at Richards' motel room. These actual circumstances — petitioner's apparent recognition of the officers combined with the easily disposable nature of the drugs — justified the officers' ultimate decision to enter without first announcing their presence and authority.

The practice of allowing magistrates to issue no-knock warrants seems entirely reasonable when sufficient cause to do so can be demonstrated ahead of time. But, as the facts of this case demonstrate, a magistrate's decision not to authorize a no-knock entry should not be interpreted to remove the officers' authority to exercise independent judgment concerning the wisdom of a no-knock entry at the time the warrant is being executed.

In its most recent cases concerning the knock and announce requirement, the Court has been deferential to law enforcement. In United States v. Banks, 540 U.S. 31 (2004), the Court held that the police did not violate the Fourth Amendment when they waited only 15-20 seconds if they had reason to believe that waiting longer would provide the opportunity for the suspects to destroy contraband.

More dramatically and more importantly, in Hudson v. Michigan, 126 S. Ct. 2159 (2006), the Court held that the exclusionary rule does not apply to evidence gained after police violate the knock and announce requirement.

Hudson is presented in the next chapter, Chapter 3, which considers the exclusionary rule. A crucial question will be whether police have sufficient incentives to comply with the knock and announce requirement since violations do not result in the suppression of evidence.

c.   What If There Are Unforeseen Circumstances or Mistakes While Executing a Warrant?

If a mistake is made in executing a warrant, the search is permissible so long as the police action is reasonable. Maryland v. Garrison illustrates this point.

MARYLAND v. GARRISON
480 U.S. 79 (1987)

Justice STEVENS delivered the opinion of the Court.

Baltimore police officers obtained and executed a warrant to search the person of Lawrence McWebb and "the premises known as 2036 Park Avenue third floor apartment." When the police applied for the warrant and when they conducted the search pursuant to the warrant, they reasonably believed that there was only one apartment on the premises described in the warrant. In fact, the third floor was divided into two apartments, one occupied by McWebb and one by respondent Garrison. Before the officers executing the warrant became aware that they were in a separate apartment occupied by respondent, they had discovered the contraband that provided the basis for respondent's conviction for violating Maryland's Controlled Substances Act. The question presented is whether the seizure of that contraband was prohibited by the Fourth Amendment.

There is no question that the warrant was valid and was supported by probable cause. The trial court found, and the two appellate courts did not dispute, that after making a reasonable investigation, including a verification of information obtained from a reliable informant, an exterior examination of the three-story building at 2036 Park Avenue, and an inquiry of the utility company, the officer who obtained the warrant reasonably concluded that there was only one apartment on the third floor and that it was occupied by McWebb. When six Baltimore police officers executed the warrant, they fortuitously encountered McWebb in front of the building and used his key to gain admittance to the first-floor hallway and to the locked door at the top of the stairs to the third floor. As they entered the vestibule on the third floor, they encountered respondent, who was standing in the hallway area. The police could see into the interior of both McWebb's apartment to the left and respondent's to the right, for the doors to both were open. Only after respondent's apartment had been entered and heroin, cash, and drug paraphernalia had been found did any of the officers realize that the third floor contained two apartments. As soon as they became aware of that fact, the search was discontinued. All of the officers reasonably believed that they were searching McWebb's apartment. No further search of respondent's apartment was made.

In our view, the case presents two separate constitutional issues, one concerning the validity of the warrant and the other concerning the reasonableness of the manner in which it was executed. We shall discuss the questions separately.

I

The Warrant Clause of the Fourth Amendment categorically prohibits the issuance of any warrant except one "particularly describing the place to be searched and the persons or things to be seized." The manifest purpose of this particularity requirement was to prevent general searches. By limiting the authorization to search to the specific areas and things for which there is probable cause to search, the requirement ensures that the search will be carefully tailored to its justifications, and will not take on the character of the wide-ranging exploratory searches the Framers intended to prohibit. Thus, the scope of a lawful search is "defined by the object of the search and the places in which there is probable cause to believe that it may be found. Just as probable cause to believe that a stolen lawnmower may be found in a garage will not support a warrant to search an upstairs bedroom, probable cause to believe that undocumented aliens are being transported in a van will not justify a warrantless search of a suitcase."

In this case there is no claim that the "persons or things to be seized" were inadequately described or that there was no probable cause to believe that those things might be found in "the place to be searched" as it was described in the warrant. With the benefit of hindsight, however, we now know that the description of that place was broader than appropriate because it was based on the mistaken belief that there was only one apartment on the third floor of the building at 2036 Park Avenue. The question is whether that factual mistake invalidated a warrant that undoubtedly would have been valid if it had reflected a completely accurate understanding of the building's floor plan.

Plainly, if the officers had known, or even if they should have known, that there were two separate dwelling units on the third floor of 2036 Park Avenue, they would have been obligated to exclude respondent's apartment from the scope of the requested warrant. But we must judge the constitutionality of their conduct in light of the information available to them at the time they acted. Those items of evidence that emerge after the warrant is issued have no bearing on whether or not a warrant was validly issued. Just as the discovery of contraband cannot validate a warrant invalid when issued, so is it equally clear that the discovery of facts demonstrating that a valid warrant was unnecessarily broad does not retroactively invalidate the warrant. The validity of the warrant must be assessed on the basis of the information that the officers disclosed, or had a duty to discover and to disclose, to the issuing Magistrate. On the basis of that information, we agree with the conclusion of all three Maryland courts that the warrant, insofar as it authorized a search that turned out to be ambiguous in scope, was valid when it issued.

II

The question whether the execution of the warrant violated respondent's constitutional right to be secure in his home is somewhat less clear. We have no difficulty concluding that the officers' entry into the third-floor common area was legal; they carried a warrant for those premises, and they were accompanied by McWebb, who provided the key that they used to open the door giving access to the third-floor common area. If the officers had known, or should have known, that the third floor contained two apartments before they entered the living quarters on the third floor, and thus had been aware of the error in the warrant, they would have been obligated to limit their search to McWebb's apartment. Moreover, as the officers recognized, they were required to discontinue the search of respondent's apartment as soon as they discovered that there were two separate units on the third floor and therefore were put on notice of the risk that they might be in a unit erroneously included within the terms of the warrant. The officers' conduct and the limits of the search were based on the information available as the search proceeded. While the purposes justifying a police search strictly limit the permissible extent of the search, the Court has also recognized the need to allow some latitude for honest mistakes that are made by officers in the dangerous and difficult process of making arrests and executing search warrants.

[T]he validity of the search of respondent's apartment pursuant to a warrant authorizing the search of the entire third floor depends on whether the officers' failure to realize the overbreadth of the warrant was objectively understandable and reasonable. Here it unquestionably was. The objective facts available to the officers at the time suggested no distinction between McWebb's apartment and the third-floor premises.

For that reason, the officers properly responded to the command contained in a valid warrant even if the warrant is interpreted as authorizing a search limited to McWebb's apartment rather than the entire third floor. Prior to the officers' discovery of the factual mistake, they perceived McWebb's apartment and the third-floor premises as one and the same; therefore their execution of the warrant reasonably included the entire third floor. Under either interpretation of the warrant, the officers' conduct was consistent with a reasonable effort to ascertain and identify the place intended to be searched within the meaning of the Fourth Amendment.

Justice BLACKMUN, with whom Justice BRENNAN and Justice MARSHALL join, dissenting.

Under this Court's precedents, the search of respondent Garrison's apartment violated the Fourth Amendment. While executing a warrant specifically limited to McWebb's residence, the officers expanded their search to include respondent's adjacent apartment, an expansion made without a warrant and in the absence of exigent circumstances. In my view, Maryland's highest court correctly concluded that the trial judge should have granted respondent's motion to suppress the evidence seized as a result of this warrantless search of his apartment. Moreover, even if I were to accept the majority's analysis of this case as one involving a mistake on the part of the police officers, I would find that the officers' error, either in obtaining or in executing the warrant, was not reasonable under the circumstances.

In applying [the Fourth Amendment's] requirement to searches aimed at residences within multiunit buildings, such as the search in the present case, courts have declared invalid those warrants that fail to describe the targeted unit with enough specificity to prevent a search of all the units. Courts have used different criteria to determine whether a warrant has identified a unit with sufficient particularity.

Applying the above principles to this case, I conclude that the search of respondent's apartment was improper. The words of the warrant were plain and distinctive: the warrant directed the officers to seize marijuana and drug paraphernalia on the person of McWebb and in McWebb's apartment, i.e., "on the premises known as 2036 Park Avenue third floor apartment." As the Court of Appeals observed, this warrant specifically authorized a search only of McWebb's — not respondent's — residence. In its interpretation of the warrant, the majority suggests that the language of this document, as well as that in the supporting affidavit, permitted a search of the entire third floor. It escapes me why the language in question, "third floor apartment," when used with reference to a single unit in a multiple-occupancy building and in the context of one person's residence, plainly has the meaning the majority discerns, rather than its apparent and, indeed, obvious signification — one apartment located on the third floor. Accordingly, if, as appears to be the case, the warrant was limited in its description to the third floor apartment of McWebb, then the search of an additional apartment — respondent's — was warrantless and is presumed unreasonable "in the absence of some one of a number of well defined 'exigent circumstances.'" Because the State has not advanced any such exception to the warrant requirement, the evidence obtained as a result of this search should have been excluded.

The willingness of the Court to excuse mistakes in executing warrants is illustrated by a recent case with egregious facts.

LOS ANGELES COUNTY, CALIFORNIA v. RETTELE

127 S. Ct. 1989 (2007)

PER CURIAM.

Deputies of the Los Angeles County Sheriff's Department obtained a valid warrant to search a house, but they were unaware that the suspects being sought had moved out three months earlier. When the deputies searched the house, they found in a bedroom two residents who were of a different race than the suspects. The deputies ordered these innocent residents, who had been sleeping unclothed, out of bed. The deputies required them to stand for a few minutes before allowing them to dress.

The residents brought suit under 42 U.S.C. § 1983, naming the deputies and other parties and accusing them of violating the Fourth Amendment right to be free from unreasonable searches and seizures. The District Court granted summary judgment to all named defendants. The Court of Appeals for the Ninth Circuit reversed, concluding both that the deputies violated the Fourth Amendment and that they were not entitled to qualified immunity because a reasonable deputy would have stopped the search upon discovering that respondents were of a different race than the suspects and because a reasonable deputy would not have ordered respondents from their bed. We grant the petition for certiorari and reverse the judgment of the Court of Appeals by this summary disposition.

I

From September to December 2001, Los Angeles County Sheriff's Department Deputy Dennis Watters investigated a fraud and identity-theft crime ring. There were four suspects of the investigation. One had registered a 9-millimeter Glock handgun. The four suspects were known to be African-Americans.

On December 11, Watters obtained a search warrant for two houses in Lancaster, California, where he believed he could find the suspects. The warrant authorized him to search the homes and three of the suspects for documents and computer files. In support of the search warrant an affidavit cited various sources showing the suspects resided at respondents' home. The sources included Department of Motor Vehicles reports, mailing address listings, an outstanding warrant, and an Internet telephone directory. In this Court respondents do not dispute the validity of the warrant or the means by which it was obtained.

What Watters did not know was that one of the houses (the first to be searched) had been sold in September to a Max Rettele. He had purchased the home and moved into it three months earlier with his girlfriend Judy Sadler and Sadler's 17-year-old son Chase Hall. All three, respondents here, are Caucasians.

On the morning of December 19, Watters briefed six other deputies in preparation for the search of the houses. Watters informed them they would be searching for three African-American suspects, one of whom owned a registered handgun. The possibility a suspect would be armed caused the deputies concern for their own safety. Watters had not obtained special permission for a night search, so he could not execute the warrant until 7 A.M. Around 7:15 Watters and six other deputies knocked on the door and announced their presence. Chase Hall answered. The deputies entered the house after ordering Hall to lie face down on the ground.

The deputies' announcement awoke Rettele and Sadler. The deputies entered their bedroom with guns drawn and ordered them to get out of their bed and to show their hands. They protested that they were not wearing clothes. Rettele stood up and attempted to put on a pair of sweatpants, but deputies told him not to move. Sadler also stood up and attempted, without success, to cover herself with a sheet. Rettele and Sadler were held at gunpoint for one to two minutes before Rettele was allowed to retrieve a robe for Sadler. He was then permitted to dress. Rettele and Sadler left the bedroom within three to four minutes to sit on the couch in the living room.

By that time the deputies realized they had made a mistake. They apologized to Rettele and Sadler, thanked them for not becoming upset, and left within five minutes. They proceeded to the other house the warrant authorized them to search, where they found three suspects. Those suspects were arrested and convicted.

Rettele and Sadler, individually and as guardians ad litem for Hall, filed this § 1983 suit against Los Angeles County, the Los Angeles County Sheriff's Department, Deputy Watters, and other members of the sheriff's department. Respondents alleged petitioners violated their Fourth Amendment rights by obtaining a warrant in reckless fashion and conducting an unreasonable search and detention. The District Court held that the warrant was obtained by proper procedures and the search was reasonable. A divided panel of the Court of Appeals for the Ninth Circuit reversed in an unpublished opinion.

II

Because respondents were of a different race than the suspects the deputies were seeking, the Court of Appeals held that "[a]fter taking one look at [respondents], the deputies should have realized that [respondents] were not the subjects of the search warrant and did not pose a threat to the deputies' safety." We need not pause long in rejecting this unsound proposition. When the deputies ordered respondents from their bed, they had no way of knowing whether the African-American suspects were elsewhere in the house. The presence of some Caucasians in the residence did not eliminate the possibility that the suspects lived there as well. As the deputies stated in their affidavits, it is not uncommon in our society for people of different races to live together. Just as people of different races live and work together, so too might they engage in joint criminal activity. The deputies, who were searching a house where they believed a suspect might be armed, possessed authority to secure the premises before deciding whether to continue with the search.

In Michigan v. Summers (1981), this Court held that officers executing a search warrant for contraband may "detain the occupants of the premises while a proper search is conducted." In executing a search warrant officers may take reasonable action to secure the premises and to ensure their own safety and the efficacy of the search. The test of reasonableness under the Fourth Amendment is an objective one. Unreasonable actions include the use of excessive force or restraints that cause unnecessary pain or are imposed for a prolonged and unnecessary period of time.

The orders by the police to the occupants, in the context of this lawful search, were permissible, and perhaps necessary, to protect the safety of the deputies. Blankets and bedding can conceal a weapon, and one of the suspects was known to own a firearm, factors which underscore this point. The Constitution does not require an officer to ignore the possibility that an armed suspect may sleep with a weapon within reach. The reports are replete with accounts of suspects sleeping close to weapons.

The deputies needed a moment to secure the room and ensure that other persons were not close by or did not present a danger. Deputies were not required to turn their backs to allow Rettele and Sadler to retrieve clothing or to cover themselves with the sheets. Rather, "[t]he risk of harm to both the police and the occupants is minimized if the officers routinely exercise unquestioned command of the situation."

This is not to say, of course, that the deputies were free to force Rettele and Sadler to remain motionless and standing for any longer than necessary. We have recognized that "special circumstances, or possibly a prolonged detention" might render a search unreasonable. There is no accusation that the detention here was prolonged. The deputies left the home less than 15 minutes after arriving. The detention was shorter and less restrictive than the 2- to 3-hour handcuff detention upheld in *Mena*. And there is no allegation that the deputies prevented Sadler and Rettele from dressing longer than necessary to protect their safety. Sadler was unclothed for no more than two minutes, and Rettele for only slightly more time than that. Sadler testified that once the police were satisfied that no immediate threat was presented, "they wanted us to get dressed and they were pressing us really fast to hurry up and get some clothes on."

The Fourth Amendment allows warrants to issue on probable cause, a standard well short of absolute certainty. Valid warrants will issue to search the innocent, and people like Rettele and Sadler unfortunately bear the cost. Officers executing search warrants on occasion enter a house when residents are engaged in private activity; and the resulting frustration, embarrassment, and humiliation may be real, as was true here. When officers execute a valid warrant and act in a reasonable manner to protect themselves from harm, however, the Fourth Amendment is not violated.

E. EXCEPTIONS TO THE WARRANT REQUIREMENT

The Supreme Court often has said that there is a warrant requirement within the Fourth Amendment and that a warrantless search is presumptively unreasonable. But many Justices have disputed this and have said that the Fourth Amendment does not require a warrant, but rather that the search be reasonable.

The Court has recognized many exceptions where searches or seizures are permissible without a warrant. As mentioned earlier, Justice Thomas said that the case law "stand[s] for the illuminating proposition that warrantless searches are per se unreasonable, except, of course, when they are not." Groh v. Ramirez, 540 U.S. 551 (2004) (Thomas, J., dissenting).

The exceptions to the warrant requirement include: searches incident to arrest; searches made in hot pursuit; searches of things in plain view; automobile searches; inventory searches; border searches and checkpoints; searches at checkpoints; searches of those on probation and parole; searches with consent; special needs situations; and exigent circumstances. Each of these has produced its own body of law. Each is reviewed below.

These exceptions, of course, are not mutually exclusive; more than one can apply in a situation. For example, screening at airports, such as through metal detectors and even physical exams, can be justified because a person consents by entering and also because there is a special need in protecting safety.

In creating the exceptions to the warrant requirement, the Court has balanced the privacy interests involved against the extent to which adhering to the warrant requirement would unduly hamper effective law enforcement. In examining the exceptions, it is important to consider whether the Court has struck the proper balance.

1. Searches Incident to Arrest

One well-established exception to the warrant requirement is the ability of police to search a person at the time of a lawful arrest.

CHIMEL v. CALIFORNIA
395 U.S. 752 (1969)

Justice STEWART delivered the opinion of the Court.

This case raises basic questions concerning the permissible scope under the Fourth Amendment of a search incident to a lawful arrest.

The relevant facts are essentially undisputed. Late in the afternoon of September 13, 1965, three police officers arrived at the Santa Ana, California, home of the petitioner with a warrant authorizing his arrest for the burglary of a coin shop. The officers knocked on the door, identified themselves to the petitioner's wife, and asked if they might come inside. She ushered them into the house, where they waited 10 or 15 minutes until the petitioner returned home from work. When the petitioner entered the house, one of the officers handed him the arrest warrant and asked for permission to "look around." The petitioner objected, but was advised that "on the basis of the lawful arrest," the officers would nonetheless conduct a search. No search warrant had been issued.

Accompanied by the petitioner's wife, the officers then looked through the entire three-bedroom house, including the attic, the garage, and a small workshop. In some rooms the search was relatively cursory. In the master bedroom and sewing room, however, the officers directed the petitioner's wife to open drawers and "to physically move contents of the drawers from side to side so that [they] might view any items that would have come from [the] burglary." After completing the search, they seized numerous items — primarily coins, but also several medals, tokens, and a few other objects. The entire search took between 45 minutes and an hour.

At the petitioner's subsequent state trial on two charges of burglary, the items taken from his house were admitted into evidence against him, over his objection that they had been unconstitutionally seized. He was convicted, and the judgments of conviction were affirmed by both the California Court of Appeal and the California Supreme Court.

Without deciding the question, we proceed on the hypothesis that the California courts were correct in holding that the arrest of the petitioner was valid under the Constitution. This brings us directly to the question whether the warrantless search of the petitioner's entire house can be constitutionally justified as incident to that arrest. The decisions of this Court bearing upon that question have been far from consistent, as even the most cursory review makes evident.

The presence of a search warrant serves a high function. Absent some grave emergency, the Fourth Amendment has interposed a magistrate between the citizen and the police. This was done not to shield criminals nor to make the home a safe haven for illegal activities. It was done so that an objective mind might weigh the need to invade that privacy in order to enforce the law. The right of privacy was deemed too precious to entrust to the discretion of those whose job is the detection of crime and the arrest of criminals. And so the Constitution requires a magistrate to pass on the desires of the police before they violate the privacy of the home. We cannot be true to that constitutional requirement and excuse the absence of a search warrant without a showing by those who seek exemption from the constitutional mandate that the exigencies of the situation made that course imperative.

When an arrest is made, it is reasonable for the arresting officer to search the person arrested in order to remove any weapons that the latter might seek to use in order to resist arrest or effect his escape. Otherwise, the officer's safety might well be endangered, and the arrest itself frustrated. In addition, it is entirely reasonable for the arresting officer to search for and seize any evidence on the arrestee's person in order to prevent its concealment or destruction. And the area into which an arrestee might reach in order to grab a weapon or evidentiary items must, of course, be governed by a like rule. A gun on a table or in a drawer in front of one who is arrested can be as dangerous to the arresting officer as one concealed in the clothing of the person arrested. There is ample justification, therefore, for a search of the arrestee's person and the area "within his immediate control" — construing that phrase to mean the area from within which he might gain possession of a weapon or destructible evidence.

There is no comparable justification, however, for routinely searching any room other than that in which an arrest occurs — or, for that matter, for searching through all the desk drawers or other closed or concealed areas in that room itself. Such searches, in the absence of well-recognized exceptions, may be made only under the authority of a search warrant. The "adherence to judicial processes" mandated by the Fourth Amendment requires no less.

It is argued in the present case that it is "reasonable" to search a man's house when he is arrested in it. But that argument is founded on little more than a subjective view regarding the acceptability of certain sorts of police conduct, and not on consideration relevant to Fourth Amendment interests. Under such an unconfined analysis, Fourth Amendment protection in this area would approach the evaporation point. It is not easy to explain why, for instance, it is less subjectively "reasonable" to search a man's house when he is arrested on his front lawn — or just down the street — than it is when he happens to be in the house at the time of arrest.

Application of sound Fourth Amendment principles to the facts of this case produces a clear result. The search here went far beyond the petitioner's person and the area from within which he might have obtained either a weapon or something that could have been used as evidence against him. There was no constitutional justification, in the absence of a search warrant, for extending the search beyond that area. The scope of the search was, therefore, "unreasonable" under the Fourth and Fourteenth Amendments and the petitioner's conviction cannot stand.

Justice WHITE, with whom Justice BLACK joins, dissenting.

The rule which has prevailed, but for very brief or doubtful periods of aberration, is that a search incident to an arrest may extend to those areas under the control of the defendant and where items subject to constitutional seizure may be found. The justification for this rule must, under the language of the Fourth Amendment, lie in the reasonableness of the rule.

In terms, then, the Court must decide whether a given search is reasonable. The Amendment does not proscribe "warrantless searches" but instead it proscribes "unreasonable searches" and this Court has never held nor does the majority today assert that warrantless searches are necessarily unreasonable.

Applying this reasonableness test to the area of searches incident to arrests, one thing is clear at the outset. Search of an arrested man and of the items within his immediate reach must in almost every case be reasonable. There is always a danger that the suspect will try to escape, seizing concealed weapons with which to overpower and injure the arresting officers, and there is a danger that he may destroy evidence vital to the prosecution. Circumstances in which these justifications would not apply are sufficiently rare that inquiry is not made into searches of this scope, which have been considered reasonable throughout.

The justifications which make such a search reasonable obviously do not apply to the search of areas to which the accused does not have ready physical access. This is not enough, however, to prove such searches unconstitutional. The Court has always held, and does not today deny, that when there is probable cause to search and it is "impracticable" for one reason or another to get a search warrant, then a warrantless search may be reasonable.

An arrested man, by definition conscious of the police interest in him, and provided almost immediately with a lawyer and a judge, is in an excellent position to dispute the reasonableness of his arrest and contemporaneous search in a full adversary proceeding. I would uphold the constitutionality of this search contemporaneous with an arrest since there were probable cause both for the search and for the arrest, exigent circumstances involving the removal or destruction of evidence, and satisfactory opportunity to dispute the issues of probable cause shortly thereafter. In this case, the search was reasonable.

In United States v. Robinson, 414 U.S. 218 (1973), the Supreme Court held that police may search a person incident to arrest regardless of the crime that led to the arrest. Robinson was stopped by police officers for driving with an expired driver's license. When Robinson got out of the car, the officer told him that he was "under arrest for 'operating after revocation and obtaining a permit by misrepresentation.' [T]he [officer then] effected a full custody arrest." The officer searched Robinson and heroin was found.

Justice Rehnquist, writing for the Court, upheld the constitutionality of the search. He began by stating the law: "It is well settled that a search incident to a lawful arrest is a traditional exception to the warrant requirement of the Fourth Amendment. This general exception has historically been formulated into two distinct propositions. The first is that a search may be made of the person of the arrestee by virtue of the lawful arrest. The second is that a search may be made of the area within the control of the arrestee."

The Court rejected the claim that only a frisk for weapons was appropriate when a person was arrested for a traffic violation and concluded that a search incident to arrest is permissible even if there is no reason to believe that the individual has weapons. Justice Rehnquist stated:

> The authority to search the person incident to a lawful custodial arrest, while based upon the need to disarm and to discover evidence, does not depend on what a court may later decide was the probability in a particular arrest situation that weapons or evidence would in fact be found upon the person of the suspect. A custodial arrest of a suspect based on probable cause is a reasonable intrusion under the Fourth Amendment; that intrusion being lawful, a search incident to the arrest requires no additional justification. It is the fact of the lawful arrest which establishes the authority to search, and we hold that in the case of a lawful custodial arrest a full search of the person is not only an exception to the warrant requirement of the Fourth Amendment, but is also a "reasonable" search under that Amendment.

However, in order for there to be a search incident to arrest, there must actually be an arrest. This was the point of the more recent decision in Knowles v. Iowa.

KNOWLES v. IOWA
525 U.S. 113 (1998)

Chief Justice REHNQUIST delivered the opinion of the Court.

An Iowa police officer stopped petitioner Knowles for speeding, but issued him a citation rather than arresting him. The question presented is whether such a procedure authorizes the officer, consistently with the Fourth Amendment, to conduct a full search of the car. We answer this question "no."

Knowles was stopped in Newton, Iowa, after having been clocked driving 43 miles per hour on a road where the speed limit was 25 miles per hour. The police officer issued a citation to Knowles, although under Iowa law he might have arrested him. The officer then conducted a full search of the car, and under the driver's seat he found a bag of marijuana and a "pot pipe." Knowles was then arrested and charged with violation of state laws dealing with controlled substances.

Before trial, Knowles moved to suppress the evidence so obtained. He argued that the search could not be sustained under the "search incident to arrest" exception recognized in United States v. Robinson (1973), because he had not been placed under arrest. At the hearing on the motion to suppress, the police officer conceded that he had neither Knowles' consent nor probable cause to conduct the search. He relied on Iowa law dealing with such searches. Iowa Code Ann. § 321.485(1)(a) provides that Iowa peace officers having cause to believe that a person has violated any traffic or motor vehicle equipment law may arrest the person and immediately take the person before a magistrate. Iowa law also authorizes the far more usual practice of issuing a citation in lieu of arrest or in lieu of continued custody after an initial arrest. Section 805.1(4) provides that the issuance of a citation in lieu of an arrest "does not affect the officer's authority to conduct an otherwise lawful search." The Iowa Supreme Court has interpreted this provision as providing authority to officers to conduct a full-blown search of an automobile and driver in those cases where police elect not to make a custodial arrest and instead issue a citation — that is, a search incident to citation.

In *Robinson*, we noted the two historical rationales for the "search incident to arrest" exception: (1) the need to disarm the suspect in order to take him into custody, and (2) the need to preserve evidence for later use at trial. But neither of these underlying rationales for the search incident to arrest exception is sufficient to justify the search in the present case.

We have recognized that the first rationale — officer safety — is "'both legitimate and weighty.'" The threat to officer safety from issuing a traffic citation, however, is a good deal less than in the case of a custodial arrest. In *Robinson*, we stated that a custodial arrest involves "danger to an officer" because of "the extended exposure which follows the taking of a suspect into custody and transporting him to the police station." A routine traffic stop, on the other hand, is a relatively brief encounter and "is more analogous to a so-called '*Terry* stop' . . . than to a formal arrest." This is not to say that the concern for officer safety is absent in the case of a routine traffic stop. It plainly is not. But while the concern for officer safety in this context may justify the "minimal" additional intrusion of ordering a driver and passengers out of the car, it does not by itself justify the often considerably greater intrusion attending a full field-type search. Even without the search authority Iowa urges, officers have other, independent bases to search for weapons and protect themselves from danger. For example, they may order out of a vehicle both the driver, and any passengers; perform a "patdown" of a driver and any passengers upon reasonable suspicion that they may be armed and dangerous; conduct a patdown of the passenger compartment of a vehicle upon reasonable suspicion that an occupant is dangerous and may gain immediate control of a weapon, and even conduct a full search of the passenger compartment, including any containers therein, pursuant to a custodial arrest.

Nor has Iowa shown the second justification for the authority to search incident to arrest — the need to discover and preserve evidence. Once Knowles was stopped for speeding and issued a citation, all the evidence necessary to prosecute that offense had been obtained. No further evidence of excessive speed was going to be found either on the person of the offender or in the passenger compartment of the car.

Iowa nevertheless argues that a "search incident to citation" is justified because a suspect who is subject to a routine traffic stop may attempt to hide or destroy evidence related to his identity (e.g., a driver's license or vehicle registration), or destroy evidence of another, as yet undetected crime. As for the destruction of evidence relating to identity, if a police officer is not satisfied with the identification furnished by the driver, this may be a basis for arresting him rather than merely issuing a citation. As for destroying evidence of other crimes, the possibility that an officer would stumble onto evidence wholly unrelated to the speeding offense seems remote.

In *Robinson*, we held that the authority to conduct a full field search as incident to an arrest was a "bright-line rule," which was based on the concern for officer safety and destruction or loss of evidence, but which did not depend in every case upon the existence of either concern. Here we are asked to extend that "bright-line rule" to a situation where the concern for officer safety is not present to the same extent and the concern for destruction or loss of evidence is not present at all. We decline to do so.

2.   Searches Made in Hot Pursuit

The Supreme Court has been most insistent on a warrant requirement when there are searches of a home, even going so far as to say that warrantless searches and seizures in homes are presumptively invalid. But the Court has recognized an exception to this when the police enter a home in "hot pursuit" of a suspected felon.

WARDEN, MD. PENITENTIARY v. HAYDEN

387 U.S. 294 (1967)

About 8 A.M. on March 17, 1962, an armed robber entered the business premises of the Diamond Cab Company in Baltimore, Maryland. He took some $363 and ran. Two cab drivers in the vicinity, attracted by shouts of "Holdup," followed the man to 2111 Cocoa Lane. One driver notified the company dispatcher by radio that the man was a Negro about 5'8" tall, wearing a light cap and dark jacket, and that he had entered the house on Cocoa Lane. The dispatcher relayed the information to police who were proceeding to the scene of the robbery. Within minutes, police arrived at the house in a number of patrol cars. An officer knocked and announced their presence. Mrs. Hayden answered, and the officers told her they believed that a robber had entered the house, and asked to search the house. She offered no objection.

The officers spread out through the first and second floors and the cellar in search of the robber. Hayden was found in an upstairs bedroom feigning sleep. He was arrested when the officers on the first floor and in the cellar reported that no other man was in the house. Meanwhile an officer was attracted to an adjoining bathroom by the noise of running water, and discovered a shotgun and a pistol in a flush tank; another officer who, according to the District Court, "was searching the cellar for a man or the money" found in a washing machine a jacket and trousers of the type the fleeing man was said to have worn. A clip of ammunition for the pistol and a cap were found under the mattress of Hayden's bed, and ammunition for the shotgun was found in a bureau drawer in Hayden's room. All these items of evidence were introduced against respondent at his trial.

We agree with the Court of Appeals that neither the entry without warrant to search for the robber, nor the search for him without warrant was invalid. Under the circumstances of this case, the exigencies of the situation made that course imperative. The police were informed that an armed robbery had taken place, and that the suspect had entered 2111 Cocoa Lane less than five minutes before they reached it. They acted reasonably when they entered the house and began to search for a man of the description they had been given and for weapons which he had used in the robbery or might use against them. The Fourth Amendment does not require police officers to delay in the course of an investigation if to do so would gravely endanger their lives or the lives of others. Speed here was essential, and only a thorough search of the house for persons and weapons could have insured that Hayden was the only man present and that the police had control of all weapons which could be used against them or to effect an escape.

Here, the seizures occurred prior to or immediately contemporaneous with Hayden's arrest, as part of an effort to find a suspected felon, armed, within the house into which he had run only minutes before the police arrived. The permissible scope of search must, therefore, at the least, be as broad as may reasonably be necessary to prevent the dangers that the suspect at large in the house may resist or escape.

But Payton v. New York is important in making clear that police cannot enter a home without a warrant to make a routine arrest.

PAYTON v. NEW YORK
445 U.S. 573 (1980)

Justice STEVENS delivered the opinion of the Court.

These appeals challenge the constitutionality of New York statutes that authorize police officers to enter a private residence without a warrant and with force, if necessary, to make a routine felony arrest.

We hold that the Fourth Amendment to the United States Constitution prohibits the police from making a warrantless and nonconsensual entry into a suspect's home in order to make a routine felony arrest.

On January 14, 1970, after two days of intensive investigation, New York detectives had assembled evidence sufficient to establish probable cause to believe that Theodore Payton had murdered the manager of a gas station two days earlier. At about 7:30 A.M. on January 15, six officers went to Payton's apartment in the Bronx, intending to arrest him. They had not obtained a warrant. Although light and music emanated from the apartment, there was no response to their knock on the metal door. They summoned emergency assistance and, about 30 minutes later, used crowbars to break open the door and enter the apartment. No one was there. In plain view, however, was a .30-caliber shell casing that was seized and later admitted into evidence at Payton's murder trial. In due course Payton surrendered to the police, was indicted for murder, and moved to suppress the evidence taken from his apartment.

It is familiar history that indiscriminate searches and seizures conducted under the authority of "general warrants" were the immediate evils that motivated the framing and adoption of the Fourth Amendment. It is perfectly clear that the evil the Amendment was designed to prevent was broader than the abuse of a general warrant. Unreasonable searches or seizures conducted without any warrant at all are condemned by the plain language of the first clause of the Amendment. The simple language of the Amendment applies equally to seizures of persons and to seizures of property. As the Court reiterated just a few years ago, the "physical entry of the home is the chief evil against which the wording of the Fourth Amendment is directed." And we have long adhered to the view that the warrant procedure minimizes the danger of needless intrusions of that sort.

It is a "basic principle of Fourth Amendment law" that searches and seizures inside a home without a warrant are presumptively unreasonable.

The Fourth Amendment protects the individual's privacy in a variety of settings. In none is the zone of privacy more clearly defined than when bounded by the unambiguous physical dimensions of an individual's home — a zone that finds its roots in clear and specific constitutional terms: "The right of the people to be secure in their . . . houses . . . shall not be violated." That language unequivocally establishes the proposition that "[a]t the very core [of the Fourth Amendment] stands the right of a man to retreat into his own home and there be free from unreasonable governmental intrusion." In terms that apply equally to seizures of property and to seizures of persons, the Fourth Amendment has drawn a firm line at the entrance to the house. Absent exigent circumstances, that threshold may not reasonably be crossed without a warrant.

Justice WHITE, with whom THE CHIEF JUSTICE and Justice REHNQUIST join, dissenting.

The Court today holds that absent exigent circumstances officers may never enter a home during the daytime to arrest for a dangerous felony unless they have first obtained a warrant. This hard-and-fast rule, founded on erroneous assumptions concerning the intrusiveness of home arrest entries, finds little or no support in the common law or in the text and history of the Fourth Amendment. I respectfully dissent.

As the Court notes, the common law of searches and seizures, as evolved in England, as transported to the Colonies, and as developed among the States, is highly relevant to the present scope of the Fourth Amendment. Today's decision virtually ignores these centuries of common-law development, and distorts the historical meaning of the Fourth Amendment, by proclaiming for the first time a rigid warrant requirement for all nonexigent home arrest entries.

The history of the Fourth Amendment does not support the rule announced today. At the time that Amendment was adopted the constable possessed broad inherent powers to arrest. The limitations on those powers derived, not from a warrant "requirement," but from the generally ministerial nature of the constable's office at common law. Far from restricting the constable's arrest power, the institution of the warrant was used to expand that authority by giving the constable delegated powers of a superior officer such as a justice of the peace. Hence at the time of the Bill of Rights, the warrant functioned as a powerful tool of law enforcement rather than as a protection for the rights of criminal suspects.

In fact, it was the abusive use of the warrant power, rather than any excessive zeal in the discharge of peace officers' inherent authority, that precipitated the Fourth Amendment. That Amendment grew out of colonial opposition to the infamous general warrants known as writs of assistance, which empowered customs officers to search at will, and to break open receptacles or packages, wherever they suspected uncustomed goods to be. The writs did not specify where searches could occur and they remained effective throughout the sovereign's lifetime. In effect, the writs placed complete discretion in the hands of executing officials.

That the Fourth Amendment was directed toward safeguarding the rights at common law, and restricting the warrant practice which gave officers vast new powers beyond their inherent authority, is evident from the legislative history of that provision. As originally drafted by James Madison, it was directed only at warrants; so deeply ingrained was the basic common-law premise that it was not even expressed: "The rights of the people to be secured in their persons[,] their houses, their papers, and their other property, from all unreasonable searches and seizures, shall not be violated by warrants issued without probable cause, supported by oath or affirmation, or not particularly describing the places to be searched, or the persons or things to be seized."

In sum, the background, text, and legislative history of the Fourth Amendment demonstrate that the purpose was to restrict the abuses that had developed with respect to warrants; the Amendment preserved common-law rules of arrest. Because it was not considered generally unreasonable at common law for officers to break doors to effect a warrantless felony arrest, I do not believe that the Fourth Amendment was intended to outlaw the types of police conduct at issue in the present cases.

While exaggerating the invasion of personal privacy involved in home arrests, the Court fails to account for the danger that its rule will "severely hamper effective law enforcement." The policeman on his beat must now make subtle discriminations that perplex even judges in their chambers. Further, police officers will often face the difficult task of deciding whether the circumstances are sufficiently exigent to justify their entry to arrest without a warrant. This is a decision that must be made quickly in the most trying of circumstances. If the officers mistakenly decide that the circumstances are exigent, the arrest will be invalid and any evidence seized incident to the arrest or in plain view will be excluded at trial. On the other hand, if the officers mistakenly determine that exigent circumstances are lacking, they may refrain from making the arrest, thus creating the possibility that a dangerous criminal will escape into the community. The police could reduce the likelihood of escape by staking out all possible exits until the circumstances become clearly exigent or a warrant is obtained. But the costs of such a stakeout seem excessive in an era of rising crime and scarce police resources.

The uncertainty inherent in the exigent-circumstances determination burdens the judicial system as well. In the case of searches, exigent circumstances are sufficiently unusual that this Court has determined that the benefits of a warrant outweigh the burdens imposed, including the burdens on the judicial system. In contrast, arrests recurringly involve exigent circumstances, and this Court has heretofore held that a warrant can be dispensed with without undue sacrifice in Fourth Amendment values. The situation should be no different with respect to arrests in the home. Under today's decision, whenever the police have made a warrantless home arrest there will be the possibility of "endless litigation with respect to the existence of exigent circumstances, whether it was practicable to get a warrant, whether the suspect was about to flee, and the like."

Our cases establish that the ultimate test under the Fourth Amendment is one of "reasonableness." I cannot join the Court in declaring unreasonable a practice which has been thought entirely reasonable by so many for so long. It would be far preferable to adopt a clear and simple rule: After knocking and announcing their presence, police may enter the home to make a daytime arrest without a warrant when there is probable cause to believe that the person to be arrested committed a felony and is present in the house. This rule would best comport with the common-law background, with the traditional practice in the States, and with the history and policies of the Fourth Amendment. Accordingly, I respectfully dissent.

3. Plain View

If officers are lawfully present in a place, they may use all of their senses. For example, imagine that an officer has a warrant to search a home for child pornography. After lawfully entering the home, the officer sees illegal drugs on a table. They may be seized and used as evidence. In fact, the same is true if the officer is lawfully in the place for any reason.

Coolidge v. New Hampshire provides the classic articulation of the plain view exception to the warrant requirement. Justice Stewart wrote for the Court.

COOLIDGE v. NEW HAMPSHIRE, 403 U.S. 443 (1971): It is well established that under certain circumstances the police may seize evidence in plain view without a warrant. But it is important to keep in mind that, in the vast majority of cases, any evidence seized by the police will be in plain view, at least at the moment of seizure. The problem with the "plain view" doctrine has been to identify the circumstances in which plain view has legal significance rather than being simply the normal concomitant of any search, legal or illegal.

An example of the applicability of the "plain view" doctrine is the situation in which the police have a warrant to search a given area for specified objects, and in the course of the search come across some other article of incriminating character. Where the initial intrusion that brings the police within plain view of such an article is supported, not by a warrant, but by one of the recognized exceptions to the warrant requirement, the seizure is also legitimate. Thus the police may inadvertently come across evidence while in "hot pursuit" of a fleeing suspect. And an object that comes into view during a search incident to arrest that is appropriately limited in scope under existing law may be seized without a warrant. Finally, the "plain view" doctrine has been applied where a police officer is not searching for evidence against the accused, but nonetheless inadvertently comes across an incriminating object.

What the "plain view" cases have in common is that the police officer in each of them had a prior justification for an intrusion in the course of which he came inadvertently across a piece of evidence incriminating the accused. The doctrine serves to supplement the prior justification — whether it be a warrant for another object, hot pursuit, search incident to lawful arrest, or some other legitimate reason for being present unconnected with a search directed against the accused — and permits the warrantless seizure. Of course, the extension of the original justification is legitimate only where it is immediately apparent to the police that they have evidence before them; the "plain view" doctrine may not be used to extend a general exploratory search from one object to another until something incriminating at last emerges.

The rationale for the "plain view" exception is evident if we keep in mind the two distinct constitutional protections served by the warrant requirement. First, the magistrate's scrutiny is intended to eliminate altogether searches not based on probable cause. The premise here is that any intrusion in the way of search or seizure is an evil, so that no intrusion at all is justified without a careful prior determination of necessity. The second, distinct objective is that those searches deemed necessary should be as limited as possible. Here, the specific evil is the "general warrant" abhorred by the colonists, and the problem is not that of intrusion per se, but of a general, exploratory rummaging in a person's belongings. The warrant accomplishes this second objective by requiring a "particular description" of the things to be seized.

The "plain view" doctrine is not in conflict with the first objective because plain view does not occur until a search is in progress. In each case, this initial intrusion is justified by a warrant or by an exception such as "hot pursuit" or search incident to a lawful arrest, or by an extraneous valid reason for the officer's presence. And, given the initial intrusion, the seizure of an object in plain view is consistent with the second objective, since it does not convert the search into a general or exploratory one. As against the minor peril to Fourth Amendment protections, there is a major gain in effective law enforcement. Where, once an otherwise lawful search is in progress, the police inadvertently come upon a piece of evidence, it would often be a needless inconvenience, and sometimes dangerous — to the evidence or to the police themselves — to require them to ignore it until they have obtained a warrant particularly describing it.

The limits on the doctrine are implicit in the statement of its rationale. The first of these is that plain view alone is never enough to justify the warrantless seizure of evidence. This is simply a corollary of the familiar principle discussed above, that no amount of probable cause can justify a warrantless search or seizure absent "exigent circumstances." Incontrovertible testimony of the senses that an incriminating object is on premises belonging to a criminal suspect may establish the fullest possible measure of probable cause. But even where the object is contraband, this Court has repeatedly stated and enforced the basic rule that the police may not enter and make a warrantless seizure.

The second limitation is that the discovery of evidence in plain view must be inadvertent. The rationale of the exception to the warrant requirement, as just stated, is that a plain-view seizure will not turn an initially valid (and therefore limited) search into a "general" one, while the inconvenience of procuring a warrant to cover an inadvertent discovery is great. But where the discovery is anticipated, where the police know in advance the location of the evidence and intend to seize it, the situation is altogether different. The requirement of a warrant to seize imposes no inconvenience whatever, or at least none which is constitutionally cognizable in a legal system that regards warrantless searches as "per se unreasonable" in the absence of "exigent circumstances."

If the initial intrusion is bottomed upon a warrant that fails to mention a particular object, though the police know its location and intend to seize it, then there is a violation of the express constitutional requirement of "Warrants . . . particularly describing . . . [the] things to be seized." The initial intrusion may, of course, be legitimated not by a warrant but by one of the exceptions to the warrant requirement, such as hot pursuit or search incident to lawful arrest. But to extend the scope of such an intrusion to the seizure of objects — not contraband nor stolen nor dangerous in themselves — which the police know in advance they will find in plain view and intend to seize, would fly in the face of the basic rule that no amount of probable cause can justify a warrantless seizure.

In Horton v. California, the Court considered whether inadvertence is a necessary element of the plain view exception to the warrant requirement.

HORTON v. CALIFORNIA
496 U.S. 128 (1990)

Justice STEVENS delivered the opinion of the Court.

In this case we revisit an issue that was considered, but not conclusively resolved, in Coolidge v. New Hampshire (1971): Whether the warrantless seizure of evidence of crime in plain view is prohibited by the Fourth Amendment if the discovery of the evidence was not inadvertent. We conclude that even though inadvertence is a characteristic of most legitimate "plain-view" seizures, it is not a necessary condition.

I

Petitioner was convicted of the armed robbery of Erwin Wallaker, the treasurer of the San Jose Coin Club. When Wallaker returned to his home after the Club's annual show, he entered his garage and was accosted by two masked men, one armed with a machine gun and the other with an electrical shocking device, sometimes referred to as a "stun gun." The two men shocked Wallaker, bound and handcuffed him, and robbed him of jewelry and cash. During the encounter sufficient conversation took place to enable Wallaker subsequently to identify petitioner's distinctive voice. His identification was partially corroborated by a witness who saw the robbers leaving the scene and by evidence that petitioner had attended the coin show.

Sergeant LaRault, an experienced police officer, investigated the crime and determined that there was probable cause to search petitioner's home for the proceeds of the robbery and for the weapons used by the robbers. His affidavit for a search warrant referred to police reports that described the weapons as well as the proceeds, but the warrant issued by the Magistrate only authorized a search for the proceeds, including three specifically described rings.

Pursuant to the warrant, LaRault searched petitioner's residence, but he did not find the stolen property. During the course of the search, however, he discovered the weapons in plain view and seized them. Specifically, he seized an Uzi machine gun, a .38-caliber revolver, two stun guns, a handcuff key, a San Jose Coin Club advertising brochure, and a few items of clothing identified by the victim. LaRault testified that while he was searching for the rings, he also was interested in finding other evidence connecting petitioner to the robbery. Thus, the seized evidence was not discovered "inadvertently."

The trial court refused to suppress the evidence found in petitioner's home and, after a jury trial, petitioner was found guilty and sentenced to prison. The California Court of Appeal affirmed.

The criteria that generally guide "plain-view" seizures were set forth in Coolidge v. New Hampshire (1971).

It is, of course, an essential predicate to any valid warrantless seizure of incriminating evidence that the officer did not violate the Fourth Amendment in arriving at the place from which the evidence could be plainly viewed. There are, moreover, two additional conditions that must be satisfied to justify the warrantless seizure. First, not only must the item be in plain view; its incriminating character must also be "immediately apparent." Second, not only must the officer be lawfully located in a place from which the object can be plainly seen, but he or she must also have a lawful right of access to the object itself.

The suggestion that the inadvertence requirement is necessary to prevent the police from conducting general searches, or from converting specific warrants into general warrants, is not persuasive because that interest is already served by the requirements that no warrant issue unless it "particularly describ[es] the place to be searched and the persons or things to be seized," and that a warrantless search be circumscribed by the exigencies which justify its initiation. Scrupulous adherence to these requirements serves the interests in limiting the area and duration of the search that the inadvertence requirement inadequately protects. Once those commands have been satisfied and the officer has a lawful right of access, however, no additional Fourth Amendment interest is furthered by requiring that the discovery of evidence be inadvertent. If the scope of the search exceeds that permitted by the terms of a validly issued warrant or the character of the relevant exception from the warrant requirement, the subsequent seizure is unconstitutional without more.

In this case, the scope of the search was not enlarged in the slightest by the omission of any reference to the weapons in the warrant. Indeed, if the three rings and other items named in the warrant had been found at the outset — or if petitioner had them in his possession and had responded to the warrant by producing them immediately — no search for weapons could have taken place.

Justice BRENNAN, with whom Justice MARSHALL joins, dissenting.

I remain convinced that Justice Stewart correctly articulated the plain-view doctrine in Coolidge v. New Hampshire (1971). The Fourth Amendment permits law enforcement officers to seize items for which they do not have a warrant when those items are found in plain view and (1) the officers are lawfully in a position to observe the items, (2) the discovery of the items is "inadvertent," and (3) it is immediately apparent to the officers that the items are evidence of a crime, contraband, or otherwise subject to seizure. In eschewing the inadvertent discovery requirement, the majority ignores the Fourth Amendment's express command that warrants particularly describe not only the places to be searched, but also the things to be seized. I respectfully dissent from this rewriting of the Fourth Amendment.

The discovery of evidence in pretextual searches is not "inadvertent" and should be suppressed for that reason. But even state courts that have rejected the inadvertent discovery requirement have held that the Fourth Amendment prohibits pretextual searches. The Court's opinion today does not address pretextual searches, but I have no doubt that such searches violate the Fourth Amendment.

As *Coolidge* and *Horton* make clear, it must be immediately apparent that the seized item is illegal. For example, in Arizona v. Hicks, 480 U.S. 321 (1987), police entered an apartment pursuant to a warrant and saw stereo equipment that they thought might be stolen merchandise. They did not have probable cause to support this. An officer moved the equipment, found a product identification number, and radioed it in to headquarters. It was found that the merchandise was stolen.

The Supreme Court held that the plain view doctrine did not apply here. The Court found that moving the stereo equipment was a search:

> Officer Nelson's moving of the equipment, however, did constitute a "search" separate and apart from the search for the shooter, victims, and weapons that was the lawful objective of his entry into the apartment. Merely inspecting those parts of the turntable that came into view during the latter search would not have constituted an independent search, because it would have produced no additional invasion of respondent's privacy interest. But taking action, unrelated to the objectives of the authorized intrusion, which exposed to view concealed portions of the apartment or its contents, did produce a new invasion of respondent's privacy unjustified by the exigent circumstance that validated the entry. This is why the distinction between "looking" at a suspicious object in plain view and "moving" it even a few inches is much more than trivial for purposes of the Fourth Amendment. It matters not that the search uncovered nothing of any great personal value to respondent — serial numbers rather than (what might conceivably have been hidden behind or under the equipment) letters or photographs. A search is a search, even if it happens to disclose nothing but the bottom of a turntable.

The Court explained that since it was not apparent that the item was contraband, the officers needed to have probable cause for their search. The Court stated:

> We now hold that probable cause is required. To say otherwise would be to cut the "plain view" doctrine loose from its theoretical and practical moorings. The theory

of that doctrine consists of extending to nonpublic places such as the home, where searches and seizures without a warrant are presumptively unreasonable, the police's longstanding authority to make warrantless seizures in public places of such objects as weapons and contraband. And the practical justification for that extension is the desirability of sparing police, whose viewing of the object in the course of a lawful search is as legitimate as it would have been in a public place, the inconvenience and the risk — to themselves or to preservation of the evidence — of going to obtain a warrant. Dispensing with the need for a warrant is worlds apart from permitting a lesser standard of cause for the seizure than a warrant would require, i.e., the standard of probable cause. No reason is apparent why an object should routinely be seizable on lesser grounds, during an unrelated search and seizure, than would have been needed to obtain a warrant for that same object if it had been known to be on the premises.

It must be remembered that the police are allowed to use all of their senses when they are lawfully present. Usually, sight is the most important, but it could be "plain smell" or "plain touch" that is used by the officer. Minnesota v. Dickerson involved the latter.

MINNESOTA v. DICKERSON
508 U.S. 366 (1993)

Justice WHITE delivered the opinion of the Court.

In this case, we consider whether the Fourth Amendment permits the seizure of contraband detected through a police officer's sense of touch during a protective patdown search.

I

On the evening of November 9, 1989, two Minneapolis police officers were patrolling an area on the city's north side in a marked squad car. At about 8:15 P.M., one of the officers observed respondent leaving a 12-unit apartment building on Morgan Avenue North. The officer, having previously responded to complaints of drug sales in the building's hallways and having executed several search warrants on the premises, considered the building to be a notorious "crack house." According to testimony credited by the trial court, respondent began walking toward the police but, upon spotting the squad car and making eye contact with one of the officers, abruptly halted and began walking in the opposite direction. His suspicion aroused, this officer watched as respondent turned and entered an alley on the other side of the apartment building. Based upon respondent's seemingly evasive actions and the fact that he had just left a building known for cocaine traffic, the officers decided to stop respondent and investigate further.

The officers pulled their squad car into the alley and ordered respondent to stop and submit to a patdown search. The search revealed no weapons, but the officer conducting the search did take an interest in a small lump in respondent's nylon jacket. The officer later testified: "[A]s I pat-searched the front of his body, I felt a lump, a small lump, in the front pocket. I examined it with my fingers and it slid and it felt to be a lump of crack cocaine in cellophane."

The officer then reached into respondent's pocket and retrieved a small plastic bag containing one fifth of one gram of crack cocaine. Respondent was arrested and charged in Hennepin County District Court with possession of a controlled substance.

Before trial, respondent moved to suppress the cocaine. The trial court first concluded that the officers were justified under Terry v. Ohio (1968),[7] in stopping respondent to investigate whether he might be engaged in criminal activity. The court further found that the officers were justified in frisking respondent to ensure that he was not carrying a weapon. Finally, analogizing to the "plain-view" doctrine, under which officers may make a warrantless seizure of contraband found in plain view during a lawful search for other items, the trial court ruled that the officers' seizure of the cocaine did not violate the Fourth Amendment.

His suppression motion having failed, respondent proceeded to trial and was found guilty. On appeal, the Minnesota Court of Appeals reversed. The court concluded, however, that the officers had overstepped the bounds allowed by seizing the cocaine. In doing so, the Court of Appeals "decline[d] to adopt the plain feel exception" to the warrant requirement. The Minnesota Supreme Court affirmed.

The question presented today is whether police officers may seize nonthreatening contraband detected during a protective patdown search. We think the answer is clearly that they may.

We have already held that police officers, at least under certain circumstances, may seize contraband detected during the lawful execution of a search.

Under [the plain view] doctrine, if police are lawfully in a position from which they view an object, if its incriminating character is immediately apparent, and if the officers have a lawful right of access to the object, they may seize it without a warrant.

We think that this doctrine has an obvious application by analogy to cases in which an officer discovers contraband through the sense of touch during an otherwise lawful search. The rationale of the plain-view doctrine is that if contraband is left in open view and is observed by a police officer from a lawful vantage point, there has been no invasion of a legitimate expectation of privacy and thus no "search" within the meaning of the Fourth Amendment — or at least no search independent of the initial intrusion that gave the officers their vantage point. The warrantless seizure of contraband that presents itself in this manner is deemed justified by the realization that resort to a neutral magistrate under such circumstances would often be impracticable and would do little to promote the objectives of the Fourth Amendment. The same can be said of tactile discoveries of contraband. If a police officer lawfully pats down a suspect's outer clothing and feels an object whose contour or mass makes its identity immediately apparent, there has been no invasion of the suspect's privacy beyond that already authorized by the officer's search for weapons; if the object is contraband, its warrantless seizure would be justified by the same practical considerations that inhere in the plain-view context.

It remains to apply these principles to the facts of this case. Respondent has not challenged the finding made by the trial court and affirmed by both the

---

7. Terry v. Ohio is discussed in Section G of this chapter and authorizes the police to "stop and frisk" individuals if there is a reasonable suspicion. [Footnote by casebook authors.]

Court of Appeals and the State Supreme Court that the police were justified under *Terry* in stopping him and frisking him for weapons. Thus, the dispositive question before this Court is whether the officer who conducted the search was acting within the lawful bounds at the time he gained probable cause to believe that the lump in respondent's jacket was contraband.

Under the State Supreme Court's interpretation of the record before it, it is clear that the court was correct in holding that the police officer in this case overstepped the bounds of the "strictly circumscribed" search for weapons allowed under *Terry*. Where, as here, "an officer who is executing a valid search for one item seizes a different item," this Court rightly "has been sensitive to the danger . . . that officers will enlarge a specific authorization, furnished by a warrant or an exigency, into the equivalent of a general warrant to rummage and seize at will." Here, the officer's continued exploration of respondent's pocket after having concluded that it contained no weapon was unrelated to "[t]he sole justification of the search [under *Terry*] . . . the protection of the police officer and others nearby." It therefore amounted to the sort of evidentiary search that *Terry* expressly refused to authorize and that we have condemned in subsequent cases.

4.   *The Automobile Exception*

One of the most important exceptions to the warrant requirement is for automobiles; cars and other movable vehicles can be searched without a warrant if there is probable cause. In presenting the automobile exception, first, the basic cases articulating and explaining the exception are presented. Second, the question is examined of whether police can search containers found in automobiles. Finally, the issue of the ability of the police to search automobiles after the arrest of the driver is discussed.

a.   The Exception and Its Rationale

The Court first articulated an automobile exception to the Fourth Amendment in Carroll v. United States, 267 U.S. 132 (1925). Agents of the federal Treasury Department, during the Prohibition era, had probable cause that Carroll was transporting alcoholic beverages in his car in violation of the law. They searched his vehicle without a warrant. The Court held that the search did not violate the Fourth Amendment and stressed that a warrant was not needed to search the car. Chief Justice Taft, writing for the Court, declared:

> On reason and authority the true rule is that if the search and seizure without a warrant are made upon probable cause, that is, upon a belief, reasonably arising out of circumstances known to the seizing officer, that an automobile or other vehicle contains that which by law is subject to seizure and destruction, the search and seizure are valid. The Fourth Amendment is to be construed in the light of what was deemed an unreasonable search and seizure when it was adopted, and in a manner which will conserve public interests as well as the interests and rights of individual citizens.
>
> [T]he guaranty of freedom from unreasonable searches and seizures by the Fourth Amendment has been construed, practically since the beginning of the

government, as recognizing a necessary difference between a search of a store, dwelling house, or other structure in respect of which a proper official warrant readily may be obtained and a search of a ship, motor boat, wagon, or automobile for contraband goods, where it is not practicable to secure a warrant, because the vehicle can be quickly moved out of the locality or jurisdiction in which the warrant must be sought.

The Court reaffirmed and explained the automobile exception to the Fourth Amendment in California v. Carney. The case involved a warrantless search of a mobile home. In *Carroll*, the Court stressed that the car was movable. *Carney* is a significant extension of *Carroll* because it involved a mobile home that was realistically no longer mobile. But the Court nonetheless held that the vehicle exception to the Fourth Amendment applied.

CALIFORNIA v. CARNEY
471 U.S. 386 (1985)

Chief Justice BURGER delivered the opinion of the Court.

We granted certiorari to decide whether law enforcement agents violated the Fourth Amendment when they conducted a warrantless search, based on probable cause, of a fully mobile "motor home" located in a public place.

I

On May 31, 1979, Drug Enforcement Agency Agent Robert Williams watched respondent, Charles Carney, approach a youth in downtown San Diego. The youth accompanied Carney to a Dodge Mini Motor Home parked in a nearby lot. Carney and the youth closed the window shades in the motor home, including one across the front window. Agent Williams had previously received uncorroborated information that the same motor home was used by another person who was exchanging marihuana for sex. Williams, with assistance from other agents, kept the motor home under surveillance for the entire one and one-quarter hours that Carney and the youth remained inside. When the youth left the motor home, the agents followed and stopped him. The youth told the agents that he had received marijuana in return for allowing Carney sexual contacts.

At the agents' request, the youth returned to the motor home and knocked on its door; Carney stepped out. The agents identified themselves as law enforcement officers. Without a warrant or consent, one agent entered the motor home and observed marihuana, plastic bags, and a scale of the kind used in weighing drugs on a table. Agent Williams took Carney into custody and took possession of the motor home. A subsequent search of the motor home at the police station revealed additional marihuana in the cupboards and refrigerator.

Respondent was charged with possession of marihuana for sale. Respondent [presented] his suppression motion in the Superior Court. The Superior Court also rejected the claim, holding that there was probable cause to arrest respondent, that the search of the motor home was authorized under the automobile exception to the Fourth Amendment's warrant requirement, and that the motor home itself could be seized without a warrant as an instrumentality of the crime. Respondent then pleaded nolo contendere to the charges against him, and was placed on probation for three years. The California Supreme Court reversed the conviction.

II

[The] fundamental right [protected by the Fourth Amendment] is preserved by a requirement that searches be conducted pursuant to a warrant issued by an independent judicial officer. There are, of course, exceptions to the general rule that a warrant must be secured before a search is undertaken; one is the so-called "automobile exception" at issue in this case. This exception to the warrant requirement was first set forth by the Court 60 years ago in Carroll v. United States (1925). There, the Court recognized that the privacy interests in an automobile are constitutionally protected; however, it held that the ready mobility of the automobile justifies a lesser degree of protection of those interests. However, although ready mobility alone was perhaps the original justification for the vehicle exception, our later cases have made clear that ready mobility is not the only basis for the exception. The reasons for the vehicle exception, we have said, are twofold. "Besides the element of mobility, less rigorous warrant requirements govern because the expectation of privacy with respect to one's automobile is significantly less than that relating to one's home or office."

Even in cases where an automobile was not immediately mobile, the lesser expectation of privacy resulting from its use as a readily mobile vehicle justified application of the vehicular exception. In some cases, the configuration of the vehicle contributed to the lower expectations of privacy; for example, we [have] said that, because the passenger compartment of a standard automobile is relatively open to plain view, there are lesser expectations of privacy. But even when enclosed "repository" areas have been involved, we have concluded that the lesser expectations of privacy warrant application of the exception. We have applied the exception in the context of a locked car trunk, a sealed package in a car trunk.

These reduced expectations of privacy derive not from the fact that the area to be searched is in plain view, but from the pervasive regulation of vehicles capable of traveling on the public highways. As we explained in South Dakota v. Opperman, an inventory search case: "Automobiles, unlike homes, are subjected to pervasive and continuing governmental regulation and controls, including periodic inspection and licensing requirements. As an everyday occurrence, police stop and examine vehicles when license plates or inspection stickers have expired, or if other violations, such as exhaust fumes or excessive noise, are noted, or if headlights or other safety equipment are not in proper working order."

The public is fully aware that it is accorded less privacy in its automobiles because of this compelling governmental need for regulation. Historically, "individuals always [have] been on notice that movable vessels may be stopped and searched on facts giving rise to probable cause that the vehicle contains contraband, without the protection afforded by a magistrate's prior evaluation of those facts." In short, the pervasive schemes of regulation, which necessarily lead to reduced expectations of privacy, and the exigencies attendant to ready mobility justify searches without prior recourse to the authority of a magistrate so long as the overriding standard of probable cause is met.

When a vehicle is being used on the highways, or if it is readily capable of such use and is found stationary in a place not regularly used for residential purposes — temporary or otherwise — the two justifications for the vehicle exception come into play. First, the vehicle is obviously readily mobile by the turn of an ignition key, if not actually moving. Second, there is a reduced expectation of privacy stemming from its use as a licensed motor vehicle subject to a range of police regulation inapplicable to a fixed dwelling. At least in these circumstances, the overriding societal interests in effective law enforcement justify an immediate search before the vehicle and its occupants become unavailable.

While it is true that respondent's vehicle possessed some, if not many of the attributes of a home, it is equally clear that the vehicle falls clearly within the scope of the exception laid down in *Carroll* and applied in succeeding cases. Like the automobile in *Carroll*, respondent's motor home was readily mobile. Absent the prompt search and seizure, it could readily have been moved beyond the reach of the police. Furthermore, the vehicle was licensed to "operate on public streets; [was] serviced in public places; . . . and [was] subject to extensive regulation and inspection." And the vehicle was so situated that an objective observer would conclude that it was being used not as a residence, but as a vehicle.

Respondent urges us to distinguish his vehicle from other vehicles within the exception because it was capable of functioning as a home. In our increasingly mobile society, many vehicles used for transportation can be and are being used not only for transportation but for shelter, i.e., as a "home" or "residence." To distinguish between respondent's motor home and an ordinary sedan for purposes of the vehicle exception would require that we apply the exception depending upon the size of the vehicle and the quality of its appointments. Moreover, to fail to apply the exception to vehicles such as a motor home ignores the fact that a motor home lends itself easily to use as an instrument of illicit drug traffic and other illegal activity.

However, in Chambers v. Maroney, 399 U.S. 42 (1970), the Court went even further and held that even if the automobile had been taken to the police station, and thus was not movable, the automobile exception still applies. Justice White, writing for the Court, explained:

> The principal question in this case concerns the admissibility of evidence seized from an automobile, in which petitioner was riding at the time of his arrest, after the automobile was taken to a police station and was there thoroughly searched without a warrant.

[T]he search that produced the incriminating evidence was made at the police station some time after the arrest and cannot be justified as a search incident to an arrest. In terms of the circumstances justifying a warrantless search, the Court has long distinguished between an automobile and a home or office.

Having thus established that contraband goods concealed and illegally transported in an automobile or other vehicle may be searched for without a warrant, we come now to consider under what circumstances such search may be made. . . . In enforcing the Fourth Amendment's prohibition against unreasonable searches and seizures, the Court has insisted upon probable cause as a minimum requirement for a reasonable search permitted by the Constitution. As a general rule, it has also required the judgment of a magistrate on the probable-cause issue and the issuance of a warrant before a search is made. Only in exigent circumstances will the judgment of the police as to probable cause serve as a sufficient authorization for a search. *Carroll* holds a search warrant unnecessary where there is probable cause to search an automobile stopped on the highway; the car is movable, the occupants are alerted, and the car's contents may never be found again if a warrant must be obtained. Hence an immediate search is constitutionally permissible.

Arguably, because of the preference for a magistrate's judgment, only the immobilization of the car should be permitted until a search warrant is obtained; arguably, only the "lesser" intrusion is permissible until the magistrate authorizes the "greater." But which is the "greater" and which the "lesser" intrusion is itself a debatable question and the answer may depend on a variety of circumstances. For constitutional purposes, we see no difference between on the one hand seizing and holding a car before presenting the probable cause issue to a magistrate and on the other hand carrying out an immediate search without a warrant. Given probable cause to search, either course is reasonable under the Fourth Amendment.

b. Searches of Containers in Automobiles

Does the automobile exception extend to allowing warrantless searches of containers within the car? The Court has held that containers, such as luggage, can be searched without a warrant only if there are exigent circumstances. United States v. Chadwick, 433 U.S. 1 (1977). But if there is probable cause to search a vehicle, the Court has said that the probable cause extends to the containers within it. California v. Acevedo addressed this.

CALIFORNIA v. ACEVEDO
500 U.S. 565 (1991)

Justice BLACKMUN delivered the opinion of the Court.

This case requires us once again to consider the so-called "automobile exception" to the warrant requirement of the Fourth Amendment and its application to the search of a closed container in the trunk of a car.

I

On October 28, 1987, Officer Coleman of the Santa Ana, Cal., Police Department received a telephone call from a federal drug enforcement agent in Hawaii. The agent informed Coleman that he had seized a package containing marijuana which was to have been delivered to the Federal Express Office in Santa Ana and which was addressed to J.R. Daza at 805 West Stevens Avenue in that city. The agent arranged to send the package to Coleman instead. Coleman then was to take the package to the Federal Express office and arrest the person who arrived to claim it.

Coleman received the package on October 29, verified its contents, and took it to the Senior Operations Manager at the Federal Express office. At about 10:30 A.M. on October 30, a man, who identified himself as Jamie Daza, arrived to claim the package. He accepted it and drove to his apartment on West Stevens. He carried the package into the apartment.

At 11:45 A.M., officers observed Daza leave the apartment and drop the box and paper that had contained the marijuana into a trash bin. Coleman at that point left the scene to get a search warrant. About 12:05 P.M., the officers saw Richard St. George leave the apartment carrying a blue knapsack which appeared to be half full. The officers stopped him as he was driving off, searched the knapsack, and found 1½ pounds of marijuana.

At 12:30 P.M., respondent Charles Steven Acevedo arrived. He entered Daza's apartment, stayed for about 10 minutes, and reappeared carrying a brown paper bag that looked full. The officers noticed that the bag was the size of one of the wrapped marijuana packages sent from Hawaii. Acevedo walked to a silver Honda in the parking lot. He placed the bag in the trunk of the car and started to drive away. Fearing the loss of evidence, officers in a marked police car stopped him. They opened the trunk and the bag, and found marijuana.

II

Contemporaneously with the adoption of the Fourth Amendment, the First Congress, and, later, the Second and Fourth Congresses, distinguished between the need for a warrant to search for contraband concealed in "a dwelling house or similar place" and the need for a warrant to search for contraband concealed in a movable vessel. In *Carroll*, this Court established an exception to the warrant requirement for moving vehicles, for it recognized "a necessary difference between a search of a store, dwelling house or other structure in respect of which a proper official warrant readily may be obtained, and a search of a ship, motor boat, wagon or automobile, for contraband goods, where it is not practicable to secure a warrant because the vehicle can be quickly moved out of the locality or jurisdiction in which the warrant must be sought."

It therefore held that a warrantless search of an automobile, based upon probable cause to believe that the vehicle contained evidence of crime in the light of an exigency arising out of the likely disappearance of the vehicle, did not contravene the Warrant Clause of the Fourth Amendment.

In United States v. Ross, decided in 1982, we held that a warrantless search of an automobile under the *Carroll* doctrine could include a search of a container or package found inside the car when such a search was supported by probable cause. The warrantless search of Ross' car occurred after an informant told the police that he had seen Ross complete a drug transaction using drugs stored in the trunk of his car. The police stopped the car, searched it, and discovered in the trunk a brown paper bag containing drugs. We decided that the search of Ross' car was not unreasonable under the Fourth Amendment: "The scope of a warrantless search based on probable cause is no narrower—and no broader—than the scope of a search authorized by a warrant supported by probable cause." Thus, "[i]f probable cause justifies the search of a lawfully stopped vehicle, it justifies the search of every part of the vehicle and its contents that may conceal the object of the search." In *Ross*, therefore, we clarified the scope of the *Carroll* doctrine as properly including a "probing search" of compartments and containers within the automobile so long as the search is supported by probable cause.

The facts in this case closely resemble the facts in *Ross*. In *Ross*, the police had probable cause to believe that drugs were stored in the trunk of a particular car. Here, the California Court of Appeal concluded that the police had probable cause to believe that respondent was carrying marijuana in a bag in his car's trunk. Furthermore, for what it is worth, in *Ross*, as here, the drugs in the trunk were contained in a brown paper bag.

We now must decide the question deferred in *Ross:* whether the Fourth Amendment requires the police to obtain a warrant to open the sack in a movable vehicle simply because they lack probable cause to search the entire car. We conclude that it does not.

[III]

We now agree that a container found after a general search of the automobile and a container found in a car after a limited search for the container are equally easy for the police to store and for the suspect to hide or destroy. In fact, we see no principled distinction in terms of either the privacy expectation or the exigent circumstances between the paper bag found by the police in *Ross* and the paper bag found by the police here. Furthermore, by attempting to distinguish between a container for which the police are specifically searching and a container which they come across in a car, we have provided only minimal protection for privacy and have impeded effective law enforcement.

The line between probable cause to search a vehicle and probable cause to search a package in that vehicle is not always clear, and separate rules that govern the two objects to be searched may enable the police to broaden their power to make warrantless searches and disserve privacy interests. We noted this in *Ross* in the context of a search of an entire vehicle. Recognizing that under *Carroll*, the "entire vehicle itself . . . could be searched without a warrant," we concluded that "prohibiting police from opening immediately a container in which the object of the search is most likely to be found and instead forcing them first to comb the entire vehicle would actually exacerbate the intrusion on privacy interests." At the moment when officers stop an automobile, it may be less than clear whether they suspect with a high degree of certainty that the vehicle contains drugs in a bag or simply contains drugs. If the police know that they may open a bag only if they are actually searching the entire car, they may search more extensively than they otherwise would in order to establish the general probable cause required by *Ross*.

Finally, the search of a paper bag intrudes far less on individual privacy than does the incursion sanctioned long ago in *Carroll*. In that case, prohibition agents slashed the upholstery of the automobile. This Court nonetheless found their search to be reasonable under the Fourth Amendment. If destroying the interior of an automobile is not unreasonable, we cannot conclude that looking inside a closed container is. [W]e now hold that the Fourth Amendment does not compel separate treatment for an automobile search that extends only to a container within the vehicle. The interpretation of the *Carroll* doctrine set forth in *Ross* now applies to all searches of containers found in an automobile. In other words, the police may search without a warrant if their search is supported by probable cause.

Justice STEVENS, with whom Justice MARSHALL joins, dissenting.

It is "a cardinal principle that searches conducted outside the judicial process, without prior approval by judge or magistrate, are per se unreasonable under the Fourth Amendment — subject only to a few specifically established and well-delineated exceptions." Relying on arguments that conservative judges have repeatedly rejected in past cases, the Court today — despite its disclaimer to the contrary, — enlarges the scope of the automobile exception to this "cardinal principle," which undergirded our Fourth Amendment jurisprudence prior.

Our decisions have always acknowledged that the warrant requirement imposes a burden on law enforcement. And our cases have not questioned that trained professionals normally make reliable assessments of the existence of probable cause to conduct a search. We have repeatedly held, however, that these factors are outweighed by the individual interest in privacy that is protected by advance judicial approval. The Fourth Amendment dictates that the privacy interest is paramount, no matter how marginal the risk of error might be if the legality of warrantless searches were judged only after the fact.

In its opinion today, the Court recognizes that the police did not have probable cause to search respondent's vehicle and that a search of anything but the paper bag that respondent had carried from Daza's apartment and placed in the trunk of his car would have been unconstitutional. Moreover, as I read the opinion, the Court assumes that the police could not have made a warrantless inspection of the bag before it was placed in the car. Finally, the Court also does not question the fact that, under our prior cases, it would have been lawful for the police to seize the container and detain it (and respondent) until they obtained a search warrant.

The Court does not attempt to identify any exigent circumstances that would justify its refusal to apply the general rule against warrantless searches.

Every citizen clearly has an interest in the privacy of the contents of his or her luggage, briefcase, handbag or any other container that conceals private papers and effects from public scrutiny. That privacy interest has been recognized repeatedly in cases spanning more than a century. Under the Court's holding today, the privacy interest that protects the contents of a suitcase or a briefcase from a warrantless search when it is in public view simply vanishes when its owner climbs into a taxicab. Unquestionably today's decision will result in a significant loss of individual privacy.

The Court's suggestion that [prior decisions create a] significant burden on effective law enforcement is unsupported, inaccurate, and, in any event, an insufficient reason for creating a new exception to the warrant requirement. Even if the warrant requirement does inconvenience the police to some extent, that fact does not distinguish this constitutional requirement from any other procedural protection secured by the Bill of Rights. It is merely a part of the price that our society must pay in order to preserve its freedom.

It is too early to know how much freedom America has lost today. The magnitude of the loss is, however, not nearly as significant as the Court's willingness to inflict it without even a colorable basis for its rejection of prior law.

Does the ability to search packages include the packages of the occupants of the car? Earlier, in United States v. Di Re, 332 U.S. 581 (1948), the Court held that passengers could not be searched without probable cause simply because the automobile was lawfully stopped by police. However, in Wyoming v. Houghton, 526 U.S. 295 (1999), the Court held that police do not violate the Fourth Amendment when they search a passenger's personal belongings inside an automobile that they have probable cause to believe contains contraband.

Justice Scalia, writing for the majority, stated the facts of the case:

> In the early morning hours of July 23, 1995, a Wyoming Highway Patrol officer stopped an automobile for speeding and driving with a faulty brake light. There were three passengers in the front seat of the car: David Young (the driver), his girlfriend, and respondent. While questioning Young, the officer noticed a hypodermic syringe in Young's shirt pocket. He left the occupants under the supervision of two backup officers as he went to get gloves from his patrol car. Upon his return, he instructed Young to step out of the car and place the syringe on the hood. The officer then asked Young why he had a syringe; with refreshing candor, Young replied that he used it to take drugs.
>
> At this point, the backup officers ordered the two female passengers out of the car and asked them for identification. Respondent falsely identified herself as "Sandra James" and stated that she did not have any identification. Meanwhile, in light of Young's admission, the officer searched the passenger compartment of the car for contraband. On the back seat, he found a purse, which respondent claimed as hers. He removed from the purse a wallet containing respondent's driver's license, identifying her properly as Sandra K. Houghton. When the officer asked her why she had lied about her name, she replied: "In case things went bad."
>
> Continuing his search of the purse, the officer found a brown pouch and a black wallet-type container. Respondent denied that the former was hers, and claimed ignorance of how it came to be there; it was found to contain drug paraphernalia and a syringe with 60 ccs of methamphetamine. Respondent admitted ownership of the black container, which was also found to contain drug paraphernalia, and a syringe (which respondent acknowledged was hers) with 10 ccs of methamphetamine — an amount insufficient to support the felony conviction at issue in this case. The officer also found fresh needle-track marks on respondent's arms. He placed her under arrest.

The Court held that the search of the purse did not violate the Fourth Amendment. The Court said that there was no basis for

> a distinction among packages or containers based on ownership. When there is probable cause to search for contraband in a car, it is reasonable for police officers — like customs officials in the founding era — to examine packages and containers without a showing of individualized probable cause for each one. A passenger's personal belongings, just like the driver's belongings or containers attached to the car like a glove compartment, are "in" the car, and the officer has probable cause to search for contraband in the car.

Justice Stevens dissented, joined by Justices Souter and Ginsburg. He stated:

> In all of our prior cases applying the automobile exception to the Fourth Amend-
> ment's warrant requirement, either the defendant was the operator of the vehicle
> and in custody of the object of the search, or no question was raised as to the
> defendant's ownership or custody. In the only automobile case confronting the
> search of a passenger defendant — United States v. Di Re (1948) — the Court held
> that the exception to the warrant requirement did not apply.
>
> Nor am I persuaded that the mere spatial association between a passenger and
> a driver provides an acceptable basis for presuming that they are partners in crime
> or for ignoring privacy interests in a purse. Whether or not the Fourth Amendment
> required a warrant to search Houghton's purse, at the very least the trooper in this
> case had to have probable cause to believe that her purse contained contraband.
> The Wyoming Supreme Court concluded that he did not.

c. Searches Incident to Arrest

When the police lawfully stop a vehicle, they may order the driver and the
passengers to exit. Pennsylvania v. Mimms, 496 U.S. 582 (1977) (driver);
Maryland v. Wilson, 519 U.S. 408 (1997) (passengers). If the police arrest the
driver, may they then search the vehicle as part of a search incident to arrest? In
New York v. Belton, the Supreme Court said yes.

NEW YORK v. BELTON

453 U.S. 454 (1981)

Justice STEWART delivered the opinion of the Court.

When the occupant of an automobile is subjected to a lawful custodial arrest,
does the constitutionally permissible scope of a search incident to his arrest
include the passenger compartment of the automobile in which he was riding?
That is the question at issue in the present case.

I

On April 9, 1978, Trooper Douglas Nicot, a New York State policeman driving an
unmarked car on the New York Thruway, was passed by another automobile
traveling at an excessive rate of speed. Nicot gave chase, overtook the speeding
vehicle, and ordered its driver to pull it over to the side of the road and stop.
There were four men in the car, one of whom was Roger Belton, the respondent
in this case. The policeman asked to see the driver's license and automobile
registration, and discovered that none of the men owned the vehicle or was
related to its owner. Meanwhile, the policeman had smelled burnt marihuana
and had seen on the floor of the car an envelope marked "Supergold" that he
associated with marihuana. He therefore directed the men to get out the car,
and placed them under arrest for the unlawful possession of marihuana.
He patted down each of the men and "split them up into four separate areas
of the Thruway at this time so they would not be in physical touching area of
each other." He then picked up the envelope marked "Supergold" and found

that it contained marihuana. After giving the arrestees the warnings required by Miranda v. Arizona, the state policeman searched each one of them. He then searched the passenger compartment of the car. On the back seat he found a black leather jacket belonging to Belton. He unzipped one of the pockets of the jacket and discovered cocaine. Placing the jacket in his automobile, he drove the four arrestees to a nearby police station.

Belton was subsequently indicted for criminal possession of a controlled substance. In the trial court he moved that the cocaine the trooper had seized from the jacket pocket be suppressed. The court denied the motion. Belton then pleaded guilty to a lesser included offense, but preserved his claim that the cocaine had been seized in violation of the Fourth and Fourteenth Amendments.

II

It is a first principle of Fourth Amendment jurisprudence that the police may not conduct a search unless they first convince a neutral magistrate that there is probable cause to do so. This Court has recognized, however, that "the exigencies of the situation" may sometimes make exemption from the warrant requirement "imperative." Specifically, the Court held in Chimel v. California that a lawful custodial arrest creates a situation which justifies the contemporaneous search without a warrant of the person arrested and of the immediately surrounding area. Such searches have long been considered valid because of the need "to remove any weapons that [the arrestee] might seek to use in order to resist arrest or effect his escape" and the need to prevent the concealment or destruction of evidence.

It follows from this conclusion that the police may also examine the contents of any containers found within the passenger compartment, for if the passenger compartment is within reach of the arrestee, so also will containers in it be within his reach. Such a container may, of course, be searched whether it is open or closed, since the justification for the search is not that the arrestee has no privacy interest in the container, but that the lawful custodial arrest justifies the infringement of any privacy interest the arrestee may have.[8] Thus, while the Court in *Chimel* held that the police could not search all the drawers in an arrestee's house simply because the police had arrested him at home, the Court noted that drawers within an arrestee's reach could be searched because of the danger their contents might pose to the police. It is true, of course, that these containers will sometimes be such that they could hold neither a weapon nor evidence of the criminal conduct for which the suspect was arrested.

It is not questioned that the respondent was the subject of a lawful custodial arrest on a charge of possessing marihuana. The search of the respondent's jacket followed immediately upon that arrest. The jacket was located inside the passenger compartment of the car in which the respondent had been a passenger just before he was arrested. The jacket was thus within the area

8. "Container" here denotes any object capable of holding another object. It thus includes closed or open glove compartments, consoles, or other receptacles located anywhere within the passenger compartment, as well as luggage, boxes, bags, clothing, and the like. Our holding encompasses only the interior of the passenger compartment of an automobile and does not encompass the trunk. [Footnote by the Court.]

which we have concluded was "within the arrestee's immediate control" within the meaning of the *Chimel* case. The search of the jacket, therefore, was a search incident to a lawful custodial arrest, and it did not violate the Fourth and Fourteenth Amendments.

Justice BRENNAN, with whom Justice MARSHALL joins, dissenting.

In Chimel v. California (1969), this Court carefully analyzed more than 50 years of conflicting precedent governing the permissible scope of warrantless searches incident to custodial arrest. The Court today turns its back on the product of that analysis, formulating an arbitrary "bright-line" rule applicable to "recent" occupants of automobiles that fails to reflect *Chimel*'s underlying policy justifications. While the Court claims to leave *Chimel* intact, I fear that its unwarranted abandonment of the principles underlying that decision may signal a wholesale retreat from our carefully developed search-incident-to-arrest analysis.

It has long been a fundamental principle of Fourth Amendment analysis that exceptions to the warrant requirement are to be narrowly construed. The *Chimel* exception to the warrant requirement was designed with two principal concerns in mind: the safety of the arresting officer and the preservation of easily concealed or destructible evidence. The *Chimel* standard was narrowly tailored to address these concerns: it permits police officers who have effected a custodial arrest to conduct a warrantless search "of the arrestee's person and the area 'within his immediate control' — construing that phrase to mean the area from within which he might gain possession of a weapon or destructible evidence." It thus places a temporal and a spatial limitation on searches incident to arrest, excusing compliance with the warrant requirement only when the search "'is substantially contemporaneous with the arrest and is confined to the immediate vicinity of the arrest.'" When the arrest has been consummated and the arrestee safely taken into custody, the justifications underlying *Chimel*'s limited exception to the warrant requirement cease to apply: at that point there is no possibility that the arrestee could reach weapons or contraband.

As the facts of this case make clear, the Court today substantially expands the permissible scope of searches incident to arrest by permitting police officers to search areas and containers the arrestee could not possibly reach at the time of arrest. These facts demonstrate that at the time Belton and his three companions were placed under custodial arrest — which was after they had been removed from the car, patted down, and separated — none of them could have reached the jackets that had been left on the back seat of the car.

This expansion of the *Chimel* exception is both analytically unsound and inconsistent with every significant search-incident-to-arrest case we have decided in which the issue was whether the police could lawfully conduct a warrantless search of the area surrounding the arrestee.

Belton involved the situation of officers stopping a car and then arresting the occupants. What if the car is already stopped and the driver has exited and then the arrest is made? Does *Belton* apply and can the police search the car? In United States v. Thornton, the Court said yes, even though the driver was under arrest in the squad car when the search was done. Some of the Justices urge a reconsideration of *Belton*. Of course, after *Thornton*, the issue will arise as to how long ago the person must have been in the car and how close he or she must be in proximity of the car to justify the search.

THORNTON v. UNITED STATES
541 U.S. 615 (2004)

Chief Justice REHNQUIST delivered the opinion of the Court.

In New York v. Belton (1981), we held that when a police officer has made a lawful custodial arrest of an occupant of an automobile, the Fourth Amendment allows the officer to search the passenger compartment of that vehicle as a contemporaneous incident of arrest. We have granted certiorari to determine whether *Belton*'s rule is limited to situations where the officer makes contact with the occupant while the occupant is inside the vehicle, or whether it applies as well when the officer first makes contact with the arrestee after the latter has stepped out of his vehicle. We conclude that *Belton* governs even when an officer does not make contact until the person arrested has left the vehicle.

Officer Deion Nichols of the Norfolk, Virginia, Police Department, who was in uniform but driving an unmarked police car, first noticed petitioner Marcus Thornton when petitioner slowed down so as to avoid driving next to him. Nichols suspected that petitioner knew he was a police officer and for some reason did not want to pull next to him. His suspicions aroused, Nichols pulled off onto a side street and petitioner passed him. After petitioner passed him, Nichols ran a check on petitioner's license tags, which revealed that the tags had been issued to a 1982 Chevy two-door and not to a Lincoln Town Car, the model of car petitioner was driving. Before Nichols had an opportunity to pull him over, petitioner drove into a parking lot, parked, and got out of the vehicle. Nichols saw petitioner leave his vehicle as he pulled in behind him. He parked the patrol car, accosted petitioner, and asked him for his driver's license. He also told him that his license tags did not match the vehicle that he was driving.

Petitioner appeared nervous. He began rambling and licking his lips; he was sweating. Concerned for his safety, Nichols asked petitioner if he had any narcotics or weapons on him or in his vehicle. Petitioner said no. Nichols then asked petitioner if he could pat him down, to which petitioner agreed. Nichols felt a bulge in petitioner's left front pocket and again asked him if he had any illegal narcotics on him. This time petitioner stated that he did, and he reached into his pocket and pulled out two individual bags, one containing three bags of marijuana and the other containing a large amount of crack cocaine. Nichols handcuffed petitioner, informed him that he was under arrest, and placed him in the back seat of the patrol car. He then searched petitioner's vehicle and found a BryCo 9-millimeter handgun under the driver's seat.

In all relevant aspects, the arrest of a suspect who is next to a vehicle presents identical concerns regarding officer safety and the destruction of evidence as the arrest of one who is inside the vehicle. An officer may search a suspect's vehicle under *Belton* only if the suspect is arrested. A custodial arrest is fluid and "[t]he danger to the police officer flows from the fact of the arrest, and its attendant proximity, stress, and uncertainty." The stress is no less merely because the arrestee exited his car before the officer initiated contact, nor is an arrestee less likely to attempt to lunge for a weapon or to destroy evidence if he is outside of, but still in control of, the vehicle. In either case, the officer faces a highly volatile situation. It would make little sense to apply two different rules to what is, at bottom, the same situation.

In some circumstances it may be safer and more effective for officers to conceal their presence from a suspect until he has left his vehicle. Certainly that is a judgment officers should be free to make. But under the strictures of petitioner's proposed "contact initiation" rule, officers who do so would be unable to search the car's passenger compartment in the event of a custodial arrest, potentially compromising their safety and placing incriminating evidence at risk of conceal-ment or destruction. The Fourth Amendment does not require such a gamble.

To be sure, not all contraband in the passenger compartment is likely to be readily accessible to a "recent occupant." It is unlikely in this case that petitioner could have reached under the driver's seat for his gun once he was outside of his automobile. But the firearm and the passenger compartment in general were no more inaccessible than were the contraband and the passenger compartment in *Belton*. The need for a clear rule, readily understood by police officers and not depending on differing estimates of what items were or were not within reach of an arrestee at any particular moment, justifies the sort of generalization which *Belton* enunciated. Once an officer determines that there is probable cause to make an arrest, it is reasonable to allow officers to ensure their safety and to preserve evidence by searching the entire passenger compartment.

Justice SCALIA, with whom Justice GINSBURG joins, concurring in the judgment.
When petitioner's car was searched in this case, he was neither in, nor anywhere near, the passenger compartment of his vehicle. Rather, he was hand-cuffed and secured in the back of the officer's squad car. The risk that he would nevertheless "grab a weapon or evidentiary ite[m]" from his car was remote in the extreme. The Court's effort to apply our current doctrine to this search stretches it beyond its breaking point, and for that reason I cannot join the Court's opinion.

I see three reasons why the search in this case might have been justified to protect officer safety or prevent concealment or destruction of evidence. None ultimately persuades me.

The first is that, despite being handcuffed and secured in the back of a squad car, petitioner might have escaped and retrieved a weapon or evidence from his vehicle — a theory that calls to mind Judge Goldberg's reference to the mythical arrestee "possessed of the skill of Houdini and the strength of Hercules."

The second defense of the search in this case is that, since the officer could have conducted the search at the time of arrest (when the suspect was still near the car), he should not be penalized for having taken the sensible precaution of securing the suspect in the squad car first. The weakness of this argument is that it assumes that, one way or another, the search must take place. But conducting a *Chimel* search is not the Government's right; it is an exception — justified by necessity — to a rule that would otherwise render the search unlawful. If "sensible police procedures" require that suspects be handcuffed and put in squad cars, then police should handcuff suspects, put them in squad cars, and not conduct the search. Indeed, if an officer leaves a suspect unrestrained nearby just to manufacture authority to search, one could argue that the search is unreasonable precisely because the dangerous conditions justifying it existed only by virtue of the officer's failure to follow sensible procedures.

The third defense of the search is that, even though the arrestee posed no risk here, *Belton* searches in general are reasonable, and the benefits of a bright-line rule justify upholding that small minority of searches that, on their particular facts, are not reasonable. The validity of this argument rests on the accuracy of *Belton*'s claim that the passenger compartment is "in fact generally, even if not inevitably," within the suspect's immediate control.

If *Belton* entitles an officer to search a vehicle upon arresting the driver despite having taken measures that eliminate any danger, what rational officer would not take those measures? If it was ever true that the passenger compartment is "in fact generally, even if not inevitably," within the arrestee's immediate control at the time of the search, it certainly is not true today.

If *Belton* searches are justifiable, it is not because the arrestee might grab a weapon or evidentiary item from his car, but simply because the car might contain evidence relevant to the crime for which he was arrested. But if we are going to continue to allow *Belton* searches on stare decisis grounds, we should at least be honest about why we are doing so. *Belton* cannot reasonably be explained as a mere application of *Chimel*. Rather, it is a return to the broader sort of search incident to arrest that we allowed before *Chimel*—limited, of course, to searches of motor vehicles, a category of "effects" which give rise to a reduced expectation of privacy, and heightened law enforcement needs.

I would therefore limit *Belton* searches to cases where it is reasonable to believe evidence relevant to the crime of arrest might be found in the vehicle. In this case, as in *Belton*, petitioner was lawfully arrested for a drug offense. It was reasonable for Officer Nichols to believe that further contraband or similar evidence relevant to the crime for which he had been arrested might be found in the vehicle from which he had just alighted and which was still within his vicinity at the time of arrest. I would affirm the decision below on that ground.

Justice STEVENS, with whom Justice SOUTER joins, dissenting.

A fair reading of the *Belton* opinion itself, and of the conflicting cases that gave rise to our grant of certiorari, makes clear that we were not concerned with the situation presented in this case. *Belton* was demonstrably concerned only with the narrow but common circumstance of a search occasioned by the arrest of a suspect who was seated in or driving an automobile at the time the law enforcement official approached. Normally, after such an arrest has occurred, the officer's safety is no longer in jeopardy, but he must decide what, if any, search for incriminating evidence he should conduct. *Belton* provided previously unavailable and therefore necessary guidance for that category of cases.

The bright-line rule crafted in *Belton* is not needed for cases in which the arrestee is first accosted when he is a pedestrian, because *Chimel* itself provides all the guidance that is necessary. The only genuine justification for extending *Belton* to cover such circumstances is the interest in uncovering potentially valuable evidence. In my opinion, that goal must give way to the citizen's constitutionally protected interest in privacy when there is already in place a well-defined rule limiting the permissible scope of a search of an arrested pedestrian. The *Chimel* rule should provide the same protection to a "recent occupant" of a vehicle as to a recent occupant of a house.

Unwilling to confine the *Belton* rule to the narrow class of cases it was designed to address, the Court extends *Belton*'s reach without supplying any guidance for the future application of its swollen rule. We are told that officers may search a vehicle incident to arrest "[s]o long as [the] arrestee is the sort of 'recent occupant' of a vehicle such as petitioner was here." But we are not told how recent is recent, or how close is close, perhaps because in this case "the record is not clear." Without some limiting principle, I fear that today's decision will contribute to "a massive broadening of the automobile exception," when officers have probable cause to arrest an individual but not to search his car.

5. Inventory Searches

Another exception to the warrant requirement is for inventory searches. If property is lawfully in the possession of the police, they may inventory the contents to protect the owner's property while it is in police possession. In South Dakota v. Opperman, the Court considered the ability of the police to inventory the contents of a car that had been impounded for a parking violation.

SOUTH DAKOTA v. OPPERMAN
428 U.S. 361 (1976)

Chief Justice BURGER delivered the opinion of the Court.

We review the judgment of the Supreme Court of South Dakota, holding that local police violated the Fourth Amendment to the Federal Constitution, as applicable to the States under the Fourteenth Amendment, when they conducted a routine inventory search of an automobile lawfully impounded by police for violations of municipal parking ordinances.

Local ordinances prohibit parking in certain areas of downtown Vermillion, S.D., between the hours of 2 A.M. and 6 A.M. During the early morning hours of December 10, 1973, a Vermillion police officer observed respondent's unoccupied vehicle illegally parked in the restricted zone. At approximately 3 A.M., the officer issued an overtime parking ticket and placed it on the car's windshield. The citation warned: "Vehicles in violation of any parking ordinance may be towed from the area."

At approximately 10 o'clock on the same morning, another officer issued a second ticket for an overtime parking violation. These circumstances were routinely reported to police headquarters, and after the vehicle was inspected, the car was towed to the city impound lot.

From outside the car at the impound lot, a police officer observed a watch on the dashboard and other items of personal property located on the back seat and back floorboard. At the officer's direction, the car door was then unlocked and, using a standard inventory form pursuant to standard police procedures, the officer inventoried the contents of the car, including the contents of the glove compartment which was unlocked. There he found marihuana contained in a plastic bag. All items, including the contraband, were removed to the police department for safekeeping. During the late afternoon of December 10, respondent appeared at the police department to claim his property. The marihuana was retained by police.

Respondent was subsequently arrested on charges of possession of marihuana. His motion to suppress the evidence yielded by the inventory search was denied; he was convicted after a jury trial and sentenced to a fine of $100 and 14 days' incarceration in the county jail. On appeal, the Supreme Court of South Dakota reversed the conviction. The court concluded that the evidence had been obtained in violation of the Fourth Amendment prohibition against unreasonable searches and seizures. We granted certiorari and we reverse.

This Court has traditionally drawn a distinction between automobiles and homes or offices in relation to the Fourth Amendment. Although automobiles are "effects" and thus within the reach of the Fourth Amendment, warrantless examinations of automobiles have been upheld in circumstances in which a search of a home or office would not. [T]he inherent mobility of automobiles creates circumstances of such exigency that, as a practical necessity, rigorous enforcement of the warrant requirement is impossible. Automobiles, unlike homes, are subjected to pervasive and continuing governmental regulation and controls, including periodic inspection and licensing requirements. As an everyday occurrence, police stop and examine vehicles when license plates or inspection stickers have expired, or if other violations, such as exhaust fumes or excessive noise, are noted, or if headlights or other safety equipment are not in proper working order. The expectation of privacy as to automobiles is further diminished by the obviously public nature of automobile travel.

In the interests of public safety and as part of what the Court has called "community caretaking functions," automobiles are frequently taken into police custody. Vehicle accidents present one such occasion. To permit the uninterrupted flow of traffic and in some circumstances to preserve evidence, disabled or damaged vehicles will often be removed from the highways or streets at the behest of police engaged solely in caretaking and traffic-control activities. Police will also frequently remove and impound automobiles which violate parking ordinances and which thereby jeopardize both the public safety and the efficient movement of vehicular traffic. The authority of police to seize and remove from the streets vehicles impeding traffic or threatening public safety and convenience is beyond challenge.

When vehicles are impounded, local police departments generally follow a routine practice of securing and inventorying the automobiles' contents. These procedures developed in response to three distinct needs: the protection of the owner's property while it remains in police custody; the protection of the police against claims or disputes over lost or stolen property; and the protection of the police from potential danger. The practice has been viewed as essential to respond to incidents of theft or vandalism. In addition, police frequently attempt to determine whether a vehicle has been stolen and thereafter abandoned.

In view of the noncriminal context of inventory searches, and the inapplicability in such a setting of the requirement of probable cause, courts have held and quite correctly that search warrants are not required, linked as the warrant requirement textually is to the probable-cause concept. We have frequently observed that the warrant requirement assures that legal inferences and conclusions as to probable cause will be drawn by a neutral magistrate unrelated to the criminal investigative-enforcement process. With respect to noninvestigative police inventories of automobiles lawfully within governmental custody, however, the policies underlying the warrant requirement are inapplicable.

The decisions of this Court point unmistakably to the conclusion reached by both federal and state courts that inventories pursuant to standard police procedures are reasonable. In applying the reasonableness standard adopted by the

Framers, this Court has consistently sustained police intrusions into automobiles impounded or otherwise in lawful police custody where the process is aimed at securing or protecting the car and its contents. [I]n Cady v. Dombrowski (1973), [t]he Court upheld a warrantless search of an automobile towed to a private garage even though no probable cause existed to believe that the vehicle contained fruits of a crime. The sole justification for the warrantless incursion was that it was incident to the caretaking function of the local police to protect the community's safety. Indeed, the protective search was instituted solely because the local police "were under the impression" that the incapacitated driver, a Chicago police officer, was required to carry his service revolver at all times; the police had reasonable grounds to believe a weapon might be in the car, and thus available to vandals. The Court carefully noted that the protective search was carried out in accordance with standard procedures in the local police department, a factor tending to ensure that the intrusion would be limited in scope to the extent necessary to carry out the caretaking function.

On this record we conclude that in following standard police procedures, prevailing throughout the country and approved by the overwhelming majority of courts, the conduct of the police was not "unreasonable" under the Fourth Amendment.

Justice MARSHALL, with whom Justice BRENNAN and Justice STEWART join, dissenting.

The Court today holds that the Fourth Amendment permits a routine police inventory search of the closed glove compartment of a locked automobile impounded for ordinary traffic violations. Under the Court's holding, such a search may be made without attempting to secure the consent of the owner and without any particular reason to believe the impounded automobile contains contraband, evidence, or valuables, or presents any danger to its custodians or the public.[9] Because I believe this holding to be contrary to sound elaboration of established Fourth Amendment principles, I dissent.

[T]he requirement of a warrant aside, resolution of the question whether an inventory search of closed compartments inside a locked automobile can ever be justified as a constitutionally "reasonable" search depends upon a reconciliation of the owner's constitutionally protected privacy interests against governmental intrusion, and legitimate governmental interests furthered by securing the car and its contents. The Court fails clearly to articulate the reasons for its reconciliation of these interests in this case, but it is at least clear to me that the considerations alluded to by the Court are insufficient to justify the Court's result in this case.

Contrary to the Court's assertion, however, the search of respondent's car was not in any way "prompted by the presence in plain view of a number of valuables inside the car." In fact, the record plainly states that every vehicle taken to the city impound lot was inventoried, and that as a matter of "standard procedure," "every inventory search" would involve entry into the car's closed glove compartment.

---

9. The Court does not consider, however, whether the police might open and search the glove compartment if it is locked, or whether the police might search a locked trunk or other compartment. [Footnote by Justice Marshall.]

The Court's opinion appears to suggest that its result may in any event be justified because the inventory search procedure is a "reasonable" response to "three distinct needs: the protection of the owner's property while it remains in police custody . . . ; the protection of the police against claims or disputes over lost or stolen property . . . ; and the protection of the police from potential danger." This suggestion is flagrantly misleading, however, because the record of this case explicitly belies any relevance of the last two concerns. In any event it is my view that none of these "needs," separately or together, can suffice to justify the inventory search procedure approved by the Court.

First, this search cannot be justified in any way as a safety measure, for though the Court ignores it the sole purpose given by the State for the Vermillion police's inventory procedure was to secure valuables. Nor is there any indication that the officer's search in this case was tailored in any way to safety concerns, or that ordinarily it is so circumscribed. Even aside from the actual basis for the police practice in this case, however, I do not believe that any blanket safety argument could justify a program of routine searches of the scope permitted here.

The Court suggests a further "crucial" justification for the search in this case: "protection of the Public from vandals who might find a firearm, or as here, contraband drugs." This rationale, too, is absolutely without support in this record. There is simply no indication the police were looking for dangerous items. Indeed, even though the police found shotgun shells in the interior of the car, they never opened the trunk to determine whether it might contain a shotgun. Aside from this, the suggestion is simply untenable as a matter of law. If this asserted rationale justifies search of all impounded automobiles, it must logically also justify the search of all automobiles, whether impounded or not, located in a similar area, for the argument is not based upon the custodial role of the police. But this Court has never permitted the search of any car or home on the mere undifferentiated assumption that it might be vandalized and the vandals might find dangerous weapons or substances.

Second, the Court suggests that the search for valuables in the closed glove compartment might be justified as a measure to protect the police against lost property claims. Again, this suggestion is belied by the record, since although the Court declines to discuss it the South Dakota Supreme Court's interpretation of state law explicitly absolves the police, as "gratuitous depositors," from any obligation beyond inventorying objects in plain view and locking the car.

Finally, the Court suggests that the public interest in protecting valuables that may be found inside a closed compartment of an impounded car may justify the inventory procedure. I recognize the genuineness of this governmental interest in protecting property from pilferage. But even if I assume that the posting of a guard would be fiscally impossible as an alternative means to the same protective end, I cannot agree with the Court's conclusion. The Court's result authorizes, indeed it appears to require, the routine search of nearly every car impounded. In my view, the Constitution does not permit such searches as a matter of routine; absent specific consent, such a search is permissible only in exceptional circumstances of particular necessity.

———————————

South Dakota v. Opperman involves an inventory search of a car. Illinois v. Lafayette applies this to a person's possessions.

ILLINOIS v. LAFAYETTE
462 U.S. 640 (1983)

Chief Justice BURGER delivered the opinion of the Court.

The question presented is whether, at the time an arrested person arrives at a police station, the police may, without obtaining a warrant, search a shoulder bag carried by that person.

On September 1, 1980, at about 10 P.M., Officer Maurice Mietzner of the Kankakee City Police arrived at the Town Cinema in Kankakee, Illinois, in response to a call about a disturbance. There he found respondent involved in an altercation with the theatre manager. He arrested respondent for disturbing the peace, handcuffed him, and took him to the police station. Respondent carried a purse-type shoulder bag on the trip to the station.

At the police station respondent was taken to the booking room; there, Officer Mietzner removed the handcuffs from respondent and ordered him to empty his pockets and place the contents on the counter. After doing so, respondent took a package of cigarettes from his shoulder bag and placed the bag on the counter. Mietzner then removed the contents of the bag, and found ten amphetamine pills inside a cigarette case package.

Respondent was subsequently charged with violating the Illinois Controlled Substances Act on the basis of the controlled substances found in his shoulder bag.

The question here is whether, consistent with the Fourth Amendment, it is reasonable for police to search the personal effects of a person under lawful arrest as part of the routine administrative procedure at a police stationhouse incident to booking and jailing the suspect. The justification for such searches does not rest on probable cause, and hence the absence of a warrant is immaterial to the reasonableness of the search. Indeed, we have previously established that the inventory search constitutes a well-defined exception to the warrant requirement. *See* South Dakota v. Opperman.

A so-called inventory search is not an independent legal concept but rather an incidental administrative step following arrest and preceding incarceration. To determine whether the search of respondent's shoulder bag was unreasonable we must "balanc[e] its intrusion on the individual's Fourth Amendment interests against its promotion of legitimate governmental interests." Delaware v. Prouse (1979).

In order to see an inventory search in proper perspective, it is necessary to study the evolution of interests along the continuum from arrest to incarceration. We have held that immediately upon arrest an officer may lawfully search the person of an arrestee; he may also search the area within the arrestee's immediate control.

An arrested person is not invariably taken to a police station or confined; if an arrestee is taken to the police station, that is no more than a continuation of the custody inherent in the arrest status. Nonetheless, the factors justifying a search of the person and personal effects of an arrestee upon reaching a police station but prior to being placed in confinement are somewhat different from the factors justifying an immediate search at the time and place of arrest.

The governmental interests underlying a stationhouse search of the arrestee's person and possessions may in some circumstances be even greater than those supporting a search immediately following arrest. Consequently, the scope of a stationhouse search will often vary from that made at the time of arrest. Police conduct that would be impractical or unreasonable — or embarrassingly intrusive — on the street can more readily — and privately — be performed at the station. For example, the interests supporting a search incident to arrest would hardly justify disrobing an arrestee on the street, but the practical necessities of routine jail administration may even justify taking a prisoner's clothes before confining him, although that step would be rare.

At the stationhouse, it is entirely proper for police to remove and list or inventory property found on the person or in the possession of an arrested person who is to be jailed. A range of governmental interests support an inventory process. It is not unheard of for persons employed in police activities to steal property taken from arrested persons; similarly, arrested persons have been known to make false claims regarding what was taken from their possession at the stationhouse. A standardized procedure for making a list or inventory as soon as reasonable after reaching the stationhouse not only deters false claims but also inhibits theft or careless handling of articles taken from the arrested person. Arrested persons have also been known to injure themselves — or others — with belts, knives, drugs or other items on their person while being detained. Dangerous instrumentalities — such as razor blades, bombs, or weapons — can be concealed in innocent-looking articles taken from the arrestee's possession. The bare recital of these mundane realities justifies reasonable measures by police to limit these risks — either while the items are in police possession or at the time they are returned to the arrestee upon his release. Examining all the items removed from the arrestee's person or possession and listing or inventorying them is an entirely reasonable administrative procedure. It is immaterial whether the police actually fear any particular package or container; the need to protect against such risks arises independent of a particular officer's subjective concerns. Finally, inspection of an arrestee's personal property may assist the police in ascertaining or verifying his identity. In short, every consideration of orderly police administration benefiting both police and the public points toward the appropriateness of the examination of respondent's shoulder bag prior to his incarceration.

The reasonableness of any particular governmental activity does not necessarily or invariably turn on the existence of alternative "less intrusive" means. We are hardly in a position to second-guess police departments as to what practical administrative method will best deter theft by and false claims against its employees and preserve the security of the stationhouse. It is evident that a stationhouse search of every item carried on or by a person who has lawfully been taken into custody by the police will amply serve the important and legitimate governmental interests involved.

Even if less intrusive means existed of protecting some particular types of property, it would be unreasonable to expect police officers in the everyday course of business to make fine and subtle distinctions in deciding which containers or items may be searched and which must be sealed as a unit. Applying these principles, we hold that it is not "unreasonable" for police, as part of the routine procedure incident to incarcerating an arrested person, to search any container or article in his possession, in accordance with established inventory procedures.

Justice MARSHALL, with whom Justice BRENNAN joins, concurring in the judgment.

I agree that the police do not need a warrant or probable cause to conduct an inventory search prior to incarcerating a suspect, and I therefore concur in the judgment. The practical necessities of securing persons and property in a jailhouse setting justify an inventory search as part of the standard procedure incident to incarceration.

A very different case would be presented if the State had relied solely on the fact of arrest to justify the search of respondent's shoulder bag. A warrantless search incident to arrest must be justified by a need to remove weapons or prevent the destruction of evidence. Officer Mietzner did not in fact deem it necessary to search the bag when he arrested respondent, and I seriously doubt that such a search would have been lawful. A search at the time of respondent's arrest could not have been justified by a need to prevent the destruction of evidence, for there is no evidence or fruits of the offense—disturbing the peace—of which respondent was suspected. Moreover, although a concern about weapons might have justified seizure of the bag, such a concern could not have justified the further step of searching the bag following its seizure.

6.   Border Crossing and Checkpoints

The Supreme Court has made clear that the government has broad authority to conduct warrantless searches of people, vehicles, and mail entering the border. In United States v. Montoya de Hernandez, 473 U.S 531 (1985), the Court explained: "At the border, customs officials have more than merely an investigative law enforcement role. They are also charged, along with immigration officials, with protecting this Nation from entrants who may bring anything harmful into this country, whether that be communicable diseases, narcotics, or explosives."

The government has the ability to stop all cars at the border and to conduct warrantless searches. In 2004, the Court considered whether this includes the ability to take apart a car's gas tank without a warrant, probable cause, or even reasonable suspicion.

UNITED STATES v. FLORES-MONTANO
541 U.S. 149 (2004)

Chief Justice REHNQUIST delivered the opinion of the Court.

Customs officials seized 37 kilograms—a little more than 81 pounds—of marijuana from respondent Manuel Flores-Montano's gas tank at the international border. The Court of Appeals for the Ninth Circuit held that the Fourth Amendment forbade the fuel tank search absent reasonable suspicion. We hold that the search in question did not require reasonable suspicion.

Respondent, driving a 1987 Ford Taurus station wagon, attempted to enter the United States at the Otay Mesa Port of Entry in southern California. A customs inspector conducted an inspection of the station wagon, and requested respondent to leave the vehicle. The vehicle was then taken to a secondary inspection station.

At the secondary station, a second customs inspector inspected the gas tank by tapping it, and noted that the tank sounded solid. Subsequently, the inspector requested a mechanic under contract with Customs to come to the border station to remove the tank. Within 20 to 30 minutes, the mechanic arrived. He raised the car on a hydraulic lift, loosened the straps and unscrewed the bolts holding the gas tank to the undercarriage of the vehicle, and then disconnected some hoses and electrical connections. After the gas tank was removed, the inspector hammered off bondo (a putty-like hardening substance that is used to seal openings) from the top of the gas tank. The inspector opened an access plate underneath the bondo and found 37 kilograms of marijuana bricks. The process took 15 to 25 minutes.

A grand jury for the Southern District of California indicted respondent on one count of unlawfully importing marijuana, in violation of 21 U.S.C. §952, and one count of possession of marijuana with intent to distribute, in violation of §841(a)(1). [R]espondent filed a motion to suppress the marijuana recovered from the gas tank. The Government advised the District Court that it was not relying on reasonable suspicion as a basis for denying respondent's suppression motion. The District Court held that reasonable suspicion was required to justify the search and, accordingly, granted respondent's motion to suppress. The Court of Appeals summarily affirmed and we now reverse.

The Government's interest in preventing the entry of unwanted persons and effects is at its zenith at the international border. Time and again, we have stated that "searches made at the border, pursuant to the longstanding right of the sovereign to protect itself by stopping and examining persons and property crossing into this country, are reasonable simply by virtue of the fact that they occur at the border." United States v. Ramsey (1977). Congress, since the beginning of our Government, "has granted the Executive plenary authority to conduct routine searches and seizures at the border, without probable cause or a warrant, in order to regulate the collection of duties and to prevent the introduction of contraband into this country." It is axiomatic that the United States, as sovereign, has the inherent authority to protect, and a paramount interest in protecting, its territorial integrity.

That interest in protecting the borders is illustrated in this case by the evidence that smugglers frequently attempt to penetrate our borders with contraband secreted in their automobiles' fuel tank. Over the past 5½ fiscal years, there have been 18,788 vehicle drug seizures at the southern California ports of entry. Of those 18,788, gas tank drug seizures have accounted for 4,619 of the vehicle drug seizures, or approximately 25%. In addition, instances of persons smuggled in and around gas tank compartments are discovered at the ports of entry of San Ysidro and Otay Mesa at a rate averaging 1 approximately every 10 days.

Respondent asserts two main arguments with respect to his Fourth Amendment interests. First, he urges that he has a privacy interest in his fuel tank, and that the suspicionless disassembly of his tank is an invasion of his privacy. But on many occasions, we have noted that the expectation of privacy is less at the border than it is in the interior. We have long recognized that automobiles seeking entry into this country may be searched. It is difficult to imagine how the search of a gas tank, which should be solely a repository for fuel, could be more of an invasion of privacy than the search of the automobile's passenger compartment.

Second, respondent argues that the Fourth Amendment "protects property as well as privacy," and that the disassembly and reassembly of his gas tank is a significant deprivation of his property interest because it may damage the vehicle. He does not, and on the record cannot, truly contend that the procedure of removal, disassembly, and reassembly of the fuel tank in this case or any other has resulted in serious damage to, or destruction of, the property. According to the Government, for example, in fiscal year 2003, 348 gas tank searches conducted along the southern border were negative (i.e., no contraband was found), the gas tanks were reassembled, and the vehicles continued their entry into the United States without incident.

Respondent cites not a single accident involving the vehicle or motorist in the many thousands of gas tank disassemblies that have occurred at the border. A gas tank search involves a brief procedure that can be reversed without damaging the safety or operation of the vehicle. If damage to a vehicle were to occur, the motorist might be entitled to recovery. While the interference with a motorist's possessory interest is not insignificant when the Government removes, disassembles, and reassembles his gas tank, it nevertheless is justified by the Government's paramount interest in protecting the border.

The procedure in this case took about an hour (including the wait for the mechanic). At oral argument, the Government advised us that, depending on the type of car, a search involving the disassembly and reassembly of a gas tank may take one to two hours. We think it clear that delays of one to two hours at international borders are to be expected.

For the reasons stated, we conclude that the Government's authority to conduct suspicionless inspections at the border includes the authority to remove, disassemble, and reassemble a vehicle's fuel tank. While it may be true that some searches of property are so destructive as to require a different result, this was not one of them.

The Court has said that the ability of the government to monitor the borders includes the ability to have a fixed checkpoint near the border where cars are stopped to ensure that all are lawfully in the United States. In United States v. Martinez-Fuerte, 428 U.S. 543 (1976), the Court stated:

> These cases involve criminal prosecutions for offenses relating to the transportation of illegal Mexican aliens. Each defendant was arrested at a permanent checkpoint operated by the Border Patrol away from the international border with Mexico, and each sought the exclusion of certain evidence on the ground that the operation of the checkpoint was incompatible with the Fourth Amendment. In each instance whether the Fourth Amendment was violated turns primarily on whether a vehicle may be stopped at a fixed checkpoint for brief questioning of its occupants even though there is no reason to believe the particular vehicle contains illegal aliens. We hold today that such stops are consistent with the Fourth Amendment. We also hold that the operation of a fixed checkpoint need not be authorized in advance by a judicial warrant.

The Court has extended this beyond automobiles and has held that mail entering the country can be inspected without a warrant.

UNITED STATES v. RAMSEY
431 U.S. 606 (1977)

Justice REHNQUIST delivered the opinion of the Court.

Customs officials, acting with "reasonable cause to suspect" a violation of customs laws, opened for inspection incoming international letter-class mail without first obtaining a search warrant.

Charles W. Ramsey and James W. Kelly jointly commenced a heroin-by-mail enterprise in the Washington, D.C., area. The process involved their procuring of heroin, which was mailed in letters from Bangkok, Thailand, and sent to various locations in the District of Columbia area for collection. Two of their suppliers, Sylvia Bailey and William Ward, who were located in West Germany, were engaged in international narcotics trafficking during the latter part of 1973 and the early part of 1974. West German agents, pursuant to court-authorized electronic surveillance, intercepted several trans-Atlantic conversations between Bailey and Ramsey during which their narcotics operation was discussed. By late January 1974, Bailey and Ward had gone to Thailand. Thai officials, alerted to their presence by West German authorities, placed them under surveillance. Ward was observed mailing letter-sized envelopes in six different mail boxes; five of these envelopes were recovered; and one of the addresses in Washington, D.C., was later linked to respondents. Bailey and Ward were arrested by Thai officials on February 2, 1974; among the items seized were eleven heroin-filed envelopes addressed to the Washington, D.C., area, and later connected with respondents.

Two days after this arrest of Bailey and Ward, Inspector George Kallnischkies, a United States customs officer in New York City, without any knowledge of the foregoing events, inspecting a sack of incoming international mail from Thailand, spotted eight envelopes that were bulky and which he believed might contain merchandise. The envelopes, all of which appeared to him to have been typed on the same typewriter, were addressed to four different locations in the Washington, D.C., area. Inspector Kallnischkies, based on the fact that the letters were from Thailand, a known source of narcotics, and were "rather bulky," suspected that the envelopes might contain merchandise or contraband rather than correspondence. He took the letters to an examining area in the post office, and felt one of the letters: It "felt like there was something in there, in the envelope. It was not just plain paper that the envelope is supposed to contain." He weighed one of the envelopes, and found it weighed 42 grams, some three to six times the normal weight of an airmail letter. Inspector Kallnischkies then opened that envelope.

The envelopes were then sent to Washington in a locked pouch where agents of the Drug Enforcement Administration, after obtaining a search warrant, opened the envelopes again and removed most of the heroin. The envelopes were then resealed, and six of them were delivered under surveillance. After Kelly collected the envelopes from the three different addressees, rendezvoused with Ramsey, and gave Ramsey a brown paper bag, federal agents arrested both of them. The bag contained the six envelopes with heroin, $1,100 in cash, and "cutting" material for the heroin.

Congress and the applicable postal regulations authorized the actions undertaken in this case. Title 19 U.S.C. § 482 explicitly deals with the search of an "envelope": "Any of the officers or persons authorized to board or search vessels may . . . search any trunk or envelope, wherever found, in which he may have a reasonable cause to suspect there is merchandise which was imported contrary to law . . . ." This provision authorizes customs officials to inspect, under the circumstances therein stated, incoming international mail. The "reasonable cause to suspect" test adopted by the statute is, we think, a practical test which imposes a less stringent requirement than that of "probable cause" imposed by the Fourth Amendment as a requirement for the issuance of warrants. Inspector Kallnischkies, at the time he opened the letters, knew that they were from Thailand, were bulky, were many times the weight of a normal airmail letter, and "felt like there was something in there." Under these circumstances, we have no doubt that he had reasonable "cause to suspect" that there was merchandise or contraband in the envelopes. The search, therefore, was plainly authorized by the statute.

[handwritten margin note: Reasons]

Since the search in this case was authorized by statute, we are left simply with the question of whether the search nevertheless violated the Constitution. That searches made at the border, pursuant to the long-standing right of the sovereign to protect itself by stopping and examining persons and property crossing into this country, are reasonable simply by virtue of the fact that they occur at the border, should, by now, require no extended demonstration. Border searches, then, from before the adoption of the Fourth Amendment, have been considered to be "reasonable" by the single fact that the person or item in question had entered into our country from outside. There has never been any additional requirement that the reasonableness of a border search depended on the existence of probable cause. This long-standing recognition that searches at our borders without probable cause and without a warrant are nonetheless "reasonable" has a history as old as the Fourth Amendment itself. We reaffirm it now.

The border-search exception is grounded in the recognized right of the sovereign to control, subject to substantive limitations imposed by the Constitution, who and what may enter the country. It is clear that there is nothing in the rationale behind the border-search exception which suggests that the mode of entry will be critical. It was conceded at oral argument that customs officials could search, without probable cause and without a warrant, envelopes carried by an entering traveler, whether in his luggage or on his person. Surely no different constitutional standard should apply simply because the envelopes were mailed not carried. The critical fact is that the envelopes cross the border and enter this country, not that they are brought in by one mode of transportation rather than another. It is their entry into this country from without it that makes a resulting search "reasonable."

We therefore conclude that the Fourth Amendment does not interdict the actions taken by Inspector Kallnischkies in opening and searching the eight envelopes.

Justice STEVENS, with whom Justice BRENNAN and Justice MARSHALL join, dissenting.

[The dissent disputed that the statute authorizes such warrantless searches of mail entering the country.] If the Government is allowed to exercise the power it claims, the door will be open to the wholesale, secret examination of all incoming international letter mail. No notice would be necessary either before or after the search. Until Congress has made an unambiguous policy decision that such an unprecedented intrusion upon a vital method of personal communication is in the Nation's interest, this Court should not address the serious constitutional question it decides today.

Individuals, of course, can be stopped at the border to ensure that they are lawfully entering the country. But more intrusive searches, such as body cavity searches or detentions, require at least reasonable suspicion. United States v. Montoya-Hernandez raises the question of whether people crossing the border can be detained based on reasonable suspicion to see if they are trying to smuggle drugs in their alimentary canal.

UNITED STATES v. MONTOYA-HERNANDEZ
473 U.S. 531 (1985)

Justice REHNQUIST delivered the opinion of the Court.

Respondent Rosa Elvira Montoya de Hernandez was detained by customs officials upon her arrival at the Los Angeles Airport on a flight from Bogota, Colombia. She was found to be smuggling 88 cocaine-filled balloons in her alimentary canal, and was convicted after a bench trial of various federal narcotics offenses. A divided panel of the United States Court of Appeals for the Ninth Circuit reversed her convictions, holding that her detention violated the Fourth Amendment to the United States Constitution because the customs inspectors did not have a "clear indication" of alimentary canal smuggling at the time she was detained. We now reverse.

Respondent arrived at Los Angeles International Airport shortly after midnight, March 5, 1983, on Avianca Flight 080, a direct 10-hour flight from Bogota, Colombia. Her visa was in order so she was passed through Immigration and proceeded to the customs desk. At the customs desk she encountered Customs Inspector Talamantes, who reviewed her documents and noticed from her passport that she had made at least eight recent trips to either Miami or Los Angeles. Talamantes referred respondent to a secondary customs desk for further questioning. At this desk Talamantes and another inspector asked respondent general questions concerning herself and the purpose of her trip. Respondent revealed that she spoke no English and had no family or friends in the United States. She explained in Spanish that she had come to the United States to purchase goods for her husband's store in Bogota. The customs inspectors recognized Bogota as a "source city" for narcotics. Respondent possessed $5,000 in cash, mostly $50 bills, but had no billfold. She indicated to the inspectors that she had no appointments with merchandise vendors, but planned to ride around Los Angeles in taxicabs visiting retail stores such as J.C. Penney and K-Mart in order to buy goods for her husband's store with the $5,000.

Respondent admitted that she had no hotel reservations, but stated that she planned to stay at a Holiday Inn. Respondent could not recall how her airline ticket was purchased. When the inspectors opened respondent's one small valise they found about four changes of "cold weather" clothing. Respondent had no shoes other than the high-heeled pair she was wearing. Although respondent possessed no checks, waybills, credit cards, or letters of credit, she did produce a Colombian business card and a number of old receipts, waybills, and fabric swatches displayed in a photo album.

At this point Talamantes and the other inspector suspected that respondent was a "balloon swallower," one who attempts to smuggle narcotics into this country hidden in her alimentary canal. Over the years Inspector Talamantes had apprehended dozens of alimentary canal smugglers arriving on Avianca Flight 080.

The inspectors requested a female customs inspector to take respondent to a private area and conduct a patdown and strip search. During the search the female inspector felt respondent's abdomen area and noticed a firm fullness, as if respondent were wearing a girdle. The search revealed no contraband, but the inspector noticed that respondent was wearing two pairs of elastic underpants with a paper towel lining the crotch area.

When respondent returned to the customs area and the female inspector reported her discoveries, the inspector in charge told respondent that he suspected she was smuggling drugs in her alimentary canal. Respondent agreed to the inspector's request that she be x-rayed at a hospital but in answer to the inspector's query stated that she was pregnant. She agreed to a pregnancy test before the x ray. Respondent withdrew the consent for an x ray when she learned that she would have to be handcuffed en route to the hospital. The inspector then gave respondent the option of returning to Colombia on the next available flight, agreeing to an x ray, or remaining in detention until she produced a monitored bowel movement that would confirm or rebut the inspectors' suspicions. Respondent chose the first option and was placed in a customs office under observation. She was told that if she went to the toilet she would have to use a wastebasket in the women's restroom, in order that female customs inspectors could inspect her stool for balloons or capsules carrying narcotics. The inspectors refused respondent's request to place a telephone call.

Respondent sat in the customs office, under observation, for the remainder of the night. During the night customs officials attempted to place respondent on a Mexican airline that was flying to Bogota via Mexico City in the morning. The airline refused to transport respondent because she lacked a Mexican visa necessary to land in Mexico City. Respondent was not permitted to leave, and was informed that she would be detained until she agreed to an x ray or her bowels moved. She remained detained in the customs office under observation, for most of the time curled up in a chair leaning to one side. She refused all offers of food and drink, and refused to use the toilet facilities.

At the shift change at 4 o'clock the next afternoon, almost 16 hours after her flight had landed, respondent still had not defecated or urinated or partaken of food or drink. At that time customs officials sought a court order authorizing a pregnancy test, an x ray, and a rectal examination. The Federal Magistrate issued an order just before midnight that evening, which authorized a rectal examination and involuntary x ray, provided that the physician in charge considered respondent's claim of pregnancy. Respondent was taken to a hospital and given a pregnancy test, which later turned out to be negative. Before the results of the pregnancy test were known, a physician conducted a rectal examination and removed from respondent's rectum a balloon containing a foreign substance. Respondent was then placed formally under arrest. By 4:10 A.M. respondent had passed 6 similar balloons; over the next four days she passed 88 balloons containing a total of 528 grams of 80% pure cocaine hydrochloride.

The Fourth Amendment commands that searches and seizures be reasonable. What is reasonable depends upon all of the circumstances surrounding the search or seizure and the nature of the search or seizure itself. The permissibility of a particular law enforcement practice is judged by "balancing its intrusion on the individual's Fourth Amendment interests against its promotion of legitimate governmental interests."

Here the seizure of respondent took place at the international border. Since the founding of our Republic, Congress has granted the Executive plenary authority to conduct routine searches and seizures at the border, without probable cause or a warrant, in order to regulate the collection of duties and to prevent the introduction of contraband into this country.

Consistently, therefore, with Congress' power to protect the Nation by stopping and examining persons entering this country, the Fourth Amendment's balance of reasonableness is qualitatively different at the international border than in the interior.

Balanced against the sovereign's interests at the border are the Fourth Amendment rights of respondent. Having presented herself at the border for admission, and having subjected herself to the criminal enforcement powers of the Federal Government, respondent was entitled to be free from unreasonable search and seizure. But not only is the expectation of privacy less at the border than in the interior, the Fourth Amendment balance between the interests of the Government and the privacy right of the individual is also struck much more favorably to the Government at the border.

We have not previously decided what level of suspicion would justify a seizure of an incoming traveler for purposes other than a routine border search.

We hold that the detention of a traveler at the border, beyond the scope of a routine customs search and inspection, is justified at its inception if customs agents, considering all the facts surrounding the traveler and her trip, reasonably suspect that the traveler is smuggling contraband in her alimentary canal.

The "reasonable suspicion" standard has been applied in a number of contexts and effects a needed balance between private and public interests when law enforcement officials must make a limited intrusion on less than probable cause. It thus fits well into the situations involving alimentary canal smuggling at the border: this type of smuggling gives no external signs and inspectors will rarely possess probable cause to arrest or search, yet governmental interests in stopping smuggling at the border are high indeed. Under this standard officials at the border must have a "particularized and objective basis for suspecting the particular person" of alimentary canal smuggling.

The facts, and their rational inferences, known to customs inspectors in this case clearly supported a reasonable suspicion that respondent was an alimentary canal smuggler. We need not belabor the facts, including respondent's implausible story, that supported this suspicion. The trained customs inspectors had encountered many alimentary canal smugglers and certainly had more than an "inchoate and unparticularized suspicion or 'hunch,'" that respondent was smuggling narcotics in her alimentary canal. The inspectors' suspicion was a "'common-sense conclusio[n] about human behavior' upon which 'practical people,' including government officials, are entitled to rely."

Under these circumstances, we conclude that the detention in this case was not unreasonably long. It occurred at the international border, where the Fourth Amendment balance of interests leans heavily to the Government.

At the border, customs officials have more than merely an investigative law enforcement role. They are also charged, along with immigration officials, with protecting this Nation from entrants who may bring anything harmful into this country, whether that be communicable diseases, narcotics, or explosives. In this regard the detention of a suspected alimentary canal smuggler at the border is analogous to the detention of a suspected tuberculosis carrier at the border: both are detained until their bodily processes dispel the suspicion that they will introduce a harmful agent into this country.

Respondent's detention was long, uncomfortable, indeed, humiliating; but both its length and its discomfort resulted solely from the method by which she chose to smuggle illicit drugs into this country. Here, by analogy, in the presence of articulable suspicion of smuggling in her alimentary canal, the customs officers were not required by the Fourth Amendment to pass respondent and her 88 cocaine-filled balloons into the interior. Her detention for the period of time necessary to either verify or dispel the suspicion was not unreasonable.

Justice BRENNAN, with whom Justice MARSHALL joins, dissenting.

We confront a "disgusting and saddening episode" at our Nation's border. Shortly after midnight on March 5, 1983, the respondent Rosa Elvira Montoya De Hernandez was detained by customs officers because she fit the profile of an "alimentary canal smuggler." This profile did not of course give the officers probable cause to believe that De Hernandez was smuggling drugs into the country, but at most a "reasonable suspicion" that she might be engaged in such an attempt. After a thorough strip search failed to uncover any contraband, De Hernandez agreed to go to a local hospital for an abdominal x ray to resolve the matter.

Stymied in their efforts, the officers decided on an alternative course: they would simply lock De Hernandez away in an adjacent manifest room "until her peristaltic functions produced a monitored bowel movement." The officers explained to De Hernandez that she could not leave until she had excreted by squatting over a wastebasket pursuant to the watchful eyes of two attending matrons. De Hernandez responded: "I will not submit to your degradation and I'd rather die." She was locked away with the matrons.

De Hernandez remained locked up in the room for almost 24 hours. Three shifts of matrons came and went during this time. The room had no bed or couch on which she could lie, but only hard chairs and a table. The matrons told her that if she wished to sleep she could lie down on the hard, uncarpeted floor. De Hernandez instead "sat in her chair clutching her purse," "occasionally putting her head down on the table to nap." Most of the time she simply wept and pleaded "to go home." She repeatedly begged for permission "to call my husband and tell him what you are doing to me." Permission was denied. Sobbing, she insisted that she had to "make a phone call home so that she could talk to her children and to let them know that everything was all right." Permission again was denied. In fact, the matrons considered it highly "unusual" that "each time someone entered the search room, she would take out two small pictures of her children and show them to the person." De Hernandez also demanded that her attorney be contacted. Once again, permission was denied. As far as the outside world knew, Rosa De Hernandez had simply vanished. And although she already had been stripped and searched and probed, the customs officers decided about halfway through her ordeal to repeat that process — "to ensure the safety of the surveilling officers. The result was again negative."

After almost 24 hours had passed, someone finally had the presence of mind to consult a Magistrate and to obtain a court order for an x ray and a body-cavity search. De Hernandez, "very agitated," was handcuffed and led away to the hospital. A rectal examination disclosed the presence of a cocaine-filled balloon. At approximately 3:15 on the morning of March 6, almost 27 hours after her initial detention, De Hernandez was formally placed under arrest and advised of her Miranda rights. Over the course of the next four days she excreted a total of 88 balloons.

The standards we fashion to govern the ferreting out of the guilty apply equally to the detention of the innocent, and "may be exercised by the most unfit and ruthless officers as well as by the fit and responsible." Nor is the issue whether there is a "veritable national crisis in law enforcement caused by smuggling of illicit narcotics." There is, and "[s]tern enforcement of the criminal law is the hallmark of a healthy and self-confident society." "But in our democracy such enforcement presupposes a moral atmosphere and a reliance upon intelligence whereby the effective administration of justice can be achieved with due regard for those civilized standards in the use of the criminal law which are formulated in our Bill of Rights."

The issue, instead, is simply this: Does the Fourth Amendment permit an international traveler, citizen or alien, to be subjected to the sort of treatment that occurred in this case without the sanction of a judicial officer and based on nothing more than the "reasonable suspicion" of low-ranking investigative officers that something might be amiss? The Court today concludes that the Fourth Amendment grants such sweeping and unmonitored authority to customs officials.

I dissent. Indefinite involuntary incommunicado detentions "for investigation" are the hallmark of a police state, not a free society. In my opinion, Government officials may no more confine a person at the border under such circumstances for purposes of criminal investigation than they may within the interior of the country. The nature and duration of the detention here may well have been tolerable for spoiled meat or diseased animals, but not for human beings held on simple suspicion of criminal activity. I believe such indefinite detentions can be "reasonable" under the Fourth Amendment only with the approval of a magistrate. I also believe that such approval can be given only upon a showing of probable cause.

In my opinion, allowing the Government to hold someone in indefinite, involuntary, incommunicado isolation without probable cause and a judicial warrant violates our constitutional charter whether the purpose is to extract ransom or to investigate suspected criminal activity. Nothing in the Fourth Amendment permits an exception for such actions at the Nation's border. It is tempting, of course, to look the other way in a case that so graphically illustrates the "veritable national crisis" caused by narcotics trafficking. But if there is one enduring lesson in the long struggle to balance individual rights against society's need to defend itself against lawlessness, it is that "[i]t is easy to make light of insistence on scrupulous regard for the safeguards of civil liberties when invoked on behalf of the unworthy. It is too easy. History bears testimony that by such disregard are the rights of liberty extinguished, heedlessly at first, then stealthily, and brazenly in the end."

7. Checkpoints

Of course, the police may stop a vehicle if they observe a traffic violation and may demand to see the driver's license and the vehicle's registration. But what about a checkpoint where cars are stopped for a brief period, such as to see if the driver is intoxicated? In Michigan Department of State Police v. Sitz, the Court upheld the constitutionality of such sobriety checkpoints.

MICHIGAN DEPT. OF STATE POLICE v. SITZ
496 U.S. 444 (1990)

Chief Justice Rehnquist delivered the opinion of the Court.

This case poses the question whether a State's use of highway sobriety checkpoints violates the Fourth and Fourteenth Amendments to the United States Constitution. We hold that it does not.

Petitioners, the Michigan Department of State Police and its director, established a sobriety checkpoint pilot program in early 1986. The director appointed a Sobriety Checkpoint Advisory Committee comprising representatives of the State Police force, local police forces, state prosecutors, and the University of Michigan Transportation Research Institute. Pursuant to its charge, the advisory committee created guidelines setting forth procedures governing checkpoint operations, site selection, and publicity.

Under the guidelines, checkpoints would be set up at selected sites along state roads. All vehicles passing through a checkpoint would be stopped and their drivers briefly examined for signs of intoxication. In cases where a checkpoint officer detected signs of intoxication, the motorist would be directed to a location out of the traffic flow where an officer would check the motorist's driver's license and car registration and, if warranted, conduct further sobriety tests. Should the field tests and the officer's observations suggest that the driver was intoxicated, an arrest would be made. All other drivers would be permitted to resume their journey immediately.

The first—and to date the only—sobriety checkpoint operated under the program was conducted in Saginaw County with the assistance of the Saginaw County Sheriff's Department. During the 75-minute duration of the checkpoint's operation, 126 vehicles passed through the checkpoint. The average delay for each vehicle was approximately 25 seconds. Two drivers were detained for field sobriety testing, and one of the two was arrested for driving under the influence of alcohol. A third driver who drove through without stopping was pulled over by an officer in an observation vehicle and arrested for driving under the influence.

On the day before the operation of the Saginaw County checkpoint, respondents filed a complaint in the Circuit Court of Wayne County seeking declaratory and injunctive relief from potential subjection to the checkpoints. Each of the respondents "is a licensed driver in the State of Michigan . . . who regularly travels throughout the State in his automobile."

Petitioners concede, correctly in our view, that a Fourth Amendment "seizure" occurs when a vehicle is stopped at a checkpoint. Fourth Amendment seizure occurs "when there is a governmental termination of freedom of movement through means intentionally applied." The question thus becomes whether such seizures are "reasonable" under the Fourth Amendment.

We address only the initial stop of each motorist passing through a checkpoint and the associated preliminary questioning and observation by checkpoint officers. Detention of particular motorists for more extensive field sobriety testing may require satisfaction of an individualized suspicion standard.

No one can seriously dispute the magnitude of the drunken driving problem or the States' interest in eradicating it. Media reports of alcohol-related death and mutilation on the Nation's roads are legion. The anecdotal is confirmed by the statistical. "Drunk drivers cause an annual death toll of over 25,000 and in the same time span cause nearly one million personal injuries and more than five billion dollars in property damage." For decades, this Court has "repeatedly lamented the tragedy."

Conversely, the weight bearing on the other scale — the measure of the intrusion on motorists stopped briefly at sobriety checkpoints — is slight.

"[T]he circumstances surrounding a checkpoint stop and search are far less intrusive than those attending a roving-patrol stop. Roving patrols often operate at night on seldom-traveled roads, and their approach may frighten motorists. At traffic checkpoints the motorist can see that other vehicles are being stopped, he can see visible signs of the officers' authority, and he is much less likely to be frightened or annoyed by the intrusion."

Here, checkpoints are selected pursuant to the guidelines, and uniformed police officers stop every approaching vehicle. In sum, the balance of the State's interest in preventing drunken driving, the extent to which this system can reasonably be said to advance that interest, and the degree of intrusion upon individual motorists who are briefly stopped, weighs in favor of the state program. We therefore hold that it is consistent with the Fourth Amendment.

Justice STEVENS, with whom Justice BRENNAN and Justice MARSHALL join, dissenting.

A sobriety checkpoint is usually operated at night at an unannounced location. Surprise is crucial to its method. The test operation conducted by the Michigan State Police and the Saginaw County Sheriff's Department began shortly after midnight and lasted until about 1 A.M. During that period, the 19 officers participating in the operation made two arrests and stopped and questioned 124 other unsuspecting and innocent drivers. It is, of course, not known how many arrests would have been made during that period if those officers had been engaged in normal patrol activities. However, the findings of the trial court, based on an extensive record and affirmed by the Michigan Court of Appeals, indicate that the net effect of sobriety checkpoints on traffic safety is infinitesimal and possibly negative.

Indeed, the record in this case makes clear that a decision holding these suspicionless seizures unconstitutional would not impede the law enforcement community's remarkable progress in reducing the death toll on our highways. Because the Michigan program was patterned after an older program in Maryland, the trial judge gave special attention to that State's experience. Over a period of several years, Maryland operated 125 checkpoints; of the 41,000 motorists passing through those checkpoints, only 143 persons (0.3%) were arrested. The number of man-hours devoted to these operations is not in the record, but it seems inconceivable that a higher arrest rate could not have been achieved by more conventional means. Yet, even if the 143 checkpoint arrests were assumed to involve a net increase in the number of drunken driving arrests per year, the figure would still be insignificant by comparison to the 71,000 such arrests made by Michigan State Police without checkpoints in 1984 alone. Any relationship between sobriety checkpoints and an actual reduction in highway fatalities is even less substantial than the minimal impact on arrest rates.

In light of these considerations, it seems evident that the Court today misapplies the balancing test. The Court overvalues the law enforcement interest in using sobriety checkpoints, undervalues the citizen's interest in freedom from random, unannounced investigatory seizures, and mistakenly assumes that there is "virtually no difference" between a routine stop at a permanent, fixed checkpoint and a surprise stop at a sobriety checkpoint. I believe this case is controlled by our several precedents condemning suspicionless random stops of motorists for investigatory purposes.

What if the checkpoint is not for purposes of stopping intoxicated drivers, but exists for officers to look into the cars to see whether there are visible illegal drugs in the car? In City of Indianapolis v. Edmond, the Court found this unconstitutional. In reading the decision, it is important to consider whether the distinction of *Sitz* is persuasive.

CITY OF INDIANAPOLIS v. EDMOND
531 U.S. 32 (2000)

Justice O'CONNOR delivered the opinion of the Court.

In Michigan Dept. of State Police v. Sitz (1990), and United States v. Martinez-Fuerte (1976), we held that brief, suspicionless seizures at highway checkpoints for the purposes of combating drunk driving and intercepting illegal immigrants were constitutional. We now consider the constitutionality of a highway checkpoint program whose primary purpose is the discovery and interdiction of illegal narcotics.

I

In August 1998, the city of Indianapolis began to operate vehicle checkpoints on Indianapolis roads in an effort to interdict unlawful drugs. The city conducted six such roadblocks between August and November that year, stopping 1,161 vehicles and arresting 104 motorists. Fifty-five arrests were for drug-related crimes, while 49 were for offenses unrelated to drugs. The overall "hit rate" of the program was thus approximately nine percent.

The parties stipulated to the facts concerning the operation of the checkpoints by the Indianapolis Police Department (IPD) for purposes of the preliminary injunction proceedings instituted below. At each checkpoint location, the police stop a predetermined number of vehicles. Approximately 30 officers are stationed at the checkpoint. Pursuant to written directives issued by the chief of police, at least one officer approaches the vehicle, advises the driver that he or she is being stopped briefly at a drug checkpoint, and asks the driver to produce a license and registration. The officer also looks for signs of impairment and conducts an open-view examination of the vehicle from the outside. A narcotics-detection dog walks around the outside of each stopped vehicle.

The directives instruct the officers that they may conduct a search only by consent or based on the appropriate quantum of particularized suspicion. The officers must conduct each stop in the same manner until particularized suspicion develops, and the officers have no discretion to stop any vehicle out of sequence. The city agreed in the stipulation to operate the checkpoints in such a way as to ensure that the total duration of each stop, absent reasonable suspicion or probable cause, would be five minutes or less.

Respondents James Edmond and Joell Palmer were each stopped at a narcotics checkpoint in late September 1998. Respondents then filed a lawsuit on behalf of themselves and the class of all motorists who had been stopped or were subject to being stopped in the future at the Indianapolis drug checkpoints. Respondents claimed that the roadblocks violated the Fourth Amendment of the United States Constitution and the search and seizure provision of the Indiana Constitution. Respondents requested declaratory and injunctive relief for the class, as well as damages and attorney's fees for themselves.

II

The Fourth Amendment requires that searches and seizures be reasonable. A search or seizure is ordinarily unreasonable in the absence of individualized suspicion of wrongdoing. While such suspicion is not an "irreducible" component of reasonableness, we have recognized only limited circumstances in which the usual rule does not apply.

It is well established that a vehicle stop at a highway checkpoint effectuates a seizure within the meaning of the Fourth Amendment. The fact that officers walk a narcotics-detection dog around the exterior of each car at the Indianapolis checkpoints does not transform the seizure into a search. *See* United States v. Place (1983). Just as in *Place*, an exterior sniff of an automobile does not require entry into the car and is not designed to disclose any information other than the presence or absence of narcotics. Like the dog sniff in *Place*, a sniff by a dog that simply walks around a car is "much less intrusive than a typical search." Rather, what principally distinguishes these checkpoints from those we have previously approved is their primary purpose.

As petitioners concede, the Indianapolis checkpoint program unquestionably has the primary purpose of interdicting illegal narcotics. In their stipulation of facts, the parties repeatedly refer to the checkpoints as "drug checkpoints" and describe them as "being operated by the City of Indianapolis in an effort to interdict unlawful drugs in Indianapolis."

We have never approved a checkpoint program whose primary purpose was to detect evidence of ordinary criminal wrongdoing. Rather, our checkpoint cases have recognized only limited exceptions to the general rule that a seizure must be accompanied by some measure of individualized suspicion. [E]ach of the checkpoint programs that we have approved was designed primarily to serve purposes closely related to the problems of policing the border or the necessity of ensuring roadway safety. Because the primary purpose of the Indianapolis narcotics checkpoint program is to uncover evidence of ordinary criminal wrongdoing, the program contravenes the Fourth Amendment.

The primary purpose of the Indianapolis narcotics checkpoints is in the end to advance "the general interest in crime control." We decline to suspend the usual requirement of individualized suspicion where the police seek to employ a checkpoint primarily for the ordinary enterprise of investigating crimes. We cannot sanction stops justified only by the generalized and ever-present possibility that interrogation and inspection may reveal that any given motorist has committed some crime.

Of course, there are circumstances that may justify a law enforcement checkpoint where the primary purpose would otherwise, but for some emergency, relate to ordinary crime control. For example, as the Court of Appeals noted, the Fourth Amendment would almost certainly permit an appropriately tailored roadblock set up to thwart an imminent terrorist attack or to catch a dangerous criminal who is likely to flee by way of a particular route. The exigencies created by these scenarios are far removed from the circumstances under which authorities might simply stop cars as a matter of course to see if there just happens to be a felon leaving the jurisdiction. While we do not limit the purposes that may justify a checkpoint program to any rigid set of categories, we decline to approve a program whose primary purpose is ultimately indistinguishable from the general interest in crime control.

Petitioners argue that the Indianapolis checkpoint program is justified by its lawful secondary purposes of keeping impaired motorists off the road and verifying licenses and registrations. If this were the case, however, law enforcement authorities would be able to establish checkpoints for virtually any purpose so long as they also included a license or sobriety check. For this reason, we examine the available evidence to determine the primary purpose of the checkpoint program. While we recognize the challenges inherent in a purpose inquiry, courts routinely engage in this enterprise in many areas of constitutional jurisprudence as a means of sifting abusive governmental conduct from that which is lawful. As a result, a program driven by an impermissible purpose may be proscribed while a program impelled by licit purposes is permitted, even though the challenged conduct may be outwardly similar. While reasonableness under the Fourth Amendment is predominantly an objective inquiry, our special needs and administrative search cases demonstrate that purpose is often relevant when suspicionless intrusions pursuant to a general scheme are at issue. When law enforcement authorities pursue primarily general crime control purposes at checkpoints such as here, however, stops can only be justified by some quantum of individualized suspicion.

Because the primary purpose of the Indianapolis checkpoint program is ultimately indistinguishable from the general interest in crime control, the checkpoints violate the Fourth Amendment.

Chief Justice REHNQUIST, with whom Justice THOMAS joins, and with whom Justice SCALIA joins as to Part I, dissenting.

The State's use of a drug-sniffing dog, according to the Court's holding, annuls what is otherwise plainly constitutional under our Fourth Amendment jurisprudence: brief, standardized, discretionless, roadblock seizures of automobiles, seizures which effectively serve a weighty state interest with only minimal intrusion on the privacy of their occupants. Because these seizures serve the State's accepted and significant interests of preventing drunken driving and checking for driver's licenses and vehicle registrations, and because there is nothing in the record to indicate that the addition of the dog sniff lengthens these otherwise legitimate seizures, I dissent.

As it is nowhere to be found in the Court's opinion, I begin with blackletter roadblock seizure law. Roadblock seizures are consistent with the Fourth Amendment if they are "carried out pursuant to a plan embodying explicit, neutral limitations on the conduct of individual officers." Specifically, the constitutionality of a seizure turns upon "a weighing of the gravity of the public concerns served by the seizure, the degree to which the seizure advances the public interest, and the severity of the interference with individual liberty."

Petitioners acknowledge that the "primary purpose" of these roadblocks is to interdict illegal drugs, but this fact should not be controlling. [T]he question whether a law enforcement purpose could support a roadblock seizure is not presented in this case. The District Court found that another "purpose of the checkpoints is to check driver's licenses and vehicle registrations," and the written directives state that the police officers are to "[l]ook for signs of impairment." That the roadblocks serve these legitimate state interests cannot be seriously disputed, as the 49 people arrested for offenses unrelated to drugs can attest.

Because of the valid reasons for conducting these roadblock seizures, it is constitutionally irrelevant that petitioners also hoped to interdict drugs. In Whren v. United States (1996), we held that an officer's subjective intent would not invalidate an otherwise objectively justifiable stop of an automobile. The reasonableness of an officer's discretionary decision to stop an automobile, at issue in Whren, turns on whether there is probable cause to believe that a traffic violation has occurred. The reasonableness of highway checkpoints, at issue here, turns on whether they effectively serve a significant state interest with minimal intrusion on motorists. The stop in Whren was objectively reasonable because the police officers had witnessed traffic violations; so too the roadblocks here are objectively reasonable because they serve the substantial interests of preventing drunken driving and checking for driver's licenses and vehicle registrations with minimal intrusion on motorists.

Once the constitutional requirements for a particular seizure are satisfied, the subjective expectations of those responsible for it, be it police officers or members of a city council, are irrelevant. It is the objective effect of the State's actions on the privacy of the individual that animates the Fourth Amendment.

These stops effectively serve the State's legitimate interests; they are executed in a regularized and neutral manner; and they only minimally intrude upon the privacy of the motorists. They should therefore be constitutional.

There has thus far been one other Supreme Court decision concerning checkpoints: Illinois v. Lidster, 540 U.S. 419 (2004). Justice Breyer, writing for the Court, began his opinion by stating that the case concerned "a highway checkpoint where police stopped motorists to ask them for information about a recent hit-and-run accident. We hold that the police stops were reasonable, hence, constitutional."

A hit and run accident killed a man on a bicycle. The Court described the checkpoint that was created:

About one week later at about the same time of night and at about the same place, local police set up a highway checkpoint designed to obtain more information about the accident from the motoring public. Police cars with flashing lights partially blocked the eastbound lanes of the highway. The blockage forced traffic to slow down, leading to lines of up to 15 cars in each lane. As each vehicle drew up to the checkpoint, an officer would stop it for 10 to 15 seconds, ask the occupants whether they had seen anything happen there the previous weekend, and hand each driver a flyer. The flyer said "ALERT . . . FATAL HIT & RUN ACCIDENT" and requested "ASSISTANCE IN IDENTIFYING THE VEHICLE AND DRIVER INVOLVED IN THIS ACCIDENT WHICH KILLED A 70 YEAR OLD BICYCLIST."

Robert Lidster, the respondent, drove a minivan toward the checkpoint. As he approached the checkpoint, his van swerved, nearly hitting one of the officers. The officer smelled alcohol on Lidster's breath. He directed Lidster to a side street where another officer administered a sobriety test and then arrested Lidster. Lidster was tried and convicted in Illinois state court of driving under the influence of alcohol.

The issue was whether the checkpoint violated the Fourth Amendment. The Court distinguished *Edmond:*

The checkpoint stop here differs significantly from that in *Edmond.* The stop's primary law enforcement purpose was not to determine whether a vehicle's occupants were committing a crime, but to ask vehicle occupants, as members of the public, for their help in providing information about a crime in all likelihood committed by others. The police expected the information elicited to help them apprehend, not the vehicle's occupants, but other individuals.

Neither do we believe, *Edmond* aside, that the Fourth Amendment would have us apply an *Edmond*-type rule of automatic unconstitutionality to brief, information-seeking highway stops of the kind now before us. For one thing, the fact that such stops normally lack individualized suspicion cannot by itself determine the constitutional outcome. As in *Edmond,* the stop here at issue involves a motorist. The Fourth Amendment does not treat a motorist's car as his castle. And special law enforcement concerns will sometimes justify highway stops without individualized suspicion. Moreover, unlike *Edmond,* the context here (seeking information from the public) is one in which, by definition, the concept of individualized suspicion has little role to play. Like certain other forms of police activity, say, crowd control or public safety, an information-seeking stop is not the kind of event that involves suspicion, or lack of suspicion, of the relevant individual.

For another thing, information-seeking highway stops are less likely to provoke anxiety or to prove intrusive. The stops are likely brief. The police are not likely to ask questions designed to elicit self-incriminating information. And citizens will often react positively when police simply ask for their help as "responsible citizen[s]" to "give whatever information they may have to aid in law enforcement."

Further, the law ordinarily permits police to seek the voluntary cooperation of members of the public in the investigation of a crime. "[L]aw enforcement officers do not violate the Fourth Amendment by merely approaching an individual on the street or in another public place, by asking him if he is willing to answer some questions, [or] by putting questions to him if the person is willing to listen."

Finally, we do not believe that an *Edmond*-type rule is needed to prevent an unreasonable proliferation of police checkpoints. Practical considerations — namely, limited police resources and community hostility to related traffic tieups — seem likely to inhibit any such proliferation. And, of course, the Fourth Amendment's normal insistence that the stop be reasonable in context will still provide an important legal limitation on police use of this kind of information-seeking checkpoint.

These considerations, taken together, convince us that an *Edmond*-type presumptive rule of unconstitutionality does not apply here. That does not mean the stop is automatically, or even presumptively, constitutional. It simply means that we must judge its reasonableness, hence, its constitutionality, on the basis of the individual circumstances.

The Court concluded that this checkpoint was reasonable as the police were investigating a death and had been stymied in obtaining other sources of information. The Court said that the intrusion was minimal and justified by the importance of the investigation.

8. Consent

A search is permissible without a warrant or even probable cause if there is voluntary consent. The standard for voluntariness was initially articulated in Schneckloth v. Bustamonte.

SCHNECKLOTH v. BUSTAMONTE
412 U.S. 218 (1973)

Justice STEWART delivered the opinion of the Court.

It is well settled under the Fourth and Fourteenth Amendments that a search conducted without a warrant issued upon probable cause is "per se unreasonable . . . subject only to a few specifically established and well-delineated exceptions." It is equally well settled that one of the specifically established exceptions to the requirements of both a warrant and probable cause is a search that is conducted pursuant to consent. The constitutional question in the present case concerns the definition of "consent" in this Fourth and Fourteenth Amendment context.

I

The respondent was brought to trial in a California court upon a charge of possessing a check with intent to defraud. He moved to suppress the introduction of certain material as evidence against him on the ground that the material had been acquired through an unconstitutional search and seizure. In response to the motion, the trial judge conducted an evidentiary hearing where it was established that the material in question had been acquired by the State under the following circumstances:

While on routine patrol in Sunnyvale, California, at approximately 2:40 in the morning, Police Officer James Rand stopped an automobile when he observed that one headlight and its license plate light were burned out. Six men were in the vehicle. Joe Alcala and the respondent, Robert Bustamonte, were in the front seat with Joe Gonzales, the driver. Three older men were seated in the rear. When, in response to the policeman's question, Gonzales could not produce a driver's license, Officer Rand asked if any of the other five had any evidence of identification. Only Alcala produced a license, and he explained that the car was his brother's. After the six occupants had stepped out of the car at the officer's request and after two additional policemen had arrived, Officer

Rand asked Alcala if he could search the car. Alcala replied, "Sure, go ahead." Prior to the search no one was threatened with arrest and, according to Officer Rand's uncontradicted testimony, it "was all very congenial at this time." Gonzales testified that Alcala actually helped in the search of the car, by opening the trunk and glove compartment. In Gonzales' words: "[T]he police officer asked Joe [Alcala], he goes, 'Does the trunk open?' And Joe said, 'Yes.' He went to the car and got the keys and opened up the trunk." Wadded up under the left rear seat, the police officers found three checks that had previously been stolen from a car wash.

The trial judge denied the motion to suppress, and the checks in question were admitted in evidence at Bustamonte's trial. On the basis of this and other evidence he was convicted.

II

It is important to make it clear at the outset what is not involved in this case. The respondent concedes that a search conducted pursuant to a valid consent is constitutionally permissible. And similarly the State concedes that when a prosecutor seeks to rely upon consent to justify the lawfulness of a search, he has the burden of proving that the consent was, in fact, freely and voluntarily given.

The precise question in this case, then, is what must the prosecution prove to demonstrate that a consent was "voluntarily" given.

The most extensive judicial exposition of the meaning of "voluntariness" has been developed in those cases in which the Court has had to determine the "voluntariness" of a defendant's confession for purposes of the Fourteenth Amendment.[10] In determining whether a defendant's will was overborne in a particular case, the Court has assessed the totality of all the surrounding circumstances — both the characteristics of the accused and the details of the interrogation.

Similar considerations lead us to [conclude] that the question whether a consent to a search was in fact "voluntary" or was the product of duress or coercion, express or implied, is a question of fact to be determined from the totality of all the circumstances. While knowledge of the right to refuse consent is one factor to be taken into account, the government need not establish such knowledge as the sine qua non of an effective consent. As with police questioning, two competing concerns must be accommodated in determining the meaning of a "voluntary" consent — the legitimate need for such searches and the equally important requirement of assuring the absence of coercion.

In situations where the police have some evidence of illicit activity, but lack probable cause to arrest or search, a search authorized by a valid consent may be the only means of obtaining important and reliable evidence. In the present case, for example, while the police had reason to stop the car for traffic violations, the State does not contend that there was probable cause to search the vehicle or that the search was incident to a valid arrest of any of the occupants. Yet, the search yielded tangible evidence that served as a basis for a prosecution, and

10. These cases are discussed in Chapter 4, below. [Footnote by casebook authors.]

provided some assurance that others, wholly innocent of the crime, were not mistakenly brought to trial. And in those cases where there is probable cause to arrest or search, but where the police lack a warrant, a consent search may still be valuable. If the search is conducted and proves fruitless, that in itself may convince the police that an arrest with its possible stigma and embarrassment is unnecessary, or that a far more extensive search pursuant to a warrant is not justified. In short, a search pursuant to consent may result in considerably less inconvenience for the subject of the search, and, properly conducted, is a constitutionally permissible and wholly legitimate aspect of effective police activity.

But the Fourth and Fourteenth Amendments require that a consent not be coerced, by explicit or implicit means, by implied threat or covert force. For, no matter how subtly the coercion was applied, the resulting "consent" would be no more than a pretext for the unjustified police intrusion against which the Fourth Amendment is directed.

The problem of reconciling the recognized legitimacy of consent searches with the requirement that they be free from any aspect of official coercion cannot be resolved by any infallible touchstone. To approve such searches without the most careful scrutiny would sanction the possibility of official coercion; to place artificial restrictions upon such searches would jeopardize their basic validity. Just as was true with confessions, the requirement of a "voluntary" consent reflects a fair accommodation of the constitutional requirements involved. In examining all the surrounding circumstances to determine if in fact the consent to search was coerced, account must be taken of subtly coercive police questions, as well as the possibly vulnerable subjective state of the person who consents. Those searches that are the product of police coercion can thus be filtered out without undermining the continuing validity of consent searches. In sum, there is no reason for us to depart in the area of consent searches, from the traditional definition of "voluntariness."

The approach of the Court of Appeals for the Ninth Circuit finds no support in any of our decisions that have attempted to define the meaning of "voluntariness." Its ruling, that the State must affirmatively prove that the subject of the search knew that he had a right to refuse consent, would, in practice, create serious doubt whether consent searches could continue to be conducted. There might be rare cases where it could be proved from the record that a person in fact affirmatively knew of his right to refuse — such as a case where he announced to the police that if he didn't sign the consent form, "you [police] are going to get a search warrant"; or a case where by prior experience and training a person had clearly and convincingly demonstrated such knowledge. But more commonly where there was no evidence of any coercion, explicit or implicit, the prosecution would nevertheless be unable to demonstrate that the subject of the search in fact had known of his right to refuse consent.

The very object of the inquiry — the nature of a person's subjective understanding — underlines the difficulty of the prosecution's burden under the rule applied by the Court of Appeals in this case. Any defendant who was the subject of a search authorized solely by his consent could effectively frustrate the introduction into evidence of the fruits of that search by simply failing to testify that he in fact knew he could refuse to consent. And the near impossibility of meeting this prosecutorial burden suggests why this Court has never accepted any such litmus-paper test of voluntariness.

One alternative that would go far toward proving that the subject of a search did know he had a right to refuse consent would be to advise him of that right before eliciting his consent. That, however, is a suggestion that has been almost universally repudiated by both federal and state courts, and, we think, rightly so. For it would be thoroughly impractical to impose on the normal consent search the detailed requirements of an effective warning. Consent searches are part of the standard investigatory techniques of law enforcement agencies. They normally occur on the highway, or in a person's home or office, and under informal and unstructured conditions. The circumstances that prompt the initial request to search may develop quickly or be a logical extension of investigative police questioning. The police may seek to investigate further suspicious circumstances or to follow up leads developed in questioning persons at the scene of a crime. These situations are a far cry from the structured atmosphere of a trial where, assisted by counsel if he chooses, a defendant is informed of his trial rights. And, while surely a closer question, these situations are still immeasurably, far removed from "custodial interrogation" where, in Miranda v. Arizona we found that the Constitution required certain now familiar warnings as a prerequisite to police interrogation. Indeed, in language applicable to the typical consent search, we refused to extend the need for warnings.

Consequently, we cannot accept the position of the Court of Appeals in this case that proof of knowledge of the right to refuse consent is a necessary prerequisite to demonstrating a "voluntary" consent. Rather it is only by analyzing all the circumstances of an individual consent that it can be ascertained whether in fact it was voluntary or coerced. It is this careful sifting of the unique facts and circumstances of each case that is evidenced in our prior decisions involving consent searches.

It is said, however, that a "consent" is a "waiver" of a person's rights under the Fourth and Fourteenth Amendments. The argument is that by allowing the police to conduct a search, a person "waives" whatever right he had to prevent the police from searching. It is argued that under the doctrine of *Johnson v. Zerbst* to establish such a "waiver" the State must demonstrate "an intentional relinquishment or abandonment of a known right or privilege."

But these standards were enunciated in *Johnson* in the context of the safeguards of a fair criminal trial. Our cases do not reflect an uncritical demand for a knowing and intelligent waiver in every situation where a person has failed to invoke a constitutional protection. The requirement of a "knowing" and "intelligent" waiver was articulated in a case involving the validity of a defendant's decision to forego a right constitutionally guaranteed to protect a fair trial and the reliability of the truth-determining process. *Johnson v. Zerbst* dealt with the denial of counsel in a federal criminal trial.

Almost without exception, the requirement of a knowing and intelligent waiver has been applied only to those rights which the Constitution guarantees to a criminal defendant in order to preserve a fair trial. Hence, and hardly surprisingly in view of the facts of *Johnson* itself, the standard of a knowing and intelligent waiver has most often been applied to test the validity of a waiver of counsel, either at trial, or upon a guilty plea.

Our cases concerning the validity of guilty pleas underscore the fact that the question whether a person has acted "voluntarily" is quite distinct from the question whether he has "waived" a trial right.

There is a vast difference between those rights that protect a fair criminal trial and the rights guaranteed under the Fourth Amendment. Nothing, either in the purposes behind requiring a "knowing" and "intelligent" waiver of trial rights, or in the practical application of such a requirement suggests that it ought to be extended to the constitutional guarantee against unreasonable searches and seizures.

In short, there is nothing in the purposes or application of the waiver requirements of *Johnson v. Zerbst* that justifies, much less compels, the easy equation of a knowing waiver with a consent search. To make such an equation is to generalize from the broad rhetoric of some of our decisions, and to ignore the substance of the differing constitutional guarantees.

Much of what has already been said disposes of the argument that the Court's decision in the *Miranda* case requires the conclusion that knowledge of a right to refuse is an indispensable element of a valid consent. The considerations that informed the Court's holding in *Miranda* are simply inapplicable in the present case. In this case, there is no evidence of any inherently coercive tactics — either from the nature of the police questioning or the environment in which it took place. Indeed, since consent searches will normally occur on a person's own familiar territory, the specter of incommunicado police interrogation in some remote station house is simply inapposite. There is no reason to believe, under circumstances such as are present here, that the response to a policeman's question is presumptively coerced; and there is, therefore, no reason to reject the traditional test for determining the voluntariness of a person's response.

Our decision today is a narrow one. We hold only that when the subject of a search is not in custody and the State attempts to justify a search on the basis of his consent, the Fourth and Fourteenth Amendments require that it demonstrate that the consent was in fact voluntarily given, and not the result of duress or coercion, express or implied. Voluntariness is a question of fact to be determined from all the circumstances, and while the subject's knowledge of a right to refuse is a factor to be taken into account, the prosecution is not required to demonstrate such knowledge as a prerequisite to establishing a voluntary consent.

Justice BRENNAN, dissenting.

The Court holds today that an individual can effectively waive this right even though he is totally ignorant of the fact that, in the absence of his consent, such invasions of his privacy would be constitutionally prohibited. It wholly escapes me how our citizens can meaningfully be said to have waived something as precious as a constitutional guarantee without ever being aware of its existence. In my view, the Court's conclusion is supported neither by "linguistics," nor by "epistemology," nor, indeed, by "common sense." I respectfully dissent.

Justice MARSHALL, dissenting.

I would have thought that the capacity to choose necessarily depends upon knowledge that there is a choice to be made. But today the Court reaches the curious result that one can choose to relinquish a constitutional right — the right to be free of unreasonable searches — without knowing that he has the alternative of refusing to accede to a police request to search. I cannot agree, and therefore dissent.

I believe that the Court misstates the true issue in this case. That issue is not, as the Court suggests, whether the police overbore Alcala's will in eliciting his consent, but rather, whether a simple statement of assent to search, without more, should be sufficient to permit the police to search and thus act as a relinquishment of Alcala's constitutional right to exclude the police. This Court has always scrutinized with great care claims that a person has forgone the opportunity to assert constitutional rights. I see no reason to give the claim that a person consented to a search any less rigorous scrutiny. Every case in this Court involving this kind of search has heretofore spoken of consent as a waiver.

To begin, it is important to understand that the opinion of the Court is misleading in its treatment of the issue here in three ways. First, it derives its criterion for determining when a verbal statement of assent to search operates as a relinquishment of a person's right to preclude entry from a justification of consent searches that is inconsistent with our treatment in earlier cases of exceptions to the requirements of the Fourth Amendment, and that is not responsive to the unique nature of the consent-search exception. Second, it applies a standard of voluntariness that was developed in a very different context, where the standard was based on policies different from those involved in this case. Third, it mischaracterizes our prior cases involving consent searches.

My approach to the case is straight-forward and, to me, obviously required by the notion of consent as a relinquishment of Fourth Amendment rights. I am at a loss to understand why consent "cannot be taken literally to mean a 'knowing' choice." In fact, I have difficulty in comprehending how a decision made without knowledge of available alternatives can be treated as a choice at all.

The Supreme Court has consistently reaffirmed Schneckloth v. Bustamonte. For example, in Ohio v. Robinette, 519 U.S. 33 (1996), the Court held that a person lawfully stopped by the police, but free to leave, does not need to be informed by the police of his or her ability to leave.

In the more recent case, United States v. Drayton, 536 U.S. 194 (2002), the Court reaffirmed that the test for consent is whether it is voluntary under the totality of the circumstances. Three police officers boarded a bus as part of a routine drug enforcement effort. One officer sat in the driver's seat and the other two went and asked passengers "about their travel plans and sought to match passengers with luggage in the overhead racks. To avoid blocking the aisle, [Officer] Lang stood next to or just behind each passenger with whom he spoke. According to Lang's testimony, passengers who declined to cooperate with him or who chose to exit the bus at any time would have been allowed to do so without argument. In Lang's experience, however, most people are willing to cooperate."

The Court described what happened next:

Lang approached respondents from the rear and leaned over Drayton's shoulder. He held up his badge long enough for respondents to identify him as a police officer. With his face 12 to 18 inches away from Drayton's, Lang spoke in a voice just loud enough for respondents to hear: "I'm Investigator Lang with the Tallahassee Police Department. We're conducting bus interdiction [sic], attempting to deter drugs and illegal weapons being transported on the bus. Do you have any bags on the bus?"

Both respondents pointed to a single green bag in the overhead luggage rack. Lang asked, "Do you mind if I check it?," and Brown responded, "Go ahead." Lang handed the bag to Officer Blackburn to check. The bag contained no contraband.

Officer Lang noticed that both respondents were wearing heavy jackets and baggy pants despite the warm weather. In Lang's experience drug traffickers often use baggy clothing to conceal weapons or narcotics. The officer thus asked Brown if he had any weapons or drugs in his possession. And he asked Brown: "Do you mind if I check your person?" Brown answered, "Sure," and cooperated by leaning up in his seat, pulling a cell phone out of his pocket, and opening up his jacket. Lang reached across Drayton and patted down Brown's jacket and pockets, including his waist area, sides, and upper thighs. In both thigh areas, Lang detected hard objects similar to drug packages detected on other occasions. Lang arrested and handcuffed Brown.

The issue was whether there was voluntary consent under these circumstances. The Court concluded:

There were ample grounds for the District Court to conclude that "everything that took place between Officer Lang and [respondents] suggests that it was cooperative" and that there "was nothing coercive [or] confrontational" about the encounter. There was no application of force, no intimidating movement, no overwhelming show of force, no brandishing of weapons, no blocking of exits, no threat, no command, not even an authoritative tone of voice. It is beyond question that had this encounter occurred on the street, it would be constitutional. The fact that an encounter takes place on a bus does not on its own transform standard police questioning of citizens into an illegal seizure. Indeed, because many fellow passengers are present to witness officers' conduct, a reasonable person may feel even more secure in his or her decision not to cooperate with police on a bus than in other circumstances.

The Court thus concluded that "respondents' consent to the search of their luggage and their persons was voluntary."

An issue sometimes arises as to who may give consent. In United States v. Matlock, 415 U.S. 164 (1974), the Court held that one occupant of a residence may give consent if the other is not present. But what if both occupants are present and one consents and the other, the target of the search, refuses? This was the question in Georgia v. Randolph.

GEORGIA v. RANDOLPH
547 U.S. 103 (2006)

Justice SOUTER delivered the opinion of the Court.

The Fourth Amendment recognizes a valid warrantless entry and search of premises when police obtain the voluntary consent of an occupant who shares, or is reasonably believed to share, authority over the area in common with a co-occupant who later objects to the use of evidence so obtained. The question here is whether such an evidentiary seizure is likewise lawful with the permission of one occupant when the other, who later seeks to suppress the evidence, is present at the scene and expressly refuses to consent. We hold that, in the circumstances here at issue, a physically present co-occupant's stated refusal to permit entry prevails, rendering the warrantless search unreasonable and invalid as to him.

I

Respondent Scott Randolph and his wife, Janet, separated in late May 2001, when she left the marital residence in Americus, Georgia, and went to stay with her parents in Canada, taking their son and some belongings. In July, she returned to the Americus house with the child, though the record does not reveal whether her object was reconciliation or retrieval of remaining possessions.

On the morning of July 6, she complained to the police that after a domestic dispute her husband took their son away, and when officers reached the house she told them that her husband was a cocaine user whose habit had caused financial troubles. She mentioned the marital problems and said that she and their son had only recently returned after a stay of several weeks with her parents. Shortly after the police arrived, Scott Randolph returned and explained that he had removed the child to a neighbor's house out of concern that his wife might take the boy out of the country again; he denied cocaine use, and countered that it was in fact his wife who abused drugs and alcohol.

One of the officers, Sergeant Murray, went with Janet Randolph to reclaim the child, and when they returned she not only renewed her complaints about her husband's drug use, but also volunteered that there were "items of drug evidence" in the house. Sergeant Murray asked Scott Randolph for permission to search the house, which he unequivocally refused.

The sergeant turned to Janet Randolph for consent to search, which she readily gave. She led the officer upstairs to a bedroom that she identified as Scott's, where the sergeant noticed a section of a drinking straw with a powdery residue he suspected was cocaine. He then left the house to get an evidence bag from his car and to call the district attorney's office, which instructed him to stop the search and apply for a warrant. When Sergeant Murray returned to the house, Janet Randolph withdrew her consent. The police took the straw to the police station, along with the Randolphs. After getting a search warrant, they returned to the house and seized further evidence of drug use, on the basis of which Scott Randolph was indicted for possession of cocaine.

He moved to suppress the evidence, as products of a warrantless search of his house unauthorized by his wife's consent over his express refusal. The trial court denied the motion, ruling that Janet Randolph had common authority to consent to the search.

II

To the Fourth Amendment rule ordinarily prohibiting the warrantless entry of a person's house as unreasonable per se, one "jealously and carefully drawn" exception, recognizes the validity of searches with the voluntary consent of an individual possessing authority. That person might be the householder against whom evidence is sought, or a fellow occupant who shares common authority over property, when the suspect is absent, and the exception for consent extends even to entries and searches with the permission of a co-occupant whom the police reasonably, but erroneously, believe to possess shared authority as an occupant. None of our co-occupant consent-to-search cases, however, has presented the further fact of a second occupant physically present and refusing permission to search, and later moving to suppress evidence so obtained. The significance of such a refusal turns on the underpinnings of the co-occupant consent rule, as recognized since *Matlock*.

The constant element in assessing Fourth Amendment reasonableness in the consent cases, then, is the great significance given to widely shared social expectations, which are naturally enough influenced by the law of property, but not controlled by its rules. *Matlock* accordingly not only holds that a solitary co-inhabitant may sometimes consent to a search of shared premises, but stands for the proposition that the reasonableness of such a search is in significant part a function of commonly held understanding about the authority that co-inhabitants may exercise in ways that affect each other's interests.

To begin with, it is fair to say that a caller standing at the door of shared premises would have no confidence that one occupant's invitation was a sufficiently good reason to enter when a fellow tenant stood there saying, "stay out." Without some very good reason, no sensible person would go inside under those conditions. Fear for the safety of the occupant issuing the invitation, or of someone else inside, would be thought to justify entry, but the justification then would be the personal risk, the threats to life or limb, not the disputed invitation. The visitor's reticence without some such good reason would show not timidity but a realization that when people living together disagree over the use of their common quarters, a resolution must come through voluntary accommodation, not by appeals to authority. Unless the people living together fall within some recognized hierarchy, like a household of parent and child or barracks housing military personnel of different grades, there is no societal understanding of superior and inferior, a fact reflected in a standard formulation of domestic property law, that "[e]ach cotenant . . . has the right to use and enjoy the entire property as if he or she were the sole owner, limited only by the same right in the other cotenants." The want of any recognized superior authority among disagreeing tenants is also reflected in the law's response when the disagreements cannot be resolved. The law does not ask who has the better side of the conflict; it simply provides a right to any co-tenant, even the most unreasonable, to obtain a decree partitioning the property (when the relationship is one of co-ownership) and terminating the relationship. In sum, there is no common understanding that one co-tenant generally has a right or authority to prevail over the express wishes of another, whether the issue is the color of the curtains or invitations to outsiders.

Since the co-tenant wishing to open the door to a third party has no recognized authority in law or social practice to prevail over a present and objecting co-tenant, his disputed invitation, without more, gives a police officer no better claim to reasonableness in entering than the officer would have in the absence of any consent at all. Accordingly, in the balancing of competing individual and governmental interests entailed by the bar to unreasonable searches, the cooperative occupant's invitation adds nothing to the government's side to counter the force of an objecting individual's claim to security against the government's intrusion into his dwelling place.

Disputed permission is thus no match for this central value of the Fourth Amendment, and the State's other countervailing claims do not add up to outweigh it. Yes, we recognize the consenting tenant's interest as a citizen in bringing criminal activity to light. But society can often have the benefit of these interests without relying on a theory of consent that ignores an inhabitant's refusal to allow a warrantless search. The co-tenant acting on his own initiative may be able to deliver evidence to the police, and can tell the police what he knows, for use before a magistrate in getting a warrant. Additional exigent circumstances might justify warrantless searches.

This case invites a straightforward application of the rule that a physically present inhabitant's express refusal of consent to a police search is dispositive as to him, regardless of the consent of a fellow occupant. Scott Randolph's refusal is clear, and nothing in the record justifies the search on grounds independent of Janet Randolph's consent. The State does not argue that she gave any indication to the police of a need for protection inside the house that might have justified entry into the portion of the premises where the police found the powdery straw (which, if lawfully seized, could have been used when attempting to establish probable cause for the warrant issued later). Nor does the State claim that the entry and search should be upheld under the rubric of exigent circumstances, owing to some apprehension by the police officers that Scott Randolph would destroy evidence of drug use before any warrant could be obtained.

Chief Justice ROBERTS, with whom Justice SCALIA joins, dissenting.

The Court creates constitutional law by surmising what is typical when a social guest encounters an entirely atypical situation. The rule the majority fashions does not implement the high office of the Fourth Amendment to protect privacy, but instead provides protection on a random and happenstance basis, protecting, for example, a co-occupant who happens to be at the front door when the other occupant consents to a search, but not one napping or watching television in the next room. And the cost of affording such random protection is great, as demonstrated by the recurring cases in which abused spouses seek to authorize police entry into a home they share with a nonconsenting abuser.

The correct approach to the question presented is clearly mapped out in our precedents: The Fourth Amendment protects privacy. If an individual shares information, papers, or places with another, he assumes the risk that the other person will in turn share access to that information or those papers or places with the government. And just as an individual who has shared illegal plans or incriminating documents with another cannot interpose an objection when that other person turns the information over to the government, just because the individual happens to be present at the time, so too someone who shares a place with another cannot interpose an objection when that person decides to grant access to the police, simply because the objecting individual happens to be present.

A warrantless search is reasonable if police obtain the voluntary consent of a person authorized to give it. Co-occupants have "assumed the risk that one of their number might permit [a] common area to be searched." Just as Mrs. Randolph could walk upstairs, come down, and turn her husband's cocaine straw over to the police, she can consent to police entry and search of what is, after all, her home, too.

9.   *Searches of Those on Probation and Parole*

The Supreme Court has upheld warrantless, even suspicionless searches, of those on probation and parole. In part, the Court has stressed that individuals on probation and parole often consent to such searches as a condition for release. But the Court also has emphasized the diminished expectation of privacy for such individuals and the government's interest in preventing recidivism.

UNITED STATES v. KNIGHTS
534 U.S. 112 (2001)

Chief Justice REHNQUIST delivered the opinion of the Court.

A California court sentenced respondent Mark James Knights to summary probation for a drug offense. The probation order included the following condition: that Knights would "[s]ubmit his . . . person, property, place of residence, vehicle, personal effects, to search at any time, with or without a search warrant, warrant of arrest or reasonable cause by any probation officer or law enforcement officer." Knights signed the probation order, which stated immediately above his signature that "I HAVE RECEIVED A COPY, READ AND UNDERSTAND THE ABOVE TERMS AND CONDITIONS OF PROBATION AND AGREE TO ABIDE BY SAME." In this case, we decide whether a search pursuant to this probation condition, and supported by reasonable suspicion, satisfied the Fourth Amendment.

Three days after Knights was placed on probation, a Pacific Gas & Electric (PG & E) power transformer and adjacent Pacific Bell telecommunications vault near the Napa County Airport were pried open and set on fire, causing an estimated $1.5 million in damage. Brass padlocks had been removed and a gasoline accelerant had been used to ignite the fire. This incident was the latest in more than 30 recent acts of vandalism against PG & E facilities in Napa County. Suspicion for these acts had long focused on Knights and his friend, Steven Simoneau. The incidents began after PG & E had filed a theft-of-services complaint against Knights and discontinued his electrical service for failure to pay his bill. Detective Todd Hancock of the Napa County Sheriff's Department had noticed that the acts of vandalism coincided with Knights' court appearance dates concerning the theft of PG & E services. And just a week before the arson, a sheriff's deputy had stopped Knights and Simoneau near a PG & E gas line and observed pipes and gasoline in Simoneau's pickup truck.

After the PG & E arson, a sheriff's deputy drove by Knights' residence, where he saw Simoneau's truck parked in front. The deputy felt the hood of the truck. It was warm. Detective Hancock decided to set up surveillance of Knights' apartment. At about 3:10 the next morning, Simoneau exited the apartment carrying three cylindrical items. Detective Hancock believed the items were pipe bombs. Simoneau walked across the street to the bank of the Napa River, and Hancock heard three splashes. Simoneau returned without the cylinders and drove away in his truck. Simoneau then stopped in a driveway, parked, and left the area. Detective Hancock entered the driveway and observed a number of suspicious objects in the truck: a Molotov cocktail and explosive materials, a gasoline can, and two brass padlocks that fit the description of those removed from the PG & E transformer vault.

After viewing the objects in Simoneau's truck, Detective Hancock decided to conduct a search of Knights' apartment. Detective Hancock was aware of the search condition in Knights' probation order and thus believed that a warrant was not necessary. The search revealed a detonation cord, ammunition, liquid chemicals, instruction manuals on chemistry and electrical circuitry, bolt cutters, telephone pole-climbing spurs, drug paraphernalia, and a brass padlock stamped "PG & E."

Knights was arrested, and a federal grand jury subsequently indicted him for conspiracy to commit arson, for possession of an unregistered destructive device, and for being a felon in possession of ammunition. Knights moved to suppress the evidence obtained during the search of his apartment. The District Court held that Detective Hancock had "reasonable suspicion" to believe that Knights was involved with incendiary materials. The District Court nonetheless granted the motion to suppress on the ground that the search was for "investigatory" rather than "probationary" purposes. The Court of Appeals for the Ninth Circuit affirmed.

Certainly nothing in the condition of probation suggests that it was confined to searches bearing upon probationary status and nothing more. The search condition provides that Knights will submit to a search "by any probation officer or law enforcement officer" and does not mention anything about purpose. The question then is whether the Fourth Amendment limits searches pursuant to this probation condition to those with a "probationary" purpose.

We need not decide whether Knights' acceptance of the search condition constituted consent in the sense of a complete waiver of his Fourth Amendment rights, however, because we conclude that the search of Knights was reasonable under our general Fourth Amendment approach of "examining the totality of the circumstances," with the probation search condition being a salient circumstance.

The touchstone of the Fourth Amendment is reasonableness, and the reasonableness of a search is determined "by assessing, on the one hand, the degree to which it intrudes upon an individual's privacy and, on the other, the degree to which it is needed for the promotion of legitimate governmental interests." Knights' status as a probationer subject to a search condition informs both sides of that balance. "Probation, like incarceration, is 'a form of criminal sanction imposed by a court upon an offender after verdict, finding, or plea of guilty.'" Just as other punishments for criminal convictions curtail an offender's freedoms, a court granting probation may impose reasonable conditions that deprive the offender of some freedoms enjoyed by law-abiding citizens.

The judge who sentenced Knights to probation determined that it was necessary to condition the probation on Knights' acceptance of the search provision. It was reasonable to conclude that the search condition would further the two primary goals of probation — rehabilitation and protecting society from future criminal violations. The probation order clearly expressed the search condition and Knights was unambiguously informed of it. The probation condition thus significantly diminished Knights' reasonable expectation of privacy.

In assessing the governmental interest side of the balance, it must be remembered that "the very assumption of the institution of probation" is that the probationer "is more likely than the ordinary citizen to violate the law." The recidivism rate of probationers is significantly higher than the general crime rate. And probationers have even more of an incentive to conceal their criminal activities and quickly dispose of incriminating evidence than the ordinary criminal because probationers are aware that they may be subject to supervision and face revocation of probation, and possible incarceration, in proceedings in which the trial rights of a jury and proof beyond a reasonable doubt, among other things, do not apply.

The State has a dual concern with a probationer. On the one hand is the hope that he will successfully complete probation and be integrated back into the community. On the other is the concern, quite justified, that he will be more likely to engage in criminal conduct than an ordinary member of the community. The view of the Court of Appeals in this case would require the State to shut its eyes to the latter concern and concentrate only on the former. But we hold that the Fourth Amendment does not put the State to such a choice. Its interest in apprehending violators of the criminal law, thereby protecting potential victims of criminal enterprise, may therefore justifiably focus on probationers in a way that it does not on the ordinary citizen.

We hold that the balance of these considerations requires no more than reasonable suspicion to conduct a search of this probationer's house. The degree of individualized suspicion required of a search is a determination of when there is a sufficiently high probability that criminal conduct is occurring to make the intrusion on the individual's privacy interest reasonable. Although the Fourth Amendment ordinarily requires the degree of probability embodied in the term "probable cause," a lesser degree satisfies the Constitution when the balance of governmental and private interests makes such a standard reasonable. Those interests warrant a lesser than probable-cause standard here. When an officer has reasonable suspicion that a probationer subject to a search condition is engaged in criminal activity, there is enough likelihood that criminal conduct is occurring that an intrusion on the probationer's significantly diminished privacy interests is reasonable. The same circumstances that lead us to conclude that reasonable suspicion is constitutionally sufficient also render a warrant requirement unnecessary.

SAMSON v. CALIFORNIA
126 S. Ct. 2193 (2006)

Justice THOMAS delivered the opinion of the Court.

California law provides that every prisoner eligible for release on state parole "shall agree in writing to be subject to search or seizure by a parole officer or other peace officer at any time of the day or night, with or without a search warrant and with or without cause." We granted certiorari to decide whether a suspicionless search, conducted under the authority of this statute, violates the Constitution. We hold that it does not.

I

In September 2002, petitioner Donald Curtis Samson was on state parole in California, following a conviction for being a felon in possession of a firearm. On September 6, 2002, Officer Alex Rohleder of the San Bruno Police

Department observed petitioner walking down a street with a woman and a child. Based on a prior contact with petitioner, Officer Rohleder was aware that petitioner was on parole and believed that he was facing an at large warrant. Accordingly, Officer Rohleder stopped petitioner and asked him whether he had an outstanding parole warrant. Petitioner responded that there was no outstanding warrant and that he "was in good standing with his parole agent." Officer Rohleder confirmed, by radio dispatch, that petitioner was on parole and that he did not have an outstanding warrant. Nevertheless, based solely on petitioner's status as a parolee, Officer Rohleder searched petitioner. During the search, Officer Rohleder found a cigarette box in petitioner's left breast pocket. Inside the box he found a plastic baggie containing methamphetamine.

The State charged petitioner with possession of methamphetamine. The trial court denied petitioner's motion to suppress the methamphetamine evidence. A jury convicted petitioner of the possession charge and the trial court sentenced him to seven years' imprisonment.

We granted certiorari, to answer a variation of the question this Court left open in United States v. Knights (2001) — whether a condition of release can so diminish or eliminate a released prisoner's reasonable expectation of privacy that a suspicionless search by a law enforcement officer would not offend the Fourth Amendment.

"[U]nder our general Fourth Amendment approach" we "examin[e] the totality of the circumstances" to determine whether a search is reasonable within the meaning of the Fourth Amendment. Whether a search is reasonable "is determined by assessing, on the one hand, the degree to which it intrudes upon an individual's privacy and, on the other, the degree to which it is needed for the promotion of legitimate governmental interests."

As we noted in Knights, parolees are on the "continuum" of state-imposed punishments. On this continuum, parolees have fewer expectations of privacy than probationers, because parole is more akin to imprisonment than probation is to imprisonment. California's system of parole is consistent with these observations: A California inmate may serve his parole period either in physical custody, or elect to complete his sentence out of physical custody and subject to certain conditions. Under the latter option, an inmate-turned-parolee remains in the legal custody of the California Department of Corrections through the remainder of his term, and must comply with all of the terms and conditions of parole, including mandatory drug tests, restrictions on association with felons or gang members, and mandatory meetings with parole officers.

Additionally, as we found "salient" in Knights with respect to the probation search condition, the parole search condition under California law requiring inmates who opt for parole to submit to suspicionless searches by a parole officer or other peace officer "at any time," was "clearly expressed" to petitioner. He signed an order submitting to the condition and thus was "unambiguously" aware of it. In Knights, we found that acceptance of a clear and unambiguous search condition "significantly diminished Knights' reasonable expectation of privacy."

The State's interests, by contrast, are substantial. This Court has repeatedly acknowledged that a State has an "overwhelming interest" in supervising parolees because "parolees . . . are more likely to commit future criminal offenses." Similarly, this Court has repeatedly acknowledged that a State's interests in reducing recidivism and thereby promoting reintegration and positive citizenship among probationers and parolees warrant privacy intrusions that would not otherwise be tolerated under the Fourth Amendment.

Thus, we conclude that the Fourth Amendment does not prohibit a police officer from conducting a suspicionless search of a parolee. Accordingly, we affirm the judgment of the California Court of Appeal.

Justice STEVENS, with whom Justice SOUTER and Justice BREYER join, dissenting.

Our prior cases have consistently assumed that the Fourth Amendment provides some degree of protection for probationers and parolees. The protection is not as robust as that afforded to ordinary citizens; we have held that probationers' lowered expectation of privacy may justify their warrantless search upon reasonable suspicion of wrongdoing. We have also recognized that the supervisory responsibilities of probation officers, who are required to provide "individualized counseling" and to monitor their charges' progress, and who are in a unique position to judge "how close a supervision the probationer requires," may give rise to special needs justifying departures from Fourth Amendment strictures. But [prior cases do not] support a regime of suspicionless searches, conducted pursuant to a blanket grant of discretion untethered by any procedural safeguards, by law enforcement personnel who have no special interest in the welfare of the parolee or probationer.

What the Court sanctions today is an unprecedented curtailment of liberty. Combining faulty syllogism with circular reasoning, the Court concludes that parolees have no more legitimate an expectation of privacy in their persons than do prisoners. However superficially appealing that parity in treatment may seem, it runs roughshod over our precedent. It also rests on an intuition that fares poorly under scrutiny. And once one acknowledges that parolees do have legitimate expectations of privacy beyond those of prisoners, our Fourth Amendment jurisprudence does not permit the conclusion, reached by the Court here for the first time, that a search supported by neither individualized suspicion nor "special needs" is nonetheless "reasonable."

The suspicionless search is the very evil the Fourth Amendment was intended to stamp out. Not surprisingly, the majority does not seek to justify the search of petitioner on "special needs" grounds. Although the Court has in the past relied on special needs to uphold warrantless searches of probationers, it has never gone so far as to hold that a probationer or parolee may be subjected to full search at the whim of any law enforcement officer he happens to encounter, whether or not the officer has reason to suspect him of wrongdoing.

Ignoring just how "closely guarded" is that "category of constitutionally permissible suspicionless searches," the Court for the first time upholds an entirely suspicionless search unsupported by any special need. And it goes further: In special needs cases we have at least insisted upon programmatic safeguards designed to ensure evenhandedness in application; if individualized suspicion is to be jettisoned, it must be replaced with measures to protect against the state actor's unfettered discretion.

The Court seems to acknowledge that unreasonable searches "inflic[t] dignitary harms that arouse strong resentment in parolees and undermine their ability to reintegrate into productive society." It is satisfied, however, that the California courts' prohibition against "arbitrary, capricious or harassing" searches suffices to avert those harms — which are of course counterproductive to the State's purported aim of rehabilitating former prisoners and reintegrating them into society. I am unpersuaded. The requirement of individualized suspicion, in all its iterations, is the shield the Framers selected to guard against the evils of arbitrary action, caprice, and harassment. To say that those evils may be averted without that shield is, I fear, to pay lipservice to the end while withdrawing the means.

10. Searches When There Are "Special Needs"

The Supreme Court has said that there is a category of searches where there are "special needs," where warrants do not need to be obtained and often where less than probable cause is required. There is no precise definition of the category of "special needs." Some of the examples above, such as checkpoints and border searches, could be regarded as "special needs" situations. In addition, the Court has considered this in the context of administrative inspections and also drug testing. These are considered below. The special needs category often, though not always, involves searches for reasons other than criminal law enforcement. In fact, the last case presented in this section, Ferguson v. City of Charleston, stresses that "special needs" must be more than the special need to have more effective law enforcement.

a. Administrative Searches

CAMARA v. MUNICIPAL COURT OF CITY
AND COUNTY OF SAN FRANCISCO

387 U.S. 523 (1967)

Justice WHITE delivered the opinion of the Court.

In Frank v. State of Maryland [1959], this Court upheld, by a five-to-four vote, a state court conviction of a homeowner who refused to permit a municipal health inspector to enter and inspect his premises without a search warrant. Since [that] closely divided decision, more intensive efforts at all levels of government to contain and eliminate urban blight have led to increasing use of such inspection techniques, while numerous decisions of this Court have more fully defined the Fourth Amendment's effect on state and municipal action. In view of the growing nationwide importance of the problem, we noted probable jurisdiction in this case and in See v. City of Seattle to re-examine whether administrative inspection programs, as presently authorized and conducted, violate Fourth Amendment rights as those rights are enforced against the States through the Fourteenth Amendment.

On November 6, 1963, an inspector of the Division of Housing Inspection of the San Francisco Department of Public Health entered an apartment building to make a routine annual inspection for possible violations of the city's Housing Code. The building's manager informed the inspector that appellant, lessee of the ground floor, was using the rear of his leasehold as a personal residence. Claiming that the building's occupancy permit did not allow residential use of the ground floor, the inspector confronted appellant and demanded that he permit an inspection of the premises. Appellant refused to allow the inspection because the inspector lacked a search warrant.

The inspector returned on November 8, again without a warrant, and appellant again refused to allow an inspection. A citation was then mailed ordering appellant to appear at the district attorney's office. When appellant failed to appear, two inspectors returned to his apartment on November 22. They informed appellant that he was required by law to permit an inspection under § 503 of the Housing Code. Appellant nevertheless refused the inspectors access to his apartment without a search warrant. Thereafter, a complaint was filed charging him with refusing to permit a lawful inspection. Appellant was arrested on December 2 and released on bail.

I.

The basic purpose of [the Fourth] Amendment, as recognized in countless decisions of this Court, is to safeguard the privacy and security of individuals against arbitrary invasions by governmental officials. Though there has been general agreement as to the fundamental purpose of the Fourth Amendment, translation of the abstract prohibition against "unreasonable searches and seizures" into workable guidelines for the decision of particular cases is a difficult task which has for many years divided the members of this Court. Nevertheless, one governing principle, justified by history and by current experience, has consistently been followed: except in certain carefully defined classes of cases, a search of private property without proper consent is "unreasonable" unless it has been authorized by a valid search warrant.

We may agree that a routine inspection of the physical condition of private property is a less hostile intrusion than the typical policeman's search for the fruits and instrumentalities of crime. But we cannot agree that the Fourth Amendment interests at stake in these inspection cases are merely "peripheral." It is surely anomalous to say that the individual and his private property are fully protected by the Fourth Amendment only when the individual is suspected of criminal behavior. For instance, even the most law-abiding citizen has a very tangible interest in limiting the circumstances under which the sanctity of his home may be broken by official authority, for the possibility of criminal entry under the guise of official sanction is a serious threat to personal and family security. And inspections of the kind we are here considering do in fact jeopardize "self-protection" interests of the property owner. Like most regulatory laws, fire, health, and housing codes are enforced by criminal processes. In some cities, discovery of a violation by the inspector leads to a criminal complaint. Even in cities where discovery of a violation produces only an administrative compliance order, refusal to comply is a criminal offense, and the fact of compliance is verified by a second inspection, again without a warrant. Finally, as this case demonstrates, refusal to permit an inspection is itself a crime, punishable by fine or even by jail sentence.

[T]wo other justifications for permitting administrative health and safety inspections without a warrant [are urged]. First, it is argued that these inspections are "designed to make the least possible demand on the individual occupant." The ordinances authorizing inspections are hedged with safeguards, and at any rate the argument proceeds, the warrant process could not function effectively in this field. The decision to inspect an entire municipal area is based upon legislative or administrative assessment of broad factors such as the area's age and condition. Unless the magistrate is to review such policy matters, he must issue a "rubber stamp" warrant which provides no protection at all to the property owner.

In our opinion, these arguments unduly discount the purposes behind the warrant machinery contemplated by the Fourth Amendment. Under the present system, when the inspector demands entry, the occupant has no way of knowing whether enforcement of the municipal code involved requires inspection of his premises, no way of knowing the lawful limits of the inspector's power to search, and no way of knowing whether the inspector himself is acting under proper authorization. These are questions which may be reviewed by a neutral magistrate without any reassessment of the basic agency decision to canvass an area. Yet, only by refusing entry and risking a criminal conviction can the occupant at present challenge the inspector's decision to search. And even if the occupant possesses sufficient fortitude to take this risk, as appellant did here, he may never learn any more about the reason for the inspection than that the law generally allows housing inspectors to gain entry. The practical effect of this system is to leave the occupant subject to the discretion of the official in the field. This is precisely the discretion to invade private property which we have consistently circumscribed by a requirement that a disinterested party warrant the need to search. We simply cannot say that the protections provided by the warrant procedure are not needed in this context; broad statutory safeguards are no substitute for individualized review, particularly when those safeguards may only be invoked at the risk of a criminal penalty.

The final justification suggested for warrantless administrative searches is that the public interest demands such a rule: it is vigorously argued that the health and safety of entire urban populations is dependent upon enforcement of minimum fire, housing, and sanitation standards, and that the only effective means of enforcing such codes is by routine systematized inspection of all physical structures. Of course, in applying any reasonableness standard, including one of constitutional dimension, an argument that the public interest demands a particular rule must receive careful consideration. But we think this argument misses the mark. The question is not, at this stage at least, whether these inspections may be made, but whether they may be made without a warrant. For example, to say that gambling raids may not be made at the discretion of the police without a warrant is not necessarily to say that gambling raids may never be made. In assessing whether the public interest demands creation of a general exception to the Fourth Amendment's warrant requirement, the question is not whether the public interest justifies the type of search in question, but whether the authority to search should be evidenced by a warrant, which in turn depends in part upon whether the burden of obtaining a warrant is likely to frustrate the governmental purpose behind the search. It has nowhere been urged that fire, health, and housing code inspection programs could not achieve their goals within the confines of a reasonable search warrant requirement. Thus, we do not find the public need argument dispositive.

In summary, we hold that administrative searches of the kind at issue here are significant intrusions upon the interests protected by the Fourth Amendment, that such searches when authorized and conducted without a warrant procedure lack the traditional safeguards which the Fourth Amendment guarantees to the individual, and that the reasons put forth for upholding these warrantless searches are insufficient to justify so substantial a weakening of the Fourth Amendment's protections. Because of the nature of the municipal programs under consideration, however, these conclusions must be the beginning, not the end, of our inquiry.

II.

Borrowing from more typical Fourth Amendment cases, appellant argues not only that code enforcement inspection programs must be circumscribed by a warrant procedure, but also that warrants should issue only when the inspector possesses probable cause to believe that a particular dwelling contains violations of the minimum standards prescribed by the code being enforced. We disagree.

In cases in which the Fourth Amendment requires that a warrant to search be obtained, "probable cause" is the standard by which a particular decision to search is tested against the constitutional mandate of reasonableness. To apply this standard, it is obviously necessary first to focus upon the governmental interest which allegedly justifies official intrusion upon the constitutionally protected interests of the private citizen. For example, in a criminal investigation, the police may undertake to recover specific stolen or contraband goods. But that public interest would hardly justify a sweeping search of an entire city conducted in the hope that these goods might be found. Consequently, a search for these goods, even with a warrant, is "reasonable" only when there is "probable cause" to believe that they will be uncovered in a particular dwelling.

Unlike the search pursuant to a criminal investigation, the inspection programs at issue here are aimed at securing city-wide compliance with minimum physical standards for private property. The primary governmental interest at stake is to prevent even the unintentional development of conditions which are hazardous to public health and safety. Because fires and epidemics may ravage large urban areas, because unsightly conditions adversely affect the economic values of neighboring structures, numerous courts have upheld the police power of municipalities to impose and enforce such minimum standards even upon existing structures. In determining whether a particular inspection is reasonable — and thus in determining whether there is probable cause to issue a warrant for that inspection — the need for the inspection must be weighed in terms of these reasonable goals of code enforcement.

There is unanimous agreement among those most familiar with this field that the only effective way to seek universal compliance with the minimum standards required by municipal codes is through routine periodic inspections of all structures. It is here that the probable cause debate is focused, for the agency's decision to conduct an area inspection is unavoidably based on its appraisal of conditions in the area as a whole, not on its knowledge of conditions in each particular building. Appellee contends that, if the probable cause standard urged by appellant is adopted, the area inspection will be eliminated as a means of seeking compliance with code standards and the reasonable goals of code enforcement will be dealt a crushing blow.

[W]e think that a number of persuasive factors combine to support the reasonableness of area code-enforcement inspections. First, such programs have a long history of judicial and public acceptance. Second, the public interest demands that all dangerous conditions be prevented or abated, yet it is doubtful that any other canvassing technique would achieve acceptable results. Many such conditions—faulty wiring is an obvious example—are not observable from outside the building and indeed may not be apparent to the inexpert occupant himself. Finally, because the inspections are neither personal in nature nor aimed at the discovery of evidence of crime, they involve a relatively limited invasion of the urban citizen's privacy.

Having concluded that the area inspection is a "reasonable" search of private property within the meaning of the Fourth Amendment, it is obvious that "probable cause" to issue a warrant to inspect must exist if reasonable legislative or administrative standards for conducting an area inspection are satisfied with respect to a particular dwelling. Such standards, which will vary with the municipal program being enforced, may be based upon the passage of time, the nature of the building (e.g., a multifamily apartment house), or the condition of the entire area, but they will not necessarily depend upon specific knowledge of the condition of the particular dwelling. It has been suggested that so to vary the probable cause test from the standard applied in criminal cases would be to authorize a "synthetic search warrant" and thereby to lessen the overall protections of the Fourth Amendment. But we do not agree. The warrant procedure is designed to guarantee that a decision to search private property is justified by a reasonable governmental interest. But reasonableness is still the ultimate standard. If a valid public interest justifies the intrusion contemplated, then there is probable cause to issue a suitably restricted search warrant. Such an approach neither endangers time-honored doctrines applicable to criminal investigations nor makes a nullity of the probable cause requirement in this area. It merely gives full recognition to the competing public and private interests here at stake and, in so doing, best fulfills the historic purpose behind the constitutional right to be free from unreasonable government invasions of privacy.

III.

Since our holding emphasizes the controlling standard of reasonableness, nothing we say today is intended to foreclose prompt inspections, even without a warrant, that the law has traditionally upheld in emergency situations. On the other hand, in the case of most routine area inspections, there is no compelling urgency to inspect at a particular time or on a particular day. Moreover, most citizens allow inspections of their property without a warrant. Thus, as a practical matter and in light of the Fourth Amendment's requirement that a warrant specify the property to be searched, it seems likely that warrants should normally be sought only after entry is refused unless there has been a citizen complaint or there is other satisfactory reason for securing immediate entry. Similarly, the requirement of a warrant procedure does not suggest any change in what seems to be the prevailing local policy, in most situations, of authorizing entry, but not entry by force, to inspect.

In the companion case, See v. City of Seattle, 387 U.S. 541 (1967), the Court applied *Camara* to non-residential commercial property. The Court, though, said that its decision did "not in any way imply that business premises may not reasonably be inspected in many more situations than private homes." The Court returned to the issue of administrative searches of business premises in New York v. Burger.

NEW YORK v. BURGER
482 U.S. 691 (1987)

Justice BLACKMUN delivered the opinion of the Court.

This case presents the question whether the warrantless search of an automobile junkyard, conducted pursuant to a statute authorizing such a search, falls within the exception to the warrant requirement for administrative inspections of pervasively regulated industries. The case also presents the question whether an otherwise proper administrative inspection is unconstitutional because the ultimate purpose of the regulatory statute pursuant to which the search is done — the deterrence of criminal behavior — is the same as that of penal laws, with the result that the inspection may disclose violations not only of the regulatory statute but also of the penal statutes.

I

Respondent Joseph Burger is the owner of a junkyard in Brooklyn, N.Y. His business consists, in part, of the dismantling of automobiles and the selling of their parts. His junkyard is an open lot with no buildings. A high metal fence surrounds it, wherein are located, among other things, vehicles and parts of vehicles. At approximately noon on November 17, 1982, Officer Joseph Vega and four other plainclothes officers, all members of the Auto Crimes Division of the New York City Police Department, entered respondent's junkyard to conduct an inspection pursuant to [New York law]. On any given day, the Division conducts from 5 to 10 inspections of vehicle dismantlers, automobile junkyards, and related businesses.

Upon entering the junkyard, the officers asked to see Burger's license and his "police book" — the record of the automobiles and parts in his possession. Burger replied that he had neither a license nor a police book. The officers then announced their intention to conduct a inspection. Burger did not object. In accordance with their practice, the officers copied down the Vehicle Identification Numbers (VINs) of several vehicles and parts of vehicles that were in the junkyard. After checking these numbers against a police computer, the officers determined that respondent was in possession of stolen vehicles and parts. Accordingly, Burger was arrested and charged with five counts of possession of stolen property and one count of unregistered operation as a vehicle dismantler.

II

The Court long has recognized that the Fourth Amendment's prohibition on unreasonable searches and seizures is applicable to commercial premises, as well as to private homes. An owner or operator of a business thus has an expectation of privacy in commercial property, which society is prepared to consider to be reasonable. This expectation exists not only with respect to traditional police searches conducted for the gathering of criminal evidence but also with respect to administrative inspections designed to enforce regulatory statutes. An expectation of privacy in commercial premises, however, is different from, and indeed less than, a similar expectation in an individual's home. This expectation is particularly attenuated in commercial property employed in "closely regulated" industries. The Court observed: "Certain industries have such a history of government oversight that no reasonable expectation of privacy, could exist for a proprietor over the stock of such an enterprise."

Because the owner or operator of commercial premises in a "closely regulated" industry has a reduced expectation of privacy, the warrant and probable-cause requirements, which fulfill the traditional Fourth Amendment standard of reasonableness for a government search, have lessened application in this context. Rather, we conclude that, as in other situations of "special need," where the privacy interests of the owner are weakened and the government interests in regulating particular businesses are concomitantly heightened, a warrantless inspection of commercial premises may well be reasonable within the meaning of the Fourth Amendment.

This warrantless inspection, however, even in the context of a pervasively regulated business, will be deemed to be reasonable only so long as three criteria are met. First, there must be a "substantial" government interest that informs the regulatory scheme pursuant to which the inspection is made. Second, the warrantless inspections must be "necessary to further [the] regulatory scheme." Finally, "the statute's inspection program, in terms of the certainty and regularity of its application, [must] provid[e] a constitutionally adequate substitute for a warrant." In other words, the regulatory statute must perform the two basic functions of a warrant: it must advise the owner of the commercial premises that the search is being made pursuant to the law and has a properly defined scope, and it must limit the discretion of the inspecting officers. To perform this first function, the statute must be "sufficiently comprehensive and defined that the owner of commercial property cannot help but be aware that his property will be subject to periodic inspections undertaken for specific purposes." In addition, in defining how a statute limits the discretion of the inspectors, we have observed that it must be "carefully limited in time, place, and scope."

III

Searches made pursuant to [the New York law], in our view, clearly fall within this established exception to the warrant requirement for administrative inspections in "closely regulated" businesses. First, the nature of the regulatory statute reveals that the operation of a junkyard, part of which is devoted to vehicle dismantling, is a "closely regulated" business in the State of New York. The provisions regulating the activity of vehicle dismantling are extensive. An operator cannot engage in this industry without first obtaining a license, which means that he must meet the registration requirements and must pay a fee. [T]he operator must maintain a police book recording the acquisition and disposition of motor vehicles and vehicle parts, and make such records and inventory available for inspection by the police or any agent of the Department of Motor Vehicles. The operator also must display his registration number prominently at his place of business, on business documentation, and on vehicles and parts that pass through his business. Moreover, the person engaged in this activity is subject to criminal penalties, as well as to loss of license or civil fines, for failure to comply with these provisions. That other States besides New York have imposed similarly extensive regulations on automobile junkyards further supports the "closely regulated" status of this industry.

Accordingly, in light of the regulatory framework governing his business and the history of regulation of related industries, an operator of a junkyard engaging in vehicle dismantling has a reduced expectation of privacy in this "closely regulated" business.

The New York regulatory scheme satisfies the three criteria necessary to make reasonable warrantless inspections. First, the State has a substantial interest in regulating the vehicle-dismantling and automobile-junkyard industry because motor vehicle theft has increased in the State and because the problem of theft is associated with this industry. In this day, automobile theft has become a significant social problem, placing enormous economic and personal burdens upon the citizens of different States.

Second, regulation of the vehicle-dismantling industry reasonably serves the State's substantial interest in eradicating automobile theft. It is well established that the theft problem can be addressed effectively by controlling the receiver of, or market in, stolen property. Moreover, the warrantless administrative inspections "are necessary to further [the] regulatory scheme."

Third, [the New York statute] provides a "constitutionally adequate substitute for a warrant." The statute informs the operator of a vehicle dismantling business that inspections will be made on a regular basis. Thus, the vehicle dismantler knows that the inspections to which he is subject do not constitute discretionary acts by a government official but are conducted pursuant to statute. [The law] also sets forth the scope of the inspection and, accordingly, places the operator on notice as to how to comply with the statute. In addition, it notifies the operator as to who is authorized to conduct an inspection. Finally, the "time, place, and scope" of the inspection is limited, to place appropriate restraints upon the discretion of the inspecting officers.

Justice BRENNAN, with whom Justice MARSHALL and Justice O'CONNOR join, dissenting.

Warrantless inspections of pervasively regulated businesses are valid if necessary to further an urgent state interest, and if authorized by a statute that carefully limits their time, place, and scope. I have no objection to this general rule. Today, however, the Court finds pervasive regulation in the barest of administrative schemes. Burger's vehicle-dismantling business is not closely regulated (unless most New York City businesses are), and an administrative warrant therefore was required to search it. The Court also perceives careful guidance and control of police discretion in a statute that is patently insufficient to eliminate the need for a warrant. Finally, the Court characterizes as administrative a search for evidence of only criminal wrongdoing. As a result, the Court renders virtually meaningless the general rule that a warrant is required for administrative searches of commercial property.

The provisions governing vehicle dismantling in New York simply are not extensive. A vehicle dismantler must register and pay a fee, display the registration in various circumstances, maintain a police book, and allow inspections. Of course, the inspections themselves cannot be cited as proof of pervasive regulation justifying elimination of the warrant requirement; that would be obvious bootstrapping. Nor can registration and recordkeeping requirements be characterized as close regulation. New York City, like many States and municipalities, imposes similar, and often more stringent licensing, recordkeeping, and other regulatory requirements on a myriad of trades and businesses. Few substantive qualifications are required of an aspiring vehicle dismantler; no regulation governs the condition of the premises, the method of operation, the hours of operation, the equipment utilized, etc.

Even if vehicle dismantling were a closely regulated industry, I would nonetheless conclude that this search violated the Fourth Amendment. The warrant requirement protects the owner of a business from the "unbridled discretion [of] executive and administrative officers," by ensuring that "reasonable legislative or administrative standards for conducting an . . . inspection are satisfied with respect to a particular [business]." In order to serve as the equivalent of a warrant, an administrative statute must create "a predictable and guided [governmental] presence." [The New York law] does not approach the level of "certainty and regularity of . . . application" necessary to provide "a constitutionally adequate substitute for a warrant." The statute does not inform the operator of a vehicle-dismantling business that inspections will be made on a regular basis; in fact, there is no assurance that any inspections at all will occur. There is neither an upper nor a lower limit on the number of searches that may be conducted at any given operator's establishment in any given time period. Neither the statute, nor any regulations, nor any regulatory body, provides limits or guidance on the selection of vehicle dismantlers for inspection. In fact, the State could not explain why Burger's operation was selected for inspection.

The implications of the Court's opinion, if realized, will virtually eliminate Fourth Amendment protection of commercial entities in the context of administrative searches. No State may require, as a condition of doing business, a blanket submission to warrantless searches for any purpose. I respectfully dissent.

b.   Drug Testing

When may the government require drug testing without a warrant and even without any individualized suspicion? There is no single answer to this question. To this point, the Court has considered drug testing in three contexts: employment, schools, and hospitals. It has arrived at different conclusions in each.

First, in the area of employment, in Skinner v. Railway Executives' Assn., 489 U.S. 602 (1989), the Court upheld Federal Railroad Administration regulations requiring drug testing of railroad workers involved in accidents. The Fourth Amendment applied because it was a federal government requirement for testing by private railroads of their employees. The Court stressed the "special needs": the need to ensure the safety of the traveling public. The Court said that the privacy expectations of the employees were diminished by their working in "an industry that is regulated pervasively to ensure safety." The Court explained that there was virtually no discretion in the requirement so that there was nothing for a neutral magistrate to evaluate and further that drugs or alcohol could dissipate from an employee's body before a warrant could be obtained.

In National Treasury Employees Union v. Von Raab, 489 U.S. 656 (1989), the Court upheld the United States Customs Service program requiring drug testing through urinalysis for customs workers upon their transfer or promotion to positions having a direct involvement in drug interdiction or requiring the carrying of firearms. The Court struck down the requirement as applied to those who would be handling classified documents.

Unlike *Skinner*, results could not be turned over to law enforcement authorities for criminal prosecutions. The Court stressed the "Government's compelling interests in preventing the promotions of drug users to positions where they might endanger the integrity of our Nation's borders or the life of the citizenry." The Court stressed the special need to ensure that those handling weapons or involved in drug interdiction themselves be free of drugs.

But not all drug testing in the employment context is allowed. In Chandler v. Miller, 520 U.S. 305 (1997), the Court struck down a Georgia statute requiring that candidates for state office pass a drug test. The law required that candidates for office submit to drug testing within 30 days of qualifying for nomination or election. A candidate who refused or tested positive for illegal drugs could not be placed on the ballot. The Court found that this "did not fit within the closely guarded category of constitutionally permissible suspicionless searches." The Court stressed that "Georgia asserts no evidence of a drug problem among the State's elected officials, those officials do not typically perform high-risk, safety-sensitive tasks, and the required certification immediately aids to interdiction effort. The need revealed, in short, is symbolic, not 'special' as that term draws meaning from our caselaw."

A second area where the Court considered and approved drug testing is in schools, for student athletes and for students participating in extracurricular activities. In reading these cases, it is important to note that the Court generally has relaxed the usual Fourth Amendment requirements for searches of students in schools. In New Jersey v. T.L.O., 469 U.S. 325 (1985), the Court held that school officials could search a student's purse based on reasonable suspicion; there did not need to be a warrant or probable cause. The Court said that "the Fourth Amendment [is] applicable to the activities of civil as well as criminal authorities."

But the Court said that it was sufficient under the Fourth Amendment that there be "reasonable grounds for suspecting that the search will turn up evidence that the student has violated or is violating either the law or the rules of the school." The Court came to this conclusion by balancing the diminished expectation of privacy of students in schools and the need for schools to maintain discipline and order. The Court stressed that the search must be reasonable in scope. It explained that "the measures adopted are reasonably related to the objectives of the search and not excessively intrusive in light of the age and sex of the student and the nature of the infraction."

In Vernonia School Dist. 47J v. Acton, the Court upheld random drug testing for students participating in athletic events, and in Board of Education of Independent School District No. 92 of Pottawatomie County v. Earls, the Court upheld random drug testing for students participating in extracurricular activities. In reading these cases, it is worth considering whether there are any limits on the ability of schools to require random drug testing. Could a school require drug testing of all students?

VERNONIA SCHOOL DIST. 47J v. ACTON
515 U.S. 646 (1995)

Justice SCALIA delivered the opinion of the Court.

The Student Athlete Drug Policy adopted by School District 47J in the town of Vernonia, Oregon, authorizes random urinalysis drug testing of students who participate in the District's school athletics programs. We granted certiorari to decide whether this violates the Fourth and Fourteenth Amendments to the United States Constitution.

I

Petitioner Vernonia School District 47J (District) operates one high school and three grade schools in the logging community of Vernonia, Oregon. As elsewhere in small-town America, school sports play a prominent role in the town's life, and student athletes are admired in their schools and in the community.

Drugs had not been a major problem in Vernonia schools. In the mid-to-late 1980's, however, teachers and administrators observed a sharp increase in drug use. Students began to speak out about their attraction to the drug culture, and to boast that there was nothing the school could do about it. Along with more drugs came more disciplinary problems. Between 1988 and 1989 the number of disciplinary referrals in Vernonia schools rose to more than twice the number reported in the early 1980's, and several students were suspended. Students became increasingly rude during class; outbursts of profane language became common.

Not only were student athletes included among the drug users but, as the District Court found, athletes were the leaders of the drug culture. This caused the District's administrators particular concern, since drug use increases the risk of sports-related injury. Expert testimony at the trial confirmed the deleterious effects of drugs on motivation, memory, judgment, reaction, coordination, and performance. The high school football and wrestling coach witnessed a severe sternum injury suffered by a wrestler, and various omissions of safety procedures and misexecutions by football players, all attributable in his belief to the effects of drug use.

Initially, the District responded to the drug problem by offering special classes, speakers, and presentations designed to deter drug use. It even brought in a specially trained dog to detect drugs, but the drug problem persisted. At that point, District officials began considering a drug-testing program. They held a parent "input night" to discuss the proposed Student Athlete Drug Policy (Policy), and the parents in attendance gave their unanimous approval. The school board approved the Policy for implementation in the fall of 1989. Its expressed purpose is to prevent student athletes from using drugs, to protect their health and safety, and to provide drug users with assistance programs.

The Policy applies to all students participating in interscholastic athletics. Students wishing to play sports must sign a form consenting to the testing and must obtain the written consent of their parents. Athletes are tested at the beginning of the season for their sport. In addition, once each week of the season the names of the athletes are placed in a "pool" from which a student, with the supervision of two adults, blindly draws the names of 10% of the athletes for random testing. Those selected are notified and tested that same day, if possible.

The student to be tested completes a specimen control form which bears an assigned number. Prescription medications that the student is taking must be identified by providing a copy of the prescription or a doctor's authorization. The student then enters an empty locker room accompanied by an adult monitor of the same sex. Each boy selected produces a sample at a urinal, remaining fully clothed with his back to the monitor, who stands approximately 12 to 15 feet behind the student. Monitors may (though do not always) watch the student while he produces the sample, and they listen for normal sounds of urination. Girls produce samples in an enclosed bathroom stall, so that they can be heard but not observed. After the sample is produced, it is given to the monitor, who checks it for temperature and tampering and then transfers it to a vial.

The samples are sent to an independent laboratory, which routinely tests them for amphetamines, cocaine, and marijuana. Other drugs, such as LSD, may be screened at the request of the District, but the identity of a particular student does not determine which drugs will be tested. The laboratory's procedures are 99.94% accurate. The District follows strict procedures regarding the chain of custody and access to test results. The laboratory does not know the identity of the students whose samples it tests. It is authorized to mail written test reports only to the superintendent and to provide test results to District personnel by telephone only after the requesting official recites a code confirming his authority. Only the superintendent, principals, vice-principals, and athletic directors have access to test results, and the results are not kept for more than one year.

If a sample tests positive, a second test is administered as soon as possible to confirm the result. If the second test is negative, no further action is taken. If the second test is positive, the athlete's parents are notified, and the school principal convenes a meeting with the student and his parents, at which the student is given the option of (1) participating for six weeks in an assistance program that includes weekly urinalysis, or (2) suffering suspension from athletics for the remainder of the current season and the next athletic season. The student is then retested prior to the start of the next athletic season for which he or she is eligible. The Policy states that a second offense results in automatic imposition of option (2); a third offense in suspension for the remainder of the current season and the next two athletic seasons.

In the fall of 1991, respondent James Acton, then a seventh grader, signed up to play football at one of the District's grade schools. He was denied participation, however, because he and his parents refused to sign the testing consent forms. The Actons filed suit, seeking declaratory and injunctive relief from enforcement of the Policy on the grounds that it violated the Fourth and Fourteenth Amendments to the United States Constitution and Article I, § 9, of the Oregon Constitution.

II

As the text of the Fourth Amendment indicates, the ultimate measure of the constitutionality of a governmental search is "reasonableness." At least in a case such as this, where there was no clear practice, either approving or disapproving the type of search at issue, at the time the constitutional provision was enacted, whether a particular search meets the reasonableness standard "'is judged by balancing its intrusion on the individual's Fourth Amendment interests against its promotion of legitimate governmental interests.'" Where a search is undertaken by law enforcement officials to discover evidence of criminal wrongdoing, this Court has said that reasonableness generally requires the obtaining of a judicial warrant, Warrants cannot be issued, of course, without the showing of probable cause required by the Warrant Clause. But a warrant is not required to establish the reasonableness of all government searches; and when a warrant is not required (and the Warrant Clause therefore not applicable), probable cause is not invariably required either. A search unsupported by probable cause can be constitutional, we have said, "when special needs, beyond the normal need for law enforcement, make the warrant and probable-cause requirement impracticable."

We have found such "special needs" to exist in the public school context. There, the warrant requirement "would unduly interfere with the maintenance of the swift and informal disciplinary procedures [that are] needed," and "strict adherence to the requirement that searches be based upon probable cause" would undercut "the substantial need of teachers and administrators for freedom to maintain order in the schools." New Jersey v. T.L.O.

III

The first factor to be considered is the nature of the privacy interest upon which the search here at issue intrudes.

Fourth Amendment rights, no less than First and Fourteenth Amendment rights, are different in public schools than elsewhere; the "reasonableness" inquiry cannot disregard the schools' custodial and tutelary responsibility for children. For their own good and that of their classmates, public school children are routinely required to submit to various physical examinations, and to be vaccinated against various diseases. Particularly with regard to medical examinations and procedures, therefore, "students within the school environment have a lesser expectation of privacy than members of the population generally."

Legitimate privacy expectations are even less with regard to student athletes. School sports are not for the bashful. They require "suiting up" before each practice or event, and showering and changing afterwards. Public school locker rooms, the usual sites for these activities, are not notable for the privacy they afford. The locker rooms in Vernonia are typical: No individual dressing rooms are provided; shower heads are lined up along a wall, unseparated by any sort of partition or curtain; not even all the toilet stalls have doors.

There is an additional respect in which school athletes have a reduced expectation of privacy. By choosing to "go out for the team," they voluntarily subject themselves to a degree of regulation even higher than that imposed on students generally. In Vernonia's public schools, they must submit to a preseason physical exam (James testified that his included the giving of a urine sample), they must acquire adequate insurance coverage or sign an insurance waiver, maintain a minimum grade point average, and comply with any "rules of conduct, dress, training hours and related matters as may be established for each sport by the head coach and athletic director with the principal's approval." Somewhat like adults who choose to participate in a "closely regulated industry," students who voluntarily participate in school athletics have reason to expect intrusions upon normal rights and privileges, including privacy.

IV

Having considered the scope of the legitimate expectation of privacy at issue here, we turn next to the character of the intrusion that is complained of. We recognized in *Skinner* that collecting the samples for urinalysis intrudes upon "an excretory function traditionally shielded by great privacy." We noted, however, that the degree of intrusion depends upon the manner in which production of the urine sample is monitored. Under the District's Policy, male students produce samples at a urinal along a wall. They remain fully clothed and are only observed from behind, if at all. Female students produce samples in an enclosed stall, with a female monitor standing outside listening only for sounds of tampering. These conditions are nearly identical to those typically encountered in public restrooms, which men, women, and especially school-children use daily. Under such conditions, the privacy interests compromised by the process of obtaining the urine sample are in our view negligible.

The other privacy-invasive aspect of urinalysis is, of course, the information it discloses concerning the state of the subject's body, and the materials he has ingested. In this regard it is significant that the tests at issue here look only for drugs, and not for whether the student is, for example, epileptic, pregnant, or diabetic. Moreover, the drugs for which the samples are screened are standard, and do not vary according to the identity of the student. And finally, the results of the tests are disclosed only to a limited class of school personnel who have a need to know; and they are not turned over to law enforcement authorities or used for any internal disciplinary function.

V

Finally, we turn to consider the nature and immediacy of the governmental concern at issue here, and the efficacy of this means for meeting it. In both *Skinner* and *Von Raab*, we characterized the government interest motivating the search as "compelling." It is a mistake, however, to think that the phrase "compelling state interest," in the Fourth Amendment context, describes a fixed, minimum quantum of governmental concern, so that one can dispose of a case by answering in isolation the question: Is there a compelling state interest here? Rather, the phrase describes an interest that appears important enough to justify the particular search at hand, in light of other factors that show the search to be relatively intrusive upon a genuine expectation of privacy. Whether that relatively high degree of government concern is necessary in this case or not, we think it is met.

That the nature of the concern is important — indeed, perhaps compelling — can hardly be doubted. Deterring drug use by our Nation's schoolchildren is at least as important as enhancing efficient enforcement of the Nation's laws against the importation of drugs, which was the governmental concern in *Von Raab*, or deterring drug use by engineers and trainmen, which was the governmental concern in *Skinner*. School years are the time when the physical, psychological, and addictive effects of drugs are most severe. "Maturing nervous systems are more critically impaired by intoxicants than mature ones are; childhood losses in learning are lifelong and profound"; "children grow chemically dependent more quickly than adults, and their record of recovery is depressingly poor." And of course the effects of a drug-infested school are visited not just upon the users, but upon the entire student body and faculty, as the educational process is disrupted. In the present case, moreover, the necessity for the State to act is magnified by the fact that this evil is being visited not just upon individuals at large, but upon children for whom it has undertaken a special responsibility of care and direction. Finally, it must not be lost sight of that this program is directed more narrowly to drug use by school athletes, where the risk of immediate physical harm to the drug user or those with whom he is playing his sport is particularly high. Apart from psychological effects, which include impairment of judgment, slow reaction time, and a lessening of the perception of pain, the particular drugs screened by the District's Policy have been demonstrated to pose substantial physical risks to athletes.

As for the immediacy of the District's concerns: We are not inclined to question — indeed, we could not possibly find clearly erroneous — the District Court's conclusion that "a large segment of the student body, particularly those involved in interscholastic athletics, was in a state of rebellion," that "[d]isciplinary actions had reached 'epidemic proportions,'" and that "the rebellion was being fueled by alcohol and drug abuse as well as by the student's misperceptions about the drug culture." That is an immediate crisis of greater proportions than existed in *Skinner*, where we upheld the Government's drug-testing program based on findings of drug use by railroad employees nationwide, without proof that a problem existed on the particular railroads whose employees were subject to the test. And of much greater proportions than existed in *Von Raab*, where there was no documented history of drug use by any customs officials.

As to the efficacy of this means for addressing the problem: It seems to us self-evident that a drug problem largely fueled by the "role model" effect of athletes' drug use, and of particular danger to athletes, is effectively addressed by making sure that athletes do not use drugs. Respondents argue that a "less intrusive means to the same end" was available, namely, "drug testing on suspicion of drug use." We have repeatedly refused to declare that only the "least intrusive" search practicable can be reasonable under the Fourth Amendment. Respondents' alternative entails substantial difficulties — if it is indeed practicable at all. It may be impracticable, for one thing, simply because the parents who are willing to accept random drug testing for athletes are not willing to accept accusatory drug testing for all students, which transforms the process into a badge of shame. Respondents' proposal brings the risk that teachers will impose testing arbitrarily upon troublesome but not drug-likely students. It generates the expense of defending lawsuits that charge such arbitrary imposition, or that simply demand greater process before accusatory drug testing is imposed.

And not least of all, it adds to the ever-expanding diversionary duties of school-teachers the new function of spotting and bringing to account drug abuse, a task for which they are ill prepared, and which is not readily compatible with their vocation.

VI

Taking into account all the factors we have considered above — the decreased expectation of privacy, the relative unobtrusiveness of the search, and the severity of the need met by the search — we conclude Vernonia's Policy is reasonable and hence constitutional.

We caution against the assumption that suspicionless drug testing will readily pass constitutional muster in other contexts. The most significant element in this case is the first we discussed: that the Policy was undertaken in furtherance of the government's responsibilities, under a public school system, as guardian and tutor of children entrusted to its care. Just as when the government conducts a search in its capacity as employer (a warrantless search of an absent employee's desk to obtain an urgently needed file, for example), the relevant question is whether that intrusion upon privacy is one that a reasonable employer might engage in; so also when the government acts as guardian and tutor the relevant question is whether the search is one that a reasonable guardian and tutor might undertake. Given the findings of need made by the District Court, we conclude that in the present case it is.

Justice O'CONNOR, with whom Justice STEVENS and Justice SOUTER join, dissenting.

The population of our Nation's public schools, grades 7 through 12, numbers around 18 million. By the reasoning of today's decision, the millions of these students who participate in interscholastic sports, an overwhelming majority of whom have given school officials no reason whatsoever to suspect they use drugs at school, are open to an intrusive bodily search.

In justifying this result, the Court dispenses with a requirement of individualized suspicion on considered policy grounds. First, it explains that precisely because every student athlete is being tested, there is no concern that school officials might act arbitrarily in choosing whom to test. Second, a broad-based search regime, the Court reasons, dilutes the accusatory nature of the search. In making these policy arguments, of course, the Court sidesteps powerful, countervailing privacy concerns. Blanket searches, because they can involve "thousands or millions" of searches, "pos[e] a greater threat to liberty" than do suspicion-based ones, which "affec[t] one person at a time." Searches based on individualized suspicion also afford potential targets considerable control over whether they will, in fact, be searched because a person can avoid such a search by not acting in an objectively suspicious way. And given that the surest way to avoid acting suspiciously is to avoid the underlying wrongdoing, the costs of such a regime, one would think, are minimal.

But whether a blanket search is "better" than a regime based on individualized suspicion is not a debate in which we should engage. In my view, it is not open to judges or government officials to decide on policy grounds which is better and which is worse. For most of our constitutional history, mass, suspicionless searches have been generally considered per se unreasonable within the meaning of the Fourth Amendment. And we have allowed exceptions in recent years only where it has been clear that a suspicion-based regime would be ineffectual. Because that is not the case here, I dissent.

One searches today's majority opinion in vain for recognition that history and precedent establish that individualized suspicion is "usually required" under the Fourth Amendment (regardless of whether a warrant and probable cause are also required) and that, in the area of intrusive personal searches, the only recognized exception is for situations in which a suspicion-based scheme would be likely ineffectual. Far from acknowledging anything special about individualized suspicion, the Court treats a suspicion-based regime as if it were just any run-of-the-mill, less intrusive alternative — that is, an alternative that officials may bypass if the lesser intrusion, in their reasonable estimation, is outweighed by policy concerns unrelated to practicability.

In addition to overstating its concerns with a suspicion-based program, the District seems to have understated the extent to which such a program is less intrusive of students' privacy. By invading the privacy of a few students rather than many (nationwide, of thousands rather than millions), and by giving potential search targets substantial control over whether they will, in fact, be searched, a suspicion-based scheme is significantly less intrusive.

In any event, whether the Court is right that the District reasonably weighed the lesser intrusion of a suspicion-based scheme against its policy concerns is beside the point. As stated, a suspicion-based search regime is not just any less intrusive alternative; the individualized suspicion requirement has a legal pedigree as old as the Fourth Amendment itself, and it may not be easily cast aside in the name of policy concerns. It may only be forsaken, our cases in the personal search context have established, if a suspicion-based regime would likely be ineffectual.

But having misconstrued the fundamental role of the individualized suspicion requirement in Fourth Amendment analysis, the Court never seriously engages the practicality of such a requirement in the instant case. And that failure is crucial because nowhere is it less clear that an individualized suspicion requirement would be ineffectual than in the school context. In most schools, the entire pool of potential search targets — students — is under constant supervision by teachers and administrators and coaches, be it in classrooms, hallways, or locker rooms.

I recognize that a suspicion-based scheme, even where reasonably effective in controlling in-school drug use, may not be as effective as a mass, suspicionless testing regime. In one sense, that is obviously true, just as it is obviously true that suspicion-based law enforcement is not as effective as mass, suspicionless enforcement might be. "But there is nothing new in the realization" that Fourth Amendment protections come with a price. Indeed, the price we pay is higher in the criminal context, given that police do not closely observe the entire class of potential search targets (all citizens in the area) and must ordinarily adhere to the rigid requirements of a warrant and probable cause.

The principal counterargument to all this, central to the Court's opinion, is that the Fourth Amendment is more lenient with respect to school searches. That is no doubt correct, for, as the Court explains, schools have traditionally had special guardian-like responsibilities for children that necessitate a degree of constitutional leeway. This principle explains the considerable Fourth

Amendment leeway we gave school officials in *T.L.O.* In that case, we held that children at school do not enjoy two of the Fourth Amendment's traditional categorical protections against unreasonable searches and seizures: the warrant requirement and the probable cause requirement. And this was true even though the same children enjoy such protections "in a nonschool setting."

The instant case, however, asks whether the Fourth Amendment is even more lenient than that, i.e., whether it is so lenient that students may be deprived of the Fourth Amendment's only remaining, and most basic, categorical protection: its strong preference for an individualized suspicion requirement, with its accompanying antipathy toward personally intrusive, blanket searches of mostly innocent people. Thus, if we are to mean what we often proclaim — that students do not "shed their constitutional rights . . . at the schoolhouse gate," — the answer must plainly be no.

It cannot be too often stated that the greatest threats to our constitutional freedoms come in times of crisis. But we must also stay mindful that not all government responses to such times are hysterical overreactions; some crises are quite real, and when they are, they serve precisely as the compelling state interest that we have said may justify a measured intrusion on constitutional rights. The only way for judges to mediate these conflicting impulses is to do what they should do anyway: stay close to the record in each case that appears before them, and make their judgments based on that alone. Having reviewed the record here, I cannot avoid the conclusion that the District's suspicionless policy of testing all student athletes sweeps too broadly, and too imprecisely, to be reasonable under the Fourth Amendment.

What, though, if the school has no evidence of a drug problem and the program applies not just to athletes, but to all students participating in extracurricular activities?

BOARD OF EDUCATION OF INDEPENDENT SCHOOL DISTRICT NO. 92 OF POTTAWATOMIE COUNTY v. EARLS

536 U.S. 822 (2002)

Justice THOMAS delivered the opinion of the Court.

The Student Activities Drug Testing Policy implemented by the Board of Education of Independent School District No. 92 of Pottawatomie County (School District) requires all students who participate in competitive extracurricular activities to submit to drug testing. Because this Policy reasonably serves the School District's important interest in detecting and preventing drug use among its students, we hold that it is constitutional.

I

The city of Tecumseh, Oklahoma, is a rural community located approximately 40 miles southeast of Oklahoma City. The School District administers all Tecumseh public schools. In the fall of 1998, the School District adopted the

Student Activities Drug Testing Policy (Policy), which requires all middle and high school students to consent to drug testing in order to participate in any extracurricular activity. In practice, the Policy has been applied only to competitive extracurricular activities sanctioned by the Oklahoma Secondary Schools Activities Association, such as the Academic Team, Future Farmers of America, Future Homemakers of America, band, choir, pom-pom, cheerleading, and athletics. Under the Policy, students are required to take a drug test before participating in an extracurricular activity, must submit to random drug testing while participating in that activity, and must agree to be tested at any time upon reasonable suspicion. The urinalysis tests are designed to detect only the use of illegal drugs, including amphetamines, marijuana, cocaine, opiates, and barbituates, not medical conditions or the presence of authorized prescription medications.

At the time of their suit, both respondents attended Tecumseh High School. Respondent Lindsay Earls was a member of the show choir, the marching band, the Academic Team, and the National Honor Society. Respondent Daniel James sought to participate in the Academic Team. Together with their parents, Earls and James brought a 42 U.S.C. § 1983, action against the School District, challenging the Policy both on its face and as applied to their participation in extracurricular activities. They alleged that the Policy violates the Fourth Amendment as incorporated by the Fourteenth Amendment and requested injunctive and declarative relief. They also argued that the School District failed to identify a special need for testing students who participate in extracurricular activities, and that the "Drug Testing Policy neither addresses a proven problem nor promises to bring any benefit to students or the school."

II

Searches by public school officials, such as the collection of urine samples, implicate Fourth Amendment interests. We must therefore review the School District's Policy for "reasonableness," which is the touchstone of the constitutionality of a governmental search.

In the criminal context, reasonableness usually requires a showing of probable cause. The probable-cause standard, however, "is peculiarly related to criminal investigations" and may be unsuited to determining the reasonableness of administrative searches where the "Government seeks to prevent the development of hazardous conditions." The Court has also held that a warrant and finding of probable cause are unnecessary in the public school context because such requirements "would unduly interfere with the maintenance of the swift and informal disciplinary procedures [that are] needed."

Given that the School District's Policy is not in any way related to the conduct of criminal investigations, respondents do not contend that the School District requires probable cause before testing students for drug use. Respondents instead argue that drug testing must be based at least on some level of individualized suspicion. It is true that we generally determine the reasonableness of a search by balancing the nature of the intrusion on the individual's privacy against the promotion of legitimate governmental interests. But we have long held that "the Fourth Amendment imposes no irreducible requirement of [individualized] suspicion." "[I]n certain limited circumstances, the Government's need to discover such latent or hidden conditions, or to prevent their development, is sufficiently compelling to justify the intrusion on privacy entailed by conducting such searches without any measure of individualized suspicion." Therefore, in the context of safety and administrative regulations, a search unsupported by probable cause may be reasonable "when 'special needs, beyond the normal need for law enforcement, make the warrant and probable-cause requirement impracticable.'"

Significantly, this Court has previously held that "special needs" inhere in the public school context. While schoolchildren do not shed their constitutional rights when they enter the schoolhouse, "Fourth Amendment rights . . . are different in public schools than elsewhere; the 'reasonableness' inquiry cannot disregard the schools' custodial and tutelary responsibility for children." In particular, a finding of individualized suspicion may not be necessary when a school conducts drug testing.

We first consider the nature of the privacy interest allegedly compromised by the drug testing. As in *Vernonia*, the context of the public school environment serves as the backdrop for the analysis of the privacy interest at stake and the reasonableness of the drug testing policy in general. A student's privacy interest is limited in a public school environment where the State is responsible for maintaining discipline, health, and safety. Schoolchildren are routinely required to submit to physical examinations and vaccinations against disease. Securing order in the school environment sometimes requires that students be subjected to greater controls than those appropriate for adults.

Respondents argue that because children participating in nonathletic extracurricular activities are not subject to regular physicals and communal undress, they have a stronger expectation of privacy than the athletes tested in *Vernonia*. This distinction, however, was not essential to our decision in *Vernonia*, which depended primarily upon the school's custodial responsibility and authority.

In any event, students who participate in competitive extracurricular activities voluntarily subject themselves to many of the same intrusions on their privacy as do athletes. Some of these clubs and activities require occasional off-campus travel and communal undress. All of them have their own rules and requirements for participating students that do not apply to the student body as a whole.

Next, we consider the character of the intrusion imposed by the Policy. Urination is "an excretory function traditionally shielded by great privacy." But the "degree of intrusion" on one's privacy caused by collecting a urine sample "depends upon the manner in which production of the urine sample is monitored." Under the Policy, a faculty monitor waits outside the closed restroom stall for the student to produce a sample and must "listen for the normal sounds of urination in order to guard against tampered specimens and to insure an accurate chain of custody." The monitor then pours the sample into two bottles that are sealed and placed into a mailing pouch along with a consent form signed by the student. This procedure is virtually identical to that reviewed in *Vernonia*, except that it additionally protects privacy by allowing male students to produce their samples behind a closed stall. Given that we considered the method of collection in *Vernonia* a "negligible" intrusion, the method here is even less problematic. In addition, the Policy clearly requires that the test results be kept in confidential files separate from a student's other educational records and released to school personnel only on a "need to know" basis.

Moreover, the test results are not turned over to any law enforcement authority. Nor do the test results here lead to the imposition of discipline or have any academic consequences. Rather, the only consequence of a failed drug test is to limit the student's privilege of participating in extracurricular activities. Indeed, a student may test positive for drugs twice and still be allowed to participate in extracurricular activities. After the first positive test, the school contacts the student's parent or guardian for a meeting. The student may continue to participate in the activity if within five days of the meeting the student shows proof of receiving drug counseling and submits to a second drug test in two weeks. For the second positive test, the student is suspended from participation in all extracurricular activities for 14 days, must complete four hours of substance abuse counseling, and must submit to monthly drug tests. Only after a third positive test will the student be suspended from participating in any extra-curricular activity for the remainder of the school year, or 88 school days, whichever is longer.

Given the minimally intrusive nature of the sample collection and the limited uses to which the test results are put, we conclude that the invasion of students' privacy is not significant.

Finally, this Court must consider the nature and immediacy of the government's concerns and the efficacy of the Policy in meeting them. This Court has already articulated in detail the importance of the governmental concern in preventing drug use by schoolchildren. The drug abuse problem among our Nation's youth has hardly abated since *Vernonia* was decided in 1995. In fact, evidence suggests that it has only grown worse. As in *Vernonia*, "the necessity for the State to act is magnified by the fact that this evil is being visited not just upon individuals at large, but upon children for whom it has undertaken a special responsibility of care and direction." The health and safety risks identified in *Vernonia* apply with equal force to Tecumseh's children. Indeed, the nationwide drug epidemic makes the war against drugs a pressing concern in every school.

Additionally, the School District in this case has presented specific evidence of drug use at Tecumseh schools. Teachers testified that they had seen students who appeared to be under the influence of drugs and that they had heard students speaking openly about using drugs. A drug dog found marijuana cigarettes near the school parking lot. Police officers once found drugs or drug paraphernalia in a car driven by a Future Farmers of America member. And the school board president reported that people in the community were calling the board to discuss the "drug situation." We decline to second-guess the finding of the District Court that "[v]iewing the evidence as a whole, it cannot be reasonably disputed that the [School District] was faced with a 'drug problem' when it adopted the Policy."

Respondents consider the proffered evidence insufficient and argue that there is no "real and immediate interest" to justify a policy of drug testing nonathletes. We have recognized, however, that "[a] demonstrated problem of drug abuse . . . [is] not in all cases necessary to the validity of a testing regime," but that some showing does "shore up an assertion of special need for a suspicionless general search program." The School District has provided sufficient evidence to shore up the need for its drug testing program. Furthermore, this Court has not required a particularized or pervasive drug problem before allowing the government to conduct suspicionless drug testing.

Given the nationwide epidemic of drug use, and the evidence of increased drug use in Tecumseh schools, it was entirely reasonable for the School District to enact this particular drug testing policy.

Respondents also argue that the testing of nonathletes does not implicate any safety concerns, and that safety is a "crucial factor" in applying the special needs framework. They contend that there must be "surpassing safety interests," or "extraordinary safety and national security hazards," in order to override the usual protections of the Fourth Amendment. Respondents are correct that safety factors into the special needs analysis, but the safety interest furthered by drug testing is undoubtedly substantial for all children, athletes and nonathletes alike. We know all too well that drug use carries a variety of health risks for children, including death from overdose.

We also reject respondents' argument that drug testing must presumptively be based upon an individualized reasonable suspicion of wrongdoing because such a testing regime would be less intrusive. In this context, the Fourth Amendment does not require a finding of individualized suspicion, and we decline to impose such a requirement on schools attempting to prevent and detect drug use by students. Moreover, we question whether testing based on individualized suspicion in fact would be less intrusive. Such a regime would place an additional burden on public school teachers who are already tasked with the difficult job of maintaining order and discipline. A program of individualized suspicion might unfairly target members of unpopular groups. The fear of lawsuits resulting from such targeted searches may chill enforcement of the program, rendering it ineffective in combating drug use. In any case, this Court has repeatedly stated that reasonableness under the Fourth Amendment does not require employing the least intrusive means, because "[t]he logic of such elaborate less-restrictive-alternative arguments could raise insuperable barriers to the exercise of virtually all search-and-seizure powers."

Finally, we find that testing students who participate in extracurricular activities is a reasonably effective means of addressing the School District's legitimate concerns in preventing, deterring, and detecting drug use. While in *Vernonia* there might have been a closer fit between the testing of athletes and the trial court's finding that the drug problem was "fueled by the 'role model' effect of athletes' drug use," such a finding was not essential to the holding. *Vernonia* did not require the school to test the group of students most likely to use drugs, but rather considered the constitutionality of the program in the context of the public school's custodial responsibilities. Evaluating the Policy in this context, we conclude that the drug testing of Tecumseh students who participate in extracurricular activities effectively serves the School District's interest in protecting the safety and health of its students.

III

Within the limits of the Fourth Amendment, local school boards must assess the desirability of drug testing schoolchildren. In upholding the constitutionality of the Policy, we express no opinion as to its wisdom. Rather, we hold only that Tecumseh's Policy is a reasonable means of furthering the School District's important interest in preventing and deterring drug use among its schoolchildren.

Justice BREYER, concurring.

I agree with the Court that Vernonia School Dist. 47J v. Acton (1995) governs this case and requires reversal of the Tenth Circuit's decision. The school's drug testing program addresses a serious national problem by focusing upon demand, avoiding the use of criminal or disciplinary sanctions, and relying upon professional counseling and treatment. In my view, this program does not violate the Fourth Amendment's prohibition of "unreasonable searches and seizures." I reach this conclusion primarily for the reasons given by the Court, but I would emphasize several underlying considerations, which I under-stand to be consistent with the Court's opinion.

I

In respect to the school's need for the drug testing program, I would emphasize the following: First, the drug problem in our Nation's schools is serious in terms of size, the kinds of drugs being used, and the consequences of that use both for our children and the rest of us.

Second, the government's emphasis upon supply side interdiction apparently has not reduced teenage use in recent years.

Third, public school systems must find effective ways to deal with this problem. Today's public expects its schools not simply to teach the fundamentals, but "to shoulder the burden of feeding students breakfast and lunch, offering before and after school child care services, and providing medical and psychological services," all in a school environment that is safe and encourages learning.

Fourth, the program at issue here seeks to discourage demand for drugs by changing the school's environment in order to combat the single most important factor leading schoolchildren to take drugs, namely, peer pressure. It offers the adolescent a nonthreatening reason to decline his friend's drug-use invitations, namely, that he intends to play baseball, participate in debate, join the band, or engage in any one of half a dozen useful, interesting, and important activities.

II

In respect to the privacy-related burden that the drug testing program imposes upon students, I would emphasize the following: First, not everyone would agree with this Court's characterization of the privacy-related significance of urine sampling as "negligible." Some find the procedure no more intrusive than a routine medical examination, but others are seriously embarrassed by the need to provide a urine sample with someone listening "outside the closed restroom stall." When trying to resolve this kind of close question involving the interpre-tation of constitutional values, I believe it important that the school board provided an opportunity for the airing of these differences at public meetings designed to give the entire community "the opportunity to be able to partici-pate" in developing the drug policy.

Second, the testing program avoids subjecting the entire school to testing. And it preserves an option for a conscientious objector. He can refuse testing while paying a price (nonparticipation) that is serious, but less severe than expulsion from the school.

Third, a contrary reading of the Constitution, as requiring "individualized suspicion" in this public school context, could well lead schools to push the boundaries of "individualized suspicion" to its outer limits, using subjective criteria that may "unfairly target members of unpopular groups," or leave those whose behavior is slightly abnormal stigmatized in the minds of others. If so, direct application of the Fourth Amendment's prohibition against "unreasonable searches and seizures" will further that Amendment's liberty-protecting objectives at least to the same extent as application of the mediating "individualized suspicion" test, where, as here, the testing program is neither criminal nor disciplinary in nature.

I cannot know whether the school's drug testing program will work. But, in my view, the Constitution does not prohibit the effort. Emphasizing the considerations I have mentioned, along with others to which the Court refers, I conclude that the school's drug testing program, constitutionally speaking, is not "unreasonable." And I join the Court's opinion.

Justice GINSBURG, with whom Justice STEVENS, Justice O'CONNOR, and Justice SOUTER join, dissenting.

Seven years ago, in Vernonia School Dist. 47J v. Acton (1995), this Court determined that a school district's policy of randomly testing the urine of its student athletes for illicit drugs did not violate the Fourth Amendment. In so ruling, the Court emphasized that drug use "increase[d] the risk of sports-related injury" and that Vernonia's athletes were the "leaders" of an aggressive local "drug culture" that had reached "'epidemic proportions.'" Today, the Court relies upon *Vernonia* to permit a school district with a drug problem its superintendent repeatedly described as "not . . . major," to test the urine of an academic team member solely by reason of her participation in a nonathletic, competitive extracurricular activity—participation associated with neither special dangers from, nor particular predilections for, drug use.

Although "special needs inhere in the public school context," those needs are not so expansive or malleable as to render reasonable any program of student drug testing a school district elects to install. The particular testing program upheld today is not reasonable; it is capricious, even perverse: Petitioners' policy targets for testing a student population least likely to be at risk from illicit drugs and their damaging effects. I therefore dissent.

It is a sad irony that the petitioning School District seeks to justify its edict here by trumpeting "the schools' custodial and tutelary responsibility for children." In regulating an athletic program or endeavoring to combat an exploding drug epidemic, a school's custodial obligations may permit searches that would otherwise unacceptably abridge students' rights. When custodial duties are not ascendant, however, schools' tutelary obligations to their students require them to "teach by example" by avoiding symbolic measures that diminish constitutional protections. "That [schools] are educating the young for citizenship is reason for scrupulous protection of Constitutional freedoms of the individual, if we are not to strangle the free mind at its source and teach youth to discount important principles of our government as mere platitudes." West Virginia Bd. of Ed. v. Barnette (1943).

The Court has considered drug testing in a third context besides employees and students: hospitals. Specifically, in Ferguson v. City of Charleston, the Court considered whether a city could require drug testing of pregnant women, with results to be used for law enforcement purposes. The Court held that this does not fit within the "special needs" exception.

FERGUSON v. CITY OF CHARLESTON
532 U.S. 67 (2001)

Justice STEVENS delivered the opinion of the Court.

In this case, we must decide whether a state hospital's performance of a diagnostic test to obtain evidence of a patient's criminal conduct for law enforcement purposes is an unreasonable search if the patient has not consented to the procedure. More narrowly, the question is whether the interest in using the threat of criminal sanctions to deter pregnant women from using cocaine can justify a departure from the general rule that an official nonconsensual search is unconstitutional if not authorized by a valid warrant.

I

In the fall of 1988, staff members at the public hospital operated in the city of Charleston by the Medical University of South Carolina (MUSC) became concerned about an apparent increase in the use of cocaine by patients who were receiving prenatal treatment. In response to this perceived increase, as of April 1989, MUSC began to order drug screens to be performed on urine samples from maternity patients who were suspected of using cocaine. If a patient tested positive, she was then referred by MUSC staff to the county substance abuse commission for counseling and treatment. However, despite the referrals, the incidence of cocaine use among the patients at MUSC did not appear to change.

Some four months later, Nurse Shirley Brown, the case manager for the MUSC obstetrics department, heard a news broadcast reporting that the police in Greenville, South Carolina, were arresting pregnant users of cocaine on the theory that such use harmed the fetus and was therefore child abuse. Nurse Brown discussed the story with MUSC's general counsel, Joseph C. Good, Jr., who then contacted Charleston Solicitor Charles Condon in order to offer MUSC's cooperation in prosecuting mothers whose children tested positive for drugs at birth.[11]

II

Petitioners are 10 women who received obstetrical care at MUSC and who were arrested after testing positive for cocaine. Four of them were arrested during the

---

11. Under South Carolina law, a viable fetus has historically been regarded as a person; in 1995, the South Carolina Supreme Court held that the ingestion of cocaine during the third trimester of pregnancy constitutes criminal child neglect. [Footnote by the Court.]

initial implementation of the policy; they were not offered the opportunity to receive drug treatment as an alternative to arrest. The others were arrested after the policy was modified in 1990; they either failed to comply with the terms of the drug treatment program or tested positive for a second time.

Petitioners' complaint challenged the validity of the policy under various theories, including the claim that warrantless and nonconsensual drug tests conducted for criminal investigatory purposes were unconstitutional searches.

[III]

Because MUSC is a state hospital, the members of its staff are government actors, subject to the strictures of the Fourth Amendment. Moreover, the urine tests conducted by those staff members were indisputably searches within the meaning of the Fourth Amendment. Neither the District Court nor the Court of Appeals concluded that any of the nine criteria used to identify the women to be searched provided either probable cause to believe that they were using cocaine, or even the basis for a reasonable suspicion of such use. Rather, the District Court and the Court of Appeals viewed the case as one involving MUSC's right to conduct searches without warrants or probable cause. Furthermore, given the posture in which the case comes to us, we must assume for purposes of our decision that the tests were performed without the informed consent of the patients.

Because the hospital seeks to justify its authority to conduct drug tests and to turn the results over to law enforcement agents without the knowledge or consent of the patients, this case differs from the four previous cases in which we have considered whether comparable drug tests "fit within the closely guarded category of constitutionally permissible suspicionless searches."

In each of those cases, we employed a balancing test that weighed the intrusion on the individual's interest in privacy against the "special needs" that supported the program. As an initial matter, we note that the invasion of privacy in this case is far more substantial than in those cases. In the previous four cases, there was no misunderstanding about the purpose of the test or the potential use of the test results, and there were protections against the dissemination of the results to third parties. The use of an adverse test result to disqualify one from eligibility for a particular benefit, such as a promotion or an opportunity to participate in an extracurricular activity, involves a less serious intrusion on privacy than the unauthorized dissemination of such results to third parties. The reasonable expectation of privacy enjoyed by the typical patient undergoing diagnostic tests in a hospital is that the results of those tests will not be shared with nonmedical personnel without her consent. In none of our prior cases was there any intrusion upon that kind of expectation.

The critical difference between those four drug-testing cases and this one, however, lies in the nature of the "special need" asserted as justification for the warrantless searches. In each of those earlier cases, the "special need" that was advanced as a justification for the absence of a warrant or individualized suspicion was one divorced from the State's general interest in law enforcement. In this case, however, the central and indispensable feature of the policy from its inception was the use of law enforcement to coerce the patients into substance abuse treatment. This fact distinguishes this case from circumstances in which physicians or psychologists, in the course of ordinary medical procedures aimed at helping the patient herself, come across information that under rules of law or ethics is subject to reporting requirements, which no one has challenged here.

Respondents argue in essence that their ultimate purpose — namely, protecting the health of both mother and child — is a beneficent one. In this case, a review of the M-7 policy plainly reveals that the purpose actually served by the MUSC searches "is ultimately indistinguishable from the general interest in crime control." In looking to the programmatic purpose, we consider all the available evidence in order to determine the relevant primary purpose. Tellingly, the document codifying the policy incorporates the police's operational guidelines. It devotes its attention to the chain of custody, the range of possible criminal charges, and the logistics of police notification and arrests. Nowhere, however, does the document discuss different courses of medical treatment for either mother or infant, aside from treatment for the mother's addiction.

Moreover, throughout the development and application of the policy, the Charleston prosecutors and police were extensively involved in the day-to-day administration of the policy. Police and prosecutors decided who would receive the reports of positive drug screens and what information would be included with those reports. Law enforcement officials also helped determine the procedures to be followed when performing the screens. Police took pains to coordinate the timing and circumstances of the arrests with MUSC staff, and, in particular, Nurse Brown.

While the ultimate goal of the program may well have been to get the women in question into substance abuse treatment and off of drugs, the immediate objective of the searches was to generate evidence for law enforcement purposes in order to reach that goal. The threat of law enforcement may ultimately have been intended as a means to an end, but the direct and primary purpose of MUSC's policy was to ensure the use of those means. In our opinion, this distinction is critical. Because law enforcement involvement always serves some broader social purpose or objective, under respondents' view, virtually any nonconsensual suspicionless search could be immunized under the special needs doctrine by defining the search solely in terms of its ultimate, rather than immediate, purpose. Such an approach is inconsistent with the Fourth Amendment. Given the primary purpose of the Charleston program, which was to use the threat of arrest and prosecution in order to force women into treatment, and given the extensive involvement of law enforcement officials at every stage of the policy, this case simply does not fit within the closely guarded category of "special needs."

Justice SCALIA, with whom THE CHIEF JUSTICE and Justice THOMAS join, dissenting.

There is always an unappealing aspect to the use of doctors and nurses, ministers of mercy, to obtain incriminating evidence against the supposed objects of their ministration — although here, it is correctly pointed out, the doctors and nurses were ministering not just to the mothers but also to the children whom their cooperation with the police was meant to protect. But whatever may be the correct social judgment concerning the desirability of what occurred here, that is not the issue in the present case. The Constitution does not resolve all difficult social questions, but leaves the vast majority of them to resolution by debate and the democratic process — which would produce a decision by the citizens of

Charleston, through their elected representatives, to forbid or permit the police action at issue here. The question before us is a narrower one: whether, whatever the desirability of this police conduct, it violates the Fourth Amendment's prohibition of unreasonable searches and seizures. In my view, it plainly does not.

The first step in Fourth Amendment analysis is to identify the search or seizure at issue. What petitioners, the Court, and to a lesser extent the concurrence really object to is not the urine testing, but the hospital's reporting of positive drug-test results to police. But the latter is obviously not a search. At most it may be a "derivative use of the product of a past unlawful search," which, of course, "work[s] no new Fourth Amendment wrong" and "presents a question, not of rights, but of remedies." There is only one act that could conceivably be regarded as a search of petitioners in the present case: the taking of the urine sample. I suppose the testing of that urine for traces of unlawful drugs could be considered a search of sorts, but the Fourth Amendment protects only against searches of citizens' "persons, houses, papers, and effects"; and it is entirely unrealistic to regard urine as one of the "effects" (i.e., part of the property) of the person who has passed and abandoned it. Some would argue, I suppose, that testing of the urine is prohibited by some generalized privacy right "emanating" from the "penumbras" of the Constitution (a question that is not before us); but it is not even arguable that the testing of urine that has been lawfully obtained is a Fourth Amendment search. (I may add that, even if it were, the factors legitimizing the taking of the sample, which I discuss below, would likewise legitimize the testing of it.)

It is rudimentary Fourth Amendment law that a search which has been consented to is not unreasonable. There is no contention in the present case that the urine samples were extracted forcibly. The only conceivable bases for saying that they were obtained without consent are the contentions (1) that the consent was coerced by the patients' need for medical treatment, (2) that the consent was uninformed because the patients were not told that the tests would include testing for drugs, and (3) that the consent was uninformed because the patients were not told that the results of the tests would be provided to the police.

Until today, we have never held — or even suggested — that material which a person voluntarily entrusts to someone else cannot be given by that person to the police, and used for whatever evidence it may contain. Without so much as discussing the point, the Court today opens a hole in our Fourth Amendment jurisprudence, the size and shape of which is entirely indeterminate. I would adhere to our established law, which says that information obtained through violation of a relationship of trust is obtained consensually, and is hence not a search.

I think it clear, therefore, that there is no basis for saying that obtaining of the urine sample was unconstitutional. The special-needs doctrine is thus quite irrelevant, since it operates only to validate searches and seizures that are otherwise unlawful. In the ensuing discussion, however, I shall assume (contrary to legal precedent) that the taking of the urine sample was (either because of the patients' necessitous circumstances, or because of failure to disclose that the urine would be tested for drugs, or because of failure to disclose that the results of the test would be given to the police) coerced. Indeed, I shall even assume (contrary to common sense) that the testing of the urine constituted an unconsented search of the patients' effects. On those assumptions, the special-needs doctrine would become relevant; and, properly applied, would validate what was done here.

The conclusion of the Court that the special-needs doctrine is inapplicable rests upon its contention that respondents "undert[ook] to obtain [drug] evidence from their patients" not for any medical purpose, but "for the specific purpose of incriminating those patients." In other words, the purported medical rationale was merely a pretext; there was no special need. This contention contradicts the District Court's finding of fact that the goal of the testing policy "was not to arrest patients but to facilitate their treatment and protect both the mother and unborn child." This finding is binding upon us unless clearly erroneous. Not only do I find it supportable; I think any other finding would have to be overturned.

In sum, there can be no basis for the Court's purported ability to "distinguis[h] this case from circumstances in which physicians or psychologists, in the course of ordinary medical procedures aimed at helping the patient herself, come across information that . . . is subject to reporting requirements," unless it is this: That the addition of a law-enforcement-related purpose to a legitimate medical purpose destroys applicability of the "special-needs" doctrine. But that is quite impossible, since the special-needs doctrine was developed, and is ordinarily employed, precisely to enable searches by law enforcement officials who, of course, ordinarily have a law enforcement objective.

As I indicated at the outset, it is not the function of this Court — at least not in Fourth Amendment cases — to weigh petitioners' privacy interest against the State's interest in meeting the crisis of "crack babies" that developed in the late 1980's. I cannot refrain from observing, however, that the outcome of a wise weighing of those interests is by no means clear. The initial goal of the doctors and nurses who conducted cocaine testing in this case was to refer pregnant drug addicts to treatment centers, and to prepare for necessary treatment of their possibly affected children. When the doctors and nurses agreed to the program providing test results to the police, they did so because (in addition to the fact that child abuse was required by law to be reported) they wanted to use the sanction of arrest as a strong incentive for their addicted patients to undertake drug-addiction treatment. And the police themselves used it for that benign purpose, as is shown by the fact that only 30 of 253 women testing positive for cocaine were ever arrested, and only 2 of those prosecuted. It would not be unreasonable to conclude that today's judgment, authorizing the assessment of damages against the county solicitor and individual doctors and nurses who participated in the program, proves once again that no good deed goes unpunished.

But as far as the Fourth Amendment is concerned: There was no unconsented search in this case. And if there was, it would have been validated by the special-needs doctrine. For these reasons, I respectfully dissent.

11.   Exigent Circumstances

In an emergency, the police can search without a warrant if there is probable cause. This is often referred to as exigent circumstances. The ability of the police to enter a home when in hot pursuit of a felon is an example of this. For this exception to apply, it must be an emergency situation justifying warrantless activity and there must be probable cause. The Court clarified the requirements for "exigent circumstances" in Welsh v. Wisconsin.

WELSH v. WISCONSIN
466 U.S. 740 (1984)

Justice BRENNAN delivered the opinion of the Court.

Payton v. New York (1980), held that, absent probable cause and exigent circumstances, warrantless arrests in the home are prohibited by the Fourth Amendment. But the Court in that case explicitly refused "to consider the sort of emergency or dangerous situation, described in our cases as 'exigent circumstances,' that would justify a warrantless entry into a home for the purpose of either arrest or search." Certiorari was granted in this case to decide whether, and if so under what circumstances, the Fourth Amendment prohibits the police from making a warrantless night entry of a person's home in order to arrest him for a nonjailable traffic offense.

I

Shortly before 9 o'clock on the rainy night of April 24, 1978, a lone witness, Randy Jablonic, observed a car being driven erratically. After changing speeds and veering from side to side, the car eventually swerved off the road and came to a stop in an open field. No damage to any person or property occurred. Concerned about the driver and fearing that the car would get back on the highway, Jablonic drove his truck up behind the car so as to block it from returning to the road. Another passerby also stopped at the scene, and Jablonic asked her to call the police. Before the police arrived, however, the driver of the car emerged from his vehicle, approached Jablonic's truck, and asked Jablonic for a ride home. Jablonic instead suggested that they wait for assistance in removing or repairing the car. Ignoring Jablonic's suggestion, the driver walked away from the scene.

A few minutes later, the police arrived and questioned Jablonic. He told one officer what he had seen, specifically noting that the driver was either very inebriated or very sick. The officer checked the motor vehicle registration of the abandoned car and learned that it was registered to the petitioner, Edward G. Welsh. In addition, the officer noted that the petitioner's residence was a short distance from the scene, and therefore easily within walking distance.

Without securing any type of warrant, the police proceeded to the petitioner's home, arriving about 9 P.M. When the petitioner's stepdaughter answered the door, the police gained entry into the house. Proceeding upstairs to the petitioner's bedroom, they found him lying naked in bed. At this point, the petitioner was placed under arrest for driving or operating a motor vehicle while under the influence of an intoxicant. The petitioner was taken to the police station, where he refused to submit to a breath-analysis test.

As a result of these events, the petitioner was subjected to two separate but related proceedings: one concerning his refusal to submit to a breath test and the other involving the alleged code violation for driving while intoxicated. Under the Wisconsin Vehicle Code in effect in April 1978, one arrested for driving while intoxicated could be requested by a law enforcement officer to provide breath, blood, or urine samples for the purpose of determining the presence or quantity of alcohol. If such a request was made, the arrestee was required to submit to the appropriate testing or risk a revocation of operating privileges.

It is axiomatic that the "physical entry of the home is the chief evil against which the wording of the Fourth Amendment is directed." And a principal protection against unnecessary intrusions into private dwellings is the warrant requirement imposed by the Fourth Amendment on agents of the government who seek to enter the home for purposes of search or arrest. It is not surprising, therefore, that the Court has recognized, as

> a "basic principle of Fourth Amendment law[,]" that searches and seizures inside a home without a warrant are presumptively unreasonable.
>
> Even if one were to conclude that urgent circumstances might justify a forced entry without a warrant, no such emergency was present in this case. This method of law enforcement displays a shocking lack of all sense of proportion. Whether there is reasonable necessity for a search without waiting to obtain a warrant certainly depends somewhat upon the gravity of the offense thought to be in progress as well as the hazards of the method of attempting to reach it. . . . It is to me a shocking proposition that private homes, even quarters in a tenement, may be indiscriminately invaded at the discretion of any suspicious police officer engaged in following up offenses that involve no violence or threats of it. While I should be human enough to apply the letter of the law with some indulgence to officers acting to deal with threats or crimes of violence which endanger life or security, it is notable that few of the searches found by this Court to be unlawful dealt with that category of crime. . . . While the enterprise of parting fools from their money by the "numbers" lottery is one that ought to be suppressed, I do not think its suppression is more important to society than the security of the people against unreasonable searches and seizures. When an officer undertakes to act as his own magistrate, he ought to be in a position to justify it by pointing to some real immediate and serious consequences if he postponed action to get a warrant.

We therefore conclude that the common-sense approach utilized by most lower courts is required by the Fourth Amendment prohibition on "unreasonable searches and seizures," and hold that an important factor to be considered when determining whether any exigency exists is the gravity of the underlying offense for which the arrest is being made. Moreover, although no exigency is created simply because there is probable cause to believe that a serious crime has been committed, application of the exigent-circumstances exception in the context of a home entry should rarely be sanctioned when there is probable cause to believe that only a minor offense, such as the kind at issue in this case, has been committed.

Application of this principle to the facts of the present case is relatively straightforward. The petitioner was arrested in the privacy of his own bedroom for a noncriminal, traffic offense. The State attempts to justify the arrest by relying on the hot-pursuit doctrine, on the threat to public safety, and on the need to preserve evidence of the petitioner's blood-alcohol level. On the facts of this case, however, the claim of hot pursuit is unconvincing because there was no immediate or continuous pursuit of the petitioner from the scene of a crime. Moreover, because the petitioner had already arrived home, and had abandoned his car at the scene of the accident, there was little remaining threat to the public safety. Hence, the only potential emergency claimed by the State was the need to ascertain the petitioner's blood-alcohol level.

The Court generally has been reluctant to find exigent circumstances. For example, in Mincey v. Arizona, 437 U.S. 385 (1978), the Court rejected a claim that there should be a blanket exception to the warrant requirement for all murder scenes. But police may act without a warrant if it is an emergency and the police believe that entering premises will provide protection. This was made clear in the recent decision, Brigham City, Utah v. Stuart.

BRIGHAM CITY, UTAH v. STUART
126 S. Ct. 1943 (2006)

Chief Justice ROBERTS delivered the opinion of the Court.

In this case we consider whether police may enter a home without a warrant when they have an objectively reasonable basis for believing that an occupant is seriously injured or imminently threatened with such injury. We conclude that they may.

I

This case arises out of a melee that occurred in a Brigham City, Utah, home in the early morning hours of July 23, 2000. At about 3 A.M., four police officers responded to a call regarding a loud party at a residence. Upon arriving at the house, they heard shouting from inside, and proceeded down the driveway to investigate. There, they observed two juveniles drinking beer in the backyard. They entered the backyard, and saw — through a screen door and windows — an altercation taking place in the kitchen of the home. According to the testimony of one of the officers, four adults were attempting, with some difficulty, to restrain a juvenile. The juvenile eventually "broke free, swung a fist and struck one of the adults in the face." The officer testified that he observed the victim of the blow spitting blood into a nearby sink. The other adults continued to try to restrain the juvenile, pressing him up against a refrigerator with such force that the refrigerator began moving across the floor. At this point, an officer opened the screen door and announced the officers' presence. Amid the tumult, nobody noticed. The officer entered the kitchen and again cried out, and as the occupants slowly became aware that the police were on the scene, the altercation ceased.

The officers subsequently arrested respondents and charged them with contributing to the delinquency of a minor, disorderly conduct, and intoxication. In the trial court, respondents filed a motion to suppress all evidence obtained after the officers entered the home, arguing that the warrantless entry violated the Fourth Amendment. The court granted the motion, and the Utah Court of Appeals affirmed.

II

It is a "basic principle of Fourth Amendment law that searches and seizures inside a home without a warrant are presumptively unreasonable." Nevertheless, because the ultimate touchstone of the Fourth Amendment is "reasonableness," the warrant requirement is subject to certain exceptions.

One exigency obviating the requirement of a warrant is the need to assist persons who are seriously injured or threatened with such injury. "The need to protect or preserve life or avoid serious injury is justification for what would be otherwise illegal absent an exigency or emergency." Accordingly, law enforcement officers may enter a home without a warrant to render emergency assistance to an injured occupant or to protect an occupant from imminent injury.

Respondents do not take issue with these principles, but instead advance two reasons why the officers' entry here was unreasonable. First, they argue that the officers were more interested in making arrests than quelling violence. They urge us to consider, in assessing the reasonableness of the entry, whether the officers were "indeed motivated primarily by a desire to save lives and property."

Our cases have repeatedly rejected this approach. An action is "reasonable" under the Fourth Amendment, regardless of the individual officer's state of mind, "as long as the circumstances, viewed objectively, justify [the] action." The officer's subjective motivation is irrelevant.

Respondents further contend that their conduct was not serious enough to justify the officers' intrusion into the home. They rely on Welsh v. Wisconsin (1984), in which we held that "an important factor to be considered when determining whether any exigency exists is the gravity of the underlying offense for which the arrest is being made." This contention, too, is misplaced. *Welsh* involved a warrantless entry by officers to arrest a suspect for driving while intoxicated. There, the "only potential emergency" confronting the officers was the need to preserve evidence (i.e., the suspect's blood-alcohol level) — an exigency that we held insufficient under the circumstances to justify entry into the suspect's home. Here, the officers were confronted with ongoing violence occurring within the home. Welsh did not address such a situation.

We think the officers' entry here was plainly reasonable under the circumstances. The officers were responding, at 3 o'clock in the morning, to complaints about a loud party. As they approached the house, they could hear from within "an altercation occurring, some kind of a fight." "It was loud and it was tumultuous." The officers heard "thumping and crashing" and people yelling "stop, stop" and "get off me." As the trial court found, "it was obvious that . . . knocking on the front door" would have been futile. The noise seemed to be coming from the back of the house; after looking in the front window and seeing nothing, the officers proceeded around back to investigate further. They found two juveniles drinking beer in the backyard. From there, they could see that a fracas was taking place inside the kitchen. A juvenile, fists clenched, was being held back by several adults. As the officers watch, he breaks free and strikes one of the adults in the face, sending the adult to the sink spitting blood.

In these circumstances, the officers had an objectively reasonable basis for believing both that the injured adult might need help and that the violence in the kitchen was just beginning. Nothing in the Fourth Amendment required them to wait until another blow rendered someone "unconscious" or "semiconscious" or worse before entering. The role of a peace officer includes preventing violence and restoring order, not simply rendering first aid to casualties; an officer is not like a boxing (or hockey) referee, poised to stop a bout only if it becomes too one-sided.

The manner of the officers' entry was also reasonable. After witnessing the punch, one of the officers opened the screen door and "yelled in police." When nobody heard him, he stepped into the kitchen and announced himself again. Only then did the tumult subside. The officer's announcement of his presence was at least equivalent to a knock on the screen door. Indeed, it was probably the only option that had even a chance of rising above the din. Under these circumstances, there was no violation of the Fourth Amendment's knock-and-announce rule. Furthermore, once the announcement was made, the officers were free to enter; it would serve no purpose to require them to stand dumbly at the door awaiting a response while those within brawled on, oblivious to their presence.

F.   SEIZURES AND ARRESTS

The Fourth Amendment, of course, applies to seizures, whether of a person or of his or her property. Arrests must be based on probable cause, though as discussed in Section G, a person may be stopped by the police with just reasonable suspicion. Both arrests and stops are seizures within the meaning of the Fourth Amendment. Also, an illegal arrest or stop generally requires the exclusion of the evidence gained as its result. (The exclusionary rule is discussed in Chapter 3.)

Three questions seem particularly important with regard to seizures. First, is a warrant needed for arrests? Second, when does a seizure occur? Finally, is an arrest permissible for a minor offense that does not carry with it the possibility of a prison term? Each of these is discussed in turn.

1.   Is a Warrant Needed for Arrests?

Although the Court has expressed a preference for warrants, it also has been clear that a warrant is not required for an arrest so long as there is probable cause.

UNITED STATES v. WATSON
423 U.S. 411 (1976)

Justice WHITE delivered the opinion of the Court.

This case presents questions under the Fourth Amendment as to the legality of a warrantless arrest and of an ensuing search of the arrestee's automobile carried out with his purported consent.

I

The relevant events began on August 17, 1972, when an informant, one Khoury, telephoned a postal inspector informing him that respondent Watson was in possession of a stolen credit card and had asked Khoury to cooperate in using the card to their mutual advantage. On five to 10 previous occasions Khoury had provided the inspector with reliable information on postal inspection matters, some involving Watson. Later that day Khoury delivered the card to the inspector. On learning that Watson had agreed to furnish additional cards, the inspector asked Khoury to arrange to meet with Watson. Khoury did so, a meeting being scheduled for August 22. Watson canceled that engagement, but at noon on August 23, Khoury met with Watson at a restaurant designated by the latter. Khoury had been instructed that if Watson had additional stolen credit cards, Khoury was to give a designated signal. The signal was given, the officers closed in, and Watson was forthwith arrested. He was removed from the restaurant to the street where he was given the warnings required by Miranda v. Arizona (1966). A search having revealed that Watson had no credit cards on his person, the inspector asked if he could look inside Watson's car, which was standing within view. Watson said, "Go ahead," and repeated these words when the inspector cautioned that "[i]f I find anything, it is going to go against you." Using keys furnished by Watson, the inspector entered the car and found under the floor mat an envelop containing two credit cards in the names of other persons. These cards were the basis for two counts of a four-count indictment charging Watson with possessing stolen mail.

Prior to trial, Watson moved to suppress the cards, claiming that his arrest was illegal for want of probable cause and an arrest warrant and that his consent to search the car was involuntary and ineffective because he had not been told that he could withhold consent. The motion was denied, and Watson was convicted of illegally possessing the two cards seized from his car.

II

Contrary to the Court of Appeals' view, Watson's arrest was not invalid because executed without a warrant. Title 18 U.S.C. § 3061(a)(3) expressly empowers the Board of Governors of the Postal Service to authorize Postal Service officers and employees "performing duties related to the inspection of postal matters" to "make arrests without warrant for felonies cognizable under the laws of the United States if they have reasonable grounds to believe that the person to be arrested has committed or is committing such a felony." Because there was probable cause in this case to believe that Watson had violated § 1708, the inspector and his subordinates, in arresting Watson, were acting strictly in accordance with the governing statute and regulations.

Section 3061 represents a judgment by Congress that it is not unreasonable under the Fourth Amendment for postal inspectors to arrest without a warrant provided they have probable cause to do so. This was not an isolated or quixotic judgment of the legislative branch. Other federal law enforcement officers have been expressly authorized by statute for many years to make felony arrests on probable cause but without a warrant. This is true of United States marshals, and of agents of the Federal Bureau of Investigation, the Drug Enforcement Administration, the Secret Service, and the Customs Service.

Because there is a "strong presumption of constitutionality due to an Act of Congress, especially when it turns on what is 'reasonable,'" "[o]bviously the Court should be reluctant to decide that a search thus authorized by Congress was unreasonable and that the Act was therefore unconstitutional." Moreover, there is nothing in the Court's prior cases indicating that under the Fourth Amendment a warrant is required to make a valid arrest for a felony. Indeed, the relevant prior decisions are uniformly to the contrary.

"The usual rule is that a police officer may arrest without warrant one believed by the officer upon reasonable cause to have been guilty of a felony . . . ." The cases construing the Fourth Amendment thus reflect the ancient common-law rule that a peace officer was permitted to arrest without a warrant for a misdemeanor or felony committed in his presence as well as for a felony not committed in his presence if there was reasonable ground for making the arrest. This has also been the prevailing rule under state constitutions and statutes. "The rule of the common law, that a peace officer or a private citizen may arrest a felon without a warrant, has been generally held by the courts of the several States to be in force in cases of felony punishable by the civil tribunals." Kurtz v. Moffitt (1885).

Watson's arrest did not violate the Fourth Amendment, and the Court of Appeals erred in holding to the contrary. Because our judgment is that Watson's arrest comported with the Fourth Amendment, Watson's consent to the search of his car was not the product of an illegal arrest.

Justice MARSHALL, with whom Justice BRENNAN joins, dissenting.

By granting police broad powers to make warrantless arrests, the Court today sharply reverses the course of our modern decisions construing the Warrant Clause of the Fourth Amendment.

I

Before addressing what the Court does today, I note what it does not do. It does not decide this case on the narrow question that is presented. That is unfortunate for this is, fundamentally, a simple case.

On the afternoon of August 23, 1972, Awad Khoury, an informant of proved reliability, met with respondent Watson at a public restaurant under the surveillance of two postal inspectors. Khoury was under instructions to light a cigarette as a signal to the watching agents if Watson was in possession of stolen credit cards. Khoury lit a cigarette, and the postal inspectors moved in, made the arrest, and, ultimately, discovered under the floor mat of Watson's automobile the stolen credit cards that formed the basis of Watson's conviction and this appeal.

The signal of the reliable informant that Watson was in possession of stolen credit cards gave the postal inspectors probable cause to make the arrest. This probable cause was separate and distinct from the probable cause relating to the offense six days earlier, and provided an adequate independent basis for the arrest. Whether or not a warrant ordinarily is required prior to making an arrest, no warrant is required when exigent circumstances are present. When law enforcement officers have probable cause to believe that an offense is taking place in their presence and that the suspect is at that moment in possession of the evidence, exigent circumstances exist. Delay could cause the escape of the suspect or the destruction of the evidence. Accordingly, Watson's warrantless arrest was valid under the recognized exigent-circumstances exception to the warrant requirement, and the Court has no occasion to consider whether a warrant would otherwise be necessary.

This conclusion should properly dispose of the case before us.

Since, for reasons it leaves unexpressed, the Court does not take this traditional course, I am constrained to express my views on the issues it unnecessarily decides. The Court reaches its conclusion that a warrant is not necessary for a police officer to make an arrest in a public place, so long as he has probable cause to believe a felony has been committed, on the basis of its views of precedent and history. [A]n examination of the history relied on by the Court shows that it does not support the conclusion laid upon it.

There is no doubt that by the reference to the seizure of persons, the Fourth Amendment was intended to apply to arrests. Indeed, we have often considered whether arrests were made in conformity with the Fourth Amendment. Admittedly, as the Court observes, some of our decisions make passing reference to the common-law rule on arrests. However, none of the cases cited by the Court, nor any other warrantless arrest case in this Court, mandates the decision announced today. Frequently exigent circumstances were present, so that the warrantless arrest was proper even if a warrant ordinarily may be required. Many cases have invalidated arrests as not based on probable cause, thereby bypassing the need to reach the warrant question. Elsewhere the Court has simply assumed the propriety of the arrest and resolved the case before it on other grounds.

The Court next turns to history. It relies on the English common-law rule of arrest and the many state and federal statutes following it. There are two serious flaws in this approach. First, as a matter of factual analysis, the substance of the ancient common-law rule provides no support for the far-reaching modern rule that the Court fashions on its model. Second, as a matter of doctrine, the long-standing existence of a Government practice does not immunize the practice from scrutiny under the mandate of our Constitution.

In sum, the Court's opinion is without foundation. It relies on precedents that are not precedents. It relies on history that offers no clear rule to impose, but only conflicting interests to balance. It relies on statutes that constitute, at best, no more than an aid to construction. The Court never grapples with the warrant requirement of the Fourth Amendment and the cases construing it. It simply announces, by ipse dixit, a rule squarely rejecting the warrant requirement we have favored for so long.

The Court has typically engaged in a two-part analysis in deciding whether the presumption favoring a warrant should be given effect in situations where a warrant has not previously been clearly required. Utilizing that approach we must now consider (1) whether the privacy of our citizens will be better protected by ordinarily requiring a warrant to be issued before they may be arrested; and (2) whether a warrant requirement would unduly burden legitimate governmental interests.

The first question is easily answered. Of course, the privacy of our citizens will be better protected by a warrant requirement. We have recognized that "the Fourth Amendment protects people, not places." Indeed, the privacy guaranteed by the Fourth Amendment is quintessentially personal. Thus a warrant is required in search situations not because of some high regard for property, but because of our regard for the individual, and his interest in his possessions and person.

Not only is the Fourth Amendment directly addressed to the privacy of our citizens, but it speaks in indistinguishable terms about the freedom of both persons and property from unreasonable seizures. A warrant is required in the search situation to protect the privacy of the individual, but there can be no less invasion of privacy when the individual himself, rather than his property, is searched and seized. Indeed, an unjustified arrest that forces the individual temporarily to forfeit his right to control his person and movements and interrupts the course of his daily business may be more intrusive than an unjustified search.

A warrant requirement for arrests would, of course, minimize the possibility that such an intrusion into the individual's sacred sphere of personal privacy would occur on less than probable cause. Primarily for this reason, a warrant is required for searches. Surely there is no reason to place greater trust in the partisan assessment of a police officer that there is probable cause for an arrest than in his determination that probable cause exists for a search.

We come then to the second part of the warrant test: whether a warrant requirement would unduly burden legitimate law enforcement interests. I believe, however, that the suggested concerns are wholly illusory. Indeed, the argument that a warrant requirement for arrests would be an onerous chore for the police seems somewhat anomalous in light of the Government's concession that "it is the standard practice of the Federal Bureau of Investigation (FBI) to present its evidence to the United States Attorney, and to obtain a warrant, before making an arrest." In the past, the practice and experience of the FBI have been taken as a substantial indication that no intolerable burden would be presented by a proposed rule of procedure. Miranda v. Arizona (1966). There is no reason to accord less deference to the FBI practice here.

The Government's assertion that a warrant requirement would impose an intolerable burden stems, in large part, from the specious supposition that procurement of an arrest warrant would be necessary as soon as probable cause ripens. There is no requirement that a search warrant be obtained the moment police have probable cause to search. The rule is only that present probable cause be shown and a warrant obtained before a search is undertaken. The same rule should obtain for arrest warrants, where it may even make more sense. Certainly, there is less need for prompt procurement of a warrant in the arrest situation. Unlike probable cause to search, probable cause to arrest, once formed will continue to exist for the indefinite future, at least if no intervening exculpatory facts come to light.

This sensible approach obviates most of the difficulties that have been suggested with an arrest warrant rule. Police would not have to cut their investigation short the moment they obtain probable cause to arrest, nor would undercover agents be forced suddenly to terminate their work and forfeit their covers. Moreover, if in the course of the continued police investigation exigent circumstances develop that demand an immediate arrest, the arrest may be made without fear of unconstitutionality, so long as the exigency was unanticipated and not used to avoid the arrest warrant requirement. Likewise, if in the course of the continued investigation police uncover evidence tying the suspect to another crime, they may immediately arrest him for that crime if exigency demands it, and still be in full conformity with the warrant rule. This is why the arrest in this case was not improper. Other than where police attempt to evade the warrant requirement, the rule would invalidate an arrest only in the obvious situation: where police, with probable cause but without exigent circumstances, set out to arrest a suspect. Such an arrest must be void, even if exigency develops in the course of the arrest that would ordinarily validate it; otherwise the warrant requirement would be reduced to a toothless prescription.

2.   When Is a Person Seized?

What constitutes a seizure for purposes of the Fourth Amendment? If a person is arrested, then there are significant consequences for both the police and the individual. For example, if there is an arrest, as explained above, police may conduct a search incident to the arrest.

In some instances, it is obvious when a person has been arrested, such as when the police tell a person, "You are under arrest," and put on the handcuffs. A seizure also can occur if a person is stopped pursuant to a "stop and frisk," which is discussed in the next section. The Supreme Court has held, such as in United States v. Mendenhall, that a person is seized if a reasonable person under the circumstances would believe that he or she was not free to leave.

UNITED STATES v. MENDENHALL
446 U.S. 544 (1980)

Justice STEWART announced the judgment of the Court.

The respondent was brought to trial in the United States District Court for the Eastern District of Michigan on a charge of possessing heroin with intent to distribute it. She moved to suppress the introduction at trial of the heroin as evidence against her on the ground that it had been acquired from her through an unconstitutional search and seizure by agents of the Drug Enforcement Administration (DEA). The District Court denied the respondent's motion, and she was convicted after a trial upon stipulated facts. The Court of Appeals reversed, finding the search of the respondent's person to have been unlawful.

I

At the hearing in the trial court on the respondent's motion to suppress, it was established how the heroin she was charged with possessing had been obtained from her. The respondent arrived at the Detroit Metropolitan Airport on a commercial airline flight from Los Angeles early in the morning on February 10, 1976. As she disembarked from the airplane, she was observed by two agents of the DEA, who were present at the airport for the purpose of detecting unlawful traffic in narcotics. After observing the respondent's conduct, which appeared to the agents to be characteristic of persons unlawfully carrying narcotics, the agents approached her as she was walking through the concourse, identified themselves as federal agents, and asked to see her identification and airline ticket. The respondent produced her driver's license, which was in the name of Sylvia Mendenhall, and, in answer to a question of one of the agents, stated that she resided at the address appearing on the license. The airline ticket was issued in the name of "Annette Ford." When asked why the ticket bore a name different from her own, the respondent stated that she "just felt like using that name." In response to a further question, the respondent indicated that she had been in California only two days. Agent Anderson then specifically identified himself as a federal narcotics agent and, according to his testimony, the respondent "became quite shaken, extremely nervous. She had a hard time speaking."

After returning the airline ticket and driver's license to her, Agent Anderson asked the respondent if she would accompany him to the airport DEA office for further questions. She did so, although the record does not indicate a verbal response to the request. The office, which was located up one flight of stairs about 50 feet from where the respondent had first been approached, consisted of a reception area adjoined by three other rooms. At the office the agent asked the respondent if she would allow a search of her person and handbag and told her that she had the right to decline the search if she desired. She responded: "Go ahead." She then handed Agent Anderson her purse, which contained a receipt for an airline ticket that had been issued to "F. Bush" three days earlier for a flight from Pittsburgh through Chicago to Los Angeles. The agent asked whether this was the ticket that she had used for her flight to California, and the respondent stated that it was.

A female police officer then arrived to conduct the search of the respondent's person. She asked the agents if the respondent had consented to be searched. The agents said that she had, and the respondent followed the policewoman into a private room. There the policewoman again asked the respondent if she consented to the search, and the respondent replied that she did. The policewoman explained that the search would require that the respondent remove her clothing. The respondent stated that she had a plane to catch and was assured by the policewoman that if she were carrying no narcotics, there would be no problem. The respondent then began to disrobe without further comment. As the respondent removed her clothing, she took from her undergarments two small packages, one of which appeared to contain heroin, and handed both to the policewoman. The agents then arrested the respondent for possessing heroin.

It was on the basis of this evidence that the District Court denied the respondent's motion to suppress. The court concluded that the agents' conduct in initially approaching the respondent and asking to see her ticket and identification was a permissible investigative stop, finding that this conduct was based on specific and articulable facts that justified a suspicion of criminal activity. The court also found that the respondent had not been placed under arrest or otherwise detained when she was asked to accompany the agents to the DEA office, but had accompanied the agents "voluntarily in a spirit of apparent cooperation." It was the court's view that no arrest occurred until after the heroin had been found. Finally, the trial court found that the respondent "gave her consent to the search [in the DEA office] and . . . such consent was freely and voluntarily given."

II

Here the Government concedes that its agents had neither a warrant nor probable cause to believe that the respondent was carrying narcotics when the agents conducted a search of the respondent's person. It is the Government's position, however, that the search was conducted pursuant to the respondent's consent, and thus was excepted from the requirements of both a warrant and probable cause.

A

The Fourth Amendment's requirement that searches and seizures be founded upon an objective justification, governs all seizures of the person, including seizures that involve only a brief detention short of traditional arrest. Accordingly, if the respondent was "seized" when the DEA agents approached her on the concourse and asked questions of her, the agents' conduct in doing so was constitutional only if they reasonably suspected the respondent of wrongdoing. But "[o]bviously, not all personal intercourse between policemen and citizens involves 'seizures' of persons. Only when the officer, by means of physical force or show of authority, has in some way restrained the liberty of a citizen may we conclude that a 'seizure' has occurred."

We adhere to the view that a person is "seized" only when, by means of physical force or a show of authority, his freedom of movement is restrained. Only when such restraint is imposed is there any foundation whatever for invoking constitutional safeguards. The purpose of the Fourth Amendment is not to eliminate all contact between the police and the citizenry, but "to prevent arbitrary and oppressive interference by enforcement officials with the privacy and personal security of individuals." As long as the person to whom questions are put remains free to disregard the questions and walk away, there has been no intrusion upon that person's liberty or privacy as would under the Constitution require some particularized and objective justification.

Moreover, characterizing every street encounter between a citizen and the police as a "seizure," while not enhancing any interest secured by the Fourth Amendment, would impose wholly unrealistic restrictions upon a wide variety of legitimate law enforcement practices. The Court has on other occasions referred to the acknowledged need for police questioning as a tool in the effective enforcement of the criminal laws. Without such investigation, those who were innocent might be falsely accused, those who were guilty might wholly escape prosecution, and many crimes would go unsolved. In short, the security of all would be diminished.

We conclude that a person has been "seized" within the meaning of the Fourth Amendment only if, in view of all of the circumstances surrounding the incident, a reasonable person would have believed that he was not free to leave. Examples of circumstances that might indicate a seizure, even where the person did not attempt to leave, would be the threatening presence of several officers, the display of a weapon by an officer, some physical touching of the person of the citizen, or the use of language or tone of voice indicating that compliance with the officer's request might be compelled. In the absence of some such evidence, otherwise inoffensive contact between a member of the public and the police cannot, as a matter of law, amount to a seizure of that person.

Reaching

On the facts of this case, no "seizure" of the respondent occurred. The events took place in the public concourse. The agents wore no uniforms and displayed no weapons. They did not summon the respondent to their presence, but instead approached her and identified themselves as federal agents. They requested, but did not demand to see the respondent's identification and ticket. Such conduct without more, did not amount to an intrusion upon any constitutionally protected interest. The respondent was not seized simply by reason of the fact that the agents approached her, asked her if she would show them her ticket and identification, and posed to her a few questions. Nor was it enough to establish a seizure that the person asking the questions was a law enforcement official. In short, nothing in the record suggests that the respondent had any objective reason to believe that she was not free to end the conversation in the concourse and proceed on her way, and for that reason we conclude that the agents' initial approach to her was not a seizure.

Our conclusion that no seizure occurred is not affected by the fact that the respondent was not expressly told by the agents that she was free to decline to cooperate with their inquiry, for the voluntariness of her responses does not depend upon her having been so informed. We also reject the argument that the only inference to be drawn from the fact that the respondent acted in a manner so contrary to her self-interest is that she was compelled to answer the agents' questions. It may happen that a person makes statements to law enforcement officials that he later regrets, but the issue in such cases is not whether the statement was self-protective, but rather whether it was made voluntarily.

B

Although we have concluded that the initial encounter between the DEA agents and the respondent on the concourse at the Detroit Airport did not constitute an unlawful seizure, it is still arguable that the respondent's Fourth Amendment protections were violated when she went from the concourse to the DEA office. Such a violation might in turn infect the subsequent search of the respondent's person.

The District Court specifically found that the respondent accompanied the agents to the office "'voluntarily in a spirit of apparent cooperation.'" The question whether the respondent's consent to accompany the agents was in fact voluntary or was the product of duress or coercion, express or implied, is to be determined by the totality of all the circumstances and is a matter which the Government has the burden of proving.

On the other hand, it is argued that the incident would reasonably have appeared coercive to the respondent, who was 22 years old and had not been graduated from high school. It is additionally suggested that the respondent, a female and a Negro, may have felt unusually threatened by the officers, who were white males. While these factors were not irrelevant, neither were they decisive, and the totality of the evidence in this case was plainly adequate to support the District Court's finding that the respondent voluntarily consented to accompany the officers to the DEA office.

C

Because the search of the respondent's person was not preceded by an impermissible seizure of her person, it cannot be contended that her apparent consent to the subsequent search was infected by an unlawful detention. We conclude that the District Court's determination that the respondent consented to the search of her person "freely and voluntarily" was sustained by the evidence and that the Court of Appeals was, therefore, in error in setting it aside.

Justice WHITE, with whom Justice BRENNAN, Justice MARSHALL, and Justice STEVENS join, dissenting.

The Court today concludes that agents of the Drug Enforcement Administration (DEA) acted lawfully in stopping a traveler changing planes in an airport terminal and escorting her to a DEA office for a strip-search of her person. The Court then concludes, based on the absence of evidence that Ms. Mendenhall resisted her detention, that she voluntarily consented to being taken to the DEA office, even though she in fact had no choice in the matter. This conclusion is inconsistent with our recognition that consent cannot be presumed from a showing of acquiescence to authority.

Beginning with Terry v. Ohio (1968), the Court has recognized repeatedly that the Fourth Amendment's proscription of unreasonable "seizures" protects individuals during encounters with police that do not give rise to an arrest.

Throughout the lower court proceedings in this case, the Government never questioned that the initial stop of Ms. Mendenhall was a "seizure" that required reasonable suspicion. Rather, the Government sought to justify the stop by arguing that Ms. Mendenhall's behavior had given rise to reasonable suspicion because it was consistent with portions of the so-called "drug courier profile," an informal amalgam of characteristics thought to be associated with persons carrying illegal drugs. Having failed to convince the Court of Appeals that the DEA agents had reasonable suspicion for the stop, the Government seeks reversal here by arguing for the first time that no "seizure" occurred, an argument that Justice Stewart now accepts, thereby pretermitting the question whether there was reasonable suspicion to stop Ms. Mendenhall. Justice Stewart's opinion not only is inconsistent with our usual refusal to reverse judgments on grounds not raised below, but it also addresses a fact-bound question with a totality-of-circumstances assessment that is best left in the first instance to the trial court, particularly since the question was not litigated below and hence we cannot be sure is adequately addressed by the record before us.

Justice Stewart believes that a "seizure" within the meaning of the Fourth Amendment occurs when an individual's freedom of movement is restrained by means of physical force or a show of authority. Although it is undisputed that Ms. Mendenhall was not free to leave after the DEA agents stopped her and inspected her identification, Justice Stewart concludes that she was not "seized" because he finds that, under the totality of the circumstances, a reasonable person would have believed that she was free to leave. While basing this finding on an alleged absence from the record of objective evidence indicating that Ms. Mendenhall was not free to ignore the officer's inquiries and continue on her way, Justice Stewart's opinion brushes off the fact that this asserted evidentiary deficiency may be largely attributable to the fact that the "seizure" question was never raised below. In assessing what the record does reveal, the opinion discounts certain objective factors that would tend to support a "seizure" finding, while relying on contrary factors inconclusive even under its own illustrations of how a "seizure" may be established. Moreover, although Justice Stewart's opinion purports to make its "seizure" finding turn on objective factors known to the person accosted, in distinguishing prior decisions holding that investigatory stops constitute "seizures," it does not rely on differences in the extent to which persons accosted could reasonably believe that they were free to leave.

II

Assuming, as we should, that Ms. Mendenhall was "seized" within the meaning of the Fourth Amendment when she was stopped by the DEA agents, the legality of that stop turns on whether there were reasonable grounds for suspecting her of criminal activity at the time of the stop. To establish that there was reasonable suspicion for the stop, it was necessary for the police at least to "be able to point to specific and articulable facts which, taken together with rational inferences from those facts, reasonably warrant that intrusion."

At the time they stopped Ms. Mendenhall, the DEA agents' suspicion that she was engaged in criminal activity was based solely on their brief observations of her conduct at the airport. The officers had no advance information that Ms. Mendenhall, or anyone on her flight, would be carrying drugs. What the agents observed Ms. Mendenhall do in the airport was not "unusual conduct" which would lead an experienced officer reasonably to conclude that criminal activity was afoot, but rather the kind of behavior that could reasonably be expected of anyone changing planes in an airport terminal.

None of the aspects of Ms. Mendenhall's conduct, either alone or in combination, were sufficient to provide reasonable suspicion that she was engaged in criminal activity. The fact that Ms. Mendenhall was the last person to alight from a flight originating in Los Angeles was plainly insufficient to provide a basis for stopping her. Nor was the fact that her flight originated from a "major source city," for the mere proximity of a person to areas with a high incidence of drug activity or to persons known to be drug addicts, does not provide the necessary reasonable suspicion for an investigatory stop.

III

Whatever doubt there may be concerning whether Ms. Mendenhall's Fourth Amendment interests were implicated during the initial stages of her confrontation with the DEA agents, she undoubtedly was "seized" within the meaning of the Fourth Amendment when the agents escorted her from the public area of the terminal to the DEA office for questioning and a strip-search of her person. Although Ms. Mendenhall was not told that she was under arrest, she in fact was not free to refuse to go to the DEA office and was not told that she was. Furthermore, once inside the office, Ms. Mendenhall would not have been permitted to leave without submitting to a strip-search.

Because Ms. Mendenhall was being illegally detained at the time of the search of her person, her suppression motion should have been granted in the absence of evidence to dissipate the taint.

_____

On many subsequent occasions, the Supreme Court reaffirmed and applied the *Mendenhall* definition of a seizure. In Florida v. Bostick, 501 U.S. 429 (1991), the Court considered whether there was a seizure when police boarded a bus and asked passengers for permission to search their luggage. Passengers on the bus are generally not "free to leave" when this happens. The police officers asked Terrance Bostick for permission to search his luggage. Bostick consented and cocaine was found.

The Court said that the test was not whether a reasonable person in his situation would have felt free to leave, but whether a person would "feel free to decline the officers' requests or otherwise terminate the encounter." The Court remanded the case to determine whether there was a seizure under that standard.

As explained above, in the subsequent case, United States v. Drayton, 536 U.S. 194 (2002), the Court found that there was not a seizure when three police officers boarded a bus and asked the passengers permission to search their bags. One officer sat in the driver's seat and the other two went down the aisle, though the Court stressed that the aisle was not blocked and no one told the passengers that they were required to remain. The Court said: "If a reasonable person would feel free to terminate the encounter, then or she has not been seized. The reasonable person test is objective and presupposes an innocent person."

Most recently, in Brendlin v. California, 127 S. Ct. 2400 (2007), the Supreme Court expressly applied *Mendenhall* and concluded that passengers are seized when they are riding in a car stopped by police officers. Justice Souter, writing for a unanimous Court, stated: "When a police officer makes a traffic stop, the driver of the car is seized within the meaning of the Fourth Amendment. The question in this case is whether the same is true of a passenger. We hold that a passenger is seized as well and so may challenge the constitutionality of the stop." *Brendlin* is presented in detail in Chapter 3, which focuses on the exclusionary rule, because the effect of finding a seizure is that the passenger can invoke the exclusionary rule by arguing that the police acted illegally.

Under this test is there a seizure if police officers chase someone? At what point does that become a seizure? That was the issue addressed by the Court in California v. Hodari D.

CALIFORNIA v. HODARI D.
499 U.S. 621 (1991)

Justice SCALIA delivered the opinion of the Court.

Late one evening in April 1988, Officers Brian McColgin and Jerry Pertoso were on patrol in a high-crime area of Oakland, California. They were dressed in street clothes but wearing jackets with "Police" embossed on both front and back. Their unmarked car proceeded west on Foothill Boulevard, and turned south onto 63rd Avenue. As they rounded the corner, they saw four or five youths huddled around a small red car parked at the curb. When the youths saw the officers' car approaching they apparently panicked, and took flight. The respondent here, Hodari D., and one companion ran west through an alley; the others fled south. The red car also headed south, at a high rate of speed.

The officers were suspicious and gave chase. McColgin remained in the car and continued south on 63rd Avenue; Pertoso left the car, ran back north along 63rd, then west on Foothill Boulevard, and turned south on 62nd Avenue.

Hodari, meanwhile, emerged from the alley onto 62nd and ran north. Looking behind as he ran, he did not turn and see Pertoso until the officer was almost upon him, whereupon he tossed away what appeared to be a small rock. A moment later, Pertoso tackled Hodari, handcuffed him, and radioed for assistance. Hodari was found to be carrying $130 in cash and a pager; and the rock he had discarded was found to be crack cocaine.

In the juvenile proceeding brought against him, Hodari moved to suppress the evidence relating to the cocaine. The court denied the motion without opinion. The California Court of Appeal reversed, holding that Hodari had been "seized" when he saw Officer Pertoso running towards him, that this seizure was unreasonable under the Fourth Amendment, and that the evidence of cocaine had to be suppressed as the fruit of that illegal seizure. As this case comes to us, the only issue presented is whether, at the time he dropped the drugs, Hodari had been "seized" within the meaning of the Fourth Amendment. If so, respondent argues, the drugs were the fruit of that seizure and the evidence concerning them was properly excluded. If not, the drugs were abandoned by Hodari and lawfully recovered by the police, and the evidence should have been admitted. (In addition, of course, Pertoso's seeing the rock of cocaine, at least if he recognized it as such, would provide reasonable suspicion for the unquestioned seizure that occurred when he tackled Hodari.

We have long understood that the Fourth Amendment's protection against "unreasonable . . . seizures" includes seizure of the person. From the time of the founding to the present, the word "seizure" has meant a "taking possession." For most purposes at common law, the word connoted not merely grasping, or applying physical force to, the animate or inanimate object in question, but actually bringing it within physical control. A ship still fleeing, even though under attack, would not be considered to have been seized as a war prize. A res capable of manual delivery was not seized until "tak[en] into custody." To constitute an arrest, however — the quintessential "seizure of the person" under our Fourth Amendment jurisprudence — the mere grasping or application of physical force with lawful authority, whether or not it succeeded in subduing the arrestee, was sufficient.

To say that an arrest is effected by the slightest application of physical force, despite the arrestee's escape, is not to say that for Fourth Amendment purposes there is a continuing arrest during the period of fugitivity. If, for example, Pertoso had laid his hands upon Hodari to arrest him, but Hodari had broken away and had then cast away the cocaine, it would hardly be realistic to say that that disclosure had been made during the course of an arrest. The present case, however, is even one step further removed. It does not involve the application of any physical force; Hodari was untouched by Officer Pertoso at the time he discarded the cocaine. His defense relies instead upon the proposition that a seizure occurs "when the officer, by means of physical force or show of authority, has in some way restrained the liberty of a citizen." Hodari contends (and we accept as true for purposes of this decision) that Pertoso's pursuit qualified as a "show of authority" calling upon Hodari to halt. The narrow question before us is whether, with respect to a show of authority as with respect to application of physical force, a seizure occurs even though the subject does not yield. We hold that it does not.

The language of the Fourth Amendment, of course, cannot sustain respondent's contention. The word "seizure" readily bears the meaning of a laying on of hands or application of physical force to restrain movement, even when it is ultimately unsuccessful. ("She seized the purse-snatcher, but he broke out of her grasp.") It does not remotely apply, however, to the prospect of a policeman yelling "Stop, in the name of the law!" at a fleeing form that continues to flee. That is no seizure. Nor can the result respondent wishes to achieve be produced—indirectly, as it were—by suggesting that Pertoso's uncomplied-with show of authority was a common-law arrest, and then appealing to the principle that all common-law arrests are seizures. An arrest requires either physical force (as described above) or, where that is absent, submission to the assertion of authority.

We do not think it desirable, even as a policy matter, to stretch the Fourth Amendment beyond its words and beyond the meaning of arrest, as respondent urges. Street pursuits always place the public at some risk, and compliance with police orders to stop should therefore be encouraged. Only a few of those orders, we must presume, will be without adequate basis, and since the addressee has no ready means of identifying the deficient ones it almost invariably is the responsible course to comply. Unlawful orders will not be deterred, moreover, by sanctioning through the exclusionary rule those of them that are not obeyed. Since policemen do not command "Stop!" expecting to be ignored, or give chase hoping to be outrun, it fully suffices to apply the deterrent to their genuine, successful seizures.

Respondent contends that his position is sustained by the so-called *Mendenhall* test: "[A] person has been 'seized' within the meaning of the Fourth Amendment only if, in view of all the circumstances surrounding the incident, a reasonable person would have believed that he was not free to leave." In seeking to rely upon that test here, respondent fails to read it carefully. It says that a person has been seized "only if," not that he has been seized "whenever"; it states a necessary, but not a sufficient, condition for seizure—or, more precisely, for seizure effected through a "show of authority." *Mendenhall* establishes that the test for existence of a "show of authority" is an objective one: not whether the citizen perceived that he was being ordered to restrict his movement, but whether the officer's words and actions would have conveyed that to a reasonable person.

In sum, assuming that Pertoso's pursuit in the present case constituted a "show of authority" enjoining Hodari to halt, since Hodari did not comply with that injunction he was not seized until he was tackled. The cocaine abandoned while he was running was in this case not the fruit of a seizure, and his motion to exclude evidence of it was properly denied.

Justice STEVENS, with whom Justice MARSHALL joins, dissenting.

The Court's narrow construction of the word "seizure" represents a significant, and in my view, unfortunate, departure from prior case law construing the Fourth Amendment. Almost a quarter of a century ago, in two landmark cases— one broadening the protection of individual privacy, and the other broadening the powers of law enforcement officers—we rejected the method of Fourth Amendment analysis that today's majority endorses. In particular, the Court now adopts a definition of "seizure" that is unfaithful to a long line of Fourth Amendment cases. Even if the Court were defining seizure for the first time, which it is not, the definition that it chooses today is profoundly unwise. In its decision, the Court assumes, without acknowledging, that a police officer may now fire his weapon at an innocent citizen and not implicate the Fourth Amendment — as long as he misses his target.

In *United States v. Mendenhall* (1980), the Court "adhere[d] to the view that a person is 'seized' only when, by means of physical force or a show of authority, his freedom of movement is restrained." The Court looked to whether the citizen who is questioned "remains free to disregard the questions and walk away," and if he or she is able to do so, then "there has been no intrusion upon that person's liberty or privacy" that would require some "particularized and objective justification" under the Constitution. The test for a "seizure," as formulated by the Court in *Mendenhall*, was whether, "in view of all of the circumstances surrounding the incident, a reasonable person would have believed that he was not free to leave." Examples of seizures include "the threatening presence of several officers, the display of a weapon by an officer, some physical touching of the person of the citizen, or the use of language or tone of voice indicating that compliance with the officer's request might be compelled." The Court's unwillingness today to adhere to the "reasonable person" standard, as formulated by Justice Stewart in *Mendenhall*, marks an unnecessary departure from Fourth Amendment case law.

The Court today draws the novel conclusion that even though no seizure can occur unless the *Mendenhall* reasonable person standard is met, the fact that the standard has been met does not necessarily mean that a seizure has occurred.

Even though momentary, a seizure occurs whenever an objective evaluation of a police officer's show of force conveys the message that the citizen is not entirely free to leave — in other words, that his or her liberty is being restrained in a significant way. [T]he Court understood the *Mendenhall* definition as both necessary and sufficient to describe a Fourth Amendment seizure.

Whatever else one may think of today's decision, it unquestionably represents a departure from earlier Fourth Amendment case law. The notion that our prior cases contemplated a distinction between seizures effected by a touching on the one hand, and those effected by a show of force on the other hand, and that all of our repeated descriptions of the *Mendenhall* test stated only a necessary, but not a sufficient, condition for finding seizures in the latter category, is nothing if not creative lawmaking. Moreover, by narrowing the definition of the term seizure, instead of enlarging the scope of reasonable justifications for seizures, the Court has significantly limited the protection provided to the ordinary citizen by the Fourth Amendment.

In this case the officer's show of force — taking the form of a head-on chase — adequately conveyed the message that respondent was not free to leave. Whereas in *Mendenhall*, there was "nothing in the record [to] sugges[t] that the respondent had any objective reason to believe that she was not free to end the conversation in the concourse and proceed on her way," here, respondent attempted to end "the conversation" before it began and soon found himself literally "not free to leave" when confronted by an officer running toward him head-on who eventually tackled him to the ground. There was an interval of time between the moment that respondent saw the officer fast approaching and the moment when he was tackled, and thus brought under the control of the officer. The question is whether the Fourth Amendment was implicated at the earlier or the later moment.

It is too early to know the consequences of the Court's holding. If carried to its logical conclusion, it will encourage unlawful displays of force that will frighten countless innocent citizens into surrendering whatever privacy rights they may still have. The message that today's literal-minded majority conveys is that the common law, rather than our understanding of the Fourth Amendment as it has developed over the last quarter of a century, defines, and limits, the scope of a seizure. The Court today defines a seizure as commencing, not with egregious police conduct, but rather with submission by the citizen. Thus, it both delays the point at which "the Fourth Amendment becomes relevant" to an encounter and limits the range of encounters that will come under the heading of "seizure." Today's qualification of the Fourth Amendment means that innocent citizens may remain "secure in their persons . . . against unreasonable searches and seizures" only at the discretion of the police.

3.   For What Crimes May a Person Be Arrested?

May the police arrest a person for a crime that has no possibility of a prison sentence? The Court said yes in Atwater v. Lago Vista, a case that produced a vehement dissent and attracted a great deal of media attention.

ATWATER v. CITY OF LAGO VISTA
532 U.S. 318 (2001)

Justice SOUTER delivered the opinion of the Court.

The question is whether the Fourth Amendment forbids a warrantless arrest for a minor criminal offense, such as a misdemeanor seatbelt violation punishable only by a fine. We hold that it does not.

I

In Texas, if a car is equipped with safety belts, a front-seat passenger must wear one, and the driver must secure any small child riding in front. Violation of either provision is "a misdemeanor punishable by a fine not less than $25 or more than $50." Texas law expressly authorizes "[a]ny peace officer [to] arrest without warrant a person found committing a violation" of these seatbelt laws, although it permits police to issue citations in lieu of arrest.

In March 1997, petitioner Gail Atwater was driving her pickup truck in Lago Vista, Texas, with her 3-year-old son and 5-year-old daughter in the front seat. None of them was wearing a seatbelt. Respondent Bart Turek, a Lago Vista police officer at the time, observed the seatbelt violations and pulled Atwater over. According to Atwater's complaint (the allegations of which we assume to be true for present purposes), Turek approached the truck and "yell[ed]" something to the effect of "[w]e've met before" and "[y]ou're going to jail." He then called for backup and asked to see Atwater's driver's license and insurance documentation, which state law required her to carry. When Atwater told Turek that she did not have the papers because her purse had been stolen the day before, Turek said that he had "heard that story two-hundred times."

Atwater asked to take her "frightened, upset, and crying" children to a friend's house nearby, but Turek told her, "[y]ou're not going anywhere."

As it turned out, Atwater's friend learned what was going on and soon arrived to take charge of the children. Turek then handcuffed Atwater, placed her in his squad car, and drove her to the local police station, where booking officers had her remove her shoes, jewelry, and eyeglasses, and empty her pockets. Officers took Atwater's "mug shot" and placed her, alone, in a jail cell for about one hour, after which she was taken before a magistrate and released on $310 bond.

Atwater was charged with driving without her seatbelt fastened, failing to secure her children in seatbelts, driving without a license, and failing to provide proof of insurance. She ultimately pleaded no contest to the misdemeanor seatbelt offenses and paid a $50 fine; the other charges were dismissed.

Atwater and her husband, petitioner Michael Haas, filed suit in a Texas state court under 42 U.S.C. § 1983 against Turek and respondents City of Lago Vista and Chief of Police Frank Miller. So far as concerns us, petitioners (whom we will simply call Atwater) alleged that respondents (for simplicity, the City) had violated Atwater's Fourth Amendment "right to be free from unreasonable seizure," and sought compensatory and punitive damages.

II

In reading the [Fourth] Amendment, we are guided by "the traditional protections against unreasonable searches and seizures afforded by the common law at the time of the framing," since "[a]n examination of the common-law understanding of an officer's authority to arrest sheds light on the obviously relevant, if not entirely dispositive, consideration of what the Framers of the Amendment might have thought to be reasonable." Thus, the first step here is to assess Atwater's claim that peace officers' authority to make warrantless arrests for misdemeanors was restricted at common law (whether "common law" is understood strictly as law judicially derived or, instead, as the whole body of law extant at the time of the framing). Atwater's specific contention is that "founding-era common-law rules" forbade peace officers to make warrantless misdemeanor arrests except in cases of "breach of the peace," a category she claims was then understood narrowly as covering only those nonfelony offenses "involving or tending toward violence."

Although her historical argument is by no means insubstantial, it ultimately fails. We begin with the state of pre-founding English common law and find that, even after making some allowance for variations in the common-law usage of the term "breach of the peace," the "founding-era common-law rules" were not nearly as clear as Atwater claims; on the contrary, the common-law commentators (as well as the sparsely reported cases) reached divergent conclusions with respect to officers' warrantless misdemeanor arrest power. Moreover, in the years leading up to American independence, Parliament repeatedly extended express warrantless arrest authority to cover misdemeanor-level offenses not amounting to or involving any violent breach of the peace. [The Court reviewed in detail English common law decisions.] We find disagreement, not unanimity, among both the common-law jurists and the text writers who sought to pull the cases together and summarize accepted practice. Having reviewed the relevant English decisions, as well as English and colonial American legal treatises, legal dictionaries, and procedure manuals, we simply are not convinced that Atwater's is the correct, or even necessarily the better, reading of the common-law history.

A second, and equally serious, problem for Atwater's historical argument is posed by the "divers Statutes," enacted by Parliament well before this Republic's founding that authorized warrantless misdemeanor arrests without reference to violence or turmoil.

An examination of specifically American evidence is to the same effect. Neither the history of the framing era nor subsequent legal development indicates that the Fourth Amendment was originally understood, or has traditionally been read, to embrace Atwater's position.

To begin with, Atwater has cited no particular evidence that those who framed and ratified the Fourth Amendment sought to limit peace officers' warrantless misdemeanor arrest authority to instances of actual breach of the peace, and our own review of the recent and respected compilations of framing-era documentary history has likewise failed to reveal any such design. Nor have we found in any of the modern historical accounts of the Fourth Amendment's adoption any substantial indication that the Framers intended such a restriction. Indeed, to the extent these modern histories address the issue, their conclusions are to the contrary.

The evidence of actual practice also counsels against Atwater's position. During the period leading up to and surrounding the framing of the Bill of Rights, colonial and state legislatures, like Parliament before them, regularly authorized local peace officers to make warrantless misdemeanor arrests without conditioning statutory authority on breach of the peace.

Nor does Atwater's argument from tradition pick up any steam from the historical record as it has unfolded since the framing, there being no indication that her claimed rule has ever become "woven . . . into the fabric" of American law. The story, on the contrary, is of two centuries of uninterrupted (and largely unchallenged) state and federal practice permitting warrantless arrests for misdemeanors not amounting to or involving breach of the peace.

Small wonder, then, that today statutes in all 50 States and the District of Columbia permit warrantless misdemeanor arrests by at least some (if not all) peace officers without requiring any breach of the peace, as do a host of congressional enactments.

III

While it is true here that history, if not unequivocal, has expressed a decided, majority view that the police need not obtain an arrest warrant merely because a misdemeanor stopped short of violence or a threat of it, Atwater does not wager all on history. Instead, she asks us to mint a new rule of constitutional law on the understanding that when historical practice fails to speak conclusively to a claim grounded on the Fourth Amendment, courts are left to strike a current balance between individual and societal interests by subjecting particular contemporary circumstances to traditional standards of reasonableness. Atwater accordingly argues for a modern arrest rule, one not necessarily requiring violent breach of the peace, but nonetheless forbidding custodial arrest, even upon probable cause, when conviction could not ultimately carry any jail time and when the government shows no compelling need for immediate detention.

If we were to derive a rule exclusively to address the uncontested facts of this case, Atwater might well prevail. She was a known and established resident of

Lago Vista with no place to hide and no incentive to flee, and common sense says she would almost certainly have buckled up as a condition of driving off with a citation. In her case, the physical incidents of arrest were merely gratuitous humiliations imposed by a police officer who was (at best) exercising extremely poor judgment. Atwater's claim to live free of pointless indignity and confinement clearly outweighs anything the City can raise against it specific to her case.

But we have traditionally recognized that a responsible Fourth Amendment balance is not well served by standards requiring sensitive, case-by-case determinations of government need, lest every discretionary judgment in the field be converted into an occasion for constitutional review. Often enough, the Fourth Amendment has to be applied on the spur (and in the heat) of the moment, and the object in implementing its command of reasonableness is to draw standards sufficiently clear and simple to be applied with a fair prospect of surviving judicial second-guessing months and years after an arrest or search is made. Courts attempting to strike a reasonable Fourth Amendment balance thus credit the government's side with an essential interest in readily administrable rules.

At first glance, Atwater's argument may seem to respect the values of clarity and simplicity, so far as she claims that the Fourth Amendment generally forbids warrantless arrests for minor crimes not accompanied by violence or some demonstrable threat of it (whether "minor crime" be defined as a fine-only traffic offense, a fine-only offense more generally, or a misdemeanor). But the claim is not ultimately so simple, nor could it be, for complications arise the moment we begin to think about the possible applications of the several criteria Atwater proposes for drawing a line between minor crimes with limited arrest authority and others not so restricted.

One line, she suggests, might be between "jailable" and "fine-only" offenses, between those for which conviction could result in commitment and those for which it could not. The trouble with this distinction, of course, is that an officer on the street might not be able to tell. It is not merely that we cannot expect every police officer to know the details of frequently complex penalty schemes, but that penalties for ostensibly identical conduct can vary on account of facts difficult (if not impossible) to know at the scene of an arrest. Is this the first offense or is the suspect a repeat offender? Is the weight of the marijuana a gram above or a gram below the fine-only line? Where conduct could implicate more than one criminal prohibition, which one will the district attorney ultimately decide to charge? And so on.

But Atwater's refinements would not end there. She represents that if the line were drawn at nonjailable traffic offenses, her proposed limitation should be qualified by a proviso authorizing warrantless arrests where "necessary for enforcement of the traffic laws or when [an] offense would otherwise continue and pose a danger to others on the road." (Were the line drawn at misdemeanors generally, a comparable qualification would presumably apply.) The proviso only compounds the difficulties. Would, for instance, either exception apply to speeding? But is it not fair to expect that the chronic speeder will speed again despite a citation in his pocket, and should that not qualify as showing that the "offense would . . . continue" under Atwater's rule? And why, as a constitutional matter, should we assume that only reckless driving will "pose a danger to others on the road" while speeding will not?

There is no need for more examples to show that Atwater's general rule and limiting proviso promise very little in the way of administrability. It is no answer that the police routinely make judgments on grounds like risk of immediate repetition; they surely do and should. But there is a world of difference between making that judgment in choosing between the discretionary leniency of a summons in place of a clearly lawful arrest, and making the same judgment when the question is the lawfulness of the warrantless arrest itself. It is the difference between no basis for legal action challenging the discretionary judgment, on the one hand, and the prospect of evidentiary exclusion or (as here) personal § 1983 liability for the misapplication of a constitutional standard, on the other. Atwater's rule therefore would not only place police in an almost impossible spot but would guarantee increased litigation over many of the arrests that would occur. For all these reasons, Atwater's various distinctions between permissible and impermissible arrests for minor crimes strike us as "very unsatisfactory line[s]" to require police officers to draw on a moment's notice.

Accordingly, we confirm today what our prior cases have intimated: the standard of probable cause "applie[s] to all arrests, without the need to 'balance' the interests and circumstances involved in particular situations." If an officer has probable cause to believe that an individual has committed even a very minor criminal offense in his presence, he may, without violating the Fourth Amendment, arrest the offender.

Atwater's arrest satisfied constitutional requirements. There is no dispute that Officer Turek had probable cause to believe that Atwater had committed a crime in his presence. She admits that neither she nor her children were wearing seatbelts, as required. Turek was accordingly authorized (not required, but authorized) to make a custodial arrest without balancing costs and benefits or determining whether or not Atwater's arrest was in some sense necessary.

Justice O'CONNOR, with whom Justice STEVENS, Justice GINSBURG, and Justice BREYER join, dissenting.

The Fourth Amendment guarantees the right to be free from "unreasonable searches and seizures." The Court recognizes that the arrest of Gail Atwater was a "pointless indignity" that served no discernible state interest, and yet holds that her arrest was constitutionally permissible. Because the Court's position is inconsistent with the explicit guarantee of the Fourth Amendment, I dissent.

I

A full custodial arrest, such as the one to which Ms. Atwater was subjected, is the quintessential seizure. When a full custodial arrest is effected without a warrant, the plain language of the Fourth Amendment requires that the arrest be reasonable. It is beyond cavil that "[t]he touchstone of our analysis under the Fourth Amendment is always 'the reasonableness in all the circumstances of the particular governmental invasion of a citizen's personal security.'"

We have "often looked to the common law in evaluating the reasonableness, for Fourth Amendment purposes, of police activity." But history is just one of the tools we use in conducting the reasonableness inquiry. And when history is inconclusive, as the majority amply demonstrates it is in this case, we will "evaluate the search or seizure under traditional standards of reasonableness by assessing, on the one hand, the degree to which it intrudes upon an individual's privacy and, on the other, the degree to which it is needed for the promotion of legitimate governmental interests."

The majority gives a brief nod to this bedrock principle of our Fourth Amendment jurisprudence, and even acknowledges that "Atwater's claim to live free of pointless indignity and confinement clearly outweighs anything the City can raise against it specific to her case." But instead of remedying this imbalance, the majority allows itself to be swayed by the worry that "every discretionary judgment in the field [will] be converted into an occasion for constitutional review." It therefore mints a new rule that "[i]f an officer has probable cause to believe that an individual has committed even a very minor criminal offense in his presence, he may, without violating the Fourth Amendment, arrest the offender." This rule is not only unsupported by our precedent, but runs contrary to the principles that lie at the core of the Fourth Amendment.

As the majority tacitly acknowledges, we have never considered the precise question presented here, namely, the constitutionality of a warrantless arrest for an offense punishable only by fine. Indeed, on the rare occasions that Members of this Court have contemplated such an arrest, they have indicated disapproval.

A custodial arrest exacts an obvious toll on an individual's liberty and privacy, even when the period of custody is relatively brief. The arrestee is subject to a full search of her person and confiscation of her possessions. If the arrestee is the occupant of a car, the entire passenger compartment of the car, including packages therein, is subject to search as well. The arrestee may be detained for up to 48 hours without having a magistrate determine whether there in fact was probable cause for the arrest. See County of Riverside v. McLaughlin (1991). Because people arrested for all types of violent and nonviolent offenses may be housed together awaiting such review, this detention period is potentially dangerous. And once the period of custody is over, the fact of the arrest is a permanent part of the public record.

We have said that "the penalty that may attach to any particular offense seems to provide the clearest and most consistent indication of the State's interest in arresting individuals suspected of committing that offense." If the State has decided that a fine, and not imprisonment, is the appropriate punishment for an offense, the State's interest in taking a person suspected of committing that offense into custody is surely limited, at best. This is not to say that the State will never have such an interest. A full custodial arrest may on occasion vindicate legitimate state interests, even if the crime is punishable only by fine. Arrest is the surest way to abate criminal conduct. It may also allow the police to verify the offender's identity and, if the offender poses a flight risk, to ensure her appearance at trial. But when such considerations are not present, a citation or summons may serve the State's remaining law enforcement interests every bit as effectively as an arrest.

Because a full custodial arrest is such a severe intrusion on an individual's liberty, its reasonableness hinges on "the degree to which it is needed for the promotion of legitimate governmental interests." In light of the availability of citations to promote a State's interests when a fine-only offense has been committed, I cannot concur in a rule which deems a full custodial arrest to be reasonable in every circumstance. Giving police officers constitutional carte blanche to effect an arrest whenever there is probable cause to believe a fine-only misdemeanor has been committed is irreconcilable with the Fourth

Amendment's command that seizures be reasonable. Instead, I would require that when there is probable cause to believe that a fine-only offense has been committed, the police officer should issue a citation unless the officer is "able to point to specific and articulable facts which, taken together with rational inferences from those facts, reasonably warrant [the additional] intrusion" of a full custodial arrest.

The record in this case makes it abundantly clear that Ms. Atwater's arrest was constitutionally unreasonable. While Turek was justified in stopping Atwater, neither law nor reason supports his decision to arrest her instead of simply giving her a citation. The officer's actions cannot sensibly be viewed as a permissible means of balancing Atwater's Fourth Amendment interests with the State's own legitimate interests.

There is no question that Officer Turek's actions severely infringed Atwater's liberty and privacy. Turek was loud and accusatory from the moment he approached Atwater's car. Atwater's young children were terrified and hysterical. Yet when Atwater asked Turek to lower his voice because he was scaring the children, he responded by jabbing his finger in Atwater's face and saying, "You're going to jail." Having made the decision to arrest, Turek did not inform Atwater of her right to remain silent. He instead asked for her license and insurance information.

Atwater asked if she could at least take her children to a friend's house down the street before going to the police station. But Turek — who had just castigated Atwater for not caring for her children — refused and said he would take the children into custody as well. Only the intervention of neighborhood children who had witnessed the scene and summoned one of Atwater's friends saved the children from being hauled to jail with their mother.

With the children gone, Officer Turek handcuffed Ms. Atwater with her hands behind her back, placed her in the police car, and drove her to the police station. Ironically, Turek did not secure Atwater in a seatbelt for the drive. At the station, Atwater was forced to remove her shoes, relinquish her possessions, and wait in a holding cell for about an hour. A judge finally informed Atwater of her rights and the charges against her, and released her when she posted bond. Atwater returned to the scene of the arrest, only to find that her car had been towed.

Ms. Atwater ultimately pleaded no contest to violating the seatbelt law and was fined $50. The city's justifications fall far short of rationalizing the extraordinary intrusion on Gail Atwater and her children. Measuring "the degree to which [Atwater's custodial arrest was] needed for the promotion of legitimate governmental interests," against "the degree to which it intrud[ed] upon [her] privacy," it can hardly be doubted that Turek's actions were disproportionate to Atwater's crime. The majority's assessment that "Atwater's claim to live free of pointless indignity and confinement clearly outweighs anything the City can raise against it specific to her case," is quite correct. In my view, the Fourth Amendment inquiry ends there.

The Court's error, however, does not merely affect the disposition of this case. The per se rule that the Court creates has potentially serious consequences for the everyday lives of Americans. A broad range of conduct falls into the category of fine-only misdemeanors. In Texas alone, for example, disobeying any sort of traffic warning sign is a misdemeanor punishable only by fine, as is failing to pay a highway toll, and driving with expired license plates. Nor are fine-only crimes limited to the traffic context. In several States, for example, littering is a criminal offense punishable only by fine.

To be sure, such laws are valid and wise exercises of the States' power to protect the public health and welfare. My concern lies not with the decision to enact or enforce these laws, but rather with the manner in which they may be enforced. Under today's holding, when a police officer has probable cause to believe that a fine-only misdemeanor offense has occurred, that officer may stop the suspect, issue a citation, and let the person continue on her way. Or, if a traffic violation, the officer may stop the car, arrest the driver, search the driver, search the entire passenger compartment of the car including any purse or package inside, and impound the car and inventory all of its contents.

Although the Fourth Amendment expressly requires that the latter course be a reasonable and proportional response to the circumstances of the offense, the majority gives officers unfettered discretion to choose that course without articulating a single reason why such action is appropriate. Such unbounded discretion carries with it grave potential for abuse. After today, the arsenal available to any officer extends to a full arrest and the searches permissible concomitant to that arrest. The Court neglects the Fourth Amendment's express command in the name of administrative ease. In so doing, it cloaks the pointless indignity that Gail Atwater suffered with the mantle of reasonableness.

G. STOP AND FRISK

The prior section discusses seizures under the Fourth Amendment, whether in an arrest or in a police stop. There is, though, an important difference between arrests and stops under the Fourth Amendment. For example, for an arrest there must be probable cause, but for a stop there only has to be reasonable suspicion. If a person is arrested, police can do a search incident to the arrest. But if a person is stopped, there can be a frisk only if there is reasonable suspicion that the person has a weapon that might endanger the police. If a person driving a car is arrested based on probable cause, the police may search the car (New York v. Belton, above); but if a person is stopped, there can be an inspection only of the area where the driver might obtain a weapon after returning to the car (Michigan v. Long, below).

This section examines the topic of stops and frisks. First, the authority for police stops and frisks is presented. Second, the distinction between stops and arrests is considered. Third, there is discussion of what police may do when they stop an individual. Finally, the important question of what is sufficient for reasonable suspicion is examined.

1. The Authority for Police to Stop and Frisk

The seminal case granting police the power to stop and frisk individuals based on reasonable suspicion (as opposed to probable cause) is Terry v. Ohio.

TERRY v. OHIO
392 U.S. 1 (1968)

Chief Justice WARREN delivered the opinion of the Court.

This case presents serious questions concerning the role of the Fourth Amendment in the confrontation on the street between the citizen and the policeman investigating suspicious circumstances.

Petitioner Terry was convicted of carrying a concealed weapon and sentenced to the statutorily prescribed term of one to three years in the penitentiary. Following the denial of a pretrial motion to suppress, the prosecution introduced in evidence two revolvers and a number of bullets seized from Terry and a codefendant, Richard Chilton, by Cleveland Police Detective Martin McFadden. At the hearing on the motion to suppress this evidence, Officer McFadden testified that while he was patrolling in plain clothes in downtown Cleveland at approximately 2:30 in the afternoon of October 31, 1963, his attention was attracted by two men, Chilton and Terry, standing on the corner of Huron Road and Euclid Avenue. He had never seen the two men before, and he was unable to say precisely what first drew his eye to them. However, he testified that he had been a policeman for 39 years and a detective for 35 and that he had been assigned to patrol this vicinity of downtown Cleveland for shoplifters and pick-pockets for 30 years. He explained that he had developed routine habits of observation over the years and that he would "stand and watch people or walk and watch people at many intervals of the day." He added: "Now, in this case when I looked over they didn't look right to me at the time."

His interest aroused, Officer McFadden took up a post of observation in the entrance to a store 300 to 400 feet away from the two men. "I get more purpose to watch them when I see their movements," he testified. He saw one of the men leave the other one and walk southwest on Huron Road, past some stores. The man paused for a moment and looked in a store window, then walked on a short distance, turned around and walked back toward the corner, pausing once again to look in the same store window. He rejoined his companion at the corner, and the two conferred briefly. Then the second man went through the same series of motions, strolling down Huron Road, looking in the same window, walking on a short distance, turning back, peering in the store window again, and returning to confer with the first man at the corner. The two men repeated this ritual alternately between five and six times apiece — in all, roughly a dozen trips. At one point, while the two were standing together on the corner, a third man approached them and engaged them briefly in conversation. This man then left the two others and walked west on Euclid Avenue. Chilton and Terry resumed their measured pacing, peering and conferring. After this had gone on for 10 to 12 minutes, the two men walked off together, heading west on Euclid Avenue, following the path taken earlier by the third man.

By this time Officer McFadden had become thoroughly suspicious. He testified that after observing their elaborately casual and oft-repeated reconnaissance of the store window on Huron Road, he suspected the two men of "casing a job, a stick-up," and that he considered it his duty as a police officer to investigate further. He added that he feared "they may have a gun." Thus, Officer McFadden followed Chilton and Terry and saw them stop in front of Zucker's store to talk to the same man who had conferred with them earlier on the street corner. Deciding that the situation was ripe for direct action, Officer McFadden approached the three men, identified himself as a police officer and asked for their names. At this point his knowledge was confined to what he had observed. He was not acquainted with any of the three men by name or by sight, and he had received no information concerning them from any other source. When the men "mumbled something" in response to his inquiries, Officer McFadden grabbed petitioner Terry, spun him around so that they were facing the other two, with Terry between McFadden and the others, and patted down the outside of his clothing. In the left breast pocket of Terry's overcoat Officer McFadden felt a pistol. He reached inside the overcoat pocket, but was unable to remove the gun. At this point, keeping Terry between himself and the others, the officer ordered all three men to enter Zucker's store. As they went in, he removed Terry's overcoat completely, removed a .38-caliber revolver from the pocket and ordered all three men to face the wall with their hands raised. Officer McFadden proceeded to pat down the outer clothing of Chilton and the third man, Katz. He discovered another revolver in the outer pocket of Chilton's overcoat, but no weapons were found on Katz. The officer testified that he only patted the men down to see whether they had weapons, and that he did not put his hands beneath the outer garments of either Terry or Chilton until he felt their guns. So far as appears from the record, he never placed his hands beneath Katz' outer garments. Officer McFadden seized Chilton's gun, asked the proprietor of the store to call a police wagon, and took all three men to the station, where Chilton and Terry were formally charged with carrying concealed weapons.

On the motion to suppress the guns the prosecution took the position that they had been seized following a search incident to a lawful arrest. The trial court rejected this theory, stating that it "would be stretching the facts beyond reasonable comprehension" to find that Officer McFadden had had probable cause to arrest the men before he patted them down for weapons. However, the court denied the defendants' motion on the ground that Officer McFadden, on the basis of his experience, "had reasonable cause to believe that the defendants were conducting themselves suspiciously, and some interrogation should be made of their action." Purely for his own protection, the court held, the officer had the right to pat down the outer clothing of these men, who he had reasonable cause to believe might be armed. The court distinguished between an investigatory "stop" and an arrest, and between a "frisk" of the outer clothing for weapons and a full-blown search for evidence of crime. The frisk, it held, was essential to the proper performance of the officer's investigatory duties, for without it "the answer to the police officer may be a bullet, and a loaded pistol discovered during the frisk is admissible." After the court denied their motion to suppress, Chilton and Terry waived jury trial and pleaded not guilty. The court adjudged them guilty, and the Court of Appeals for the Eighth Judicial District, Cuyahoga County, affirmed. We affirm the conviction.

I.

The Fourth Amendment provides that "the right of the people to be secure in their persons, houses, papers, and effects, against unreasonable searches and seizures, shall not be violated." This inestimable right of personal security belongs as much to the citizen on the streets of our cities as to the homeowner closeted in his study to dispose of his secret affairs.

We would be less than candid if we did not acknowledge that this question thrusts to the fore difficult and troublesome issues regarding a sensitive area of police activity—issues which have never before been squarely presented to this Court. Reflective of the tensions involved are the practical and constitutional arguments pressed with great vigor on both sides of the public debate over the power of the police to "stop and frisk"—as it is sometimes euphemistically termed—suspicious persons.

On the one hand, it is frequently argued that in dealing with the rapidly unfolding and often dangerous situations on city streets the police are in need of an escalating set of flexible responses, graduated in relation to the amount of information they possess. For this purpose it is urged that distinctions should be made between a "stop" and an "arrest" (or a "seizure" of a person), and between a "frisk" and a "search." Thus, it is argued, the police should be allowed to "stop" a person and detain him briefly for questioning upon suspicion that he may be connected with criminal activity. Upon suspicion that the person may be armed, the police should have the power to "frisk" him for weapons. If the "stop" and the "frisk" give rise to probable cause to believe that the suspect has committed a crime, then the police should be empowered to make a formal "arrest," and a full incident "search" of the person. This scheme is justified in part upon the notion that a "stop" and a "frisk" amount to a mere "minor inconvenience and petty indignity," which can properly be imposed upon the citizen in the interest of effective law enforcement on the basis of a police officer's suspicion.

On the other side the argument is made that the authority of the police must be strictly circumscribed by the law of arrest and search as it has developed to date in the traditional jurisprudence of the Fourth Amendment. It is contended with some force that there is not—and cannot be—a variety of police activity which does not depend solely upon the voluntary cooperation of the citizen and yet which stops short of an arrest based upon probable cause to make such an arrest. The heart of the Fourth Amendment, the argument runs, is a severe requirement of specific justification for any intrusion upon protected personal security, coupled with a highly developed system of judicial controls to enforce upon the agents of the State the commands of the Constitution. Acquiescence by the courts in the compulsion inherent in the field interrogation practices at issue here, it is urged, would constitute an abdication of judicial control over, and indeed an encouragement of, substantial interference with liberty and personal security by police officers whose judgment is necessarily colored by their primary involvement in "the often competitive enterprise of ferreting out crime." This, it is argued, can only serve to exacerbate police-community tensions in the crowded centers of our Nation's cities.

Having thus roughly sketched the perimeters of the constitutional debate over the limits on police investigative conduct in general and the background against which this case presents itself, we turn our attention to the quite narrow question posed by the facts before us: whether it is always unreasonable for a policeman to seize a person and subject him to a limited search for weapons unless there is probable cause for an arrest. Given the narrowness of this question, we have no occasion to canvass in detail the constitutional limitations upon the scope of a policeman's power when he confronts a citizen without probable cause to arrest him.

II.

Our first task is to establish at what point in this encounter the Fourth Amendment becomes relevant. That is, we must decide whether and when Officer McFadden "seized" Terry and whether and when he conducted a "search." There is some suggestion in the use of such terms as "stop" and "frisk" that such police conduct is outside the purview of the Fourth Amendment because neither action rises to the level of a "search" or "seizure" within the meaning of the Constitution. We emphatically reject this notion. It is quite plain that the Fourth Amendment governs "seizures" of the person which do not eventuate in a trip to the station house and prosecution for crime — "arrests" in traditional terminology. It must be recognized that whenever a police officer accosts an individual and restrains his freedom to walk away, he has "seized" that person. And it is nothing less than sheer torture of the English language to suggest that a careful exploration of the outer surfaces of a person's clothing all over his or her body in an attempt to find weapons is not a "search." Moreover, it is simply fantastic to urge that such a procedure performed in public by a policeman while the citizen stands helpless, perhaps facing a wall with his hands raised, is a "petty indignity." It is a serious intrusion upon the sanctity of the person, which may inflict great indignity and arouse strong resentment, and it is not to be undertaken lightly.

We have noted that the abusive practices which play a major, though by no means exclusive, role in creating this friction are not susceptible of control by means of the exclusionary rule, and cannot properly dictate our decision with respect to the powers of the police in genuine investigative and preventive situations. However, the degree of community resentment aroused by particular practices is clearly revelant to an assessment of the quality of the intrusion upon reasonable expectations of personal security caused by those practices.

The danger in the logic which proceeds upon distinctions between a "stop" and an "arrest," or "seizure" of the person, and between a "frisk" and a "search" is twofold. It seeks to isolate from constitutional scrutiny the initial stages of the contact between the policeman and the citizen. And by suggesting a rigid all-or-nothing model of justification and regulation under the Amendment, it obscures the utility of limitations upon the scope, as well as the initiation, of police action as a means of constitutional regulation. The scope of the search must be "strictly tied to and justified by" the circumstances which rendered its initiation permissible.

In our view the sounder course is to recognize that the Fourth Amendment governs all intrusions by agents of the public upon personal security, and to make the scope of the particular intrusion, in light of all the exigencies of the case, a central element in the analysis of reasonableness. This seems preferable to an approach which attributes too much significance to an overly technical definition of "search," and which turns in part upon a judge-made hierarchy of legislative enactments in the criminal sphere. Focusing the inquiry squarely on the dangers and demands of the particular situation also seems more likely to produce rules which are intelligible to the police and the public alike than requiring the officer in the heat of an unfolding encounter on the street to make a judgment as to which laws are "of limited public consequence."

The distinctions of classical "stop-and-frisk" theory thus serve to divert attention from the central inquiry under the Fourth Amendment — the reasonableness in all the circumstances of the particular governmental invasion of a citizen's personal security. "Search" and "seizure" are not talismans. We therefore reject the notions that the Fourth Amendment does not come into play at all as a limitation upon police conduct if the officers stop short of something called a "technical arrest" or a "full-blown search."

In this case there can be no question, then, that Officer McFadden "seized" petitioner and subjected him to a "search" when he took hold of him and patted down the outer surfaces of his clothing. We must decide whether at that point it was reasonable for Officer McFadden to have interfered with petitioner's personal security as he did. And in determining whether the seizure and search were "unreasonable" our inquiry is a dual one — whether the officer's action was justified at its inception, and whether it was reasonably related in scope to the circumstances which justified the interference in the first place.

III.

If this case involved police conduct subject to the Warrant Clause of the Fourth Amendment, we would have to ascertain whether "probable cause" existed to justify the search and seizure which took place. However, that is not the case. We do not retreat from our holdings that the police must, whenever practicable, obtain advance judicial approval of searches and seizures through the warrant procedure, or that in most instances failure to comply with the warrant requirement can only be excused by exigent circumstances. But we deal here with an entire rubric of police conduct — necessarily swift action predicated upon the on-the-spot observations of the officer on the beat — which historically has not been, and as a practical matter could not be, subjected to the warrant procedure. Instead, the conduct involved in this case must be tested by the Fourth Amendment's general proscription against unreasonable searches and seizures.

Nonetheless, the notions which underlie both the warrant procedure and the requirement of probable cause remain fully relevant in this context. In order to assess the reasonableness of Officer McFadden's conduct as a general proposition, it is necessary "first to focus upon the governmental interest which allegedly justifies official intrusion upon the constitutionally protected interests of the private citizen," for there is "no ready test for determining reasonableness other than by balancing the need to search (or seize) against the invasion which the search (or seizure) entails." And in justifying the particular intrusion the police officer must be able to point to specific and articulable facts which, taken together with rational inferences from those facts, reasonably warrant that intrusion. The scheme of the Fourth Amendment becomes meaningful only when it is assured that at some point the conduct of those charged with enforcing the laws can be subjected to the more detached, neutral scrutiny of a judge who must evaluate the reasonableness of a particular search or seizure in light of the particular circumstances. And in making that assessment it is imperative that the facts be judged against an objective standard: would the facts available to the officer at the moment of the seizure or the search "warrant a man of reasonable caution in the belief" that the action taken was appropriate? Anything less would invite intrusions upon constitutionally guaranteed rights based on nothing more substantial than inarticulate hunches, a result this Court has consistently refused to sanction. And simple "good faith on the part of the arresting officer is not enough." If subjective good faith alone were the test, the protections of the Fourth Amendment would evaporate, and the people would be "secure in their persons, houses, papers and effects," only in the discretion of the police.

Applying these principles to this case, we consider first the nature and extent of the governmental interests involved. One general interest is of course that of effective crime prevention and detection; it is this interest which underlies the recognition that a police officer may in appropriate circumstances and in an appropriate manner approach a person for purposes of investigating possibly criminal behavior even though there is no probable cause to make an arrest. It was this legitimate investigative function Officer McFadden was discharging when he decided to approach petitioner and his companions. He had observed Terry, Chilton, and Katz go through a series of acts, each of them perhaps innocent in itself, but which taken together warranted further investigation. There is nothing unusual in two men standing together on a street corner, perhaps waiting for someone. Nor is there anything suspicious about people in such circumstances strolling up and down the street, singly or in pairs. Store windows, moreover, are made to be looked in. But the story is quite different where, as here, two men hover about a street corner for an extended period of time, at the end of which it becomes apparent that they are not waiting for anyone or anything; where these men pace alternately along an identical route, pausing to stare in the same store window roughly 24 times; where each completion of this route is followed immediately by a conference between the two men on the corner; where they are joined in one of these conferences by a third man who leaves swiftly; and where the two men finally follow the third and rejoin him a couple of blocks away. It would have been poor police work indeed for an officer of 30 years'' experience in the detection of thievery from stores in this same neighborhood to have failed to investigate this behavior further.

The crux of this case, however, is not the propriety of Officer McFadden's taking steps to investigate petitioner's suspicious behavior, but rather, whether there was justification for McFadden's invasion of Terry's personal security by searching him for weapons in the course of that investigation. We are now concerned with more than the governmental interest in investigating crime; in addition, there is the more immediate interest of the police officer in taking steps to assure himself that the person with whom he is dealing is not armed with a weapon that could unexpectedly and fatally be used against him. Certainly it would be unreasonable to require that police officers take unnecessary risks in the performance of their duties. American criminals have a long tradition of armed violence, and every year in this country many law enforcement officers are killed in the line of duty, and thousands more are wounded. Virtually all of these deaths and a substantial portion of the injuries are inflicted with guns and knives.

The easy availability of firearms to potential criminals in this country is well known and has provoked much debate. Whatever the merits of gun-control proposals, this fact is relevant to an assessment of the need for some form of self-protective search power.

In view of these facts, we cannot blind ourselves to the need for law enforcement officers to protect themselves and other prospective victims of violence in situations where they may lack probable cause for an arrest. When an officer is justified in believing that the individual whose suspicious behavior he is investigating at close range is armed and presently dangerous to the officer or to others, it would appear to be clearly unreasonable to deny the officer the power to take necessary measures to determine whether the person is in fact carrying a weapon and to neutralize the threat of physical harm.

We must still consider, however, the nature and quality of the intrusion on individual rights which must be accepted if police officers are to be conceded the right to search for weapons in situations where probable cause to arrest for crime is lacking. Even a limited search of the outer clothing for weapons constitutes a severe, though brief, intrusion upon cherished personal security, and it must surely be an annoying, frightening, and perhaps humiliating experience. Petitioner contends that such an intrusion is permissible only incident to a lawful arrest, either for a crime involving the possession of weapons or for a crime the commission of which led the officer to investigate in the first place.

Our evaluation of the proper balance that has to be struck in this type of case leads us to conclude that there must be a narrowly drawn authority to permit a reasonable search for weapons for the protection of the police officer, where he has reason to believe that he is dealing with an armed and dangerous individual, regardless of whether he has probable cause to arrest the individual for a crime. The officer need not be absolutely certain that the individual is armed; the issue is whether a reasonably prudent man in the circumstances would be warranted in the belief that his safety or that of others was in danger. And in determining whether the officer acted reasonably in such circumstances, due weight must be given, not to his inchoate and unparticularized suspicion or "hunch," but to the specific reasonable inferences which he is entitled to draw from the facts in light of his experience.

We need not develop at length in this case, however, the limitations which the Fourth Amendment places upon a protective seizure and search for weapons. These limitations will have to be developed in the concrete factual circumstances of individual cases. Suffice it to note that such a search, unlike a search without a warrant incident to a lawful arrest, is not justified by any need to prevent the disappearance or destruction of evidence of crime. The sole justification of the search in the present situation is the protection of the police officer and others nearby, and it must therefore be confined in scope to an intrusion reasonably designed to discover guns, knives, clubs, or other hidden instruments for the assault of the police officer.

The scope of the search in this case presents no serious problem in light of these standards. Officer McFadden patted down the outer clothing of petitioner and his two companions. He did not place his hands in their pockets or under the outer surface of their garments until he had felt weapons, and then he merely reached for and removed the guns. He never did invade Katz' person beyond the outer surfaces of his clothes, since he discovered nothing in his patdown which might have been a weapon. Officer McFadden confined his search strictly to what was minimally necessary to learn whether the men were armed and to disarm them once he discovered the weapons. He did not conduct a general exploratory search for whatever evidence of criminal activity he might find.

V.

We conclude that the revolver seized from Terry was properly admitted in evidence against him. At the time he seized petitioner and searched him for weapons, Officer McFadden had reasonable grounds to believe that petitioner was armed and dangerous, and it was necessary for the protection of himself and others to take swift measures to discover the true facts and neutralize the threat of harm if it materialized. The policeman carefully restricted his search to what was appropriate to the discovery of the particular items which he sought. Each case of this sort will, of course, have to be decided on its own facts. We merely hold today that where a police officer observes unusual conduct which leads him reasonably to conclude in light of his experience that criminal activity may be afoot and that the persons with whom he is dealing may be armed and presently dangerous, where in the course of investigating this behavior he identifies himself as a policeman and makes reasonable inquiries, and where nothing in the initial stages of the encounter serves to dispel his reasonable fear for his own or others' safety, he is entitled for the protection of himself and others in the area to conduct a carefully limited search of the outer clothing of such persons in an attempt to discover weapons which might be used to assault him. Such a search is a reasonable search under the Fourth Amendment, and any weapons seized may properly be introduced in evidence against the person from whom they were taken.

Justice DOUGLAS, dissenting.

I agree that petitioner was "seized" within the meaning of the Fourth Amendment. I also agree that frisking petitioner and his companions for guns was a "search." But it is a mystery how that "search" and that "seizure" can be constitutional by Fourth Amendment standards, unless there was "probable cause" to believe that (1) a crime had been committed or (2) a crime was in the process of being committed or (3) a crime was about to be committed.

The opinion of the Court disclaims the existence of "probable cause." If loitering were in issue and that was the offense charged, there would be "probable cause" shown. But the crime here is carrying concealed weapons; and there is no basis for concluding that the officer had "probable cause" for believing that that crime was being committed. Had a warrant been sought, a magistrate would, therefore, have been unauthorized to issue one, for he can act only if there is a showing of "probable cause." We hold today that the police have greater authority to make a "seizure" and conduct a "search" than a judge has to authorize such action. We have said precisely the opposite over and over again.

[P]olice officers up to today have been permitted to effect arrests or searches without warrants only when the facts within their personal knowledge would satisfy the constitutional standard of probable cause. At the time of their "seizure" without a warrant they must possess facts concerning the person arrested that would have satisfied a magistrate that "probable cause" was indeed present. The term "probable cause" rings a bell of certainty that is not sounded by phrases such as "reasonable suspicion." Moreover, the meaning of "probable cause" is deeply imbedded in our constitutional history.

To give the police greater power than a magistrate is to take a long step down the totalitarian path. Perhaps such a step is desirable to cope with modern forms of lawlessness. But if it is taken, it should be the deliberate choice of the people through a constitutional amendment. Until the Fourth Amendment, which is closely allied with the Fifth, is rewritten, the person and the effects of the individual are beyond the reach of all government agencies until there are reasonable grounds to believe (probable cause) that a criminal venture has been launched or is about to be launched.

There have been powerful hydraulic pressures throughout our history that bear heavily on the Court to water down constitutional guarantees and give the police the upper hand. That hydraulic pressure has probably never been greater than it is today.

Yet if the individual is no longer to be sovereign, if the police can pick him up whenever they do not like the cut of his jib, if they can "seize" and "search" him in their discretion, we enter a new regime. The decision to enter it should be made only after a full debate by the people of this country.

In assessing *Terry*, it is important to consider a key problem that Chief Justice Warren's majority opinion acknowledged: the likelihood that police may use race as a factor in stopping individuals. African Americans and Latinos frequently describe being stopped by police solely for "driving while black" or "driving while brown." There have been widely reported incidents of famous athletes and actors being stopped seemingly solely for driving a nice car in a predominately white area. Many studies have documented racial disparities in the frequency of stops. *See, e.g.*, David A. Harris, *The Stories, the Statistics, and the Law: Why "Driving While Black" Matters*, 84 Minn. L. Rev. 265 (1999). Although the Supreme Court has not yet decided a case dealing directly with "racial profiling," some cities and states have attempted to outlaw it. It is important to consider whether *Terry* exacerbated the problem of racial profiling and if limits, constitutional or statutory, are possible.

2. The Distinction Between Stops and Arrests

Under Terry v. Ohio, both stops and arrests are seizures within the meaning of the Fourth Amendment. Arrests, though, must be based on probable cause, while stops require only reasonable suspicion. There is often not a bright line to distinguish when a stop becomes an arrest.

The Court has made clear that if a person is detained for sustained interrogation that is an arrest within the meaning of the Fourth Amendment. For example, an arrest has occurred if police officers take a suspect to the station house for questioning. In Dunaway v. New York, 442 U.S. 200 (1979), the Court stated: "[D]etention for custodial interrogation — regardless of its label — intrudes so severely on interests protected by the Fourth Amendment as necessarily to trigger the traditional safeguards against illegal arrest." The Court said that "any exception that could cover a seizure as intrusive as that in this case would threaten to swallow the general rule that the Fourth Amendment seizures are reasonable only if based upon probable cause."

In Florida v. Royer, 460 U.S. 491 (1983), the Court held that taking a suspect from the public area of an airport into a small room constituted an arrest. Justice White, writing for the plurality, clarified the distinction between stops and arrests:

The scope of the intrusion permitted will vary to some extent with the particular facts and circumstances of each case. This much, however, is clear: an investigative detention must be temporary and last no longer than is necessary to effectuate the purpose of the stop. Similarly, the investigative methods employed should be the least intrusive means reasonably available to verify or dispel the officer's suspicion in a short period of time. It is the State's burden to demonstrate that the seizure it seeks to justify on the basis of a reasonable suspicion was sufficiently limited in scope and duration to satisfy the conditions of an investigative seizure.

Similarly, in Hayes v. Florida, 470 U.S. 811 (1985), the Court held that taking a suspect to the police station house for fingerprinting was an arrest and had to be based upon probable cause. Earlier in Davis v. Mississippi, 394 U.S. 21 (1969), the Court found that the Fourth Amendment was violated when police finger-printed and questioned 25 African-American men to match fingerprints found at a rape scene. Neither of these cases, though, hold that fingerprinting, if done in the field as part of a brief encounter, always constitute an arrest.

The duration of the detention also matters in determining whether there has been a stop or an arrest. In United States v. Place, 462 U.S. 696 (1983), the Court found that detaining a person's luggage for 90 minutes was a seizure under the Fourth Amendment. The Court explained that the "limitations applicable to investigative detentions of the person should define the permissible scope of the person's luggage on less than probable cause." The Court noted that it had "never approved a seizure of the person for the prolonged 90 minute period involved here."

But the Court has not imposed rigid time limits in determining when a stop becomes an arrest. In United States v. Sharpe, 470 U.S. 675 (1985), a police officer detained the suspects between 30 and 40 minutes while waiting for the arrival of a Drug Enforcement Agent. The Court ruled that this was a stop, not an arrest. The Court said that "if an investigative stop continues indefinitely, at some point it can no longer be justified as an investigative stop." But the Court said that there is no "hard-and-fast time limit." The Court emphasized that there was no delay "unnecessary to the legitimate investigation of the law enforcement officers." The Court acknowledged the "difficult linedrawing pro-blems in distinguishing an investigative stop from a de facto arrest."

3. What May Police Do When They Stop an Individual?

Terry v. Ohio says that police may frisk an individual if there are reasonable grounds for believing that the person has a weapon that might endanger the officers. In Michigan v. Long, 463 U.S. 1032 (1983), the Court said that if the police reasonably believe that a person might be dangerous, they can conduct a limited investigation of an area from which a person could obtain a weapon. The Court thus said that it was permissible for the police to inspect the areas of the car from which the suspect could obtain a weapon after the stop was completed.

Similarly, the Court has held that when the police arrest a person, they may conduct a prospective sweep of the premises if they have reasonable suspicion that a person might be there who poses a threat to them. In Michigan v. Buie, 494 U.S. 325 (1990), the Court said that such a sweep "may extend only to a cursory inspection of those places where a person may be found."

When the police frisk a person, they may seize any evidence that is apparent to their experienced "plain feel." Minnesota v. Dickerson, 508 U.S. 366 (1993), which is presented above, drew a distinction between "plain touch," which is allowed, and the police manipulating the lining of a person's clothes to look for evidence, which is not permitted.

The Supreme Court recently confronted the question of whether the police may require that a person identify him- or herself when stopped.

HIIBEL v. SIXTH JUDICIAL DIST. COURT OF NEVADA
542 U.S. 177 (2004)

Justice KENNEDY delivered the opinion of the Court.

The petitioner was arrested and convicted for refusing to identify himself during a stop allowed by Terry v. Ohio (1968). He challenges his conviction under the Fourth and Fifth Amendments to the United States Constitution, applicable to the States through the Fourteenth Amendment.

I

The sheriff's department in Humboldt County, Nevada, received an afternoon telephone call reporting an assault. The caller reported seeing a man assault a woman in a red and silver GMC truck on Grass Valley Road. Deputy Sheriff Lee Dove was dispatched to investigate. When the officer arrived at the scene, he found the truck parked on the side of the road. A man was standing by the truck, and a young woman was sitting inside it. The officer observed skid marks in the gravel behind the vehicle, leading him to believe it had come to a sudden stop.

The officer approached the man and explained that he was investigating a report of a fight. The man appeared to be intoxicated. The officer asked him if he had "any identification on [him]," which we understand as a request to produce a driver's license or some other form of written identification. The man refused and asked why the officer wanted to see identification. The officer responded that he was conducting an investigation and needed to see some identification. The unidentified man became agitated and insisted he had done nothing wrong. The officer explained that he wanted to find out who the man was and what he was doing there. After continued refusals to comply with the officer's request for identification, the man began to taunt the officer by placing his hands behind his back and telling the officer to arrest him and take him to jail. This routine kept up for several minutes: The officer asked for identification 11 times and was refused each time. After warning the man that he would be arrested if he continued to refuse to comply, the officer placed him under arrest.

We now know that the man arrested on Grass Valley Road is Larry Dudley Hiibel. Hiibel was charged with "willfully resist[ing], delay[ing] or obstruct[ing] a public officer in discharging or attempting to discharge any legal duty of his office" in violation of Nev. Rev. Stat. (NRS) § 199.280 (2003). The government reasoned that Hiibel had obstructed the officer in carrying out his duties under § 171.123, a Nevada statute that defines the legal rights and duties of a police officer in the context of an investigative stop. Section 171.123 provides in relevant part:

1. Any peace officer may detain any person whom the officer encounters under circumstances which reasonably indicate that the person has committed, is committing or is about to commit a crime.

3. The officer may detain the person pursuant to this section only to ascertain his identity and the suspicious circumstances surrounding his presence abroad. Any person so detained shall identify himself, but may not be compelled to answer any other inquiry of any peace officer.

Hiibel was tried in the Justice Court of Union Township. The court agreed that Hiibel's refusal to identify himself as required by § 171.123 "obstructed and delayed Dove as a public officer in attempting to discharge his duty" in violation of § 199.280. Hiibel was convicted and fined $250.

II

NRS § 171.123(3) is an enactment sometimes referred to as a "stop and identify" statute.

Stop and identify statutes often combine elements of traditional vagrancy laws with provisions intended to regulate police behavior in the course of investigatory stops. The statutes vary from State to State, but all permit an officer to ask or require a suspect to disclose his identity. A few States model their statutes on the Uniform Arrest Act, a model code that permits an officer to stop a person reasonably suspected of committing a crime and "demand of him his name, address, business abroad and whither he is going." In some States, a suspect's refusal to identify himself is a misdemeanor offense or civil violation; in others, it is a factor to be considered in whether the suspect has violated loitering laws. In other States, a suspect may decline to identify himself without penalty.

The present case begins where our prior cases left off. Here there is no question that the initial stop was based on reasonable suspicion, satisfying the Fourth Amendment requirements. Further, the petitioner has not alleged that the statute is unconstitutionally vague. [T]he Nevada Supreme Court has interpreted NRS § 171.123(3) to require only that a suspect disclose his name. As we understand it, the statute does not require a suspect to give the officer a driver's license or any other document. Provided that the suspect either states his name or communicates it to the officer by other means — a choice, we assume, that the suspect may make — the statute is satisfied and no violation occurs.

III

Hiibel argues that his conviction cannot stand because the officer's conduct violated his Fourth Amendment rights. We disagree.

Asking questions is an essential part of police investigations. In the ordinary course a police officer is free to ask a person for identification without implicating the Fourth Amendment. "[I]nterrogation relating to one's identity or a request for identification by the police does not, by itself, constitute a Fourth Amendment seizure." Beginning with Terry v. Ohio (1968), the Court has recognized that a law enforcement officer's reasonable suspicion that a person may be involved in criminal activity permits the officer to stop the person for a brief time and take additional steps to investigate further. To ensure that the resulting seizure is constitutionally reasonable, a *Terry* stop must be limited. The officer's action must be "'justified at its inception, and . . . reasonably related in scope to the circumstances which justified the interference in the first place.'" For example, the seizure can not continue for an excessive period of time, or resemble a traditional arrest.

Our decisions make clear that questions concerning a suspect's identity are a routine and accepted part of many *Terry* stops.

Obtaining a suspect's name in the course of a *Terry* stop serves important government interests. Knowledge of identity may inform an officer that a suspect is wanted for another offense, or has a record of violence or mental disorder. On the other hand, knowing identity may help clear a suspect and allow the police to concentrate their efforts elsewhere. Identity may prove particularly important in cases such as this, where the police are investigating what appears to be a domestic assault. Officers called to investigate domestic disputes need to know whom they are dealing with in order to assess the situation, the threat to their own safety, and possible danger to the potential victim.

Although it is well established that an officer may ask a suspect to identify himself in the course of a *Terry* stop, it has been an open question whether the suspect can be arrested and prosecuted for refusal to answer.

The principles of *Terry* permit a State to require a suspect to disclose his name in the course of a *Terry* stop. The reasonableness of a seizure under the Fourth Amendment is determined "by balancing its intrusion on the individual's Fourth Amendment interests against its promotion of legitimate government interests." The Nevada statute satisfies that standard. The request for identity has an immediate relation to the purpose, rationale, and practical demands of a *Terry* stop. The threat of criminal sanction helps ensure that the request for identity does not become a legal nullity. On the other hand, the Nevada statute does not alter the nature of the stop itself: it does not change its duration or its location. A state law requiring a suspect to disclose his name in the course of a valid *Terry* stop is consistent with Fourth Amendment prohibitions against unreasonable searches and seizures.

Petitioner argues that the Nevada statute circumvents the probable-cause requirement, in effect allowing an officer to arrest a person for being suspicious. According to petitioner, this creates a risk of arbitrary police conduct that the Fourth Amendment does not permit. These are familiar concerns. Petitioner's concerns are met by the requirement that a *Terry* stop must be justified at its inception and "reasonably related in scope to the circumstances which justified" the initial stop. Under these principles, an officer may not arrest a suspect for failure to identify himself if the request for identification is not reasonably related to the circumstances justifying the stop.

It is clear in this case that the request for identification was "reasonably related in scope to the circumstances which justified" the stop. The officer's request was a commonsense inquiry, not an effort to obtain an arrest for failure to identify after a *Terry* stop yielded insufficient evidence. The stop, the request, and the State's requirement of a response did not contravene the guarantees of the Fourth Amendment.

[The Court then rejected the argument that requiring a person to identify him- or herself in such circumstances violates the Fifth Amendment privilege against self-incrimination.]

[Justice Stevens dissented on the grounds that there was a Fifth Amendment violation.]

Justice BREYER, with whom Justice SOUTER and Justice GINSBURG join, dissenting.
[T]his Court's Fourth Amendment precedents make clear that police may conduct a *Terry* stop only within circumscribed limits. And one of those limits invalidates laws that compel responses to police questioning.

There is no good reason now to reject this generation-old statement of the law. There are sound reasons rooted in Fifth Amendment considerations for adhering to this Fourth Amendment legal condition circumscribing police authority to stop an individual against his will. Administrative considerations also militate against change. Can a State, in addition to requiring a stopped individual to answer "What's your name?" also require an answer to "What's your license number?" or "Where do you live?" Can a police officer, who must know how to make a *Terry* stop, keep track of the constitutional answers? After all, answers to any of these questions may, or may not, incriminate, depending upon the circumstances.

The majority presents no evidence that the rule which for nearly a generation has set forth a settled *Terry* stop condition, has significantly interfered with law enforcement. Nor has the majority presented any other convincing justification for change. I would not begin to erode a clear rule with special exceptions.

4. What Is Sufficient for Reasonable Suspicion?

Terry v. Ohio draws a distinction between reasonable suspicion and probable cause. This, of course, is a distinction that appears elsewhere in the law of the Fourth Amendment. For example, as explained earlier, in New Jersey v. T.L.O., 469 U.S. 325 (1969), the Court held that school officials may search a student's purse based on reasonable suspicion.

But phrases like "reasonable suspicion" and "probable cause" do not lend themselves to precise definitions. There is no bright-line rule for determining what is sufficient for reasonable suspicion. But the Supreme Court has considered this question in a number of contexts. A few of these are presented below: reasonable suspicion for stopping cars; reasonable suspicion based on informants' tips; reasonable suspicion based on a person's trying to avoid a police officer; and reasonable suspicions based on profiles. This, of course, is not an exhaustive list, but these are some of the key situations so far in which the Court has confronted the question of what is enough for reasonable suspicion.

a. Reasonable Suspicion for Stopping Cars

Can many facts, which themselves are not evidence of any crime, be taken together to create reasonable suspicion to stop a car?

UNITED STATES v. ARVIZU
534 U.S. 266 (2002)

Chief Justice REHNQUIST delivered the opinion of the Court.
Respondent Ralph Arvizu was stopped by a border patrol agent while driving on an unpaved road in a remote area of southeastern Arizona. A search of his

vehicle turned up more than 100 pounds of marijuana. The District Court for the District of Arizona denied respondent's motion to suppress, but the Court of Appeals for the Ninth Circuit reversed. In the course of its opinion, it categorized certain factors relied upon by the District Court as simply out of bounds in deciding whether there was "reasonable suspicion" for the stop. We hold that the Court of Appeals' methodology was contrary to our prior decisions and that it reached the wrong result in this case.

On an afternoon in January 1998, Agent Clinton Stoddard was working at a border patrol checkpoint along U.S. Highway 191 approximately 30 miles north of Douglas, Arizona. Douglas has a population of about 13,000 and is situated on the United States-Mexico border in the southeastern part of the State. Only two highways lead north from Douglas. Highway 191 leads north to Interstate 10, which passes through Tucson and Phoenix. State Highway 80 heads northeast through less populated areas toward New Mexico, skirting south and east of the portion of the Coronado National Forest that lies approximately 20 miles northeast of Douglas.

The checkpoint is located at the intersection of 191 and Rucker Canyon Road, an unpaved east-west road that connects 191 and the Coronado National Forest. When the checkpoint is operational, border patrol agents stop the traffic on 191 as part of a coordinated effort to stem the flow of illegal immigration and smuggling across the international border. Agents use roving patrols to apprehend smugglers trying to circumvent the checkpoint by taking the backroads, including those roads through the sparsely populated area between Douglas and the national forest. Magnetic sensors, or "intrusion devices," facilitate agents' efforts in patrolling these areas. Directionally sensitive, the sensors signal the passage of traffic that would be consistent with smuggling activities.

Around 2:15 P.M., Stoddard received a report via Douglas radio that a Leslie Canyon Road sensor had been triggered. This was significant to Stoddard for two reasons. First, it suggested to him that a vehicle might be trying to circumvent the checkpoint. Second, the timing coincided with the point when agents begin heading back to the checkpoint for a shift change, which leaves the area unpatrolled. Stoddard knew that alien smugglers did extensive scouting and seemed to be most active when agents were en route back to the checkpoint. Another border patrol agent told Stoddard that the same sensor had gone off several weeks before and that he had apprehended a minivan using the same route and witnessed the occupants throwing bundles of marijuana out the door.

Stoddard drove eastbound on Rucker Canyon Road to investigate. As he did so, he received another radio report of sensor activity. It indicated that the vehicle that had triggered the first sensor was heading westbound on Rucker Canyon Road. He saw the dust trail of an approaching vehicle about a half mile away. Stoddard had not seen any other vehicles and, based on the timing, believed that this was the one that had tripped the sensors. He pulled off to the side of the road at a slight slant so he could get a good look at the oncoming vehicle as it passed by.

It was a minivan, a type of automobile that Stoddard knew smugglers used. As it approached, it slowed dramatically, from about 50-55 to 25-30 miles per hour. He saw five occupants inside. An adult man was driving, an adult woman sat in the front passenger seat, and three children were in the back. The driver appeared stiff and his posture very rigid. He did not look at Stoddard and seemed to be trying to pretend that Stoddard was not there. Stoddard thought this suspicious because in his experience on patrol most persons look over and see what is going on, and in that area most drivers give border patrol agents a friendly wave. Stoddard noticed that the knees of the two children sitting in the very back seat were unusually high, as if their feet were propped up on some cargo on the floor.

At that point, Stoddard decided to get a closer look, so he began to follow the vehicle as it continued westbound on Rucker Canyon Road toward Kuykendall Cutoff Road. Shortly thereafter, all of the children, though still facing forward, put their hands up at the same time and began to wave at Stoddard in an abnormal pattern. It looked to Stoddard as if the children were being instructed. Their odd waving continued on and off for about four to five minutes.

Several hundred feet before the Kuykendall Cutoff Road intersection, the driver signaled that he would turn. At one point, the driver turned the signal off, but just as he approached the intersection he put it back on and abruptly turned north onto Kuykendall. The turn was significant to Stoddard because it was made at the last place that would have allowed the minivan to avoid the checkpoint. Also, Kuykendall, though passable by a sedan or van, is rougher than either Rucker Canyon or Leslie Canyon Roads, and the normal traffic is four-wheel-drive vehicles. Stoddard did not recognize the minivan as part of the local traffic agents encounter on patrol and he did not think it likely that the minivan was going to or coming from a picnic outing. He was not aware of any picnic grounds on Turkey Creek, which could be reached by following Kuykendall Cutoff all the way up.

Stoddard radioed for a registration check and learned that the minivan was registered to an address in Douglas that was four blocks north of the border in an area notorious for alien and narcotics smuggling. After receiving the information, Stoddard decided to make a vehicle stop. He approached the driver and learned that his name was Ralph Arvizu. Stoddard asked if respondent would mind if he looked inside and searched the vehicle. Respondent agreed, and Stoddard discovered marijuana in a black duffel bag under the feet of the two children in the back seat. Another bag containing marijuana was behind the rear seat. *Id.*, at 46. In all, the van contained 128.85 pounds of marijuana, worth an estimated $99,080.

Respondent was charged with possession with intent to distribute marijuana. He moved to suppress the marijuana, arguing among other things that Stoddard did not have reasonable suspicion to stop the vehicle as required by the Fourth Amendment.

The Fourth Amendment prohibits "unreasonable searches and seizures" by the Government, and its protections extend to brief investigatory stops of persons or vehicles that fall short of traditional arrest. Because the "balance between the public interest and the individual's right to personal security," tilts in favor of a standard less than probable cause in such cases, the Fourth Amendment is satisfied if the officer's action is supported by reasonable suspicion to believe that criminal activity "may be afoot."

When discussing how reviewing courts should make reasonable-suspicion determinations, we have said repeatedly that they must look at the "totality of the circumstances" of each case to see whether the detaining officer has a "particularized and objective basis" for suspecting legal wrongdoing. This process allows officers to draw on their own experience and specialized training to make inferences from and deductions about the cumulative information available to them that "might well elude an untrained person." Although an officer's reliance on a mere "hunch" is insufficient to justify a stop, the likelihood of criminal activity need not rise to the level required for probable cause, and it falls considerably short of satisfying a preponderance of the evidence standard.

Our cases have recognized that the concept of reasonable suspicion is somewhat abstract. But we have deliberately avoided reducing it to "a neat set of legal rules."

We think that the approach taken by the Court of Appeals here departs sharply from the teachings of these cases. The court's evaluation and rejection of seven of the listed factors in isolation from each other does not take into account the "totality of the circumstances," as our cases have understood that phrase. The court appeared to believe that each observation by Stoddard that was by itself readily susceptible to an innocent explanation was entitled to "no weight." *Terry,* however, precludes this sort of divide and conquer analysis. The officer in *Terry* observed the petitioner and his companions repeatedly walk back and forth, look into a store window, and confer with one another. Although each of the series of acts was "perhaps innocent in itself," we held that, taken together, they "warranted further investigation."

Having considered the totality of the circumstances and given due weight to the factual inferences drawn by the law enforcement officer and District Court Judge, we hold that Stoddard had reasonable suspicion to believe that respondent was engaged in illegal activity. It was reasonable for Stoddard to infer from his observations, his registration check, and his experience as a border patrol agent that respondent had set out from Douglas along a little-traveled route used by smugglers to avoid the 191 checkpoint. Stoddard's knowledge further supported a commonsense inference that respondent intended to pass through the area at a time when officers would be leaving their backroads patrols to change shifts. The likelihood that respondent and his family were on a picnic outing was diminished by the fact that the minivan had turned away from the known recreational areas accessible to the east on Rucker Canyon Road. Corroborating this inference was the fact that recreational areas farther to the north would have been easier to reach by taking 191, as opposed to the 40-to-50-mile trip on unpaved and primitive roads. The children's elevated knees suggested the existence of concealed cargo in the passenger compartment. Finally, for the reasons we have given, Stoddard's assessment of respondent's reactions upon seeing him and the children's mechanical-like waving, which continued for a full four to five minutes, were entitled to some weight.

Respondent argues that we must rule in his favor because the facts suggested a family in a minivan on a holiday outing. A determination that reasonable suspicion exists, however, need not rule out the possibility of innocent conduct. Undoubtedly, each of these factors alone is susceptible of innocent explanation, and some factors are more probative than others. Taken together, we believe they sufficed to form a particularized and objective basis for Stoddard's stopping the vehicle, making the stop reasonable within the meaning of the Fourth Amendment.

b.   Reasonable Suspicion Based on Informants' Tips

In *Illinois v. Gates,* 462 U.S. 213 (1983), presented above, the Court considered when an informant's tip is sufficient for probable cause. What is a sufficient tip to meet the standard of reasonable suspicion? In assessing this, compare the following two cases, Alabama v. White and Florida v. J.L.

ALABAMA v. WHITE
496 U.S. 325 (1990)

Justice WHITE delivered the opinion of the Court.

Based on an anonymous telephone tip, police stopped respondent's vehicle. A consensual search of the car revealed drugs. The issue is whether the tip, as corroborated by independent police work, exhibited sufficient indicia of reliability to provide reasonable suspicion to make the investigatory stop. We hold that it did.

On April 22, 1987, at approximately 3 P.M., Corporal B. H. Davis of the Montgomery Police Department received a telephone call from an anonymous person, stating that Vanessa White would be leaving 235-C Lynwood Terrace Apartments at a particular time in a brown Plymouth station wagon with the right taillight lens broken, that she would be going to Dobey's Motel, and that she would be in possession of about an ounce of cocaine inside a brown attaché case.

Corporal Davis and his partner, Corporal P. A. Reynolds, proceeded to the Lynwood Terrace Apartments. The officers saw a brown Plymouth station wagon with a broken right taillight in the parking lot in front of the 235 building. The officers observed respondent leave the 235 building, carrying nothing in her hands, and enter the station wagon. They followed the vehicle as it drove the most direct route to Dobey's Motel. When the vehicle reached the Mobile Highway, on which Dobey's Motel is located, Corporal Reynolds requested a patrol unit to stop the vehicle. The vehicle was stopped at approximately 4:18 P.M., just short of Dobey's Motel. Corporal Davis asked respondent to step to the rear of her car, where he informed her that she had been stopped because she was suspected of carrying cocaine in the vehicle. He asked if they could look for cocaine, and respondent said they could look. The officers found a locked brown attaché case in the car, and, upon request, respondent provided the combination to the lock. The officers found marijuana in the attaché case and placed respondent under arrest. During processing at the station, the officers found three milligrams of cocaine in respondent's purse.

Respondent was charged in Montgomery County Court with possession of marijuana and possession of cocaine. The trial court denied respondent's motion to suppress, and she pleaded guilty to the charges, reserving the right to appeal the denial of her suppression motion. The Court of Criminal Appeals of Alabama held that the officers did not have the reasonable suspicion necessary under Terry v. Ohio (1968), to justify the investigatory stop of respondent's car, and that the marijuana and cocaine were fruits of respondent's unconstitutional detention.

Adams v. Williams (1972), sustained a *Terry* stop and frisk undertaken on the basis of a tip given in person by a known informant who had provided information in the past. We concluded that, while the unverified tip may have been insufficient to support an arrest or search warrant, the information carried sufficient "indicia of reliability" to justify a forcible stop. We did not address the issue of anonymous tips in *Adams*, except to say that "[t]his is a stronger case than obtains in the case of an anonymous telephone tip."

Illinois v. Gates (1983), dealt with an anonymous tip in the probable-cause context. The Court there abandoned the "two-pronged test" of Aguilar v. Texas (1964), and Spinelli v. United States (1969), in favor of a "totality of the circumstances" approach to determining whether an informant's tip establishes probable cause. *Gates* made clear, however, that those factors that had been considered critical under *Aguilar* and *Spinelli*—an informant's "veracity," "reliability," and "basis of knowledge"—remain "highly relevant in determining the value of his report." These factors are also relevant in the reasonable-suspicion context, although allowance must be made in applying them for the lesser showing required to meet that standard.

The opinion in *Gates* recognized that an anonymous tip alone seldom demonstrates the informant's basis of knowledge or veracity inasmuch as ordinary citizens generally do not provide extensive recitations of the basis of their everyday observations and given that the veracity of persons supplying anonymous tips is "by hypothesis largely unknown, and unknowable." This is not to say that an anonymous caller could never provide the reasonable suspicion necessary for a *Terry* stop.

Simply put, a tip such as this one, standing alone, would not "'warrant a man of reasonable caution in the belief' that [a stop] was appropriate." As there was in *Gates*, however, in this case there is more than the tip itself. The tip was not as detailed, and the corroboration was not as complete, as in *Gates*, but the required degree of suspicion was likewise not as high. Reasonable suspicion is a less demanding standard than probable cause not only in the sense that reasonable suspicion can be established with information that is different in quantity or content than that required to establish probable cause, but also in the sense that reasonable suspicion can arise from information that is less reliable than that required to show probable cause. Adams v. Williams demonstrates as much. We there assumed that the unverified tip from the known informant might not have been reliable enough to establish probable cause, but nevertheless found it sufficiently reliable to justify a *Terry* stop. Reasonable suspicion, like probable cause, is dependent upon both the content of information possessed by police and its degree of reliability. Both factors—quantity and quality—are considered in the "totality of the circumstances—the whole picture," that must be taken into account when evaluating whether there is reasonable suspicion. Thus, if a tip has a relatively low degree of reliability, more information will be required to establish the requisite quantum of suspicion than would be required if the tip were more reliable. The *Gates* Court applied its totality-of-the-circumstances approach in this manner, taking into account the facts known to the officers from personal observation, and giving the anonymous tip the weight it deserved in light of its indicia of reliability as established through independent police work. The same approach applies in the reasonable-suspicion context, the only difference being the level of suspicion that must be established.

Contrary to the court below, we conclude that when the officers stopped respondent, the anonymous tip had been sufficiently corroborated to furnish reasonable suspicion that respondent was engaged in criminal activity and that the investigative stop therefore did not violate the Fourth Amendment.

We think it also important that, as in *Gates*, "the anonymous [tip] contained a range of details relating not just to easily obtained facts and conditions existing at the time of the tip, but to future actions of third parties ordinarily not easily predicted." The fact that the officers found a car precisely matching the caller's description in front of the 235 building is an example of the former. Anyone could have "predicted" that fact because it was a condition presumably existing at the time of the call. What was important was the caller's ability to predict respondent's future behavior, because it demonstrated inside information — a special familiarity with respondent's affairs. The general public would have had no way of knowing that respondent would shortly leave the building, get in the described car, and drive the most direct route to Dobey's Motel. Because only a small number of people are generally privy to an individual's itinerary, it is reasonable for police to believe that a person with access to such information is likely to also have access to reliable information about that individual's illegal activities. When significant aspects of the caller's predictions were verified, there was reason to believe not only that the caller was honest but also that he was well informed, at least well enough to justify the stop.

Although it is a close case, we conclude that under the totality of the circumstances the anonymous tip, as corroborated, exhibited sufficient indicia of reliability to justify the investigatory stop of respondent's car.

Justice STEVENS, with whom Justice BRENNAN and Justice MARSHALL join, dissenting.

Millions of people leave their apartments at about the same time every day carrying an attaché case and heading for a destination known to their neighbors. Usually, however, the neighbors do not know what the briefcase contains. An anonymous neighbor's prediction about somebody's time of departure and probable destination is anything but a reliable basis for assuming that the commuter is in possession of an illegal substance — particularly when the person is not even carrying the attaché case described by the tipster.

The record in this case does not tell us how often respondent drove from the Lynwood Terrace Apartments to Dobey's Motel; for all we know, she may have been a room clerk or telephone operator working the evening shift. It does not tell us whether Officer Davis made any effort to ascertain the informer's identity, his reason for calling, or the basis of his prediction about respondent's destination. Indeed, for all that this record tells us, the tipster may well have been another police officer who had a "hunch" that respondent might have cocaine in her attaché case.

Anybody with enough knowledge about a given person to make her the target of a prank, or to harbor a grudge against her, will certainly be able to formulate a tip about her like the one predicting Vanessa White's excursion. In addition, under the Court's holding, every citizen is subject to being seized and questioned by any officer who is prepared to testify that the warrantless stop was based on an anonymous tip predicting whatever conduct the officer just observed. Fortunately, the vast majority of those in our law enforcement community would not adopt such a practice. But the Fourth Amendment was intended to protect the citizen from the overzealous and unscrupulous officer as well as from those who are conscientious and truthful. This decision makes a mockery of that protection.

FLORIDA v. J.L.
529 U.S. 266 (2000)

Justice GINSBURG delivered the opinion of the Court.

The question presented in this case is whether an anonymous tip that a person is carrying a gun is, without more, sufficient to justify a police officer's stop and frisk of that person. We hold that it is not.

I

On October 13, 1995, an anonymous caller reported to the Miami-Dade Police that a young black male standing at a particular bus stop and wearing a plaid shirt was carrying a gun. So far as the record reveals, there is no audio recording of the tip, and nothing is known about the informant. Sometime after the police received the tip — the record does not say how long — two officers were instructed to respond. They arrived at the bus stop about six minutes later and saw three black males "just hanging out [there]." One of the three, respondent J.L., was wearing a plaid shirt. Apart from the tip, the officers had no reason to suspect any of the three of illegal conduct. The officers did not see a firearm, and J.L. made no threatening or otherwise unusual movements.

One of the officers approached J.L., told him to put his hands up on the bus stop, frisked him, and seized a gun from J.L.'s pocket. The second officer frisked the other two individuals, against whom no allegations had been made, and found nothing.

J.L., who was at the time of the frisk "10 days shy of his 16th birth[day]," was charged under state law with carrying a concealed firearm without a license and possessing a firearm while under the age of 18. He moved to suppress the gun as the fruit of an unlawful search, and the trial court granted his motion. The intermediate appellate court reversed, but the Supreme Court of Florida quashed that decision and held the search invalid under the Fourth Amendment.

II

In the instant case, the officers' suspicion that J.L. was carrying a weapon arose not from any observations of their own but solely from a call made from an unknown location by an unknown caller. Unlike a tip from a known informant whose reputation can be assessed and who can be held responsible if her allegations turn out to be fabricated, *see* Adams v. Williams (1972), "an anonymous tip alone seldom demonstrates the informant's basis of knowledge or veracity." As we have recognized, however, there are situations in which an anonymous tip, suitably corroborated, exhibits "sufficient indicia of reliability to provide reasonable suspicion to make the investigatory stop." The question we here confront is whether the tip pointing to J.L. had those indicia of reliability.

The tip in the instant case lacked the moderate indicia of reliability present in *White* and essential to the Court's decision in that case. The anonymous call concerning J.L. provided no predictive information and therefore left the police without means to test the informant's knowledge or credibility. That the allegation about the gun turned out to be correct does not suggest that the officers, prior to the frisks, had a reasonable basis for suspecting J.L. of engaging in unlawful conduct: The reasonableness of official suspicion must be measured by what the officers knew before they conducted their search. All the police had to go on in this case was the bare report of an unknown, unaccountable informant who neither explained how he knew about the gun nor supplied any basis for believing he had inside information about J.L. If *White* was a close case on the reliability of anonymous tips, this one surely falls on the other side of the line.

Florida contends that the tip was reliable because its description of the suspect's visible attributes proved accurate: There really was a young black male wearing a plaid shirt at the bus stop. These contentions misapprehend the reliability needed for a tip to justify a *Terry* stop.

An accurate description of a subject's readily observable location and appearance is of course reliable in this limited sense: It will help the police correctly identify the person whom the tipster means to accuse. Such a tip, however, does not show that the tipster has knowledge of concealed criminal activity. The reasonable suspicion here at issue requires that a tip be reliable in its assertion of illegality, not just in its tendency to identify a determinate person.

A second major argument advanced by Florida and the United States as amicus is, in essence, that the standard *Terry* analysis should be modified to license a "firearm exception." Under such an exception, a tip alleging an illegal gun would justify a stop and frisk even if the accusation would fail standard presearch reliability testing. We decline to adopt this position.

Firearms are dangerous, and extraordinary dangers sometimes justify unusual precautions. Our decisions recognize the serious threat that armed criminals pose to public safety; *Terry*'s rule, which permits protective police searches on the basis of reasonable suspicion rather than demanding that officers meet the higher standard of probable cause, responds to this very concern. But an automatic firearm exception to our established reliability analysis would rove too far. Such an exception would enable any person seeking to harass another to set in motion an intrusive, embarrassing police search of the targeted person simply by placing an anonymous call falsely reporting the target's unlawful carriage of a gun. Nor could one securely confine such an exception to allegations involving firearms. If police officers may properly conduct *Terry* frisks on the basis of bare-boned tips about guns, it would be reasonable to maintain that the police should similarly have discretion to frisk based on bare-boned tips about narcotics.

The facts of this case do not require us to speculate about the circumstances under which the danger alleged in an anonymous tip might be so great as to justify a search even without a showing of reliability. We do not say, for example, that a report of a person carrying a bomb need bear the indicia of reliability we demand for a report of a person carrying a firearm before the police can constitutionally conduct a frisk. Nor do we hold that public safety officials in quarters where the reasonable expectation of Fourth Amendment privacy is diminished, such as airports and schools, cannot conduct protective searches on the basis of information insufficient to justify searches elsewhere.

Finally, the requirement that an anonymous tip bear standard indicia of reliability in order to justify a stop in no way diminishes a police officer's prerogative, in accord with *Terry*, to conduct a protective search of a person who has already been legitimately stopped. We speak in today's decision only of cases in which the officer's authority to make the initial stop is at issue. In that context, we hold that an anonymous tip lacking indicia of reliability of the kind contemplated in *Adams* and *White* does not justify a stop and frisk whenever and however it alleges the illegal possession of a firearm.

c.   Reasonable Suspicion Based on a Person's Trying to Avoid a Police Officer

Is it sufficient to create reasonable suspicion that a person sees a police officer and then walks in the opposite direction to avoid contact or even passing the officer?

ILLINOIS v. WARDLOW

528 U.S. 119 (2000)

Chief Justice R EHNQUIST delivered the opinion of the Court.

Respondent Wardlow fled upon seeing police officers patrolling an area known for heavy narcotics trafficking. Two of the officers caught up with him, stopped him and conducted a protective patdown search for weapons. Discovering a .38-caliber handgun, the officers arrested Wardlow. We hold that the officers' stop did not violate the Fourth Amendment to the United States Constitution.

On September 9, 1995, Officers Nolan and Harvey were working as uniformed officers in the special operations section of the Chicago Police Department. The officers were driving the last car of a four car caravan converging on an area known for heavy narcotics trafficking in order to investigate drug transactions. The officers were traveling together because they expected to find a crowd of people in the area, including lookouts and customers.

As the caravan passed 4035 West Van Buren, Officer Nolan observed respondent Wardlow standing next to the building holding an opaque bag. Respondent looked in the direction of the officers and fled. Nolan and Harvey turned their car southbound, watched him as he ran through the gangway and an alley, and eventually cornered him on the street. Nolan then exited his car and stopped respondent. He immediately conducted a protective patdown search for weapons because in his experience it was common for there to be weapons in the near vicinity of narcotics transactions. During the frisk, Officer Nolan squeezed the bag respondent was carrying and felt a heavy, hard object similar to the shape of a gun. The officer then opened the bag and discovered a .38-caliber handgun with five live rounds of ammunition. The officers arrested Wardlow.

The Illinois trial court denied respondent's motion to suppress, finding the gun was recovered during a lawful stop and frisk. Following a stipulated bench trial, Wardlow was convicted of unlawful use of a weapon by a felon. The Illinois Appellate Court reversed Wardlow's conviction, concluding that the gun should have been suppressed because Officer Nolan did not have reasonable suspicion sufficient to justify an investigative stop pursuant to Terry v. Ohio (1968). The Illinois Supreme Court agreed.

This case, involving a brief encounter between a citizen and a police officer on a public street, is governed by the analysis we first applied in *Terry*. In *Terry*, we held that an officer may, consistent with the Fourth Amendment, conduct a brief, investigatory stop when the officer has a reasonable, articulable suspicion that criminal activity is afoot.[12] While "reasonable suspicion" is a less demanding standard than probable cause and requires a showing considerably less than preponderance of the evidence, the Fourth Amendment requires at least a minimal level of objective justification for making the stop. The officer must be able to articulate more than an "inchoate and unparticularized suspicion or 'hunch'" of criminal activity.

Nolan and Harvey were among eight officers in a four-car caravan that was converging on an area known for heavy narcotics trafficking, and the officers

---

12. We granted certiorari solely on the question whether the initial stop was supported by reasonable suspicion. Therefore, we express no opinion as to the lawfulness of the frisk independently of the stop. [Footnote by the Court.]

anticipated encountering a large number of people in the area, including drug customers and individuals serving as lookouts. It was in this context that Officer Nolan decided to investigate Wardlow after observing him flee. An individual's presence in an area of expected criminal activity, standing alone, is not enough to support a reasonable, particularized suspicion that the person is committing a crime. But officers are not required to ignore the relevant characteristics of a location in determining whether the circumstances are sufficiently suspicious to warrant further investigation. Accordingly, we have previously noted the fact that the stop occurred in a "high crime area" among the relevant contextual considerations in a *Terry* analysis.

In this case, moreover, it was not merely respondent's presence in an area of heavy narcotics trafficking that aroused the officers' suspicion, but his unprovoked flight upon noticing the police. Our cases have also recognized that nervous, evasive behavior is a pertinent factor in determining reasonable suspicion. Headlong flight—wherever it occurs—is the consummate act of evasion: It is not necessarily indicative of wrongdoing, but it is certainly suggestive of such. In reviewing the propriety of an officer's conduct, courts do not have available empirical studies dealing with inferences drawn from suspicious behavior, and we cannot reasonably demand scientific certainty from judges or law enforcement officers where none exists. Thus, the determination of reasonable suspicion must be based on commonsense judgments and inferences about human behavior. We conclude Officer Nolan was justified in suspecting that Wardlow was involved in criminal activity, and, therefore, in investigating further.

Respondent and amici also argue that there are innocent reasons for flight from police and that, therefore, flight is not necessarily indicative of ongoing criminal activity. This fact is undoubtedly true, but does not establish a violation of the Fourth Amendment. Even in *Terry*, the conduct justifying the stop was ambiguous and susceptible of an innocent explanation. The officer observed two individuals pacing back and forth in front of a store, peering into the window and periodically conferring. All of this conduct was by itself lawful, but it also suggested that the individuals were casing the store for a planned robbery. *Terry* recognized that the officers could detain the individuals to resolve the ambiguity.

In allowing such detentions, *Terry* accepts the risk that officers may stop innocent people. Indeed, the Fourth Amendment accepts that risk in connection with more drastic police action; persons arrested and detained on probable cause to believe they have committed a crime may turn out to be innocent. The *Terry* stop is a far more minimal intrusion, simply allowing the officer to briefly investigate further. If the officer does not learn facts rising to the level of probable cause, the individual must be allowed to go on his way. But in this case the officers found respondent in possession of a handgun, and arrested him for violation of an Illinois firearms statute. No question of the propriety of the arrest itself is before us.

Justice STEVENS, with whom Justice SOUTER, Justice GINSBURG, and Justice BREYER join, concurring in part and dissenting in part.

The State of Illinois asks this Court to announce a "bright-line rule" authorizing the temporary detention of anyone who flees at the mere sight of a police officer. Respondent counters by asking us to adopt the opposite per se rule — that the fact that a person flees upon seeing the police can never, by itself, be sufficient to justify a temporary investigative stop of the kind authorized by Terry v. Ohio.

I.

The Court today wisely endorses neither per se rule. Instead, it rejects the proposition that "flight is . . . necessarily indicative of ongoing criminal activity," adhering to the view that "[t]he concept of reasonable suspicion . . . is not readily, or even usefully, reduced to a neat set of legal rules," but must be determined by looking to "the totality of the circumstances — the whole picture." Abiding by this framework, the Court concludes that "Officer Nolan was justified in suspecting that Wardlow was involved in criminal activity."

Although I agree with the Court's rejection of the per se rules proffered by the parties, unlike the Court, I am persuaded that in this case the brief testimony of the officer who seized respondent does not justify the conclusion that he had reasonable suspicion to make the stop.

The question in this case concerns "the degree of suspicion that attaches to" a person's flight — or, more precisely, what "commonsense conclusions" can be drawn respecting the motives behind that flight. A pedestrian may break into a run for a variety of reasons — to catch up with a friend a block or two away, to seek shelter from an impending storm, to arrive at a bus stop before the bus leaves, to get home in time for dinner, to resume jogging after a pause for rest, to avoid contact with a bore or a bully, or simply to answer the call of nature — any of which might coincide with the arrival of an officer in the vicinity. A pedestrian might also run because he or she has just sighted one or more police officers. In the latter instance, the State properly points out "that the fleeing person may be (1) an escapee from jail; (2) wanted on a warrant; (3) in possession of contraband (i.e. drugs, weapons, stolen goods, etc.); or (4) someone who has just committed another type of crime." In short, there are unquestionably circumstances in which a person's flight is suspicious, and undeniably instances in which a person runs for entirely innocent reasons.

Given the diversity and frequency of possible motivations for flight, it would be profoundly unwise to endorse either per se rule. The inference we can reasonably draw about the motivation for a person's flight, rather, will depend on a number of different circumstances. Factors such as the time of day, the number of people in the area, the character of the neighborhood, whether the officer was in uniform, the way the runner was dressed, the direction and speed of the flight, and whether the person's behavior was otherwise unusual might be relevant in specific cases. This number of variables is surely sufficient to preclude either a bright-line rule that always justifies, or that never justifies, an investigative stop based on the sole fact that flight began after a police officer appeared nearby.

Among some citizens, particularly minorities and those residing in high crime areas, there is also the possibility that the fleeing person is entirely innocent, but, with or without justification, believes that contact with the police can itself be dangerous, apart from any criminal activity associated with the officer's sudden presence. For such a person, unprovoked flight is neither "aberrant" nor "abnormal." Moreover, these concerns and fears are known to the police officers themselves, and are validated by law enforcement investigations into their own practices.

"Unprovoked flight," in short, describes a category of activity too broad and varied to permit a per se reasonable inference regarding the motivation for the activity. While the innocent explanations surely do not establish that the Fourth Amendment is always violated whenever someone is stopped solely on the basis of an unprovoked flight, neither do the suspicious motivations establish that the Fourth Amendment is never violated when a *Terry* stop is predicated on that fact alone. For these reasons, the Court is surely correct in refusing to embrace either per se rule advocated by the parties. The totality of the circumstances, as always, must dictate the result.

II

Guided by that totality-of-the-circumstances test, the Court concludes that Officer Nolan had reasonable suspicion to stop respondent. In this respect, my view differs from the Court's. The entire justification for the stop is articulated in the brief testimony of Officer Nolan. Some facts are perfectly clear; others are not. This factual insufficiency leads me to conclude that the Court's judgment is mistaken.

Officer Nolan and his partner were in the last of the four patrol cars that "were all caravaning eastbound down Van Buren." Nolan first observed respondent "in front of 4035 West Van Buren." Wardlow "looked in our direction and began fleeing." Nolan then "began driving southbound down the street observing [respondent] running through the gangway and the alley southbound," and observed that Wardlow was carrying a white, opaque bag under his arm. After the car turned south and intercepted respondent as he "ran right towards us," Officer Nolan stopped him and conducted a "protective search," which revealed that the bag under respondent's arm contained a loaded handgun.

This terse testimony is most noticeable for what it fails to reveal. Though asked whether he was in a marked or unmarked car, Officer Nolan could not recall the answer. He was not asked whether any of the other three cars in the caravan were marked, or whether any of the other seven officers were in uniform. Though he explained that the size of the caravan was because "[n]ormally in these different areas there's an enormous amount of people, sometimes lookouts, customers," Officer Nolan did not testify as to whether anyone besides Wardlow was nearby 4035 West Van Buren. Nor is it clear that that address was the intended destination of the caravan. As the Appellate Court of Illinois interpreted the record, "it appears that the officers were simply driving by, on their way to some unidentified location, when they noticed defendant standing at 4035 West Van Buren." Officer Nolan's testimony also does not reveal how fast the officers were driving. It does not indicate whether he saw respondent notice the other patrol cars. And it does not say whether the caravan, or any part of it, had already passed Wardlow by before he began to run.

Indeed, the Appellate Court thought the record was even "too vague to support the inference that . . . defendant's flight was related to his expectation of police focus on him." Presumably, respondent did not react to the first three cars, and we cannot even be sure that he recognized the occupants of the fourth as police officers. The adverse inference is based entirely on the officer's statement: "He looked in our direction and began fleeing."

No other factors sufficiently support a finding of reasonable suspicion. Though respondent was carrying a white, opaque bag under his arm, there is nothing at all suspicious about that. Certainly the time of day—shortly after noon—does not support Illinois' argument. Nor were the officers "responding to any call or report of suspicious activity in the area." Officer Nolan did testify that he expected to find "an enormous amount of people," including drug customers or lookouts, and the Court points out that "[i]t was in this context that Officer Nolan decided to investigate Wardlow after observing him flee." This observation, in my view, lends insufficient weight to the reasonable suspicion analysis; indeed, in light of the absence of testimony that anyone else was nearby when respondent began to run, this observation points in the opposite direction.

The State, along with the majority of the Court, relies as well on the assumption that this flight occurred in a high crime area. Even if that assumption is accurate, it is insufficient because even in a high crime neighborhood unprovoked flight does not invariably lead to reasonable suspicion. On the contrary, because many factors providing innocent motivations for unprovoked flight are concentrated in high crime areas, the character of the neighborhood arguably makes an inference of guilt less appropriate, rather than more so. Like unprovoked flight itself, presence in a high crime neighborhood is a fact too generic and susceptible to innocent explanation to satisfy the reasonable suspicion inquiry.

It is the State's burden to articulate facts sufficient to support reasonable suspicion. In my judgment, Illinois has failed to discharge that burden. I am not persuaded that the mere fact that someone standing on a sidewalk looked in the direction of a passing car before starting to run is sufficient to justify a forcible stop and frisk.

d. Reasonable Suspicion Based on Profiles

Can the use of profiles by the police be sufficient for reasonable suspicion? In United States v. Sokolow, the Court found that the use of a drug courier profile in an airport provided reasonable suspicion for a stop under Terry v. Ohio.

UNITED STATES v. SOKOLOW
490 U.S. 1 (1989)

Chief Justice REHNQUIST delivered the opinion of the Court.

Respondent Andrew Sokolow was stopped by Drug Enforcement Administration (DEA) agents upon his arrival at Honolulu International Airport. The agents found 1,063 grams of cocaine in his carry-on luggage. When respondent was stopped, the agents knew that (1) he paid $2,100 for two airplane tickets from a roll of $20 bills; (2) he traveled under a name that did not match the name under which his telephone number was listed; (3) his original destination was Miami, a source city for illicit drugs; (4) he stayed in Miami for only 48 hours, even though a round-trip flight from Honolulu to Miami takes 20 hours; (5) he appeared nervous during his trip; and (6) he checked none of his luggage. A divided panel of the United States Court of Appeals for the Ninth Circuit held that the DEA agents did not have a reasonable suspicion to stop respondent, as required by the Fourth Amendment. We take the contrary view.

This case involves a typical attempt to smuggle drugs through one of the Nation's airports. On a Sunday in July 1984, respondent went to the United Airlines ticket counter at Honolulu Airport, where he purchased two round-trip tickets for a flight to Miami leaving later that day. The tickets were purchased in the names of "Andrew Kray" and "Janet Norian" and had open return dates. Respondent paid $2,100 for the tickets from a large roll of $20 bills, which appeared to contain a total of $4,000. He also gave the ticket agent his home telephone number. The ticket agent noticed that respondent seemed nervous; he was about 25 years old; he was dressed in a black jumpsuit and wore gold jewelry; and he was accompanied by a woman, who turned out to be Janet Norian. Neither respondent nor his companion checked any of their four pieces of luggage.

After the couple left for their flight, the ticket agent informed Officer John McCarthy of the Honolulu Police Department of respondent's cash purchase of tickets to Miami. Officer McCarthy determined that the telephone number respondent gave to the ticket agent was subscribed to a "Karl Herman," who resided at 348-A Royal Hawaiian Avenue in Honolulu. Unbeknownst to McCarthy (and later to the DEA agents), respondent was Herman's roommate. The ticket agent identified respondent's voice on the answering machine at Herman's number. Officer McCarthy was unable to find any listing under the name "Andrew Kray" in Hawaii. McCarthy subsequently learned that return reservations from Miami to Honolulu had been made in the names of Kray and Norian, with their arrival scheduled for July 25, three days after respondent and his companion had left. He also learned that Kray and Norian were scheduled to make stopovers in Denver and Los Angeles.

On July 25, during the stopover in Los Angeles, DEA agents identified respondent. He "appeared to be very nervous and was looking all around the waiting area." Later that day, at 6:30 P.M., respondent and Norian arrived in Honolulu. As before, they had not checked their luggage. Respondent was still wearing a black jumpsuit and gold jewelry. The couple proceeded directly to the street and tried to hail a cab, where Agent Richard Kempshall and three other DEA agents approached them. Kempshall displayed his credentials, grabbed respondent by the arm, and moved him back onto the sidewalk. Kempshall asked respondent for his airline ticket and identification; respondent said that he had neither. He told the agents that his name was "Sokolow," but that he was traveling under his mother's maiden name, "Kray."

Respondent and Norian were escorted to the DEA office at the airport. There, the couple's luggage was examined by "Donker," a narcotics detector dog, which alerted on respondent's brown shoulder bag. The agents arrested respondent. He was advised of his constitutional rights and declined to make any statements. The agents obtained a warrant to search the shoulder bag. They found no illicit drugs, but the bag did contain several suspicious documents indicating respondent's involvement in drug trafficking. The agents had Donker reexamine the remaining luggage, and this time the dog alerted on a medium-sized Louis Vuitton bag. By now, it was 9:30 P.M., too late for the agents to obtain a second warrant. They allowed respondent to leave for the night, but kept his luggage. The next morning, after a second dog confirmed Donker's alert, the agents obtained a warrant and found 1,063 grams of cocaine inside the bag.

Respondent was indicted for possession with the intent to distribute cocaine in violation of 21 U.S.C. § 841(a)(1). The United States District Court for Hawaii denied his motion to suppress the cocaine and other evidence seized from his luggage, finding that the DEA agents had a reasonable suspicion that he was involved in drug trafficking when they stopped him at the airport. Respondent then entered a conditional plea of guilty to the offense charged.

The United States Court of Appeals for the Ninth Circuit reversed respondent's conviction by a divided vote, holding that the DEA agents did not have a reasonable suspicion to justify the stop.

The Court of Appeals held that the DEA agents seized respondent when they grabbed him by the arm and moved him back onto the sidewalk. The Government does not challenge that conclusion, and we assume — without deciding — that a stop occurred here. Our decision, then, turns on whether the agents had a reasonable suspicion that respondent was engaged in wrongdoing when they encountered him on the sidewalk. In Terry v. Ohio (1968), we held that the police can stop and briefly detain a person for investigative purposes if the officer has a reasonable suspicion supported by articulable facts that criminal activity "may be afoot," even if the officer lacks probable cause.

The officer, of course, must be able to articulate something more than an "inchoate and unparticularized suspicion or 'hunch.'" The Fourth Amendment requires "some minimal level of objective justification" for making the stop. That level of suspicion is considerably less than proof of wrongdoing by a preponderance of the evidence. We have held that probable cause means "a fair probability that contraband or evidence of a crime will be found," and the level of suspicion required for a Terry stop is obviously less demanding than that for probable cause.

The concept of reasonable suspicion, like probable cause, is not "readily, or even usefully, reduced to a neat set of legal rules."

Paying $2,100 in cash for two airplane tickets is out of the ordinary, and it is even more out of the ordinary to pay that sum from a roll of $20 bills containing nearly twice that amount of cash. Most business travelers, we feel confident, purchase airline tickets by credit card or check so as to have a record for tax or business purposes, and few vacationers carry with them thousands of dollars in $20 bills. We also think the agents had a reasonable ground to believe that respondent was traveling under an alias; the evidence was by no means conclusive, but it was sufficient to warrant consideration. While a trip from Honolulu to Miami, standing alone, is not a cause for any sort of suspicion, here there was more: surely few residents of Honolulu travel from that city for 20 hours to spend 48 hours in Miami during the month of July.

Any one of these factors is not by itself proof of any illegal conduct and is quite consistent with innocent travel. But we think taken together they amount to reasonable suspicion. Indeed, Terry itself involved "a series of acts, Rets, each of them perhaps innocent" if viewed separately, "but which taken together warranted further investigation." We noted in Gates that "innocent behavior will frequently provide the basis for a showing of probable cause," and that "[i]n making a determination of probable cause the relevant inquiry is not whether particular conduct is 'innocent' or 'guilty,' but the degree of suspicion that attaches to particular types of noncriminal acts." That principle applies equally well to the reasonable suspicion inquiry.

We do not agree with respondent that our analysis is somehow changed by the agents' belief that his behavior was consistent with one of the DEA's "drug courier profiles." A court sitting to determine the existence of reasonable suspicion must require the agent to articulate the factors leading to that conclusion, but the fact that these factors may be set forth in a "profile" does not somehow detract from their evidentiary significance as seen by a trained agent.

Respondent also contends that the agents were obligated to use the least intrusive means available to verify or dispel their suspicions that he was smuggling narcotics. In respondent's view, the agents should have simply approached and spoken with him, rather than forcibly detaining him. The reasonableness of the officer's decision to stop a suspect does not turn on the availability of less intrusive investigatory techniques. Such a rule would unduly hamper the police's ability to make swift, on-the-spot decisions — here, respondent was about to get into a taxicab — and it would require courts to "indulge in 'unrealistic second-guessing.'"

We hold that the agents had a reasonable basis to suspect that respondent was transporting illegal drugs on these facts.

Justice MARSHALL, with whom Justice BRENNAN joins, dissenting.

Because the strongest advocates of Fourth Amendment rights are frequently criminals, it is easy to forget that our interpretations of such rights apply to the innocent and the guilty alike. In the present case, the chain of events set in motion when respondent Andrew Sokolow was stopped by Drug Enforcement Administration (DEA) agents at Honolulu International Airport led to the discovery of cocaine and, ultimately, to Sokolow's conviction for drug trafficking. But in sustaining this conviction on the ground that the agents reasonably suspected Sokolow of ongoing criminal activity, the Court diminishes the rights of all citizens "to be secure in their persons," as they traverse the Nation's airports. Finding this result constitutionally impermissible, I dissent.

[T]he facts about Andrew Sokolow known to the DEA agents at the time they stopped him fall short of reasonably indicating that he was engaged at the time in criminal activity. It is highly significant that the DEA agents stopped Sokolow because he matched one of the DEA's "profiles" of a paradigmatic drug courier. In my view, a law enforcement officer's mechanistic application of a formula of personal and behavioral traits in deciding whom to detain can only dull the officer's ability and determination to make sensitive and fact-specific inferences "in light of his experience," particularly in ambiguous or borderline cases. Reflexive reliance on a profile of drug courier characteristics runs a far greater risk than does ordinary, case-by-case police work of subjecting innocent individuals to unwarranted police harassment and detention. This risk is enhanced by the profile's "chameleon-like way of adapting to any particular set of observations." In asserting that it is not "somehow" relevant that the agents who stopped Sokolow did so in reliance on a prefabricated profile of criminal characteristics, the majority thus ducks serious issues relating to a questionable law enforcement practice, to address the validity of which we granted certiorari in this case.

The remaining circumstantial facts known about Sokolow, considered either singly or together, are scarcely indicative of criminal activity. [T]he fact that

Sokolow took a brief trip to a resort city for which he brought only carry-on luggage also "describe[s] a very large category of presumably innocent travelers." That Sokolow embarked from Miami, "a source city for illicit drugs," is no more suggestive of illegality; thousands of innocent persons travel from "source cities" every day and, judging from the DEA's testimony in past cases, nearly every major city in the country may be characterized as a source or distribution city. That Sokolow had his phone listed in another person's name also does not support the majority's assertion that the DEA agents reasonably believed Sokolow was using an alias; it is commonplace to have one's phone registered in the name of a roommate, which, it later turned out, was precisely what Sokolow had done. That Sokolow was dressed in a black jumpsuit and wore gold jewelry also provides no grounds for suspecting wrongdoing, the majority's repeated and unexplained allusions to Sokolow's style of dress notwithstanding. For law enforcement officers to base a search, even in part, on a "pop" guess that persons dressed in a particular fashion are likely to commit crimes not only stretches the concept of reasonable suspicion beyond recognition, but also is inimical to the self-expression which the choice of wardrobe may provide.

Finally, that Sokolow paid for his tickets in cash indicates no imminent or ongoing criminal activity. The majority "feel[s] confident" that "[m]ost business travelers . . . purchase airline tickets by credit card or check." Why the majority confines its focus only to "business travelers" I do not know, but I would not so lightly infer ongoing crime from the use of legal tender. Making major cash purchases, while surely less common today, may simply reflect the traveler's aversion to, or inability to obtain, plastic money. Moreover, it is unreasonable to suggest that, had Sokolow left the airport, he would have been gone forever and thus immune from subsequent investigation. Sokolow, after all, had given the airline his phone number, and the DEA, having ascertained that it was indeed Sokolow's voice on the answering machine at that number, could have learned from that information where Sokolow resided.

The fact is that, unlike the taking of patently evasive action, the use of an alias, the casing of a store, or the provision of a reliable report from an informant that wrongdoing is imminent, nothing about the characteristics shown by airport traveler Sokolow reasonably suggests that criminal activity is afoot. The majority's hasty conclusion to the contrary serves only to indicate its willingness, when drug crimes or antidrug policies are at issue, to give short shrift to constitutional rights.

H.   ELECTRONIC SURVEILLANCE

It is now clearly established that electronic surveillance, such as wiretapping and interception of electronic communications, is a search and governed by Fourth Amendment principles. It is a bit different than other aspects of the Fourth Amendment because electronic surveillance by law enforcement officials is governed by specific statutes that define the procedures to be used. The result is that electronic surveillance is less likely than other forms of searches to lead to litigation and decisions under the Fourth Amendment, but there have been many decisions interpreting the statutes.

Subsection 1 briefly describes how the Supreme Court initially rejected viewing surveillance as a search, but then changed course and applied the Fourth Amendment. Subsection 2 describes the statutes governing electronic eavesdropping by federal officials. Finally, subsection 3 considers whether the President has the power to authorize warrantless wiretapping for national security purposes.

1.   Is Electronic Eavesdropping a Search?

In Olmstead v. United States, 277 U.S. 438 (1928), the Supreme Court held that wiretapping was not a search because the wires were tapped outside of the suspect's property and thus there was not a physical trespass. The Court explained: "The insertions were made without trespass upon any property of the defendants. They were made in the basement of the large office building. The taps from house lines were made in the streets near the houses." Chief Justice Taft, writing for the Court, said: "The language of the amendment cannot be extended and expanded to include telephone wires, reaching to the whole world from the defendant's house or office. The intervening wires are not part of his house or office, any more than are the highways along which they are stretched."

The Court concluded:

> Congress may, of course, protect the secrecy of telephone messages by making them, when intercepted, inadmissible in evidence in federal criminal trials, by direct legislation, and thus depart from the common law of evidence. But the courts may not adopt such a policy by attributing an enlarged and unusual meaning to the Fourth Amendment. The reasonable view is that one who installs in his house a telephone instrument with connecting wires intends to project his voice to those quite outside, and that the wires beyond his house, and messages while passing over them, are not within the protection of the Fourth Amendment. Here those who intercepted the projected voices were not in the house of either party to the conversation.

Justice Brandeis dissented and wrote an opinion that remains influential for articulating the right to privacy as a core of the Fourth Amendment. He stated:

> The makers of our Constitution undertook to secure conditions favorable to the pursuit of happiness. They recognized the significance of man's spiritual nature, of his feelings and of his intellect. They knew that only a part of the pain, pleasure and satisfactions of life are to be found in material things. They sought to protect Americans in their beliefs, their thoughts, their emotions and their sensations. They conferred, as against the government, the right to be let alone — the most comprehensive of rights and the right most valued by civilized men. To protect that right, every unjustifiable intrusion by the government upon the privacy of the individual, whatever the means employed, must be deemed a violation of the Fourth Amendment.

In words that seem particularly apt today, Justice Brandeis declared:

> It is, of course, immaterial where the physical connection with the telephone wires leading into the defendants' premises was made. And it is also immaterial that the

intrusion was in aid of law enforcement. Experience should teach us to be most on our guard to protect liberty when the government's purposes are beneficent. Men born to freedom are naturally alert to repel invasion of their liberty by evil-minded rulers. The greatest dangers to liberty lurk in insidious encroachment by men of zeal, well-meaning but without understanding.

For several decades, the Supreme Court adhered to the *Olmstead* view that electronic eavesdropping is not a search so long as there is no physical trespass. For example, in Goldman v. United States, 316 U.S. 129 (1942), the Court held that there was not a search when police placed a listening device against an office wall because they had not entered the premises of the office. By contrast, in Silverman v. United States, 365 U.S. 505 (1961), the Court found that there was a Fourth Amendment violation when police inserted an electric device (a "spike mike") into the shared wall of a person's apartment.

In 1967, the Court abandoned the *Olmstead* approach and said that the Fourth Amendment is about protecting a reasonable expectation of privacy, not simply stopping trespassing by law enforcement. In Berger v. United States, 388 U.S. 41 (1967), the Court found that the New York procedures for electronic eavesdropping lacked sufficient procedural protections to comply with the Fourth Amendment. The Court explained:

> The Fourth Amendment commands that a warrant issue not only upon probable cause supported by oath or affirmation, but also "particularly describing the place to be searched, and the persons or things to be seized." New York's statute lacks this particularization. It merely says that a warrant may issue on reasonable ground to believe that evidence of crime may be obtained by the eavesdrop. It lays down no requirement for particularity in the warrant as to what specific crime has been or is being committed, nor "the place to be searched," or "the persons or things to be seized" as specifically required by the Fourth Amendment. The need for particularity and evidence of reliability in the showing required when judicial authorization of a search is sought is especially great in the case of eavesdropping. By its very nature eavesdropping involves an intrusion on privacy that is broad in scope.
>
> First, as we have mentioned, eavesdropping is authorized without requiring belief that any particular offense has been or is being committed; nor that the "property" sought, the conversations, be particularly described. The purpose of the probable cause requirement of the Fourth Amendment, to keep the state out of constitutionally protected areas until it has reason to believe that a specific crime has been or is being committed, is thereby wholly aborted. Likewise the statute's failure to describe with particularity the conversations sought gives the officer a roving commission to "seize" any and all conversations. It is true that the statute requires the naming of "the person or persons whose communications, conversations or discussions are to be overheard or recorded." But this does no more than identify the person whose constitutionally protected area is to be invaded rather than "particularly describing" the communications, conversations, or discussions to be seized. As with general warrants this leaves too much to the discretion of the officer executing the order. Secondly, authorization of eavesdropping for a two-month period is the equivalent of a series of intrusions, searches, and seizures pursuant to a single showing of probable cause. Prompt execution is also avoided. During such a long and continuous (24 hours a day) period the conversations of any and all persons coming into the area covered by the device will be seized indiscriminately and without regard to their connection with the crime under investigation. Moreover, the statute permits, and there were authorized here, extensions of the original two-month period — presumably for two months

each—on a mere showing that such extension is "in the public interest." Apparently the original grounds on which the eavesdrop order was initially issued also form the basis of the renewal. This we believe insufficient without a showing of present probable cause for the continuance of the eavesdrop. Third, the statute places no termination date on the eavesdrop once the conversation sought is seized. This is left entirely in the discretion of the officer. Finally, the statute's procedure, necessarily because its success depends on secrecy, has no requirement for notice as do conventional warrants, nor does it overcome this defect by requiring some showing of special facts. On the contrary, it permits uncontested entry without any showing of exigent circumstances. Such a showing of exigency, in order to avoid notice would appear more important in eavesdropping, with its inherent dangers, than that required when conventional procedures of search and seizure are utilized. Nor does the statute provide for a return on the warran[t,] thereby leaving full discretion in the officer as to the use of seized conversations of innocent as well as guilty parties. In short, the statute's blanket grant of permission to eavesdrop is without adequate judicial supervision or protective procedures.

It is said with fervor that electronic eavesdropping is a most important technique of law enforcement and that outlawing it will severely cripple crime detection. In any event we cannot forgive the requirements of the Fourth Amendment in the name of law enforcement. This is no formality that we require today but a fundamental rule that has long been recognized as basic to the privacy of every home in America. Few threats to liberty exist which are greater than that posed by the use of eavesdropping devices. Some may claim that without the use of such devices crime detection in certain areas may suffer some delays since eavesdropping is quicker, easier, and more certain. However, techniques and practices may well be developed that will operate just as speedily and certainly and—what is more important—without attending illegality.

A few months after *Berger*, the Supreme Court expressly repudiated the trespass test of *Olmstead*. In United States v. Katz, presented at the beginning of this chapter, the Court held that the Fourth Amendment was violated by the warrantless wiretapping of a phone booth. The Court held that the Fourth Amendment protects reasonable expectations of privacy and that electronic eavesdropping is a search. The Court said that the Amendment governs "not only the seizure of tangible items, but extends as well to the recording of oral statements . . . without any technical trespass under . . . local property law."

2. Statutory Requirements

The year after *Katz* and *Berger*, Congress adopted Title III of the Omnibus Crime Control and Safe Streets Act of 1968 to regulate electronic eavesdropping. 18 U.S.C. § 2510, *et seq.* The statute addresses the procedural requirements that the Court articulated in *Berger*. The law was adopted under Congress' Commerce Clause power and regulates eavesdropping by government officials at all levels (federal, state, and local) and also private actors. In other words, the law is significantly broader than the Fourth Amendment in its regulating private behavior where the Constitution does not apply. The law was amended by the Electronic Communications Privacy Act of 1964 and the Digital Telephony Act of 1994. As amended, Title III covers the intentional interception by any means of wire, oral, and electronic communications. The Act defines interception as "the aural acquisition or other acquisition of the contents of any wire, electronic, or oral communication through the use of any electronic, mechanical, or other device."

The statute provides that no information gained in violation of statute, and no evidence derived as a result, may be admitted in any court proceeding. 18 U.S.C. § 2515. The statute provides that a court order may be obtained authorizing interception for any one of a long list of specified crimes. The application for a warrant must state with particularity the basis for probable cause, a description of the type of communications sought to be intercepted, the identity of the person (if known) whose communications are to be intercepted, whether other investigative techniques have been used, and a statement of the period of time during which interception will occur.

The statute provides that the court may issue an order authorizing interception if it finds (a) there is probable cause to believe that an individual is committing, has committed, or is about to commit an enumerated offense; (b) there is probable cause to believe that the communications concerning that offense will be obtained through the interception; and (c) "normal investigative procedures have been tried and failed or reasonably appear to be unlikely to succeed if tried or to be too dangerous." The court order must enumerate this and be specific as to whose communications may be intercepted, by what specific agency, and for what period of time. Generally, the court order must specify which specific communications media are to be monitored (such as what phone number), but the Act now allows "roving wiretaps," where all communication devices used by a person will be subject to surveillance, if there is a showing that a stationary wiretap will not be sufficient.

The Act is specific that the order cannot authorize interception "for any period longer than necessary to achieve the objective of the authorization, nor in any event longer than 30 days." Extensions may be granted, but only upon applications demonstrating necessity.

Title III requires that interception "shall be conducted in a way as to minimize the interception of communications." "Minimization" requires that law enforcement stop monitoring a communication when it becomes apparent that it is not about criminal activity. For example, if police obtain a court order to wiretap a phone for evidence of illegal drug transactions, they must stop listening when they realize that the conversation involves the suspect's child talking with a friend about unrelated matters.

The Act allows interception without a court order in emergency situations. Specifically, the Act provides that for a period not to exceed 48 hours, there can be interception if a specifically designated law enforcement official determines that "(a) an emergency situation exists that involves (i) immediate danger of death or serious physical injury to any person, (ii) conspiratorial activities threatening the national security interest, or (iii) conspiratorial activities characteristic of organized crime, that require a wire, oral, or electronic communication to be intercepted before an order authorizing such interception with due diligence can be obtained, and (b) there are grounds upon which an order can be entered." Also, Title III says that it does not limit the power of the President to obtain foreign intelligence information that is essential to the security of the United States.

The Act requires that a person whose communications were intercepted be notified in a reasonable period, not to exceed 90 days. The court may make available for inspection "such portions of the intercepted communications, applications and orders as the judge determines to be in the interests of justice."

As mentioned above, Title III provides for the exclusion of evidence obtained in violation of its provisions. It also provides criminal and civil penalties against those who violate it, although good faith reliance on a court order or legislative authorization is a complete defense to criminal or civil liability.

In 1978, Congress adopted the Foreign Intelligence Surveillance Act (FISA), 50 U.S.C. § 1801, *et seq.* FISA creates a special court comprised of 11 federal district court judges, chosen by the Chief Justice, to hear requests for eavesdropping under it. The FISA court operates in secret. Appeals are heard by a panel of federal court of appeals judges designated by the Chief Justice.

FISA, as amended, applies if a significant purpose of the interception is the gathering of foreign intelligence information. As originally adopted, FISA applied only to electronic interceptions, but later was amended to include physical searches. The government, to obtain a FISA warrant, need not show probable cause that a crime has been or will be committed. Rather, the government must show that "the target of the electronic surveillance is a foreign power or an agent of a foreign power." Unlike interceptions pursuant to Title III, the government never is required to notify the target if the Attorney General determines that it is in the interests of national security to keep this secret. The government can engage in interceptions without a court order in exigent circumstances for up to 72 hours.

The USA Patriot Act, adopted soon after the attacks of September 11, 2001, amended provisions of FISA in several important ways. Previously, the law applied only if the purpose was foreign intelligence gathering and not if it was for purposes of a criminal prosecution. But under the Patriot Act, FISA procedures can be used so long as a significant purpose is foreign intelligence gathering. The Patriot Act also provides for the sharing of information gained for intelligence purposes with law enforcement officials. Such sharing of information is allowed if it will "assist the official who is to receive that information in the performance of his duties." The Act authorizes "roving wiretaps" where all phones used by a person can be monitored.

The Patriot Act also modifies provisions of Title III. For example, it authorizes so-called sneak and peak warrants where the government may engage in searches or interceptions without notifying the target if there is reason to believe that giving notice will create an "adverse result" in the form of danger to persons or evidence. The Act allows for nationwide warrants for searching of stored electronic communications and for pen registers to monitor from whom a person is calling or receiving calls, or sending or receiving e-mail communication.

3. Warrantless Eavesdropping

The Foreign Intelligence Security Act provides that all interception by law enforcement officials must be done in compliance either with Title III or FISA. The exclusivity provision states that Title III and FISA "shall be the exclusive means by which electronic surveillance, as defined in section 101 of [FISA], and the interception of domestic wire, oral, and electronic communications may be conducted." 18 U.S.C. § 2511(2)(f). But does the President have the inherent power to authorize electronic surveillance for security purposes? There is just one Supreme Court decision concerning this and it held that there is no such authority for eavesdropping for *domestic* security purposes. The Court expressly said that it was not considering the President's authority when *foreign* threats were involved.

UNITED STATES v. UNITED STATES DISTRICT COURT FOR THE EASTERN DISTRICT OF MICHIGAN

407 U.S. 297 (1972)

Justice POWELL delivered the opinion of the Court.

The issue before us is an important one for the people of our country and their Government. It involves the delicate question of the President's power, acting through the Attorney General, to authorize electronic surveillance in internal security matters without prior judicial approval. Successive Presidents for more than one-quarter of a century have authorized such surveillance in varying degrees, without guidance from the Congress or a definitive decision of this Court. This case brings the issue here for the first time. Its resolution is a matter of national concern, requiring sensitivity both to the Government's right to protect itself from unlawful subversion and attack and to the citizen's right to be secure in his privacy against unreasonable Government intrusion.

This case arises from a criminal proceeding in the United States District Court for the Eastern District of Michigan, in which the United States charged three defendants with conspiracy to destroy Government property in violation of 18 U.S.C. § 371. One of the defendants, Plamondon, was charged with the dynamite bombing of an office of the Central Intelligence Agency in Ann Arbor, Michigan.

During pretrial proceedings, the defendants moved to compel the United States to disclose certain electronic surveillance information and to conduct a hearing to determine whether this information "tainted" the evidence on which the indictment was based or which the Government intended to offer at trial. In response, the Government filed an affidavit of the Attorney General, acknowledging that its agents had overheard conversations in which Plamondon had participated. On the basis of the Attorney General's affidavit and the sealed exhibit, the Government asserted that the surveillance was lawful, though conducted without prior judicial approval, as a reasonable exercise of the President's power (exercised through the Attorney General) to protect the national security. The District Court held that the surveillance violated the Fourth Amendment, and ordered the Government to make full disclosure to Plamondon of his overheard conversations.

Title III of the Omnibus Crime Control and Safe Streets Act authorizes the use of electronic surveillance for classes of crimes carefully specified. Such surveillance is subject to prior court order. The Act represents a comprehensive attempt by Congress to promote more effective control of crime while protecting the privacy of individual thought and expression. Much of Title III was drawn to meet the constitutional requirements for electronic surveillance enunciated by this Court in Berger v. New York (1967), and Katz v. United States (1967).

Together with the elaborate surveillance requirements in Title III, there is the following proviso: "Nothing contained in this chapter or in section 605 of the Communications Act of 1934 shall limit the constitutional power of the President to take such measures as he deems necessary to protect the Nation against actual or potential attack or other hostile acts of a foreign power, to obtain foreign intelligence information deemed essential to the security of the United States, or to protect national security information against foreign intelligence activities. Nor shall anything contained in this chapter be deemed to limit the constitutional power of the President to take such measures as he deems necessary to protect the United States against the overthrow of the Government by force or other unlawful means, or against any other clear and present danger to the structure or existence of the Government. The contents of any wire or oral communication intercepted by authority of the President in the exercise of the foregoing powers may be received in evidence in any trial hearing, or other proceeding only where such interception was reasonable, and shall not be otherwise used or disclosed except as is necessary to implement that power."

The Government argues that "in excepting national security surveillances from the Act's warrant requirement Congress recognized the President's authority to conduct such surveillances without prior judicial approval. We think the language of 2511(3), as well as the legislative history of the statute, refutes this interpretation. The relevant language is that: "Nothing contained in this chapter . . . shall limit the constitutional power of the President to take such measures as he deems necessary to protect . . ." against the dangers specified. At most, this is an implicit recognition that the President does have certain powers in the specified areas. Few would doubt this, as the section refers — among other things — to protection "against actual or potential attack or other hostile acts of a foreign power." But so far as the use of the President's electronic surveillance power is concerned, the language is essentially neutral.

Section 2511(3) certainly confers no power, as the language is wholly inappropriate for such a purpose. It merely provides that the Act shall not be interpreted to limit or disturb such power as the President may have under the Constitution. In short, Congress simply left presidential powers where it found them.

In view of these and other interrelated provisions delineating permissible interceptions of particular criminal activity upon carefully specified conditions, it would have been incongruous for Congress to have legislated with respect to the important and complex area of national security in a single brief and nebulous paragraph. This would not comport with the sensitivity of the problem involved or with the extraordinary care Congress exercised in drafting other sections of the Act. We therefore think the conclusion inescapable that Congress only intended to make clear that the Act simply did not legislate with respect to national security surveillances.

It is important at the outset to emphasize the limited nature of the question before the Court. This case raises no constitutional challenge to electronic surveillance as specifically authorized by Title III of the Omnibus Crime Control and Safe Streets Act of 1968. Nor is there any question or doubt as to the necessity of obtaining a warrant in the surveillance of crimes unrelated to the national security interest. Further, the instant case requires no judgment on the scope of the President's surveillance power with respect to the activities of foreign powers, within or without this country. The Attorney General's affidavit in this case states that the surveillances were "deemed necessary to protect the nation from attempts of domestic organizations to attack and subvert the existing structure of Government." There is no evidence of any involvement, directly or indirectly, of a foreign power.

We begin the inquiry by noting that the President of the United States has the fundamental duty, under Art. II, § 1, of the Constitution, to "preserve, protect and defend the Constitution of the United States." Implicit in that duty is the power to protect our Government against those who would subvert or overthrow it by unlawful means. In the discharge of this duty, the President—through the Attorney General—may find it necessary to employ electronic surveillance to obtain intelligence information on the plans of those who plot unlawful acts against the Government. The use of such surveillance in internal security cases has been sanctioned more or less continuously by various Presidents and Attorneys General since July 1946.

Though the Government and respondents debate their seriousness and magnitude, threats and acts of sabotage against the Government exist in sufficient number to justify investigative powers with respect to them. The covertness and complexity of potential unlawful conduct against the Government and the necessary dependency of many conspirators upon the telephone make electronic surveillance an effective investigatory instrument in certain circumstances. The marked acceleration in technological developments and sophistication in their use have resulted in new techniques for the planning, commission, and concealment of criminal activities. It would be contrary to the public interest for Government to deny to itself the prudent and lawful employment of those very techniques which are employed against the Government and its law-abiding citizens.

But a recognition of these elementary truths does not make the employment by Government of electronic surveillance a welcome development—even when employed with restraint and under judicial supervision. There is, understandably, a deep-seated uneasiness and apprehension that this capability will be used to intrude upon cherished privacy of law-abiding citizens. We look to the Bill of Rights to safeguard this privacy. Though physical entry of the home is the chief evil against which the wording of the Fourth Amendment is directed, its broader spirit now shields private speech from unreasonable surveillance.

National security cases, moreover, often reflect a convergence of First and Fourth Amendment values not present in cases of "ordinary" crime. Though the investigative duty of the executive may be stronger in such cases, so also is there greater jeopardy to constitutionally protected speech. Fourth Amendment protections become the more necessary when the targets of official surveillance may be those suspected of unorthodoxy in their political beliefs. The danger to political dissent is acute where the Government attempts to act under so vague a concept as the power to protect "domestic security." Given the difficulty of defining the domestic security interest, the danger of abuse in acting to protect that interest becomes apparent.

The price of lawful public dissent must not be a dread of subjection to an unchecked surveillance power. Nor must the fear of unauthorized official eavesdropping deter vigorous citizen dissent and discussion of Government action in private conversation. For private dissent, no less than open public discourse, is essential to our free society.

As the Fourth Amendment is not absolute in its terms, our task is to examine and balance the basic values at stake in this case: the duty of Government to protect the domestic security, and the potential danger posed by unreasonable surveillance to individual privacy and free expression. If the legitimate need of Government to safeguard domestic security requires the use of electronic surveillance, the question is whether the needs of citizens for privacy and the free expression may not be better protected by requiring a warrant before such surveillance is undertaken. We must also ask whether a warrant requirement would unduly frustrate the efforts of Government to protect itself from acts of subversion and overthrow directed against it.

Though the Fourth Anendment speaks broadly of "unreasonable searches and seizures," the definition of "reasonableness" turns, at least in part, on the more specific commands of the warrant clause. Some have argued that "[t]he relevant test is not whether it is reasonable to procure a search warrant, but whether the search was reasonable." This view, however, overlooks the second clause of the Amendment. The warrant clause of the Fourth Amendment is not dead language. Rather, it has been "a valued part of our constitutional law for decades, and it has determined the result in scores and scores of cases in courts all over this country. It is not an inconvenience to be somehow 'weighed' against the claims of police efficiency. It is, or should be, an important working part of our machinery of government, operating as a matter of course to check the 'well-intentioned but mistakenly over-zealous executive officers' who are a party of any system of law enforcement."

These Fourth Amendment freedoms cannot properly be guaranteed if domestic security surveillances may be conducted solely within the discretion of the Executive Branch. The Fourth Amendment does not contemplate the executive officers of Government as neutral and disinterested magistrates. Their duty and responsibility are to enforce the laws, to investigate, and to prosecute. But those charged with this investigative and prosecutorial duty should not be the sole judges of when to utilize constitutionally sensitive means in pursuing their tasks. The historical judgment, which the Fourth Amendment accepts, is that unreviewed executive discretion may yield too readily to pressures to obtain incriminating evidence and overlook potential invasions of privacy and protected speech.

It may well be that, in the instant case, the Government's surveillance of Plamondon's conversations was a reasonable one which readily would have gained prior judicial approval. But this Court "has never sustained a search upon the sole ground that officers reasonably expected to find evidence of a particular crime and voluntarily confined their activities to the least intrusive means consistent with that end." The Fourth Amendment contemplates a prior judicial judgment, not the risk that executive discretion may be reasonably exercised. This judicial role accords with our basic constitutional doctrine that individual freedoms will best be preserved through a separation of powers and division of functions among the different branches and levels of Government. The independent check upon executive discretion is not satisfied, as the Government argues, by "extremely limited" post-surveillance judicial review. Indeed, post-surveillance review would never reach the surveillances which failed to result in prosecutions. Prior review by a neutral and detached magistrate is the time-tested means of effectuating Fourth Amendment rights.

It is true that there have been some exceptions to the warrant requirement. But those exceptions are few in number and carefully delineated; in general, they serve the legitimate needs of law enforcement officers to protect their own well-being and preserve evidence from destruction. Even while carving out those exceptions, the Court has reaffirmed the principle that the "police must, whenever practicable, obtain advance judicial approval of searches and seizures through the warrant procedure."

The Government argues that the special circumstances applicable to domestic security surveillances necessitate a further exception to the warrant requirement. It is urged that the requirement of prior judicial review would obstruct the President in the discharge of his constitutional duty to protect domestic security. We are told further that these surveillances are directed primarily to the collecting and maintaining of intelligence with respect to subversive forces, and are not an attempt to gather evidence for specific criminal prosecutions. It is said that this type of surveillance should not be subject to traditional warrant requirements which were established to govern investigation of criminal activity, not ongoing intelligence gathering.

The Government further insists that courts "as a practical matter would have neither the knowledge nor the techniques necessary to determine whether there was probable cause to believe that surveillance was necessary to protect national security." These security problems, the Government contends, involve "a large number of complex and subtle factors" beyond the competence of courts to evaluate.

As a final reason for exemption from a warrant requirement, the Government believes that disclosure to a magistrate of all or even a significant portion of the information involved in domestic security surveillances "would create serious potential dangers to the national security and to the lives of informants and agents. . . . Secrecy is the essential ingredient in intelligence gathering; requiring prior judicial authorization would create a greater 'danger of leaks . . . , because in addition to the judge, you have the clerk, the stenographer and some other officer like a law assistant or bailiff who may be apprised of the nature' of the surveillance."

These contentions in behalf of a complete exemption from the warrant requirement, when urged on behalf of the President and the national security in its domestic implications, merit the most careful consideration. We certainly do not reject them lightly, especially at a time of worldwide ferment and when civil disorders in this country are more prevalent than in the less turbulent periods of our history. There is, no doubt, pragmatic force to the Government's position.

But we do not think a case has been made for the requested departure from Fourth Amendment standards. The circumstances described do not justify complete exemption of domestic security surveillance from prior judicial scrutiny. Official surveillance, whether its purpose be criminal investigation or ongoing intelligence gathering, risks infringement of constitutionally protected privacy of speech. Security surveillances are especially sensitive because of the inherent vagueness of the domestic security concept, the necessarily broad and continuing nature of intelligence gathering, and the temptation to utilize such surveillances to oversee political dissent. We recognize, as we have before, the constitutional basis of the President's domestic security role, but we think it must be exercised in a manner compatible with the Fourth Amendment. In this case *holding* we hold that this requires an appropriate prior warrant procedure.

We cannot accept the Government's argument that internal security matters are too subtle and complex for judicial evaluation. Courts regularly deal with the most difficult issues of our society. There is no reason to believe that federal judges will be insensitive to or uncomprehending of the issues involved in domestic security cases. Certainly courts can recognize that domestic security surveillance involves different considerations from the surveillance of "ordinary crime." If the threat is too subtle or complex for our senior law enforcement officers to convey its significance to a court, one may question whether there is probable cause for surveillance.

Nor do we believe prior judicial approval will fracture the secrecy essential to official intelligence gathering. The investigation of criminal activity has long involved imparting sensitive information to judicial officers who have respected the confidentialities involved. Judges may be counted upon to be especially conscious of security requirements in national security cases. Title III of the Omnibus Crime Control and Safe Streets Act already has imposed this responsibility on the judiciary in connection with such crimes as espionage, sabotage, and treason, each of which may involve domestic as well as foreign security threats. Moreover, a warrant application involves no public or adversary proceedings: it is an ex parte request before a magistrate or judge. Whatever security dangers clerical and secretarial personnel may pose can be minimized by proper administrative measures, possibly to the point of allowing the Government itself to provide the necessary clerical assistance.

Thus, we conclude that the Government's concerns do not justify departure in this case from the customary Fourth Amendment requirement of judicial approval prior to initiation of a search or surveillance. Although some added burden will be imposed upon the Attorney General, this inconvenience is justified in a free society to protect constitutional values. Nor do we think the Government's domestic surveillance powers will be impaired to any significant degree. A prior warrant establishes presumptive validity of the surveillance and will minimize the burden of justification in post-surveillance judicial review. By no means of least importance will be the reassurance of the public generally that indiscriminate wiretapping and bugging of law-abiding citizens cannot occur.

We emphasize, before concluding this opinion, the scope of our decision. As stated at the outset, this case involves only the domestic aspects of national security. We have not addressed and express no opinion as to the issues which may be involved with respect to activities of foreign powers or their agents. Moreover, we do not hold that the same type of standards and procedures prescribed by Title III are necessarily applicable to this case. We recognize that domestic security surveillance may involve different policy and practical considerations from the surveillance of "ordinary crime." The gathering of security intelligence is often long range and involves the interrelation of various sources and types of information. The exact targets of such surveillance may be more difficult to identify than in surveillance operations against many types of crime specified in Title III. Often, too, the emphasis of domestic intelligence gathering is on the prevention of unlawful activity or the enhancement of the Government's preparedness for some possible future crisis or emergency. Thus, the focus of domestic surveillance may be less precise than that directed against more conventional types of crime.

Given those potential distinctions between Title III criminal surveillances and those involving the domestic security, Congress may wish to consider protective standards for the latter which differ from those already prescribed for specified crimes in Title III. Different standards may be compatible with the Fourth Amendment if they are reasonable both in relation to the legitimate need of Government for intelligence information and the protected rights of our citizens. For the warrant application may vary according to the governmental interest to be enforced and the nature of citizen rights deserving protection.

We do not attempt to detail the precise standards for domestic security warrants any more than our decision in *Katz* sought to set the refined requirements for the specified criminal surveillances which now constitute Title III. We do hold, however, that prior judicial approval is required for the type of domestic security surveillance involved in this case and that such approval may be made in accordance with such reasonable standards as the Congress may prescribe.

The Court was clear that it was not discussing whether the President has the power to authorize warrantless wiretapping directed at foreign threats to national security. The issue has arisen in recent years in connection with the Bush administration's authorization for the National Security Agency to engage in warrantless electronic eavesdropping. In December 2005, the New York Times reported that since 2002, the National Security Agency had engaged in a Terrorist Surveillance Program that included data mining and warrantless interception of telephone and e-mail communications where one party to the communication was located outside the United States and the NSA had reasonable basis to conclude that one party to the communication was connected to al Qaeda. James Risen and Eric Lichthlau, *Bush Lets U.S. Spy on Callers Without Courts*, N.Y. Times (Dec. 16, 2005). The day after this story appeared, President George W. Bush confirmed the existence of a "terrorist surveillance program" in his weekly radio address: "In the weeks following the [September 11, 2001] terrorist attacks on our Nation, I authorized the National Security Agency, consistent with U.S. law and the Constitution, to intercept the international communications of people with known links to Al Qaeda and related terrorist organizations. Before we intercept these communications, the Government must have information that establishes a clear link to these terrorist networks."

The American Civil Liberties Union filed a lawsuit on behalf of journalists, academics, and lawyers who regularly communicate with individuals located overseas, who the plaintiffs believe are the types of people the NSA suspects of being al Qaeda terrorists, affiliates, or supporters, and are therefore likely to be monitored under the TSP. The United States District Court for the Eastern District of Michigan ruled that the plaintiffs had standing and that the warrantless electronic eavesdropping violated the Constitution and the FISA statute. American Civil Liberties Union v. National Sec. Agency, 438 F. Supp. 2d 754 (E.D. Mich. 2006). The United States Court of Appeals for the Sixth Circuit, in a 2-1 decision, reversed. American Civil Liberties Union v. National Sec. Agency, 493 F.3d 644 (6th Cir. 2007). The court concluded that the plaintiffs lacked standing because they could not demonstrate that their conversations had been intercepted. The court stated: "Notably, the plaintiffs do not allege as injury that they personally, either as individuals or associations, anticipate or fear any form of direct reprisal by the government (e.g., the NSA, the Justice Department, the Department of Homeland Security, etc.), such as criminal prosecution, deportation, administrative inquiry, civil litigation, or even public exposure." The court concluded: "Based on the evidence in the record, as applied in the foregoing analysis, none of the plaintiffs in the present case is able to establish standing for any of the asserted claims."

In February 2008, the Supreme Court denied certiorari. 128 S.Ct. _____ (February 19, 2008). Although the case was resolved based on whether the plaintiffs have standing to sue, the underlying issue is of enormous importance: Does the

President have the power to authorize warrantless interception of electronic communication to protect against foreign threats to national security? The Bush administration claims that this is inherent power to protect the nation that Congress cannot constitutionally limit. Critics argue that the Fourth Amendment is based on the need for judicial approval of all searches and that warrantless searches are unnecessary and undesirable because there is no protection of privacy.

CHAPTER

3

THE EXCLUSIONARY RULE

What are the consequences if the police violate the Fourth Amendment requirements for searches and seizures described in the prior chapter? Similarly, what
are the consequences if the police violate other constitutional limits in investigations, such as interrogations that violate the privilege against self-incrimination (discussed in Chapter 4) or identification procedures that violate due
process (discussed in Chapter 5)? The most important enforcement mechanism
is the "exclusionary rule." This is the rule that material obtained in violation of
the Constitution cannot be introduced at trial against a criminal defendant.

This chapter focuses primarily on the exclusionary rule in Fourth Amendment cases. Its application to other investigative techniques, such as interrogations and identification procedures, is discussed in the following chapters.
Section A considers whether the exclusionary rule is a desirable remedy for
unconstitutional police behavior. Section B examines the cases that created
the exclusionary rule and applied it to the states. Section C examines who
can object to the introduction of illegal evidence and raise the exclusionary
rule. Section D considers the exceptions to the exclusionary rule. Finally,
Section E discusses the primary mechanism for raising the exclusionary rule:
suppression hearings.

A. IS THE EXCLUSIONARY RULE A DESIRABLE REMEDY FOR UNCONSTITUTIONAL POLICE BEHAVIOR?

The exclusionary rule is defended as a key way of deterring police misconduct.
Officers know that if they violate the Constitution, the fruits of their efforts will
be excluded. Officers, who obviously desire that their work will lead to convictions, will thus refrain from violating the Constitution. The Supreme Court
often has expressed deterrence as a key purpose of the exclusionary rule. For
example, the Court has declared that the exclusionary rule is "a judicially created remedy designed to safeguard Fourth Amendment rights through its deterrence effect." United States v. Calandra, 428 U.S. 465 (1976).

The exclusionary rule also is justified based on concerns for judicial integrity.
The view is that courts are tainted if they convict people based on illegally
obtained evidence. In some areas, the concern is that illegally obtained evidence

is unreliable and could lead to the conviction of innocent people. For example, involuntary confessions or suggestive police lineups are excluded, in part, for fear that the results are not trustworthy. On the other hand, this concern is not present when tangible evidence is gained as a result of an illegal search.

There also is a notion that the exclusionary rule sends a powerful message that the government cannot and will not benefit from wrongdoing by its officers. Justice Brennan argued that application of the exclusionary rule "assures the people — all potential victims of unlawful government conduct — that the government [will] not profit from its lawless behavior, thus minimizing the risk of seriously undermining public trust in the government." United States v. Calandra, 414 U.S. 338 (1974) (Brennan, J., dissenting).

Critics of the exclusionary rule primarily focus on its cost in letting potentially guilty people go free. Justice Cardozo captured this in his famous lament that under the exclusionary rule, "[t]he criminal is to go free because the constable has blundered." People v. Defore, 242 N.Y. 13, 21, 150 N.E. 585, 587 (1926). Indeed, the existence of the exclusionary rule may make judges less likely to find a Fourth Amendment violation since they know that the outcome of the case might be determined by the loss of key evidence.

Critics also argue that the exclusionary rule is unnecessary. In a recent majority opinion, Justice Scalia advanced these criticisms. The case, Hudson v. Michigan, 126 S. Ct. 2159 (2006),[1] involved the question of whether evidence must be excluded when police violate the requirement for "knocking" and "announcing" before executing a warrant to search a residence. The Court held that the exclusionary rule does not apply. In defending this conclusion, Justice Scalia's majority opinion presents many of the traditional arguments against the exclusionary rule.

HUDSON v. MICHIGAN
126 S. Ct. 2159 (2006)

Justice SCALIA delivered the opinion of the Court.

Suppression of evidence, however, has always been our last resort, not our first impulse. The exclusionary rule generates "substantial social costs," which sometimes include setting the guilty free and the dangerous at large. We have therefore been "cautio[us] against expanding" it, and "have repeatedly emphasized that the rule's 'costly toll' upon truth-seeking and law enforcement objectives presents a high obstacle for those urging [its] application." We have rejected "[i]ndiscriminate application" of the rule, and have held it to be applicable only "where its remedial objectives are thought most efficaciously served," — that is, "where its deterrence benefits outweigh its 'substantial social costs.'" The exclusionary rule has never been applied except "where its deterrence benefits outweigh its 'substantial social costs.'" The costs here are considerable. In addition to the grave adverse consequence that exclusion of relevant incriminating evidence always entails (viz., the risk of releasing dangerous criminals into society), imposing that massive remedy for a knock-and-announce

---

1. *Hudson* is discussed in more detail in Section D below, which considers the exceptions to the exclusionary rule and *Hudson*'s holding that the exclusionary rule does not apply if the police violate the requirements for knocking and announcing before searching a dwelling.

violation would generate a constant flood of alleged failures to observe the rule. The cost of entering this lottery would be small, but the jackpot enormous: suppression of all evidence, amounting in many cases to a get-out-of-jail-free card. Courts would experience as never before the reality that "[t]he exclusionary rule frequently requires extensive litigation to determine whether particular evidence must be excluded."

Another consequence of the incongruent remedy Hudson proposes would be police officers' refraining from timely entry after knocking and announcing. As we have observed, the amount of time they must wait is necessarily uncertain. If the consequences of running afoul of the rule were so massive, officers would be inclined to wait longer than the law requires — producing preventable violence against officers in some cases, and the destruction of evidence in many others. We deemed these consequences severe enough to produce our unanimous agreement that a mere "reasonable suspicion" that knocking and announcing "under the particular circumstances, would be dangerous or futile, or that it would inhibit the effective investigation of the crime," will cause the requirement to yield.

Next to these "substantial social costs" we must consider the deterrence benefits, existence of which is a necessary condition for exclusion. (It is not, of course, a sufficient condition: "[I]t does not follow that the Fourth Amendment requires adoption of every proposal that might deter police misconduct.") To begin with, the value of deterrence depends upon the strength of the incentive to commit the forbidden act. Viewed from this perspective, deterrence of knock-and-announce violations is not worth a lot. Violation of the warrant requirement sometimes produces incriminating evidence that could not otherwise be obtained. But ignoring knock-and-announce can realistically be expected to achieve absolutely nothing except the prevention of destruction of evidence and the avoidance of life-threatening resistance by occupants of the premises — dangers which, if there is even "reasonable suspicion" of their existence, suspend the knock-and-announce requirement anyway. Massive deterrence is hardly required.

It seems to us not even true, as Hudson contends, that without suppression there will be no deterrence of knock-and-announce violations at all. Of course even if this assertion were accurate, it would not necessarily justify suppression. Assuming (as the assertion must) that civil suit is not an effective deterrent, one can think of many forms of police misconduct that are similarly "undeterred." When, for example, a confessed suspect in the killing of a police officer, arrested (along with incriminating evidence) in a lawful warranted search, is subjected to physical abuse at the station house, would it seriously be suggested that the evidence must be excluded, since that is the only "effective deterrent"? And what, other than civil suit, is the "effective deterrent" of police violation of an already-confessed suspect's Sixth Amendment rights by denying him prompt access to counsel? Many would regard these violated rights as more significant than the right not to be intruded upon in one's nightclothes — and yet nothing but "ineffective" civil suit is available as a deterrent. And the police incentive for those violations is arguably greater than the incentive for disregarding the knock-and-announce rule.

We cannot assume that exclusion in this context is necessary deterrence simply because we found that it was necessary deterrence in different contexts and long ago. That would be forcing the public today to pay for the sins and inadequacies of a legal regime that existed almost half a century ago. Dollree Mapp could not turn to 42 U.S.C. § 1983 for meaningful relief; Monroe v. Pape (1961), which began the slow but steady expansion of that remedy, was decided the same Term as *Mapp*. It would be another 17 years before the § 1983 remedy was extended to reach the deep pocket of municipalities, Monell v. New York City Dept. of Social Servs., (1978). Citizens whose Fourth Amendment rights were violated by federal officers could not bring suit until 10 years after *Mapp*, with this Court's decision in Bivens v. Six Unknown Fed. Narcotics Agents (1971).

Hudson complains that "it would be very hard to find a lawyer to take a case such as this," but 42 U.S.C. § 1988(b) answers this objection. Since some civil-rights violations would yield damages too small to justify the expense of litigation, Congress has authorized attorney's fees for civil-rights plaintiffs. This remedy was unavailable in the heydays of our exclusionary-rule jurisprudence, because it is tied to the availability of a cause of action. For years after *Mapp*, "very few lawyers would even consider representation of persons who had civil rights claims against the police," but now "much has changed. Citizens and lawyers are much more willing to seek relief in the courts for police misconduct." M. Avery, D. Rudovsky, & K. Blum, Police Misconduct: Law and Litigation, p. v (3d ed. 2005); see generally N. Aron, Liberty and Justice for All: Public Interest Law in the 1980s and Beyond (1989) (describing the growth of public-interest law). The number of public-interest law firms and lawyers who specialize in civil-rights grievances has greatly expanded.

Hudson points out that few published decisions to date announce huge awards for knock-and-announce violations. But this is an unhelpful statistic. Even if we thought that only large damages would deter police misconduct (and that police somehow are deterred by "damages" but indifferent to the prospect of large § 1988 attorney's fees), we do not know how many claims have been settled, or indeed how many violations have occurred that produced anything more than nominal injury. It is clear, at least, that the lower courts are allowing colorable knock-and-announce suits to go forward, unimpeded by assertions of qualified immunity. As far as we know, civil liability is an effective deterrent here, as we have assumed it is in other contexts.

Another development over the past half-century that deters civil-rights violations is the increasing professionalism of police forces, including a new emphasis on internal police discipline. Even as long ago as 1980 we felt it proper to "assume" that unlawful police behavior would "be dealt with appropriately" by the authorities, but we now have increasing evidence that police forces across the United States take the constitutional rights of citizens seriously. There have been "wide-ranging reforms in the education, training, and supervision of police officers." Numerous sources are now available to teach officers and their supervisors what is required of them under this Court's cases, how to respect constitutional guarantees in various situations, and how to craft an effective regime for internal discipline. Moreover, modern police forces are staffed with professionals; it is not credible to assert that internal discipline, which can limit successful careers, will not have a deterrent effect. There is also evidence that the increasing use of various forms of citizen review can enhance police accountability.

In sum, the social costs of applying the exclusionary rule to knock-and-announce violations are considerable; the incentive to such violations is minimal to begin with, and the extant deterrences against them are substantial — incomparably greater than the factors deterring warrantless entries when *Mapp* was decided. Resort to the massive remedy of suppressing evidence of guilt is unjustified.

It is striking that Justice Scalia's arguments are not simply reasons for an exception to the exclusionary rule for knock and announce violations; they are arguments against the existence of the exclusionary rule. They prompted Justice Kennedy, who concurred in Justice Scalia's opinion, to declare: "[T]he continued operation of the exclusionary rule, as settled and defined by our precedents, is not in doubt." Yet, *Hudson* suggests that there may be four votes on the current Court — Chief Justice Roberts and Justices Scalia, Thomas, and Alito — to eliminate the exclusionary rule and that it will continue to exist, and exceptions will be created, to the extent Justice Kennedy wishes.

Justice Scalia's majority opinion in *Hudson* argues that the costs of the exclusionary rule outweigh its benefits. The primary cost, of course, is allowing guilty people to go free. He argues that deterring police misconduct, the central benefit of the exclusionary rule, does not warrant its existence. He says that civil suits for damages against the police who violate the Fourth Amendment are an adequate deterrent. He also maintains that increased professionalization of police forces makes the exclusionary rule unnecessary.

There long has been a debate over whether money damages against police officers for Fourth Amendment violations are a sufficient deterrent. Those who take this view, like Justice Scalia in *Hudson*, argue that the ability to sue police officers makes the exclusionary rule unnecessary.[2]

Others argue that such suits have so little chance of success that there will be little deterrence without the exclusionary rule.[3] Juries are unlikely to find against the police in favor of convicted criminals and if they did, any damages would be nominal. Justice Breyer, in dissent in *Hudson*, makes these points in response to the majority opinion:

> What reason is there to believe that those remedies (such as private damages actions under 42 U.S.C. § 1983), which the Court found inadequate in *Mapp*, can adequately deter unconstitutional police behavior here?
>
> The cases reporting knock-and-announce violations are legion. Indeed, these cases of reported violations seem sufficiently frequent and serious as to indicate "a widespread pattern." Yet the majority, like Michigan and the United States, has failed to cite a single reported case in which a plaintiff has collected more than nominal damages solely as a result of a knock-and-announce violation. Even Michigan concedes that, "in cases like the present one . . . , damages may be virtually non-existent." And Michigan's amici further concede that civil immunities prevent tort law from being an effective substitute for the exclusionary rule at this time.

---

2. *See, e.g.*, Christopher Slobogin, *Why Liberals Should Chuck the Exclusionary Rule*, 1999 Univ. Ill. L. Rev. 363.

3. *See, e.g.*, Yale Kamisar, *In Defense of the Search and Seizure Exclusionary Rule*, 26 Harv. J.L. & Pub. Pol'y 119, 126-129 (2003) (arguing that "five decades of post-*Weeks* 'freedom' from the inhibiting effect of the federal exclusionary rule failed to produce any meaningful alternative to the exclusionary rule in any jurisdiction" and that there is no evidence that "times have changed" post-*Mapp*).

As Justice Stewart, the author of a number of significant Fourth Amendment opinions, explained, the deterrent effect of damage actions "can hardly be said to be great," as such actions are "expensive, time-consuming, not readily available, and rarely successful." The upshot is that the need for deterrence — the critical factor driving this Court's Fourth Amendment cases for close to a century — argues with at least comparable strength for evidentiary exclusion here.

There may be instances in the law where text or history or tradition leaves room for a judicial decision that rests upon little more than an unvarnished judicial instinct. But this is not one of them. Rather, our Fourth Amendment traditions place high value upon protecting privacy in the home. They emphasize the need to assure that its constitutional protections are effective, lest the Amendment "sound the word of promise to the ear but break it to the hope." They include an exclusionary principle, which since *Weeks* has formed the centerpiece of the criminal law's effort to ensure the practical reality of those promises. That is why the Court should assure itself that any departure from that principle is firmly grounded in logic, in history, in precedent, and in empirical fact. It has not done so. That is why, with respect, I dissent.

B. THE ORIGINS OF THE EXCLUSIONARY RULE

The Court first invoked the exclusionary rule as a remedy for Fourth Amendment violations in Weeks v. United States in 1914.

WEEKS v. UNITED STATES
232 U.S. 383 (1914)

Justice DAY delivered the opinion of the Court:

An indictment was returned against the defendant in the district court of the United States for the western district of Missouri, containing nine counts. The seventh count, upon which a conviction was had, charged the use of the mails for the purpose of transporting certain coupons or tickets representing chances or shares in a lottery or gift enterprise, in violation of § 213 of the Criminal Code. Sentence of fine and imprisonment was imposed.

The defendant was arrested by a police officer, so far as the record shows, without warrant, at the Union Station in Kansas City, Missouri, where he was employed by an express company. Other police officers had gone to the house of the defendant, and being told by a neighbor where the key was kept, found it and entered the house. They searched the defendant's room and took possession of various papers and articles found there, which were afterwards turned over to the United States marshal. Later in the same day police officers returned with the marshal, who thought he might find additional evidence, and, being admitted by someone in the house, probably a boarder, in response to a rap, the marshal searched the defendant's room and carried away certain letters and envelops found in the drawer of a chiffonier. Neither the marshal nor the police officer had a search warrant.

After the jury had been sworn and before any evidence had been given, the defendant urged his petition for the return of his property, which was denied by the court. Upon the introduction of such papers during the trial, the defendant objected on the ground that the papers had been obtained without a search warrant, and by breaking open his home, in violation of the 4th and 5th Amendments to the Constitution of the United States, which objection was overruled by the court. Among the papers retained and put in evidence were a number of lottery tickets and statements with reference to the lottery, taken at the first visit of the police to the defendant's room, and a number of letters written to the defendant in respect to the lottery, taken by the marshal upon his search of defendant's room.

The defendant assigns error, among other things, in the court's refusal to grant his petition for the return of his property, and in permitting the papers to be used at the trial.

It is thus apparent that the question presented involves the determination of the duty of the court with reference to the motion made by the defendant for the return of certain letters, as well as other papers, taken from his room by the United States marshal, who, without authority of process, if any such could have been legally issued, visited the room of the defendant for the declared purpose of obtaining additional testimony to support the charge against the accused, and, having gained admission to the house, took from the drawer of a chiffonier there found certain letters written to the defendant, tending to show his guilt. These letters were placed in the control of the district attorney, and were subsequently produced by him and offered in evidence against the accused at the trial. The defendant contends that such appropriation of his private correspondence was in violation of rights secured to him by the 4th and 5th Amendments to the Constitution of the United States. We shall deal with the 4th Amendment.

The effect of the 4th Amendment is to put the courts of the United States and Federal officials, in the exercise of their power and authority, under limitations and restraints as to the exercise of such power and authority, and to forever secure the people, their persons, houses, papers, and effects, against all unreasonable searches and seizures under the guise of law. This protection reaches all alike, whether accused of crime or not, and the duty of giving to it force and effect is obligatory upon all intrusted under our Federal system with the enforcement of the laws. The tendency of those who execute the criminal laws of the country to obtain conviction by means of unlawful seizures and enforced confessions, the latter often obtained after subjecting accused persons to unwarranted practices destructive of rights secured by the Federal Constitution, should find no sanction in the judgments of the courts, which are charged at all times with the support of the Constitution, and to which people of all conditions have a right to appeal for the maintenance of such fundamental rights.

If letters and private documents can thus be seized and held and used in evidence against a citizen accused of an offense, the protection of the 4th Amendment, declaring his right to be secure against such searches and seizures, is of no value, and, so far as those thus placed are concerned, might as well be stricken from the Constitution. The efforts of the courts and their officials to bring the guilty to punishment, praiseworthy as they are, are not to be aided by the sacrifice of those great principles established by years of endeavor and suffering which have resulted in their embodiment in the fundamental law of the land. The United States marshal could only have invaded the house of the accused when armed with a warrant issued as required by the Constitution, upon sworn information, and describing with reasonable particularity the thing for which the search was to be made. Instead, he acted without sanction of law, doubtless prompted by the desire to bring further proof to the aid of the government, and under color of his office undertook to make a seizure of private papers in direct violation of the constitutional prohibition against such action. Under such circumstances, without sworn information and particular description, not even an order of court would have justified such procedure; much less was it within the authority of the United States marshal to thus invade the house and privacy of the accused.

The court before which the application was made in this case recognized the illegal character of the seizure, and ordered the return of property not in its judgment competent to be offered at the trial, but refused the application of the accused to turn over the letters, which were afterwards put in evidence on behalf of the government.

We therefore reach the conclusion that the letters in question were taken from the house of the accused by an official of the United States, acting under color of his office, in direct violation of the constitutional rights of the defendant; that having made a seasonable application for their return, which was heard and passed upon by the court, there was involved in the order refusing the application a denial of the constitutional rights of the accused, and that the court should have restored these letters to the accused. In holding them and permitting their use upon the trial, we think prejudicial error was committed. As to the papers and property seized by the policemen, it does not appear that they acted under any claim of Federal authority such as would make the amendment applicable to such unauthorized seizures. The record shows that what they did by way of arrest and search and seizure was done before the finding of the indictment in the Federal court; under what supposed right or authority does not appear. What remedies the defendant may have against them we need not inquire, as the 4th Amendment is not directed to individual misconduct of such officials. Its limitations reach the Federal government and its agencies.

Weeks involves the application of the exclusionary rule to the federal government. The Court initially considered and rejected the application of the exclusionary rule to the states in Wolf v. Colorado, 338 U.S. 25 (1949). Although the Court in *Wolf* said that "[t]he security of one's privacy against arbitrary intrusion by the police ... is ... implicit in 'the concept of ordered liberty' and as such enforceable against the States through the Due Process Clause," the Court held that the exclusionary rule is not enforceable against the States as "an essential ingredient of the right." The Court concluded: "We hold, therefore, that in a prosecution in a State court for a State crime the Fourteenth Amendment does not forbid the admission of evidence obtained by an unreasonable search and seizure." As explained in Chapter 1, *Wolf* was decided at a time when there was intense debate over whether the Bill of Rights should be applied to the states and when a majority of the Court was generally reluctant to apply Bill of Rights provisions to the states.

This changed with the Warren Court, which found almost all of the Bill of Rights to be incorporated and to apply to the states. In 1961, the Supreme Court overruled *Wolf* and held that the exclusionary rule applies to the states in the landmark decision of Mapp v. Ohio.

MAPP v. OHIO

367 U.S. 643 (1961)

Justice CLARK delivered the opinion of the Court.

Appellant stands convicted of knowingly having had in her possession and under her control certain lewd and lascivious books, pictures, and photographs in violation of § 2905.34 of Ohio's Revised Code. As officially stated in the syllabus to its opinion, the Supreme Court of Ohio found that her conviction was valid though "based primarily upon the introduction in evidence of lewd and lascivious books and pictures unlawfully seized during an unlawful search of defendant's home."

On May 23, 1957, three Cleveland police officers arrived at appellant's residence in that city pursuant to information that "a person [was] hiding out in the home, who was wanted for questioning in connection with a recent bombing, and that there was a large amount of policy paraphernalia being hidden in the home." Miss Mapp and her daughter by a former marriage lived on the top floor of the two-family dwelling. Upon their arrival at that house, the officers knocked on the door and demanded entrance but appellant, after telephoning her attorney, refused to admit them without a search warrant. They advised their headquarters of the situation and undertook a surveillance of the house.

The officers again sought entrance some three hours later when four or more additional officers arrived on the scene. When Miss Mapp did not come to the door immediately, at least one of the several doors to the house was forcibly opened and the policemen gained admittance. Meanwhile Miss Mapp's attorney arrived, but the officers, having secured their own entry, and continuing in their defiance of the law, would permit him neither to see Miss Mapp nor to enter the house. It appears that Miss Mapp was halfway down the stairs from the upper floor to the front door when the officers, in this highhanded manner, broke into the hall. She demanded to see the search warrant. A paper, claimed to be a warrant, was held up by one of the officers. She grabbed the "warrant" and placed it in her bosom. A struggle ensued in which the officers recovered the piece of paper and as a result of which they handcuffed appellant because she had been "belligerent" in resisting their official rescue of the "warrant" from her person. Running roughshod over appellant, a policeman "grabbed" her, "twisted [her] hand," and she "yelled [and] pleaded with him" because "it was hurting." Appellant, in handcuffs, was then forcibly taken upstairs to her bedroom where the officers searched a dresser, a chest of drawers, a closet and some suitcases. They also looked into a photo album and through personal papers belonging to the appellant. The search spread to the rest of the second floor including the child's bedroom, the living room, the kitchen and a dinette. The basement of the building and a trunk found therein were also searched. The obscene materials for possession of which she was ultimately convicted were discovered in the course of that widespread search.

At the trial no search warrant was produced by the prosecution, nor was the failure to produce one explained or accounted for. At best, "There is, in the record, considerable doubt as to whether there ever was any warrant for the search of defendant's home."

The State says that even if the search were made without authority, or otherwise unreasonably, it is not prevented from using the unconstitutionally seized evidence at trial, citing Wolf v. People of State of Colorado (1949).

There are in the cases of this Court some passing references to the *Weeks* rule as being one of evidence. But the plain and unequivocal language of *Weeks*—and its later paraphrase in *Wolf*—to the effect that the *Weeks* rule is of constitutional origin, remains entirely undisturbed.

Since the Fourth Amendment's right of privacy has been declared enforceable against the States through the Due Process Clause of the Fourteenth, it is enforceable against them by the same sanction of exclusion as is used against the Federal Government. Were it otherwise, then just as without the *Weeks* rule the assurance against unreasonable federal searches and seizures would be "a form of words," valueless and undeserving of mention in a perpetual charter of inestimable human liberties, so too, without that rule the freedom from state invasions of privacy would be so ephemeral and so neatly severed from its conceptual nexus with the freedom from all brutish means of coercing evidence as not to merit this Court's high regard as a freedom "implicit in 'the concept of ordered liberty.'" At the time that the Court held in *Wolf* that the Amendment was applicable to the States through the Due Process Clause, the cases of this Court had steadfastly held that as to federal officers the Fourth Amendment included the exclusion of the evidence seized in violation of its provisions. Even *Wolf* "stoutly adhered" to that proposition. The right to privacy, when conceded operatively enforceable against the States, was not susceptible of destruction by avulsion of the sanction upon which its protection and enjoyment had always been deemed dependent. Therefore, in extending the substantive protections of due process to all constitutionally unreasonable searches — state or federal — it was logically and constitutionally necessary that the exclusion doctrine — an essential part of the right to privacy — be also insisted upon as an essential ingredient of the right newly recognized by the *Wolf* case. In short, the admission of the new constitutional right by *Wolf* could not consistently tolerate denial of its most important constitutional privilege, namely, the exclusion of the evidence which an accused had been forced to give by reason of the unlawful seizure. To hold otherwise is to grant the right but in reality to withhold its privilege and enjoyment. Only last year the Court itself recognized that the purpose of the exclusionary rule "is to deter — to compel respect for the constitutional guaranty in the only effectively available way — by removing the incentive to disregard it."

Indeed, we are aware of no restraint, similar to that rejected today, conditioning the enforcement of any other basic constitutional right. The right to privacy, no less important than any other right carefully and particularly reserved to the people, would stand in marked contrast to all other rights declared as "basic to a free society." This Court has not hesitated to enforce as strictly against the States as it does against the Federal Government the rights of free speech and of a free press, the rights to notice and to a fair, public trial, including, as it does, the right not to be convicted by use of a coerced confession, however logically relevant it be, and without regard to its reliability. And nothing could be more certain than that when a coerced confession is involved, "the relevant rules of evidence" are overridden without regard to "the incidence of such conduct by the police," slight or frequent. Why should not the same rule apply to what is tantamount to coerced testimony by way of unconstitutional seizure of goods, papers, effect, documents, etc.? We find that, as to the Federal Government, the Fourth and Fifth Amendments and, as to the States, the freedom from unconscionable invasions of privacy and the freedom from convictions based upon coerced confessions do enjoy an "intimate relation" in their perpetuation of "principles of humanity and civil liberty (secured) . . . only after years of struggle." They express "supplementing phases of the same constitutional purpose — to maintain inviolate large areas of personal privacy." The philosophy of each Amendment and of each freedom is complementary to, although not dependent upon, that of the other in its sphere of influence — the very least that together they assure in either sphere is that no man is to be convicted on unconstitutional evidence.

Moreover, our holding that the exclusionary rule is an essential part of both the Fourth and Fourteenth Amendments is not only the logical dictate of prior cases, but it also makes very good sense. There is no war between the Constitution and common sense. Presently, a federal prosecutor may make no use of evidence illegally seized, but a State's attorney across the street may, although he supposedly is operating under the enforceable prohibitions of the same Amendment. Thus the State, by admitting evidence unlawfully seized, serves to encourage disobedience to the Federal Constitution which it is bound to uphold.

In non-exclusionary States, federal officers, being human, were by it invited to and did, as our cases indicate, step across the street to the State's attorney with their unconstitutionally seized evidence. Prosecution on the basis of that evidence was then had in a state court in utter disregard of the enforceable Fourth Amendment. If the fruits of an unconstitutional search had been inadmissible in both state and federal courts, this inducement to evasion would have been sooner eliminated. There would be no need to reconcile such cases as *Rea* and *Schnettler*, each pointing up the hazardous uncertainties of our heretofore ambivalent approach.

Federal-state cooperation in the solution of crime under constitutional standards will be promoted, if only by recognition of their now mutual obligation to respect the same fundamental criteria in their approaches. "However much in a particular case insistence upon such rules may appear as a technicality that inures to the benefit of a guilty person, the history of the criminal law proves that tolerance of shortcut methods in law enforcement impairs its enduring effectiveness." Denying shortcuts to only one of two cooperating law enforcement agencies tends naturally to breed legitimate suspicion of "working arrangements" whose results are equally tainted.

There are those who say, as did Justice (then Judge) Cardozo, that under our constitutional exclusionary doctrine "[t]he criminal is to go free because the constable has blundered." In some cases this will undoubtedly be the result. But, "there is another consideration — the imperative of judicial integrity." The criminal goes free, if he must, but it is the law that sets him free. Nothing can destroy a government more quickly than its failure to observe its own laws, or worse, its disregard of the charter of its own existence. As Mr. Justice Brandeis, dissenting, said in Olmstead v. United States, 1928: "Our government is the potent, the omnipresent teacher. For good or for ill, it teaches the whole people by its example. . . . If the government becomes a lawbreaker, it breeds contempt for law; it invites every man to become a law unto himself; it invites anarchy."

Nor can it lightly be assumed that, as a practical matter, adoption of the exclusionary rule fetters law enforcement. Only last year this Court expressly considered that contention and found that "pragmatic evidence of a sort" to the contrary was not wanting.

The ignoble shortcut to conviction left open to the State tends to destroy the entire system of constitutional restraints on which the liberties of the people rest. Having once recognized that the right to privacy embodied in the Fourth Amendment is enforceable against the States, and that the right to be secure against rude invasions of privacy by state officers is, therefore, constitutional in origin, we can no longer permit that right to remain an empty promise. Because it is enforceable in the same manner and to like effect as other basic rights secured by the Due Process Clause, we can no longer permit it to be revocable at the whim of any police officer who, in the name of law enforcement itself, chooses to suspend its enjoyment. Our decision, founded on reason and truth, gives to the individual no more than that which the Constitution guarantees him, to the police officer no less than that to which honest law enforcement is entitled, and, to the courts, that judicial integrity so necessary in the true administration of justice.

Justice HARLAN, whom Justice FRANKFURTER and Justice WHITTAKER join, dissenting.

In overruling the *Wolf* case the Court, in my opinion, has forgotten the sense of judicial restraint which, with due regard for stare decisis, is one element that should enter into deciding whether a past decision of this Court should be overruled. Apart from that I also believe that the *Wolf* rule represents sounder Constitutional doctrine than the new rule which now replaces it.

Essential to the majority's argument against *Wolf* is the proposition that the rule of Weeks v. United States excluding in federal criminal trials the use of evidence obtained in violation of the Fourth Amendment, derives not from the "supervisory power" of this Court over the federal judicial system, but from Constitutional requirement. This is so because no one, I suppose, would suggest that this Court possesses any general supervisory power over the state courts. Although I entertain considerable doubt as to the soundness of this foundational proposition of the majority, I shall assume, for present purposes, that the *Weeks* rule "is of constitutional origin."

At the heart of the majority's opinion in this case is the following syllogism: (1) the rule excluding in federal criminal trials evidence which is the product of all illegal search and seizure is a "part and parcel" of the Fourth Amendment; (2) *Wolf* held that the "privacy" assured against federal action by the Fourth Amendment is also protected against state action by the Fourteenth Amendment; and (3) it is therefore "logically and constitutionally necessary" that the *Weeks* exclusionary rule should also be enforced against the States.

This reasoning ultimately rests on the unsound premise that because *Wolf* carried into the States, as part of "the concept of ordered liberty" embodied in the Fourteenth Amendment, the principle of "privacy" underlying the Fourth Amendment, it must follow that whatever configurations of the Fourth Amendment have been developed in the particularizing federal precedents are likewise to be deemed a part of "ordered liberty," and as such are enforceable against the States. For me, this does not follow at all.

It cannot be too much emphasized that what was recognized in *Wolf* was not that the Fourth Amendment as such is enforceable against the States as a facet of due process, a view of the Fourteenth Amendment which, as *Wolf* itself pointed out, has long since been discredited, but the principle of privacy "which is at the core of the Fourth Amendment." It would not be proper to expect or impose any precise equivalence, either as regards the scope of the right or the means of its implementation, between the requirements of the Fourth and Fourteenth Amendments.

Thus, even in a case which presented simply the question of whether a particular search and seizure was constitutionally "unreasonable" — say in a tort action against state officers — we would not be true to the Fourteenth Amendment were we merely to stretch the general principle of individual privacy on a Procrustean bed of federal precedents under the Fourth Amendment. But in this instance more than that is involved, for here we are reviewing not a determination that what the state police did was Constitutionally permissible (since the state court quite evidently assumed that it was not), but a determination that appellant was properly found guilty of conduct which, for present purposes, it is to be assumed the State could Constitutionally punish. Since there is not the slightest suggestion that Ohio's policy is "affirmatively to sanction . . . police incursion into privacy" what the Court is now doing is to impose upon the States not only federal substantive standards of "search and seizure" but also the basic federal remedy for violation of those standards. For I think it entirely clear that the *Weeks* exclusionary rule is but a remedy which, by penalizing past official misconduct, is aimed at deterring such conduct in the future.

I would not impose upon the States this federal exclusionary remedy. The reasons given by the majority for now suddenly turning its back on *Wolf* seem to me notably unconvincing. The preservation of a proper balance between state and federal responsibility in the administration of criminal justice demands patience on the part of those who might like to see things move faster among the States in this respect. Problems of criminal law enforcement vary widely from State to State. One State, in considering the totality of its legal picture, may conclude that the need for embracing the *Weeks* rule is pressing because other remedies are unavailable or inadequate to secure compliance with the substantive Constitutional principle involved. Another, though equally solicitous of Constitutional rights, may choose to pursue one purpose at a time, allowing all evidence relevant to guilt to be brought into a criminal trial, and dealing with Constitutional infractions by other means. Still another may consider the exclusionary rule too rough-and-ready a remedy, in that it reaches only unconstitutional intrusions which eventuate in criminal prosecution of the victims. Further, a State after experimenting with the *Weeks* rule for a time may, because of unsatisfactory experience with it, decide to revert to a non-exclusionary rule.

A state conviction comes to us as the complete product of a sovereign judicial system. Typically a case will have been tried in a trial court, tested in some final appellate court, and will go no further. In the comparatively rare instance when a conviction is reviewed by us on due process grounds we deal then with a finished product in the creation of which we are allowed no hand, and our task, far from being one of over-all supervision, is, speaking generally, restricted to a determination of whether the prosecution was Constitutionally fair. The specifics of trial procedure, which in every mature legal system will vary greatly in detail, are within the sole competence of the States. I do not see how it can be said that a trial becomes unfair simply because a State determines that evidence may be considered by the trier of fact, regardless of how it was obtained, if it is relevant to the one issue with which the trial is concerned, the guilt or innocence of the accused. Of course, a court may use its procedures as an incidental means of pursuing other ends than the correct resolution of the controversies before it. Such indeed is the *Weeks* rule, but if a State does not choose to use its courts in this way, I do not believe that this Court is empowered to impose this much-debated procedure on local courts, however efficacious we may consider the *Weeks* rule to be as a means of securing Constitutional rights.

I regret that I find so unwise in principle and so inexpedient in policy a decision motivated by the high purpose of increasing respect for Constitutional rights. But in the last analysis I think this Court can increase respect for the Constitution only if it rigidly respects the limitations which the Constitution places upon it, and respects as well the principles inherent in its own processes. In the present case I think we exceed both, and that our voice becomes only a voice of power, not of reason.

C. WHO CAN OBJECT TO THE INTRODUCTION OF EVIDENCE AND RAISE THE EXCLUSIONARY RULE?

In Jones v. United States, 362 U.S. 257 (1960), the Supreme Court took a broad view of who could object to the introduction of evidence and raise the exclusionary rule. The Court said that a person who "was aggrieved by an unlawful search or seizure" had standing to challenge it. The Court said that "[i]n order to qualify as a 'person aggrieved by an unlawful search and seizure' one must have been a victim of a search or seizure, one against whom the search was directed, as distinguished from one who claims prejudice only through the use of evidence gathered as a consequence of a search or seizure directed at someone else." The Court concluded that "anyone legitimately on premises where a search occurs may challenge its legality by way of a motion to suppress, when its fruits are proposed to be used against him."

In Rakas v. Illinois, below, the Court changed the approach to determining who may raise the exclusionary rule. The Court held that only those whose Fourth Amendment rights were violated may raise the exclusionary rule. In other words, a person cannot raise the exclusionary rule just because he or she is "aggrieved" by an illegal search; to raise the exclusionary rule a person must show a violation of his or her Fourth Amendment rights.

RAKAS v. ILLINOIS
439 U.S. 128 (1978)

Justice REHNQUIST delivered the opinion of the Court.

Petitioners were convicted of armed robbery in the Circuit Court of Kankakee County, Ill., and their convictions were affirmed on appeal. At their trial, the prosecution offered into evidence a sawed-off rifle and rifle shells that had been seized by police during a search of an automobile in which petitioners had been passengers. Neither petitioner is the owner of the automobile and neither has ever asserted that he owned the rifle or shells seized. The Illinois Appellate Court held that petitioners lacked standing to object to the allegedly unlawful search and seizure and denied their motion to suppress the evidence.

I

Because we are not here concerned with the issue of probable cause, a brief description of the events leading to the search of the automobile will suffice. A police officer on a routine patrol received a radio call notifying him of a robbery of a clothing store in Bourbonnais, Ill., and describing the getaway car. Shortly thereafter, the officer spotted an automobile which he thought might be the getaway car. After following the car for some time and after the arrival of assistance, he and several other officers stopped the vehicle. The occupants of the automobile, petitioners and two female companions, were ordered out of the car and, after the occupants had left the car, two officers searched the interior of the vehicle. They discovered a box of rifle shells in the glove compartment, which had been locked, and a sawed-off rifle under the front passenger seat. After discovering the rifle and the shells, the officers took petitioners to the station and placed them under arrest.

Before trial petitioners moved to suppress the rifle and shells seized from the car on the ground that the search violated the Fourth and Fourteenth Amendments. They conceded that they did not own the automobile and were simply passengers; the owner of the car had been the driver of the vehicle at the time of the search. Nor did they assert that they owned the rifle or the shells seized. The prosecutor challenged petitioners' standing to object to the lawfulness of the search of the car because neither the car, the shells nor the rifle belonged to them. The trial court agreed that petitioners lacked standing and denied the motion to suppress the evidence. In view of this holding, the court did not determine whether there was probable cause for the search and seizure. On appeal after petitioners' conviction, the Appellate Court of Illinois, Third Judicial District, affirmed the trial court's denial of petitioners' motion to suppress because it held that "without a proprietary or other similar interest in an automobile, a mere passenger therein lacks standing to challenge the legality of the search of the vehicle."

We reject petitioners' suggestion. The proponent of a motion to suppress has the burden of establishing that his own Fourth Amendment rights were violated by the challenged search or seizure. The prosecutor argued that petitioners lacked standing to challenge the search because they did not own the rifle, the shells or the automobile. Petitioners did not contest the factual predicates of the prosecutor's argument and instead, simply stated that they were not required to prove ownership to object to the search. The prosecutor's argument gave petitioners notice that they were to be put to their proof on any issue as to which they had the burden, and because of their failure to assert ownership, we must assume, for purposes of our review, that petitioners do not own the rifle or the shells.

II

Petitioners first urge us to relax or broaden the rule of standing enunciated in Jones v. United States (1960), so that any criminal defendant at whom a search was "directed" would have standing to contest the legality of that search and object to the admission at trial of evidence obtained as a result of the search. Alternatively, petitioners argue that they have standing to object to the search under *Jones* because they were "legitimately on [the] premises" at the time of the search.

The concept of standing discussed in *Jones* focuses on whether the person seeking to challenge the legality of a search as a basis for suppressing evidence was himself the "victim" of the search or seizure. Adoption of the so-called "target" theory advanced by petitioners would in effect permit a defendant to assert that a violation of the Fourth Amendment rights of a third party entitled him to have evidence suppressed at his trial. If we reject petitioners' request for a broadened rule of standing such as this, and reaffirm the holding of *Jones* and other cases that Fourth Amendment rights are personal rights that may not be asserted vicariously, we will have occasion to re-examine the "standing" terminology emphasized in *Jones*. For we are not at all sure that the determination of a motion to suppress is materially aided by labeling the inquiry identified in *Jones* as one of standing, rather than simply recognizing it as one involving the substantive question of whether or not the proponent of the motion to suppress has had his own Fourth Amendment rights infringed by the search and seizure which he seeks to challenge.

A

We decline to extend the rule of standing in Fourth Amendment cases in the manner suggested by petitioners. As we stated in Alderman v. United States (1969), "Fourth Amendment rights are personal rights which, like some other constitutional rights, may not be vicariously asserted." A person who is aggrieved by an illegal search and seizure only through the introduction of damaging evidence secured by a search of a third person's premises or property has not had any of his Fourth Amendment rights infringed. And since the exclusionary rule is an attempt to effectuate the guarantees of the Fourth Amendment, it is proper to permit only defendants whose Fourth Amendment rights have been violated to benefit from the rule's protections. There is no reason to think that a party whose rights have been infringed will not, if evidence is used against him, have ample motivation to move to suppress it. Even if such a person is not a defendant in the action, he may be able to recover damages for the violation of his Fourth Amendment rights, or seek redress under state law for invasion of privacy or trespass.

Conferring standing to raise vicarious Fourth Amendment claims would necessarily mean a more widespread invocation of the exclusionary rule during criminal trials. The Court's opinion in *Alderman* counseled against such an extension of the exclusionary rule. Each time the exclusionary rule is applied it exacts a substantial social cost for the vindication of Fourth Amendment rights. Relevant and reliable evidence is kept from the trier of fact and the search for truth at trial is deflected. Since our cases generally have held that one whose Fourth Amendment rights are violated may successfully suppress evidence obtained in the course of an illegal search and seizure, misgivings as to the benefit of enlarging the class of persons who may invoke that rule are properly considered when deciding whether to expand standing to assert Fourth Amendment violations.

B

Had we accepted petitioners' request to allow persons other than those whose own Fourth Amendment rights were violated by a challenged search and seizure to suppress evidence obtained in the course of such police activity, it would be appropriate to retain *Jones*' use of standing in Fourth Amendment analysis.

Under petitioners' target theory, a court could determine that a defendant had standing to invoke the exclusionary rule without having to inquire into the substantive question of whether the challenged search or seizure violated the Fourth Amendment rights of that particular defendant. However, having rejected petitioners' target theory and reaffirmed the principle that the "rights assured by the Fourth Amendment are personal rights, [which] . . . may be enforced by exclusion of evidence only at the instance of one whose own protection was infringed by the search and seizure," the question necessarily arises whether it serves any useful analytical purpose to consider this principle a matter of standing, distinct from the merits of a defendant's Fourth Amendment claim. We can think of no decided cases of this Court that would have come out differently had we concluded, as we do now, that the type of standing requirement discussed in *Jones* and reaffirmed today is more properly subsumed under substantive Fourth Amendment doctrine. Rigorous application of the principle that the rights secured by this Amendment are personal, in place of a notion of "standing," will produce no additional situations in which evidence must be excluded. The inquiry under either approach is the same. But we think the better analysis forthrightly focuses on the extent of a particular defendant's rights under the Fourth Amendment, rather than on any theoretically separate, but invariably intertwined concept of standing.

Analyzed in these terms, the question is whether the challenged search or seizure violated the Fourth Amendment rights of a criminal defendant who seeks to exclude the evidence obtained during it. That inquiry in turn requires a determination of whether the disputed search and seizure has infringed an interest of the defendant which the Fourth Amendment was designed to protect. We are under no illusion that by dispensing with the rubric of standing used in *Jones* we have rendered any simpler the determination of whether the proponent of a motion to suppress is entitled to contest the legality of a search and seizure. But by frankly recognizing that this aspect of the analysis belongs more properly under the heading of substantive Fourth Amendment doctrine than under the heading of standing, we think the decision of this issue will rest on sounder logical footing.

C

Judged by the foregoing analysis, petitioners' claims must fail. They asserted neither a property nor a possessory interest in the automobile, nor an interest in the property seized. And as we have previously indicated, the fact that they were "legitimately on [the] premises" in the sense that they were in the car with the permission of its owner is not determinative of whether they had a legitimate expectation of privacy in the particular areas of the automobile searched. It is unnecessary for us to decide here whether the same expectations of privacy are warranted in a car as would be justified in a dwelling place in analogous circumstances. We have on numerous occasions pointed out that cars are not to be treated identically with houses or apartments for Fourth Amendment purposes. But here petitioners' claim is one which would fail even in an analogous situation in a dwelling place, since they made no showing that they had any legitimate expectation of privacy in the glove compartment or area under the seat of the car in which they were merely passengers. Like the trunk of an automobile, these are areas in which a passenger qua passenger simply would not normally have a legitimate expectation of privacy.

Justice WHITE, with whom Justice BRENNAN, Justice MARSHALL, and Justice STEVENS join, dissenting.

The Court today holds that the Fourth Amendment protects property, not people, and specifically that a legitimate occupant of an automobile may not invoke the exclusionary rule and challenge a search of that vehicle unless he happens to own or have a possessory interest in it. Though professing to acknowledge that the primary purpose of the Fourth Amendment's prohibition of unreasonable searches is the protection of privacy — not property — the Court nonetheless effectively ties the application of the Fourth Amendment and the exclusionary rule in this situation to property law concepts. Insofar as passengers are concerned, the Court's opinion today declares an "open season" on automobiles. However unlawful stopping and searching a car may be, absent a possessory or ownership interest, no "mere" passenger may object, regardless of his relationship to the owner. Because the majority's conclusion has no support in the Court's controlling decisions, in the logic of the Fourth Amendment, or in common sense, I must respectfully dissent. If the Court is troubled by the practical impact of the exclusionary rule, it should face the issue of that rule's continued validity squarely instead of distorting other doctrines in an attempt to reach what are perceived as the correct results in specific cases.

Two intersecting doctrines long established in this Court's opinions control here. The first is the recognition of some cognizable level of privacy in the interior of an automobile. Though the reasonableness of the expectation of privacy in a vehicle may be somewhat weaker than that in a home, "[a] search even of an automobile, is a substantial invasion of privacy. To protect that privacy from official arbitrariness, the Court always has regarded probable cause as the minimum requirement for a lawful search."

The second tenet is that when a person is legitimately present in a private place, his right to privacy is protected from unreasonable governmental interference even if he does not own the premises.

These two fundamental aspects of Fourth Amendment law demand that petitioners be permitted to challenge the search and seizure of the automobile in this case. It is of no significance that a car is different for Fourth Amendment purposes from a house, for if there is some protection for the privacy of an automobile then the only relevant analogy is between a person legitimately in someone else's vehicle and a person legitimately in someone else's home. If both strands of the Fourth Amendment doctrine adumbrated above are valid, the Court must reach a different result. Instead, it chooses to eviscerate the *Jones* principle, an action in which I am unwilling to participate.

It is true that the Court asserts that it is not limiting the Fourth Amendment bar against unreasonable searches to the protection of property rights, but in reality it is doing exactly that. Petitioners were in a private place with the permission of the owner, but the Court states that that is not sufficient to establish entitlement to a legitimate expectation of privacy. But if that is not sufficient, what would be? We are not told, and it is hard to imagine anything short of a property interest that would satisfy the majority. Insofar as the Court's rationale is concerned, no passenger in an automobile, without an ownership or possessory interest and regardless of his relationship to the owner, may claim Fourth Amendment protection against illegal stops and searches of the automobile in which he is rightfully present.

More importantly, how is the Court able to avoid answering the question why presence in a private place with the owner's permission is insufficient? If it is "tautological to fall back on the notion that those expectations of privacy which are legitimate depend primarily on cases deciding exclusionary rule issues in criminal cases," then it surely must be tautological to decide that issue simply by unadorned fiat.

As a control on governmental power, the Fourth Amendment assures that some expectations of privacy are justified and will be protected from official intrusion. That should be true in this instance, for if protected zones of privacy can only be purchased or obtained by possession of property, then much of our daily lives will be unshielded from unreasonable governmental prying, and the reach of the Fourth Amendment will have been narrowed to protect chiefly those with possessory interests in real or personal property.

At most, one could say that perhaps the Constitution provides some degree less protection for the personal freedom from unreasonable governmental intrusion when one does not have a possessory interest in the invaded private place. But that would only change the extent of the protection; it would not free police to do the unreasonable, as does the decision today. And since the accused should be entitled to litigate the application of the Fourth Amendment where his privacy interest is merely arguable, the failure to allow such litigation here is the more incomprehensible.

The Court's holding is contrary not only to our past decisions and the logic of the Fourth Amendment but also to the everyday expectations of privacy that we all share. Because of that, it is unworkable in all the various situations that arise in real life. If the owner of the car had not only invited petitioners to join her but had said to them, "I give you a temporary possessory interest in my vehicle so that you will share the right to privacy that the Supreme Court says that I own," then apparently the majority would reverse. But people seldom say such things, though they may mean their invitation to encompass them if only they had thought of the problem. If the nonowner were the spouse or child of the owner, would the Court recognize a sufficient interest? If so, would distant relatives somehow have more of an expectation of privacy than close friends? What if the nonowner were driving with the owner's permission? Would nonowning drivers have more of an expectation of privacy than mere passengers? What about a passenger in a taxicab? *Katz* expressly recognized protection for such passengers. Why should Fourth Amendment rights be present when one pays a cabdriver for a ride but be absent when one is given a ride by a friend?

The distinctions the Court would draw are based on relationships between private parties, but the Fourth Amendment is concerned with the relationship of one of those parties to the government. Divorced as it is from the purpose of the Fourth Amendment, the Court's essentially property-based rationale can satisfactorily answer none of the questions posed above. That is reason enough to reject it. The *Jones* rule is relatively easily applied by police and courts; the rule announced today will not provide law enforcement officials with a bright line between the protected and the unprotected. Only rarely will police know whether one private party has or has not been granted a sufficient possessory or other interest by another private party. Surely in this case the officers had no such knowledge. The Court's rule will ensnare defendants and police in need-less litigation over factors that should not be determinative of Fourth Amend-ment rights.

More importantly, the ruling today undercuts the force of the exclusionary rule in the one area in which its use is most certainly justified — the deterrence of bad-faith violations of the Fourth Amendment. This decision invites police to engage in patently unreasonable searches every time an automobile contains more than one occupant. Should something be found, only the owner of the vehicle, or of the item, will have standing to seek suppression, and the evidence will presumably be usable against the other occupants. The danger of such bad faith is especially high in cases such as this one where the officers are only after the passengers and can usually infer accurately that the driver is the owner. The suppression remedy for those owners in whose vehicles something is found and who are charged with crime is small consolation for all those owners and occu-pants whose privacy will be needlessly invaded by officers following mistaken hunches not rising to the level of probable cause but operated on in the knowl-edge that someone in a crowded car will probably be unprotected if contraband or incriminating evidence happens to be found. After this decision, police will have little to lose by unreasonably searching vehicles occupied by more than one person.

Of course, most police officers will decline the Court's invitation and will continue to do their jobs as best they can in accord with the Fourth Amendment. But the very purpose of the Bill of Rights was to answer the justified fear that governmental agents cannot be left totally to their own devices, and the Bill of Rights is enforceable in the courts because human experience teaches that not all such officials will otherwise adhere to the stated precepts. Some police-men simply do act in bad faith, even if for understandable ends, and some deterrent is needed. In the rush to limit the applicability of the exclusionary rule somewhere, anywhere, the Court ignores precedent, logic, and common sense to exclude the rule's operation from situations in which, paradoxically, it is justified and needed.

Rakas, then, disavows the use of the term "standing," and says instead that the focus in determining who can raise the exclusionary rule is on whether a per-son's Fourth Amendment rights were violated, which generally turns on whether a person has a reasonable expectation of privacy. For example, in Rawlings v. Kentucky, 448 U.S. 98 (1980), the Court held that a man could not raise the exclusionary rule when contraband belonging to him was found inside a woman's purse when he and the woman were visiting premises that were searched. The Court concluded that the man had no reasonable expectation of privacy under the circumstances and thus could not raise the exclusionary rule.

The Court has considered the application of *Rakas* in two situations that repeatedly occur: When can visitors in a person's home raise the exclusionary rule? When can passengers in a person's car raise the exclusionary rule? Minnesota v. Carter addresses the former and the recent decision in Brendlin v. California concerns the latter.

MINNESOTA v. CARTER
525 U.S. 83 (1998)

Chief Justice REHNQUIST delivered the opinion of the Court.

Respondents and the lessee of an apartment were sitting in one of its rooms, bagging cocaine. While so engaged they were observed by a police officer, who looked through a drawn window blind. The Supreme Court of Minnesota held that the officer's viewing was a search that violated respondents' Fourth Amendment rights. We hold that no such violation occurred.

James Thielen, a police officer in the Twin Cities' suburb of Eagan, Minnesota, went to an apartment building to investigate a tip from a confidential informant. The informant said that he had walked by the window of a ground-floor apartment and had seen people putting a white powder into bags. The officer looked in the same window through a gap in the closed blind and observed the bagging operation for several minutes. He then notified headquarters, which began preparing affidavits for a search warrant while he returned to the apartment building. When two men left the building in a previously identified Cadillac, the police stopped the car. Inside were respondents Carter and Johns. As the police opened the door of the car to let Johns out, they observed a black, zippered pouch and a handgun, later determined to be loaded, on the vehicle's floor. Carter and Johns were arrested, and a later police search of the vehicle the next day discovered pagers, a scale, and 47 grams of cocaine in plastic sandwich bags.

After seizing the car, the police returned to Apartment 103 and arrested the occupant, Kimberly Thompson, who is not a party to this appeal. A search of the apartment pursuant to a warrant revealed cocaine residue on the kitchen table and plastic baggies similar to those found in the Cadillac. Thielen identified Carter, Johns, and Thompson as the three people he had observed placing the powder into baggies. The police later learned that while Thompson was the lessee of the apartment, Carter and Johns lived in Chicago and had come to the apartment for the sole purpose of packaging the cocaine. Carter and Johns had never been to the apartment before and were only in the apartment for approximately 2 1/2 hours. In return for the use of the apartment, Carter and Johns had given Thompson one-eighth of an ounce of the cocaine.

Carter and Johns were charged with conspiracy to commit a controlled substance crime in the first degree and aiding and abetting in a controlled substance crime in the first degree, in violation of Minn. Stat. §§ 152.021. They moved to suppress all evidence obtained from the apartment and the Cadillac, as well as to suppress several postarrest incriminating statements they had made. They argued that Thielen's initial observation of their drug packaging activities was an unreasonable search in violation of the Fourth Amendment and that all evidence obtained as a result of this unreasonable search was inadmissible as fruit of the poisonous tree.

The Minnesota courts analyzed whether respondents had a legitimate expectation of privacy under the rubric of "standing" doctrine, an analysis that this Court expressly rejected 20 years ago in *Rakas*. The [Fourth] Amendment protects persons against unreasonable searches of "their persons [and] houses" and thus indicates that the Fourth Amendment is a personal right that must be invoked by an individual. *See* Katz v. United States (1967) ("[T]he Fourth Amendment protects people, not places"). But the extent to which the Fourth

Amendment protects people may depend upon where those people are. We have held that "capacity to claim the protection of the Fourth Amendment depends . . . upon whether the person who claims the protection of the Amendment has a legitimate expectation of privacy in the invaded place."

The text of the Amendment suggests that its protections extend only to people in "their" houses. But we have held that in some circumstances a person may have a legitimate expectation of privacy in the house of someone else. In Minnesota v. Olson (1990), for example, we decided that an overnight guest in a house had the sort of expectation of privacy that the Fourth Amendment protects.

In Jones v. United States (1960), the defendant seeking to exclude evidence resulting from a search of an apartment had been given the use of the apartment by a friend. He had clothing in the apartment, had slept there "maybe a night," and at the time was the sole occupant of the apartment. But while the holding of *Jones*—that a search of the apartment violated the defendant's Fourth Amendment rights—is still valid, its statement that "anyone legitimately on the premises where a search occurs may challenge its legality," was expressly repudiated in Rakas v. Illinois (1978). Thus, an overnight guest in a home may claim the protection of the Fourth Amendment, but one who is merely present with the consent of the householder may not.

Respondents here were obviously not overnight guests, but were essentially present for a business transaction and were only in the home a matter of hours. There is no suggestion that they had a previous relationship with Thompson, or that there was any other purpose to their visit. Nor was there anything similar to the overnight guest relationship in *Olson* to suggest a degree of acceptance into the household. While the apartment was a dwelling place for Thompson, it was for these respondents simply a place to do business.

Property used for commercial purposes is treated differently for Fourth Amendment purposes from residential property. "An expectation of privacy in commercial premises, however, is different from, and indeed less than, a similar expectation in an individual's home." New York v. Burger (1987). And while it was a "home" in which respondents were present, it was not their home.

If we regard the overnight guest in Minnesota v. Olson as typifying those who may claim the protection of the Fourth Amendment in the home of another, and one merely "legitimately on the premises" as typifying those who may not do so, the present case is obviously somewhere in between. But the purely commercial nature of the transaction engaged in here, the relatively short period of time on the premises, and the lack of any previous connection between respondents and the householder, all lead us to conclude that respondents' situation is closer to that of one simply permitted on the premises. We therefore hold that any search which may have occurred did not violate their Fourth Amendment rights.

Because we conclude that respondents had no legitimate expectation of privacy in the apartment, we need not decide whether the police officer's observation constituted a "search."

Justice KENNEDY, concurring.

I join the Court's opinion, for its reasoning is consistent with my view that almost all social guests have a legitimate expectation of privacy, and hence protection against unreasonable searches, in their host's home.

The Fourth Amendment protects "[t]he right of the people to be secure in their . . . houses," and it is beyond dispute that the home is entitled to special protection as the center of the private lives of our people. Security of the home must be guarded by the law in a world where privacy is diminished by enhanced surveillance and sophisticated communication systems. As is well established, however, Fourth Amendment protection, though dependent upon spatial definition, is in essence a personal right. Thus, as the Court held in Rakas v. Illinois (1978), there are limits on who may assert it.

In this case respondents have established nothing more than a fleeting and insubstantial connection with Thompson's home. For all that appears in the record, respondents used Thompson's house simply as a convenient processing station, their purpose involving nothing more than the mechanical act of chopping and packing a substance for distribution. There is no suggestion that respondents engaged in confidential communications with Thompson about their transaction. Respondents had not been to Thompson's apartment before, and they left it even before their arrest.

If respondents here had been visiting 20 homes, each for a minute or two, to drop off a bag of cocaine and were apprehended by a policeman wrongfully present in the 19th home; or if they had left the goods at a home where they were not staying and the police had seized the goods in their absence, we would have said that *Rakas* compels rejection of any privacy interest respondents might assert. So it does here, given that respondents have established no meaningful tie or connection to the owner, the owner's home, or the owner's expectation of privacy.

We cannot remain faithful to the underlying principle in *Rakas* without reversing in this case, and I am not persuaded that we need depart from it to protect the homeowner's own privacy interests. Respondents have made no persuasive argument that we need to fashion a per se rule of home protection, with an automatic right for all in the home to invoke the exclusionary rule, in order to protect homeowners and their guests from unlawful police intrusion. With these observations, I join the Court's opinion.

Justice GINSBURG, with whom Justice STEVENS and Justice SOUTER join, dissenting.

The Court's decision undermines not only the security of short-term guests, but also the security of the home resident herself. In my view, when a homeowner or lessee personally invites a guest into her home to share in a common endeavor, whether it be for conversation, to engage in leisure activities, or for business purposes licit or illicit, that guest should share his host's shelter against unreasonable searches and seizures.

I do not here propose restoration of the "legitimately on the premises" criterion stated in Jones v. United States (1960), for the Court rejected that formulation in Rakas v. Illinois (1978), as it did the "automatic standing rule." First, the disposition I would reach in this case responds to the unique importance of the home — the most essential bastion of privacy recognized by the law. Further, I would here decide only the case of the homeowner who chooses to share the privacy of her home and her company with a guest, and would not reach classroom hypotheticals like the milkman or pizza deliverer.

My concern centers on an individual's choice to share her home and her associations there with persons she selects. Our decisions indicate that people have a reasonable expectation of privacy in their homes in part because they have the prerogative to exclude others. The power to exclude implies the power to include. Our Fourth Amendment decisions should reflect these complementary prerogatives.

A homedweller places her own privacy at risk, the Court's approach indicates, when she opens her home to others, uncertain whether the duration of their stay, their purpose, and their "acceptance into the household" will earn protection. It remains textbook law that "[s]earches and seizures inside a home without a warrant are presumptively unreasonable absent exigent circumstances." The law in practice is less secure. Human frailty suggests that today's decision will tempt police to pry into private dwellings without warrant, to find evidence incriminating guests who do not rest there through the night.

Through the host's invitation, the guest gains a reasonable expectation of privacy in the home. Minnesota v. Olson (1990), so held with respect to an overnight guest. The logic of that decision extends to shorter term guests as well. One need not remain overnight to anticipate privacy in another's home, "a place where [the guest] and his possessions will not be disturbed by anyone but his host and those his host allows inside." In sum, when a homeowner chooses to share the privacy of her home and her company with a short-term guest, the twofold requirement "emerg[ing] from prior decisions" has been satisfied: Both host and guest "have exhibited an actual (subjective) expectation of privacy"; that "expectation [is] one [our] society is prepared to recognize as 'reasonable.'"

BRENDLIN v. CALIFORNIA
127 S. Ct. 2400 (2007)

Justice SOUTER delivered the opinion of the Court.

When a police officer makes a traffic stop, the driver of the car is seized within the meaning of the Fourth Amendment. The question in this case is whether the same is true of a passenger. We hold that a passenger is seized as well and so may challenge the constitutionality of the stop.

I

Early in the morning of November 27, 2001, Deputy Sheriff Robert Brokenbrough and his partner saw a parked Buick with expired registration tags. In his ensuing conversation with the police dispatcher, Brokenbrough learned that an application for renewal of registration was being processed. The officers saw the car again on the road, and this time Brokenbrough noticed its display of a temporary operating permit with the number "11," indicating it was legal to drive the car through November. The officers decided to pull the Buick over to verify that the permit matched the vehicle, even though, as Brokenbrough admitted later, there was nothing unusual about the permit or the way it was affixed. Brokenbrough asked the driver, Karen Simeroth, for her license and saw a passenger in the front seat, petitioner Bruce Brendlin, whom he recognized as "one of the Brendlin brothers." He recalled that either Scott or Bruce Brendlin had dropped out of parole supervision and asked Brendlin to identify himself.

Brokenbrough returned to his cruiser, called for backup, and verified that Brendlin was a parole violator with an outstanding no-bail warrant for his arrest. While he was in the patrol car, Brokenbrough saw Brendlin briefly open and then close the passenger door of the Buick. Once reinforcements arrived, Brokenbrough went to the passenger side of the Buick, ordered him out of the car at gunpoint, and declared him under arrest. When the police searched Brendlin incident to arrest, they found an orange syringe cap on his person. A patdown search of Simeroth revealed syringes and a plastic bag of a green leafy substance, and she was also formally arrested. Officers then searched the car and found tubing, a scale, and other things used to produce methamphetamine.

Brendlin was charged with possession and manufacture of methamphetamine, and he moved to suppress the evidence obtained in the searches of his person and the car as fruits of an unconstitutional seizure, arguing that the officers lacked probable cause or reasonable suspicion to make the traffic stop. He did not assert that his Fourth Amendment rights were violated by the search of Simeroth's vehicle, *cf.* Rakas v. Illinois (1978), but claimed only that the traffic stop was an unlawful seizure of his person. The trial court denied the suppression motion after finding that the stop was lawful and Brendlin was not seized until Brokenbrough ordered him out of the car and formally arrested him. Brendlin pleaded guilty, subject to appeal on the suppression issue, and was sentenced to four years in prison.

We granted certiorari to decide whether a traffic stop subjects a passenger, as well as the driver, to Fourth Amendment seizure.

II

A

A person is seized by the police and thus entitled to challenge the government's action under the Fourth Amendment when the officer, "by means of physical force or show of authority," terminates or restrains his freedom of movement, "through means intentionally applied." Thus, an "unintended person . . . [may be] the object of the detention," so long as the detention is "willful" and not merely the consequence of "an unknowing act." A police officer may make a seizure by a show of authority and without the use of physical force, but there is no seizure without actual submission; otherwise, there is at most an attempted seizure, so far as the Fourth Amendment is concerned.

When the actions of the police do not show an unambiguous intent to restrain or when an individual's submission to a show of governmental authority takes the form of passive acquiescence, there needs to be some test for telling when a seizure occurs in response to authority, and when it does not. The test was devised by Justice Stewart in United States v. Mendenhall (1980), who wrote that a seizure occurs if "in view of all of the circumstances surrounding the incident, a reasonable person would have believed that he was not free to leave." Later on, the Court adopted Justice Stewart's touchstone, but added that when a person "has no desire to leave" for reasons unrelated to the police presence, the "coercive effect of the encounter" can be measured better by asking whether "a reasonable person would feel free to decline the officers' requests or otherwise terminate the encounter."

The law is settled that in Fourth Amendment terms a traffic stop entails a seizure of the driver "even though the purpose of the stop is limited and the resulting detention quite brief." Delaware v. Prouse (1979). And although we have not, until today, squarely answered the question whether a passenger is also seized, we have said over and over in dicta that during a traffic stop an officer seizes everyone in the vehicle, not just the driver.

B

The State concedes that the police had no adequate justification to pull the car over, but argues that the passenger was not seized and thus cannot claim that the evidence was tainted by an unconstitutional stop. We resolve this question by asking whether a reasonable person in Brendlin's position when the car stopped would have believed himself free to "terminate the encounter" between the police and himself. We think that in these circumstances any reasonable passenger would have understood the police officers to be exercising control to the point that no one in the car was free to depart without police permission.

A traffic stop necessarily curtails the travel a passenger has chosen just as much as it halts the driver, diverting both from the stream of traffic to the side of the road, and the police activity that normally amounts to intrusion on "privacy and personal security" does not normally (and did not here) distinguish between passenger and driver. An officer who orders one particular car to pull over acts with an implicit claim of right based on fault of some sort, and a sensible person would not expect a police officer to allow people to come and go freely from the physical focal point of an investigation into faulty behavior or wrongdoing. If the likely wrongdoing is not the driving, the passenger will reasonably feel subject to suspicion owing to close association; but even when the wrongdoing is only bad driving, the passenger will expect to be subject to some scrutiny, and his attempt to leave the scene would be so obviously likely to prompt an objection from the officer that no passenger would feel free to leave in the first place.

It is also reasonable for passengers to expect that a police officer at the scene of a crime, arrest, or investigation will not let people move around in ways that could jeopardize his safety.

C

The contrary conclusion drawn by the Supreme Court of California, that seizure came only with formal arrest, reflects three premises as to which we respectfully disagree. First, the State Supreme Court reasoned that Brendlin was not seized by the stop because Deputy Sheriff Brokenbrough only intended to investigate Simeroth and did not direct a show of authority toward Brendlin. The court saw Brokenbrough's "flashing lights [as] directed at the driver," and pointed to the lack of record evidence that Brokenbrough "was even aware [Brendlin] was in the car prior to the vehicle stop." But that view of the facts ignores the objective *Mendenhall* test of what a reasonable passenger would understand. To the extent that there is anything ambiguous in the show of force (was it fairly seen as directed only at the driver or at the car and its occupants?), the test resolves the ambiguity, and here it leads to the intuitive conclusion that all the occupants were subject to like control by the successful display of authority. The State Supreme Court's approach, on the contrary, shifts the issue from the intent of the police as objectively manifested to the motive of the police for taking the intentional action to stop the car, and we have repeatedly rejected attempts to introduce this kind of subjectivity into Fourth Amendment analysis.

Second, the Supreme Court of California assumed that Brendlin, "as the passenger, had no ability to submit to the deputy's show of authority" because only the driver was in control of the moving vehicle. But what may amount to submission depends on what a person was doing before the show of authority: a fleeing man is not seized until he is physically overpowered, but one sitting in a chair may submit to authority by not getting up to run away. Here, Brendlin had no effective way to signal submission while the car was still moving on the roadway, but once it came to a stop he could, and apparently did, submit by staying inside.

Third, the State Supreme Court shied away from the rule we apply today for fear that it "would encompass even those motorists following the vehicle subject to the traffic stop who, by virtue of the original detention, are forced to slow down and perhaps even come to a halt in order to accommodate that vehicle's submission to police authority." But an occupant of a car who knows that he is stuck in traffic because another car has been pulled over (like the motorist who can't even make out why the road is suddenly clogged) would not perceive a show of authority as directed at him or his car. Such incidental restrictions on freedom of movement would not tend to affect an individual's "sense of security and privacy in traveling in an automobile." Nor would the consequential blockage call for a precautionary rule to avoid the kind of "arbitrary and oppressive interference by [law] enforcement officials with the privacy and personal security of individuals" that the Fourth Amendment was intended to limit.[4]

Indeed, the consequence to worry about would not flow from our conclusion, but from the rule that almost all courts have rejected. Holding that the passenger in a private car is not (without more) seized in a traffic stop would invite police officers to stop cars with passengers regardless of probable cause or reasonable suspicion of anything illegal. The fact that evidence uncovered as a result of an arbitrary traffic stop would still be admissible against any passengers would be a powerful incentive to run the kind of "roving patrols" that would still violate the driver's Fourth Amendment right.

Brendlin was seized from the moment Simeroth's car came to a halt on the side of the road, and it was error to deny his suppression motion on the ground that seizure occurred only at the formal arrest.

D. EXCEPTIONS TO THE EXCLUSIONARY RULE

There are several situations in which the Supreme Court has said that even though there is a Fourth Amendment violation, the exclusionary rule does not apply. In examining these exceptions, it is important to consider whether

4. California claims that, under today's rule, "all taxi cab and bus passengers would be 'seized' under the Fourth Amendment when the cab or bus driver is pulled over by the police for running a red light." But the relationship between driver and passenger is not the same in a common carrier as it is in a private vehicle, and the expectations of police officers and passengers differ accordingly. In those cases, as here, the crucial question would be whether a reasonable person in the passenger's position would feel free to take steps to terminate the encounter. [Footnote by the Court.]

they are justified or whether they unduly undercut the ability to achieve the purposes of the exclusionary rule.

1. Independent Source

Even if police obtain evidence in violation of the Fourth Amendment, it is still admissible if it is also obtained through a source independent of the police misconduct and untainted by the illegal actions of the police. In a footnote, in his dissenting opinion in Murray v. United States, below, Justice Marshall gives a clear illustration:

> The clearest case for the application of the independent source exception is when a wholly separate line of investigation, shielded from information gathered in an illegal search, turns up the same evidence through a separate, lawful search. Under these circumstances, there is little doubt that the lawful search was not connected to the constitutional violation. The exclusion of such evidence would not significantly add to the deterrence facing the law enforcement officers conducting the illegal search, because they would have little reason to anticipate the separate investigation leading to the same evidence.

For example, in Segura v. United States, 468 U.S. 796 (1984), agents unlawfully entered the defendant's apartment and remained there until a search warrant was obtained. But the Court held that the evidence found for the first time during the execution of the valid and untainted search warrant was admissible because it was discovered pursuant to an "independent source."

Murray v. United States, below, is one of the Supreme Court's most detailed examinations of the independent source exception to the exclusionary rule.

MURRAY v. UNITED STATES
487 U.S. 533 (1988)

Justice SCALIA delivered the opinion of the Court.

In Segura v. United States (1984), we held that police officers' illegal entry upon private premises did not require suppression of evidence subsequently discovered at those premises when executing a search warrant obtained on the basis of information wholly unconnected with the initial entry. In these consolidated cases we are faced with the question whether, again assuming evidence obtained pursuant to an independently obtained search warrant, the portion of such evidence that had been observed in plain view at the time of a prior illegal entry must be suppressed.

I

Both cases arise out of the conviction of petitioner Michael F. Murray, petitioner James D. Carter, and others for conspiracy to possess and distribute illegal drugs. Insofar as relevant for our purposes, the facts are as follows: Based on information received from informants, federal law enforcement agents had been surveilling petitioner Murray and several of his co-conspirators. At about 1:45 P.M. on April 6, 1983, they observed Murray drive a truck and Carter drive a green camper, into a warehouse in South Boston. When the petitioners drove the vehicles out about 20 minutes later, the surveilling agents saw within the warehouse two individuals and a tractor-trailer rig bearing a long, dark container. Murray and Carter later turned over the truck and camper to other drivers, who were in turn followed and ultimately arrested, and the vehicles lawfully seized. Both vehicles were found to contain marijuana.

After receiving this information, several of the agents converged on the South Boston warehouse and forced entry. They found the warehouse unoccupied, but observed in plain view numerous burlap-wrapped bales that were later found to contain marijuana. They left without disturbing the bales, kept the warehouse under surveillance, and did not reenter it until they had a search warrant. In applying for the warrant, the agents did not mention the prior entry, and did not rely on any observations made during that entry. When the warrant was issued — at 10:40 P.M., approximately eight hours after the initial entry — the agents immediately reentered the warehouse and seized 270 bales of marijuana and notebooks listing customers for whom the bales were destined.

Before trial, petitioners moved to suppress the evidence found in the warehouse. The District Court denied the motion, rejecting petitioners' arguments that the warrant was invalid because the agents did not inform the Magistrate about their prior warrantless entry, and that the warrant was tainted by that entry. The First Circuit affirmed, assuming for purposes of its decision that the first entry into the warehouse was unlawful.

II

The exclusionary rule prohibits introduction into evidence of tangible materials seized during an unlawful search, and of testimony concerning knowledge acquired during an unlawful search. Beyond that, the exclusionary rule also prohibits the introduction of derivative evidence, both tangible and testimonial, that is the product of the primary evidence, or that is otherwise acquired as an indirect result of the unlawful search, up to the point at which the connection with the unlawful search becomes "so attentuated as to dissipate the taint."

Almost simultaneously with our development of the exclusionary rule, in the first quarter of this century, we also announced what has come to be known as the "independent source" doctrine. See Silverthorne Lumber Co. v. United States (1920). That doctrine, which has been applied to evidence acquired not only through Fourth Amendment violations but also through Fifth and Sixth Amendment violations, has recently been described as follows: "[T]he interest of society in deterring unlawful police conduct and the public interest in having juries receive all probative evidence of a crime are properly balanced by putting the police in the same, not a worse, position that they would have been in if no police error or misconduct had occurred. . . . When the challenged evidence has an independent source, exclusion of such evidence would put the police in a worse position than they would have been in absent any error or violation." Nix v. Williams (1984).

The dispute here is over the scope of this doctrine. Petitioners contend that it applies only to evidence obtained for the first time during an independent lawful search. The Government argues that it applies also to evidence initially discovered during, or as a consequence of, an unlawful search, but later obtained independently from activities untainted by the initial illegality. We think the Government's view has better support in both precedent and policy.

Our cases have used the concept of "independent source" in a more general and a more specific sense. The more general sense identifies all evidence acquired in a fashion untainted by the illegal evidence-gathering activity. Thus, where an unlawful entry has given investigators knowledge of facts x and y, but fact z has been learned by other means, fact z can be said to be admissible because derived from an "independent source." This is how we used the term in Segura v. United States (1984).

The original use of the term, however, and its more important use for purposes of these cases, was more specific. It was originally applied in the exclusionary rule context, by Justice Holmes, with reference to that particular category of evidence acquired by an untainted search which is identical to the evidence unlawfully acquired — that is, in the example just given, to knowledge of facts x and y derived from an independent source:

> The essence of a provision forbidding the acquisition of evidence in a certain way is that not merely evidence so acquired shall not be used before the Court but that it shall not be used at all. Of course this does not mean that the facts thus obtained become sacred and inaccessible. If knowledge of them is gained from an independent source they may be proved like any others.

Petitioners' asserted policy basis for excluding evidence which is initially discovered during an illegal search, but is subsequently acquired through an independent and lawful source, is that a contrary rule will remove all deterrence to, and indeed positively encourage, unlawful police searches. As petitioners see the incentives, law enforcement officers will routinely enter without a warrant to make sure that what they expect to be on the premises is in fact there. If it is not, they will have spared themselves the time and trouble of getting a warrant; if it is, they can get the warrant and use the evidence despite the unlawful entry. We see the incentives differently. An officer with probable cause sufficient to obtain a search warrant would be foolish to enter the premises first in an unlawful manner. By doing so, he would risk suppression of all evidence on the premises, both seen and unseen, since his action would add to the normal burden of convincing a magistrate that there is probable cause the much more onerous burden of convincing a trial court that no information gained from the illegal entry affected either the law enforcement officers' decision to seek a warrant or the magistrate's decision to grant it. Nor would the officer without sufficient probable cause to obtain a search warrant have any added incentive to conduct an unlawful entry, since whatever he finds cannot be used to establish probable cause before a magistrate.

III

To apply what we have said to the present cases: Knowledge that the marijuana was in the warehouse was assuredly acquired at the time of the unlawful entry. But it was also acquired at the time of entry pursuant to the warrant, and if that later acquisition was not the result of the earlier entry there is no reason why the independent source doctrine should not apply. Invoking the exclusionary rule would put the police (and society) not in the same position they would have occupied if no violation occurred, but in a worse one.

The ultimate question, therefore, is whether the search pursuant to warrant was in fact a genuinely independent source of the information and tangible evidence at issue here. This would not have been the case if the agents' decision to seek the warrant was prompted by what they had seen during the initial entry, or if information obtained during that entry was presented to the Magistrate and affected his decision to issue the warrant. On this point the Court of Appeals said the following: "[W]e can be absolutely certain that the warrantless entry in no way contributed in the slightest either to the issuance of a warrant or to the discovery of the evidence during the lawful search that occurred pursuant to the warrant."

Although these statements can be read to provide emphatic support for the Government's position, it is the function of the District Court rather than the Court of Appeals to determine the facts, and we do not think the Court of Appeals' conclusions are supported by adequate findings. The District Court found that the agents did not reveal their warrantless entry to the Magistrate, and that they did not include in their application for a warrant any recitation of their observations in the warehouse. It did not, however, explicitly find that the agents would have sought a warrant if they had not earlier entered the warehouse. The Government concedes this in its brief. To be sure, the District Court did determine that the purpose of the warrantless entry was in part "to guard against the destruction of possibly critical evidence," and one could perhaps infer from this that the agents who made the entry already planned to obtain that "critical evidence" through a warrant-authorized search. That inference is not, however, clear enough to justify the conclusion that the District Court's findings amounted to a determination of independent source.

Accordingly, we vacate the judgment and remand these cases to the Court of Appeals with instructions that it remand to the District Court for determination whether the warrant-authorized search of the warehouse was an independent source of the challenged evidence in the sense we have described.

Justice MARSHALL, with whom Justice STEVENS and Justice O'CONNOR join, dissenting.

The Court today holds that the "independent source" exception to the exclusionary rule may justify admitting evidence discovered during an illegal warrantless search that is later "rediscovered" by the same team of investigators during a search pursuant to a warrant obtained immediately after the illegal search. I believe the Court's decision, by failing to provide sufficient guarantees that the subsequent search was, in fact, independent of the illegal search, emasculates the Warrant Clause and undermines the deterrence function of the exclusionary rule. I therefore dissent.

This Court has stated frequently that the exclusionary rule is principally designed to deter violations of the Fourth Amendment. By excluding evidence discovered in violation of the Fourth Amendment, the rule "compel[s] respect for the constitutional guaranty in the only effectively available way, by removing the incentive to disregard it." The Court has crafted exceptions to the exclusionary rule when the purposes of the rule are not furthered by the exclusion. As the Court today recognizes, the independent source exception to the exclusionary rule "allows admission of evidence that has been discovered by means wholly independent of any constitutional violation." The independent source exception, like the inevitable discovery exception, is primarily based on a practical view that under certain circumstances the beneficial deterrent effect that exclusion will have on future constitutional violations is too slight to justify the social cost of excluding probative evidence from a criminal trial. When the seizure of the evidence at issue is "wholly independent of" the constitutional violation, then exclusion arguably will have no effect on a law enforcement officer's incentive to commit an unlawful search.

Under the circumstances of these cases, the admission of the evidence "reseized" during the second search severely undermines the deterrence function of the exclusionary rule. Indeed, admission in these cases affirmatively encourages illegal searches. The incentives for such illegal conduct are clear. Obtaining a warrant is inconvenient and time consuming. Even when officers have probable cause to support a warrant application, therefore, they have an incentive first to determine whether it is worthwhile to obtain a warrant. Probable cause is much less than certainty, and many "confirmatory" searches will result in the discovery that no evidence is present, thus saving the police the time and trouble of getting a warrant. If contraband is discovered, however, the officers may later seek a warrant to shield the evidence from the taint of the illegal search. The police thus know in advance that they have little to lose and much to gain by forgoing the bother of obtaining a warrant and undertaking an illegal search.

The Court, however, "see[s] the incentives differently." Under the Court's view, today's decision does not provide an incentive for unlawful searches, because the officer undertaking the search would know that "his action would add to the normal burden of convincing a magistrate that there is probable cause the much more onerous burden of convincing a trial court that no information gained from the illegal entry affected either the law enforcement officers' decision to seek a warrant or the magistrate's decision to grant it." The Court, however, provides no hint of why this risk would actually seem significant to the officers. Under the circumstances of these cases, the officers committing the illegal search have both knowledge and control of the factors central to the trial court's determination.

The strong Fourth Amendment interest in eliminating these incentives for illegal entry should cause this Court to scrutinize closely the application of the independent source exception to evidence obtained under the circumstances of the instant cases; respect for the constitutional guarantee requires a rule that does not undermine the deterrence function of the exclusionary rule. When, as here, the same team of investigators is involved in both the first and second search, there is a significant danger that the "independence" of the source will in fact be illusory, and that the initial search will have affected the decision to obtain a warrant notwithstanding the officers' subsequent assertions to the contrary. It is therefore crucial that the factual premise of the exception — complete independence — be clearly established before the exception can justify admission of the evidence. I believe the Court's reliance on the intent of the law enforcement officers who conducted the warrantless search provides insufficient guarantees that the subsequent legal search was unaffected by the prior illegal search.

To ensure that the source of the evidence is genuinely independent, the basis for a finding that a search was untainted by a prior illegal search must focus, as with the inevitable discovery doctrine, on "demonstrated historical facts capable of ready verification or impeachment." In the instant cases, there are no "demonstrated historical facts" capable of supporting a finding that the subsequent warrant search was wholly unaffected by the prior illegal search. The same team of investigators was involved in both searches. The warrant was obtained immediately after the illegal search, and no effort was made to obtain a warrant prior to the discovery of the marijuana during the illegal search. The only evidence available that the warrant search was wholly independent is the testimony of the agents who conducted the illegal search. Under these circumstances, the threat that the subsequent search was tainted by the illegal search is too great to allow for the application of the independent source exception. The Court's contrary holding lends itself to easy abuse, and offers an incentive to bypass the constitutional requirement that probable cause be assessed by a neutral and detached magistrate before the police invade an individual's privacy.

In sum, under circumstances as are presented in these cases, when the very law enforcement officers who participate in an illegal search immediately thereafter obtain a warrant to search the same premises, I believe the evidence discovered during the initial illegal entry must be suppressed. Any other result emasculates the Warrant Clause and provides an intolerable incentive for warrantless searches. I respectfully dissent.

2. Inevitable Discovery

Closely related to the "independent source" exception is the "inevitable discovery" exception. If the police can demonstrate that they inevitably would have discovered the evidence, even without a violation of the Fourth Amendment, the exclusionary rule does not apply and the evidence is admissible. Nix v. Williams is the key case recognizing an "inevitable discovery" exception to the exclusionary rule.

NIX v. WILLIAMS

_467 U.S. 431 (1984)_

Chief Justice BURGER delivered the opinion of the Court.

We granted certiorari to consider whether, at respondent Williams' second murder trial in state court, evidence pertaining to the discovery and condition of the victim's body was properly admitted on the ground that it would ultimately or inevitably have been discovered even if no violation of any constitutional or statutory provision had taken place.

I

A

On December 24, 1968, 10-year-old Pamela Powers disappeared from a YMCA building in Des Moines, Iowa, where she had accompanied her parents to watch an athletic contest. Shortly after she disappeared, Williams was seen leaving the

YMCA carrying a large bundle wrapped in a blanket; a 14-year-old boy who had helped Williams open his car door reported that he had seen "two legs in it and they were skinny and white."

Williams' car was found the next day 160 miles east of Des Moines in Davenport, Iowa. Later several items of clothing belonging to the child, some of Williams' clothing, and an army blanket like the one used to wrap the bundle that Williams carried out of the YMCA were found at a rest stop on Interstate 80 near Grinnell, between Des Moines and Davenport. A warrant was issued for Williams' arrest.

Police surmised that Williams had left Pamela Powers or her body somewhere between Des Moines and the Grinnell rest stop where some of the young girl's clothing had been found. On December 26, the Iowa Bureau of Criminal Investigation initiated a large-scale search. Two hundred volunteers divided into teams began the search 21 miles east of Grinnell, covering an area several miles to the north and south of Interstate 80. They moved westward from Poweshiek County, in which Grinnell was located, into Jasper County. Searchers were instructed to check all roads, abandoned farm buildings, ditches, culverts, and any other place in which the body of a small child could be hidden.

Meanwhile, Williams surrendered to local police in Davenport, where he was promptly arraigned. Williams contacted a Des Moines attorney who arranged for an attorney in Davenport to meet Williams at the Davenport police station. Des Moines police informed counsel they would pick Williams up in Davenport and return him to Des Moines without questioning him. Two Des Moines detectives then drove to Davenport, took Williams into custody, and proceeded to drive him back to Des Moines.

During the return trip, one of the policemen, Detective Leaming, began a conversation with Williams, saying: "I want to give you something to think about while we're traveling down the road. . . . They are predicting several inches of snow for tonight, and I feel that you yourself are the only person that knows where this little girl's body is . . . and if you get a snow on top of it you yourself may be unable to find it. And since we will be going right past the area [where the body is] on the way into Des Moines, I feel that we could stop and locate the body, that the parents of this little girl should be entitled to a Christian burial for the little girl who was snatched away from them on Christmas [E]ve and murdered. . . . [A]fter a snow storm [we may not be] able to find it at all."

Leaming told Williams he knew the body was in the area of Mitchellville — a town they would be passing on the way to Des Moines. He concluded the conversation by saying "I do not want you to answer me. . . . Just think about it. . . ." Later, as the police car approached Grinnell, Williams asked Leaming whether the police had found the young girl's shoes. After Leaming replied that he was unsure, Williams directed the police to a point near a service station where he said he had left the shoes; they were not found. As they continued to drive to Des Moines, Williams asked whether the blanket had been found and then directed the officers to a rest area in Grinnell where he said he had disposed of the blanket; they did not find the blanket. At this point Leaming and his party were joined by the officers in charge of the search. As they approached Mitchellville, Williams, without any further conversation, agreed to direct the officers to the child's body.

The officers directing the search had called off the search at 3 P.M., when they left the Grinnell Police Department to join Leaming at the rest area. At that time, one search team near the Jasper County-Polk County line was only two and one-half miles from where Williams soon guided Leaming and his party to the body. The child's body was found next to a culvert in a ditch beside a gravel road in Polk County, about two miles south of Interstate 80, and essentially within the area to be searched.

B

First Trial

In February 1969 Williams was indicted for first-degree murder. Before trial in the Iowa court, his counsel moved to suppress evidence of the body and all related evidence including the condition of the body as shown by the autopsy. The ground for the motion was that such evidence was the "fruit" or product of Williams' statements made during the automobile ride from Davenport to Des Moines and prompted by Leaming's statements. The motion to suppress was denied.

The jury found Williams guilty of first-degree murder; the judgment of conviction was affirmed by the Iowa Supreme Court. Williams then sought release on habeas corpus in the United States District Court for the Southern District of Iowa. That court concluded that the evidence in question had been wrongly admitted at Williams' trial; a divided panel of the Court of Appeals for the Eighth Circuit agreed.

We granted certiorari, and a divided Court affirmed, holding that Detective Leaming had obtained incriminating statements from Williams by what was viewed as interrogation in violation of his right to counsel.

Second Trial

At Williams' second trial in 1977 in the Iowa court, the prosecution did not offer Williams' statements into evidence, nor did it seek to show that Williams had directed the police to the child's body. However, evidence of the condition of her body as it was found, articles and photographs of her clothing, and the results of post mortem medical and chemical tests on the body were admitted. The trial court concluded that the State had proved by a preponderance of the evidence that, if the search had not been suspended and Williams had not led the police to the victim, her body would have been discovered "within a short time" in essentially the same condition as it was actually found. The trial court also ruled that if the police had not located the body, "the search would clearly have been taken up again where it left off, given the extreme circumstances of this case and the body would [have] been found in short order."

In finding that the body would have been discovered in essentially the same condition as it was actually found, the court noted that freezing temperatures had prevailed and tissue deterioration would have been suspended. The challenged evidence was admitted and the jury again found Williams guilty of first-degree murder; he was sentenced to life in prison.

II

A

The Iowa Supreme Court correctly stated that the "vast majority" of all courts, both state and federal, recognize an inevitable discovery exception to the exclusionary rule. We are now urged to adopt and apply the so-called ultimate or inevitable discovery exception to the exclusionary rule.

Williams contends that evidence of the body's location and condition is "fruit of the poisonous tree," i.e., the "fruit" or product of Detective Leaming's plea to help the child's parents give her "a Christian burial," which this Court had already held equated to interrogation. He contends that admitting the challenged evidence violated the Sixth Amendment whether it would have been inevitably discovered or not. Williams also contends that, if the inevitable discovery doctrine is constitutionally permissible, it must include a threshold showing of police good faith.

B

The doctrine requiring courts to suppress evidence as the tainted "fruit" of unlawful governmental conduct had its genesis in Silverthorne Lumber Co. v. United States (1920); there, the Court held that the exclusionary rule applies not only to the illegally obtained evidence itself, but also to other incriminating evidence derived from the primary evidence.

The core rationale consistently advanced by this Court for extending the exclusionary rule to evidence that is the fruit of unlawful police conduct has been that this admittedly drastic and socially costly course is needed to deter police from violations of constitutional and statutory protections. This Court has accepted the argument that the way to ensure such protections is to exclude evidence seized as a result of such violations notwithstanding the high social cost of letting persons obviously guilty go unpunished for their crimes. On this rationale, the prosecution is not to be put in a better position than it would have been in if no illegality had transpired.

By contrast, the derivative evidence analysis ensures that the prosecution is not put in a worse position simply because of some earlier police error or misconduct. The independent source doctrine allows admission of evidence that has been discovered by means wholly independent of any constitutional violation. That doctrine, although closely related to the inevitable discovery doctrine, does not apply here; Williams' statements to Leaming indeed led police to the child's body, but that is not the whole story. The independent source doctrine teaches us that the interest of society in deterring unlawful police conduct and the public interest in having juries receive all probative evidence of a crime are properly balanced by putting the police in the same, not a worse, position than they would have been in if no police error or misconduct had occurred. When the challenged evidence has an independent source, exclusion of such evidence would put the police in a worse position than they would have been in absent any error or violation. There is a functional similarity between these two doctrines in that exclusion of evidence that would inevitably have been discovered would also put the government in a worse position, because the police would have obtained that evidence if no misconduct had taken place. Thus, while the independent source exception would not justify admission of evidence in this case, its rationale is wholly consistent with and justifies our adoption of the ultimate or inevitable discovery exception to the exclusionary rule.

If the prosecution can establish by a preponderance of the evidence that the information ultimately or inevitably would have been discovered by lawful means — here the volunteers' search — then the deterrence rationale has so little basis that the evidence should be received. Anything less would reject logic, experience, and common sense.

The requirement that the prosecution must prove the absence of bad faith, imposed here by the Court of Appeals, would place courts in the position of withholding from juries relevant and undoubted truth that would have been available to police absent any unlawful police activity. Of course, that view would put the police in a worse position than they would have been in if no unlawful conduct had transpired. And, of equal importance, it wholly fails to take into account the enormous societal cost of excluding truth in the search for truth in the administration of justice. Nothing in this Court's prior holdings supports any such formalistic, pointless, and punitive approach.

The Court of Appeals concluded, without analysis, that if an absence-of-bad-faith requirement were not imposed, "the temptation to risk deliberate violations of the Sixth Amendment would be too great, and the deterrent effect of the Exclusionary Rule reduced too far." We reject that view. A police officer who is faced with the opportunity to obtain evidence illegally will rarely, if ever, be in a position to calculate whether the evidence sought would inevitably be discovered.

On the other hand, when an officer is aware that the evidence will inevitably be discovered, he will try to avoid engaging in any questionable practice. In that situation, there will be little to gain from taking any dubious "shortcuts" to obtain the evidence. Significant disincentives to obtaining evidence illegally — including the possibility of departmental discipline and civil liability — also lessen the likelihood that the ultimate or inevitable discovery exception will promote police misconduct. In these circumstances, the societal costs of the exclusionary rule far outweigh any possible benefits to deterrence that a good-faith requirement might produce.

The Court of Appeals did not find it necessary to consider whether the record fairly supported the finding that the volunteer search party would ultimately or inevitably have discovered the victim's body. However, three courts independently reviewing the evidence have found that the body of the child inevitably would have been found by the searchers.

Justice STEVENS, concurring in the judgment.

This litigation is exceptional for at least three reasons. The facts are unusually tragic; it involves an unusually clear violation of constitutional rights; and it graphically illustrates the societal costs that may be incurred when police officers decide to dispense with the requirements of law. Because the Court does not adequately discuss any of these aspects of the case, I am unable to join its opinion.

The constitutional violation that gave rise to the decision in *Williams I* is neither acknowledged nor fairly explained in the Court's opinion. Yet the propriety of admitting evidence relating to the victim's body can only be evaluated if that constitutional violation is properly identified.

Before he was taken into custody, Williams, as a recent escapee from a mental hospital who had just abducted and murdered a small child, posed a special threat to public safety. Acting on his lawyer's advice, Williams surrendered to the Davenport police. The lawyer notified the Des Moines police of Williams' imminent surrender, and police officials, in the presence of Detective Leaming, agreed that Williams would not be questioned while being brought back from Davenport. Williams was advised of this agreement by his attorney. After he was arraigned in Davenport, Williams conferred with another lawyer who was acting as local counsel. This lawyer reminded Williams that he would not be questioned. When Detective Leaming arrived in Davenport, local counsel stressed that the agreement was to be carried out and that Williams was not to be questioned. Detective Leaming then took custody of respondent, and denied counsel's request to ride to Des Moines in the police car with Williams. The "Christian burial speech" occurred during the ensuing trip. As Justice Powell succinctly observed, this was a case "in which the police deliberately took advantage of an inherently coercive setting in the absence of counsel, contrary to their express agreement."

The Sixth Amendment guarantees that the conviction of the accused will be the product of an adversarial process, rather than the ex parte investigation and determination by the prosecutor.

Once the constitutional violation is properly identified, the answers to the questions presented in this case follow readily. Admission of the victim's body, if it would have been discovered anyway, means that the trial in this case was not the product of an inquisitorial process; that process was untainted by illegality. The good or bad faith of Detective Leaming is therefore simply irrelevant. If the trial process was not tainted as a result of his conduct, this defendant received the type of trial that the Sixth Amendment envisions. Generalizations about the exclusionary rule employed by the majority simply do not address the primary question in the case.

The majority is correct to insist that any rule of exclusion not provide the authorities with an incentive to commit violations of the Constitution. If the inevitable discovery rule provided such an incentive by permitting the prosecution to avoid the uncertainties inherent in its search for evidence, it would undermine the constitutional guarantee itself, and therefore be inconsistent with the deterrent purposes of the exclusionary rule. But when the burden of proof on the inevitable discovery question is placed on the prosecution, it must bear the risk of error in the determination made necessary by its constitutional violation. The uncertainty as to whether the body would have been discovered can be resolved in its favor here only because, as the Court explains, petitioner adduced evidence demonstrating that at the time of the constitutional violation an investigation was already under way which, in the natural and probable course of events, would have soon discovered the body. This is not a case in which the prosecution can escape responsibility for a constitutional violation through speculation; to the extent uncertainty was created by the constitutional violation the prosecution was required to resolve that uncertainty through proof. Even if Detective Leaming acted in bad faith in the sense that he deliberately violated the Constitution in order to avoid the possibility that the body would not be discovered, the prosecution ultimately does not avoid that risk; its burden of proof forces it to assume the risk. The need to adduce proof sufficient to discharge its burden, and the difficulty in predicting whether such proof will be available or sufficient, means that the inevitable discovery rule does not permit state officials to avoid the uncertainty they would have faced but for the constitutional violation.

Justice BRENNAN, with whom Justice MARSHALL joins, dissenting.

To the extent that today's decision adopts this "inevitable discovery" exception to the exclusionary rule, it simply acknowledges a doctrine that is akin to the "independent source" exception recognized by the Court. In particular, the

Court concludes that unconstitutionally obtained evidence may be admitted at trial if it inevitably would have been discovered in the same condition by an independent line of investigation that was already being pursued when the constitutional violation occurred. As has every Federal Court of Appeals previously addressing this issue, I agree that in these circumstances the "inevitable discovery" exception to the exclusionary rule is consistent with the requirements of the Constitution.

In its zealous efforts to emasculate the exclusionary rule, however, the Court loses sight of the crucial difference between the "inevitable discovery" doctrine and the "independent source" exception from which it is derived. When properly applied, the "independent source" exception allows the prosecution to use evidence only if it was, in fact, obtained by fully lawful means. It therefore does no violence to the constitutional protections that the exclusionary rule is meant to enforce. The "inevitable discovery" exception is likewise compatible with the Constitution, though it differs in one key respect from its next of kin: specifically, the evidence sought to be introduced at trial has not actually been obtained from an independent source, but rather would have been discovered as a matter of course if independent investigations were allowed to proceed.

In my view, this distinction should require that the government satisfy a heightened burden of proof before it is allowed to use such evidence. The inevitable discovery exception necessarily implicates a hypothetical finding that differs in kind from the factual finding that precedes application of the independent source rule. To ensure that this hypothetical finding is narrowly confined to circumstances that are functionally equivalent to an independent source, and to protect fully the fundamental rights served by the exclusionary rule, I would require clear and convincing evidence before concluding that the government had met its burden of proof on this issue. Increasing the burden of proof serves to impress the factfinder with the importance of the decision and thereby reduces the risk that illegally obtained evidence will be admitted. Because the lower courts did not impose such a requirement, I would remand this case for application of this heightened burden of proof by the lower courts in the first instance. I am therefore unable to join either the Court's opinion or its judgment.

3. Inadequate Causal Connection — Attenuation of the Taint

The exclusionary rule applies if there is a substantial causal connection between the illegal police behavior and the evidence. Indeed, the Supreme Court has made clear that all evidence that is the product of the illegal police activity — the "fruit of the poisonous tree" — must be excluded. Conversely, though, if the link between the illegal police act and the evidence is attenuated, then the evidence is admissible.

Wong Sun v. United States, 371 U.S. 471 (1963), illustrates this. Police illegally broke into Wong Sun's laundry and adjacent apartment. The police handcuffed Wong Sun and held him at gunpoint. Wong Sun made incriminating statements. Wong Sun was arrested, charged, and released on his own recognizance. Subsequently, he was questioned by an agent who informed Wong Sun of his right to remain silent and to consult with counsel. Wong Sun again gave incriminating statements.

The Supreme Court held that Wong Sun's statements to the police at the time of his arrest had to be excluded as the fruits of his unlawful arrest. By contrast, though, the Court said that Wong Sun's later confession was admissible because the connection with the earlier illegal police activity "became so attenuated as to dissipate the taint."

Brown v. Illinois, below, is one of the most widely cited cases with regard to this exception to the exclusionary rule.

BROWN v. ILLINOIS
422 U.S. 590 (1975)

Justice BLACKMUN delivered the opinion of the Court.

This case lies at the crossroads of the Fourth and the Fifth Amendments. Petitioner was arrested without probable cause and without a warrant. He was given, in full, the warnings prescribed by Miranda v. Arizona (1966). Thereafter, while in custody, he made two inculpatory statements. The issue is whether evidence of those statements was properly admitted, or should have been excluded, in petitioner's subsequent trial for murder in state court. Expressed another way, the issue is whether the statements were to be excluded as the fruit of the illegal arrest, or were admissible because the giving of the *Miranda* warnings sufficiently attenuated the taint of the arrest. *See* Wong Sun v. United States (1963).

I

As petitioner Richard Brown was climbing the last of the stairs leading to the rear entrance of his Chicago apartment in the early evening of May 13, 1968, he happened to glance at the window near the door. He saw, pointed at him through the window, a revolver held by a stranger who was inside the apartment. The man said: "Don't move, you are under arrest." Another man, also with a gun, came up behind Brown and repeated the statement that he was under arrest. It was about 7:45 P.M. The two men turned out to be Detectives William Nolan and William Lenz of the Chicago police force. It is not clear from the record exactly when they advised Brown of their identity, but it is not disputed that they broke into his apartment, searched it, and then arrested Brown, all without probable cause and without any warrant, when he arrived. They later testified that they made the arrest for the purpose of questioning Brown as part of their investigation of the murder of a man named Roger Corpus.

Corpus was murdered one week earlier, on May 6, with a .38-caliber revolver in his Chicago West Side second-floor apartment. Shortly thereafter, Detective Lenz obtained petitioners' name, among others, from Corpus' brother. Petitioner and the others were identified as acquaintances of the victim, not as suspects.

On the day of petitioner's arrest, Detectives Lenz and Nolan, armed with a photograph of Brown, and another officer arrived at petitioner's apartment about 5 P.M. While the third officer covered the front entrance downstairs, the two detectives broke into Brown's apartment and searched it. Lenz then positioned himself near the rear door and watched through the adjacent window which opened onto the back porch. Nolan sat near the front door.

As both officers held him at gunpoint, the three entered the apartment. Brown was ordered to stand against the wall and was searched. No weapon was found. He was asked his name. When he denied being Richard Brown, Detective Lenz showed him the photograph, informed him that he was under arrest for the murder of Roger Corpus, handcuffed him, and escorted him to the squad car. The two detectives took petitioner to the Maxwell Street police station. During the 20-minute drive Nolan again asked Brown, who then was sitting with him in the back seat of the car, whether his name was Richard Brown and whether he owned a 1966 Oldsmobile. Brown alternately evaded these questions or answered them falsely. Upon arrival at the station house Brown was placed in the second-floor central interrogation room. The room was bare, except for a table and four chairs. He was left alone, apparently without handcuffs, for some minutes while the officers obtained the file on the Corpus homicide. They returned with the file, sat down at the table, one across from Brown and the other to his left, and spread the file on the table in front of him.

The officers warned Brown of his rights under *Miranda*. They then informed him that they knew of an incident that had occurred in a poolroom on May 5, when Brown, angry at having been cheated at dice, fired a shot from a revolver into the ceiling. Brown answered: "Oh, you know about that." Lenz informed him that a bullet had been obtained from the ceiling of the poolroom and had been taken to the crime laboratory to be compared with bullets taken from Corpus' body. Brown responded: "Oh, you know that, too." At this point — it was about 8:45 P.M. — Lenz asked Brown whether he wanted to talk about the Corpus homicide. Petitioner answered that he did. For the next 20 to 25 minutes Brown answered questions put to him by Nolan, as Lenz typed.

This questioning produced a two-page statement in which Brown acknowledged that he and a man named Jimmy Claggett visited Corpus on the evening of May 5; that the three for some time sat drinking and smoking marihuana; that Claggett ordered him at gunpoint to bind Corpus' hands and feet with cord from the headphone of a stereo set; and that Claggett, using a .38-caliber revolver sold to him by Brown, shot Corpus three times through a pillow. The statement was signed by Brown.

About 9:30 P.M. the two detectives and Brown left the station house to look for Claggett in an area of Chicago Brown knew him to frequent. They made a tour of that area but did not locate their quarry. They then went to police headquarters where they endeavored, without success, to obtain a photograph of Claggett. They resumed their search — it was now about 11 P.M. — and they finally observed Claggett crossing at an intersection. Lenz and Nolan arrested him. All four, the two detectives and the two arrested men, returned to the Maxwell Street station about 12:15 A.M.

Brown was again placed in the interrogation room. He was given coffee and was left alone, for the most part, until 2 A.M. when Assistant State's Attorney Crilly arrived.

Crilly, too, informed Brown of his *Miranda* rights. After a half hour's conversation, a court reporter appeared. Once again the *Miranda* warnings were given. Brown gave a second statement, providing a factual account of the murder substantially in accord with his first statement, but containing factual inaccuracies with respect to his personal background. When the statement was completed, at about 3 A.M., Brown refused to sign it. An hour later he made a phone call to his mother. At 9:30 that morning, about 14 hours after his arrest, he was taken before a magistrate.

On June 20 Brown and Claggett were jointly indicted by a Cook County grand jury for Corpus' murder. Prior to trial, petitioner moved to suppress the two statements he had made. He alleged that his arrest and detention had been illegal and that the statements were taken from him in violation of his constitutional rights. After a hearing, the motion was denied.

The case proceeded to trial. The State introduced evidence of both statements. The jury found petitioner guilty of murder. He was sentenced to imprisonment for not less than 15 years nor more than 30 years. On appeal, the Supreme Court of Illinois affirmed the judgment of conviction.

II

In *Wong Sun*, the Court pronounced the principles to be applied where the issue is whether statements and other evidence obtained after an illegal arrest or search should be excluded. [We stated:] "We need not hold that all evidence is 'fruit of the poisonous tree' simply because it would not have come to light but for the illegal actions of the police. Rather, the more apt question in such a case is 'whether, granting establishment of the primary illegality, the evidence to which instant objection is made has been come at by exploitation of that illegality or instead by means sufficiently distinguishable to be purged of the primary taint.' "

The exclusionary rule thus was applied in *Wong Sun* primarily to protect Fourth Amendment rights. Protection of the Fifth Amendment right against self-incrimination was not the Court's paramount concern there. To the extent that the question whether Toy's statement was voluntary was considered, it was only to judge whether it "was sufficiently an act of free will to purge the primary taint of the unlawful invasion."

III

The Illinois courts refrained from resolving the question, as apt here as it was in *Wong Sun*, whether Brown's statements were obtained by exploitation of the illegality of his arrest. They assumed that the *Miranda* warnings, by themselves, assured that the statements (verbal acts, as contrasted with physical evidence) were of sufficient free will as to purge the primary taint of the unlawful arrest. *Wong Sun*, of course, preceded *Miranda*.

Although, almost 90 years ago, the Court observed that the Fifth Amendment is in "intimate relation" with the Fourth, the *Miranda* warnings thus far have not been regarded as a means either of remedying or deterring violations of Fourth Amendment rights. Frequently, as here, rights under the two Amendments may appear to coalesce since "the unreasonable searches and seizures condemned in the Fourth Amendment are almost always made for the purpose of compelling a man to give evidence against himself, which in criminal cases is condemned in the Fifth Amendment." The exclusionary rule, however, when utilized to effectuate the Fourth Amendment, serves interests and policies that are distinct from those it serves under the Fifth. It is directed at all unlawful searches and seizures, and not merely those that happen to produce incriminating material or testimony as fruits. In short, exclusion of a confession made without *Miranda* warnings might be regarded as necessary to effectuate the Fifth Amendment, but it would not be sufficient fully to protect the Fourth. *Miranda* warnings, and the exclusion of a confession made without them, do not alone sufficiently deter a Fourth Amendment violation.

Thus, even if the statements in this case were found to be voluntary under the Fifth Amendment, the Fourth Amendment issue remains. In order for the causal chain, between the illegal arrest and the statements made subsequent thereto, to be broken, *Wong Sun* requires not merely that the statement meet the Fifth Amendment standard of voluntariness but that it be "sufficiently an act of free will to purge the primary taint." *Wong Sun* thus mandates consideration of a statement's admissibility in light of the distinct policies and interests of the Fourth Amendment.

If *Miranda* warnings, by themselves, were held to attenuate the taint of an unconstitutional arrest, regardless of how wanton and purposeful the Fourth Amendment violation, the effect of the exclusionary rule would be substantially diluted. Arrests made without warrant or without probable cause, for questioning or "investigation," would be encouraged by the knowledge that evidence derived therefrom could well be made admissible at trial by the simple expendent of giving *Miranda* warnings. Any incentive to avoid Fourth Amendment violations would be eviscerated by making the warnings, in effect, a "cure-all," and the constitutional guarantee against unlawful searches and seizures could be said to be reduced to "a form of words."

It is entirely possible, of course, as the State here argues, that persons arrested illegally frequently may decide to confess, as an act of free will unaffected by the initial illegality. But the *Miranda* warnings, alone and per se, cannot always make the act sufficiently a product of free will to break, for Fourth Amendment purposes, the causal connection between the illegality and the confession. They cannot assure in every case that the Fourth Amendment violation has not been unduly exploited. *[State argument]*

While we therefore reject the per se rule which the Illinois courts appear to have accepted, we also decline to adopt any alternative per se or "but for" rule. The petitioner himself professes not to demand so much. The question whether a confession is the product of a free will under *Wong Sun* must be answered on the facts of each case. No single fact is dispositive. The workings of the human mind are too complex, and the possibilities of misconduct too diverse, to permit protection of the Fourth Amendment to turn on such a talismanic test. The *Miranda* warnings are an important factor, to be sure, in determining whether the confession is obtained by exploitation of an illegal arrest. But they are not the only factor to be considered. The temporal proximity of the arrest and the confession, the presence of intervening circumstances, and, particularly, the purpose and flagrancy of the official misconduct are all relevant. The voluntariness of the statement is a threshold requirement. And the burden of showing admissibility rests, of course, on the prosecution. *[factors]*

IV

Although the Illinois courts failed to undertake the inquiry mandated by *Wong Sun* to evaluate the circumstances of this case in the light of the policy served by the exclusionary rule, the trial resulted in a record of amply sufficient detail and depth from which the determination may be made. We conclude that the State failed to sustain the burden of showing that the evidence in question was admissible under *Wong Sun*.

Brown's first statement was separated from his illegal arrest by less than two hours, and there was no intervening event of significance whatsoever. In its essentials, his situation is remarkably like that of James Wah Toy in *Wong Sun*. We could hold Brown's first statement admissible only if we overrule *Wong Sun*. We decline to do so. And the second statement was clearly the result and the fruit of the first.

The illegality here, moreover, had a quality of purposefulness. The impropriety of the arrest was obvious; awareness of that fact was virtually conceded by the two detectives when they repeatedly acknowledged, in their testimony, that the purpose of their action was "for investigation" or for "questioning." The arrest, both in design and in execution, was investigatory. The detectives embarked upon this expedition for evidence in the hope that something might turn up. The manner in which Brown's arrest was affected gives the appearance of having been calculated to cause surprise, fright, and confusion.

We emphasize that our holding is a limited one. We decide only that the Illinois courts were in error in assuming that the *Miranda* warnings, by themselves, under *Wong Sun* always purge the taint of an illegal arrest.

Justice POWELL, with whom Justice REHNQUIST joins, concurring in part.

I join the Court insofar as it holds that the per se rule adopted by the Illinois Supreme Court for determining the admissibility of petitioner's two statements inadequately accommodates the diverse interests underlying the Fourth Amendment exclusionary rule. I would, however, remand the case for reconsideration under the general standards articulated in the Court's opinion and elaborated herein.

On this record, I cannot conclude as readily as the Court that admission of the statements here at issue would constitute an effective overruling of *Wong Sun*.

The notion of the "dissipation of the taint" attempts to mark the point at which the detrimental consequences of illegal police action become so attenuated that the deterrent effect of the exclusionary rule no longer justifies its cost. Application of the *Wong Sun* doctrine will generate fact-specific cases bearing distinct differences as well as similarities, and the question of attenuation inevitably is largely a matter of degree. The Court today identifies the general factors that the trial court must consider in making this determination. I think it appropriate, however, to attempt to articulate the possible relationships to those factors in particular, broad categories of cases.

All Fourth Amendment violations are, by constitutional definition, "unreasonable." There are, however, significant practical differences that distinguish among violations, differences that measurably assist in identifying the kinds of cases in which disqualifying the evidence is likely to serve the deterrent purposes of the exclusionary rule. In my view, the point at which the taint can be said to have dissipated should be related, in the absence of other controlling circumstances, to the nature of that taint.

Bearing these considerations in mind, and recognizing that the deterrent value of the Fourth Amendment exclusionary rule is limited to certain kinds of police conduct, the following general categories can be identified. Those most readily identifiable are on the extremes: the flagrantly abusive violation of Fourth Amendment rights, on the one hand, and "technical" Fourth Amendment violations, on the other. In my view, these extremes call for significantly different judicial responses.

I would require the clearest indication of attenuation in cases in which official conduct was flagrantly abusive of Fourth Amendment rights. If, for example, the factors relied on by the police in determining to make the arrest were so lacking in indicia of probable cause as to render official belief in its existence entirely unreasonable, or if the evidence clearly suggested that the arrest was effectuated as a pretext for collateral objectives, or the physical circumstances of the arrest unnecessarily intrusive on personal privacy, I would consider the equalizing potential of *Miranda* warnings rarely sufficient to dissipate the taint. In such cases the deterrent value of the exclusionary rule is most likely to be effective, and the corresponding mandate to preserve judicial integrity, most clearly demands that the fruits of official misconduct be denied. I thus would require some demonstrably effective break in the chain of events leading from the illegal arrest to the statement, such as actual consultation with counsel or the accused's presentation before a magistrate for a determination of probable cause, before the taint can be deemed removed.

At the opposite end of the spectrum lie "technical" violations of Fourth Amendment rights where, for example, officers in good faith arrest an individual in reliance on a warrant later invalidated or pursuant to a statute that subsequently is declared unconstitutional. Absent aggravating circumstances, I would consider a statement given at the station house after one has been advised of *Miranda* rights to be sufficiently removed from the immediate circumstances of the illegal arrest to justify its admission at trial.

Between these extremes lies a wide range of situations that defy ready categorization, and I will not attempt to embellish on the factors set forth in the Court's opinion other than to emphasize that the *Wong Sun* inquiry always should be conducted with the deterrent purpose of the Fourth Amendment exclusionary rule sharply in focus. And, in view of the inevitably fact-specific nature of the inquiry, we must place primary reliance on the "learning, good sense, fairness and courage" of judges who must make the determination in the first instance.

C

On the facts of record as I view them, it is possible that the police may have believed reasonably that there was probable cause for petitioner's arrest. I am not able to conclude on this record that the officers arrested petitioner solely for the purpose of questioning. To be sure, there is evidence suggesting, as the Court notes, an investigatory arrest. But the evidence is conflicting.

I would leave the question of admissibility of this statement to the lower Illinois courts. In any event, the question whether there was sufficient attenuation between the first and second statements to render the second admissible in spite of the inadmissibility of the first presents a factual issue which, like the factual issue underlying the possible admissibility of the first statement, has not been passed on by the state courts.

In other cases, the Supreme Court found that statements obtained after a Fourth Amendment violation did not have to be excluded because the taint was sufficiently attenuated. For example, in Rawlings v. Kentucky, 448 U.S. 98 (1980), the defendant was illegally detained in his home while the police went to obtain a search warrant. Rawlings made incriminating statements during this time and the issue was whether they had to be excluded. The Court, in an opinion by Justice Rehnquist, said that the taint was sufficiently attenuated so as to allow the statements to be admitted. The Court pointed to the lack of flagrant misconduct by the police, the lack of a coercive atmosphere, and the fact that the statements were a spontaneous result of the discovery of evidence.

Similarly, in New York v. Harris, 495 U.S. 14 (1990), the Court found that a statement made by a suspect at the police station house was admissible, even though it followed an illegal search of the suspect's home. The Court explained that evidence from the warrantless home search would need to be excluded, but the subsequent statement to the police — at a different place and time from the search — was admissible.

These cases focus on when statements must be excluded when they follow a violation of the Fourth Amendment. The distinct, though obviously related, question of whether statements must be excluded when they follow illegal questioning is discussed below in Chapter 4, which considers interrogations.[5]

4. The Good Faith Exception to the Exclusionary Rule

In United States v. Leon, below, the Court held that the exclusionary rule does not apply if police reasonably rely on an invalid warrant to conduct a search or seizure. This is the most hotly disputed of the exceptions to the exclusionary rule and, not surprisingly, *Leon* provided the occasion for an important debate among the Justices as to the purposes of the exclusionary rule.

UNITED STATES v. LEON

468 U.S. 897 (1984)

Justice WHITE delivered the opinion of the Court.

This case presents the question whether the Fourth Amendment exclusionary rule should be modified so as not to bar the use in the prosecution's case in chief of evidence obtained by officers acting in reasonable reliance on a search warrant issued by a detached and neutral magistrate but ultimately found to be unsupported by probable cause. To resolve this question, we must consider once again the tension between the sometimes competing goals of, on the one hand, deterring official misconduct and removing inducements to unreasonable invasions of privacy and, on the other, establishing procedures under which

---

5. Also discussed in Chapter 4 is the related question of whether physical evidence must be suppressed if it is the result of questioning without *Miranda* warnings in violation of the Fifth Amendment. In United States v. Patane, 542 U.S. 630 (2004), presented in Chapter 4, the Court held (5-4) that physical evidence gained in such circumstances need not be excluded.

criminal defendants are "acquitted or convicted on the basis of all the evidence which exposes the truth."

I

In August 1981, a confidential informant of unproven reliability informed an officer of the Burbank Police Department that two persons known to him as "Armando" and "Patsy" were selling large quantities of cocaine and methaqualone from their residence at 620 Price Drive in Burbank, Cal. The informant also indicated that he had witnessed a sale of methaqualone by "Patsy" at the residence approximately five months earlier and had observed at that time a shoebox containing a large amount of cash that belonged to "Patsy." He further declared that "Armando" and "Patsy" generally kept only small quantities of drugs at their residence and stored the remainder at another location in Burbank.

On the basis of this information, the Burbank police initiated an extensive investigation focusing first on the Price Drive residence and later on two other residences as well. Cars parked at the Price Drive residence were determined to belong to respondents Armando Sanchez, who had previously been arrested for possession of marihuana, and Patsy Stewart, who had no criminal record. During the course of the investigation, officers observed an automobile belonging to respondent Ricardo Del Castillo, who had previously been arrested for possession of 50 pounds of marihuana, arrive at the Price Drive residence. The driver of that car entered the house, exited shortly thereafter carrying a small paper sack, and drove away. A check of Del Castillo's probation records led the officers to respondent Alberto Leon, whose telephone number Del Castillo had listed as his employer's. Leon had been arrested in 1980 on drug charges, and a companion had informed the police at that time that Leon was heavily involved in the importation of drugs into this country. Before the current investigation began, the Burbank officers had learned that an informant had told a Glendale police officer that Leon stored a large quantity of methaqualone at his residence in Glendale. During the course of this investigation, the Burbank officers learned that Leon was living at 716 South Sunset Canyon in Burbank.

Subsequently, the officers observed several persons, at least one of whom had prior drug involvement, arriving at the Price Drive residence and leaving with small packages; observed a variety of other material activity at the two residences as well as at a condominium at 7902 Via Magdalena; and witnessed a variety of relevant activity involving respondents' automobiles. The officers also observed respondents Sanchez and Stewart board separate flights for Miami. The pair later returned to Los Angeles together, consented to a search of their luggage that revealed only a small amount of marihuana, and left the airport. Based on these and other observations summarized in the affidavit, Officer Cyril Rombach of the Burbank Police Department, an experienced and well-trained narcotics investigator, prepared an application for a warrant to search 620 Price Drive, 716 South Sunset Canyon, 7902 Via Magdalena, and automobiles registered to each of the respondents for an extensive list of items believed to be related to respondents' drug-trafficking activities. Officer Rombach's extensive application was reviewed by several Deputy District Attorneys.

A facially valid search warrant was issued in September 1981 by a State Superior Court Judge. The ensuing searches produced large quantities of drugs at the Via Magdalena and Sunset Canyon addresses and a small quantity at the Price Drive residence. Other evidence was discovered at each of the residences and in Stewart's and Del Castillo's automobiles. Respondents were indicted by a grand jury in the District Court for the Central District of California and charged with conspiracy to possess and distribute cocaine and a variety of substantive counts.

The respondents then filed motions to suppress the evidence seized pursuant to the warrant. The District Court held an evidentiary hearing and, while recognizing that the case was a close one, granted the motions to suppress in part. It concluded that the affidavit was insufficient to establish probable cause, but did not suppress all of the evidence as to all of the respondents because none of the respondents had standing to challenge all of the searches. In response to a request from the Government, the court made clear that Officer Rombach had acted in good faith, but it rejected the Government's suggestion that the Fourth Amendment exclusionary rule should not apply where evidence is seized in reasonable, good-faith reliance on a search warrant.

The Government's petition for certiorari expressly declined to seek review of the lower courts' determinations that the search warrant was unsupported by probable cause and presented only the question "[w]hether the Fourth Amendment exclusionary rule should be modified so as not to bar the admission of evidence seized in reasonable, good-faith reliance on a search warrant that is subsequently held to be defective." We granted certiorari to consider the propriety of such a modification. We have concluded that, in the Fourth Amendment context, the exclusionary rule can be modified somewhat without jeopardizing its ability to perform its intended functions.

II

Language in opinions of this Court and of individual Justices has sometimes implied that the exclusionary rule is a necessary corollary of the Fourth Amendment, or that the rule is required by the conjunction of the Fourth and Fifth Amendments. These implications need not detain us long. The Fifth Amendment theory has not withstood critical analysis or the test of time, and the Fourth Amendment "has never been interpreted to proscribe the introduction of illegally seized evidence in all proceedings or against all persons."

A

The Fourth Amendment contains no provision expressly precluding the use of evidence obtained in violation of its commands, and an examination of its origin and purposes makes clear that the use of fruits of a past unlawful search or seizure "work[s] no new Fourth Amendment wrong." The wrong condemned by the Amendment is "fully accomplished" by the unlawful search or seizure itself, *ibid.*, and the exclusionary rule is neither intended nor able to "cure the invasion of the defendant's rights which he has already suffered." The rule thus operates as "a judicially created remedy designed to safeguard Fourth Amendment rights generally through its deterrent effect, rather than a personal constitutional right of the party aggrieved."

Whether the exclusionary sanction is appropriately imposed in a particular case, our decisions make clear, is "an issue separate from the question whether the Fourth Amendment rights of the party seeking to invoke the rule were violated by police conduct." Only the former question is currently before us, and it must be resolved by weighing the costs and benefits of preventing the use in the prosecution's case in chief of inherently trustworthy tangible evidence obtained in reliance on a search warrant issued by a detached and neutral magistrate that ultimately is found to be defective.

The substantial social costs exacted by the exclusionary rule for the vindication of Fourth Amendment rights have long been a source of concern. "Our cases have consistently recognized that unbending application of the exclusionary sanction to enforce ideals of governmental rectitude would impede unacceptably the truth-finding functions of judge and jury." An objectionable collateral consequence of this interference with the criminal justice system's truth-finding function is that some guilty defendants may go free or receive reduced sentences as a result of favorable plea bargains.[6] Particularly when law enforcement officers have acted in objective good faith or their transgressions have been minor, the magnitude of the benefit conferred on such guilty defendants offends basic concepts of the criminal justice system. Indiscriminate application of the exclusionary rule, therefore, may well "generat[e] disrespect for the law and administration of justice." Accordingly, "[a]s with any remedial device, the application of the rule has been restricted to those areas where its remedial objectives are thought most efficaciously served."

Many of these researchers have concluded that the impact of the exclusionary rule is insubstantial, but the small percentages with which they deal mask a large absolute number of felons who are released because the cases against them were based in part on illegal searches or seizures. "[A]ny rule of evidence that denies the jury access to clearly probative and reliable evidence must bear a heavy burden of justification, and must be carefully limited to the circumstances in which it will pay its way by deterring official unlawlessness." Because we find that the rule can have no substantial deterrent effect in the sorts of situations under consideration in this case, we conclude that it cannot pay its way in those situations.

B

Close attention to those remedial objectives has characterized our recent decisions concerning the scope of the Fourth Amendment exclusionary rule. The

---

6. Researchers have only recently begun to study extensively the effects of the exclusionary rule on the disposition of felony arrests. One study suggests that the rule results in the nonprosecution or nonconviction of between 0.6% and 2.35% of individuals arrested for felonies. Davies, A Hard Look at What We Know (and Still Need to Learn) About the "Costs" of the Exclusionary Rule: The NIJ Study and Other Studies of "Lost" Arrests, 1983 A.B.F.Res.J. 611, 621. The estimates are higher for particular crimes the prosecution of which depends heavily on physical evidence. Thus, the cumulative loss due to nonprosecution or nonconviction of individuals arrested on felony drug charges is probably in the range of 2.8% to 7.1%. Davies' analysis of California data suggests that screening by police and prosecutors results in the release because of illegal searches or seizures of as many as 1.4% of all felony arrestees, id., at 650, that 0.9% of felony arrestees are released, because of illegal searches or seizures, at the preliminary hearing or after trial, id., at 653, and that roughly 0.5% of all felony arrestees benefit from reversals on appeal because of illegal searches. [Footnote by the Court.]

Court has, to be sure, not seriously questioned, "in the absence of a more efficacious sanction, the continued application of the rule to suppress evidence
from the [prosecution's] case where a Fourth Amendment violation has been
substantial and deliberate. . . ." Nevertheless, the balancing approach that has
evolved in various contexts — including criminal trials — "forcefully suggest[s]
that the exclusionary rule be more generally modified to permit the introduction of evidence obtained in the reasonable good-faith belief that a search or
seizure was in accord with the Fourth Amendment."

As cases considering the use of unlawfully obtained evidence in criminal trials
themselves make clear, it does not follow from the emphasis on the exclusionary
rule's deterrent value that "anything which deters illegal searches is thereby
commanded by the Fourth Amendment." In determining whether persons
aggrieved solely by the introduction of damaging evidence unlawfully obtained
from their co-conspirators or co-defendants could seek suppression, for
example, we found that the additional benefits of such an extension of the
exclusionary rule would not outweigh its costs. Standing to invoke the rule
has thus been limited to cases in which the prosecution seeks to use the fruits
of an illegal search or seizure against the victim of police misconduct. Rakas v.
Illinois (1978).

Even defendants with standing to challenge the introduction in their
criminal trials of unlawfully obtained evidence cannot prevent every conceivable use of such evidence. Evidence obtained in violation of the Fourth
Amendment and inadmissible in the prosecution's case in chief may be
used to impeach a defendant's direct testimony. Walder v. United States
(1954). A similar assessment of the "incremental furthering" of the ends of
the exclusionary rule led us to conclude in United States v. Havens (1980), that
evidence inadmissible in the prosecution's case in chief or otherwise as
substantive evidence of guilt may be used to impeach statements made by a
defendant in response to "proper cross-examination reasonably suggested by
the defendant's direct examination."

When considering the use of evidence obtained in violation of the Fourth
Amendment in the prosecution's case in chief, moreover, we have declined to
adopt a per se or "but for" rule that would render inadmissible any evidence
that came to light through a chain of causation that began with an illegal arrest.
We also have held that a witness' testimony may be admitted even when his
identity was discovered in an unconstitutional search. United States v. Ceccolini
(1978). The perception underlying these decisions — that the connection
between police misconduct and evidence of crime may be sufficiently attenuated to permit the use of that evidence at trial — is a product of considerations
relating to the exclusionary rule and the constitutional principles it is designed
to protect. In short, the "dissipation of the taint" concept that the Court has
applied in deciding whether exclusion is appropriate in a particular case
"attempts to mark the point at which the detrimental consequences of illegal
police action become so attenuated that the deterrent effect of the exclusionary
rule no longer justifies its cost." Not surprisingly in view of this purpose, an
assessment of the flagrancy of the police misconduct constitutes an important
step in the calculus.

As yet, we have not recognized any form of good-faith exception to the Fourth
Amendment exclusionary rule. But the balancing approach that has evolved
during the years of experience with the rule provides strong support for the

modification currently urged upon us. As we discuss below, our evaluation of the costs and benefits of suppressing reliable physical evidence seized by officers reasonably relying on a warrant issued by a detached and neutral magistrate leads to the conclusion that such evidence should be admissible in the prosecution's case in chief.

III

A

Because a search warrant "provides the detached scrutiny of a neutral magistrate, which is a more reliable safeguard against improper searches than the hurried judgment of a law enforcement officer 'engaged in the often competitive enterprise of ferreting out crime,'" we have expressed a strong preference for warrants and declared that "in a doubtful or marginal case a search under a warrant may be sustainable where without one it would fall." Reasonable minds frequently may differ on the question whether a particular affidavit establishes probable cause, and we have thus concluded that the preference for warrants is most appropriately effectuated by according "great deference" to a magistrate's determination.

Deference to the magistrate, however, is not boundless. It is clear, first, that the deference accorded to a magistrate's finding of probable cause does not preclude inquiry into the knowing or reckless falsity of the affidavit on which that determination was based. Second, the courts must also insist that the magistrate purport to "perform his 'neutral and detached' function and not serve merely as a rubber stamp for the police." A magistrate failing to "manifest that neutrality and detachment demanded of a judicial officer when presented with a warrant application" and who acts instead as "an adjunct law enforcement officer" cannot provide valid authorization for an otherwise unconstitutional search.

Third, reviewing courts will not defer to a warrant based on an affidavit that does not "provide the magistrate with a substantial basis for determining the existence of probable cause." "Sufficient information must be presented to the magistrate to allow that official to determine probable cause; his action cannot be a mere ratification of the bare conclusions of others." Even if the warrant application was supported by more than a "bare bones" affidavit, a reviewing court may properly conclude that, notwithstanding the deference that magistrates deserve, the warrant was invalid because the magistrate's probable-cause determination reflected an improper analysis of the totality of the circumstances, or because the form of the warrant was improper in some respect.

We adhere to this view and emphasize that nothing in this opinion is intended to suggest a lowering of the probable-cause standard. On the contrary, we deal here only with the remedy to be applied to a concededly unconstitutional search.

Only in the first of these three situations, however, has the Court set forth a rationale for suppressing evidence obtained pursuant to a search warrant; in the other areas, it has simply excluded such evidence without considering whether Fourth Amendment interests will be advanced. To the extent that proponents of exclusion rely on its behavioral effects on judges and magistrates in these areas, their reliance is misplaced. First, the exclusionary rule is designed to deter police misconduct rather than to punish the errors of judges and magistrates. Second, there exists no evidence suggesting that judges and magistrates are inclined to ignore or subvert the Fourth Amendment or that lawlessness among these actors requires application of the extreme sanction of exclusion.

Third, and most important, we discern no basis, and are offered none, for believing that exclusion of evidence seized pursuant to a warrant will have a significant deterrent effect on the issuing judge or magistrate. Many of the factors that indicate that the exclusionary rule cannot provide an effective "special" or "general" deterrent for individual offending law enforcement officers apply as well to judges or magistrates. And, to the extent that the rule is thought to operate as a "systemic" deterrent on a wider audience, it clearly can have no such effect on individuals empowered to issue search warrants. Judges and magistrates are not adjuncts to the law enforcement team; as neutral judicial officers, they have no stake in the outcome of particular criminal prosecutions. The threat of exclusion thus cannot be expected significantly to deter them. Imposition of the exclusionary sanction is not necessary meaningfully to inform judicial officers of their errors, and we cannot conclude that admitting evidence obtained pursuant to a warrant while at the same time declaring that the warrant was somehow defective will in any way reduce judicial officers' professional incentives to comply with the Fourth Amendment, encourage them to repeat their mistakes, or lead to the granting of all colorable warrant requests.

B

If exclusion of evidence obtained pursuant to a subsequently invalidated warrant is to have any deterrent effect, therefore, it must alter the behavior of individual law enforcement officers or the policies of their departments. One could argue that applying the exclusionary rule in cases where the police failed to demonstrate probable cause in the warrant application deters future inadequate presentations or "magistrate shopping" and thus promotes the ends of the Fourth Amendment. Suppressing evidence obtained pursuant to a technically defective warrant supported by probable cause also might encourage officers to scrutinize more closely the form of the warrant and to point out suspected judicial errors. We find such arguments speculative and conclude that suppression of evidence obtained pursuant to a warrant should be ordered only on a case-by-case basis and only in those unusual cases in which exclusion will further the purposes of the exclusionary rule.

We have frequently questioned whether the exclusionary rule can have any deterrent effect when the offending officers acted in the objectively reasonable belief that their conduct did not violate the Fourth Amendment. "No empirical researcher, proponent or opponent of the rule, has yet been able to establish with any assurance whether the rule has a deterrent effect. . . ." But even assuming that the rule effectively deters some police misconduct and provides incentives for the law enforcement profession as a whole to conduct itself in accord with the Fourth Amendment, it cannot be expected, and should not be applied, to deter objectively reasonable law enforcement activity. In short, where the officer's conduct is objectively reasonable,[7] "excluding the evidence will not further the ends of the exclusionary rule in any appreciable way; for it is painfully

_____

7. We emphasize that the standard of reasonableness we adopt is an objective one. Many objections to a good-faith exception assume that the exception will turn on the subjective good faith of

apparent that . . . the officer is acting as a reasonable officer would and should act in similar circumstances. Excluding the evidence can in no way affect his future conduct unless it is to make him less willing to do his duty."

This is particularly true, we believe, when an officer acting with objective good faith has obtained a search warrant from a judge or magistrate and acted within its scope. In most such cases, there is no police illegality and thus nothing to deter. It is the magistrate's responsibility to determine whether the officer's allegations establish probable cause and, if so, to issue a warrant comporting in form with the requirements of the Fourth Amendment. In the ordinary case, an officer cannot be expected to question the magistrate's probable-cause determination or his judgment that the form of the warrant is technically sufficient. "[O]nce the warrant issues, there is literally nothing more the policeman can do in seeking to comply with the law." Penalizing the officer for the magistrate's error, rather than his own, cannot logically contribute to the deterrence of Fourth Amendment violations.

C

We conclude that the marginal or nonexistent benefits produced by suppressing evidence obtained in objectively reasonable reliance on a subsequently invalidated search warrant cannot justify the substantial costs of exclusion. We do not suggest, however, that exclusion is always inappropriate in cases where an officer has obtained a warrant and abided by its terms. "[S]earches pursuant to a warrant will rarely require any deep inquiry into reasonableness," for "a warrant issued by a magistrate normally suffices to establish" that a law enforcement officer has "acted in good faith in conducting the search." Nevertheless, the officer's reliance on the magistrate's probable-cause determination and on the technical sufficiency of the warrant he issues must be objectively reasonable, and it is clear that in some circumstances the officer will have no reasonable grounds for believing that the warrant was properly issued.

Suppression therefore remains an appropriate remedy if the magistrate or judge in issuing a warrant was misled by information in an affidavit that the affiant knew was false or would have known was false except for his reckless disregard of the truth. The exception we recognize today will also not apply in cases where the issuing magistrate wholly abandoned his judicial role; in such circumstances, no reasonably well trained officer should rely on the warrant. Nor would an officer manifest objective good faith in relying on a warrant based on an affidavit "so lacking in indicia of probable cause as to render official belief in its existence entirely unreasonable." Finally, depending on the circumstances of the particular case, a warrant may be so facially deficient — i.e., in failing to particularize the place to be searched or the things to be seized — that the executing officers cannot reasonably presume it to be valid.

---

individual officers. "Grounding the modification in objective reasonableness, however, retains the value of the exclusionary rule as an incentive for the law enforcement profession as a whole to conduct themselves in accord with the Fourth Amendment." The objective standard we adopt, moreover, requires officers to have a reasonable knowledge of what the law prohibits. [Footnote by the Court.]

In so limiting the suppression remedy, we leave untouched the probable-cause standard and the various requirements for a valid warrant. The good-faith exception for searches conducted pursuant to warrants is not intended to signal our unwillingness strictly to enforce the requirements of the Fourth Amendment, and we do not believe that it will have this effect. As we have already suggested, the good-faith exception, turning as it does on objective reasonableness, should not be difficult to apply in practice. When officers have acted pursuant to a warrant, the prosecution should ordinarily be able to establish objective good faith without a substantial expenditure of judicial time.

IV

When the principles we have enunciated today are applied to the facts of this case, it is apparent that the judgment of the Court of Appeals cannot stand. The Court of Appeals applied the prevailing legal standards to Officer Rombach's warrant application and concluded that the application could not support the magistrate's probable-cause determination. Having determined that the warrant should not have issued, the Court of Appeals understandably declined to adopt a modification of the Fourth Amendment exclusionary rule that this Court had not previously sanctioned. Although the modification finds strong support in our previous cases, the Court of Appeals' commendable self-restraint is not to be criticized. We have now reexamined the purposes of the exclusionary rule and the propriety of its application in cases where officers have relied on a subsequently invalidated search warrant. Our conclusion is that the rule's purposes will only rarely be served by applying it in such circumstances.

In the absence of an allegation that the magistrate abandoned his detached and neutral role, suppression is appropriate only if the officers were dishonest or reckless in preparing their affidavit or could not have harbored an objectively reasonable belief in the existence of probable cause. Under these circumstances, the officers' reliance on the magistrate's determination of probable cause was objectively reasonable, and application of the extreme sanction of exclusion is inappropriate.

Justice BRENNAN, with whom Justice MARSHALL joins, dissenting.

Ten years ago, I expressed the fear that the Court's decision "may signal that a majority of my colleagues have positioned themselves to reopen the door [to evidence secured by official lawlessness] still further and abandon altogether the exclusionary rule in search-and-seizure cases." Since then, in case after case, I have witnessed the Court's gradual but determined strangulation of the rule. It now appears that the Court's victory over the Fourth Amendment is complete. That today's decisions represent the pièce de résistance of the Court's past efforts cannot be doubted, for today the Court sanctions the use in the prosecution's case in chief of illegally obtained evidence against the individual whose rights have been violated — a result that had previously been thought to be foreclosed.

The Court seeks to justify this result on the ground that the "costs" of adhering to the exclusionary rule in cases like those before us exceed the "benefits." But the language of deterrence and of cost/benefit analysis, if used indiscriminately, can have a narcotic effect. It creates an illusion of technical precision and ineluctability. It suggests that not only constitutional principle but also empirical data support the majority's result. When the Court's analysis is examined carefully, however, it is clear that we have not been treated to an honest assessment of the merits of the exclusionary rule, but have instead been drawn into a curious world where the "costs" of excluding illegally obtained evidence loom to exaggerated heights and where the "benefits" of such exclusion are made to disappear with a mere wave of the hand.

The majority ignores the fundamental constitutional importance of what is at stake here. While the machinery of law enforcement and indeed the nature of crime itself have changed dramatically since the Fourth Amendment became part of the Nation's fundamental law in 1791, what the Framers understood then remains true today — that the task of combating crime and convicting the guilty will in every era seem of such critical and pressing concern that we may be lured by the temptations of expediency into forsaking our commitment to protecting individual liberty and privacy. It was for that very reason that the Framers of the Bill of Rights insisted that law enforcement efforts be permanently and unambiguously restricted in order to preserve personal freedoms. In the constitutional scheme they ordained, the sometimes unpopular task of ensuring that the government's enforcement efforts remain within the strict boundaries fixed by the Fourth Amendment was entrusted to the courts.

A proper understanding of the broad purposes sought to be served by the Fourth Amendment demonstrates that the principles embodied in the exclusionary rule rest upon a far firmer constitutional foundation than the shifting sands of the Court's deterrence rationale. But even if I were to accept the Court's chosen method of analyzing the question posed by these cases, I would still conclude that the Court's decision cannot be justified.

I

The Court holds that physical evidence seized by police officers reasonably relying upon a warrant issued by a detached and neutral magistrate is admissible in the prosecution's case in chief, even though a reviewing court has subsequently determined either that the warrant was defective, or that those officers failed to demonstrate when applying for the warrant that there was probable cause to conduct the search. I have no doubt that these decisions will prove in time to have been a grave mistake. But, as troubling and important as today's new doctrine may be for the administration of criminal justice in this country, the mode of analysis used to generate that doctrine also requires critical examination, for it may prove in the long run to pose the greater threat to our civil liberties.

At bottom, the Court's decision turns on the proposition that the exclusionary rule is merely a " 'judicially created remedy designed to safeguard Fourth Amendment rights generally through its deterrent effect, rather than a personal constitutional right.' " The essence of this view, as expressed initially in the *Calandra* opinion and as reiterated today, is that the sole "purpose of the Fourth Amendment is to prevent unreasonable governmental intrusions into the privacy of one's person, house, papers, or effects. The wrong condemned is the unjustified governmental invasion of these areas of an individual's life. That wrong . . . is fully accomplished by the original search without probable cause." This reading of the Amendment implies that its proscriptions are directed solely at those government agents who may actually invade an individual's constitutionally protected privacy. The courts are not subject to any direct constitutional duty to exclude illegally obtained evidence, because the question of the admissibility of such evidence is not addressed by the Amendment. This view of the scope of the Amendment relegates the judiciary to the periphery. Because the only constitutionally cognizable injury has already been "fully accomplished" by the police by the time a case comes before the courts, the Constitution is not itself violated if the judge decides to admit the tainted evidence. Indeed, the most the judge can do is wring his hands and hope that perhaps by excluding such evidence he can deter future transgressions by the police.

Such a reading appears plausible, because, as critics of the exclusionary rule never tire of repeating, the Fourth Amendment makes no express provision for the exclusion of evidence secured in violation of its commands. A short answer to this claim, of course, is that many of the Constitution's most vital imperatives are stated in general terms and the task of giving meaning to these precepts is therefore left to subsequent judicial decisionmaking in the context of concrete cases.

A more direct answer may be supplied by recognizing that the Amendment, like other provisions of the Bill of Rights, restrains the power of the government as a whole; it does not specify only a particular agency and exempt all others. The judiciary is responsible, no less than the executive, for ensuring that constitutional rights are respected.

When that fact is kept in mind, the role of the courts and their possible involvement in the concerns of the Fourth Amendment comes into sharper focus. Because seizures are executed principally to secure evidence, and because such evidence generally has utility in our legal system only in the context of a trial supervised by a judge, it is apparent that the admission of illegally obtained evidence implicates the same constitutional concerns as the initial seizure of that evidence. Indeed, by admitting unlawfully seized evidence, the judiciary becomes a part of what is in fact a single governmental action prohibited by the terms of the Amendment. Once that connection between the evidence-gathering role of the police and the evidence-admitting function of the courts is acknowledged, the plausibility of the Court's interpretation becomes more suspect. Certainly nothing in the language or history of the Fourth Amendment suggests that a recognition of this evidentiary link between the police and the courts was meant to be foreclosed. It is difficult to give any meaning at all to the limitations imposed by the Amendment if they are read to proscribe only certain conduct by the police but to allow other agents of the same government to take advantage of evidence secured by the police in violation of its requirements. The Amendment therefore must be read to condemn not only the initial unconstitutional invasion of privacy — which is done, after all, for the purpose of securing evidence — but also the subsequent use of any evidence so obtained.

The Court evades this principle by drawing an artificial line between the constitutional rights and responsibilities that are engaged by actions of the police and those that are engaged when a defendant appears before the courts. According to the Court, the substantive protections of the Fourth Amendment are wholly exhausted at the moment when police unlawfully invade an individual's privacy and thus no substantive force remains to those protections at the time of trial when the government seeks to use evidence obtained by the police.

I submit that such a crabbed reading of the Fourth Amendment casts aside the teaching of those Justices who first formulated the exclusionary rule, and rests ultimately on an impoverished understanding of judicial responsibility in our constitutional scheme. For my part, "[t]he right of the people to be secure in their persons, houses, papers, and effects, against unreasonable searches and seizures" comprises a personal right to exclude all evidence secured by means of unreasonable searches and seizures. The right to be free from the initial invasion of privacy and the right of exclusion are coordinate components of the central embracing right to be free from unreasonable searches and seizures.

From the foregoing, it is clear why the question whether the exclusion of evidence would deter future police misconduct was never considered a relevant concern in the early cases from *Weeks* to *Olmstead.* In those formative decisions, the Court plainly understood that the exclusion of illegally obtained evidence was compelled not by judicially fashioned remedial purposes, but rather by a direct constitutional command.

Despite this clear pronouncement, however, the Court has gradually pressed the deterrence rationale for the rule back to center stage. The various arguments advanced by the Court in this campaign have only strengthened my conviction that the deterrence theory is both misguided and unworkable. First, the Court has frequently bewailed the "cost" of excluding reliable evidence. In large part, this criticism rests upon a refusal to acknowledge the function of the Fourth Amendment itself. If nothing else, the Amendment plainly operates to disable the government from gathering information and securing evidence in certain ways. In practical terms, of course, this restriction of official power means that some incriminating evidence inevitably will go undetected if the government obeys these constitutional restraints. It is the loss of that evidence that is the "price" our society pays for enjoying the freedom and privacy safeguarded by the Fourth Amendment. Thus, some criminals will go free not, in Justice (then Judge) Cardozo's misleading epigram, "because the constable has blundered," but rather because official compliance with Fourth Amendment requirements makes it more difficult to catch criminals. Understood in this way, the Amendment directly contemplates that some reliable and incriminating evidence will be lost to the government; therefore, it is not the exclusionary rule, but the Amendment itself that has imposed this cost.

In addition, the Court's decisions over the past decade have made plain that the entire enterprise of attempting to assess the benefits and costs of the exclusionary rule in various contexts is a virtually impossible task for the judiciary to perform honestly or accurately. Although the Court's language in those cases suggests that some specific empirical basis may support its analyses, the reality is that the Court's opinions represent inherently unstable compounds of intuition, hunches, and occasional pieces of partial and often inconclusive data. To the extent empirical data are available regarding the general costs and benefits of the exclusionary rule, such data have shown, on the one hand, as the Court acknowledges today, that the costs are not as substantial as critics have asserted in the past, and, on the other hand, that while the exclusionary rule may well have certain deterrent effects, it is extremely difficult to determine with any degree of precision whether the incidence of unlawful conduct by police is now lower than it was prior to *Mapp*. The Court has sought to turn this uncertainty to its advantage by casting the burden of proof upon proponents of the rule. "Obviously," however, "the assignment of the burden of proof on an issue where evidence does not exist and cannot be obtained is outcome determinative. [The] assignment of the burden is merely a way of announcing a predetermined conclusion." By remaining within its redoubt of empiricism and by basing the rule solely on the deterrence rationale, the Court has robbed the rule of legitimacy. A doctrine that is explained as if it were an empirical proposition but for which there is only limited empirical support is both inherently unstable and an easy mark for critics. The extent of this Court's fidelity to Fourth Amendment requirements, however, should not turn on such statistical uncertainties.

What the Framers of the Bill of Rights sought to accomplish through the express requirements of the Fourth Amendment was to define precisely the conditions under which government agents could search private property so that citizens would not have to depend solely upon the discretion and restraint of those agents for the protection of their privacy. Although the self-restraint and care exhibited by the officers in this case is commendable, that alone can never be a sufficient protection for constitutional liberties. I am convinced that it is not too much to ask that an attentive magistrate take those minimum steps necessary to ensure that every warrant he issues describes with particularity the things that his independent review of the warrant application convinces him are likely to be found in the premises. And I am equally convinced that it is not too much to ask that well-trained and experienced police officers take a moment to check that the warrant they have been issued at least describes those things for which they have sought leave to search. These convictions spring not from my own view of sound criminal law enforcement policy, but are instead compelled by the language of the Fourth Amendment and the history that led to its adoption.

III

Even if I were to accept the Court's general approach to the exclusionary rule, I could not agree with today's result. There is no question that in the hands of the present Court the deterrence rationale has proved to be a powerful tool for confining the scope of the rule.

Thus, in this bit of judicial stagecraft, while the sets sometimes change, the actors always have the same lines. Given this well-rehearsed pattern, one might have predicted with some assurance how the present case would unfold. First there is the ritual incantation of the "substantial social costs" exacted by the exclusionary rule, followed by the virtually foreordained conclusion that, given the marginal benefits, application of the rule in the circumstances of these cases is not warranted. Upon analysis, however, such a result cannot be justified even on the Court's own terms.

At the outset, the Court suggests that society has been asked to pay a high price — in terms either of setting guilty persons free or of impeding the proper functioning of trials — as a result of excluding relevant physical evidence in cases where the police, in conducting searches and seizing evidence, have made only an "objectively reasonable" mistake concerning the constitutionality of their actions. But what evidence is there to support such a claim?

Significantly, the Court points to none, and, indeed, as the Court acknowledges, recent studies have demonstrated that the "costs" of the exclusionary rule — calculated in terms of dropped prosecutions and lost convictions — are quite low. Contrary to the claims of the rule's critics that exclusion leads to "the release of countless guilty criminals," these studies have demonstrated that federal and state prosecutors very rarely drop cases because of potential search and seizure problems. For example, a 1979 study prepared at the request of Congress by the General Accounting Office reported that only 0.4% of all cases actually declined for prosecution by federal prosecutors were declined primarily because of illegal search problems. If the GAO data are restated as a percentage of all arrests, the study shows that only 0.2% of all felony arrests are declined for prosecution because of potential exclusionary rule problems. Of course, these data describe only the costs attributable to the exclusion of evidence in all cases; the costs due to the exclusion of evidence in the narrower category of cases where police have made objectively reasonable mistakes must necessarily be even smaller. The Court, however, ignores this distinction and mistakenly weighs the aggregated costs of exclusion in all cases, irrespective of the circumstances that led to exclusion, against the potential benefits associated with only those cases in which evidence is excluded because police reasonably but mistakenly believe that their conduct does not violate the Fourth Amendment. When such faulty scales are used, it is little wonder that the balance tips in favor of restricting the application of the rule.

What then supports the Court's insistence that this evidence be admitted? Apparently, the Court's only answer is that even though the costs of exclusion are not very substantial, the potential deterrent effect in these circumstances is so marginal that exclusion cannot be justified. The key to the Court's conclusion in this respect is its belief that the prospective deterrent effect of the exclusionary rule operates only in those situations in which police officers, when deciding whether to go forward with some particular search, have reason to know that their planned conduct will violate the requirements of the Fourth Amendment. If these officers in fact understand (or reasonably should understand because the law is well settled) that their proposed conduct will offend the Fourth Amendment and that, consequently, any evidence they seize will be suppressed in court, they will refrain from conducting the planned search. In those circumstances, the incentive system created by the exclusionary rule will have the hoped-for deterrent effect. But in situations where police officers reasonably (but mistakenly) believe that their planned conduct satisfies Fourth Amendment requirements — presumably either (a) because they are acting on the basis of an apparently valid warrant, or (b) because their conduct is only later determined to be invalid as a result of a subsequent change in the law or the resolution of an unsettled question of law — then such officers will have no reason to refrain from conducting the search and the exclusionary rule will have no effect.

At first blush, there is some logic to this position. Undoubtedly, in the situation hypothesized by the Court, the existence of the exclusionary rule cannot be expected to have any deterrent effect on the particular officers at the moment they are deciding whether to go forward with the search. Indeed, the subsequent exclusion of any evidence seized under such circumstances appears somehow "unfair" to the particular officers involved. As the Court suggests, these officers have acted in what they thought was an appropriate and constitutionally autho-rized manner, but then the fruit of their efforts is nullified by the application of the exclusionary rule.

The flaw in the Court's argument, however, is that its logic captures only one comparatively minor element of the generally acknowledged deterrent pur-poses of the exclusionary rule. To be sure, the rule operates to some extent to deter future misconduct by individual officers who have had evidence sup-pressed in their own cases. But what the Court overlooks is that the deterrence rationale for the rule is not designed to be, nor should it be thought of as, a form of "punishment" of individual police officers for their failures to obey the restraints imposed by the Fourth Amendment. Instead, the chief deterrent function of the rule is its tendency to promote institutional compliance with Fourth Amendment requirements on the part of law enforcement agencies generally. Thus, as the Court has previously recognized, "over the long term, [the] demonstration [provided by the exclusionary rule] that our society attaches serious consequences to violation of constitutional rights is thought to encourage those who formulate law enforcement policies, and the officers who implement them, to incorporate Fourth Amendment ideals into their value system." It is only through such an institutionwide mechanism that information concerning Fourth Amendment standards can be effectively communicated to rank-and-file officers.

If the overall educational effect of the exclusionary rule is considered, appli-cation of the rule to even those situations in which individual police officers have acted on the basis of a reasonable but mistaken belief that their conduct was authorized can still be expected to have a considerable long-term deterrent effect. If evidence is consistently excluded in these circumstances, police depart-ments will surely be prompted to instruct their officers to devote greater care and attention to providing sufficient information to establish probable cause when applying for a warrant, and to review with some attention the form of the warrant that they have been issued, rather than automatically assuming that whatever document the magistrate has signed will necessarily comport with Fourth Amendment requirements.

After today's decisions, however, that institutional incentive will be lost. Indeed, the Court's "reasonable mistake" exception to the exclusionary rule will tend to put a premium on police ignorance of the law. Armed with the assurance provided by today's decisions that evidence will always be admissible whenever an officer has "reasonably" relied upon a warrant, police departments will be encouraged to train officers that if a warrant has simply been signed, it is reasonable, without more, to rely on it. Since in close cases there will no longer be any incentive to err on the side of constitutional behavior, police would have every reason to adopt a "let's-wait-until-it's-decided" approach in situations in which there is a question about a warrant's validity or the basis for its issuance.

Although the Court brushes these concerns aside, a host of grave conse-quences can be expected to result from its decision to carve this new exception out of the exclusionary rule. A chief consequence of today's decisions will be to convey a clear and unambiguous message to magistrates that their decisions to issue warrants are now insulated from subsequent judicial review. Creation of this new exception for good-faith reliance upon a warrant implicitly tells magistrates that they need not take much care in reviewing warrant applications, since their mistakes will from now on have virtually no consequence: If their decision to issue a warrant was correct, the evidence will be admitted; if their decision was incorrect but the police relied in good faith on the warrant, the evidence will also be admitted. Inevitably, the care and attention devoted to such an inconsequential chore will dwindle. Although the Court is correct to note that magistrates do not share the same stake in the outcome of a criminal case as the police, they nevertheless need to appreciate that their role is of some moment in order to continue performing the important task of carefully reviewing warrant applications. Today's decisions effectively remove that incentive.

After today's decisions, there will be little reason for reviewing courts to conduct such a conscientious review; rather, these courts will be more likely to focus simply on the question of police good faith. Despite the Court's confident prediction that such review will continue to be conducted, it is difficult to believe that busy courts faced with heavy dockets will take the time to render essentially advisory opinions concerning the constitutionality of the magistrate's decision before considering the officer's good faith.

Moreover, the good-faith exception will encourage police to provide only the bare minimum of information in future warrant applications. The police will now know that if they can secure a warrant, so long as the circumstances of its issuance are not "entirely unreasonable," all police conduct pursuant to that warrant will be protected from further judicial review. The clear incentive that operated in the past to establish probable cause adequately because reviewing courts would examine the magistrate's judgment carefully, has now been so completely vitiated that the police need only show that it was not "entirely unreasonable" under the circumstances of a particular case for them to believe that the warrant they were issued was valid. The long-run effect unquestionably will be to undermine the integrity of the warrant process.

Justice STEVENS, dissenting.

The Court assumes that the searches in these cases violated the Fourth Amendment, yet refuses to apply the exclusionary rule because the Court concludes that it was "reasonable" for the police to conduct them. In my opinion an official search and seizure cannot be both "unreasonable" and "reasonable" at the same time. The doctrinal vice in the Court's holding is its failure to consider the separate purposes of the two prohibitory Clauses in the Fourth Amendment. The first Clause prohibits unreasonable searches and seizures and the second prohibits the issuance of warrants that are not supported by probable cause or that do not particularly describe the place to be searched and the persons or things to be seized. We have, of course, repeatedly held that warrantless searches are presumptively unreasonable, and that there are only a few carefully delineated exceptions to that basic presumption. But when such an exception has been recognized, analytically we have necessarily concluded that the warrantless activity was not "unreasonable" within the meaning of the first Clause. Thus, any Fourth Amendment case may present two separate questions: whether the search was conducted pursuant to a warrant issued in accordance with the second Clause, and, if not, whether it was nevertheless "reasonable" within the meaning of the first. On these questions, the constitutional text requires that we speak with one voice. We cannot intelligibly assume, arguendo, that a search was constitutionally unreasonable but that the seized evidence is admissible because the same search was reasonable.

Thus, if the majority's assumption is correct, that even after paying heavy deference to the magistrate's finding and resolving all doubt in its favor, there is no probable cause here, then by definition — as a matter of constitutional law — the officers' conduct was unreasonable. The Court's own hypothesis is that there was no fair likelihood that the officers would find evidence of a crime, and hence there was no reasonable law enforcement justification for their conduct.

The majority's contrary conclusion rests on the notion that it must be reasonable for a police officer to rely on a magistrate's finding. Until today that has plainly not been the law; it has been well settled that even when a magistrate issues a warrant there is no guarantee that the ensuing search and seizure is constitutionally reasonable. Law enforcement officers have long been on notice that despite the magistrate's decision a warrant will be invalidated if the officers did not provide sufficient facts to enable the magistrate to evaluate the existence of probable cause responsibly and independently. Reviewing courts have always inquired into whether the magistrate acted properly in issuing the warrant — not merely whether the officers acted properly in executing it. Thus, under our cases it has never been "reasonable" for the police to rely on the mere fact that a warrant has issued; the police have always known that if they fail to supply the magistrate with sufficient information, the warrant will be held invalid and its fruits excluded.

Today's decisions do grave damage to that deterrent function. Under the majority's new rule, even when the police know their warrant application is probably insufficient, they retain an incentive to submit it to a magistrate, on the chance that he may take the bait. No longer must they hesitate and seek additional evidence in doubtful cases.

The Court is of course correct that the exclusionary rule cannot deter when the authorities have no reason to know that their conduct is unconstitutional. But when probable cause is lacking, then by definition a reasonable person under the circumstances would not believe there is a fair likelihood that a search will produce evidence of a crime. Under such circumstances well-trained professionals must know that they are violating the Constitution. The Court's approach — which, in effect, encourages the police to seek a warrant even if they know the existence of probable cause is doubtful — can only lead to an increased number of constitutional violations.

Thus, the Court's creation of a double standard of reasonableness inevitably must erode the deterrence rationale that still supports the exclusionary rule. But we should not ignore the way it tarnishes the role of the judiciary in enforcing the Constitution.

It is of course true that the exclusionary rule exerts a high price — the loss of probative evidence of guilt. But that price is one courts have often been required to pay to serve important social goals. That price is also one the Fourth Amendment requires us to pay, assuming as we must that the Framers intended that its strictures "shall not be violated." For in all such cases, as Justice Stewart has observed, "the same extremely relevant evidence would not have been obtained had the police officer complied with the commands of the fourth amendment in the first place."

We could, of course, facilitate the process of administering justice to those who violate the criminal laws by ignoring the commands of the Fourth Amendment—indeed, by ignoring the entire Bill of Rights—but it is the very purpose of a Bill of Rights to identify values that may not be sacrificed to expediency. In a just society those who govern, as well as those who are governed, must obey the law.

The same day it decided United States v. Leon, the Court also handed down Massachusetts v. Sheppard, 468 U.S. 961 (1984). Police investigating a murder obtained a warrant to search Sheppard's residence. The officers used a pre-printed warrant form which listed "controlled substances" as the items to be seized. The judge said that he would make changes in the warrant, but the final version continued to list controlled substances as the items to be searched for and seized. Sheppard moved to suppress the evidence. The Supreme Court, however, said that the evidence did not need to be excluded because the officers reasonably relied on the warrant.[8]

Justice White, writing for the Court, said:

> Having already decided that the exclusionary rule should not be applied when the officer conducting the search acted in objectively reasonable reliance on a warrant issued by a detached and neutral magistrate that subsequently is determined to be invalid, the sole issue before us in this case is whether the officers reasonably believed that the search they conducted was authorized by a valid warrant. There is no dispute that the officers believed that the warrant authorized the search that they conducted. Thus, the only question is whether there was an objectively reasonable basis for the officers' mistaken belief. Both the trial court, and a majority of the Supreme Judicial Court, concluded that there was. We agree.

Ultimately, the disagreement over whether there should be a good faith exception is about whether there should be an exclusionary rule, what purposes the exclusionary rule serves, and what is the best way to achieve them.

5.   The Exception for Violations of the Requirement for "Knocking and Announcing"

As explained in Chapter 2, the Supreme Court has held that absent exigent circumstances, the police must knock and announce their presence before searching a residence. In Hudson v. Michigan, 126 S. Ct. 2159 (2006), the Court held that the exclusionary rule does not apply if police violate this Fourth Amendment requirement. As explained at the beginning of this chapter, Justice Scalia's majority opinion in the 5-4 decision stressed the costs of the exclusionary

---

8. The Court did not deny that there was a Fourth Amendment violation. In fact, in a subsequent case, Groh v. Ramirez, 540 U.S. 551 (2004), the Court held that the Fourth Amendment is violated if the warrant fails to list the specifics of what is to searched for and seized, even if that information is in an affidavit supporting the warrant. *Groh*, though, was a civil suit for money damages for violation of the Fourth Amendment and not an attempt to exclude evidence from use in a criminal prosecution.

rule as compared with its benefits. He also discussed the problems with applying the exclusionary rule to the knock and announce context:

> The costs here are considerable. In addition to the grave adverse consequence that exclusion of relevant incriminating evidence always entails (viz., the risk of releasing dangerous criminals into society), imposing that massive remedy for a knock-and-announce violation would generate a constant flood of alleged failures to observe the rule, and claims that any asserted *Richards* justification for a no-knock entry, had inadequate support. The cost of entering this lottery would be small, but the jackpot enormous: suppression of all evidence, amounting in many cases to a get-out-of-jail-free card. Courts would experience as never before the reality that "[t]he exclusionary rule frequently requires extensive litigation to determine whether particular evidence must be excluded." Unlike the warrant or *Miranda* requirements, compliance with which is readily determined (either there was or was not a warrant; either the *Miranda* warning was given, or it was not), what constituted a "reasonable wait time" in a particular case (or, for that matter, how many seconds the police in fact waited), or whether there was "reasonable suspicion" of the sort that would invoke the exceptions, is difficult for the trial court to determine and even more difficult for an appellate court to review.
>
> Another consequence of the incongruent remedy Hudson proposes would be police officers' refraining from timely entry after knocking and announcing. As we have observed, the amount of time they must wait is necessarily uncertain. If the consequences of running afoul of the rule were so massive, officers would be inclined to wait longer than the law requires — producing preventable violence against officers in some cases, and the destruction of evidence in many others. We deemed these consequences severe enough to produce our unanimous agreement that a mere "reasonable suspicion" that knocking and announcing "under the particular circumstances, would be dangerous or futile, or that it would inhibit the effective investigation of the crime," will cause the requirement to yield.
>
> Next to these "substantial social costs" we must consider the deterrence benefits, existence of which is a necessary condition for exclusion. (It is not, of course, a sufficient condition: "[I]t does not follow that the Fourth Amendment requires adoption of every proposal that might deter police misconduct.") To begin with, the value of deterrence depends upon the strength of the incentive to commit the forbidden act. Viewed from this perspective, deterrence of knock-and-announce violations is not worth a lot. Violation of the warrant requirement sometimes produces incriminating evidence that could not otherwise be obtained. But ignoring knock-and-announce can realistically be expected to achieve absolutely nothing except the prevention of destruction of evidence and the avoidance of life-threatening resistance by occupants of the premises — dangers which, if there is even "reasonable suspicion" of their existence, suspend the knock-and-announce requirement anyway. Massive deterrence is hardly required.

Justice Breyer, writing for the four dissenters, began his opinion by stating:

> In Wilson v. Arkansas (1995), a unanimous Court held that the Fourth Amendment normally requires law enforcement officers to knock and announce their presence before entering a dwelling. Today's opinion holds that evidence seized from a home following a violation of this requirement need not be suppressed.
>
> As a result, the Court destroys the strongest legal incentive to comply with the Constitution's knock-and-announce requirement. And the Court does so without significant support in precedent. At least I can find no such support in the many Fourth Amendment cases the Court has decided in the near century since it first set forth the exclusionary principle in Weeks v. United States (1914).

Today's opinion is thus doubly troubling. It represents a significant departure from the Court's precedents. And it weakens, perhaps destroys, much of the practical value of the Constitution's knock-and-announce protection.

The question after *Hudson* is whether police will have a sufficient incentive to comply with the knock and announce requirement knowing that evidence gained will not be excluded, and if not, whether this exception is justified by the benefits of the evidence being introduced. This, of course, is the same underlying question as to whether there should be an exclusionary rule and if so, for which exceptions should be created.

E. SUPPRESSION HEARINGS

The primary mechanism for raising the exclusionary rule is via a "suppression hearing." Generally, these occur before trial and it is the occasion for the trial court's hearing the defendant's motion that evidence was illegally obtained and should be excluded.[9] In fact, many jurisdictions require that such motions be made before trial and bar a defendant from doing so later unless there is good cause for the failure to do so.[10]

A defendant seeking to challenge the truthfulness of statements made in warrant applications must make a showing that the officers who prepared the warrant engaged in deliberate falsification or reckless disregard for the truth. In Franks v. Delaware, 438 U.S. 154 (1978), the Court stated:

> There is, of course, a presumption of validity with respect to the affidavit supporting the search warrant. To mandate an evidentiary hearing, the challenger's attack must be more than conclusory and must be supported by more than a mere desire to cross-examine. There must be allegations of deliberate falsehood or of reckless disregard for the truth, and those allegations must be accompanied by an offer of proof. They should point out specifically the portion of the warrant affidavit that is claimed to be false; and they should be accompanied by a statement of supporting reasons. Affidavits or sworn or otherwise reliable statements of witnesses should be furnished, or their absence satisfactorily explained. Allegations of negligence or innocent mistake are insufficient. The deliberate falsity or reckless disregard whose impeachment is permitted today is only that of the affiant, not of any nongovernmental informant.

The Court in *Franks* went on to emphasize that even if these requirements are met, no hearing is required if there is sufficient other content in the warrant application to support its issuance. The Court explained:

> Finally, if these requirements are met, and if, when material that is the subject of the alleged falsity or reckless disregard is set to one side, there remains sufficient

---

9. Defendants also can raise Fourth Amendment violations by bringing a motion for the return of illegally obtained evidence.

10. For example, Federal Rule of Criminal Procedure 12(h)(3)(c) provides that motions to suppress must be made before trial unless there is good cause.

content in the warrant affidavit to support a finding of probable cause, no hearing is required. On the other hand, if the remaining content is insufficient, the defendant is entitled, under the Fourth and Fourteenth Amendments, to his hearing. Whether he will prevail at that hearing is, of course, another issue.

The suppression motion occurs outside the presence of the jury. The ordinary rules of evidence do not apply at suppression hearings. In United States v. Matlock, 415 U.S. 164 (1974), the Court held that judges can rely on hearsay evidence at suppression hearings. The Court declared: "[I]n proceedings where the judge himself is considering the admissibility of evidence, the exclusionary rules, aside from rules of privilege, should not be applicable, and the judge should receive the evidence and give it such weight as his judgment and experience counsel."

Many have raised concerns that police officers sometimes do not tell the truth at suppression hearings, instead saying what is necessary to make their conduct seem lawful and to gain use of the illegally obtained evidence. *See* Christopher Slobogin, *Testilying: Police Perjury and What to Do About It*, 67 Colo. L. Rev. 1037 (1996); Donald Dripps, *The Case for the Contingent Exclusionary Rule*, 38 Am. Crim. L. Rev. 1 (2001). Often the only witnesses to the police violation are the defendant and the officers, and the concern is that officers sometimes lie to avoid the exclusionary rule. When it is the officer's word against a criminal defendant caught with contraband, courts tend to believe the officer. The concern is that officers violate the Fourth Amendment and then lie in court to ensure that the fruit of their illegal search is admitted. There is, of course, no agreement as to how often this occurs, or, if it is a problem, what to do about it.

CHAPTER

4

POLICE INTERROGATION AND THE PRIVILEGE AGAINST SELF-INCRIMINATION

The Fifth Amendment provides, in part, "No person . . . shall be compelled in any criminal case to be a witness against himself." This is referred to as the privilege against self-incrimination and is a crucial protection provided to suspects and criminal defendants in the criminal justice system.

The privilege against self-incrimination arises in many contexts, including during police interrogation. Police questioning of suspects is a crucial investigative tool. The problem, though, is that police questioning can be coercive, physically or psychologically, and false confessions can result. One study estimated that there are over 6,000 false confessions each year in the United States.[1] A recent study of cases where there were false confessions found that often these lead to conviction of innocent people. Obviously, a confession is very powerful evidence at trial. Professors Drizin and Leo explained: "[C]onfession evidence is inherently prejudicial and highly damaging to a defendant, even if it is the product of coercive interrogation, even if it is supported by no other evidence, and even if it is proven false beyond any reasonable doubt."[2]

The Supreme Court has dealt with issues of police interrogation for over a century. In examining the law in this area, this chapter is divided into three parts. First, Section A examines the requirement under the Due Process Clause that any statement introduced against a criminal defendant be "voluntary." Whether the interrogation by the police is in-custody or not, a statement that is deemed "involuntary" will be excluded from being used against a criminal defendant as being a violation of due process of law. Second, Section B examines the protections accorded to suspects during in-custodial interrogation under Miranda v. Arizona, 384 U.S. 436 (1966). A large body of case law has developed concerning when *Miranda* applies, when it is waived, and remedies for its violation. All of these are examined in Section B. Section C then considers the Sixth

---

1. Jerome H. Skolnick & James J. Frye, Above the Law: The Police and the Excessive Use of Force 63 (1987).
2. Steven A. Drizen & Richard A. Leo, *The Problem of False Confessions in the Post-DNA World*, 82 N.C. L. Rev. 891 (2004).

Amendment right to counsel, which also provides protection during some police interrogations. Finally, Section D looks at the privilege against self-incrimination in other contexts besides police interrogation.

A. DUE PROCESS AND THE REQUIREMENT FOR VOLUNTARINESS

1. The Requirement for Voluntariness

The Supreme Court first discussed limits on the admissibility of confessions in Hopt v. People of Territory of Utah, 110 U.S. 574 (1884). The Court said that "a confession . . . should not go to the jury unless it appears to the court to have been voluntary." The Court based its decision on English common law and not the Constitution, but it made clear that involuntary confessions are unreliable and should not be admissible as evidence:

> But the presumption upon which weight is given to such evidence, namely, that one who is innocent will not imperil his safety or prejudice his interests by an untrue statement, ceases when the confession appears to have been made either in consequence of inducements of a temporal nature, held out by one in authority, touching the charge preferred, or because of a threat or promise by or in the presence of such person, which, operating upon the fears or hopes of the accused, in reference to the charge, deprive him of that freedom of will or self-control essential to make his confession voluntary within the meaning of the law.

In Bram v. United States, 168 U.S. 532 (1897), the Supreme Court first found that involuntary confessions violate the privilege against self-incrimination under the Fifth Amendment. The Court stated:

> In criminal trials, in the courts of the United States, wherever a question arises whether a confession is incompetent because not voluntary, the issue is controlled by that portion of the fifth amendment to the constitution of the United States commanding that no person "shall be compelled in any criminal case to be a witness against himself." The legal principle by which the admissibility of the confession of an accused person is to be determined is expressed in the textbooks. [I]t is stated as follows: "But a confession, in order to be admissible, must be free and voluntary; that is, must not be extracted by any sort of threats or violence, nor obtained by any direct or implied promises, however slight, nor by the exertion of any improper influence. . . . A confession can never be received in evidence where the prisoner has been influenced by any threat or promise; for the law cannot measure the force of the influence used, or decide upon its effect upon the mind of the prisoner, and therefore excludes the declaration if any degree of influence has been exerted."

Brown v. Mississippi is a crucial case holding that confessions gained involuntarily are inadmissible as violating the Fifth Amendment's privilege against self-incrimination.

BROWN v. MISSISSIPPI
297 U.S. 278 (1936)

Chief Justice HUGHES delivered the opinion of the Court.

The question in this case is whether convictions, which rest solely upon confessions shown to have been extorted by officers of the state by brutality and violence, are consistent with the due process of law required by the Fourteenth Amendment of the Constitution of the United States.

Petitioners were indicted for the murder of one Raymond Stewart, whose death occurred on March 30, 1934. They were indicted on April 4, 1934, and were then arraigned and pleaded not guilty. Counsel were appointed by the court to defend them. Trial was begun the next morning and was concluded on the following day, when they were found guilty and sentenced to death.

Aside from the confessions, there was no evidence sufficient to warrant the submission of the case to the jury. After a preliminary inquiry, testimony as to the confessions was received over the objection of defendants' counsel. Defendants then testified that the confessions were false and had been procured by physical torture.

There is no dispute as to the facts upon this point, and as they are clearly and adequately stated in the dissenting opinion of Judge Griffith showing both the extreme brutality of the measures to extort the confessions and the participation of the state authorities, we quote this part of his opinion in full, as follows: "The crime with which these defendants, all ignorant negroes, are charged, was discovered about 1 o'clock P.M. on Friday, March 30, 1934. On that night one Dial, a deputy sheriff, accompanied by others, came to the home of Ellington, one of the defendants, and requested him to accompany them to the house of the deceased, and there a number of white men were gathered, who began to accuse the defendant of the crime. Upon his denial they seized him, and with the participation of the deputy they hanged him by a rope to the limb of a tree, and, having let him down, they hung him again, and when he was let down the second time, and he still protested his innocence, he was tied to a tree and whipped, and, still declining to accede to the demands that he confess, he was finally released, and he returned with some difficulty to his home, suffering intense pain and agony. The record of the testimony shows that the signs of the rope on his neck were plainly visible during the so-called trial. A day or two thereafter the said deputy, accompanied by another, returned to the home of the said defendant and arrested him, and departed with the prisoner towards the jail in an adjoining county, but went by a route which led into the state of Alabama; and while on the way, in that state, the deputy stopped and again severely whipped the defendant, declaring that he would continue the whipping until he confessed, and the defendant then agreed to confess to such a statement as the deputy would dictate, and he did so, after which he was delivered to jail.

The other two defendants, Ed Brown and Henry Shields, were also arrested and taken to the same jail. On Sunday night, April 1, 1934, the same deputy, accompanied by a number of white men, one of whom was also an officer, and by the jailer, came to the jail, and the two last named defendants were made to strip and they were laid over chairs and their backs were cut to pieces with a leather strap with buckles on it, and they were likewise made by the said deputy definitely to understand that the whipping would be continued unless and until they confessed, and not only confessed, but confessed in every matter of detail as demanded by those present; and in this manner the defendants confessed the crime, and, as the whippings progressed and were repeated, they changed or adjusted their confession in all particulars of detail so as to conform to the demands of their torturers. When the confessions had been obtained in the exact form and contents as desired by the mob, they left with the parting admonition and warning that, if the defendants changed their story at any time in any respect from that last stated, the perpetrators of the outrage would administer the same or equally effective treatment."

The state is free to regulate the procedure of its courts in accordance with its own conceptions of policy, unless in so doing it "offends some principle of justice so rooted in the traditions and conscience of our people as to be ranked as fundamental." But the freedom of the state in establishing its policy is the freedom of constitutional government and is limited by the requirement of due process of law. Because a state may dispense with a jury trial, it does not follow that it may substitute trial by ordeal. The rack and torture chamber may not be substituted for the witness stand. The state may not permit an accused to be hurried to conviction under mob domination—where the whole proceeding is but a mask—without supplying corrective process. The state may not deny to the accused the aid of counsel. Nor may a state, through the action of its officers, contrive a conviction through the pretense of a trial which in truth is "but used as a means of depriving a defendant of liberty through a deliberate deception of court and jury by the presentation of testimony known to be perjured." And the trial equally is a mere pretense where the state authorities have contrived a conviction resting solely upon confessions obtained by violence. The due process clause requires "that state action, whether through one agency or another, shall be consistent with the fundamental principles of liberty and justice which lie at the base of all our civil and political institutions." It would be difficult to conceive of methods more revolting to the sense of justice than those taken to procure the confessions of these petitioners, and the use of the confessions thus obtained as the basis for conviction and sentence was a clear denial of due process.

Over 30 years, between when *Brown* was decided in 1936 and when Miranda v. Arizona was decided in 1966, the Supreme Court decided a large number of cases concerning when confessions are voluntary. As discussed below in Section B, after *Miranda*, there is a presumption of the admissibility of confessions if police follow *Miranda*'s dictates. But even after *Miranda*, due process requires that any confession be voluntary in order to be admissible as evidence. For example, as explained below, *Miranda* applies only to interrogations while a person is in police custody. The key protection for questioning that occurs when a person is not in police custody is that any confession must be voluntary. Also, a person can waive his or her rights under *Miranda*, but even if there is a waiver, a confession is not admissible unless it is voluntary.

2.   *Determining Whether a Confession Is Voluntary*

The Supreme Court has held that the prosecution has the burden of proving that a confession is voluntary in order to admit it into evidence. Jackson v. Denno, 378 U.S. 368 (1964). Of course, even if the judge deems the confession to be voluntary and it is admitted, a defendant still can argue to the jury that the confession was obtained under circumstances and conditions that make it unreliable. Crane v. Kentucky, 476 U.S. 683 (1986). Ultimately, the Court has been clear that voluntariness is to be determined by the "totality of the circumstances."

The Court has considered a number of factors in assessing the voluntariness of confessions based on the totality of the circumstances.

The Length of the Interrogation and Whether the Defendant Was Deprived of Basic Bodily Functions. If an interrogation went on over a very long period of time, it is more likely to be deemed involuntary, especially where a suspect has been denied sleep, food, water, and/or access to a restroom. For example, in Ashcraft v. Tennessee, 322 U.S. 143 (1944), a confession was deemed involuntary when a suspect was not permitted to sleep for 36 hours during which the interrogation occurred. In Payne v. Arkansas, 356 U.S. 560 (1958), the fact that the suspect was given no food for 24 hours was important to the Court's conclusion that the confession was involuntary.

The Use of Force and Threats of Force. A confession obtained after a defendant is physically coerced, as in Brown v. Mississippi, or threatened with physical force, is not voluntary. In *Payne*, the suspect was told that a mob of 30 to 40 people were waiting outside the station to get him unless he confessed. Arizona v. Fulminante is an important, relatively recent case in which a confession was deemed involuntary because of the threat of force against a criminal suspect.

ARIZONA v. FULMINANTE
499 U.S. 279 (1991)

Justice WHITE delivered an opinion, Parts I and II, which are the opinion of the Court.[3]

The Arizona Supreme Court ruled in this case that respondent Oreste Fulminante's confession, received in evidence at his trial for murder, had been coerced and that its use against him was barred by the Fifth and Fourteenth Amendments to the United States Constitution.

I

Early in the morning of September 14, 1982, Fulminante called the Mesa, Arizona, Police Department to report that his 11-year-old stepdaughter, Jeneane Michelle Hunt, was missing. He had been caring for Jeneane while his wife,

---

3. Justices Brennan, Marshall, Stevens, and Scalia joined Parts I and II of the opinion, which are included here. The remainder of the opinion, which is not included, concerns whether harmless error analysis should apply to confessions that are deemed involuntary. [Footnote by casebook authors.]

Jeneane's mother, was in the hospital. Two days later, Jeneane's body was found in the desert east of Mesa. She had been shot twice in the head at close range with a large caliber weapon, and a ligature was around her neck. Because of the decomposed condition of the body, it was impossible to tell whether she had been sexually assaulted.

Fulminante's statements to police concerning Jeneane's disappearance and his relationship with her contained a number of inconsistencies, and he became a suspect in her killing. When no charges were filed against him, Fulminante left Arizona for New Jersey. Fulminante was later convicted in New Jersey on federal charges of possession of a firearm by a felon.

Fulminante was incarcerated in the Ray Brook Federal Correctional Institution in New York. There he became friends with another inmate, Anthony Sarivola, then serving a 60-day sentence for extortion. The two men came to spend several hours a day together. Sarivola, a former police officer, had been involved in loansharking for organized crime but then became a paid informant for the Federal Bureau of Investigation. While at Ray Brook, he masqueraded as an organized crime figure. After becoming friends with Fulminante, Sarivola heard a rumor that Fulminante was suspected of killing a child in Arizona. Sarivola then raised the subject with Fulminante in several conversations, but Fulminante repeatedly denied any involvement in Jeneane's death. During one conversation, he told Sarivola that Jeneane had been killed by bikers looking for drugs; on another occasion, he said he did not know what had happened. Sarivola passed this information on to an agent of the Federal Bureau of Investigation, who instructed Sarivola to find out more.

Sarivola learned more one evening in October 1983, as he and Fulminante walked together around the prison track. Sarivola said that he knew Fulminante was "starting to get some tough treatment and whatnot" from other inmates because of the rumor. Sarivola offered to protect Fulminante from his fellow inmates, but told him, " 'You have to tell me about it,' you know. I mean, in other words, 'For me to give you any help.'" *Ibid.* Fulminante then admitted to Sarivola that he had driven Jeneane to the desert on his motorcycle, where he choked her, sexually assaulted her, and made her beg for her life, before shooting her twice in the head.

Sarivola was released from prison in November 1983. Fulminante was released the following May, only to be arrested the next month for another weapons violation. On September 4, 1984, Fulminante was indicted in Arizona for the first-degree murder of Jeneane.

Prior to trial, Fulminante moved to suppress the statement he had given Sarivola in prison, as well as a second confession he had given to Donna Sarivola, then Anthony Sarivola's fiancée and later his wife, following his May 1984 release from prison. He asserted that the confession to Sarivola was coerced, and that the second confession was the "fruit" of the first. Following the hearing, the trial court denied the motion to suppress, specifically finding that, based on the stipulated facts, the confessions were voluntary. The State introduced both confessions as evidence at trial, and on December 19, 1985, Fulminante was convicted of Jeneane's murder. He was subsequently sentenced to death.

Fulminante appealed, arguing, among other things, that his confession to Sarivola was the product of coercion and that its admission at trial violated his rights to due process under the Fifth and Fourteenth Amendments to the United States Constitution. After considering the evidence at trial as well as the stipulated facts before the trial court on the motion to suppress, the Arizona Supreme Court held that the confession was coerced, but initially determined that the admission of the confession at trial was harmless error, because of the overwhelming nature of the evidence against Fulminante. Upon Fulminante's motion for reconsideration, however, the court ruled that this Court's precedent precluded the use of the harmless-error analysis in the case of a coerced confession. The court therefore reversed the conviction and ordered that Fulminante be retried without the use of the confession to Sarivola.

II

We deal first with the State's contention that the court below erred in holding Fulminante's confession to have been coerced. We normally give great deference to the factual findings of the state court. Nevertheless, "the ultimate issue of 'voluntariness' is a legal question requiring independent federal determination."

Although the question is a close one, we agree with the Arizona Supreme Court's conclusion that Fulminante's confession was coerced. The Arizona Supreme Court found a credible threat of physical violence unless Fulminante confessed. Our cases have made clear that a finding of coercion need not depend upon actual violence by a government agent; a credible threat is sufficient. As we have said, "coercion can be mental as well as physical, and . . . the blood of the accused is not the only hallmark of an unconstitutional inquisition." Blackburn v. Alabama (1960). As in *Payne*, where the Court found that a confession was coerced because the interrogating police officer had promised that if the accused confessed, the officer would protect the accused from an angry mob outside the jailhouse door, so too here, the Arizona Supreme Court found that it was fear of physical violence, absent protection from his friend (and Government agent) Sarivola, which motivated Fulminante to confess. Accepting the Arizona court's finding, permissible on this record, that there was a credible threat of physical violence, we agree with its conclusion that Fulminante's will was overborne in such a way as to render his confession the product of coercion.

Chief Justice REHNQUIST, with whom Justices O'CONNOR, KENNEDY, and SOUTER join, dissenting.

The Court today properly concludes that the admission of an "involuntary" confession at trial is subject to harmless error analysis. Nonetheless, the independent review of the record which we are required to make shows that respondent Fulminante's confession was not in fact involuntary.

The admissibility of a confession such as that made by respondent Fulminante depends upon whether it was voluntarily made. "The ultimate test remains that which has been the only clearly established test in Anglo-American courts for two hundred years: the test of voluntariness. Is the confession the product of an essentially free and unconstrained choice by its maker? If it is, if he has willed to confess, it may be used against him. If it is not, if his will has been overborne and his capacity for self-determination critically impaired, the use of his confession offends due process." *Culombe v. Connecticut*, 367 U.S. 568 (1961).

Exercising our responsibility to make the independent examination of the record necessary to decide this federal question, I am at a loss to see how the

Supreme Court of Arizona reached the conclusion that it did. Fulminante offered no evidence that he believed that his life was in danger or that he in fact confessed to Sarivola in order to obtain the proffered protection. Indeed, he had stipulated that "[a]t no time did the defendant indicate he was in fear of other inmates nor did he ever seek Mr. Sarivola's 'protection.'" Sarivola's testimony that he told Fulminante that "if [he] would tell the truth, he could be protected," adds little if anything to the substance of the parties' stipulation. The decision of the Supreme Court of Arizona rests on an assumption that is squarely contrary to this stipulation, and one that is not supported by any testimony of Fulminante.

The facts of record in the present case are quite different from those present in cases where we have found confessions to be coerced and involuntary. Since Fulminante was unaware that Sarivola was an FBI informant, there existed none of "the danger of coercion result[ing] from the interaction of custody and official interrogation." The fact that Sarivola was a Government informant does not by itself render Fulminante's confession involuntary, since we have consistently accepted the use of informants in the discovery of evidence of a crime as a legitimate investigatory procedure consistent with the Constitution. The conversations between Sarivola and Fulminante were not lengthy, and the defendant was free at all times to leave Sarivola's company. Sarivola at no time threatened him or demanded that he confess; he simply requested that he speak the truth about the matter. Fulminante was an experienced habitue of prisons, and presumably able to fend for himself. In concluding on these facts that Fulminante's confession was involuntary, the Court today embraces a more expansive definition of that term than is warranted by any of our decided cases.

Psychological Pressure Tactics. Coercion obviously can be psychological as well as physical. It is difficult, though, to define when psychological pressure is sufficient to rise to the level of coercion. The most famous Supreme Court case on this is Spano v. New York.

SPANO v. NEW YORK
360 U.S. 315 (1959)

Chief Justice WARREN delivered the opinion of the Court.

This is another in the long line of cases presenting the question whether a confession was properly admitted into evidence under the Fourteenth Amendment. As in all such cases, we are forced to resolve a conflict between two fundamental interests of society; its interest in prompt and efficient law enforcement, and its interest in preventing the rights of its individual members from being abridged by unconstitutional methods of law enforcement. Because of the delicate nature of the constitutional determination which we must make, we cannot escape the responsibility of making our own examination of the record.

The State's evidence reveals the following: Petitioner Vincent Joseph Spano is a derivative citizen of this country, having been born in Messina, Italy. He was 25 years old at the time of the shooting in question and had graduated from junior high school. He had a record of regular employment. The shooting took place on January 22, 1957.

On that day, petitioner was drinking in a bar. The decedent, a former professional boxer weighing almost 200 pounds who had fought in Madison Square

Garden, took some of petitioner's money from the bar. Petitioner followed him out of the bar to recover it. A fight ensued, with the decedent knocking petitioner down and then kicking him in the head three or four times. Shock from the force of these blows caused petitioner to vomit. After the bartender applied some ice to his head, petitioner left the bar, walked to his apartment, secured a gun, and walked eight or nine blocks to a candy store where the decedent was frequently to be found. He entered the store in which decedent, three friends of decedent, at least two of whom were ex-convicts, and a boy who was supervising the store were present. He fired five shots, two of which entered the decedent's body, causing his death. The boy was the only eyewitness; the three friends of decedent did not see the person who fired the shot. Petitioner then disappeared for the next week or so.

On February 1, 1957, the Bronx County Grand Jury returned an indictment for first-degree murder against petitioner. Accordingly, a bench warrant was issued for his arrest. On February 3, 1957, petitioner called one Gaspar Bruno, a close friend of 8 or 10 years' standing who had attended school with him. Bruno was a fledgling police officer, having at that time not yet finished attending police academy. According to Bruno's testimony, petitioner told him "that he took a terrific beating, that the deceased hurt him real bad and he dropped him a couple of times and he was dazed; he didn't know what he was doing and that he went and shot at him." Petitioner told Bruno that he intended to get a lawyer and give himself up. Bruno relayed this information to his superiors.

The following day, February 4, at 7:10 P.M., petitioner, accompanied by counsel, surrendered himself to the authorities in front of the Bronx County Building, where both the office of the Assistant District Attorney who ultimately prosecuted his case and the court-room in which he was ultimately tried were located. His attorney had cautioned him to answer no questions, and left him in the custody of the officers. He was promptly taken to the office of the Assistant District Attorney and at 7:15 P.M. the questioning began, being conducted by Assistant District Attorney Goldsmith, Lt. Gannon, Detectives Farrell, Lehrer and Motta, and Sgt. Clarke. The record reveals that the questioning was both persistent and continuous. Petitioner, in accordance with his attorney's instructions, steadfastly refused to answer. Detective Motta testified: "He refused to talk to me." "He just looked up to the ceiling and refused to talk to me."

At 12:15 A.M. on the morning of February 5, after five hours of questioning in which it became evident that petitioner was following his attorney's instructions, on the Assistant District Attorney's orders petitioner was transferred to the 46th Squad, Ryer Avenue Police Station. The Assistant District Attorney also went to the police station and to some extent continued to participate in the interrogation. Petitioner arrived at 12:30 and questioning was resumed at 12:40. But petitioner persisted in his refusal to answer, and again requested permission to see his attorney, this time from Detective Lehrer. His request was again denied.

It was then that those in charge of the investigation decided that petitioner's close friend, Bruno, could be of use. He had been called out on the case around 10 or 11 P.M., although he was not connected with the 46th Squad or Precinct in any way. Although, in fact, his job was in no way threatened, Bruno was told to tell petitioner that petitioner's telephone call had gotten him "in a lot of trouble, and that he should seek to extract sympathy from petitioner for Bruno's pregnant wife and three children. Bruno developed this theme with petitioner without success, and petitioner, also without success, again sought to see his attorney, a request which Bruno relayed unavailingly to his superiors. After this first session with petitioner, Bruno was again directed by Lt. Gannon to play on petitioner's sympathies, but again no confession was forthcoming. But the Lieutenant a third time ordered Bruno falsely to importune his friend to confess but again petitioner clung to his attorney's advice. Inevitably, in the fourth such session directed by the Lieutenant, lasting a full hour, petitioner succumbed to his friend's prevarications and agreed to make a statement. Accordingly, at 3:25 A.M. the Assistant District Attorney, a stenographer, and several other law enforcement officials entered the room where petitioner was being questioned, and took his statement in question and answer form with the Assistant District Attorney asking the questions. The statement was completed at 4:05 A.M.

But this was not the end. At 4:30 A.M. three detectives took petitioner to Police Headquarters in Manhattan. On the way they attempted to find the bridge from which petitioner said he had thrown the murder weapon. They crossed the Triborough Bridge into Manhattan, arriving at Police Headquarters at 5 A.M., and left Manhattan for the Bronx at 5:40 A.M. via the Willis Avenue Bridge. When petitioner recognized neither bridge as the one from which he had thrown the weapon, they re-entered Manhattan via the Third Avenue Bridge, which petitioner stated was the right one, and then returned to the Bronx well after 6 A.M. During that trip the officers also elicited a statement from petitioner that the deceased was always "on [his] back," "always pushing" him and that he was "not sorry" he had shot the deceased. All three detectives testified to that statement at the trial. Court opened at 10 A.M. that morning, and petitioner was arraigned at 10:15.

At the trial, the confession was introduced in evidence over appropriate objections. The jury was instructed that it could rely on it only if it was found to be voluntary. The jury returned a guilty verdict and petitioner was sentenced to death.

We find use of the confession obtained here inconsistent with the Fourteenth Amendment under traditional principles. The abhorrence of society to the use of involuntary confessions does not turn alone on their inherent untrustworthiness. It also turns on the deep-rooted feeling that the police must obey the law while enforcing the law; that in the end life and liberty can be as much endangered from illegal methods used to convict those thought to be criminals as from the actual criminals themselves. Accordingly, the actions of police in obtaining confessions have come under scrutiny in a long series of cases. Those cases suggest that in recent years law enforcement officials have become increasingly aware of the burden which they share, along with our courts, in protecting fundamental rights of our citizenry, including that portion of our citizenry suspected of crime. The facts of no case recently in this Court have quite approached the brutal beatings in Brown v. State of Mississippi (1936), or the 36 consecutive hours of questioning present in Ashcraft v. State of Tennessee (1944). But as law enforcement officers become more responsible, and the methods used to extract confessions more sophisticated, our duty to enforce federal constitutional protections does not cease. It only becomes more difficult because of the more delicate judgments to be made. Our judgment here is that, on all the facts, this conviction cannot stand.

Petitioner was a foreign-born young man of 25 with no past history of law violation or of subjection to official interrogation, at least insofar as the record shows. He had progressed only one-half year into high school and the record indicates that he had a history of emotional instability. He did not make a narrative statement, but was subject to the leading questions of a skillful prosecutor in a question and answer confession. He was subjected to questioning not by a few men, but by many. They included Assistant District Attorney Goldsmith, one Hyland of the District Attorney's Office, Deputy Inspector Halks, Lieutenant Gannon, Detective Ciccone, Detective Motta, Detective Lehrer, Detective Marshal, Detective Farrell, Detective Leira, Detective Murphy, Detective Murtha, Sergeant Clarke, Patrolman Bruno and Stenographer Baldwin. All played some part, and the effect of such massive official interrogation must have been felt. Petitioner was questioned for virtually eight straight hours before he confessed, with his only respite being a transfer to an arena presumably considered more appropriate by the police for the task at hand. Nor was the questioning conducted during normal business hours, but began in early evening, continued into the night, and did not bear fruition until the not-too-early morning. The drama was not played out, with the final admissions obtained, until almost sunrise. In such circumstances slowly mounting fatigue does, and is calculated to, play its part. The questioners persisted in the face of his repeated refusals to answer on the advice of his attorney, and they ignored his reasonable requests to contact the local attorney whom he had already retained and who had personally delivered him into the custody of these officers in obedience to the bench warrant.

The use of Bruno, characterized in this Court by counsel for the State as a "childhood friend" of petitioner's, is another factor which deserves mention in the totality of the situation. Bruno's was the one face visible to petitioner in which he could put some trust. There was a bond of friendship between them going back a decade into adolescence. It was with this material that the officers felt that they could overcome petitioner's will. They instructed Bruno falsely to state that petitioner's telephone call had gotten him into trouble, that his job was in jeopardy, and that loss of his job would be disastrous to his three children, his wife and his unborn child. And Bruno played this part of a worried father, harried by his superiors, in not one, but four different acts, the final one lasting an hour. Petitioner was apparently unaware of John Gay's famous couplet: "An open foe may prove a curse, But a pretended friend is worse," and he yielded to his false friend's entreaties.

We conclude that petitioner's will was overborne by official pressure, fatigue and sympathy falsely aroused after considering all the facts in their post-indictment setting.

Deception. In Lynumn v. Illinois, 372 U.S. 528 (1963), a suspect was told that if she cooperated and answered the questions from the police officers, she would not be prosecuted for participating in a marijuana sale. But she was told that if she did not cooperate, she would face ten years in prison and have her children taken away from her. She told the police that she would say whatever they wanted. They told her to admit the marijuana sale and she did. The Court held that is "clear that a confession made under such circumstances must not be deemed voluntary."

Although deception can make a confession involuntary, the Court has been tolerant of many police techniques. For example, in Leyra v. Dennis, 347 U.S.

556 (1954), the Court found that a confession was voluntary, even though the police lied to the suspect and told a suspect that his accomplice had already confessed. In Frazier v. Cupp, 394 U.S. 731 (1969), the Court found that an officer acting as a friend to a suspect and expressing sympathy for his or her plight is not deception requiring suppression of a confession.

   The Age, Level of Education, and Mental Condition of a Suspect. For example, in Payne v. Arkansas, the Court, in finding a confession involuntary, stressed that the suspect had a fifth-grade education. In *Spano*, above, the Court focused on the defendant's level of education as a factor in determining his confession to be involuntary. In Culombe v. Connecticut, 367 U.S. 568 (1961), the Court emphasized that the suspect was illiterate and of low intelligence. By contrast, in finding a confession to be voluntary in Crooker v. California, 357 U.S. 433 (1958), the Court noted that the suspect had completed a year of law school.

   However, in Colorado v. Connelly, below, the Court imposed a major limit on consideration of a defendant's mental condition in determining whether a confession is voluntary. The Court held that a confession is to be deemed involuntary, regardless of the defendant's mental condition, only if it is the product of police misconduct. The contrast between Chief Justice Rehnquist's majority opinion and Justice Brennan's dissent is important in illuminating different views about the voluntariness requirement and the privilege against self-incrimination.

COLORADO v. CONNELLY
479 U.S. 157 (1986)

   Chief Justice REHNQUIST delivered the opinion of the Court.
   In this case, the Supreme Court of Colorado held that the United States Constitution requires a court to suppress a confession when the mental state of the defendant, at the time he made the confession, interfered with his "rational intellect" and his "free will." We conclude that the admissibility of this kind of statement is governed by state rules of evidence, rather than by our previous decisions regarding coerced confessions and *Miranda* waivers. We therefore reverse.

I

On August 18, 1983, Officer Patrick Anderson of the Denver Police Department was in uniform, working in an off-duty capacity in downtown Denver. Respondent Francis Connelly approached Officer Anderson and, without any prompting, stated that he had murdered someone and wanted to talk about it. Anderson immediately advised respondent that he had the right to remain silent, that anything he said could be used against him in court, and that he had the right to an attorney prior to any police questioning. *See* Miranda v. Arizona (1966). Respondent stated that he understood these rights but he still wanted to talk about the murder. Understandably bewildered by this confession, Officer Anderson asked respondent several questions. Connelly denied that he had been drinking, denied that he had been taking any drugs, and stated that, in the past, he had been a patient in several mental hospitals. Officer Anderson again told Connelly that he was under no obligation to say anything. Connelly replied that it was "all right," and that he would talk to

Officer Anderson because his conscience had been bothering him. To Officer Anderson, respondent appeared to understand fully the nature of his acts.

Shortly thereafter, Homicide Detective Stephen Antuna arrived. Respondent was again advised of his rights, and Detective Antuna asked him "what he had on his mind." Respondent answered that he had come all the way from Boston to confess to the murder of Mary Ann Junta, a young girl whom he had killed in Denver sometime during November 1982. Respondent was taken to police headquarters, and a search of police records revealed that the body of an unidentified female had been found in April 1983. Respondent openly detailed his story to Detective Antuna and Sergeant Thomas Haney, and readily agreed to take the officers to the scene of the killing. Under Connelly's sole direction, the two officers and respondent proceeded in a police vehicle to the location of the crime. Respondent pointed out the exact location of the murder. Throughout this episode, Detective Antuna perceived no indication whatsoever that respondent was suffering from any kind of mental illness.

Respondent was held overnight. During an interview with the public defender's office the following morning, he became visibly disoriented. He began giving confused answers to questions, and for the first time, stated that "voices" had told him to come to Denver and that he had followed the directions of these voices in confessing. Respondent was sent to a state hospital for evaluation. He was initially found incompetent to assist in his own defense. By March 1984, however, the doctors evaluating respondent determined that he was competent to proceed to trial.

At a preliminary hearing, respondent moved to suppress all of his statements. Dr. Jeffrey Metzner, a psychiatrist employed by the state hospital, testified that respondent was suffering from chronic schizophrenia and was in a psychotic state at least as of August 17, 1983, the day before he confessed. Metzner's interviews with respondent revealed that respondent was following the "voice of God." This voice instructed respondent to withdraw money from the bank, to buy an airplane ticket, and to fly from Boston to Denver. When respondent arrived from Boston, God's voice became stronger and told respondent either to confess to the killing or to commit suicide. Reluctantly following the command of the voices, respondent approached Officer Anderson and confessed. Dr. Metzner testified that, in his expert opinion, respondent was experiencing "command hallucinations." This condition interfered with respondent's "volitional abilities; that is, his ability to make free and rational choices." Dr. Metzner further testified that Connelly's illness did not significantly impair his cognitive abilities. Thus, respondent understood the rights he had when Officer Anderson and Detective Antuna advised him that he need not speak. Dr. Metzner admitted that the "voices" could in reality be Connelly's interpretation of his own guilt, but explained that in his opinion, Connelly's psychosis motivated his confession. On the basis of this evidence the Colorado trial court decided that respondent's statements must be suppressed because they were "involuntary." The Colorado Supreme Court affirmed.

II

The Due Process Clause of the Fourteenth Amendment provides that no State shall "deprive any person of life, liberty, or property, without due process of law." [W]e have held that by virtue of the Due Process Clause "certain interrogation techniques, either in isolation or as applied to the unique characteristics of a particular suspect, are so offensive to a civilized system of justice that they must be condemned." Indeed, coercive government misconduct was the catalyst for this Court's seminal confession case, Brown v. Mississippi (1936).

Thus the cases considered by this Court over the 50 years since Brown v. Mississippi have focused upon the crucial element of police overreaching. While each confession case has turned on its own set of factors justifying the conclusion that police conduct was oppressive, all have contained a substantial element of coercive police conduct. Absent police conduct causally related to the confession, there is simply no basis for concluding that any state actor has deprived a criminal defendant of due process of law. Respondent correctly notes that as interrogators have turned to more subtle forms of psychological persuasion, courts have found the mental condition of the defendant a more significant factor in the "voluntariness" calculus. *See* Spano v. New York (1959). But this fact does not justify a conclusion that a defendant's mental condition, by itself and apart from its relation to official coercion, should ever dispose of the inquiry into constitutional "voluntariness."

Our "involuntary confession" jurisprudence is entirely consistent with the settled law requiring some sort of "state action" to support a claim of violation of the Due Process Clause of the Fourteenth Amendment. The Colorado trial court, of course, found that the police committed no wrongful acts, and that finding has been neither challenged by respondent nor disturbed by the Supreme Court of Colorado.

The difficulty with the approach of the Supreme Court of Colorado is that it fails to recognize the essential link between coercive activity of the State, on the one hand, and a resulting confession by a defendant, on the other. The flaw in respondent's constitutional argument is that it would expand our previous line of "voluntariness" cases into a far-ranging requirement that courts must divine a defendant's motivation for speaking or acting as he did even though there be no claim that governmental conduct coerced his decision.

The most outrageous behavior by a private party seeking to secure evidence against a defendant does not make that evidence inadmissible under the Due Process Clause. We have also observed that "[j]urists and scholars uniformly have recognized that the exclusionary rule imposes a substantial cost on the societal interest in law enforcement by its proscription of what concededly is relevant evidence." Moreover, suppressing respondent's statements would serve absolutely no purpose in enforcing constitutional guarantees. The purpose of excluding evidence seized in violation of the Constitution is to substantially deter future violations of the Constitution. Only if we were to establish a brand new constitutional right — the right of a criminal defendant to confess to his crime only when totally rational and properly motivated — could respondent's present claim be sustained.

We have previously cautioned against expanding "currently applicable exclusionary rules by erecting additional barriers to placing truthful and probative evidence before state juries. . . ." We abide by that counsel now. "[T]he central purpose of a criminal trial is to decide the factual question of the defendant's guilt or innocence," and while we have previously held that exclusion of evidence may be necessary to protect constitutional guarantees, both the necessity for the collateral inquiry and the exclusion of evidence deflect a criminal trial from its basic purpose. Respondent would now have us require sweeping inquiries into the state of mind of a criminal defendant who has confessed, inquiries quite divorced from any coercion brought to bear on the defendant by the State. We think the Constitution rightly leaves this sort of inquiry to be resolved by state laws governing the admission of evidence and erects no standard of its own in this area. A statement rendered by one in the condition of respondent might be proved to be quite unreliable, but this is a matter to be governed by the evidentiary laws of the forum, and not by the Due Process Clause of the Fourteenth Amendment. "The aim of the requirement of due process is not to exclude presumptively false evidence, but to prevent fundamental unfairness in the use of evidence, whether true or false."

We hold that coercive police activity is a necessary predicate to the finding that a confession is not "voluntary" within the meaning of the Due Process Clause of the Fourteenth Amendment. We also conclude that the taking of respondent's statements, and their admission into evidence, constitute no violation of that Clause.

Justice BRENNAN, with whom Justice MARSHALL joins, dissenting.

Today the Court denies Mr. Connelly his fundamental right to make a vital choice with a sane mind, involving a determination that could allow the State to deprive him of liberty or even life. This holding is unprecedented: "Surely in the present stage of our civilization a most basic sense of justice is affronted by the spectacle of incarcerating a human being upon the basis of a statement he made while insane. . . ." Blackburn v. Alabama (1960). Because I believe that the use of a mentally ill person's involuntary confession is antithetical to the notion of fundamental fairness embodied in the Due Process Clause, I dissent.

I

The respondent's seriously impaired mental condition is clear on the record of this case. At the time of his confession, Mr. Connelly suffered from a "long-standing severe mental disorder," diagnosed as chronic paranoid schizophrenia. He had been hospitalized for psychiatric reasons five times prior to his confession; his longest hospitalization lasted for seven months. Mr. Connelly heard imaginary voices and saw nonexistent objects. He believed that his father was God, and that he was a reincarnation of Jesus.

At the time of his confession, Mr. Connelly's mental problems included "grandiose and delusional thinking." He had a known history of "thought withdrawal and insertion." Although physicians had treated Mr. Connelly "with a wide variety of medications in the past including antipsychotic medications," he had not taken any antipsychotic medications for at least six months prior to his confession. Following his arrest, Mr. Connelly initially was found incompetent to stand trial because the court-appointed psychiatrist, Dr. Metzner, "wasn't very confident that he could consistently relate accurate information." Dr. Metzner testified that Mr. Connelly was unable "to make free and rational choices" due to auditory hallucinations: "[W]hen he was read his *Miranda* rights, he probably had the capacity to know that he was being read his *Miranda* rights [but] he wasn't able to use that information because of the command hallucinations that he had experienced." He achieved competency to stand trial only after six months of hospitalization and treatment with antipsychotic and sedative medications.

The state trial court found that the "overwhelming evidence presented by the Defense" indicated that the prosecution did not meet its burden of demonstrating by a preponderance of the evidence that the initial statement to Officer Anderson was voluntary.

II

The absence of police wrongdoing should not, by itself, determine the voluntariness of a confession by a mentally ill person. The requirement that a confession be voluntary reflects a recognition of the importance of free will and of reliability in determining the admissibility of a confession, and thus demands an inquiry into the totality of the circumstances surrounding the confession.

Today's decision restricts the application of the term "involuntary" to those confessions obtained by police coercion. Confessions by mentally ill individuals or by persons coerced by parties other than police officers are now considered "voluntary." The Court's failure to recognize all forms of involuntariness or coercion as antithetical to due process reflects a refusal to acknowledge free will as a value of constitutional consequence. But due process derives much of its meaning from a conception of fundamental fairness that emphasizes the right to make vital choices voluntarily: "The Fourteenth Amendment secures against state invasion . . . the right of a person to remain silent unless he chooses to speak in the unfettered exercise of his own will. . . ." Malloy v. Hogan (1964). This right requires vigilant protection if we are to safeguard the values of private conscience and human dignity.

This Court's assertion that we would be required "to establish a brand new constitutional right" to recognize the respondent's claim, ignores 200 years of constitutional jurisprudence.

A true commitment to fundamental fairness requires that the inquiry be "not whether the conduct of state officers in obtaining the confession is shocking, but whether the confession was 'free and voluntary'. . . ." Malloy v. Hogan.

We have never confined our focus to police coercion, because the value of freedom of will has demanded a broader inquiry. While it is true that police overreaching has been an element of every confession case to date, it is also true that in every case the Court has made clear that ensuring that a confession is a product of free will is an independent concern. The fact that involuntary confessions have always been excluded in part because of police overreaching signifies only that this is a case of first impression. Until today, we have never upheld the admission of a confession that does not reflect the exercise of free will.

Since the Court redefines voluntary confessions to include confessions by mentally ill individuals, the reliability of these confessions becomes a central concern. A concern for reliability is inherent in our criminal justice system, which relies upon accusatorial rather than inquisitorial practices. While an inquisitorial system prefers obtaining confessions from criminal defendants, an accusatorial system must place its faith in determinations of "guilt by evidence independently and freely secured."

Our distrust for reliance on confessions is due, in part, to their decisive impact upon the adversarial process. Triers of fact accord confessions such heavy weight in their determinations that "the introduction of a confession makes the other aspects of a trial in court superfluous, and the real trial, for all practical purposes, occurs when the confession is obtained." No other class of evidence is so profoundly prejudicial.

Because the admission of a confession so strongly tips the balance against the defendant in the adversarial process, we must be especially careful about a confession's reliability. We have to date not required a finding of reliability for involuntary confessions only because all such confessions have been excluded upon a finding of involuntariness, regardless of reliability. The Court's adoption today of a restrictive definition of an "involuntary" confession will require heightened scrutiny of a confession's reliability.

Minimum standards of due process should require that the trial court find substantial indicia of reliability, on the basis of evidence extrinsic to the confession itself, before admitting the confession of a mentally ill person into evidence. I would require the trial court to make such a finding on remand. To hold otherwise allows the State to imprison and possibly to execute a mentally ill defendant based solely upon an inherently unreliable confession.

3.   Is the Voluntariness Test Desirable?

The voluntariness test has the advantage that it focuses on the totality of the circumstances in deciding whether a confession should be admitted into evidence. Underlying the voluntariness test, and often expressed by the Supreme Court, is a concern for the reliability of a confession. Obviously, a confession gained through violence and threats of violence, or when a person has been deprived sleep and food for over a day, is unreliable. But the Court is explicit, in cases such as *Spano* above, that reliability is not the only concern; certain police techniques are repugnant and override free will and thus are not to be tolerated.

On the other hand, the voluntariness test provides relatively little in the way of clear guidance to police officers as to what they can and cannot do in questioning a suspect. Judges inherently have great discretion under a "totality of the circumstances" test. Critics argue that police, who question suspects literally every day, need more instructions than a voluntariness test can provide. In fact, some police organizations have come to support the requirements imposed under Miranda v. Arizona because they provide clear and simple requirements for police to follow with the knowledge that if they do so, there is a presumption that any confession obtained will be deemed voluntary.

4.   Coercive Questioning, Torture, and the War on Terrorism

The issue of coercive questioning techniques has arisen as part of the war on terror. In a famous memorandum, since repudiated, high-level legal advisors within the Bush administration urged that the President has the authority to override treaties and statutes prohibiting torture and that the definition of torture should be limited to pain and suffering causing failure of bodily organs or similar to that suffered when there is the failure of major bodily organs. The Bush administration, in response to great pressure, repudiated that, but has continued to argue that while torture is prohibited, coercive questioning is allowed and necessary in fighting terrorism.

The Military Commission Act of 2006, Pub. L. No. 109-366, 120 Stat. 2600 (2006), follows this distinction. The Act provides for military commissions to try non-citizens accused of terrorism and prohibits the admissibility of statements gained through torture. The Act provides that in determining whether a statement is admissible before a military commission, the tribunal should consider whether under the totality of the circumstances the statement should be deemed reliable, whether the interests of justice would be served by admission of the statement, and whether the methods used to gain the statement amount to "cruel, inhuman, or degrading treatment."

As a constitutional matter, there is the question of whether due process applies to non-citizens held and questioned outside the United States. As a practical matter, there is the issue of whether statements made after coercive questioning ever can be sufficiently reliable to justify the practice. As an ethical matter, there is the question of whether coercive questioning is ever acceptable.

B. FIFTH AMENDMENT LIMITS ON IN-CUSTODIAL INTERROGATION: MIRANDA v. ARIZONA

1. Miranda v. Arizona and Its Affirmation by the Supreme Court

Probably the most famous Supreme Court case dealing with criminal procedure, and one of the most famous Supreme Court decisions of all time, is Miranda v. Arizona. The Court spoke of the inherently coercive nature of in-custodial interrogation and as a solution required that every suspect questioned by the police be given certain warnings. A key difference between the majority and the dissent is whether more than a voluntariness test is needed to protect criminal suspects: The majority believes that more than a voluntariness test is essential; the dissent argues that the voluntariness test is sufficient.

In reading the decision, it also is important to note that the majority opinion was written by Chief Justice Earl Warren. He had been a district attorney, the Attorney General of California, and the Governor of California before becoming Chief Justice. This may have been important in providing additional credibility for a particularly controversial decision.

MIRANDA v. ARIZONA

384 U.S. 436 (1966)

Chief Justice WARREN delivered the opinion of the Court.

The cases before us raise questions which go to the roots of our concepts of American criminal jurisprudence: the restraints society must observe consistent with the Federal Constitution in prosecuting individuals for crime. More specifically, we deal with the admissibility of statements obtained from an individual who is subjected to custodial police interrogation and the necessity for procedures which assure that the individual is accorded his privilege under the Fifth Amendment to the Constitution not to be compelled to incriminate himself.

We dealt with certain phases of this problem recently in Escobedo v. State of Illinois (1964). There, as in the four cases before us, law enforcement officials took the defendant into custody and interrogated him in a police station for the purpose of obtaining a confession. The police did not effectively advise him of his right to remain silent or of his right to consult with his attorney. Rather, they confronted him with an alleged accomplice who accused him of having perpetrated a murder. When the defendant denied the accusation and said "I didn't shoot Manuel, you did it," they handcuffed him and took him to an interrogation room. There, while handcuffed and standing, he was questioned for four hours until he confessed. During this interrogation, the police denied his request to speak to his attorney, and they prevented his retained attorney, who had come to the police station, from consulting with him. At his trial, the State, over his objection, introduced the confession against him. We held that the statements thus made were constitutionally inadmissible.

This case has been the subject of judicial interpretation and spirited legal debate since it was decided two years ago.

We start here, as we did in *Escobedo*, with the premise that our holding is not an innovation in our jurisprudence, but is an application of principles long recognized and applied in other settings. We have undertaken a thorough re-examination of the *Escobedo* decision and the principles it announced, and we reaffirm it. That case was but an explication of basic rights that are enshrined in our Constitution — that "No person . . . shall be compelled in any criminal case to be a witness against himself," and that "the accused shall . . . have the Assistance of Counsel" — rights which were put in jeopardy in that case through official overbearing. These precious rights were fixed in our Constitution only after centuries of persecution and struggle.

Our holding will be spelled out with some specificity in the pages which follow but briefly stated it is this: the prosecution may not use statements, whether exculpatory or inculpatory, stemming from custodial interrogation of the defendant unless it demonstrates the use of procedural safeguards effective to secure the privilege against self-incrimination. By custodial interrogation, we mean questioning initiated by law enforcement officers after a person has been taken into custody or otherwise deprived of his freedom of action in any significant way. As for the procedural safeguards to be employed, unless other fully effective means are devised to inform accused persons of their right of silence and to assure a continuous opportunity to exercise it, the following measures are required. Prior to any questioning, the person must be warned that he has a right to remain silent, that any statement he does make may be used as evidence against him, and that he has a right to the presence of an attorney, either retained or appointed. The defendant may waive effectuation of these rights, provided the waiver is made voluntarily, knowingly and intelligently. If, however, he indicates in any manner and at any stage of the process that he wishes to consult with an attorney before speaking there can be no questioning. Likewise, if the individual is alone and indicates in any manner that he does not wish to be interrogated, the police may not question him. The mere fact that he may have answered some questions or volunteered some statements on his own does not deprive him of the right to refrain from answering any further inquiries until he has consulted with an attorney and thereafter consents to be questioned.

I.

The constitutional issue we decide in each of these cases is the admissibility of statements obtained from a defendant questioned while in custody or otherwise deprived of his freedom of action in any significant way. In each, the defendant was questioned by police officers, detectives, or a prosecuting attorney in a room in which he was cut off from the outside world. In none of these cases was the defendant given a full and effective warning of his rights at the outset of the interrogation process. In all the cases, the questioning elicited oral admissions, and in three of them, signed statements as well which were admitted at their trials. They all thus share salient features — incommunicado interrogation of individuals in a police-dominated atmosphere, resulting in self-incriminating statements without full warnings of constitutional rights.

An understanding of the nature and setting of this in-custody interrogation is essential to our decisions today. The difficulty in depicting what transpires at such interrogations stems from the fact that in this country they have largely taken place incommunicado. From extensive factual studies undertaken in the early 1930's, including the famous Wickersham Report to Congress by a Presidential Commission, it is clear that police violence and the "third degree" flourished at that time. In a series of cases decided by this Court long after these studies, the police resorted to physical brutality — beatings, hanging, whipping — and to sustained and protracted questioning incommunicado in order to extort confessions. The use of physical brutality and violence is not, unfortunately, relegated to the past or to any part of the country. Only recently in Kings County, New York, the police brutally beat, kicked and placed lighted cigarette butts on the back of a potential witness under interrogation for the purpose of securing a statement incriminating a third party.

The examples given above are undoubtedly the exception now, but they are sufficiently widespread to be the object of concern. Unless a proper limitation upon custodial interrogation is achieved — such as these decisions will advance — there can be no assurance that practices of this nature will be eradicated in the foreseeable future.

Again we stress that the modern practice of in-custody interrogation is psychologically rather than physically oriented. As we have stated before, this Court has recognized that coercion can be mental as well as physical, and that the blood of the accused is not the only hallmark of an unconstitutional inquisition. Interrogation still takes place in privacy. Privacy results in secrecy and this in turn results in a gap in our knowledge as to what in fact goes on in the interrogation rooms. A valuable source of information about present police practices, however, may be found in various police manuals and texts which document procedures employed with success in the past, and which recommend various other effective tactics. These texts are used by law enforcement agencies themselves as guides. It should be noted that these texts professedly present the most enlightened and effective means presently used to obtain statements through custodial interrogation. By considering these texts and other data, it is possible to describe procedures observed and noted around the country.

The officers are told by the manuals that the "principal psychological factor contributing to a successful interrogation is privacy — being alone with the person under interrogation." To highlight the isolation and unfamiliar surroundings, the manuals instruct the police to display an air of confidence in the suspect's guilt and from outward appearance to maintain only an interest in confirming certain details. The guilt of the subject is to be posited as a fact. The interrogator should direct his comments toward the reasons why the subject committed the act, rather than court failure by asking the subject whether he did it. Like other men, perhaps the subject has had a bad family life, had an unhappy childhood, had too much to drink, had an unrequited desire for women. The officers are instructed to minimize the moral seriousness of the offense, to cast blame on the victim or on society. These tactics are designed to put the subject in a psychological state where his story is but an elaboration of what the police purport to know already — that he is guilty. Explanations to the contrary are dismissed and discouraged. The texts thus stress that the major qualities an interrogator should possess are patience and perseverance.

When the techniques described above prove unavailing, the texts recommend they be alternated with a show of some hostility. One ploy often used has been termed the "friendly-unfriendly" or the "Mutt and Jeff" act.

The interrogators sometimes are instructed to induce a confession out of trickery. The technique here is quite effective in crimes which require identification or which run in series. In the identification situation, the interrogator may take a break in his questioning to place the subject among a group of men in a line-up. "The witness or complainant (previously coached, if necessary) studies the line-up and confidently points out the subject as the guilty party." Then the questioning resumes "as though there were now no doubt about the guilt of the subject."

The manuals also contain instructions for police on how to handle the individual who refuses to discuss the matter entirely, or who asks for an attorney or relatives. The examiner is to concede him the right to remain silent. "This usually has a very undermining effect. First of all, he is disappointed in his expectation of an unfavorable reaction on the part of the interrogator. Secondly, a concession of this right to remain silent impresses the subject with the apparent fairness of his interrogator." After this psychological conditioning, however, the officer is told to point out the incriminating significance of the suspect's refusal to talk. Few will persist in their initial refusal to talk, it is said, if this monologue is employed correctly.

From these representative samples of interrogation techniques, the setting prescribed by the manuals and observed in practice becomes clear. In essence, it is this: To be alone with the subject is essential to prevent distraction and to deprive him of any outside support. The aura of confidence in his guilt undermines his will to resist. He merely confirms the preconceived story the police seek to have him describe. Patience and persistence, at times relentless questioning, are employed. To obtain a confession, the interrogator must "patiently maneuver himself or his quarry into a position from which the desired objective may be attained." When normal procedures fail to produce the needed result, the police may resort to deceptive stratagems such as giving false legal advice. It is important to keep the subject off balance, for example, by trading on his insecurity about himself or his surroundings. The police then persuade, trick, or cajole him out of exercising his constitutional rights.

Even without employing brutality, the "third degree" or the specific stratagems described above, the very fact of custodial interrogation exacts a heavy toll on individual liberty and trades on the weakness of individuals.

In the cases before us today, given this background, we concern ourselves primarily with this interrogation atmosphere and the evils it can bring.

In No. 759, Miranda v. Arizona, the police arrested the defendant and took him to a special interrogation room where they secured a confession. In No. 760, Vignera v. New York, the defendant made oral admissions to the police after interrogation in the afternoon, and then signed an inculpatory statement upon being questioned by an assistant district attorney later the same evening. In No. 761, Westover v. United States, the defendant was handed over to the Federal Bureau of Investigation by local authorities after they had detained and interrogated him for a lengthy period, both at night and the following morning. After some two hours of questioning, the federal officers had obtained signed statements from the defendant. Lastly, in No. 584, California v. Stewart, the local police held the defendant five days in the station and interrogated him on nine separate occasions before they secured his inculpatory statement.

In these cases, we might not find the defendants' statements to have been involuntary in traditional terms. Our concern for adequate safeguards to protect precious Fifth Amendment rights is, of course, not lessened in the slightest. In each of the cases, the defendant was thrust into an unfamiliar atmosphere and run through menacing police interrogation procedures. The potentiality for compulsion is forcefully apparent, for example, in *Miranda*, where the indigent Mexican defendant was a seriously disturbed individual with pronounced sexual fantasies, and in *Stewart*, in which the defendant was an indigent Los Angeles Negro who had dropped out of school in the sixth grade. To be sure, the records do not evince overt physical coercion or patent psychological ploys. The fact remains that in none of these cases did the officers undertake to afford appropriate safeguards at the outset of the interrogation to insure that the statements were truly the product of free choice.

It is obvious that such an interrogation environment is created for no purpose other than to subjugate the individual to the will of his examiner. This atmosphere carries its own badge of intimidation. To be sure, this is not physical intimidation, but it is equally destructive of human dignity. The current practice of incommunicado interrogation is at odds with one of our Nation's most cherished principles — that the individual may not be compelled to incriminate himself. Unless adequate protective devices are employed to dispel the compulsion inherent in custodial surroundings, no statement obtained from the defendant can truly be the product of his free choice.

II.

We sometimes forget how long it has taken to establish the privilege against self-incrimination, the sources from which it came and the fervor with which it was defended. Its roots go back into ancient times. [W]e may view the historical development of the privilege as one which groped for the proper scope of governmental power over the citizen.

The question in these cases is whether the privilege is fully applicable during a period of custodial interrogation. We are satisfied that all the principles embodied in the privilege apply to informal compulsion exerted by law-enforcement officers during in-custody questioning. An individual swept from familiar surroundings into police custody, surrounded by antagonistic forces, and subjected to the techniques of persuasion described above cannot be otherwise than under compulsion to speak. As a practical matter, the compulsion to speak in the isolated setting of the police station may well be greater than in courts or other official investigations, where there are often impartial observers to guard against intimidation or trickery.

III.

Today, then, there can be no doubt that the Fifth Amendment privilege is available outside of criminal court proceedings and serves to protect persons in all settings in which their freedom of action is curtailed in any significant way from being compelled to incriminate themselves. We have concluded that without proper safeguards the process of in-custody interrogation of persons suspected or accused of crime contains inherently compelling pressures which work to undermine the individual's will to resist and to compel him to speak where he would not otherwise do so freely. In order to combat these pressures and to permit a full opportunity to exercise the privilege against self-incrimination, the accused must be adequately and effectively apprised of his rights and the exercise of those rights must be fully honored.

It is impossible for us to foresee the potential alternatives for protecting the privilege which might be devised by Congress or the States in the exercise of their creative rule-making capacities. Therefore we cannot say that the Constitution necessarily requires adherence to any particular solution for the inherent compulsions of the interrogation process as it is presently conducted. Our decision in no way creates a constitutional straitjacket which will handicap sound efforts at reform, nor is it intended to have this effect. We encourage Congress and the States to continue their laudable search for increasingly effective ways of protecting the rights of the individual while promoting efficient enforcement of our criminal laws. However, unless we are shown other procedures which are at least as effective in apprising accused persons of their right of silence and in assuring a continuous opportunity to exercise it, the following safeguards must be observed.

At the outset, if a person in custody is to be subjected to interrogation, he must first be informed in clear and unequivocal terms that he has the right to remain silent. For those unaware of the privilege, the warning is needed simply to make them aware of it — the threshold requirement for an intelligent decision as to its exercise. More important, such a warning is an absolute prerequisite in overcoming the inherent pressures of the interrogation atmosphere. It is not just the subnormal or woefully ignorant who succumb to an interrogator's imprecations, whether implied or expressly stated, that the interrogation will continue until a confession is obtained or that silence in the face of accusation is itself damning and will bode ill when presented to a jury. Further, the warning will show the individual that his interrogators are prepared to recognize his privilege should he choose to exercise it.

In accord with our decision today, it is impermissible to penalize an individual for exercising his Fifth Amendment privilege when he is under police custodial interrogation. The prosecution may not, therefore, use at trial the fact that he stood mute or claimed his privilege in the face of accusation.

The Fifth Amendment privilege is so fundamental to our system of constitutional rule and the expedient of giving an adequate warning as to the availability of the privilege so simple, we will not pause to inquire in individual cases whether the defendant was aware of his rights without a warning being given. Assessments of the knowledge the defendant possessed, based on information as to his age, education, intelligence, or prior contact with authorities, can never be more than speculation; a warning is a clearcut fact. More important, whatever the background of the person interrogated, a warning at the time of the interrogation is indispensable to overcome its pressures and to insure that the individual knows he is free to exercise the privilege at that point in time.

The warning of the right to remain silent must be accompanied by the explanation that anything said can and will be used against the individual in court. This warning is needed in order to make him aware not only of the privilege, but also of the consequences of forgoing it. It is only through an awareness of these consequences that there can be any assurance of real understanding and intelligent exercise of the privilege. Moreover, this warning may serve to make the individual more acutely aware that he is faced with a phase of the adversary system — that he is not in the presence of persons acting solely in his interest.

The circumstances surrounding in-custody interrogation can operate very quickly to overbear the will of one merely made aware of his privilege by his interrogators. Therefore, the right to have counsel present at the interrogation is indispensable to the protection of the Fifth Amendment privilege under the system we delineate today. Our aim is to assure that the individual's right to choose between silence and speech remains unfettered throughout the interrogation process. A once-stated warning, delivered by those who will conduct the interrogation, cannot itself suffice to that end among those who most require knowledge of their rights. A mere warning given by the interrogators is not alone sufficient to accomplish that end. Prosecutors themselves claim that the admonishment of the right to remain silent without more "will benefit only the recidivist and the professional." Thus, the need for counsel to protect the Fifth Amendment privilege comprehends not merely a right to consult with counsel prior to questioning, but also to have counsel present during any questioning if the defendant so desires.

The presence of counsel at the interrogation may serve several significant subsidiary functions as well. If the accused decides to talk to his interrogators, the assistance of counsel can mitigate the dangers of untrustworthiness. With a lawyer present the likelihood that the police will practice coercion is reduced, and if coercion is nevertheless exercised the lawyer can testify to it in court. The presence of a lawyer can also help to guarantee that the accused gives a fully accurate statement to the police and that the statement is rightly reported by the prosecution at trial.

An individual need not make a pre-interrogation request for a lawyer. While such request affirmatively secures his right to have one, his failure to ask for a lawyer does not constitute a waiver. No effective waiver of the right to counsel during interrogation can be recognized unless specifically made after the warnings we here delineate have been given. The accused who does not know his rights and therefore does not make a request may be the person who most needs counsel.

Accordingly we hold that an individual held for interrogation must be clearly informed that he has the right to consult with a lawyer and to have the lawyer with him during interrogation under the system for protecting the privilege we delineate today. As with the warnings of the right to remain silent and that anything stated can be used in evidence against him, this warning is an absolute prerequisite to interrogation. No amount of circumstantial evidence that the person may have been aware of this right will suffice to stand in its stead. Only through such a warning is there ascertainable assurance that the accused was aware of this right.

If an individual indicates that he wishes the assistance of counsel before any interrogation occurs, the authorities cannot rationally ignore or deny his request on the basis that the individual does not have or cannot afford a retained attorney. The financial ability of the individual has no relationship to the scope of the rights involved here. The privilege against self-incrimination secured by the Constitution applies to all individuals. The need for counsel in order to protect the privilege exists for the indigent as well as the affluent. In fact, were we to limit these constitutional rights to those who can retain an attorney, our decisions today would be of little significance. The cases before us as well as the vast majority of confession cases with which we have dealt in the past involve those unable to retain counsel. While authorities are not required to relieve the accused of his poverty, they have the obligation not to take advantage of indigence in the administration of justice. Denial of counsel to the indigent at the time of interrogation while allowing an attorney to those who can afford one would be no more supportable by reason or logic than the similar situation at trial and on appeal struck down in Gideon v. Wainwright (1963) and Douglas v. People of State of California (1963).

In order fully to apprise a person interrogated of the extent of his rights under this system then, it is necessary to warn him not only that he has the right to consult with an attorney, but also that if he is indigent a lawyer will be appointed to represent him. Without this additional warning, the admonition of the right to consult with counsel would often be understood as meaning only that he can consult with a lawyer if he has one or has the funds to obtain one. The warning of a right to counsel would be hollow if not couched in terms that would convey to the indigent — the person most often subjected to interrogation — the knowledge that he too has a right to have counsel present. As with the warnings of the right to remain silent and of the general right to counsel, only by effective and express explanation to the indigent of this right can there be assurance that he was truly in a position to exercise it.

Once warnings have been given, the subsequent procedure is clear. If the individual indicates in any manner, at any time prior to or during questioning, that he wishes to remain silent, the interrogation must cease. At this point he has shown that he intends to exercise his Fifth Amendment privilege; any statement taken after the person invokes his privilege cannot be other than the product of compulsion, subtle or otherwise. Without the right to cut off questioning, the setting of in-custody interrogation operates on the individual to overcome free choice in producing a statement after the privilege has been once invoked. If the individual states that he wants an attorney, the interrogation must cease until an attorney is present. At that time, the individual must have an opportunity to confer with the attorney and to have him present during any subsequent questioning. If the individual cannot obtain an attorney and he indicates that he wants one before speaking to police, they must respect his decision to remain silent.

This does not mean, as some have suggested, that each police station must have a "station house lawyer" present at all times to advise prisoners. It does mean, however, that if police propose to interrogate a person they must make known to him that he is entitled to a lawyer and that if he cannot afford one, a lawyer will be provided for him prior to any interrogation. If authorities conclude that they will not provide counsel during a reasonable period of time in which investigation in the field is carried out, they may refrain from doing so without violating the person's Fifth Amendment privilege so long as they do not question him during that time.

If the interrogation continues without the presence of an attorney and a statement is taken, a heavy burden rests on the government to demonstrate that the defendant knowingly and intelligently waived his privilege against self-incrimination and his right to retained or appointed counsel. This Court has always set high standards of proof for the waiver of constitutional rights, and we reassert these standards as applied to in-custody interrogation. Since the State is responsible for establishing the isolated circumstances under which the interrogation takes place and has the only means of making available corroborated evidence of warnings given during incommunicado interrogation, the burden is rightly on its shoulders.

An express statement that the individual is willing to make a statement and does not want an attorney followed closely by a statement could constitute a waiver. But a valid waiver will not be presumed simply from the silence of the accused after warnings are given or simply from the fact that a confession was in fact eventually obtained.

Whatever the testimony of the authorities as to waiver of rights by an accused, the fact of lengthy interrogation or incommunicado incarceration before a statement is made is strong evidence that the accused did not validly waive his rights. In these circumstances the fact that the individual eventually made a statement is consistent with the conclusion that the compelling influence of the interrogation finally forced him to do so. It is inconsistent with any notion of a voluntary relinquishment of the privilege. Moreover, any evidence that the accused was threatened, tricked, or cajoled into a waiver will, of course, show that the defendant did not voluntarily waive his privilege. The requirement of warnings and waiver of rights is a fundamental with respect to the Fifth Amendment privilege and not simply a preliminary ritual to existing methods of interrogation.

The principles announced today deal with the protection which must be given to the privilege against self-incrimination when the individual is first subjected to police interrogation while in custody at the station or otherwise deprived of his freedom of action in any significant way. It is at this point that our adversary system of criminal proceedings commences, distinguishing itself at the outset from the inquisitorial system recognized in some countries. Under the system of warnings we delineate today or under any other system which may be devised and found effective, the safeguards to be erected about the privilege must come into play at this point.

Our decision is not intended to hamper the traditional function of police officers in investigating crime. When an individual is in custody on probable cause, the police may, of course, seek out evidence in the field to be used at trial against him. Such investigation may include inquiry of persons not under restraint. General on-the-scene questioning as to facts surrounding a crime or other general questioning of citizens in the fact-finding process is not affected by our holding. It is an act of responsible citizenship for individuals to give whatever information they may have to aid in law enforcement. In such situations the compelling atmosphere inherent in the process of in-custody interrogation is not necessarily present.

In dealing with statements obtained through interrogation, we do not purport to find all confessions inadmissible. Confessions remain a proper element in law enforcement. Any statement given freely and voluntarily without any compelling influences is, of course, admissible in evidence. The fundamental import of the privilege while an individual is in custody is not whether he is allowed to talk to the police without the benefit of warnings and counsel, but whether he can be interrogated. There is no requirement that police stop a person who enters a police station and states that he wishes to confess to a crime, or a person who calls the police to offer a confession or any other statement he desires to make. Volunteered statements of any kind are not barred by the Fifth Amendment and their admissibility is not affected by our holding today.

To summarize, we hold that when an individual is taken into custody or otherwise deprived of his freedom by the authorities in any significant way and is subjected to questioning, the privilege against self-incrimination is jeopardized. Procedural safeguards must be employed to protect the privilege and unless other fully effective means are adopted to notify the person of his right of silence and to assure that the exercise of the right will be scrupulously honored, the following measures are required. He must be warned prior to any questioning that he has the right to remain silent, that anything he says can be used against him in a court of law, that he has the right to the presence of an attorney, and that if he cannot afford an attorney one will be appointed for him prior to any questioning if he so desires. Opportunity to exercise these rights must be afforded to him throughout the interrogation. After such warnings have been given, and such opportunity afforded him, the individual may knowingly and intelligently waive these rights and agree to answer questions or make a statement. But unless and until such warnings and waiver are demonstrated by the prosecution at trial, no evidence obtained as a result of interrogation can be used against him.

IV.

A recurrent argument made in these cases is that society's need for interrogation outweighs the privilege. This argument is not unfamiliar to this Court. The whole thrust of our foregoing discussion demonstrates that the Constitution has prescribed the rights of the individual when confronted with the power of government when it provided in the Fifth Amendment that an individual cannot be compelled to be a witness against himself. That right cannot be abridged. In this connection, one of our country's distinguished jurists has pointed out: "The quality of a nation's civilization can be largely measured by the methods it uses in the enforcement of its criminal law."

In announcing these principles, we are not unmindful of the burdens which law enforcement officials must bear, often under trying circumstances. We also fully recognize the obligation of all citizens to aid in enforcing the criminal laws. This Court, while protecting individual rights, has always given ample latitude to law enforcement agencies in the legitimate exercise of their duties. The limits we have placed on the interrogation process should not constitute an undue interference with a proper system of law enforcement. As we have noted, our decision does not in any way preclude police from carrying out their traditional investigatory functions. Although confessions may play an important role in some convictions, the cases before us present graphic examples of the overstatement of the "need" for confessions. In each case authorities conducted interrogations ranging up to five days in duration despite the presence, through standard investigating practices, of considerable evidence against each defendant.

Over the years the Federal Bureau of Investigation has compiled an exemplary record of effective law enforcement while advising any suspect or arrested person, at the outset of an interview, that he is not required to make a statement, that any statement may be used against him in court, that the individual may obtain the services of an attorney of his own choice and, more recently, that he has a right to free counsel if he is unable to pay. The practice of the FBI can readily be emulated by state and local enforcement agencies. The argument that the FBI deals with different crimes than are dealt with by state authorities does not mitigate the significance of the FBI experience.

The experience in some other countries also suggests that the danger to law enforcement in curbs on interrogation is overplayed. The English procedure since 1912 under the Judges' Rules is significant. As recently strengthened, the Rules require that a cautionary warning be given an accused by a police officer as soon as he has evidence that affords reasonable grounds for suspicion; they also require that any statement made be given by the accused without questioning by police. The right of the individual to consult with an attorney during this period is expressly recognized.

The safeguards present under Scottish law may be even greater than in England. Scottish judicial decisions bar use in evidence of most confessions obtained through police interrogation. In India, confessions made to police not in the presence of a magistrate have been excluded by rule of evidence since 1872, at a time when it operated under British law. Identical provisions appear in the Evidence Ordinance of Ceylon, enacted in 1895.

Justice CLARK, dissenting.

It is with regret that I find it necessary to write in these cases. However, I am unable to join the majority because its opinion goes too far on too little, while my dissenting brethren do not go quite far enough. Nor can I join in the Court's criticism of the present practices of police and investigatory agencies as to custodial interrogation. The materials it refers to as "police manuals" are, as I read them, merely writings in this filed by professors and some police officers. Not one is shown by the record here to be the official manual of any police department, much less in universal use in crime detection. Moreover the examples of police brutality mentioned by the Court are rare exceptions to the thousands of cases that appear every year in the law reports. The police agencies — all the way from municipal and state forces to the federal bureaus — are responsible for law enforcement and public safety in this country. I am proud of their efforts, which in my view are not fairly characterized by the Court's opinion.

I would continue to follow th[e] rule [that the use of involuntary confessions as evidence violates due process]. Under the "totality of circumstances" rule, I would consider in each case whether the police officer prior to custodial interrogation added the warning that the suspect might have counsel present at the interrogation and, further, that a court would appoint one at his request if he was too poor to employ counsel. In the absence of warnings, the burden would be on the State to prove that counsel was knowingly and intelligently waived or that in the totality of the circumstances, including the failure to give the necessary warnings, the confession was clearly voluntary.

Rather than employing the arbitrary Fifth Amendment rule which the Court lays down I would follow the more pliable dictates of the Due Process Clauses of the Fifth and Fourteenth Amendments which we are accustomed to administering and which we know from our cases are effective instruments in protecting persons in police custody. In this way we would not be acting in the dark nor in one full sweep changing the traditional rules of custodial interrogation which this Court has for so long recognized as a justifiable and proper tool in balancing individual rights against the rights of society. It will be soon enough to go further when we are able to appraise with somewhat better accuracy the effect of such a holding.

Justice HARLAN, whom Justice STEWART and Justice WHITE join, dissenting.

I believe the decision of the Court represents poor constitutional law and entails harmful consequences for the country at large. How serious these consequences may prove to be only time can tell. But the basic flaws in the Court's justification seem to me readily apparent now once all sides of the problem are considered.

I. INTRODUCTION

At the outset, it is well to note exactly what is required by the Court's new constitutional code of rules for confessions. The foremost requirement, upon which later admissibility of a confession depends, is that a fourfold warning be given to a person in custody before he is questioned, namely, that he has a right to remain silent, that anything he says may be used against him, that he has a right to have present an attorney during the questioning, and that if indigent he has a right to a lawyer without charge. To forgo these rights, some affirmative statement of rejection is seemingly required, and threats, tricks, or cajolings to obtain this waiver are forbidden. If before or during questioning the suspect seeks to invoke his right to remain silent, interrogation must be forgone or cease; a request for counsel brings about the same result until a lawyer is procured. Finally, there are a miscellany of minor directives, for example, the burden of proof of waiver is on the State, admissions and exculpatory statements are treated just like confessions, withdrawal of a waiver is always permitted, and so forth.

While the fine points of this scheme are far less clear than the Court admits, the tenor is quite apparent. The new rules are not designed to guard against police brutality or other unmistakably banned forms of coercion. Those who use third-degree tactics and deny them in court are equally able and destined to lie as skillfully about warnings and waivers. Rather, the thrust of the new rules is to negate all pressures, to reinforce the nervous or ignorant suspect, and ultimately to discourage any confession at all. The aim in short is toward "voluntariness" in a utopian sense, or to view it from a different angle, voluntariness with a vengeance.

To incorporate this notion into the Constitution requires a strained reading of history and precedent and a disregard of the very pragmatic concerns that alone may on occasion justify such strains. I believe that reasoned examination will show that the Due Process Clauses provide an adequate tool for coping with confessions and that, even if the Fifth Amendment privilege against self-incrimination be invoked, its precedents taken as a whole do not sustain the present rules. Viewed as a choice based on pure policy, these new rules prove to be a highly debatable, if not one-sided, appraisal of the competing interests, imposed over widespread objection, at the very time when judicial restraint is most called for by the circumstances.

II. CONSTITUTIONAL PREMISES

It is most fitting to begin an inquiry into the constitutional precedents by surveying the limits on confessions the Court has evolved under the Due Process Clause of the Fourteenth Amendment. This is so because these cases show that there exists a workable and effective means of dealing with confessions in a judicial manner; because the cases are the baseline from which the Court now departs and so serve to measure the actual as opposed to the professed distance it travels; and because examination of them helps reveal how the Court has coasted into its present position. [Justice Harlan then reviewed the prior decisions holding that involuntary confessions are inadmissible as evidence under the Due Process Clause.]

There are several relevant lessons to be drawn from this constitutional history. The first is that with over 25 years of precedent the Court has developed an elaborate, sophisticated, and sensitive approach to admissibility of confessions. It is "judicial" in its treatment of one case at a time, flexible in its ability to respond to the endless mutations of fact presented, and ever more familiar to the lower courts.

The second point is that in practice and from time to time in principle, the Court has given ample recognition to society's interest in suspect questioning as an instrument of law enforcement. Cases countenancing quite significant pressures can be cited without difficulty, and the lower courts may often have been yet more tolerant. Of course the limitations imposed today were rejected by necessary implication in case after case, the right to warnings having been explicitly rebuffed in this Court many years ago.

Finally, the cases disclose that the language in many of the opinions overstates the actual course of decision. It has been said, for example, that an admissible confession must be made by the suspect "in the unfettered exercise of his own will," and that "a prisoner is not to be made the deluded instrument of his own conviction." Though often repeated, such principles are rarely observed in full measure. Even the word "voluntary" may be deemed somewhat misleading, especially when one considers many of the confessions that have been brought under its umbrella.

I turn now to the Court's asserted reliance on the Fifth Amendment, an approach which I frankly regard as a trompe l'oeil. The Court's opinion in my view reveals no adequate basis for extending the Fifth Amendment's privilege against self-incrimination to the police station. Far more important, it fails to show that the Court's new rules are well supported, let alone compelled, by Fifth Amendment precedents. Instead, the new rules actually derive from quotation and analogy drawn from precedents under the Sixth Amendment, which should properly have no bearing on police interrogation.

The Court's opening contention, that the Fifth Amendment governs police station confessions, is perhaps not an impermissible extension of the law but it has little to commend itself in the present circumstances. Historically, the privilege against self-incrimination did not bear at all on the use of extra-legal confessions. Even those who would readily enlarge the privilege must concede some linguistic difficulties since the Fifth Amendment in terms proscribes only compelling any person "in any criminal case to be a witness against himself."

Having decided that the Fifth Amendment privilege does apply in the police station, the Court reveals that the privilege imposes more exacting restrictions than does the Fourteenth Amendment's voluntariness test. It then emerges from a discussion of *Escobedo* that the Fifth Amendment requires for an admissible confession that it be given by one distinctly aware of his right not to speak and shielded from "the compelling atmosphere" of interrogation.

The more important premise is that pressure on the suspect must be eliminated though it be only the subtle influence of the atmosphere and surroundings. The Fifth Amendment, however, has never been thought to forbid all pressure to incriminate one's self in the situations covered by it. This is not to say that short of jail or torture any sanction is permissible in any case; policy and history alike may impose sharp limits. However, the Court's unspoken assumption that any pressure violates the privilege is not supported by the precedents and it has failed to show why the Fifth Amendment prohibits that relatively mild pressure the Due Process Clause permits.

The Court appears similarly wrong in thinking that precise knowledge of one's rights is a settled prerequisite under the Fifth Amendment to the loss of its protections. There might of course be reasons apart from Fifth Amendment precedent for requiring warning or any other safeguard on questioning but that is a different matter entirely.

A closing word must be said about the Assistance of Counsel Clause of the Sixth Amendment, which is never expressly relied on by the Court but whose judicial precedents turn out to be linchpins of the confession rules announced today. The only attempt in this Court to carry the right to counsel into the station house occurred in *Escobedo*, the Court repeating several times that that stage was no less "critical" than trial itself. This is hardly persuasive when we consider that a grand jury inquiry, the filing of a certiorari petition, and certainly the purchase of narcotics by an undercover agent from a prospective defendant may all be equally "critical" yet provision of counsel and advice on the score have never been thought compelled by the Constitution in such cases. The sound reason why this right is so freely extended for a criminal trial is the severe injustice risked by confronting an untrained defendant with a range of technical points of law, evidence, and tactics familiar to the prosecutor but not to himself. This danger shrinks markedly in the police station where indeed the lawyer in fulfilling his professional responsibilities of necessity may become an obstacle to truthfinding.

III. Policy Considerations

Examined as an expression of public policy, the Court's new regime proves so dubious that there can be no due compensation for its weakness in constitutional law. The foregoing discussion has shown, I think, how mistaken is the Court in implying that the Constitution has struck the balance in favor of the approach the Court takes. Rather, precedent reveals that the Fourteenth Amendment in practice has been construed to strike a different balance, that the Fifth Amendment gives the Court little solid support in this context, and that the Sixth Amendment should have no bearing at all. Legal history has been stretched before to satisfy deep needs of society. In this instance, however, the Court has not and cannot make the powerful showing that its new rules are plainly desirable in the context of our society, something which is surely demanded before those rules are engrafted onto the Constitution and imposed on every State and county in the land.

Without at all subscribing to the generally black picture of police conduct painted by the Court, I think it must be frankly recognized at the outset that police questioning allowable under due process precedents may inherently entail some pressure on the suspect and may seek advantage in his ignorance or weaknesses. The atmosphere and questioning techniques, proper and fair though they be, can in themselves exert a tug on the suspect to confess. The Court's new rules aim to offset these minor pressures and disadvantages intrinsic to any kind of police interrogation. The rules do not serve due process interests in preventing blatant coercion since, as I noted earlier, they do nothing to contain the policeman who is prepared to lie from the start. The rules work for reliability in confessions almost only in the Pickwickian sense that they can prevent some from being given at all. In short, the benefit of this new regime is simply to lessen or wipe out the inherent compulsion and inequalities to which the Court devotes some nine pages of description.

What the Court largely ignores is that its rules impair, if they will not eventually serve wholly to frustrate, an instrument of law enforcement that has long and quite reasonably been thought worth the price paid for it. There can be little doubt that the Court's new code would markedly decrease the number of confessions. To warn the suspect that he may remain silent and remind him that his confession may be used in court are minor obstructions. To require also an express waiver by the suspect and an end to questioning whenever he demurs must heavily handicap questioning. And to suggest or provide counsel for the suspect simply invites the end of the interrogation.

How much harm this decision will inflict on law enforcement cannot fairly be predicted with accuracy. Evidence on the role of confessions is notoriously incomplete, and little is added by the Court's reference to the FBI experience and the resources believed wasted in interrogation. We do know that some crimes cannot be solved without confessions, that ample expert testimony attests to their importance in crime control, and that the Court is taking a real risk with society's welfare in imposing its new regime on the country. The social costs of crime are too great to call the new rules anything but a hazardous experimentation.

In conclusion: Nothing in the letter or the spirit of the Constitution or in the precedents squares with the heavy-handed and one-sided action that is so precipitously taken by the Court in the name of fulfilling its constitutional responsibilities. The foray which the Court makes today brings to mind the wise and farsighted words of Justice Jackson: "This Court is forever adding new stories to the temples of constitutional law, and the temples have a way of collapsing when one story too many is added."

Miranda v. Arizona was enormously controversial when it was decided. The arguments for and against *Miranda* are described below. In 2000, the Supreme Court had the occasion to reconsider the decision and in a 7-2 decision emphatically reaffirmed it. United States v. Dickerson arose in an unusual procedural context. In 1968, two years after *Miranda*, Congress adopted a statute that provided that confessions shall be admissible as evidence in federal court, notwithstanding the failure to properly administer warnings, so long as the confession was voluntary. 18 U.S.C. §3501. From the Nixon administration through the Clinton presidency, every Justice Department, whether under a Democratic or a Republican President, refused to invoke this statute because of a belief that it was unconstitutional.

In *Dickerson*, a confession was excluded by the federal district court for failure to properly administer *Miranda* warnings. The government appealed. The United States Court of Appeals for the Fourth Circuit, on its own, raised §3501, asked for briefing as to its constitutionality, upheld the law, and held the confession was admissible because it was voluntary. The Supreme Court granted certiorari and reconsidered *Miranda* and its constitutional status.

DICKERSON v. UNITED STATES
530 U.S. 428 (2000)

Chief Justice REHNQUIST delivered the opinion of the Court.

In *Miranda v. Arizona* (1966), we held that certain warnings must be given before a suspect's statement made during custodial interrogation could be admitted in evidence. In the wake of that decision, Congress enacted 18 U.S.C. §3501, which in essence laid down a rule that the admissibility of such statements should turn only on whether or not they were voluntarily made. We hold that *Miranda*, being a constitutional decision of this Court, may not be in effect overruled by an Act of Congress, and we decline to overrule *Miranda* ourselves. We therefore hold that *Miranda* and its progeny in this Court govern the admissibility of statements made during custodial interrogation in both state and federal courts.

Given §3501's express designation of voluntariness as the touchstone of admissibility, its omission of any warning requirement, and the instruction for trial courts to consider a nonexclusive list of factors relevant to the circumstances of a confession, we agree with the Court of Appeals that Congress intended by its enactment to overrule *Miranda*. Because of the obvious conflict between our decision in *Miranda* and §3501, we must address whether Congress has constitutional authority to thus supersede *Miranda*. If Congress has such authority, §3501's totality-of-the-circumstances approach must prevail over *Miranda*'s requirement of warnings; if not, that section must yield to *Miranda*'s more specific requirements.

The law in this area is clear. This Court has supervisory authority over the federal courts, and we may use that authority to prescribe rules of evidence and procedure that are binding in those tribunals. However, the power to judicially create and enforce nonconstitutional "rules of procedure and evidence for the federal courts exists only in the absence of a relevant Act of Congress." Congress retains the ultimate authority to modify or set aside any judicially created rules of evidence and procedure that are not required by the Constitution.

But Congress may not legislatively supersede our decisions interpreting and applying the Constitution. This case therefore turns on whether the *Miranda* Court announced a constitutional rule or merely exercised its supervisory authority to regulate evidence in the absence of congressional direction.

[T]he Court of Appeals concluded that the protections announced in *Miranda* are not constitutionally required. We disagree with the Court of Appeals' conclusion, although we concede that there is language in some of our opinions that supports the view taken by that court. But first and foremost of the factors on the other side — that *Miranda* is a constitutional decision — is that both *Miranda* and two of its companion cases applied the rule to proceedings in state courts. Since that time, we have consistently applied *Miranda*'s rule to prosecutions arising in state courts. It is beyond dispute that we do not hold a supervisory power over the courts of the several States.

Additional support for our conclusion that *Miranda* is constitutionally based is found in the *Miranda* Court's invitation for legislative action to protect the constitutional right against coerced self-incrimination. However, the Court emphasized that it could not foresee "the potential alternatives for protecting the privilege which might be devised by Congress or the States," and it accordingly opined that the Constitution would not preclude legislative solutions that differed from the prescribed *Miranda* warnings but which were "at least as effective in apprising accused persons of their right of silence and in assuring a continuous opportunity to exercise it."

Miranda requires procedures that will warn a suspect in custody of his right to remain silent and which will assure the suspect that the exercise of that right will be honored. As discussed above, § 3501 explicitly eschews a requirement of preinterrogation warnings in favor of an approach that looks to the administration of such warnings as only one factor in determining the voluntariness of a suspect's confession.

The dissent argues that it is judicial overreaching for this Court to hold § 3501 unconstitutional unless we hold that the *Miranda* warnings are required by the Constitution, in the sense that nothing else will suffice to satisfy constitutional requirements. But we need not go further than *Miranda* to decide this case. In *Miranda*, the Court noted that reliance on the traditional totality-of-the-circumstances test raised a risk of overlooking an involuntary custodial confession, a risk that the Court found unacceptably great when the confession is offered in the case in chief to prove guilt. The Court therefore concluded that something more than the totality test was necessary. As discussed above, § 3501 reinstates the totality test as sufficient. Section 3501 therefore cannot be sustained if *Miranda* is to remain the law.

Whether or not we would agree with *Miranda*'s reasoning and its resulting rule, were we addressing the issue in the first instance, the principles of stare decisis weigh heavily against overruling it now. While "'stare decisis is not an inexorable command,'" particularly when we are interpreting the Constitution, "even in constitutional cases, the doctrine carries such persuasive force that we have always required a departure from precedent to be supported by some 'special justification.'"

We do not think there is such justification for overruling *Miranda*. *Miranda* has become embedded in routine police practice to the point where the warnings have become part of our national culture. While we have overruled our precedents when subsequent cases have undermined their doctrinal underpinnings, we do not believe that this has happened to the *Miranda* decision. If anything, our subsequent cases have reduced the impact of the *Miranda* rule on legitimate law enforcement while reaffirming the decision's core ruling that unwarned statements may not be used as evidence in the prosecution's case in chief.

The disadvantage of the *Miranda* rule is that statements which may be by no means involuntary, made by a defendant who is aware of his "rights," may nonetheless be excluded and a guilty defendant go free as a result. But experience suggests that the totality-of-the-circumstances test which § 3501 seeks to revive is more difficult than *Miranda* for law enforcement officers to conform to, and for courts to apply in a consistent manner.

In sum, we conclude that *Miranda* announced a constitutional rule that Congress may not supersede legislatively. Following the rule of stare decisis, we decline to overrule *Miranda* ourselves.

Justice SCALIA, with whom Justice THOMAS joins, dissenting.

Those to whom judicial decisions are an unconnected series of judgments that produce either favored or disfavored results will doubtless greet today's decision as a paragon of moderation, since it declines to overrule Miranda v. Arizona (1966). Those who understand the judicial process will appreciate that today's decision is not a reaffirmation of *Miranda*, but a radical revision of the most significant element of *Miranda* (as of all cases): the rationale that gives it a permanent place in our jurisprudence.

Marbury v. Madison (1803), held that an Act of Congress will not be enforced by the courts if what it prescribes violates the Constitution of the United States. That was the basis on which *Miranda* was decided. One will search today's opinion in vain, however, for a statement (surely simple enough to make) that what 18 U.S.C. § 3501 prescribes — the use at trial of a voluntary confession, even when a *Miranda* warning or its equivalent has failed to be given — violates the Constitution. The reason the statement does not appear is not only (and perhaps not so much) that it would be absurd, inasmuch as § 3501 excludes from trial precisely what the Constitution excludes from trial, viz., compelled confessions; but also that Justices whose votes are needed to compose today's majority are on record as believing that a violation of *Miranda* is not a violation of the Constitution.

And so, to justify today's agreed-upon result, the Court must adopt a significant new, if not entirely comprehensible, principle of constitutional law. As the Court chooses to describe that principle, statutes of Congress can be disregarded, not only when what they prescribe violates the Constitution, but when what they prescribe contradicts a decision of this Court that "announced a constitutional rule." [T]he only thing that can possibly mean in the context of this case is that this Court has the power, not merely to apply the Constitution but to expand it, imposing what it regards as useful "prophylactic" restrictions upon Congress and the States. That is an immense and frightening antidemocratic power, and it does not exist.

It takes only a small step to bring today's opinion out of the realm of power-judging and into the mainstream of legal reasoning: The Court need only go beyond its carefully couched iterations that "*Miranda* is a constitutional decision," that "*Miranda* is constitutionally based," that *Miranda* has "constitutional underpinnings," and come out and say quite clearly: "We reaffirm today that custodial interrogation that is not preceded by *Miranda* warnings or their equivalent violates the Constitution of the United States." It cannot say that, because a majority of the Court does not believe it. The Court therefore acts in plain violation of the Constitution when it denies effect to this Act of Congress.

I dissent from today's decision, and, until § 3501 is repealed, will continue to apply it in all cases where there has been a sustainable finding that the defendant's confession was voluntary.

———————

Despite the reaffirmation of *Miranda* in *Dickerson*, there remained an unanswered constitutional question. Is *Miranda* simply a rule of evidence that has no application until and unless a prosecutor seeks to admit a confession into evidence? Or is it a rule concerning police behavior under the Fifth Amendment? The Court confronted that question in deciding whether an individual could sue police officers for damages for a violation of *Miranda*. In Chavez v. Martinez, 538 U.S. 760 (2003), four Justices took the former view of *Miranda*, but five rejected that position. Nonetheless, the Court held that there cannot be civil suits for violation of *Miranda*'s requirements. The case involved a man who was shot by the police and was questioned without *Miranda* warnings while being rushed to the hospital and in the emergency room. He sued for excessive force, which was handled separately, and also for the questioning without proper administration of *Miranda* warnings.

Justice Thomas, writing for a plurality of four (joined by Chief Justice Rehnquist and Justices O'Connor and Scalia), stated that the Fifth Amendment applied only if there is a criminal case and

> [i]n our view, a "criminal case" at the very least requires the initiation of legal proceedings. We need not decide today the precise moment when a "criminal case" commences; it is enough to say that police questioning does not constitute a "case" any more than a private investigator's precomplaint activities constitute a "civil case." Statements compelled by police interrogations of course may not be used against a defendant at trial, but it is not until their use in a criminal case that a violation of the Self-Incrimination Clause occurs. The text of the Self-Incrimination Clause simply cannot support the view that the mere use of compulsive questioning, without more, violates the Constitution.

Justices Souter and Breyer disagreed with this conclusion, but said that money damages are not necessary to enforce *Miranda*; the exclusionary rule is a sufficient enforcement mechanism. Justice Souter wrote:

> I do not, however, believe that Martinez can make the "powerful showing," subject to a realistic assessment of costs and risks, necessary to expand protection of the privilege against compelled self-incrimination to the point of the civil liability he asks us to recognize here. The most obvious drawback inherent in Martinez's purely Fifth Amendment claim to damages is its risk of global application in every instance of interrogation producing a statement inadmissible under Fifth and Fourteenth Amendment principles, or violating one of the complementary rules we have accepted in aid of the privilege against evidentiary use. If obtaining Martinez's statement is to be treated as a stand-alone violation of the privilege subject to compensation, why should the same not be true whenever the police obtain any involuntary self-incriminating statement, or whenever the government so much as threatens a penalty in derogation of the right to immunity, or whenever the police fail to honor *Miranda*? Martinez offers no limiting principle or reason to foresee a stopping place short of liability in all such cases.

Justices Stevens, Kennedy, and Ginsburg dissented. They also believed that the Fifth Amendment privilege against self-incrimination applies even if no statement is used as evidence against a defendant and they believed that a damage remedy should be allowed for violations of the Fifth Amendment's requirements by the police. Justice Stevens wrote: "As a matter of fact, the interrogation of respondent was the functional equivalent of an attempt to obtain an involuntary confession from a prisoner by torturous methods. As a matter of law, that type of brutal police conduct constitutes an immediate deprivation of the prisoner's constitutionally protected interest in liberty. Because these propositions are so clear [Martinez should be entitled to damages for violation of his Fifth Amendment rights.]" Justice Kennedy stated: "A constitutional right is traduced the moment torture or its close equivalents are brought to bear. Constitutional protection for a tortured suspect is not held in abeyance until some later criminal proceeding takes place." Justice Ginsburg declared: "I would hold that the Self-Incrimination Clause applies at the time and place police use severe compulsion to extract a statement from a suspect."

The issue of whether the privilege against self-incrimination applies only as a rule of evidence at trial is of great importance. For instance, may a person invoke the privilege against self-incrimination in a civil deposition or before a grand jury? The law is clear that the privilege can be invoked in these contexts. But under Justice Thomas's view, the privilege would not apply then and could not be invoked until and unless the prosecutor attempted to use the statements at trial against the defendant.

Given the importance of the issue and the closeness of the vote in Chavez v. Martinez, it is likely that the Court will return to the question in the years ahead.

2.   Is Miranda Desirable?

The debate over Miranda began when it was decided and continues to this day. Three very different criticisms have been advanced. First, some argue that Miranda is ineffective; it does not succeed in curing the inherently coercive nature of in-custodial interrogation. Some studies seem to confirm this criticism. For example, a study was done by Yale law students of the impact of Miranda in New Haven, Connecticut soon after the decision.[4] The study found that administering the warnings caused a person to stop the questioning in only 8 of 81 cases. Another study found that Miranda had little impact because virtually the same percentage of people talked to the police after receiving warnings as did without warnings.[5] Perhaps the lack of effect is because of the ability of police to undermine the warnings or perhaps it is just that in-custodial interrogation is inherently coercive and having the police read warnings cannot lessen that.

A second criticism of Miranda is exactly the opposite: Miranda prevents police from gaining confessions and it allows guilty people to go free. Law professor and former federal district court judge, Paul Cassell, is the leading advocate of

---

4. Michael Wald, et al., *Interrogations in New Haven: The Impact of Miranda*, 76 Yale L.J. 1519 (1967).

5. Richard J. Medalie, *Custodial Police Interrogation in Our Nation's Capital: The Attempt to Implement Miranda*, 66 Mich. L. Rev. 1347 (1968) (44 percent who received warnings talked to the police; whereas 42 percent who did not receive warnings talked to the police).

this view. Cassell reexamined the data and concluded that *Miranda* resulted in the loss of confessions in 3.8 percent of cases involving serious crimes and has led to guilty people escaping punishment.[6]

A third criticism of *Miranda* is based on constitutional interpretation and the role of the judiciary. Critics, including the dissenters in *Miranda* and *Dickerson*, argue that neither the text nor the history of the Fifth Amendment support the Court's requiring warnings be administered or a right to counsel during interrogation.[7]

On the other hand, *Miranda* has its defenders. They dispute that *Miranda* has had a significant effect in hampering law enforcement. Professor Stephen Schulhofer has responded at length to Judge Cassell, criticized his methodology, and concluded that "*Miranda*'s empirically detectable net damage to law enforcement is zero."[8] Professor Schulhofer also argues that *Miranda* is consistent with the original purpose of the Self-Incrimination Clause of the Fifth Amendment. He explains that the "privilege was intended primarily to bar pretrial examination by magistrates, the only form of pretrial interrogation known at the time."[9]

Defenders of *Miranda* argue that it provides clear guidance to police: Administer the simple warnings and follow the procedures outlines and there is a presumption that any confession is admissible. The Supreme Court has declared:

> *Miranda*'s holding has the virtue of informing police and prosecutors with specificity as to what they may do in conducting custodial interrogation, and of informing courts under what circumstances statements obtained during such interrogation are not admissible. This gain in specificity, which benefits the accused and the State alike, has been thought to outweigh the burdens that the decision in *Miranda* imposes on law enforcement agencies and the courts by requiring the suppression of trustworthy and highly probative evidence even though the confession might be voluntary under traditional Fifth Amendment analysis.

Fare v. Michael C., 442 U.S. 707 (1979).

Professor Richard Leo has argued that *Miranda* has had a significant effect in increasing professional behavior by police officers and enhancing the public's awareness of constitutional rights.[10] As Chief Justice Rehnquist stated in *Dickerson*, "*Miranda* has become embedded in routine police practice to the point where the warnings have become part of our national culture."

What, if anything, needs to be done obviously depends on one's views of this debate. Critics who believe that *Miranda* hampers law enforcement would like to see it overruled. Critics who think that *Miranda* has not done enough to protect suspects would like to see additional protections, such as a requirement that all in-custodial interrogations be videotaped. Ultimately, the underlying issue is the same as in examining all police investigative techniques: how to balance the need for effective law enforcement tools with the desire to prevent police

---

6. Paul G. Cassell, *Miranda's Social Costs: An Empirical Reassessment*, 90 Nw. L. Rev. 387 (1996).
7. *See, e.g.*, Joseph Grano, Confessions, Truth, and the Law 106 (1993).
8. Stephen Schulhofer, *Miranda's Practical Effect: "Substantial Benefits and Surprisingly Small Costs,"* 90 Nw. U. L. Rev. 500 (1996).
9. Stephen Schulhofer, *Reconsidering Miranda and the Fifth Amendment*, in The Bill of Rights: Original Meaning and Original Understanding 289 (Eugene W. Hickok, Jr., ed. 1991).
10. Richard A. Leo, *The Impact of Miranda Revisited*, 86 J. Crim. L. & Criminology 621 (1996).

abuse, protect the dignity of the individual, and lessen the likelihood that innocent people will be convicted.

3. What Are the Requirements for Miranda to Apply?

Miranda requires that during in-custodial interrogation police administer the prescribed warnings, make counsel available, and behave as described in the decision. Therefore, three key questions arise in applying Miranda: (1) When is a person "in custody"? (2) What is interrogation? (3) What police actions are sufficient to meet the requirements of Miranda?

a. When Is a Person "In Custody"?

The Supreme Court in Miranda focused on the coercion inherent to in-custodial interrogation. The Court repeatedly has reaffirmed that this is a requirement in order for Miranda to apply. For example, soon after Miranda, in Orozco v. Texas, 394 U.S. 324 (1969), the Court found that a person who has been arrested is in custody and Miranda warnings must be given, even if the questioning occurs in a person's home. In Orozco, man was a suspect in a murder. Justice Black describes what happened:

> At about 4 A.M. four police officers arrived at petitioner's boardinghouse, were admitted by an unidentified woman, and were told that petitioner was asleep in the bedroom. All four officers entered the bedroom and began to question petitioner. From the moment he gave his name, according to the testimony of one of the officers, petitioner was not free to go where he pleased but was "under arrest." The officers asked him if he had been to the El Farleto restaurant that night and when he answered "yes" he was asked if he owned a pistol. Petitioner admitted owning one. After being asked a second time where the pistol was located, he admitted that it was in the washing machine in a backroom of the boardinghouse. Ballistics tests indicated that the gun found in the washing machine was the gun that fired the fatal shot. The trial testimony clearly shows that the officers questioned petitioner about incriminating facts without first informing him of his right to remain silent, his right to have the advice of a lawyer before making any statement, and his right to have a lawyer appointed to assist him if he could not afford to hire one.

The Court concluded: "[W]e hold that the use of these admissions obtained in the absence of the required warnings was a flat violation of the Self-Incrimination Clause of the Fifth Amendment as construed in Miranda." The Court explained:

> The State has argued here that since petitioner was interrogated on his own bed, in familiar surroundings, our Miranda holding should not apply. It is true that the Court did say in Miranda that "compulsion to speak in the isolated setting of the police station may well be greater than in courts or other official investigations, where there are often impartial observers to guard against intimidation or trickery." But the opinion iterated and reiterated the absolute necessity for officers interrogating people "in custody" to give the described warnings. According to the officer's testimony, petitioner was under arrest and not free to leave when he was

questioned in his bedroom in the early hours of the morning. The *Miranda* opinion declared that the warnings were required when the person being interrogated was "in custody at the station or otherwise deprived of his freedom of action in any significant way." We do not, as the dissent implies, expand or extend to the slightest extent our *Miranda* decision. We do adhere to our well-considered holding in that case and therefore reverse the conviction below.

By contrast, a person who is free to leave is not in custody and no *Miranda* warnings are required. Oregon v. Mathiason expresses this.

OREGON v. MATHIASON
429 U.S. 492 (1977)

PER CURIAM.

Respondent Carl Mathiason was convicted of first-degree burglary after a bench trial in which his confession was critical to the State's case. At trial he moved to suppress the confession as the fruit of questioning by the police not preceded by the warnings required in Miranda v. Arizona (1966).

The Supreme Court of Oregon described the factual situation surrounding the confession as follows: "An officer of the State Police investigated a theft at a residence near Pendleton. He asked the lady of the house which had been burglarized if she suspected anyone. She replied that the defendant was the only one she could think of. The defendant was a parolee and a 'close associate' of her son. The officer tried to contact defendant on three or four occasions with no success. Finally, about 25 days after the burglary, the officer left his card at defendant's apartment with a note asking him to call because 'I'd like to discuss something with you.' The next afternoon the defendant did call. The officer asked where it would be convenient to meet. The defendant had no preference; so the officer asked if the defendant could meet him at the state patrol office in about an hour and a half, about 5:00 P.M. The patrol office was about two blocks from defendant's apartment. The building housed several state agencies.

"The officer met defendant in the hallway, shook hands and took him into an office. The defendant was told he was not under arrest. The door was closed. The two sat across a desk. The police radio in another room could be heard. The officer told defendant he wanted to talk to him about a burglary and that his truthfulness would possibly be considered by the district attorney or judge. The officer further advised that the police believed defendant was involved in the burglary and [falsely stated that] defendant's fingerprints were found at the scene. The defendant sat for a few minutes and then said he had taken the property. This occurred within five minutes after defendant had come to the office. The officer then advised defendant of his *Miranda* rights and took a taped confession.

"At the end of the taped conversation the officer told defendant he was not arresting him at this time; he was released to go about his job and return to his family. The officer said he was referring the case to the district attorney for him to determine whether criminal charges would be brought. It was 5:30 P.M. when the defendant left the office."

Our decision in *Miranda* set forth rules of police procedure applicable to "custodial interrogation." "By custodial interrogation, we mean questioning initiated by law enforcement officers after a person has been taken into custody or otherwise deprived of his freedom of action in any significant way." Subsequently we have found the *Miranda* principle applicable to questioning which takes place in a prison setting during a suspect's term of imprisonment on a separate offense, Mathis v. United States (1968), and to questioning taking place in a suspect's home, after he has been arrested and is no longer free to go where he pleases, Orozco v. Texas (1969).

In the present case, however, there is no indication that the questioning took place in a context where respondent's freedom to depart was restricted in any way. He came voluntarily to the police station, where he was immediately informed that he was not under arrest. At the close of a ½-hour interview respondent did in fact leave the police station without hindrance. It is clear from these facts that Mathiason was not in custody "or otherwise deprived of his freedom of action in any significant way."

Such a noncustodial situation is not converted to one in which *Miranda* applies simply because a reviewing court concludes that, even in the absence of any formal arrest or restraint on freedom of movement, the questioning took place in a "coercive environment." Any interview of one suspected of a crime by a police officer will have coercive aspects to it, simply by virtue of the fact that the police officer is part of a law enforcement system which may ultimately cause the suspect to be charged with a crime. But police officers are not required to administer *Miranda* warnings to everyone whom they question. Nor is the requirement of warnings to be imposed simply because the questioning takes place in the station house, or because the questioned person is one whom the police suspect. *Miranda* warnings are required only where there has been such a restriction on a person's freedom as to render him "in custody." It was that sort of coercive environment to which *Miranda* by its terms was made applicable, and to which it is limited.

Justice MARSHALL, dissenting.

The respondent in this case was interrogated behind closed doors at police headquarters in connection with a burglary investigation. He had been named by the victim of the burglary as a suspect, and was told by the police that they believed he was involved. He was falsely informed that his fingerprints had been found at the scene, and in effect was advised that by cooperating with the police he could help himself. Not until after he had confessed was he given the warnings set forth in Miranda v. Arizona (1966).

The Court today holds that for constitutional purposes all this is irrelevant because respondent had not " 'been taken into custody or otherwise deprived of his freedom of action in any significant way.' " I do not believe that such a determination is possible on the record before us. It is true that respondent was not formally placed under arrest, but surely formalities alone cannot control. At the very least, if respondent entertained an objectively reasonable belief that he was not free to leave during the questioning, then he was "deprived of his freedom of action in a significant way." Plainly the respondent could have so believed, after being told by the police that they thought he was involved in a burglary and that his fingerprints had been found at the scene.

In my view, even if respondent were not in custody, the coercive elements in the instant case were so pervasive as to require *Miranda*-type warnings. Respondent was interrogated in "privacy" and in "unfamiliar surroundings," factors on which *Miranda* places great stress. The investigation had focused on respondent. And respondent was subjected to some of the "deceptive stratagems," which called forth the *Miranda* decision. I therefore agree with the Oregon Supreme Court that to excuse the absence of warnings given these facts is "contrary to the rationale expressed in *Miranda*."

Similarly, in Beckwith v. United States, 425 U.S. 341 (1976), the Court held that a special agent of the Internal Revenue Service, investigating potential criminal income tax violations, in an interview with a taxpayer, not in custody, is not required to give the warnings called for in Miranda v. Arizona. The Court explained: "An interview with Government agents in a situation such as the one shown by this record simply does not present the elements which the *Miranda* Court found so inherently coercive as to require its holding. Although the 'focus' of an investigation may indeed have been on Beckwith at the time of the interview in the sense that it was his tax liability which was under scrutiny, he hardly found himself in the custodial situation described by the *Miranda* Court as the basis for its holding." Likewise, in Minnesota v. Murphy, 465 U.S. 420 (1984), the Court held that statements made in a meeting with a person's probation officer were not uttered in a custodial context and no *Miranda* warnings were required. Although a person on probation is deemed to be in custody for some purposes, the Court explained that "[u]nder the narrower standard appropriate in the *Miranda* context, it is clear that Murphy was not 'in custody' for purposes of receiving *Miranda* protection since there was no 'formal arrest or restraint on freedom of movement' of the degree associated with a formal arrest."

The Supreme Court has emphasized that the determination of whether a person is in custody is an objective one, not a subjective one focusing on the individual's or the officer's state of mind. For example, in Stansbury v. California, 511 U.S. 318 (1994), the Court held that "an officer's subjective and undisclosed view concerning whether the person being interrogated is a suspect is irrelevant to the assessment whether the person is in custody." The Court said that "[o]ur decisions make clear that the initial determination of custody depends on the objective circumstances of the interrogation, not on the subjective views harbored by either the interrogating officers or the person being questioned."

The Court recently reaffirmed this in Yarborough v. Alvarado.

YARBOROUGH v. ALVARADO
541 U.S. 652 (2004)

Justice KENNEDY delivered the opinion of the Court.

I

Paul Soto and respondent Michael Alvarado attempted to steal a truck in the parking lot of a shopping mall in Santa Fe Springs, California. Soto and Alvarado were part of a larger group of teenagers at the mall that night. Soto decided to steal the truck, and Alvarado agreed to help. Soto pulled out a .357 Magnum and approached the driver, Francisco Castaneda, who was standing near the truck emptying trash into a dumpster. Soto demanded money and the ignition keys from Castaneda. Alvarado, then five months short of his 18th birthday, approached the passenger side door of the truck and crouched down. When Castaneda refused to comply with Soto's demands, Soto shot Castaneda, killing him. Alvarado then helped hide Soto's gun.

Los Angeles County Sheriff's detective Cheryl Comstock led the investigation into the circumstances of Castaneda's death. About a month after the shooting, Comstock left word at Alvarado's house and also contacted Alvarado's mother at work with the message that she wished to speak with Alvarado. Alvarado's parents brought him to the Pico Rivera Sheriff's Station to be interviewed around lunchtime. They waited in the lobby while Alvarado went with Comstock to be interviewed. Alvarado contends that his parents asked to be present during the interview but were rebuffed.

Comstock brought Alvarado to a small interview room and began interviewing him at about 12:30 P.M. The interview lasted about two hours, and was recorded by Comstock with Alvarado's knowledge. Only Comstock and Alvarado were present. Alvarado was not given a warning under Miranda v. Arizona (1966). Comstock began the interview by asking Alvarado to recount the events on the night of the shooting. On that night, Alvarado explained, he had been drinking alcohol at a friend's house with some other friends and acquaintances. After a few hours, part of the group went home and the rest walked to a nearby mall to use its public telephones. In Alvarado's initial telling, that was the end of it. The group went back to the friend's home and "just went to bed."

Unpersuaded, Comstock pressed on. Alvarado slowly began to change his story. First he acknowledged being present when the carjacking occurred but claimed that he did not know what happened or who had a gun. When he hesitated to say more, Comstock tried to encourage Alvarado to discuss what happened by appealing to his sense of honesty and the need to bring the man who shot Castaneda to justice. Alvarado then admitted he had helped the other man try to steal the truck by standing near the passenger side door. Next he admitted that the other man was Paul Soto, that he knew Soto was armed, and that he had helped hide the gun after the murder. Alvarado explained that he had expected Soto to scare the driver with the gun, but that he did not expect Soto to kill anyone. Toward the end of the interview, Comstock twice asked Alvarado if he needed to take a break. Alvarado declined. When the interview was over, Comstock returned with Alvarado to the lobby of the sheriff's station where his parents were waiting. Alvarado's father drove him home.

A few months later, the State of California charged Soto and Alvarado with first-degree murder and attempted robbery. Citing *Miranda*, Alvarado moved to suppress his statements from the Comstock interview. The trial court denied the motion on the ground that the interview was noncustodial. The jury convicted Soto and Alvarado of first-degree murder and attempted robbery. The trial judge later reduced Alvarado's conviction to second-degree murder for his comparatively minor role in the offense. The judge sentenced Soto to life in prison and Alvarado to 15-years-to-life.

[After the conviction was upheld on appeal, Alvarado filed a habeas corpus petition, which was denied by the federal district court.] The Court of Appeals for the Ninth Circuit reversed. [T]he Court of Appeals held that the state court erred in failing to account for Alvarado's youth and inexperience when evaluating whether a reasonable person in his position would have felt free to leave. It noted that this Court has considered a suspect's juvenile status when evaluating the voluntariness of confessions and the waiver of the privilege against self-incrimination. The Court of Appeals held that in light of these authorities, Alvarado's age and experience must be a factor in the *Miranda* custody inquiry.

II

Our more recent cases instruct that custody must be determined based on how a reasonable person in the suspect's situation would perceive his circumstances. Based on these principles, we conclude that the state court's application of our clearly established law was reasonable. [I]t can be said that fairminded jurists could disagree over whether Alvarado was in custody. On one hand, certain facts weigh against a finding that Alvarado was in custody. The police did not transport Alvarado to the station or require him to appear at a particular time. They did not threaten him or suggest he would be placed under arrest. Alvarado's parents remained in the lobby during the interview, suggesting that the interview would be brief. In fact, according to trial counsel for Alvarado, he and his parents were told that the interview was "not going to be long." During the interview, Comstock focused on Soto's crimes rather than Alvarado's. Instead of pressuring Alvarado with the threat of arrest and prosecution, she appealed to his interest in telling the truth and being helpful to a police officer. In addition, Comstock twice asked Alvarado if he wanted to take a break. At the end of the interview, Alvarado went home. All of these objective facts are consistent with an interrogation environment in which a reasonable person would have felt free to terminate the interview and leave.

Other facts point in the opposite direction. Comstock interviewed Alvarado at the police station. The interview lasted two hours, four times longer than the 30-minute interview in *Mathiason*. Unlike the officer in *Mathiason*, Comstock did not tell Alvarado that he was free to leave. Alvarado was brought to the police station by his legal guardians rather than arriving on his own accord, making the extent of his control over his presence unclear. Counsel for Alvarado alleges that Alvarado's parents asked to be present at the interview but were rebuffed, a fact that — if known to Alvarado — might reasonably have led someone in Alvarado's position to feel more restricted than otherwise. These facts weigh in favor of the view that Alvarado was in custody.

These differing indications lead us to hold that the state court's application of our custody standard was reasonable. The Court of Appeals was nowhere close to the mark when it concluded otherwise. Although the question of what an "unreasonable application" of law might be is difficult in some cases, it is not difficult here. The custody test is general, and the state court's application of our law fits within the matrix of our prior decisions.

III

The Court of Appeals reached the opposite result by placing considerable reliance on Alvarado's age and inexperience with law enforcement. Our Court has not stated that a suspect's age or experience is relevant to the *Miranda* custody analysis. According to the Court of Appeals, however, our Court's emphasis on juvenile status in other contexts demanded consideration of Alvarado's age and inexperience here.

Our opinions applying the *Miranda* custody test have not mentioned the suspect's age, much less mandated its consideration. The only indications in the Court's opinions relevant to a suspect's experience with law enforcement have rejected reliance on such factors.

There is an important conceptual difference between the Miranda custody test and the line of cases from other contexts considering age and experience. The objective test furthers "the clarity of [*Miranda*'s] rule," ensuring that the police do not need "to make guesses as to [the circumstances] at issue before deciding how they may interrogate the suspect." To be sure, the line between permissible objective facts and impermissible subjective experiences can be indistinct in some cases. It is possible to subsume a subjective factor into an objective test by making the latter more specific in its formulation. Thus the Court of Appeals styled its inquiry as an objective test by considering what a "reasonable 17-year-old, with no prior history of arrest or police interviews," would perceive.

At the same time, the objective *Miranda* custody inquiry could reasonably be viewed as different from doctrinal tests that depend on the actual mindset of a particular suspect, where we do consider a suspect's age and experience. For example, the voluntariness of a statement is often said to depend on whether "the defendant's will was overborne," a question that logically can depend on "the characteristics of the accused." The characteristics of the accused can include the suspect's age, education, and intelligence, as well as a suspect's prior experience with law enforcement. In concluding that there was "no principled reason" why such factors should not also apply to the *Miranda* custody inquiry, the Court of Appeals ignored the argument that the custody inquiry states an objective rule designed to give clear guidance to the police, while consideration of a suspect's individual characteristics — including his age — could be viewed as creating a subjective inquiry. For these reasons, the state court's failure to consider Alvarado's age does not provide a proper basis for finding that the state court's decision was an unreasonable application of clearly established law.

Justice O'CONNOR, concurring.

I join the opinion of the Court, but write separately to express an additional reason for reversal. There may be cases in which a suspect's age will be relevant to the "custody" inquiry under Miranda v. Arizona (1966). In this case, however, Alvarado was almost 18 years old at the time of his interview. It is difficult to expect police to recognize that a suspect is a juvenile when he is so close to the age of majority. Even when police do know a suspect's age, it may be difficult for them to ascertain what bearing it has on the likelihood that the suspect would feel free to leave. That is especially true here; 17½-year-olds vary widely in their reactions to police questioning, and many can be expected to behave as adults. Given these difficulties, I agree that the state court's decision in this case cannot be called an unreasonable application of federal law simply because it failed explicitly to mention Alvarado's age.

Justice BREYER, with whom Justice STEVENS, Justice SOUTER, and Justice GINSBURG join, dissenting.

In my view, Michael Alvarado clearly was "in custody" when the police questioned him (without *Miranda* warnings) about the murder of Francisco Castaneda. To put the question in terms of federal law's well-established legal standards: Would a "reasonable person" in Alvarado's "position" have felt he was "at liberty to terminate the interrogation and leave"? A court must answer this question in light of "all of the circumstances surrounding the interrogation." And the obvious answer here is "no."

The law in this case asks judges to apply, not arcane or complex legal directives, but ordinary common sense. Would a reasonable person in Alvarado's position have felt free simply to get up and walk out of the small room in the station house at will during his 2-hour police interrogation? I ask the reader to put himself, or herself, in Alvarado's circumstances and then answer that question: Alvarado hears from his parents that he is needed for police questioning. His parents take him to the station. On arrival, a police officer separates him from his parents. His parents ask to come along, but the officer says they may not. Another officer says, "What do we have here; we are going to question a suspect."

The police take Alvarado to a small interrogation room, away from the station's public area. A single officer begins to question him, making clear in the process that the police have evidence that he participated in an attempted carjacking connected with a murder. When he says that he never saw any shooting, the officer suggests that he is lying, while adding that she is "giving [him] the opportunity to tell the truth" and "tak[e] care of [him]self." Toward the end of the questioning, the officer gives him permission to take a bathroom or water break. After two hours, by which time he has admitted he was involved in the attempted theft, knew about the gun, and helped to hide it, the questioning ends.

What reasonable person in the circumstances — brought to a police station by his parents at police request, put in a small interrogation room, questioned for a solid two hours, and confronted with claims that there is strong evidence that he participated in a serious crime, could have thought to himself, "Well, anytime I want to leave I can just get up and walk out"? If the person harbored any doubts, would he still think he might be free to leave once he recalls that the police officer has just refused to let his parents remain with him during questioning? Would he still think that he, rather than the officer, controls the situation?

There is only one possible answer to these questions. A reasonable person would not have thought he was free simply to pick up and leave in the middle of the interrogation. I believe the California courts were clearly wrong to hold the contrary, and the Ninth Circuit was right in concluding that those state courts unreasonably applied clearly established federal law.

What about Alvarado's youth? The majority suggests that the law might prevent a judge from taking account of the fact that Alvarado was 17. I can find nothing in the law that supports that conclusion. Our cases do instruct lower courts to apply a "reasonable person" standard. But the "reasonable person" standard does not require a court to pretend that Alvarado was a 35-year-old with aging parents whose middle-aged children do what their parents ask only out of respect. Nor does it say that a court should pretend that Alvarado was the statistically determined "average person" — a working, married, 35-year-old white female with a high school degree.

Rather, the precise legal definition of "reasonable person" may, depending on legal context, appropriately account for certain personal characteristics. In negligence suits, for example, the question is what would a "reasonable person" do "under the same or similar circumstances." In answering that question, courts enjoy "latitude" and may make "allowance not only for external facts, but sometimes for certain characteristics of the actor himself," including physical disability, youth, or advanced age.

In the present context, that of *Miranda*'s "in custody" inquiry, the law has introduced the concept of a "reasonable person" to avoid judicial inquiry into subjective states of mind, and to focus the inquiry instead upon objective circumstances that are known to both the officer and the suspect and that are likely relevant to the way a person would understand his situation. This focus helps to keep *Miranda* a workable rule.

In this case, Alvarado's youth is an objective circumstance that was known to the police. It is not a special quality, but rather a widely shared characteristic that generates commonsense conclusions about behavior and perception. To focus on the circumstance of age in a case like this does not complicate the "in custody" inquiry. And to say that courts should ignore widely shared, objective characteristics, like age, on the ground that only a (large) minority of the population possesses them would produce absurd results, the present instance being a case in point. I am not surprised that the majority points to no case suggesting any such limitation. Nor am I surprised that the majority makes no real argument at all explaining why any court would believe that the objective fact of a suspect's age could never be relevant.

The cases thus establish that a person is in custody if from an objective perspective the person is under arrest or otherwise not free to leave. What, then, about questioning when there is a traffic stop? A person certainly does not feel free to just drive away, but is the person in custody for purposes of *Miranda*?

BERKEMER v. MCCARTY
468 U.S. 420 (1984)

Justice MARSHALL delivered the opinion of the Court.

This case presents two related questions: First, does our decision in Miranda v. Arizona (1966), govern the admissibility of statements made during custodial interrogation by a suspect accused of a misdemeanor traffic offense? Second, does the roadside questioning of a motorist detained pursuant to a traffic stop constitute custodial interrogation for the purposes of the doctrine enunciated in *Miranda*?

I

The parties have stipulated to the essential facts. On the evening of March 31, 1980, Trooper Williams of the Ohio State Highway Patrol observed respondent's car weaving in and out of a lane on Interstate Highway 270. After following the car for two miles, Williams forced respondent to stop and asked him to get out of the vehicle. When respondent complied, Williams noticed that he was having difficulty standing. At that point, "Williams concluded that [respondent] would be charged with a traffic offense and, therefore, his freedom to leave the scene was terminated." However, respondent was not told that he would be taken into custody. Williams then asked respondent to perform a field sobriety test, commonly known as a "balancing test." Respondent could not do so without falling.

While still at the scene of the traffic stop, Williams asked respondent whether he had been using intoxicants. Respondent replied that "he had consumed two beers and had smoked several joints of marijuana a short time before." Respondent's speech was slurred, and Williams had difficulty understanding him. Williams thereupon formally placed respondent under arrest and transported him in the patrol car to the Franklin County Jail.

At the jail, respondent was given an intoxilyzer test to determine the concentration of alcohol in his blood. The test did not detect any alcohol whatsoever in respondent's system. Williams then resumed questioning respondent in order to obtain information for inclusion in the State Highway Patrol Alcohol Influence Report. Respondent answered affirmatively a question whether he had been drinking. When then asked if he was under the influence of alcohol, he said, "I guess, barely." Williams next asked respondent to indicate on the form whether the marihuana he had smoked had been treated with any chemicals. In the section of the report headed "Remarks," respondent wrote, "No ang[el] dust or PCP in the pot. Rick McCarty."

At no point in this sequence of events did Williams or anyone else tell respondent that he had a right to remain silent, to consult with an attorney, and to have an attorney appointed for him if he could not afford one.

Respondent was charged with operating a motor vehicle while under the influence of alcohol and/or drugs in violation of Ohio Rev. Code Ann. § 4511.19. Under Ohio law, that offense is a first-degree misdemeanor and is punishable by fine or imprisonment for up to six months.

Respondent moved to exclude the various incriminating statements he had made to Trooper Williams on the ground that introduction into evidence of those statements would violate the Fifth Amendment insofar as he had not been informed of his constitutional rights prior to his interrogation. When the trial court denied the motion, respondent pleaded "no contest" and was found guilty. He was sentenced to 90 days in jail, 80 of which were suspended, and was fined $300, $100 of which were suspended.

II

In the years since the decision in *Miranda*, we have frequently reaffirmed the central principle established by that case: if the police take a suspect into custody and then ask him questions without informing him of the rights enumerated above, his responses cannot be introduced into evidence to establish his guilt. Petitioner asks us to carve an exception out of the foregoing principle. When the police arrest a person for allegedly committing a misdemeanor traffic offense and then ask him questions without telling him his constitutional rights, petitioner argues, his responses should be admissible against him. We cannot agree.

One of the principal advantages of the doctrine that suspects must be given warnings before being interrogated while in custody is the clarity of that rule.

The exception to *Miranda* proposed by petitioner would substantially undermine this crucial advantage of the doctrine. The police often are unaware when they arrest a person whether he may have committed a misdemeanor or a felony.

It might be argued that the police would not need to make such guesses; whenever in doubt, they could ensure compliance with the law by giving the full *Miranda* warnings. It cannot be doubted, however, that in some cases a desire to induce a suspect to reveal information he might withhold if informed of his rights would induce the police not to take the cautious course.

Equally importantly, the doctrinal complexities that would confront the courts if we accepted petitioner's proposal would be Byzantine. Difficult questions quickly spring to mind: For instance, investigations into seemingly minor offenses sometimes escalate gradually into investigations into more serious matters; at what point in the evolution of an affair of this sort would the police be obliged to give *Miranda* warnings to a suspect in custody? What evidence would be necessary to establish that an arrest for a misdemeanor offense was merely a pretext to enable the police to interrogate the suspect (in hopes of obtaining information about a felony) without providing him the safeguards prescribed by *Miranda*? The litigation necessary to resolve such matters would be time-consuming and disruptive of law enforcement. And the end result would be an elaborate set of rules, interlaced with exceptions and subtle distinctions, discriminating between different kinds of custodial interrogations. Neither the police nor criminal defendants would benefit from such a development.

We do not suggest that there is any reason to think improper efforts were made in this case to induce respondent to make damaging admissions. More generally, we have no doubt that, in conducting most custodial interrogations of persons arrested for misdemeanor traffic offenses, the police behave responsibly and do not deliberately exert pressures upon the suspect to confess against his will. But the same might be said of custodial interrogations of persons arrested for felonies. The purposes of the safeguards prescribed by *Miranda* are to ensure that the police do not coerce or trick captive suspects into confessing, to relieve the " 'inherently compelling pressures' " generated by the custodial setting itself, "which work to undermine the individual's will to resist," and as much as possible to free courts from the task of scrutinizing individual cases to try to determine, after the fact, whether particular confessions were voluntary. Those purposes are implicated as much by in-custody questioning of persons suspected of misdemeanors as they are by questioning of persons suspected of felonies.

Petitioner's second argument is that law enforcement would be more expeditious and effective in the absence of a requirement that persons arrested for traffic offenses be informed of their rights. Again, we are unpersuaded. The occasions on which the police arrest and then interrogate someone suspected only of a misdemeanor traffic offense are rare. The police are already well accustomed to giving *Miranda* warnings to persons taken into custody. Adherence to the principle that all suspects must be given such warnings will not significantly hamper the efforts of the police to investigate crimes.

We hold therefore that a person subjected to custodial interrogation is entitled to the benefit of the procedural safeguards enunciated in *Miranda*, regardless of the nature or severity of the offense of which he is suspected or for which he was arrested.

III

To assess the admissibility of the self-incriminating statements made by respondent prior to his formal arrest, we are obliged to address a second issue concerning the scope of our decision in *Miranda*: whether the roadside questioning of a motorist detained pursuant to a routine traffic stop should be considered "custodial interrogation." Respondent urges that it should, on the ground that *Miranda* by its terms applies whenever "a person has been taken into custody or otherwise deprived of his freedom of action in any significant way." Petitioner contends that a holding that every detained motorist must be advised of his rights before being questioned would constitute an unwarranted extension of the *Miranda* doctrine.

It must be acknowledged at the outset that a traffic stop significantly curtails the "freedom of action" of the driver and the passengers, if any, of the detained vehicle. Under the law of most States, it is a crime either to ignore a policeman's signal to stop one's car or, once having stopped, to drive away without permission. Certainly few motorists would feel free either to disobey a directive to pull over or to leave the scene of a traffic stop without being told they might do so. Partly for these reasons, we have long acknowledged that "stopping an automobile and detaining its occupants constitute a 'seizure' within the meaning of [the Fourth] Amendmen[t], even though the purpose of the stop is limited and the resulting detention quite brief."

However, we decline to accord talismanic power to the phrase in the *Miranda* opinion emphasized by respondent. Fidelity to the doctrine announced in *Miranda* requires that it be enforced strictly, but only in those types of situations in which the concerns that powered the decision are implicated. Thus, we must decide whether a traffic stop exerts upon a detained person pressures that sufficiently impair his free exercise of his privilege against self-incrimination to require that he be warned of his constitutional rights.

Two features of an ordinary traffic stop mitigate the danger that a person questioned will be induced "to speak where he would not otherwise do so freely," Miranda v. Arizona. First, detention of a motorist pursuant to a traffic stop is presumptively temporary and brief. The vast majority of roadside detentions last only a few minutes.

Second, circumstances associated with the typical traffic stop are not such that the motorist feels completely at the mercy of the police. To be sure, the aura of authority surrounding an armed, uniformed officer and the knowledge that the officer has some discretion in deciding whether to issue a citation, in combination, exert some pressure on the detainee to respond to questions. But other aspects of the situation substantially offset these forces. Perhaps most importantly, the typical traffic stop is public, at least to some degree. Passersby, on foot or in other cars, witness the interaction of officer and motorist. This exposure to public view both reduces the ability of an unscrupulous policeman to use illegitimate means to elicit self-incriminating statements and diminishes the motorist's fear that, if he does not cooperate, he will be subjected to abuse. The fact that the detained motorist typically is confronted by only one or at most two policemen further mutes his sense of vulnerability. In short, the atmosphere surrounding an ordinary traffic stop is substantially less "police dominated" than that surrounding the kinds of interrogation at issue in *Miranda* itself, and in the subsequent cases in which we have applied *Miranda*.

In both of these respects, the usual traffic stop is more analogous to a so-called "*Terry* stop," *see* Terry v. Ohio (1968), than to a formal arrest. Under the Fourth Amendment, we have held, a policeman who lacks probable cause but whose "observations lead him reasonably to suspect" that a particular person has committed, is committing, or is about to commit a crime, may detain that person briefly in order to "investigate the circumstances that provoke suspicion." "[T]he stop and inquiry must be 'reasonably related in scope to the justification for their initiation.'" Typically, this means that the officer may ask the detainee a moderate number of questions to determine his identity and to try to obtain information confirming or dispelling the officer's suspicions. But the detainee is not obliged to respond. And, unless the detainee's answers provide the officer with probable cause to arrest him, he must then be released. The comparatively nonthreatening character of detentions of this sort explains the absence of any suggestion in our opinions that *Terry* stops are subject to the dictates of *Miranda*. The similarly noncoercive aspect of ordinary traffic stops prompts us to hold that persons temporarily detained pursuant to such stops are not "in custody" for the purposes of *Miranda*.

b.   What Is an "Interrogation"?

Miranda applies only if the police engage in interrogation. This, of course, is not an issue in the vast majority of cases. If police are questioning a person, that is an interrogation; if a person blurts out something to the police without being questioned, that is not an interrogation. Sometimes, though, the question of whether there is an interrogation is crucial in determining whether a confession is to be admitted. Rhode Island v. Innis is the leading case in defining what is an interrogation.

RHODE ISLAND v. INNIS

446 U.S. 291 (1980)

Justice STEWART delivered the opinion of the Court.
In Miranda v. Arizona (1966), the Court held that, once a defendant in custody asks to speak with a lawyer, all interrogation must cease until a lawyer is present. The issue in this case is whether the respondent was "interrogated" in violation of the standards promulgated in the *Miranda* opinion.

I

On the night of January 12, 1975, John Mulvaney, a Providence, R.I., taxicab driver, disappeared after being dispatched to pick up a customer. His body was discovered four days later buried in a shallow grave in Coventry, R.I. He had died from a shotgun blast aimed at the back of his head.
On January 17, 1975, shortly after midnight, the Providence police received a telephone call from Gerald Aubin, also a taxicab driver, who reported that he had just been robbed by a man wielding a sawed-off shotgun. Aubin further reported that he had dropped off his assailant near Rhode Island College in

a section of Providence known as Mount Pleasant. While at the Providence police station waiting to give a statement, Aubin noticed a picture of his assailant on a bulletin board. Aubin so informed one of the police officers present. The officer prepared a photo array, and again Aubin identified a picture of the same person. That person was the respondent. Shortly thereafter, the Providence police began a search of the Mount Pleasant area.

At approximately 4:30 A.M. on the same date, Patrolman Lovell, while cruising the streets of Mount Pleasant in a patrol car, spotted the respondent standing in the street facing him. When Patrolman Lovell stopped his car, the respondent walked towards it. Patrolman Lovell then arrested the respondent, who was unarmed, and advised him of his so-called *Miranda* rights. While the two men waited in the patrol car for other police officers to arrive, Patrolman Lovell did not converse with the respondent other than to respond to the latter's request for a cigarette.

Within minutes, Sergeant Sears arrived at the scene of the arrest, and he also gave the respondent the *Miranda* warnings. Immediately thereafter, Captain Leyden and other police officers arrived. Captain Leyden advised the respondent of his *Miranda* rights. The respondent stated that he understood those rights and wanted to speak with a lawyer. Captain Leyden then directed that the respondent be placed in a "caged wagon," a four-door police car with a wire screen mesh between the front and rear seats, and be driven to the central police station. Three officers, Patrolmen Gleckman, Williams, and McKenna, were assigned to accompany the respondent to the central station. They placed the respondent in the vehicle and shut the doors. Captain Leyden then instructed the officers not to question the respondent or intimidate or coerce him in any way. The three officers then entered the vehicle, and it departed.

While en route to the central station, Patrolman Gleckman initiated a conversation with Patrolman McKenna concerning the missing shotgun. As Patrolman Gleckman later testified:

A.   At this point, I was talking back and forth with Patrolman McKenna stating that I frequent this area while on patrol and [that because a school for handicapped children is located nearby,] there's a lot of handicapped children running around in this area, and God forbid one of them might find a weapon with shells and they might hurt themselves.

Patrolman McKenna apparently shared his fellow officer's concern:

A.   I more or less concurred with him [Gleckman] that it was a safety factor and that we should, you know, continue to search for the weapon and try to find it.

While Patrolman Williams said nothing, he overheard the conversation between the two officers:

A.   He [Gleckman] said it would be too bad if the little — I believe he said a girl — would pick up the gun, maybe kill herself.

The respondent then interrupted the conversation, stating that the officers should turn the car around so he could show them where the gun was located. At this point, Patrolman McKenna radioed back to Captain Leyden that they were returning to the scene of the arrest and that the respondent would inform them of the location of the gun. At the time the respondent indicated that the officers should turn back, they had traveled no more than a mile, a trip encompassing only a few minutes.

The police vehicle then returned to the scene of the arrest where a search for the shotgun was in progress. There, Captain Leyden again advised the respondent of his *Miranda* rights. The respondent replied that he understood those rights but that he "wanted to get the gun out of the way because of the kids in the area in the school." The respondent then led the police to a nearby field, where he pointed out the shotgun under some rocks by the side of the road.

On March 20, 1975, a grand jury returned an indictment charging the respondent with the kidnaping, robbery, and murder of John Mulvaney. Before trial, the respondent moved to suppress the shotgun and the statements he had made to the police regarding it. After an evidentiary hearing at which the respondent elected not to testify, the trial judge found that the respondent had been "repeatedly and completely advised of his *Miranda* rights." He further found that it was "entirely understandable that [the officers in the police vehicle] would voice their concern [for the safety of the handicapped children] to each other." Thus, without passing on whether the police officers had in fact "interrogated" the respondent, the trial court sustained the admissibility of the shotgun and testimony related to its discovery. That evidence was later introduced at the respondent's trial, and the jury returned a verdict of guilty on all counts.

On appeal, the Rhode Island Supreme Court, in a 3-2 decision, set aside the respondent's conviction. [T]he court concluded that the respondent had invoked his *Miranda* right to counsel and that, contrary to *Miranda*'s mandate that, in the absence of counsel, all custodial interrogation then cease, the police officers in the vehicle had "interrogated" the respondent without a valid waiver of his right to counsel. We granted certiorari to address for the first time the meaning of "interrogation" under Miranda v. Arizona.

II

In its *Miranda* opinion, the Court concluded that in the context of "custodial interrogation" certain procedural safeguards are necessary to protect a defendant's Fifth and Fourteenth Amendment privilege against compulsory self-incrimination. In the present case, the parties are in agreement that the respondent was fully informed of his *Miranda* rights and that he invoked his *Miranda* right to counsel when he told Captain Leyden that he wished to consult with a lawyer. It is also uncontested that the respondent was "in custody" while being transported to the police station. The issue, therefore, is whether the respondent was "interrogated" by the police officers in violation of the respondent's undisputed right under *Miranda* to remain silent until he had consulted with a lawyer. In resolving this issue, we first define the term "interrogation" under *Miranda* before turning to a consideration of the facts of this case.

The starting point for defining "interrogation" in this context is, of course, the Court's *Miranda* opinion. There the Court observed that "[b]y custodial interrogation, we mean questioning initiated by law enforcement officers after a person has been taken into custody or otherwise deprived of his freedom of action in any significant way." This passage and other references throughout the opinion to "questioning" might suggest that the *Miranda* rules were to apply only to those police interrogation practices that involve express questioning of a defendant while in custody.

We do not, however, construe the *Miranda* opinion so narrowly. The concern of the Court in *Miranda* was that the "interrogation environment" created by the interplay of interrogation and custody would "subjugate the individual to the will of his examiner" and thereby undermine the privilege against compulsory self-incrimination. The police practices that evoked this concern included several that did not involve express questioning. For example, one of the practices discussed in *Miranda* was the use of line-ups in which a coached witness would pick the defendant as the perpetrator. This was designed to establish that the defendant was in fact guilty as a predicate for further interrogation. The Court in *Miranda* also included in its survey of interrogation practices the use of psychological ploys, such as to "posi[t]" "the guilt of the subject," to "minimize the moral seriousness of the offense," and "to cast blame on the victim or on society." It is clear that these techniques of persuasion, no less than express questioning, were thought, in a custodial setting, to amount to interrogation.

This is not to say, however, that all statements obtained by the police after a person has been taken into custody are to be considered the product of interrogation. As the Court in *Miranda* noted: "Confessions remain a proper element in law enforcement. Any statement given freely and voluntarily without any compelling influences is, of course, admissible in evidence. The fundamental import of the privilege while an individual is in custody is not whether he is allowed to talk to the police without the benefit of warnings and counsel, but whether he can be interrogated. . . . Volunteered statements of any kind are not barred by the Fifth Amendment and their admissibility is not affected by our holding today."

It is clear therefore that the special procedural safeguards outlined in *Miranda* are required not where a suspect is simply taken into custody, but rather where a suspect in custody is subjected to interrogation. "Interrogation," as conceptualized in the *Miranda* opinion, must reflect a measure of compulsion above and beyond that inherent in custody itself.

We conclude that the *Miranda* safeguards come into play whenever a person in custody is subjected to either express questioning or its functional equivalent. That is to say, the term "interrogation" under *Miranda* refers not only to express questioning, but also to any words or actions on the part of the police (other than those normally attendant to arrest and custody) that the police should know are reasonably likely to elicit an incriminating response from the suspect. The latter portion of this definition focuses primarily upon the perceptions of the suspect, rather than the intent of the police. This focus reflects the fact that the *Miranda* safeguards were designed to vest a suspect in custody with an added measure of protection against coercive police practices, without regard to objective proof of the underlying intent of the police. A practice that the police should know is reasonably likely to evoke an incriminating response from a suspect thus amounts to interrogation. But, since the police surely cannot be held accountable for the unforeseeable results of their words or actions, the definition of interrogation can extend only to words or actions on the part of police officers that they should have known were reasonably likely to elicit an incriminating response.

Turning to the facts of the present case, we conclude that the respondent was not "interrogated" within the meaning of *Miranda*. It is undisputed that the first prong of the definition of "interrogation" was not satisfied, for the conversation between Patrolmen Gleckman and McKenna included no express questioning of the respondent. Rather, that conversation was, at least in form, nothing more than a dialogue between the two officers to which no response from the respondent was invited.

Moreover, it cannot be fairly concluded that the respondent was subjected to the "functional equivalent" of questioning. It cannot be said, in short, that Patrolmen Gleckman and McKenna should have known that their conversation was reasonably likely to elicit an incriminating response from the respondent. There is nothing in the record to suggest that the officers were aware that the respondent was peculiarly susceptible to an appeal to his conscience concerning the safety of handicapped children. Nor is there anything in the record to suggest that the police knew that the respondent was unusually disoriented or upset at the time of his arrest.

The case thus boils down to whether, in the context of a brief conversation, the officers should have known that the respondent would suddenly be moved to make a self-incriminating response. Given the fact that the entire conversation appears to have consisted of no more than a few off hand remarks, we cannot say that the officers should have known that it was reasonably likely that Innis would so respond. This is not a case where the police carried on a lengthy harangue in the presence of the suspect. Nor does the record support the respondent's contention that, under the circumstances, the officers' comments were particularly "evocative." It is our view, therefore, that the respondent was not subjected by the police to words or actions that the police should have known were reasonably likely to elicit an incriminating response from him.

Justice MARSHALL, with whom Justice BRENNAN joins, dissenting.

I am substantially in agreement with the Court's definition of "interrogation" within the meaning of Miranda v. Arizona (1966). In my view, the *Miranda* safeguards apply whenever police conduct is intended or likely to produce a response from a suspect in custody. As I read the Court's opinion, its definition of "interrogation" for *Miranda* purposes is equivalent, for practical purposes, to my formulation, since it contemplates that "where a police practice is designed to elicit an incriminating response from the accused, it is unlikely that the practice will not also be one which the police should have known was reasonably likely to have that effect." Thus, the Court requires an objective inquiry into the likely effect of police conduct on a typical individual, taking into account any special susceptibility of the suspect to certain kinds of pressure of which the police know or have reason to know.

I am utterly at a loss, however, to understand how this objective standard as applied to the facts before us can rationally lead to the conclusion that there was no interrogation. Innis was arrested at 4:30 A.M., handcuffed, searched, advised of his rights, and placed in the back seat of a patrol car. Within a short time he had been twice more advised of his rights and driven away in a four-door sedan with three police officers. Two officers sat in the front seat and one sat beside Innis in the back seat. Since the car traveled no more than a mile before Innis agreed to point out the location of the murder weapon, Officer Gleckman must have begun almost immediately to talk about the search for the shotgun.

The Court attempts to characterize Gleckman's statements as "no more than a few off hand remarks" which could not reasonably have been expected to elicit a response. If the statements had been addressed to respondent, it would be impossible to draw such a conclusion. The simple message of the "talking back and forth" between Gleckman and McKenna was that they had to find the shotgun to avert a child's death.

One can scarcely imagine a stronger appeal to the conscience of a suspect — any suspect — than the assertion that if the weapon is not found an innocent person will be hurt or killed. And not just any innocent person, but an innocent child — a little girl — a helpless, handicapped little girl on her way to school. The notion that such an appeal could not be expected to have any effect unless the suspect were known to have some special interest in handicapped children verges on the ludicrous. As a matter of fact, the appeal to a suspect to confess for the sake of others, to "display some evidence of decency and honor," is a classic interrogation technique.

Gleckman's remarks would obviously have constituted interrogation if they had been explicitly directed to respondent, and the result should not be different because they were nominally addressed to McKenna. This is not a case where police officers speaking among themselves are accidentally overheard by a suspect. These officers were "talking back and forth" in close quarters with the handcuffed suspect, traveling past the very place where they believed the weapon was located. They knew respondent would hear and attend to their conversation, and they are chargeable with knowledge of and responsibility for the pressures to speak which they created.

I firmly believe that this case is simply an aberration, and that in future cases the Court will apply the standard adopted today in accordance with its plain meaning.

Justice STEVENS, dissenting.

In my opinion the state court's conclusion that there was interrogation rests on a proper interpretation of both the facts and the law; thus, its determination that the products of the interrogation were inadmissible at trial should be affirmed.

In short, in order to give full protection to a suspect's right to be free from any interrogation at all, the definition of "interrogation" must include any police statement or conduct that has the same purpose or effect as a direct question. Statements that appear to call for a response from the suspect, as well as those that are designed to do so, should be considered interrogation. By prohibiting only those relatively few statements or actions that a police officer should know are likely to elicit an incriminating response, the Court today accords a suspect considerably less protection. Indeed, since I suppose most suspects are unlikely to incriminate themselves even when questioned directly, this new definition will almost certainly exclude every statement that is not punctuated with a question mark from the concept of "interrogation."

In subsequent cases, the Supreme Court continued to adhere to the narrow view of what constitutes interrogation that it used in Rhode Island v. Innis. For example, in Arizona v. Mauro, 481 U.S. 520 (1987), an individual was in police custody and indicated that he did not wish to answer any questions until a lawyer was present. The question was whether the officers interrogated the individual in violation of the Fifth and Fourteenth Amendments when they allowed him to speak with his wife in the presence of a police officer.

Justice Powell, writing for the Court in a 5-4 decision, held that there was not an interrogation. He stated:

> The sole issue, then, is whether the officers' subsequent actions rose to the level of interrogation — that is, in the language of *Innis*, whether they were the "functional equivalent" of police interrogation. We think it is clear under both *Miranda* and *Innis* that Mauro was not interrogated. The tape recording of the conversation between Mauro and his wife shows that Detective Manson asked Mauro no questions about the crime or his conduct. Nor is it suggested — or supported by any evidence — that Sergeant Allen's decision to allow Mauro's wife to see him was the kind of psychological ploy that properly could be treated as the functional equivalent of interrogation.

Justice Powell stressed that the purposes of *Miranda* did not call for finding this to be interrogation:

> In deciding whether particular police conduct is interrogation, we must remember the purpose behind our decisions: preventing government officials from using the coercive nature of confinement to extract confessions that would not be given in an unrestrained environment. The government actions in this case do not implicate this purpose in any way. Police departments need not adopt inflexible rules barring suspects from speaking with their spouses, nor must they ignore legitimate security concerns by allowing spouses to meet in private. In this situation, the Federal Constitution does not forbid use of Mauro's subsequent statements at his criminal trial.

Justice Stevens, writing for the four dissenters, took a very different view of what had transpired:

> The record indicates, however, that the police employed a powerful psychological ploy; they failed to give respondent any advance warning that Mrs. Mauro was coming to talk to him, that a police officer would accompany her, or that their conversation would be recorded. As the transcript of the conversation reveals, respondent would not have freely chosen to speak with her. These facts compel the conclusion that the police took advantage of Mrs. Mauro's request to visit her husband, setting up a confrontation between them at a time when he manifestly desired to remain silent. Because they allowed respondent's conversation with his wife to commence at a time when they knew it was reasonably likely to produce an incriminating statement, the police interrogated him. The Court's opposite conclusion removes an important brick from the wall of protection against police overreaching that surrounds the Fifth Amendment rights of suspects in custody.

The issue of what is interrogation also arises in the context when the police use an informant who speaks to a person who is in custody. When, if at all, should this be regarded as "interrogation"?

ILLINOIS v. PERKINS
496 U.S. 292 (1990)

Justice KENNEDY delivered the opinion of the Court.

An undercover government agent was placed in the cell of respondent Perkins, who was incarcerated on charges unrelated to the subject of the agent's investigation. Respondent made statements that implicated him in the crime that the agent sought to solve. Respondent claims that the statements should be inadmissible because he had not been given *Miranda* warnings by the agent. We hold that the statements are admissible. *Miranda* warnings are not required when the suspect is unaware that he is speaking to a law enforcement officer and gives a voluntary statement.

I

In November 1984, Richard Stephenson was murdered in a suburb of East St. Louis, Illinois. The murder remained unsolved until March 1986, when one Donald Charlton told police that he had learned about a homicide from a fellow inmate at the Graham Correctional Facility, where Charlton had been serving a sentence for burglary. The fellow inmate was Lloyd Perkins, who is the respondent here. Charlton told police that, while at Graham, he had befriended respondent, who told him in detail about a murder that respondent had committed in East St. Louis. On hearing Charlton's account, the police recognized details of the Stephenson murder that were not well known, and so they treated Charlton's story as a credible one.

By the time the police heard Charlton's account, respondent had been released from Graham, but police traced him to a jail in Montgomery County, Illinois, where he was being held pending trial on a charge of aggravated battery, unrelated to the Stephenson murder. The police wanted to investigate further respondent's connection to the Stephenson murder, but feared that the use of an eavesdropping device would prove impracticable and unsafe. They decided instead to place an undercover agent in the cellblock with respondent and Charlton. The plan was for Charlton and undercover agent John Parisi to pose as escapees from a work release program who had been arrested in the course of a burglary. Parisi and Charlton were instructed to engage respondent in casual conversation and report anything he said about the Stephenson murder.

Parisi, using the alias "Vito Bianco," and Charlton, both clothed in jail garb, were placed in the cellblock with respondent at the Montgomery County jail. The cellblock consisted of 12 separate cells that opened onto a common room. Respondent greeted Charlton who, after a brief conversation with respondent, introduced Parisi by his alias. Parisi told respondent that he "wasn't going to do any more time" and suggested that the three of them escape. Respondent replied that the Montgomery County jail was "rinky-dink" and that they could "break out." The trio met in respondent's cell later that evening, after the other inmates were asleep, to refine their plan. Respondent said that his girlfriend could smuggle in a pistol. Charlton said: "Hey, I'm not a murderer, I'm a burglar. That's your guys' profession." After telling Charlton that he would be responsible for any murder that occurred, Parisi asked respondent if he had ever "done" anybody. Respondent said that he had and proceeded to describe at length the events of the Stephenson murder. Parisi and respondent then engaged in some casual conversation before respondent went to sleep. Parisi did not give respondent *Miranda* warnings before the conversations.

Respondent was charged with the Stephenson murder. Before trial, he moved to suppress the statements made to Parisi in the jail. The trial court granted the motion to suppress, and the State appealed. The Appellate Court of Illinois affirmed. We granted certiorari to decide whether an undercover law enforcement officer must give *Miranda* warnings to an incarcerated suspect before asking him questions that may elicit an incriminating response. We now reverse.

II

Conversations between suspects and undercover agents do not implicate the concerns underlying *Miranda.* The essential ingredients of a "police-dominated atmosphere" and compulsion are not present when an incarcerated person speaks freely to someone whom he believes to be a fellow inmate. Coercion is determined from the perspective of the suspect. When a suspect considers himself in the company of cellmates and not officers, the coercive atmosphere is lacking. There is no empirical basis for the assumption that a suspect speaking to those whom he assumes are not officers will feel compelled to speak by the fear of reprisal for remaining silent or in the hope of more lenient treatment should he confess.

It is the premise of *Miranda* that the danger of coercion results from the interaction of custody and official interrogation. We reject the argument that *Miranda* warnings are required whenever a suspect is in custody in a technical sense and converses with someone who happens to be a government agent. Questioning by captors, who appear to control the suspect's fate, may create mutually reinforcing pressures that the Court has assumed will weaken the suspect's will, but where a suspect does not know that he is conversing with a government agent, these pressures do not exist. The state court here mistakenly assumed that because the suspect was in custody, no undercover questioning could take place. When the suspect has no reason to think that the listeners have official power over him, it should not be assumed that his words are motivated by the reaction he expects from his listeners. "[W]hen the agent carries neither badge nor gun and wears not 'police blue,' but the same prison gray" as the suspect, there is no "interplay between police interrogation and police custody."

Miranda forbids coercion, not mere strategic deception by taking advantage of a suspect's misplaced trust in one he supposes to be a fellow prisoner. As we recognized in *Miranda*: "[C]onfessions remain a proper element in law enforcement. Any statement given freely and voluntarily without any compelling influences is, of course, admissible in evidence." Ploys to mislead a suspect or lull him into a false sense of security that do not rise to the level of compulsion or coercion to speak are not within *Miranda*'s concerns.

Miranda was not meant to protect suspects from boasting about their criminal activities in front of persons whom they believe to be their cellmates. This case is illustrative. Respondent had no reason to feel that undercover agent Parisi had any legal authority to force him to answer questions or that Parisi could affect respondent's future treatment. Respondent viewed the cellmate-agent as an equal and showed no hint of being intimidated by the atmosphere of the jail. In recounting the details of the Stephenson murder, respondent was motivated solely by the desire to impress his fellow inmates. He spoke at his own peril.

The tactic employed here to elicit a voluntary confession from a suspect does not violate the Self-Incrimination Clause. We held in Hoffa v. United States (1966), that placing an undercover agent near a suspect in order to gather incriminating information was permissible under the Fifth Amendment.

We hold that an undercover law enforcement officer posing as a fellow inmate need not give *Miranda* warnings to an incarcerated suspect before asking questions that may elicit an incriminating response. The statements at issue in this case were voluntary, and there is no federal obstacle to their admissibility at trial.

Justice MARSHALL, dissenting.

This Court clearly and simply stated its holding in Miranda v. Arizona (1966): "[T]he prosecution may not use statements, whether exculpatory or inculpatory, stemming from custodial interrogation of the defendant unless it demonstrates the use of procedural safeguards effective to secure the privilege against self-incrimination." The conditions that require the police to apprise a defendant of his constitutional rights — custodial interrogation conducted by an agent of the police — were present in this case. Because Lloyd Perkins received no *Miranda* warnings before he was subjected to custodial interrogation, his confession was not admissible.

The Court reaches the contrary conclusion by fashioning an exception to the *Miranda* rule that applies whenever "an undercover law enforcement officer posing as a fellow inmate . . . ask[s] questions that may elicit an incriminating response" from an incarcerated suspect. This exception is inconsistent with the rationale supporting *Miranda* and allows police officers intentionally to take advantage of suspects unaware of their constitutional rights. I therefore dissent.

The Court does not dispute that the police officer here conducted a custodial interrogation of a criminal suspect. Perkins was incarcerated in county jail during the questioning at issue here; under these circumstances, he was in custody as that term is defined in *Miranda*.

While Perkins was confined, an undercover police officer, with the help of a police informant, questioned him about a serious crime. Although the Court does not dispute that Perkins was interrogated, it downplays the nature of the 35-minute questioning by disingenuously referring to it as a "conversatio[n]." The officer's narration of the "conversation" at Perkins' suppression hearing however, reveals that it clearly was an interrogation.

The police officer continued the inquiry, asking a series of questions designed to elicit specific information about the victim, the crime scene, the weapon, Perkins' motive, and his actions during and after the shooting. This interaction was not a "conversation"; Perkins, the officer, and the informant were not equal participants in a free-ranging discussion, with each man offering his views on different topics. Rather, it was an interrogation: Perkins was subjected to express questioning likely to evoke an incriminating response.

Because Perkins was interrogated by police while he was in custody, *Miranda* required that the officer inform him of his rights. In rejecting that conclusion, the Court finds that "conversations" between undercover agents and suspects are devoid of the coercion inherent in station house interrogations conducted by law enforcement officials who openly represent the State. *Miranda* was not, however, concerned solely with police coercion. It dealt with any police tactics that may operate to compel a suspect in custody to make incriminating statements without full awareness of his constitutional rights. Thus, when a law enforcement agent structures a custodial interrogation so that a suspect feels compelled to reveal incriminating information, he must inform the suspect of his constitutional rights and give him an opportunity to decide whether or not to talk. The compulsion proscribed by *Miranda* includes deception by the police.

Even if *Miranda*, as interpreted by the Court, would not permit such obviously compelled confessions, the ramifications of today's opinion are still disturbing. The exception carved out of the *Miranda* doctrine today may well result in a proliferation of departmental policies to encourage police officers to conduct interrogations of confined suspects through undercover agents, thereby circumventing the need to administer *Miranda* warnings. Indeed, if *Miranda* now requires a police officer to issue warnings only in those situations in which the suspect might feel compelled "to speak by the fear of reprisal for remaining silent or in the hope of more lenient treatment should he confess," presumably it allows custodial interrogation by an undercover officer posing as a member of the clergy or a suspect's defense attorney. Although such abhorrent tricks would play on a suspect's need to confide in a trusted adviser, neither would cause the suspect to "think that the listeners have official power over him." The Court's adoption of the "undercover agent" exception to the *Miranda* rule thus is necessarily also the adoption of a substantial loophole in our jurisprudence protecting suspects' Fifth Amendment rights.

c.   What Is Required of the Police?

As explained above, *Miranda* has been defended, in part, based on the argument that it is clear in terms of what is required of the police: They must administer the prescribed warnings; they must provide an attorney if one is requested; they must stop questioning a suspect who is in custody if the suspect requests an attorney or says that he does not wish to answer further questions. But what deviations from this are allowed without their being deemed to be a violation of the Fifth Amendment? The following two decisions, California v. Prysock and Duckworth v. Eagan, address that question.

CALIFORNIA v. PRYSOCK

453 U.S. 355 (1981)

PER CURIAM.

This case presents the question whether the warnings given to respondent prior to a recorded conversation with a police officer satisfied the requirements of Miranda v. Arizona (1966). Although ordinarily this Court would not be inclined to review a case involving application of that precedent to a particular set of facts, the opinion of the California Court of Appeal essentially laid down a flat rule requiring that the content of *Miranda* warnings be a virtual incantation of the precise language contained in the *Miranda* opinion. Because such a rigid rule was not mandated by *Miranda* or any other decision of this Court, and is not required to serve the purposes of *Miranda*, we reverse.

On January 30, 1978, Mrs. Donna Iris Erickson was brutally murdered. Later that evening respondent and a codefendant were apprehended for commission of the offense. Respondent was brought to a substation of the Tulare County Sheriff's Department and advised of his *Miranda* rights. He declined to talk and, since he was a minor, his parents were notified. Respondent's parents arrived and after meeting with them respondent decided to answer police questions. An officer questioned respondent, on tape, with respondent's parents present. The tape reflects that the following warnings were given prior to any questioning:

Sgt. Byrd.   . . . Mr. Randall James Prysock, earlier today I advised you of your legal rights and at that time you advised me you did not wish to talk to me, is that correct?

Randall P.   Yeh.

Sgt. Byrd.   And, uh, during, at the first interview your folks were not present, they are now present. I want to go through your legal rights again with you and after each legal right I would like for you to answer whether you understand it or not. . . . Your legal rights, Mr. Prysock, is [sic] follows: Number One, you have the right to remain silent. This means you don't have to talk to me at all unless you so desire. Do you understand this?

Randall P.   Yeh.

Sgt. Byrd.   If you give up your right to remain silent, anything you say can and will be used as evidence against you in a court of law. Do you understand this?

Randall P.   Yes.

Sgt. Byrd.   You have the right to talk to a lawyer before you are questioned, have him present with you while you are being questioned, and all during the questioning. Do you understand this?

Randall P.   Yes.

Sgt. Byrd.   You also, being a juvenile, you have the right to have your parents present, which they are. Do you understand this?

Randall P.   Yes.

Sgt. Byrd.   Even if they weren't here, you'd have this right. Do you understand this?

Randall P.   Yes.

Sgt. Byrd.   You all, uh, — if, — you have the right to have a lawyer appointed to represent you at no cost to yourself. Do you understand this?

Randall P.   Yes.

Sgt. Byrd.   Now, having all these legal rights in mind, do you wish to talk to me at this time?

Randall P.   Yes.

At this point, at the request of Mrs. Prysock, a conversation took place with the tape recorder turned off. According to Sgt. Byrd, Mrs. Prysock asked if respondent could still have an attorney at a later time if he gave a statement now without one. Sgt. Byrd assured Mrs. Prysock that respondent would have an attorney when he went to court and that "he could have one at this time if he wished one."

At trial in the Superior Court of Tulare County the court denied respondent's motion to suppress the taped statement. Respondent was convicted by a jury of first-degree murder with two special circumstances — torture and robbery. The Court of Appeal for the Fifth Appellate District reversed respondent's convictions and ordered a new trial because of what it thought to be error under *Miranda.* The Court of Appeal ruled that respondent's recorded incriminating statements, given with his parents present, had to be excluded from consideration by the jury because respondent was not properly advised of his right to the services of a free attorney before and during interrogation. Although respondent was indisputably informed that he had "the right to talk to a lawyer before you are questioned, have him present with you while you are being questioned, and all during the questioning," and further informed that he had "the right to have a lawyer appointed to represent you at no cost to yourself," the Court of Appeal ruled that these warnings were inadequate because respondent was not explicitly informed of his right to have an attorney appointed before further questioning. The Court of Appeal stated that "[o]ne of [Miranda's] virtues is its precise requirements which are so easily met," and that " 'the rigidity of the Miranda rules and the way in which they are to be applied was conceived of and continues to be recognized as the decision's greatest strength.' "

This Court has never indicated that the "rigidity" of Miranda extends to the precise formulation of the warnings given a criminal defendant. This Court and others have stressed as one virtue of Miranda the fact that the giving of the warnings obviates the need for a case-by-case inquiry into the actual voluntariness of the admissions of the accused. Nothing in these observations suggests any desirable rigidity in the form of the required warnings. Quite the contrary, Miranda itself indicated that no talismanic incantation was required to satisfy its strictures.

[N]othing in the warnings given respondent suggested any limitation on the right to the presence of appointed counsel different from the clearly conveyed rights to a lawyer in general, including the right "to a lawyer before you are questioned, . . . while you are being questioned, and all during the questioning."

It is clear that the police in this case fully conveyed to respondent his rights as required by Miranda. He was told of his right to have a lawyer present prior to and during interrogation, and his right to have a lawyer appointed at no cost if he could not afford one. These warnings conveyed to respondent his right to have a lawyer appointed if he could not afford one prior to and during interrogation. The Court of Appeal erred in holding that the warnings were inadequate simply because of the order in which they were given.

Justice STEVENS, with whom Justice BRENNAN and Justice MARSHALL join, dissenting.

A juvenile informed by police that he has a right to counsel may understand that right to include one or more of three options: (1) that he has a right to have a lawyer represent him if he or his parents are able and willing to hire one; (2) that, if he cannot afford to hire an attorney, he has a right to have a lawyer represent him without charge at trial, even if his parents are unwilling to spend money on his behalf; or (3) that, if he is unable to afford an attorney, he has a right to consult a lawyer without charge before he decides whether to talk to the police, even if his parents decline to pay for such legal representation. All three of these options are encompassed within the right to counsel possessed by a juvenile charged with a crime. In this case, the first two options were explained to respondent, but the third was not.

The California Court of Appeal in this case analyzed the warning given respondent, and concluded that he had not been adequately informed of this crucial right. The police sergeant informed respondent that he had the right to have counsel present during questioning and, after a brief interlude, informed him that he had the right to appointed counsel. The Court of Appeal concluded that this warning was constitutionally inadequate, not because it deviated from the precise language of Miranda, but because "[u]nfortunately, the minor was not given the crucial information that the services of the free attorney were available prior to the impending questioning."

There can be no question that Miranda requires, as a matter of federal constitutional law, that an accused effectively be provided with this "crucial information" in some form. The Court's demonstration that the Constitution does not require that the precise language of *Miranda* be recited to an accused simply fails to come to terms with the express finding of the California Court of Appeal that respondent was not given this information. The warning recited by the police sergeant is sufficiently ambiguous on its face to provide adequate support for the California court's finding. That court's conclusion is at least reasonable, and is clearly not so patently erroneous as to warrant summary reversal.

DUCKWORTH v. EAGAN
492 U.S. 195 (1989)

Chief Justice REHNQUIST delivered the opinion of the Court.

Respondent confessed to stabbing a woman nine times after she refused to have sexual relations with him, and he was convicted of attempted murder. Before confessing, respondent was given warnings by the police, which included the advice that a lawyer would be appointed "if and when you go to court." The United States Court of Appeals for the Seventh Circuit held that such advice did not comply with the requirements of Miranda v. Arizona (1966). We disagree and reverse.

Late on May 16, 1982, respondent contacted a Chicago police officer he knew to report that he had seen the naked body of a dead woman lying on a Lake Michigan beach. Respondent denied any involvement in criminal activity. He then took several Chicago police officers to the beach, where the woman was crying for help. When she saw respondent, the woman exclaimed: "Why did you stab me? Why did you stab me?" Respondent told the officers that he had been with the woman earlier that night, but that they had been attacked by several men who abducted the woman in a van.

The next morning, after realizing that the crime had been committed in Indiana, the Chicago police turned the investigation over to the Hammond, Indiana, Police Department. Respondent repeated to the Hammond police officers his story that he had been attacked on the lakefront, and that the woman had been abducted by several men. After he filled out a battery complaint at a local police station, respondent agreed to go to the Hammond police headquarters for further questioning.

At about 11 A.M., the Hammond police questioned respondent. Before doing so, the police read to respondent a waiver form, entitled "Voluntary Appearance; Advice of Rights," and they asked him to sign it. The form provided: "Before we ask you any questions, you must understand your rights. You have the right to remain silent. Anything you say can be used against you in court. You have a right to talk to a lawyer for advice before we ask you any questions, and to have him with you during questioning. You have this right to the advice and presence of a lawyer even if you cannot afford to hire one. We have no way of giving you a lawyer, but one will be appointed for you, if you wish, if and when you go to court. If you wish to answer questions now without a lawyer present, you have the right to stop answering questions at any time. You also have the right to stop answering at any time until you've talked to a lawyer." Respondent signed the form and repeated his exculpatory explanation for his activities of the previous evening.

Respondent was then placed in the "lock up" at the Hammond police head-quarters. Some 29 hours later, at about 4 P.M. on May 18, the police again inter-viewed respondent. Before this questioning, one of the officers read the following waiver form to respondent:

"1. Before making this statement, I was advised that I have the right to remain silent and that anything I might say may or will be used against me in a court of law.

"2. That I have the right to consult with an attorney of my own choice before saying anything, and that an attorney may be present while I am making any statement or throughout the course of any conversation with any police officer if I so choose.

"3. That I can stop and request an attorney at any time during the course of the taking of any statement or during the course of any such conversation.

"4. That in the course of any conversation I can refuse to answer any further questions and remain silent, thereby terminating the conversation.

"5. That if I do not hire an attorney, one will be provided for me."

Respondent read the form back to the officers and signed it. He proceeded to confess to stabbing the woman. The next morning, respondent led the officers to the Lake Michigan beach where they recovered the knife he had used in the stabbing and several items of clothing.

At trial, over respondent's objection, the state court admitted his confession, his first statement denying any involvement in the crime, the knife, and the clothing. The jury found respondent guilty of attempted murder, but acquitted him of rape. He was sentenced to 35 years' imprisonment. The conviction was upheld on appeal.

Respondent sought a writ of habeas corpus in the United States District Court for the Northern District of Indiana, claiming, inter alia, that his confession was inadmissible because the first waiver form did not comply with *Miranda*. The District Court denied the petition. A divided United States Court of Appeals for the Seventh Circuit reversed. The majority held that the advice that counsel would be appointed "if and when you go to court," which was included in the first warnings given to respondent, was "constitutionally defective because it denies an accused indigent a clear and unequivocal warning of the right to appointed counsel before any interrogation," and "link[s] an indigent's right to counsel before interrogation with a future event."

In Miranda v. Arizona (1966), the Court established certain procedural safe-guards that require police to advise criminal suspects of their rights under the Fifth and Fourteenth Amendments before commencing custodial interroga-tion. We have never insisted that *Miranda* warnings be given in the exact form described in that decision. In *Miranda* itself, the Court said that "[t]he warnings required and the waiver necessary in accordance with our opinion today are, in the absence of a fully effective equivalent, prerequisites to the admissibility of any statement made by a defendant." Reviewing courts therefore need not examine *Miranda* warnings as if construing a will or defining the terms of an easement. The inquiry is simply whether the warnings reasonably "conve[y] to [a suspect] his rights as required by *Miranda*."

We think the initial warnings given to respondent touched all of the bases required by *Miranda*. The police told respondent that he had the right to remain silent, that anything he said could be used against him in court, that he had the right to speak to an attorney before and during questioning, that he had "this right to the advice and presence of a lawyer even if [he could] not afford to hire one," and that he had the "right to stop answering at any time until [he] talked to a lawyer." As noted, the police also added that they could not provide respondent with a lawyer, but that one would be appointed "if and when you go to court." The Court of Appeals thought this "if and when you go to court" language suggested that "only those accused who can afford an attorney have the right to have one present before answering any questions," and "implie[d] that if the accused does not 'go to court,' i.e.[,] the government does not file charges, the accused is not entitled to [counsel] at all."

In our view, the Court of Appeals misapprehended the effect of the inclusion of "if and when you go to court" language in *Miranda* warnings. First, this instruction accurately described the procedure for the appointment of counsel in Indiana. Under Indiana law, counsel is appointed at the defendant's initial appearance in court, and formal charges must be filed at or before that hearing. We think it must be relatively commonplace for a suspect, after receiving *Miranda* warnings, to ask when he will obtain counsel. The "if and when you go to court" advice simply anticipates that question. Second, *Miranda* does not require that attorneys be producible on call, but only that the suspect be informed, as here, that he has the right to an attorney before and during questioning, and that an attorney would be appointed for him if he could not afford one. The Court in *Miranda* emphasized that it was not suggesting that "each police station must have a 'station house lawyer' present at all times to advise prisoners." If the police cannot provide appointed counsel, *Miranda* requires only that the police not question a suspect unless he waives his right to counsel. Here, respondent did just that.

Justice MARSHALL, with whom Justice BRENNAN joins, and with whom Justice BLACKMUN and Justice STEVENS join, dissenting.

The majority holds today that a police warning advising a suspect that he is entitled to an appointed lawyer only "if and when he goes to court" satisfies the requirements of *Miranda v. Arizona* (1966). The majority reaches this result by seriously mischaracterizing that decision. Under *Miranda*, a police warning must "clearly infor[m]" a suspect taken into custody "that if he cannot afford an attorney one will be appointed for him prior to any questioning if he so desires." A warning qualified by an "if and when you go to court" caveat does nothing of the kind; instead, it leads the suspect to believe that a lawyer will not be provided until some indeterminate time in the future after questioning. I refuse to acquiesce in the continuing debasement of this historic precedent and therefore dissent.

Miranda mandated no specific verbal formulation that police must use, but the Court, speaking through Chief Justice Warren, emphasized repeatedly that the offer of appointed counsel must be "effective and express." In concluding that the first warning given to respondent Eagan, satisfies the dictates of *Miranda*, the majority makes a mockery of that decision. Eagan was initially advised that he had the right to the presence of counsel before and during questioning. But in the very next breath, the police informed Eagan that, if he could not afford a lawyer, one would be appointed to represent him only "if and when" he went to court. As the Court of Appeals found, Eagan could easily have concluded from the "if and when" caveat that only "those accused who can afford an attorney have the right to have one present before answering any questions; those who are not so fortunate must wait." Eagan was, after all, never told that questioning would be delayed until a lawyer was appointed "if and when" Eagan did, in fact, go to court. Thus, the "if and when" caveat may well have had the effect of negating the initial promise that counsel could be present. At best, a suspect like Eagan "would not know . . . whether or not he had a right to the services of a lawyer."

In lawyerlike fashion, the Chief Justice parses the initial warnings given Eagan and finds that the most plausible interpretation is that Eagan would not be questioned until a lawyer was appointed when he later appeared in court. What goes wholly overlooked in the Chief Justice's analysis is that the recipients of police warnings are often frightened suspects unlettered in the law, not lawyers or judges or others schooled in interpreting legal or semantic nuance. Such suspects can hardly be expected to interpret, in as facile a manner as the Chief Justice, "the pretzel-like warnings here — intertwining, contradictory, and ambiguous as they are."

Even if the typical suspect could draw the inference the majority does — that questioning will not commence until a lawyer is provided at a later court appearance — a warning qualified by an "if and when" caveat still fails to give a suspect any indication of when he will be taken to court. Upon hearing the warnings given in this case, a suspect would likely conclude that no lawyer would be provided until trial. In common parlance, "going to court" is synonymous with "going to trial." Furthermore, the negative implication of the caveat is that, if the suspect is never taken to court, he "is not entitled to an attorney at all." An unwitting suspect harboring uncertainty on this score is precisely the sort of person who may feel compelled to talk "voluntarily" to the police, without the presence of counsel, in an effort to extricate himself from his predicament.

It poses no great burden on law enforcement officers to eradicate the confusion stemming from the "if and when" caveat. Deleting the sentence containing the offending language is all that needs to be done. Purged of this language, the warning tells the suspect in a straightforward fashion that he has the right to the presence of a lawyer before and during questioning, and that a lawyer will be appointed if he cannot afford one. The suspect is given no reason to believe that the appointment of an attorney may come after interrogation.

4.   What Are the Consequences of a Violation of Miranda?

Miranda is clear that a confession obtained in violation of its requirements, as well as a confession deemed involuntary, must be excluded from evidence. The more difficult question concerns the extent to which the police may use the knowledge that they gain from questioning in violation of *Miranda* or whether the use of such information must be suppressed as the "fruit of the poisonous tree."

The Supreme Court first addressed this in Michigan v. Tucker, 417 U.S. 433 (1974). The police questioned a suspect without properly administering *Miranda* warnings and during this interrogation learned the identity of a key witness. The issue was whether the prosecutor could use this witness at trial. The Court stressed that the interrogation occurred prior to its decision in Miranda v. Arizona, but it nonetheless addressed the broader issue as to the consequences of violations of *Miranda*'s requirements.

Justice Rehnquist, writing for the Court, said that in deciding what should be excluded courts must consider the underlying purpose of the exclusionary rule. He wrote:

> The deterrent purpose of the exclusionary rule necessarily assumes that the police have engaged in willful, or at the very least negligent, conduct which has deprived the defendant of some right. By refusing to admit evidence gained as a result of such conduct, the courts hope to instill in those particular investigating officers, or in their future counterparts, a greater degree of care toward the rights of an accused. Where the official action was pursued in complete good faith, however, the deterrence rationale loses much of its force.

Justice Rehnquist said that balancing the competing interests warranted allowing the use of the witness at trial:

> In summary, we do not think that any single reason supporting exclusion of this witness' testimony, or all of them together, are very persuasive. By contrast, we find the arguments in favor of admitting the testimony quite strong. For, when balancing the interests involved, we must weigh the strong interest under any system of justice of making available to the trier of fact all concededly relevant and trustworthy evidence which either party seeks to adduce. In this particular case we also "must consider society's interest in the effective prosecution of criminals in light of the protection our pre-*Miranda* standards afford criminal defendants." These interests may be outweighed by the need to provide an effective sanction to a constitutional right, but they must in any event be valued. Here respondent's own statement, which might have helped the prosecution show respondent's guilty conscience at trial, had already been excised from the prosecution's case pursuant to this Court's *Johnson* decision. To extend the excision further under the circumstances of this case and exclude relevant testimony of a third-party witness would require far more persuasive arguments than those advanced by respondent.

Justice Brennan, in dissent, criticized the Court for reaching the question as to remedy at all since this case involved questioning that occurred prior to *Miranda*. He wrote:

> The Court finds it unnecessary to decide "the broad question" of whether the fruits of "statements taken in violation of the *Miranda* rules must be excluded regardless of when the interrogation took place," since respondent's interrogation occurred prior to our decision in Miranda v. Arizona (1966). In my view, however, it is unnecessary, too, for the Court to address the narrower question of whether the principles of *Miranda* require that fruits be excluded when obtained as a result of a pre-*Miranda* interrogation without the requisite prior warnings.

Until the decisions in two recent cases, Oregon v. Elstad was the leading decision concerning the admissibility of evidence gained as the "fruits" of a *Miranda* violation.

OREGON v. ELSTAD
470 U.S. 298 (1985)

Justice O'CONNOR delivered the opinion of the Court.

This case requires us to decide whether an initial failure of law enforcement officers to administer the warnings required by Miranda v. Arizona (1966), without more, "taints" subsequent admissions made after a suspect has been fully advised of and has waived his *Miranda* rights. Respondent, Michael James Elstad, was convicted of burglary by an Oregon trial court. The Oregon Court of Appeals reversed, holding that respondent's signed confession, although voluntary, was rendered inadmissible by a prior remark made in response to questioning without benefit of *Miranda* warnings.

I

In December 1981, the home of Mr. and Mrs. Gilbert Gross, in the town of Salem, Polk County, Ore., was burglarized. Missing were art objects and furnishings valued at $150,000. A witness to the burglary contacted the Polk County Sheriff's office, implicating respondent Michael Elstad, an 18-year-old neighbor and friend of the Grosses' teenage son. Thereupon, Officers Burke and McAllister went to the home of respondent Elstad, with a warrant for his arrest. Elstad's mother answered the door. She led the officers to her son's room where he lay on his bed, clad in shorts and listening to his stereo. The officers asked him to get dressed and to accompany them into the living room. Officer McAllister asked respondent's mother to step into the kitchen, where he explained that they had a warrant for her son's arrest for the burglary of a neighbor's residence. Officer Burke remained with Elstad in the living room. He later testified: "I sat down with Mr. Elstad and I asked him if he was aware of why Detective McAllister and myself were there to talk with him. He stated no, he had no idea why we were there. I then asked him if he knew a person by the name of Gross, and he said yes, he did, and also added that he heard that there was a robbery at the Gross house. And at that point I told Mr. Elstad that I felt he was involved in that, and he looked at me and stated, 'Yes, I was there.' "

Elstad was transported to the Sheriff's headquarters and approximately one hour later, Officers Burke and McAllister joined him in McAllister's office. McAllister then advised respondent for the first time of his *Miranda* rights, reading from a standard card. Respondent indicated he understood his rights, and, having these rights in mind, wished to speak with the officers. Elstad gave a full statement, explaining that he had known that the Gross family was out of town and had been paid to lead several acquaintances to the Gross residence and show them how to gain entry through a defective sliding glass door. The statement was typed, reviewed by respondent, read back to him for correction, initialed and signed by Elstad and both officers. As an afterthought, Elstad added and initialed the sentence, "After leaving the house Robby & I went back to [the] van & Robby handed me a small bag of grass." Respondent concedes that the officers made no threats or promises either at his residence or at the Sheriff's office.

Respondent was charged with first-degree burglary. Respondent moved at once to suppress his oral statement and signed confession. He contended that the statement he made in response to questioning at his house "let the cat out of the bag," and tainted the subsequent confession as "fruit of the poisonous tree." The judge ruled that the statement, "I was there," had to be excluded because the defendant had not been advised of his *Miranda* rights. The written confession taken after Elstad's arrival at the Sheriff's office, however, was admitted in evidence.

II

The arguments advanced in favor of suppression of respondent's written confession rely heavily on metaphor. One metaphor, familiar from the Fourth Amendment context, would require that respondent's confession, regardless of its integrity, voluntariness, and probative value, be suppressed as the "tainted fruit of the poisonous tree" of the *Miranda* violation. A second metaphor questions whether a confession can be truly voluntary once the "cat is out of the bag." Taken out of context, each of these metaphors can be misleading. They should not be used to obscure fundamental differences between the role of the Fourth Amendment exclusionary rule and the function of *Miranda* in guarding against the prosecutorial use of compelled statements as prohibited by the Fifth Amendment. The Oregon court assumed and respondent here contends that a failure to administer *Miranda* warnings necessarily breeds the same consequences as police infringement of a constitutional right, so that evidence uncovered following an unwarned statement must be suppressed as "fruit of the poisonous tree." We believe this view misconstrues the nature of the protections afforded by *Miranda* warnings and therefore misreads the consequences of police failure to supply them.

A

Respondent's contention that his confession was tainted by the earlier failure of the police to provide *Miranda* warnings and must be excluded as "fruit of the poisonous tree" assumes the existence of a constitutional violation. This figure of speech is drawn from Wong Sun v. United States (1963), in which the Court held that evidence and witnesses discovered as a result of a search in violation of the Fourth Amendment must be excluded from evidence. The *Wong Sun* doctrine applies as well when the fruit of the Fourth Amendment violation is a confession.

But a procedural *Miranda* violation differs in significant respects from violations of the Fourth Amendment, which have traditionally mandated a broad application of the "fruits" doctrine. The purpose of the Fourth Amendment exclusionary rule is to deter unreasonable searches, no matter how probative their fruits.

The *Miranda* exclusionary rule, however, serves the Fifth Amendment and sweeps more broadly than the Fifth Amendment itself. It may be triggered even in the absence of a Fifth Amendment violation. The Fifth Amendment prohibits use by the prosecution in its case in chief only of compelled testimony. Failure to administer *Miranda* warnings creates a presumption of compulsion. Consequently, unwarned statements that are otherwise voluntary within the meaning of the Fifth Amendment must nevertheless be excluded from evidence under *Miranda*. Thus, in the individual case, *Miranda*'s preventive medicine provides a remedy even to the defendant who has suffered no identifiable constitutional harm.

But the *Miranda* presumption, though irrebuttable for purposes of the prosecution's case in chief, does not require that the statements and their fruits be discarded as inherently tainted. Despite the fact that patently voluntary statements taken in violation of *Miranda* must be excluded from the prosecution's case, the presumption of coercion does not bar their use for impeachment purposes on cross-examination. Harris v. New York (1971).

In Michigan v. Tucker, the Court was asked to extend the *Wong Sun* fruits doctrine to suppress the testimony of a witness for the prosecution whose identity was discovered as the result of a statement taken from the accused without benefit of full *Miranda* warnings. The Court concluded that the unwarned questioning "did not abridge respondent's constitutional privilege . . . but departed only from the prophylactic standards later laid down by this Court in *Miranda* to safeguard that privilege." Since there was no actual infringement of the suspect's constitutional rights, the case was not controlled by the doctrine expressed in *Wong Sun* that fruits of a constitutional violation must be suppressed. In deciding "how sweeping the judicially imposed consequences" of a failure to administer *Miranda* warnings should be, the *Tucker* Court noted that neither the general goal of deterring improper police conduct nor the Fifth Amendment goal of assuring trustworthy evidence would be served by suppression of the witness' testimony.

We believe that this reasoning applies with equal force when the alleged "fruit" of a noncoercive *Miranda* violation is neither a witness nor an article of evidence but the accused's own voluntary testimony. As in *Tucker*, the absence of any coercion or improper tactics undercuts the twin rationales—trustworthiness and deterrence—for a broader rule. Once warned, the suspect is free to exercise his own volition in deciding whether or not to make a statement to the authorities.

Because *Miranda* warnings may inhibit persons from giving information, this Court has determined that they need be administered only after the person is taken into "custody" or his freedom has otherwise been significantly restrained. Unfortunately, the task of defining "custody" is a slippery one, and "policemen investigating serious crimes [cannot realistically be expected to] make no errors whatsoever." If errors are made by law enforcement officers in administering the prophylactic *Miranda* procedures, they should not breed the same irremediable consequences as police infringement of the Fifth Amendment itself. It is an unwarranted extension of *Miranda* to hold that a simple failure to administer the warnings, unaccompanied by any actual coercion or other circumstances calculated to undermine the suspect's ability to exercise his free will, so taints the investigatory process that a subsequent voluntary and informed waiver is ineffective for some indeterminate period. Though *Miranda* requires that the unwarned admission must be suppressed, the admissibility of any subsequent statement should turn in these circumstances solely on whether it is knowingly and voluntarily made.

B

The Oregon court, however, believed that the unwarned remark compromised the voluntariness of respondent's later confession. It was the court's view that the prior answer and not the unwarned questioning impaired respondent's ability to give a valid waiver and that only lapse of time and change of place could dissipate what it termed the "coercive impact" of the inadmissible statement. When a prior statement is actually coerced, the time that passes between confessions, the change in place of interrogations, and the change in identity of the interrogators all bear on whether that coercion has carried over into the second confession.

The Oregon court nevertheless identified a subtle form of lingering compulsion, the psychological impact of the suspect's conviction that he has let the cat out of the bag and, in so doing, has sealed his own fate. But endowing the psychological effects of voluntary unwarned admissions with constitutional implications would, practically speaking, disable the police from obtaining the suspect's informed cooperation even when the official coercion proscribed by the Fifth Amendment played no part in either his warned or unwarned confessions.

This Court has never held that the psychological impact of voluntary disclosure of a guilty secret qualifies as state compulsion or compromises the voluntariness of a subsequent informed waiver. The Oregon court, by adopting this expansive view of Fifth Amendment compulsion, effectively immunizes a suspect who responds to pre-*Miranda* warning questions from the consequences of his subsequent informed waiver of the privilege of remaining silent. This immunity comes at a high cost to legitimate law enforcement activity, while adding little desirable protection to the individual's interest in not being compelled to testify against himself. When neither the initial nor the subsequent admission is coerced, little justification exists for permitting the highly probative evidence of a voluntary confession to be irretrievably lost to the factfinder.

We must conclude that, absent deliberately coercive or improper tactics in obtaining the initial statement, the mere fact that a suspect has made an unwarned admission does not warrant a presumption of compulsion. A subsequent administration of *Miranda* warnings to a suspect who has given a voluntary but unwarned statement ordinarily should suffice to remove the conditions that precluded admission of the earlier statement. In such circumstances, the finder of fact may reasonably conclude that the suspect made a rational and intelligent choice whether to waive or invoke his rights.

Justice BRENNAN, with whom Justice MARSHALL joins, dissenting.

The Self-Incrimination Clause of the Fifth Amendment guarantees every individual that, if taken into official custody, he shall be informed of important constitutional rights and be given the opportunity knowingly and voluntarily to waive those rights before being interrogated about suspected wrongdoing. Miranda v. Arizona. This guarantee embodies our society's conviction that "no system of criminal justice can, or should, survive if it comes to depend for its continued effectiveness on the citizens' abdication through unawareness of their constitutional rights." Escobedo v. Illinois (1964).

Even while purporting to reaffirm these constitutional guarantees, the Court has engaged of late in a studied campaign to strip the *Miranda* decision piecemeal and to undermine the rights *Miranda* sought to secure. Today's decision not only extends this effort a further step, but delivers a potentially crippling blow to *Miranda* and the ability of courts to safeguard the rights of persons accused of crime. For at least with respect to successive confessions, the Court today appears to strip remedies for *Miranda* violations of the "fruit of the poisonous tree" doctrine prohibiting the use of evidence presumptively derived from official illegality.

Two major premises undergird the Court's decision. The Court rejects as nothing more than "speculative" the long-recognized presumption that an illegally extracted confession causes the accused to confess again out of the mistaken belief that he already has sealed his fate, and it condemns as "extravagant" the requirement that the prosecution affirmatively rebut the presumption before the subsequent confession may be admitted. The Court instead adopts a new rule that, so long as the accused is given the usual *Miranda* warnings before further interrogation, the taint of a previous confession obtained in violation of *Miranda* "ordinarily" must be viewed as automatically dissipated.

In the alternative, the Court asserts that neither the Fifth Amendment itself nor the judicial policy of deterring illegal police conduct requires the suppression of the "fruits" of a confession obtained in violation of *Miranda*, reasoning that to do otherwise would interfere with "legitimate law enforcement activity." As the Court surely understands, however, "[t]o forbid the direct use of methods . . . but to put no curb on their full indirect use would only invite the very methods deemed 'inconsistent with ethical standards and destructive of personal liberty.'" If violations of constitutional rights may not be remedied through the well-established rules respecting derivative evidence, as the Court has held today, there is a critical danger that the rights will be rendered nothing more than a mere "form of words."

The Court's decision says much about the way the Court currently goes about implementing its agenda. In imposing its new rule, for example, the Court mischaracterizes our precedents, obfuscates the central issues, and altogether ignores the practical realities of custodial interrogation that have led nearly every lower court to reject its simplistic reasoning. Moreover, the Court adopts startling and unprecedented methods of construing constitutional guarantees. Finally the Court reaches out once again to address issues not before us. For example, although the State of Oregon has conceded that the arresting officers broke the law in this case, the Court goes out of its way to suggest that they may have been objectively justified in doing so.

Today's decision, in short, threatens disastrous consequences far beyond the outcome in this case. The threshold question is this: What effect should an admission or confession of guilt obtained in violation of an accused's *Miranda* rights be presumed to have upon the voluntariness of subsequent confessions that are preceded by *Miranda* warnings? The correct approach, administered for almost 20 years by most courts with no untoward results, is to presume that an admission or confession obtained in violation of *Miranda* taints a subsequent confession unless the prosecution can show that the taint is so attenuated as to justify admission of the subsequent confession. Until today the Court has recognized that the dissipation inquiry requires the prosecution to demonstrate that the official illegality did not taint the challenged confession, and we have rejected the simplistic view that abstract notions of "free will" are alone sufficient to dissipate the challenged taint.

The Supreme Court returned to the issue of when information gained in violation of *Miranda* can be used as evidence in two decisions in 2004. In one, Missouri v. Seibert, the Court held that subsequent statements must be excluded, even if *Miranda* warnings were given before the statements were repeated. But in United States v. Patane, the Court said that tangible evidence could be introduced even if it resulted from violations of *Miranda*. In reading these cases, it is important to consider whether there is a meaningful distinction between these two cases. Interestingly, eight of the nine Justices saw no difference; only Justice Kennedy was in the majority in both decisions. Four Justices—Chief Justice Rehnquist and Justices O'Connor, Scalia, and

Thomas—would have allowed both the statement in *Seibert* and the gun in *Patane* to be admitted notwithstanding the failure to properly administer *Miranda* warnings. On the other hand, there also were four Justices—Justices Stevens, Souter, Ginsburg, and Breyer—who would have excluded both as the fruits of violations of *Miranda*. Justice Kennedy, though, determined the outcome of both cases by voting for the exclusion of the subsequent statement in *Seibert*, but not the gun in *Patane*. Also, in considering Missouri v. Seibert, it is important to consider whether there is a meaningful distinction between it and the earlier decision in Oregon v. Elstad.

MISSOURI v. SEIBERT
542 U.S. 600 (2004)

Justice SOUTER announced the judgment of the Court and delivered an opinion, in which Justice STEVENS, Justice GINSBURG, and Justice BREYER join.

This case tests a police protocol for custodial interrogation that calls for giving no warnings of the rights to silence and counsel until interrogation has produced a confession. Although such a statement is generally inadmissible, since taken in violation of Miranda v. Arizona (1966), the interrogating officer follows it with *Miranda* warnings and then leads the suspect to cover the same ground a second time. The question here is the admissibility of the repeated statement. Because this midstream recitation of warnings after interrogation and unwarned confession could not effectively comply with *Miranda*'s constitutional requirement, we hold that a statement repeated after a warning in such circumstances is inadmissible.

I

Respondent Patrice Seibert's 12-year-old son Jonathan had cerebral palsy, and when he died in his sleep she feared charges of neglect because of bedsores on his body. In her presence, two of her teenage sons and two of their friends devised a plan to conceal the facts surrounding Jonathan's death by incinerating his body in the course of burning the family's mobile home, in which they planned to leave Donald Rector, a mentally ill teenager living with the family, to avoid any appearance that Jonathan had been unattended. Seibert's son Darian and a friend set the fire, and Donald died.

Five days later, the police awakened Seibert at 3 A.M. at a hospital where Darian was being treated for burns. In arresting her, Officer Kevin Clinton followed instructions from Rolla, Missouri, Officer Richard Hanrahan that he refrain from giving *Miranda* warnings. After Seibert had been taken to the police station and left alone in an interview room for 15 to 20 minutes, Officer Hanrahan questioned her without *Miranda* warnings for 30 to 40 minutes, squeezing her arm and repeating "Donald was also to die in his sleep." After Seibert finally admitted she knew Donald was meant to die in the fire, she was given a 20-minute coffee and cigarette break. Officer Hanrahan then turned on a tape recorder, gave Seibert the *Miranda* warnings, and obtained a signed waiver of rights from her. He resumed the questioning with "Ok, 'Trice, we've been talking for a little while about what happened on Wednesday the twelfth, haven't we?", and confronted her with her prewarning statements:

Hanrahan. Now, in discussion you told us, you told us that there was a[n] understanding about Donald.
Seibert. Yes.
Hanrahan. Did that take place earlier that morning?
Seibert. Yes.
Hanrahan. And what was the understanding about Donald?
Seibert. If they could get him out of the trailer, to take him out of the trailer.
Hanrahan. And if they couldn't?
Seibert. I, I never even thought about it. I just figured they would.
Hanrahan. Trice, didn't you tell me that he was supposed to die in his sleep?
Seibert. If that would happen, 'cause he was on that new medicine, you know'. . . .
Hanrahan. The Prozac? And it makes him sleepy. So he was supposed to die in his sleep?
Seibert. Yes.

After being charged with first-degree murder for her role in Donald's death, Seibert sought to exclude both her prewarning and postwarning statements. At the suppression hearing, Officer Hanrahan testified that he made a "conscious decision" to withhold *Miranda* warnings, thus resorting to an interrogation technique he had been taught: question first, then give the warnings, and then repeat the question "until I get the answer that she's already provided once." He acknowledged that Seibert's ultimate statement was "largely a repeat of information . . . obtained" prior to the warning.

The trial court suppressed the prewarning statement but admitted the responses given after the *Miranda* recitation. A jury convicted Seibert of second degree murder. On appeal, the Missouri Court of Appeals affirmed, treating this case as indistinguishable from Oregon v. Elstad (1985). The Supreme Court of Missouri reversed, holding that "[i]n the circumstances here, where the interrogation was nearly continuous, . . . the second statement, clearly the product of the invalid first statement, should have been suppressed."

[II]

The technique of interrogating in successive, unwarned and warned phases raises a new challenge to *Miranda*. Although we have no statistics on the frequency of this practice, it is not confined to Rolla, Missouri. An officer of that police department testified that the strategy of withholding *Miranda* warnings until after interrogating and drawing out a confession was promoted not only by his own department, but by a national police training organization and other departments in which he had worked. Consistently with the officer's testimony, the Police Law Institute, for example, instructs that "officers may conduct a two-stage interrogation. . . . At any point during the pre-*Miranda* interrogation, usually after arrestees have confessed, officers may then read the *Miranda* warnings and ask for a waiver. If the arrestees waive their *Miranda* rights, officers will be able to repeat any subsequent incriminating statements later in court."

The object of question-first is to render *Miranda* warnings ineffective by waiting for a particularly opportune time to give them, after the suspect has already confessed. Just as "no talismanic incantation [is] required to satisfy [*Miranda's*] strictures," California v. Prysock (1981), it would be absurd to think that mere recitation of the litany suffices to satisfy *Miranda* in every conceivable circumstance. The threshold issue when interrogators question first and warn later is thus whether it would be reasonable to find that in these circumstances the warnings could function "effectively" as *Miranda* requires. Could the warnings effectively advise the suspect that he had a real choice about giving an admissible statement at that juncture? Could they reasonably convey that he could choose to stop talking even if he had talked earlier? For unless the warnings could place a suspect who has just been interrogated in a position to make such an informed choice, there is no practical justification for accepting the formal warnings as compliance with *Miranda*, or for treating the second stage of interrogation as distinct from the first, unwarned and inadmissible segment.

There is no doubt about the answer that proponents of question-first give to this question about the effectiveness of warnings given only after successful interrogation, and we think their answer is correct. By any objective measure, applied to circumstances exemplified here, it is likely that if the interrogators employ the technique of withholding warnings until after interrogation succeeds in eliciting a confession, the warnings will be ineffective in preparing the suspect for successive interrogation, close in time and similar in content. After all, the reason that question-first is catching on is as obvious as its manifest purpose, which is to get a confession the suspect would not make if he understood his rights at the outset; the sensible underlying assumption is that with one confession in hand before the warnings, the interrogator can count on getting its duplicate, with trifling additional trouble. Upon hearing warnings only in the aftermath of interrogation and just after making a confession, a suspect would hardly think he had a genuine right to remain silent, let alone persist in so believing once the police began to lead him over the same ground again. A more likely reaction on a suspect's part would be perplexity about the reason for discussing rights at that point, bewilderment being an unpromising frame of mind for knowledgeable decision. What is worse, telling a suspect that "anything you say can and will be used against you," without expressly excepting the statement just given, could lead to an entirely reasonable inference that what he has just said will be used, with subsequent silence being of no avail. Thus, when *Miranda* warnings are inserted in the midst of coordinated and continuing interrogation, they are likely to mislead and "depriv[e] a defendant of knowledge essential to his ability to understand the nature of his rights and the consequences of abandoning them." By the same token, it would ordinarily be unrealistic to treat two spates of integrated and proximately conducted questioning as independent interrogations subject to independent evaluation simply because *Miranda* warnings formally punctuate them in the middle.

Missouri argues that a confession repeated at the end of an interrogation sequence envisioned in a question-first strategy is admissible on the authority of Oregon v. Elstad (1985), but the argument disfigures that case. In *Elstad*, the police went to the young suspect's house to take him into custody on a charge of burglary. Before the arrest, one officer spoke with the suspect's mother, while the other one joined the suspect in a "brief stop in the living room," where the officer said he "felt" the young man was involved in a burglary. The suspect acknowledged he had been at the scene. This Court noted that the pause in the living room "was not to interrogate the suspect but to notify his mother of the reason for his arrest," and described the incident as having "none of the ear-marks of coercion." The Court, indeed, took care to mention that the officer's initial failure to warn was an "oversight" that "may have been the result of confusion as to whether the brief exchange qualified as 'custodial interrogation' or . . . may simply have reflected . . . reluctance to initiate an alarming police procedure before [an officer] had spoken with respondent's mother." At the outset of a later and systematic station house interrogation going well beyond the scope of the laconic prior admission, the suspect was given *Miranda* warnings and made a full confession. In holding the second statement admissible and voluntary, *Elstad* rejected the "cat out of the bag" theory that any short, earlier admission, obtained in arguably innocent neglect of *Miranda*, determined the character of the later, warned confession; on the facts of that case, the Court thought any causal connection between the first and second responses to the police was "speculative and attenuated." Although the *Elstad* Court expressed no explicit conclusion about either officer's state of mind, it is fair to read *Elstad* as treating the living room conversation as a good-faith *Miranda* mistake, not only open to correction by careful warnings before systematic questioning in that particular case, but posing no threat to warn-first practice generally.

The contrast between *Elstad* and this case reveals a series of relevant facts that bear on whether *Miranda* warnings delivered midstream could be effective enough to accomplish their object: the completeness and detail of the questions and answers in the first round of interrogation, the overlapping content of the two statements, the timing and setting of the first and the second, the continuity of police personnel, and the degree to which the interrogator's questions treated the second round as continuous with the first. In *Elstad*, it was not unreasonable to see the occasion for questioning at the station house as pre-senting a markedly different experience from the short conversation at home; since a reasonable person in the suspect's shoes could have seen the station house questioning as a new and distinct experience, the *Miranda* warnings could have made sense as presenting a genuine choice whether to follow up on the earlier admission.

At the opposite extreme are the facts here, which by any objective measure reveal a police strategy adapted to undermine the *Miranda* warnings. The unwarned interrogation was conducted in the station house, and the question-ing was systematic, exhaustive, and managed with psychological skill. When the police were finished there was little, if anything, of incriminating potential left unsaid. The warned phase of questioning proceeded after a pause of only 15 to 20 minutes, in the same place as the unwarned segment. When the same officer who had conducted the first phase recited the *Miranda* warnings, he said nothing to counter the probable misimpression that the advice that anything Seibert said could be used against her also applied to the details of the incul-patory statement previously elicited. In particular, the police did not advise that her prior statement could not be used. Nothing was said or done to dispel the oddity of warning about legal rights to silence and counsel right after the police had led her through a systematic interrogation, and any uncertainty on her part about a right to stop talking about matters previously discussed would only have been aggravated by the way Officer Hanrahan set the scene by saying "we've been talking for a little while about what happened on Wednesday the twelfth, haven't we?" The impression that the further questioning was a mere continu-ation of the earlier questions and responses was fostered by references back to the confession already given. It would have been reasonable to regard the two sessions as parts of a continuum, in which it would have been unnatural to refuse to repeat at the second stage what had been said before. These circumstances must be seen as challenging the comprehensibility and efficacy of the *Miranda* warnings to the point that a reasonable person in the suspect's shoes would not have understood them to convey a message that she retained a choice about continuing to talk.

Strategists dedicated to draining the substance out of *Miranda* cannot accomplish by training instructions what *Dickerson* held Congress could not do by statute. Because the question-first tactic effectively threatens to thwart *Miranda*'s purpose of reducing the risk that a coerced confession would be admitted, and because the facts here do not reasonably support a conclusion that the warnings given could have served their purpose, Seibert's postwarning statements are inadmissible.

Justice BREYER, concurring.

In my view, the following simple rule should apply to the two-stage interrogation technique: Courts should exclude the "fruits" of the initial unwarned questioning unless the failure to warn was in good faith. I believe this is a sound and workable approach to the problem this case presents. Prosecutors and judges have long understood how to apply the "fruits" approach, which they use in other areas of law. And in the workaday world of criminal law enforcement the administrative simplicity of the familiar has significant advantages over a more complex exclusionary rule.

Justice KENNEDY, concurring in the judgment.

The interrogation technique used in this case is designed to circumvent Miranda v. Arizona (1966). It undermines the *Miranda* warning and obscures its meaning. The plurality opinion is correct to conclude that statements obtained through the use of this technique are inadmissible. Although I agree with much in the careful and convincing opinion for the plurality, my approach does differ in some respects, requiring this separate statement.

In my view, *Elstad* was correct in its reasoning and its result. *Elstad* reflects a balanced and pragmatic approach to enforcement of the *Miranda* warning. An officer may not realize that a suspect is in custody and warnings are required. The officer may not plan to question the suspect or may be waiting for a more appropriate time. Skilled investigators often interview suspects multiple times, and good police work may involve referring to prior statements to test their veracity or to refresh recollection. In light of these realities it would be extravagant to treat the presence of one statement that cannot be admitted under *Miranda* as sufficient reason to prohibit subsequent statements preceded by a proper warning.

This case presents different considerations. The police used a two-step questioning technique based on a deliberate violation of *Miranda*. The *Miranda* warning was withheld to obscure both the practical and legal significance of the admonition when finally given. The strategy is based on the assumption that *Miranda* warnings will tend to mean less when recited midinterrogation, after inculpatory statements have already been obtained. This tactic relies on an intentional misrepresentation of the protection that *Miranda* offers and does not serve any legitimate objectives that might otherwise justify its use.

Further, the interrogating officer here relied on the defendant's prewarning statement to obtain the postwarning statement used against her at trial. The postwarning interview resembled a cross-examination. The officer confronted the defendant with her inadmissible prewarning statements and pushed her to acknowledge them. This shows the temptations for abuse inherent in the two-step technique. Reference to the prewarning statement was an implicit suggestion that the mere repetition of the earlier statement was not independently incriminating. The implicit suggestion was false.

The technique used in this case distorts the meaning of *Miranda* and furthers no legitimate countervailing interest. The *Miranda* rule would be frustrated were we to allow police to undermine its meaning and effect. The technique simply creates too high a risk that postwarning statements will be obtained when a suspect was deprived of "knowledge essential to his ability to understand the nature of his rights and the consequences of abandoning them." When an interrogator uses this deliberate, two-step strategy, predicated upon violating *Miranda* during an extended interview, postwarning statements that are related to the substance of prewarning statements must be excluded absent specific, curative steps.

The plurality concludes that whenever a two-stage interview occurs, admissibility of the postwarning statement should depend on "whether [the] *Miranda* warnings delivered midstream could have been effective enough to accomplish their object" given the specific facts of the case. This test envisions an objective inquiry from the perspective of the suspect, and applies in the case of both intentional and unintentional two-stage interrogations. In my view, this test cuts too broadly. *Miranda*'s clarity is one of its strengths, and a multifactor test that applies to every two-stage interrogation may serve to undermine that clarity. I would apply a narrower test applicable only in the infrequent case, such as we have here, in which the two-step interrogation technique was used in a calculated way to undermine the *Miranda* warning.

The admissibility of postwarning statements should continue to be governed by the principles of *Elstad* unless the deliberate two-step strategy was employed. If the deliberate two-step strategy has been used, postwarning statements that are related to the substance of prewarning statements must be excluded unless curative measures are taken before the postwarning statement is made. Curative measures should be designed to ensure that a reasonable person in the suspect's situation would understand the import and effect of the *Miranda* warning and of the *Miranda* waiver. For example, a substantial break in time and circumstances between the prewarning statement and the *Miranda* warning may suffice in most circumstances, as it allows the accused to distinguish the two contexts and appreciate that the interrogation has taken a new turn. Alternatively, an additional warning that explains the likely inadmissibility of the prewarning custodial statement may be sufficient. No curative steps were taken in this case, however, so the postwarning statements are inadmissible and the conviction cannot stand.

Justice O'CONNOR, with whom THE CHIEF JUSTICE, Justice SCALIA, and Justice THOMAS join, dissenting.

The plurality devours Oregon v. Elstad (1985), even as it accuses petitioner's argument of "disfigur[ing]" that decision. I believe that we are bound by *Elstad* to reach a different result.

I believe that the approach espoused by Justice Kennedy is ill advised. Justice Kennedy would extend *Miranda*'s exclusionary rule to any case in which the use of the "two-step interrogation technique" was "deliberate" or "calculated." This approach untethers the analysis from facts knowable to, and therefore having any potential directly to affect, the suspect. Far from promoting "clarity," the approach will add a third step to the suppression inquiry. In virtually every two-stage interrogation case, in addition to addressing the standard *Miranda* and voluntariness questions, courts will be forced to conduct the kind of difficult, state-of-mind inquiry that we normally take pains to avoid.

UNITED STATES v. PATANE

542 U.S. 630 (2004)

Justice THOMAS announced the judgment of the Court and delivered an opinion, in which THE CHIEF JUSTICE and Justice SCALIA join.

In this case we must decide whether a failure to give a suspect the warnings prescribed by Miranda v. Arizona (1966), requires suppression of the physical fruits of the suspect's unwarned but voluntary statements. Because the *Miranda* rule protects against violations of the Self-Incrimination Clause, which, in turn, is not implicated by the introduction at trial of physical evidence resulting from voluntary statements, we answer the question presented in the negative.

I

In June 2001, respondent, Samuel Francis Patane, was arrested for harassing his ex-girlfriend, Linda O'Donnell. He was released on bond, subject to a temporary restraining order that prohibited him from contacting O'Donnell. Respondent apparently violated the restraining order by attempting to telephone O'Donnell. On June 6, 2001, Officer Tracy Fox of the Colorado Springs Police Department began to investigate the matter. On the same day, a county probation officer informed an agent of the Bureau of Alcohol, Tobacco and Firearms (ATF), that respondent, a convicted felon, illegally possessed a .40 Glock pistol. The ATF relayed this information to Detective Josh Benner, who worked closely with the ATF. Together, Detective Benner and Officer Fox proceeded to respondent's residence.

After reaching the residence and inquiring into respondent's attempts to contact O'Donnell, Officer Fox arrested respondent for violating the restraining order. Detective Benner attempted to advise respondent of his *Miranda* rights but got no further than the right to remain silent. At that point, respondent interrupted, asserting that he knew his rights, and neither officer attempted to complete the warning.[11]

Detective Benner then asked respondent about the Glock. Respondent was initially reluctant to discuss the matter, stating: "I am not sure I should tell you anything about the Glock because I don't want you to take it away from me." Detective Benner persisted, and respondent told him that the pistol was in his

---

11. The Government concedes that respondent's answers to subsequent on-the-scene questioning are inadmissible at trial under Miranda v. Arizona despite the partial warning and respondent's assertions that he knew his rights. [Footnote by the Court.]

bedroom. Respondent then gave Detective Benner permission to retrieve the pistol. Detective Benner found the pistol and seized it.

A grand jury indicted respondent for possession of a firearm by a convicted felon, in violation of 18 U.S.C. §922(g)(1). The District Court granted respondent's motion to suppress the firearm, reasoning that the officers lacked probable cause to arrest respondent for violating the restraining order. It therefore declined to rule on respondent's alternative argument that the gun should be suppressed as the fruit of an unwarned statement.

The Court of Appeals reversed the District Court's ruling with respect to probable cause but affirmed the suppression order on respondent's alternative theory.

As we explain below, the *Miranda* rule is a prophylactic employed to protect against violations of the Self-Incrimination Clause. The Self-Incrimination Clause, however, is not implicated by the admission into evidence of the physical fruit of a voluntary statement. Accordingly, there is no justification for extending the *Miranda* rule to this context. And just as the Self-Incrimination Clause primarily focuses on the criminal trial, so too does the *Miranda* rule. The *Miranda* rule is not a code of police conduct, and police do not violate the Constitution (or even the *Miranda* rule, for that matter) by mere failures to warn. For this reason, the exclusionary rule articulated in cases such as *Wong Sun* does not apply.

II

The Self-Incrimination Clause provides: "No person . . . shall be compelled in any criminal case to be a witness against himself." We need not decide here the precise boundaries of the Clause's protection. For present purposes, it suffices to note that the core protection afforded by the Self-Incrimination Clause is a prohibition on compelling a criminal defendant to testify against himself at trial. To be sure, the Court has recognized and applied several prophylactic rules designed to protect the core privilege against self-incrimination. For example, although the text of the Self-Incrimination Clause at least suggests that "its coverage [is limited to] compelled testimony that is used against the defendant in the trial itself," potential suspects may, at times, assert the privilege in proceedings in which answers might be used to incriminate them in a subsequent criminal case.

Similarly, in *Miranda*, the Court concluded that the possibility of coercion inherent in custodial interrogations unacceptably raises the risk that a suspect's privilege against self-incrimination might be violated. To protect against this danger, the *Miranda* rule creates a presumption of coercion, in the absence of specific warnings, that is generally irrebuttable for purposes of the prosecution's case in chief.

But because these prophylactic rules (including the *Miranda* rule) necessarily sweep beyond the actual protections of the Self-Incrimination Clause, any further extension of these rules must be justified by its necessity for the protection of the actual right against compelled self-incrimination.

Our cases also make clear the related point that a mere failure to give *Miranda* warnings does not, by itself, violate a suspect's constitutional rights or even the *Miranda* rule. It follows that police do not violate a suspect's constitutional rights (or the *Miranda* rule) by negligent or even deliberate failures to provide the suspect with the full panoply of warnings prescribed by *Miranda*. Potential violations occur, if at all, only upon the admission of unwarned statements into evidence at trial. And, at that point, "[t]he exclusion of unwarned statements . . . is a complete and sufficient remedy" for any perceived *Miranda* violation.

Thus, unlike unreasonable searches under the Fourth Amendment or actual violations of the Due Process Clause or the Self-Incrimination Clause, there is, with respect to mere failures to warn, nothing to deter. There is therefore no reason to apply the "fruit of the poisonous tree" doctrine. It is not for this Court to impose its preferred police practices on either federal law enforcement officials or their state counterparts.

The Court of Appeals ascribed significance to the fact that, in this case, there might be "little [practical] difference between [respondent's] confessional statement" and the actual physical evidence. But, putting policy aside, we have held that "[t]he word 'witness' in the constitutional text limits the" scope of the Self-Incrimination Clause to testimonial evidence. The Constitution itself makes the distinction. And although it is true that the Court requires the exclusion of the physical fruit of actually coerced statements, it must be remembered that statements taken without sufficient *Miranda* warnings are presumed to have been coerced only for certain purposes and then only when necessary to protect the privilege against self-incrimination. For the reasons discussed above, we decline to extend that presumption further.

Justice KENNEDY, with whom Justice O'CONNOR joins, concurring in the judgment.

In Oregon v. Elstad (1984) and Harris v. New York (1971), evidence obtained following an unwarned interrogation was held admissible. This result was based in large part on our recognition that the concerns underlying the Miranda v. Arizona (1966), rule must be accommodated to other objectives of the criminal justice system. Here, it is sufficient to note that the Government presents an even stronger case for admitting the evidence obtained as the result of Patane's unwarned statement. Admission of nontestimonial physical fruits (the Glock in this case), even more so than the postwarning statements to the police in *Elstad* and Michigan v. Tucker (1974), does not run the risk of admitting into trial an accused's coerced incriminating statements against himself. In light of the important probative value of reliable physical evidence, it is doubtful that exclusion can be justified by a deterrence rationale sensitive to both law enforcement interests and a suspect's rights during an in-custody interrogation. Unlike the plurality, however, I find it unnecessary to decide whether the detective's failure to give Patane the full *Miranda* warnings should be characterized as a violation of the *Miranda* rule itself, or whether there is "[any]thing to deter" so long as the unwarned statements are not later introduced at trial.

Justice SOUTER, with whom Justice STEVENS and Justice GINSBURG join, dissenting.

The plurality repeatedly says that the Fifth Amendment does not address the admissibility of nontestimonial evidence, an overstatement that is beside the point. The issue actually presented today is whether courts should apply the fruit of the poisonous tree doctrine lest we create an incentive for the police to omit *Miranda* warnings, before custodial interrogation. In closing their eyes to the consequences of giving an evidentiary advantage to those who ignore *Miranda,* the plurality adds an important inducement for interrogators to ignore the rule in that case.

Miranda rested on insight into the inherently coercive character of custodial interrogation and the inherently difficult exercise of assessing the voluntariness of any confession resulting from it. Unless the police give the prescribed warnings meant to counter the coercive atmosphere, a custodial confession is inadmissible, there being no need for the previous time-consuming and difficult enquiry into voluntariness. That inducement to forestall involuntary statements and troublesome issues of fact can only atrophy if we turn around and recognize an evidentiary benefit when an unwarned statement leads investigators to tangible evidence. There is, of course, a price for excluding evidence, but the Fifth Amendment is worth a price, and in the absence of a very good reason, the logic of *Miranda* should be followed: a *Miranda* violation raises a presumption of coercion, and the Fifth Amendment privilege against compelled self-incrimination extends to the exclusion of derivative evidence. That should be the end of this case.

There is no way to read this case except as an unjustifiable invitation to law enforcement officers to flout *Miranda* when there may be physical evidence to be gained. The incentive is an odd one, coming from the Court on the same day it decides Missouri v. Seibert.

Justice BREYER, dissenting.

For reasons similar to those set forth in Justice Souter's dissent and in my concurring opinion in Missouri v. Seibert, I would extend to this context the "fruit of the poisonous tree" approach, which I believe the Court has come close to adopting in *Seibert.* Under that approach, courts would exclude physical evidence derived from unwarned questioning unless the failure to provide Miranda v. Arizona warnings was in good faith.

5.   *What Are the Exceptions to* **Miranda?**

Under what circumstances can a statement from a criminal defendant be used against him or her at trial despite the failure to properly administer *Miranda* warnings where they are required?. There are four major exceptions:

(1)   if the statements are used for impeachment purposes;
(2)   if the statements were obtained in an emergency situation;
(3)   if the statements were made at the time of booking the suspect in response to routine questions by the police; or
(4)   if the suspect waived his or her rights under *Miranda.*

a.   Impeachment

In Harris v. New York, the Court held that statements gained from a criminal defendant are admissible for impeachment purposes if the defendant chooses to testify at trial. In reading *Harris*, it is important to consider the competing views of *Miranda* and the exclusionary rule. Chief Justice Burger's majority opinion emphasizes the need to protect the integrity of trials by allowing prior statements to the police to be used to impeach a criminal defendant who takes the stand and does not tell the truth. Justice Brennan's dissent, by contrast, focuses especially on the concern that allowing impermissibly obtained statements to be used for impeachment will give police an incentive to ignore *Miranda*, knowing that the statements they obtain still can be used for impeachment.[12]

HARRIS v. NEW YORK
401 U.S. 222 (1971)

Chief Justice BURGER delivered the opinion of the Court.

We granted the writ in this case to consider petitioner's claim that a statement made by him to police under circumstances rendering it inadmissible to establish the prosecution's case in chief under Miranda v. Arizona (1966), may not be used to impeach his credibility.

The State of New York charged petitioner in a two-count indictment with twice selling heroin to an undercover police officer. At a subsequent jury trial the officer was the State's chief witness, and he testified as to details of the two sales. A second officer verified collateral details of the sales, and a third offered testimony about the chemical analysis of the heroin.

Petitioner took the stand in his own defense. He admitted knowing the undercover police officer but denied a sale on January 4, 1966. He admitted making a sale of contents of a glassine bag to the officer on January 6 but claimed it was baking powder and part of a scheme to defraud the purchaser.

On cross-examination petitioner was asked seriatim whether he had made specified statements to the police immediately following his arrest on January 7 — statements that partially contradicted petitioner's direct testimony at trial. In response to the cross-examination, petitioner testified that he could not remember virtually any of the questions or answers recited by the prosecutor. At the request of petitioner's counsel the written statement from which the prosecutor had read questions and answers in his impeaching process was placed in the record for possible use on appeal; the statement was not shown to the jury.

The trial judge instructed the jury that the statements attributed to petitioner by the prosecution could be considered only in passing on petitioner's credibility and not as evidence of guilt. In closing summations both counsel argued the substance of the impeaching statements. The jury then found petitioner guilty on the second count of the indictment. The New York Court of Appeals affirmed in a per curiam opinion.

At trial the prosecution made no effort in its case in chief to use the statements allegedly made by petitioner, conceding that they were inadmissible under Miranda v. Arizona (1966). The transcript of the interrogation used in the

---

12. For an excellent discussion of police intentionally questioning "outside *Miranda*," *see* Charles Weisselberg, *Saving Miranda*, 84 Cornell L. Rev. 109 (1998) (collecting California training materials encouraging questioning "outside *Miranda*").

impeachment, but not given to the jury, shows that no warning of a right to appointed counsel was given before questions were put to petitioner when he was taken into custody. Petitioner makes no claim that the statements made to the police were coerced or involuntary.

Some comments in the *Miranda* opinion can indeed be read as indicating a bar to use of an uncounseled statement for any purpose, but discussion of that issue was not at all necessary to the Court's holding and cannot be regarded as controlling. *Miranda* barred the prosecution from making its case with statements of an accused made while in custody prior to having or effectively waiving counsel. It does not follow from *Miranda* that evidence inadmissible against an accused in the prosecution's case in chief is barred for all purposes, provided of course that the trustworthiness of the evidence satisfies legal standards.

Petitioner's testimony in his own behalf concerning the events of January 7 contrasted sharply with what he told the police shortly after his arrest. The impeachment process here undoubtedly provided valuable aid to the jury in assessing petitioner's credibility, and the benefits of this process should not be lost, in our view, because of the speculative possibility that impermissible police conduct will be encouraged thereby. Assuming that the exclusionary rule has a deterrent effect on proscribed police conduct, sufficient deterrence flows when the evidence in question is made unavailable to the prosecution in its case in chief.

Every criminal defendant is privileged to testify in his own defense, or to refuse to do so. But that privilege cannot be construed to include the right to commit perjury. Having voluntarily taken the stand, petitioner was under an obligation to speak truthfully and accurately, and the prosecution here did no more than utilize the traditional truth-testing devices of the adversary process. Had inconsistent statements been made by the accused to some third person, it could hardly be contended that the conflict could not be laid before the jury by way of cross-examination and impeachment.

The shield provided by *Miranda* cannot be perverted into a license to use perjury by way of a defense, free from the risk of confrontation with prior inconsistent utterances. We hold, therefore, that petitioner's credibility was appropriately impeached by use of his earlier conflicting statements.

Justice BRENNAN, with whom Justice DOUGLAS and Justice MARSHALL join, dissenting.

It is conceded that the question-and-answer statement used to impeach petitioner's direct testimony was, under Miranda v. Arizona (1966), constitutionally inadmissible as part of the State's direct case against petitioner. I think that the Constitution also denied the State the use of the statement on cross-examination to impeach the credibility of petitioner's testimony given in his own defense.

The prosecution's use of the tainted statement cuts down on the privilege by making its assertion costly. Thus, the accused is denied an "unfettered" choice when the decision whether to take the stand is burdened by the risk that an illegally obtained prior statement may be introduced to impeach his direct testimony denying complicity in the crime charged against him. We settled this proposition in *Miranda* where we said:

An incriminating statement is as incriminating when used to impeach credibility as it is when used as direct proof of guilt and no constitutional distinction can legitimately be drawn. The objective of deterring improper police conduct is only part of the larger objective of safeguarding the integrity of our adversary system. The "essential mainstay" of that system, is the privilege against self-incrimination, which for that reason has occupied a central place in our jurisprudence since before the Nation's birth. Moreover, "we may view the historical development of the privilege as one which groped for the proper scope of governmental power over the citizen. . . . All these policies point to one overriding thought: the constitutional foundation underlying the privilege is the respect a government . . . must accord to the dignity and integrity of its citizens.

These values are plainly jeopardized if an exception against admission of tainted statements is made for those used for impeachment purposes. Moreover, it is monstrous that courts should aid or abet the law-breaking police officer. It is abiding truth that "[N]othing can destroy a government more quickly than its failure to observe its own laws, or worse, its disregard of the charter of its own existence." Mapp v. Ohio (1961). Thus even to the extent that *Miranda* was aimed at deterring police practices in disregard of the Constitution, I fear that today's holding will seriously undermine the achievement of that objective. The Court today tells the police that they may freely interrogate an accused incommunicado and without counsel and know that although any statement they obtain in violation of *Miranda* cannot be used on the State's direct case, it may be introduced if the defendant has the temerity to testify in his own defense. This goes far toward undoing much of the progress made in conforming police methods to the Constitution.

b. Emergencies

In New York v. Quarles, the Supreme Court held that statements obtained by police from suspects during emergency situations could be used against a criminal defendant even if *Miranda* warnings were not properly administered. In assessing *Quarles*, it is important to consider whether there should be such an exception and, if so, what is sufficient to constitute such an emergency.

NEW YORK v. QUARLES
467 U.S. 649 (1984)

Justice REHNQUIST delivered the opinion of the Court.

Respondent Benjamin Quarles was charged in the New York trial court with criminal possession of a weapon. The trial court suppressed the gun in question, and a statement made by respondent, because the statement was obtained by police before they read respondent his "*Miranda* rights." That ruling was affirmed on appeal through the New York Court of Appeals. We granted certiorari and we now reverse. We conclude that under the circumstances involved in this case, overriding considerations of public safety justify the officer's failure to provide *Miranda* warnings before he asked questions devoted to locating the abandoned weapon.

On September 11, 1980, at approximately 12:30 A.M., Officer Frank Kraft and Officer Sal Scarring were on road patrol in Queens, N.Y., when a young woman approached their car. She told them that she had just been raped by a black male, approximately six feet tall, who was wearing a black jacket with the name "Big Ben" printed in yellow letters on the back. She told the officers that the man had just entered an A & P supermarket located nearby and that the man was carrying a gun.

The officers drove the woman to the supermarket, and Officer Kraft entered the store while Officer Scarring radioed for assistance. Officer Kraft quickly spotted respondent, who matched the description given by the woman, approaching a checkout counter. Apparently upon seeing the officer, respondent turned and ran toward the rear of the store, and Officer Kraft pursued him with a drawn gun. When respondent turned the corner at the end of an aisle, Officer Kraft lost sight of him for several seconds, and upon regaining sight of respondent, ordered him to stop and put his hands over his head.

Although more than three other officers had arrived on the scene by that time, Officer Kraft was the first to reach respondent. He frisked him and discovered that he was wearing a shoulder holster which was then empty. After handcuffing him, Officer Kraft asked him where the gun was. Respondent nodded in the direction of some empty cartons and responded, "the gun is over there." Officer Kraft thereafter retrieved a loaded .38-caliber revolver from one of the cartons, formally placed respondent under arrest, and read him his *Miranda* rights from a printed card. Respondent indicated that he would be willing to answer questions without an attorney present. Officer Kraft then asked respondent if he owned the gun and where he had purchased it. Respondent answered that he did own it and that he had purchased it in Miami, Fla.

In the subsequent prosecution of respondent for criminal possession of a weapon, the judge excluded the statement, "the gun is over there," and the gun because the officer had not given respondent the warnings required by our decision in Miranda v. Arizona (1966), before asking him where the gun was located. The judge excluded the other statements about respondent's ownership of the gun and the place of purchase, as evidence tainted by the prior *Miranda* violation.

In this case we have before us no claim that respondent's statements were actually compelled by police conduct which overcame his will to resist. Thus the only issue before us is whether Officer Kraft was justified in failing to make available to respondent the procedural safeguards associated with the privilege against compulsory self-incrimination since *Miranda*.[13]

The New York Court of Appeals was undoubtedly correct in deciding that the facts of this case come within the ambit of the *Miranda* decision as we have subsequently interpreted it. We agree that respondent was in police custody because we have noted that "the ultimate inquiry is simply whether there is a 'formal arrest or restraint on freedom of movement' of the degree associated

---

13. The dissent curiously takes us to task for "endors[ing] the introduction of coerced self-incriminating statements in criminal prosecutions," and for "sanction[ing] sub silentio criminal prosecutions based on compelled self-incriminating statements." Of course our decision today does nothing of the kind. As the *Miranda* Court itself recognized, the failure to provide *Miranda* warnings in and of itself does not render a confession involuntary, and respondent is certainly free on remand to argue that his statement was coerced under traditional due process standards. Today we merely reject the only argument that respondent has raised to support the exclusion of his statement, that the statement must be presumed compelled because of Officer Kraft's failure to read him his *Miranda* warnings. [Footnote by Justice Rehnquist.]

with a formal arrest." Here Quarles was surrounded by at least four police officers and was handcuffed when the questioning at issue took place.

We hold that on these facts there is a "public safety" exception to the requirement that *Miranda* warnings be given before a suspect's answers may be admitted into evidence, and that the availability of that exception does not depend upon the motivation of the individual officers involved. In a kaleidoscopic situation such as the one confronting these officers, where spontaneity rather than adherence to a police manual is necessarily the order of the day, the application of the exception which we recognize today should not be made to depend on post hoc findings at a suppression hearing concerning the subjective motivation of the arresting officer. Undoubtedly most police officers, if placed in Officer Kraft's position, would act out of a host of different, instinctive, and largely unverifiable motives — their own safety, the safety of others, and perhaps as well the desire to obtain incriminating evidence from the suspect.

Whatever the motivation of individual officers in such a situation, we do not believe that the doctrinal underpinnings of *Miranda* require that it be applied in all its rigor to a situation in which police officers ask questions reasonably prompted by a concern for the public safety. The *Miranda* decision was based in large part on this Court's view that the warnings which it required police to give to suspects in custody would reduce the likelihood that the suspects would fall victim to constitutionally impermissible practices of police interrogation in the presumptively coercive environment of the station house.

The police in this case, in the very act of apprehending a suspect, were confronted with the immediate necessity of ascertaining the whereabouts of a gun which they had every reason to believe the suspect had just removed from his empty holster and discarded in the supermarket. So long as the gun was concealed somewhere in the supermarket, with its actual whereabouts unknown, it obviously posed more than one danger to the public safety: an accomplice might make use of it, a customer or employee might later come upon it.

In such a situation, if the police are required to recite the familiar *Miranda* warnings before asking the whereabouts of the gun, suspects in Quarles' position might well be deterred from responding. Procedural safeguards which deter a suspect from responding were deemed acceptable in *Miranda* in order to protect the Fifth Amendment privilege; when the primary social cost of those added protections is the possibility of fewer convictions, the *Miranda* majority was willing to bear that cost. Here, had *Miranda* warnings deterred Quarles from responding to Officer Kraft's question about the whereabouts of the gun, the cost would have been something more than merely the failure to obtain evidence useful in convicting Quarles. Officer Kraft needed an answer to his question not simply to make his case against Quarles but to insure that further danger to the public did not result from the concealment of the gun in a public area.

We conclude that the need for answers to questions in a situation posing a threat to the public safety outweighs the need for the prophylactic rule protecting the Fifth Amendment's privilege against self-incrimination. We decline to place officers such as Officer Kraft in the untenable position of having to consider, often in a matter of seconds, whether it best serves society for them to ask the necessary questions without the *Miranda* warnings and render whatever probative evidence they uncover inadmissible, or for them to give the warnings in order to preserve the admissibility of evidence they might uncover but possibly damage or destroy their ability to obtain that evidence and neutralize the volatile situation confronting them.[14]

As we have in other contexts, we recognize here the importance of a workable rule "to guide police officers, who have only limited time and expertise to reflect on and balance the social and individual interests involved in the specific circumstances they confront." But as we have pointed out, we believe that the exception which we recognize today lessens the necessity of that on-the-scene balancing process. The exception will not be difficult for police officers to apply because in each case it will be circumscribed by the exigency which justifies it. We think police officers can and will distinguish almost instinctively between questions necessary to secure their own safety or the safety of the public and questions designed solely to elicit testimonial evidence from a suspect.

We hold that the Court of Appeals in this case erred in excluding the statement, "the gun is over there," and the gun because of the officer's failure to read respondent his *Miranda* rights before attempting to locate the weapon. Accordingly we hold that it also erred in excluding the subsequent statements as illegal fruits of a *Miranda* violation.

Justice O'CONNOR, concurring in the judgment in part and dissenting in part.

In Miranda v. Arizona (1966), the Court held unconstitutional, because inherently compelled, the admission of statements derived from in-custody questioning not preceded by an explanation of the privilege against self-incrimination and the consequences of forgoing it. Today, the Court concludes that overriding considerations of public safety justify the admission of evidence — oral statements and a gun — secured without the benefit of such warnings. In so holding, the Court acknowledges that it is departing from prior precedent, and that it is "lessen[ing] the desirable clarity of [the *Miranda*] rule." Were the Court writing from a clean slate, I could agree with its holding. But *Miranda* is now the law and, in my view, the Court has not provided sufficient justification for departing from it or for blurring its now clear strictures. Accordingly, I would require suppression of the initial statement taken from respondent in this case. On the other hand, nothing in *Miranda* or the privilege itself requires exclusion of nontestimonial evidence derived from informal custodial interrogation, and I therefore agree with the Court that admission of the gun in evidence is proper.

In my view, a "public safety" exception unnecessarily blurs the edges of the clear line heretofore established and makes *Miranda*'s requirements more difficult to understand. In some cases, police will benefit because a reviewing court will find that an exigency excused their failure to administer the required warnings. But in other cases, police will suffer because, though they thought an exigency excused their noncompliance, a reviewing court will view the "objective" circumstances differently and require exclusion of admissions thereby obtained. The end result will be a finespun new doctrine on public

14. The dissent argues that a public safety exception to *Miranda* is unnecessary because in every case an officer can simply ask the necessary questions to protect himself or the public, and then the prosecution can decline to introduce any incriminating responses at a subsequent trial. But absent actual coercion by the officer, there is no constitutional imperative requiring the exclusion of the evidence that results from police inquiry of this kind; and we do not believe that the doctrinal underpinnings of *Miranda* require us to exclude the evidence, thus penalizing officers for asking the very questions which are the most crucial to their efforts to protect themselves and the public. [Footnote by Justice Rehnquist.]

safety exigencies incident to custodial interrogation, complete with the hair-splitting distinctions that currently plague our Fourth Amendment jurisprudence. "While the rigidity of the prophylactic rules was a principal weakness in the view of dissenters and critics outside the Court, . . . that rigidity [has also been called a] strength of the decision. It [has] afforded police and courts clear guidance on the manner in which to conduct a custodial investigation: if it was rigid, it was also precise. . . . [T]his core virtue of *Miranda* would be eviscerated if the prophylactic rules were freely [ignored] by . . . courts under the guise of [reinterpreting] *Miranda* . . . ."

The justification the Court provides for upsetting the equilibrium that has finally been achieved — that police cannot and should not balance considerations of public safety against the individual's interest in avoiding compulsory testimonial self-incrimination — really misses the critical question to be decided. *Miranda* has never been read to prohibit the police from asking questions to secure the public safety. Rather, the critical question *Miranda* addresses is who shall bear the cost of securing the public safety when such questions are asked and answered: the defendant or the State. *Miranda*, for better or worse, found the resolution of that question implicit in the prohibition against compulsory self-incrimination and placed the burden on the State. When police ask custodial questions without administering the required warnings, *Miranda* quite clearly requires that the answers received be presumed compelled and that they be excluded from evidence at trial.

The Court concedes, as it must, both that respondent was in "custody" and subject to "interrogation" and that his statement "the gun is over there" was compelled within the meaning of our precedent. In my view, since there is nothing about an exigency that makes custodial interrogation any less compelling, a principled application of *Miranda* requires that respondent's statement be suppressed.

The court below assumed, without discussion, that the privilege against self-incrimination required that the gun derived from respondent's statement also be suppressed, whether or not the State could independently link it to him. That conclusion was, in my view, incorrect.

The gun respondent was compelled to supply is clearly evidence of the "real or physical" sort. What makes the question of its admissibility difficult is the fact that, in asking respondent to produce the gun, the police also "compelled" him, in the *Miranda* sense, to create an incriminating testimonial response. In other words, the case is problematic because police compelled respondent not only to provide the gun but also to admit that he knew where it was and that it was his.

To be sure, admission of nontestimonial evidence secured through informal custodial interrogation will reduce the incentives to enforce the *Miranda* code. But that fact simply begs the question of how much enforcement is appropriate. There are some situations, as the Court's struggle to accommodate a "public safety" exception demonstrates, in which the societal cost of administering the *Miranda* warnings is very high indeed. The *Miranda* decision quite practically does not express any societal interest in having those warnings administered for their own sake. Rather, the warnings and waiver are only required to ensure that "testimony" used against the accused at trial is voluntarily given. Therefore, if the testimonial aspects of the accused's custodial communications are suppressed, the failure to administer the *Miranda* warnings should cease to be of concern. The harm caused by failure to administer *Miranda* warnings relates only to admission of testimonial self-incriminations, and the suppression of such incriminations should by itself produce the optimal enforcement of the *Miranda* rule.

Justice MARSHALL, with whom Justice BRENNAN and Justice STEVENS join, dissenting.

The police in this case arrested a man suspected of possessing a firearm in violation of New York law. Once the suspect was in custody and found to be unarmed, the arresting officer initiated an interrogation. Without being advised of his right not to respond, the suspect incriminated himself by locating the gun. The majority concludes that the State may rely on this incriminating statement to convict the suspect of possessing a weapon. I disagree. The arresting officers had no legitimate reason to interrogate the suspect without advising him of his rights to remain silent and to obtain assistance of counsel. By finding on these facts justification for unconsented interrogation, the majority abandons the clear guidelines enunciated in Miranda v. Arizona (1966), and condemns the American judiciary to a new era of post hoc inquiry into the propriety of custodial interrogations. More significantly and in direct conflict with this Court's longstanding interpretation of the Fifth Amendment, the majority has endorsed the introduction of coerced self-incriminating statements in criminal prosecutions. I dissent.

The majority contends that the law, as it currently stands, places police officers in a dilemma whenever they interrogate a suspect who appears to know of some threat to the public's safety. If the police interrogate the suspect without advising him of his rights, the suspect may reveal information that the authorities can use to defuse the threat, but the suspect's statements will be inadmissible at trial. If, on the other hand, the police advise the suspect of his rights, the suspect may be deterred from responding to the police's questions, and the risk to the public may continue unabated. According to the majority, the police must now choose between establishing the suspect's guilt and safeguarding the public from danger.

The majority proposes to eliminate this dilemma by creating an exception to Miranda v. Arizona for custodial interrogations concerning matters of public safety. Under the majority's exception, police would be permitted to interrogate suspects about such matters before the suspects have been advised of their constitutional rights. Without being "deterred" by the knowledge that they have a constitutional right not to respond, these suspects will be likely to answer the questions. Should the answers also be incriminating, the State would be free to introduce them as evidence in a criminal prosecution. Through this "narrow exception to the *Miranda* rule," the majority proposes to protect the public's safety without jeopardizing the prosecution of criminal defendants. I find in this reasoning an unwise and unprincipled departure from our Fifth Amendment precedents.

Before today's opinion, the procedures established in Miranda v. Arizona had "the virtue of informing police and prosecutors with specificity as to what they may do in conducting custodial interrogation, and of informing courts under what circumstances statements obtained during such interrogation are not admissible." In a chimerical quest for public safety, the majority has abandoned the rule that brought 18 years of doctrinal tranquility to the field of custodial interrogations. As the majority candidly concedes, a public-safety exception destroys forever the clarity of *Miranda* for both law enforcement officers and members of the judiciary. The Court's candor cannot mask what a serious loss the administration of justice has incurred.

This case is illustrative of the chaos the "public-safety" exception will unlease. The circumstances of Quarles' arrest have never been in dispute. After the benefit of briefing and oral argument, the New York Court of Appeals, as previously noted, concluded that there was "no evidence in the record before us that there were exigent circumstances posing a risk to the public safety." Upon reviewing the same facts and hearing the same arguments, a majority of this Court has come to precisely the opposite conclusion: "So long as the gun was concealed somewhere in the supermarket, with its actual whereabouts unknown, it obviously posed more than one danger to the public safety. . . ."

If after plenary review two appellate courts so fundamentally differ over the threat to public safety presented by the simple and uncontested facts of this case, one must seriously question how law enforcement officers will respond to the majority's new rule in the confusion and haste of the real world.

Though unfortunate, the difficulty of administering the "public-safety" exception is not the most profound flaw in the majority's decision. The majority has lost sight of the fact Miranda v. Arizona and our earlier custodial-interrogation cases all implemented a constitutional privilege against self-incrimination. The rules established in these cases were designed to protect criminal defendants against prosecutions based on coerced self-incriminating statements. The majority today turns its back on these constitutional considerations, and invites the government to prosecute through the use of what necessarily are coerced statements.

The "public-safety" exception is efficacious precisely because it permits police officers to coerce criminal defendants into making involuntary statements. Indeed, in the efficacy of the "public-safety" exception lies a fundamental and constitutional defect. Until today, this Court could truthfully state that the Fifth Amendment is given "broad scope" "[w]here there has been genuine compulsion of testimony." Coerced confessions were simply inadmissible in criminal prosecutions. The "public-safety" exception departs from this principle by expressly inviting police officers to coerce defendants into making incriminating statements, and then permitting prosecutors to introduce those statements at trial. Though the majority's opinion is cloaked in the beguiling language of utilitarianism, the Court has sanctioned sub silentio criminal prosecutions based on compelled self-incriminating statements. I find this result in direct conflict with the Fifth Amendment's dictate that "[n]o person . . . shall be compelled in any criminal case to be a witness against himself."

The irony of the majority's decision is that the public's safety can be perfectly well protected without abridging the Fifth Amendment. If a bomb is about to explode or the public is otherwise imminently imperiled, the police are free to interrogate suspects without advising them of their constitutional rights. Such unconsented questioning may take place not only when police officers act on instinct but also when higher faculties lead them to believe that advising a suspect of his constitutional rights might decrease the likelihood that the suspect would reveal life-saving information. If trickery is necessary to protect the public, then the police may trick a suspect into confessing. While the Fourteenth Amendment sets limits on such behavior, nothing in the Fifth Amendment or our decision in Miranda v. Arizona proscribes this sort of emergency questioning. All the Fifth Amendment forbids is the introduction of coerced statements at trial.

Having determined that the Fifth Amendment renders inadmissible Quarles' response to Officer Kraft's questioning, I have no doubt that our precedents require that the gun discovered as a direct result of Quarles' statement must be presumed inadmissible as well. The gun was the direct product of a coercive custodial interrogation. In Silverthorne Lumber Co. v. United States (1920), and Wong Sun v. United States (1963), this Court held that the Government may not introduce incriminating evidence derived from an illegally obtained source.

c.   Booking Exception

The Supreme Court has held that the police can ask a person questions when taking a person into custody that are needed in the booking process, such as name, address, date of birth, height, and weight. The Court has said that the answers to these questions are admissible, even without administration of *Miranda* warnings. In Pennsylvania v. Muniz, 496 U.S. 583 (1990), the Court considered whether "various incriminating utterances of a drunken-driving suspect, made while performing a series of sobriety tests, constitute testimonial responses to custodial interrogation for purposes of the Self-Incrimination Clause of the Fifth Amendment." The suspect was taken to the booking station and "was not at this time (nor had he been previously) advised of his rights under Miranda v. Arizona." The officer asked Muniz "his name, address, height, weight, eye color, date of birth, and current age. He responded to each of these questions, stumbling over his address and age. The officer then asked Muniz, 'Do you know what the date was of your sixth birthday?' After Muniz offered an inaudible reply, the officer repeated, 'When you turned six years old, do you remember what the date was?' Muniz responded, 'No, I don't.'"

The Court held that the slurred speech that was evident on the videotape did not violate the privilege against self-incrimination because it was not testimonial. As explained below, in Section D of this chapter, the privilege against self-incrimination applies only if a person is compelled to make statements; physical evidence or observation of physical characteristics are not testimonial. As to the questions asking him for identifying information, the Court held that these fell within the "booking exception" to *Miranda.* Justice Brennan, writing for the Court, stated:

> Muniz's answers to these first seven questions are nonetheless admissible because the questions fall within a "routine booking question" exception which exempts from *Miranda*'s coverage questions to secure the biographical data necessary to complete booking or pretrial services. The state court found that the first seven questions were "requested for record-keeping purposes only," and therefore the questions appear reasonably related to the police's administrative concerns. In this context, therefore, the first seven questions asked at the booking center fall outside the protections of *Miranda* and the answers thereto need not be suppressed.

The Court, however, found that asking the suspect the date of his sixth birthday did not fit within the booking exception and had to be suppressed.

d. Waiver

In *Miranda,* the Court recognized that individuals may waive their right to remain silent and their right to counsel. However, the Court said that the government would have a "heavy burden" of demonstrating "that the defendant knowingly and intelligently waived his privilege against self-incrimination and his right to retained or appointed counsel." The Court said that "a valid waiver will not be presumed from the silence of the accused after warnings are given or simply from the fact that a confession was in fact eventually obtained."

What Is Sufficient to Constitute a Waiver? Must a waiver be express or are implied waivers permissible? The Court resolved this in United States v. Butler by holding that implied waivers are allowed.

NORTH CAROLINA v. BUTLER
441 U.S. 369 (1979)

Justice STEWART delivered the opinion of the Court.

In evident conflict with the present view of every other court that has considered the issue, the North Carolina Supreme Court has held that Miranda v. Arizona requires that no statement of a person under custodial interrogation may be admitted in evidence against him unless, at the time the statement was made, he explicitly waived the right to the presence of a lawyer.

The respondent was convicted in a North Carolina trial court of kidnaping, armed robbery, and felonious assault. The evidence at his trial showed that he and a man named Elmer Lee had robbed a gas station in Goldsboro, N. C., in December 1976, and had shot the station attendant as he was attempting to escape. The attendant was paralyzed, but survived to testify against the respondent. The prosecution also produced evidence of incriminating statements made by the respondent shortly after his arrest by Federal Bureau of Investigation agents in the Bronx, N. Y., on the basis of a North Carolina fugitive warrant. Outside the presence of the jury, FBI Agent Martinez testified that at the time of the arrest he fully advised the respondent of the rights delineated in the *Miranda* case. According to the uncontroverted testimony of Martinez, the agents then took the respondent to the FBI office in nearby New Rochelle, N. Y. There, after the agents determined that the respondent had an 11th grade education and was literate, he was given the Bureau's "Advice of Rights" form which he read. When asked if he understood his rights, he replied that he did. The respondent refused to sign the waiver at the bottom of the form. He was told that he need neither speak nor sign the form, but that the agents would like him to talk to them. The respondent replied: "I will talk to you but I am not signing any form." He then made inculpatory statements. Agent Martinez testified that the respondent said nothing when advised of his right to the assistance of a lawyer. At no time did the respondent request counsel or attempt to terminate the agents' questioning.

At the conclusion of this testimony the respondent moved to suppress the evidence of his incriminating statements on the ground that he had not waived his right to the assistance of counsel at the time the statements were made. On appeal, the North Carolina Supreme Court reversed the convictions and ordered a new trial. It found that the statements had been admitted in violation of the requirements of the *Miranda* decision, noting that the respondent had refused to waive in writing his right to have counsel present and that there had not been a specific oral waiver.

We conclude that the North Carolina Supreme Court erred in its reading of the *Miranda* opinion. An express written or oral statement of waiver of the right to remain silent or of the right to counsel is usually strong proof of the validity of that waiver, but is not inevitably either necessary or sufficient to establish waiver. The question is not one of form, but rather whether the defendant in fact knowingly and voluntarily waived the rights delineated in the *Miranda* case. As was unequivocally said in *Miranda,* mere silence is not enough. That does not mean that the defendant's silence, coupled with an understanding of his rights and a course of conduct indicating waiver, may never support a conclusion that a defendant has waived his rights. The courts must presume that a defendant did not waive his rights; the prosecution's burden is great; but in at least some cases waiver can be clearly inferred from the actions and words of the person interrogated.

The per se rule that the North Carolina Supreme Court has found in *Miranda* does not speak to these concerns. There is no doubt that this respondent was adequately and effectively apprised of his rights. The only question is whether he waived the exercise of one of those rights, the right to the presence of a lawyer. Neither the state court nor the respondent has offered any reason why there must be a negative answer to that question in the absence of an express waiver.

Justice BRENNAN, with whom Justice MARSHALL and Justice STEVENS join, dissenting.

There is no allegation of an affirmative waiver in this case. As the Court concedes, the respondent here refused to sign the waiver form, and "said nothing when advised of his right to the assistance of a lawyer." In the absence of an "affirmative waiver" in the form of an express written or oral statement, the Supreme Court of North Carolina correctly granted a new trial. I would, therefore, affirm its decision.

The rule announced by the Court today allows a finding of waiver based upon "infer[ence] from the actions and words of the person interrogated." The Court thus shrouds in half-light the question of waiver, allowing courts to construct inferences from ambiguous words and gestures. But the very premise of *Miranda* requires that ambiguity be interpreted against the interrogator. That premise is the recognition of the "compulsion inherent in custodial" interrogation, and of its purpose "to subjugate the individual to the will of [his] examiner." Under such conditions, only the most explicit waivers of rights can be considered knowingly and freely given.

The Supreme Court has ruled that whether there was a waiver is to be determined from the totality of the circumstances. In Fare v. Michael C., 442 U.S. 507 (1979), the Court said that the "totality of the circumstances approach is adequate to determine whether there has been a waiver even when interrogation of juveniles is involved." This includes considering the "juvenile's age, experience, education, background, and intelligence, and into whether he has the capacity to understand the warnings given him, the nature of his Fifth Amendment rights, and the consequences of waiving those rights."

However, the Court has stressed that these factors are relevant only as they relate to determining whether there was impermissible police behavior in obtaining incriminating statements. In Colorado v. Connelly, which is presented at the beginning of this chapter, the Court rejected the argument that a waiver of *Miranda* rights was invalid because the defendant was suffering from psychosis that prevented him from making free and voluntary choices. The Court explained that "*Miranda* protects defendants from government coercion, [but] goes no further than that." The Court said that "voluntariness of a waiver has always depended on the absence of police overreaching, not on 'free choice' in any broader sense of the word."

Can there be a knowing and voluntary waiver if police withhold from a suspect the information that an attorney sought to consult with him? This knowledge and the resulting consultation might well have prevented the incriminating statements. In Moran v. Burbine, 475 U.S. 412 (1986), the Court resolved this issue in favor of the police. A suspect in a murder case waived his *Miranda* rights, including his right to counsel, and confessed. The suspect's sister had hired an attorney who telephoned the police station and was told that no interrogation would occur until the next day. At no point was the suspect told that there was an attorney who had been retained and wanted to see him. The Court found no constitutional violation and said that "events occurring outside of the presence of the suspect and entirely unknown to him can have no bearing on the capacity to comprehend and knowingly relinquish a constitutional right." Although the Court criticized the police conduct as "inimical to the Fifth Amendment['s] values," it nonetheless found no constitutional violation.

Similarly, in Spring v. Colorado, 479 U.S. 564 (1987), the Court ruled that the police had no duty to inform a suspect of the nature of the crime for which he or she is under suspicion. The Court explained that "the additional information could affect only the wisdom of a *Miranda* waiver, not its essentially voluntary and knowing nature."

How Is a Waiver After the Assertion of Rights Treated? If a suspect asserts his or her rights under *Miranda*, how is a subsequent waiver handled? The Court here has drawn a distinction between the two key rights specified in *Miranda*: the right to remain silent and the right to counsel. As for the former, the Court has been willing to find waivers in these situations where the defendant speaks to police after initially invoking the right to remain silent. Michigan v. Mosley is the key case.

MICHIGAN v. MOSLEY

423 U.S. 96 (1975)

Justice STEWART delivered the opinion of the Court.

The respondent, Richard Bert Mosley, was arrested in Detroit, Mich., in the early afternoon of April 8, 1971, in connection with robberies that had recently occurred at the Blue Goose Bar and the White Tower Restaurant on that city's lower east side. The arresting officer, Detective James Cowie of the Armed Robbery Section of the Detroit Police Department, was acting on a tip implicating Mosley and three other men in the robberies. After effecting the arrest,

Detective Cowie brought Mosley to the Robbery, Breaking and Entering Bureau of the Police Department, located on the fourth floor of the departmental headquarters building. The officer advised Mosley of his rights under this Court's decision in Miranda v. Arizona and had him read and sign the department's constitutional rights notification certificate. After filling out the necessary arrest papers, Cowie began questioning Mosley about the robbery of the White Tower Restaurant. When Mosley said he did not want to answer any questions about the robberies, Cowie promptly ceased the interrogation. The completion of the arrest papers and the questioning of Mosley together took approximately 20 minutes. At no time during the questioning did Mosley indicate a desire to consult with a lawyer, and there is no claim that the procedures followed to this point did not fully comply with the strictures of the *Miranda* opinion. Mosley was then taken to a ninth-floor cell block.

Shortly after 6 P.M., Detective Hill of the Detroit Police Department Homicide Bureau brought Mosley from the cell block to the fifth-floor office of the Homicide Bureau for questioning about the fatal shooting of a man named Leroy Williams. Williams had been killed on January 9, 1971, during a holdup attempt outside the 101 Ranch Bar in Detroit. Mosley had not been arrested on this charge or interrogated about it by Detective Cowie. Before questioning Mosley about this homicide, Detective Hill carefully advised him of his "*Miranda* rights." Mosley read the notification form both silently and aloud, and Detective Hill then read and explained the warnings to him and had him sign the form. Mosley at first denied any involvement in the Williams murder, but after the officer told him that Anthony Smith had confessed to participating in the slaying and had named him as the "shooter," Mosley made a statement implicating himself in the homicide. The interrogation by Detective Hill lasted approximately 15 minutes, and at no time during its course did Mosley ask to consult with a lawyer or indicate that he did not want to discuss the homicide. In short, there is no claim that the procedures followed during Detective Hill's interrogation of Mosley, standing alone, did not fully comply with the strictures of the *Miranda* opinion.

Mosley was subsequently charged in a one-count information with first-degree murder. Before the trial he moved to suppress his incriminating statement on a number of grounds, among them the claim that under the doctrine of the *Miranda* case it was constitutionally impermissible for Detective Hill to question him about the Williams murder after he had told Detective Cowie that he did not want to answer any questions about the robberies. The trial court denied the motion to suppress after an evidentiary hearing, and the incriminating statement was subsequently introduced in evidence against Mosley at his trial. The jury convicted Mosley of first-degree murder, and the court imposed a mandatory sentence of life imprisonment.

The issue in this case, rather, is whether the conduct of the Detroit police that led to Mosley's incriminating statement did in fact violate the *Miranda* "guidelines," so as to render the statement inadmissible in evidence against Mosley at his trial.

[*Miranda*] states that "the interrogation must cease" when the person in custody indicates that "he wishes to remain silent." It does not state under what circumstances, if any, a resumption of questioning is permissible. The passage could be literally read to mean that a person who has invoked his "right to silence" can never again be subjected to custodial interrogation by any police officer at any time or place on any subject. Another possible construction of the passage would characterize "any statement taken after the person invokes his privilege" as "the product of compulsion" and would therefore mandate its exclusion from evidence, even if it were volunteered by the person in custody without any further interrogation whatever. Or the passage could be interpreted to require only the immediate cessation of questioning, and to permit a resumption of interrogation after a momentary respite.

It is evident that any of these possible literal interpretations would lead to absurd and unintended results. To permit the continuation of custodial interrogation after a momentary cessation would clearly frustrate the purposes of *Miranda* by allowing repeated rounds of questioning to undermine the will of the person being questioned. At the other extreme, a blanket prohibition against the taking of voluntary statements or a permanent immunity from further interrogation, regardless of the circumstances, would transform the *Miranda* safeguards into wholly irrational obstacles to legitimate police investigative activity, and deprive suspects of an opportunity to make informed and intelligent assessments of their interests. Clearly, therefore, neither this passage nor any other passage in the *Miranda* opinion can sensibly be read to create a per se proscription of indefinite duration upon any further questioning by any police officer on any subject, once the person in custody has indicated a desire to remain silent.

A reasonable and faithful interpretation of the *Miranda* opinion must rest on the intention of the Court in that case to adopt "fully effective means . . . to notify the person of his right of silence and to assure that the exercise of the right will be scrupulously honored . . . ." The critical safeguard identified in the passage at issue is a person's "right to cut off questioning." Through the exercise of his option to terminate questioning he can control the time at which questioning occurs, the subjects discussed, and the duration of the interrogation. The requirement that law enforcement authorities must respect a person's exercise of that option counteracts the coercive pressures of the custodial setting. We therefore conclude that the admissibility of statements obtained after the person in custody has decided to remain silent depends under *Miranda* on whether his "right to cut off questioning" was "scrupulously honored."

This is not a case, therefore, where the police failed to honor a decision of a person in custody to cut off questioning, either by refusing to discontinue the interrogation upon request or by persisting in repeated efforts to wear down his resistance and make him change his mind. In contrast to such practices, the police here immediately ceased the interrogation, resumed questioning only after the passage of a significant period of time and the provision of a fresh set of warnings, and restricted the second interrogation to a crime that had not been a subject of the earlier interrogation.

For these reasons, we conclude that the admission in evidence of Mosley's incriminating statement did not violate the principles of Miranda v. Arizona.

Justice BRENNAN, with whom Justice MARSHALL joins, dissenting.

In formulating its procedural safeguard, the Court skirts the problem of compulsion and thereby fails to join issue with the dictates of *Miranda*. The language which the Court finds controlling in this case teaches that renewed questioning itself is part of the process which invariably operates to overcome the will of a suspect. That teaching is embodied in the form of a proscription on any further questioning once the suspect has exercised his right to remain silent. Today's decision uncritically abandons that teaching. The Court assumes, contrary to the controlling language, that "scrupulously honoring" an initial exercise of the right to remain silent preserves the efficaciousness of initial and future warnings despite the fact that the suspect has once been subjected to interrogation and then has been detained for a lengthy period of time.

Observing that the suspect can control the circumstances of interrogation "[t]hrough the exercise of his option to terminate questioning," the Court concludes "that the admissibility of statements obtained after the person in custody has decided to remain silent depends . . . on whether his 'right to cut off questioning' was 'scrupulously honored.'" But scrupulously honoring exercises of the right to cut off questioning is only meaningful insofar as the suspect's will to exercise that right remains wholly unfettered. The Court's formulation thus assumes the very matter at issue here: whether renewed questioning following a lengthy period of detention acts to overbear the suspect's will, irrespective of giving the *Miranda* warnings a second time (and scrupulously honoring them), thereby rendering inconsequential any failure to exercise the right to remain silent. For the Court it is enough conclusorily to assert that "[t]he subsequent questioning did not undercut Mosley's previous decision not to answer Detective Cowie's inquiries." Under *Miranda*, however, Mosley's failure to exercise the right upon renewed questioning is presumptively the consequence of an overbearing in which detention and that subsequent questioning played central roles.

I agree that *Miranda* is not to be read, on the one hand, to impose an absolute ban on resumption of questioning "at any time or place on any subject," or on the other hand, "to permit a resumption of interrogation after a momentary respite." But this surely cannot justify adoption of a vague and ineffective procedural standard that falls somewhere between those absurd extremes, for *Miranda* in flat and unambiguous terms requires that questioning "cease" when a suspect exercises the right to remain silent. *Miranda*'s terms, however, are not so uncompromising as to preclude the fashioning of guidelines to govern this case. Those guidelines must, of course, necessarily be sensitive to the reality that "[a]s a practical matter, the compulsion to speak in the isolated setting of the police station may well be greater than in courts or other official investigations, where there are often impartial observers to guard against intimidation or trickery."

However, the Court has treated a defendant's invocation of the right to counsel differently. If a defendant invokes the right to counsel, then the police cannot initiate further interrogation unless the suspect initiates the communications. Edwards v. Arizona, an especially important decision in this area, articulated the rule here.

EDWARDS v. ARIZONA
451 U.S. 477 (1981)

Justice WHITE delivered the opinion of the Court.

We granted certiorari in this case, limited to whether the Fifth, Sixth, and Fourteenth Amendments require suppression of a post-arrest confession, which was obtained after Edwards had invoked his right to consult counsel before further interrogation.

I

On January 19, 1976, a sworn complaint was filed against Edwards in Arizona state court charging him with robbery, burglary, and first-degree murder. An arrest warrant was issued pursuant to the complaint, and Edwards was arrested at his home later that same day. At the police station, he was informed of his rights as required by Miranda v. Arizona. Petitioner stated that he understood his rights, and was willing to submit to questioning. After being told that another suspect already in custody had implicated him in the crime, Edwards denied involvement and gave a taped statement presenting an alibi defense. He then sought to "make a deal." The interrogating officer told him that he wanted a statement, but that he did not have the authority to negotiate a deal. The officer provided Edwards with the telephone number of a county attorney. Petitioner made the call, but hung up after a few moments. Edwards then said: "I want an attorney before making a deal." At that point, questioning ceased and Edwards was taken to county jail.

At 9:15 the next morning, two detectives, colleagues of the officer who had interrogated Edwards the previous night, came to the jail and asked to see Edwards. When the detention officer informed Edwards that the detectives wished to speak with him, he replied that he did not want to talk to anyone. The guard told him that "he had" to talk and then took him to meet with the detectives. The officers identified themselves, stated they wanted to talk to him, and informed him of his *Miranda* rights. Edwards was willing to talk, but he first wanted to hear the taped statement of the alleged accomplice who had implicated him. After listening to the tape for several minutes, petitioner said that he would make a statement so long as it was not tape-recorded. The detectives informed him that the recording was irrelevant since they could testify in court concerning whatever he said. Edwards replied: "I'll tell you anything you want to know, but I don't want it on tape." He thereupon implicated himself in the crime.

Prior to trial, Edwards moved to suppress his confession on the ground that his *Miranda* rights had been violated when the officers returned to question him after he had invoked his right to counsel.

II

Edwards insists that having exercised his right on the 19th to have counsel present during interrogation, he did not validly waive that right on the 20th. For the following reasons, we agree.

First, the Arizona Supreme Court applied an erroneous standard for determining waiver where the accused has specifically invoked his right to counsel. It is reasonably clear under our cases that waivers of counsel must not only be voluntary, but must also constitute a knowing and intelligent relinquishment or abandonment of a known right or privilege, a matter which depends in each case "upon the particular facts and circumstances surrounding that case, including the background, experience, and conduct of the accused."

Considering the proceedings in the state courts in the light of this standard, we note that in denying petitioner's motion to suppress, the trial court found the admission to have been "voluntary," without separately focusing on whether Edwards had knowingly and intelligently relinquished his right to counsel. Here, however sound the conclusion of the state courts as to the voluntariness of Edwards' admission may be, neither the trial court nor the Arizona Supreme Court undertook to focus on whether Edwards understood his right to counsel and intelligently and knowingly relinquished it. It is thus apparent that the decision below misunderstood the requirement for finding a valid waiver of the right to counsel, once invoked.

Second, although we have held that after initially being advised of his *Miranda* rights, the accused may himself validly waive his rights and respond to interrogation, see North Carolina v. Butler, the Court has strongly indicated that additional safeguards are necessary when the accused asks for counsel; and we now hold that when an accused has invoked his right to have counsel present during custodial interrogation, a valid waiver of that right cannot be established by showing only that he responded to further police-initiated custodial interrogation even if he has been advised of his rights. We further hold that an accused, such as Edwards, having expressed his desire to deal with the police only through counsel, is not subject to further interrogation by the authorities until counsel has been made available to him, unless the accused himself initiates further communication, exchanges, or conversations with the police.

Miranda itself indicated that the assertion of the right to counsel was a significant event and that once exercised by the accused, "the interrogation must cease until an attorney is present." Our later cases have not abandoned that view.

Justice POWELL, with whom Justice REHNQUIST joins, concurring in the result.

Although I agree that the judgment of the Arizona Supreme Court must be reversed, I do not join the Court's opinion because I am not sure what it means. I have thought it settled law, as these cases tell us, that one accused of crime may waive any of the constitutional safeguards — including the right to remain silent, to jury trial, to call witnesses, to cross-examine one's accusers, to testify in one's own behalf, and — of course — to have counsel. Whatever the right, the standard for waiver is whether the actor fully understands the right in question and voluntarily intends to relinquish it.

In its opinion today, however, the Court — after reiterating the familiar principles of waiver — goes on to say: "We further hold that an accused, such as Edwards, having expressed his desire to deal with the police only through counsel, is not subject to further interrogation by the authorities until counsel has been made available to him, unless the accused [has] himself initiate[d] further communication, exchanges, or conversations with the police."

In view of the emphasis placed on "initiation," I find the Court's opinion unclear. If read to create a new per se rule, requiring a threshold inquiry as to precisely who opened any conversation between an accused and state officials, I cannot agree. I would not superimpose a new element of proof on the established doctrine of waiver of counsel.

In sum, once warnings have been given and the right to counsel has been invoked, the relevant inquiry — whether the suspect now desires to talk to police without counsel — is a question of fact to be determined in light of all of the circumstances. Who "initiated" a conversation may be relevant to the question of waiver, but it is not the sine qua non to the inquiry. The ultimate question is whether there was a free and knowing waiver of counsel before interrogation commenced.

The Court often has reaffirmed and applied the holding of *Edwards*. In Michigan v. Jackson, 475 U.S. 625 (1986), the Court ruled that "if the police initiate interrogation after a defendant's assertion, at arraignment or similar proceeding, of the right to counsel, any waiver of the defendant's right to counsel for that police-initiated interrogation is invalid." Minnick v. Mississippi is a particularly important affirmation and application of *Edwards*.

MINNICK v. MISSISSIPPI

498 U.S. 146 (1990)

Justice KENNEDY delivered the opinion of the Court.

To protect the privilege against self-incrimination guaranteed by the Fifth Amendment, we have held that the police must terminate interrogation of an accused in custody if the accused requests the assistance of counsel. Miranda v. Arizona (1966). We reinforced the protections of *Miranda* in Edwards v. Arizona (1981), which held that once the accused requests counsel, officials may not reinitiate questioning "until counsel has been made available" to him. The issue in the case before us is whether *Edwards*' protection ceases once the suspect has consulted with an attorney.

Petitioner Robert Minnick and fellow prisoner James Dyess escaped from a county jail in Mississippi and, a day later, broke into a mobile home in search of weapons. In the course of the burglary they were interrupted by the arrival of the trailer's owner, Ellis Thomas, accompanied by Lamar Lafferty and Lafferty's infant son. Dyess and Minnick used the stolen weapons to kill Thomas and the senior Lafferty. Minnick's story is that Dyess murdered one victim and forced Minnick to shoot the other. Before the escapees could get away, two young women arrived at the mobile home. They were held at gunpoint, then bound hand and foot. Dyess and Minnick fled in Thomas' truck, abandoning the vehicle in New Orleans. The fugitives continued to Mexico, where they fought, and Minnick then proceeded alone to California. Minnick was arrested in Lemon Grove, California, on a Mississippi warrant, some four months after the murders.

The confession at issue here resulted from the last interrogation of Minnick while he was held in the San Diego jail, but we first recount the events which preceded it. Minnick was arrested on Friday, August 22, 1986. Petitioner testified that he was mistreated by local police during and after the arrest. The day following the arrest, Saturday, two Federal Bureau of Investigation (FBI) agents came to the jail to interview him. Petitioner testified that he refused to go to the interview, but was told he would "have to go down or else." The FBI report indicates that the agents read petitioner his *Miranda* warnings, and that he acknowledged he understood his rights. He refused to sign a rights waiver form, however, and said he would not answer "very many" questions. Minnick told the agents about the jailbreak and the flight, and described how Dyess threatened and beat him. Early in the interview, he sobbed "[i]t was my life or theirs," but otherwise he hesitated to tell what happened at the trailer. The agents reminded him he did not have to answer questions without a lawyer present. According to the report, "Minnick stated 'Come back Monday when I have a lawyer,' and stated that he would make a more complete statement then with his lawyer present." The FBI interview ended.

After the FBI interview, an appointed attorney met with petitioner. Petitioner spoke with the lawyer on two or three occasions, though it is not clear from the record whether all of these conferences were in person.

On Monday, August 25, Deputy Sheriff J.C. Denham of Clarke County, Mississippi, came to the San Diego jail to question Minnick. Minnick testified that his jailers again told him he would "have to talk" to Denham and that he "could not refuse." Denham advised petitioner of his rights, and petitioner again declined to sign a rights waiver form. Petitioner told Denham about the escape and then proceeded to describe the events at the mobile home. According to petitioner, Dyess jumped out of the mobile home and shot the first of the two victims, once in the back with a shotgun and once in the head with a pistol. Dyess then handed the pistol to petitioner and ordered him to shoot the other victim, holding the shotgun on petitioner until he did so. Petitioner also said that when the two girls arrived, he talked Dyess out of raping or otherwise hurting them.

Minnick was tried for murder in Mississippi. He moved to suppress all statements given to the FBI or other police officers, including Denham. The trial court denied the motion with respect to petitioner's statements to Denham, but suppressed his other statements. Petitioner was convicted on two counts of capital murder and sentenced to death.

Edwards is "designed to prevent police from badgering a defendant into waiving his previously asserted *Miranda* rights." The rule ensures that any statement made in subsequent interrogation is not the result of coercive pressures. *Edwards* conserves judicial resources which would otherwise be expended in making difficult determinations of voluntariness, and implements the protections of *Miranda* in practical and straightforward terms.

The merit of the *Edwards* decision lies in the clarity of its command and the certainty of its application. We have confirmed that the *Edwards* rule provides " 'clear and unequivocal' guidelines to the law enforcement profession."

We do not interpret [*Edwards*] to mean, as the Mississippi court thought, that the protection of *Edwards* terminates once counsel has consulted with the suspect. In context, the requirement that counsel be "made available" to the accused refers to more than an opportunity to consult with an attorney outside the interrogation room.

In *Edwards*, we focused on *Miranda*'s instruction that when the accused invokes his right to counsel, "the interrogation must cease until an attorney is present," agreeing with Edwards' contention that he had not waived his right "to have counsel present during custodial interrogation."

Our emphasis on counsel's presence at interrogation is not unique to *Edwards*. It derives from *Miranda*, where we said that in the cases before us "[t]he presence of counsel . . . would be the adequate protective device necessary to make the process of police interrogation conform to the dictates of the [Fifth Amendment] privilege. His presence would insure that statements made in the government-established atmosphere are not the product of compulsion." In our view, a fair reading of *Edwards* and subsequent cases demonstrates that we have interpreted the rule to bar police-initiated interrogation unless the accused has counsel with him at the time of questioning. Whatever the ambiguities of our earlier cases on this point, we now hold that when counsel is requested, interrogation must cease, and officials may not reinitiate interrogation without counsel present, whether or not the accused has consulted with his attorney.

We consider our ruling to be an appropriate and necessary application of the *Edwards* rule. A single consultation with an attorney does not remove the suspect from persistent attempts by officials to persuade him to waive his rights, or from the coercive pressures that accompany custody and that may increase as custody is prolonged.

The case before us well illustrates the pressures, and abuses, that may be concomitants of custody. Petitioner testified that though he resisted, he was required to submit to both the FBI and the Denham interviews. In the latter instance, the compulsion to submit to interrogation followed petitioner's unequivocal request during the FBI interview that questioning cease until counsel was present. The case illustrates also that consultation is not always effective in instructing the suspect of his rights. One plausible interpretation of the record is that petitioner thought he could keep his admissions out of evidence by refusing to sign a formal waiver of rights. If the authorities had complied with Minnick's request to have counsel present during interrogation, the attorney could have corrected Minnick's misunderstanding, or indeed counseled him that he need not make a statement at all. We decline to remove protection from police-initiated questioning based on isolated consultations with counsel who is absent when the interrogation resumes.

Edwards does not foreclose finding a waiver of Fifth Amendment protections after counsel has been requested, provided the accused has initiated the conversation or discussions with the authorities; but that is not the case before us. There can be no doubt that the interrogation in question was initiated by the police; it was a formal interview which petitioner was compelled to attend. Since petitioner made a specific request for counsel before the interview, the police-initiated interrogation was impermissible. Petitioner's statement to Denham was not admissible at trial.

Justice SCALIA, with whom THE CHIEF JUSTICE joins, dissenting.

The Court today establishes an irrebuttable presumption that a criminal suspect, after invoking his *Miranda* right to counsel, can never validly waive that right during any police-initiated encounter, even after the suspect has been provided multiple *Miranda* warnings and has actually consulted his attorney. Because I see no justification for applying the *Edwards* irrebuttable presumption when a criminal suspect has actually consulted with his attorney, I respectfully dissent.

In this case, of course, we have not been called upon to reconsider *Edwards*, but simply to determine whether its irrebuttable presumption should continue after a suspect has actually consulted with his attorney. Whatever justifications might support *Edwards* are even less convincing in this context.

Most of the Court's discussion of *Edwards*—which stresses repeatedly, in various formulations, the case's emphasis upon the "right 'to have counsel present during custodial interrogation,' " — is beside the point. The existence and the importance of the *Miranda*-created right "to have counsel present" are unquestioned here. What is questioned is why a State should not be given the opportunity to prove that the right was voluntarily waived by a suspect who, after having been read his *Miranda* rights twice and having consulted with counsel at least twice, chose to speak to a police officer (and to admit his involvement in two murders) without counsel present.

Edwards did not assert the principle that no waiver of the *Miranda* right "to have counsel present" is possible. It simply adopted the presumption that no waiver is voluntary in certain circumstances, and the issue before us today is how broadly those circumstances are to be defined. They should not, in my view, extend beyond the circumstances present in *Edwards* itself—where the suspect in custody asked to consult an attorney and was interrogated before that attorney had ever been provided. In those circumstances, the *Edwards* rule rests upon an assumption similar to that of *Miranda* itself: that when a suspect in police custody is first questioned he is likely to be ignorant of his rights and to feel isolated in a hostile environment. This likelihood is thought to justify special protection against unknowing or coerced waiver of rights. After a suspect has seen his request for an attorney honored, however, and has actually spoken with that attorney, the probabilities change. The suspect then knows that he has an advocate on his side, and that the police will permit him to consult that advocate. He almost certainly also has a heightened awareness (above what the *Miranda* warning itself will provide) of his right to remain silent—since at the earliest opportunity "any lawyer worth his salt will tell the suspect in no uncertain terms to make no statement to the police under any circumstances."

Under these circumstances, an irrebuttable presumption that any police-prompted confession is the result of ignorance of rights, or of coercion, has no genuine basis in fact.

One should not underestimate the extent to which the Court's expansion of *Edwards* constricts law enforcement. Today's ruling, that the invocation of a right to counsel permanently prevents a police-initiated waiver, makes it largely impossible for the police to urge a prisoner who has initially declined to confess to change his mind—or indeed, even to ask whether he has changed his mind. Many persons in custody will invoke the *Miranda* right to counsel during the first interrogation, so that the permanent prohibition will attach at once. Those who do not do so will almost certainly request or obtain counsel at arraignment.

Today's extension of the *Edwards* prohibition is the latest stage of prophylaxis built upon prophylaxis, producing a veritable fairyland castle of imagined constitutional restriction upon law enforcement. It seems obvious to me that, even in *Edwards* itself but surely in today's decision, we have gone far beyond any genuine concern about suspects who do not know their right to remain silent, or who have been coerced to abandon it. Both holdings are explicable, in my view, only as an effort to protect suspects against what is regarded as their own folly. The sharp-witted criminal would know better than to confess; why should the dull-witted suffer for his lack of mental endowment? Providing him an attorney at every stage where he might be induced or persuaded (though not coerced) to incriminate himself will even the odds. Apart from the fact that this protective enterprise is beyond our authority under the Fifth Amendment or any other provision of the Constitution, it is unwise. The procedural protections of the Constitution protect the guilty as well as the innocent, but it is not their objective to set the guilty free. That some clever criminals may employ those protections to their advantage is poor reason to allow criminals who have not done so to escape justice.

Thus, even if I were to concede that an honest confession is a foolish mistake, I would welcome rather than reject it; a rule that foolish mistakes do not count would leave most offenders not only unconvicted but undetected. More fundamentally, however, it is wrong, and subtly corrosive of our criminal justice system, to regard an honest confession as a "mistake." While every person is entitled to stand silent, it is more virtuous for the wrongdoer to admit his offense and accept the punishment he deserves. Not only for society, but for the wrongdoer himself, "admissio[n] of guilt . . . , if not coerced, [is] inherently desirable" because it advances the goals of both "justice and rehabilitation." We should, then, rejoice at an honest confession, rather than pity the "poor fool" who has made it; and we should regret the attempted retraction of that good act, rather than seek to facilitate and encourage it. To design our laws on premises contrary to these is to abandon belief in either personal responsibility or the moral claim of just government to obedience. Today's decision is misguided.

What, though, of the situation where a suspect's request for counsel is equivocal or unclear? Do the police in such situations have the obligation to stop questioning or at least clarify the suspect's desires? In Davis v. United States, the Court resolved this in favor of the police and held that "the suspect must unambiguously request counsel."

DAVIS v. UNITED STATES
512 U.S. 452 (1994)

Justice O'CONNOR delivered the opinion of the Court.

In Edwards v. Arizona (1981), we held that law enforcement officers must immediately cease questioning a suspect who has clearly asserted his right to have counsel present during custodial interrogation. In this case we decide how law enforcement officers should respond when a suspect makes a reference to counsel that is insufficiently clear to invoke the *Edwards* prohibition on further questioning.

I

Pool brought trouble — not to River City, but to the Charleston Naval Base. Petitioner, a member of the United States Navy, spent the evening of October 2, 1988, shooting pool at a club on the base. Another sailor, Keith Shackleton, lost a game and a $30 wager to petitioner, but Shackleton refused to pay. After the club closed, Shackleton was beaten to death with a pool cue on a loading dock behind the commissary. The body was found early the next morning.

The investigation by the Naval Investigative Service (NIS) gradually focused on petitioner. Investigative agents determined that petitioner was at the club that evening, and that he was absent without authorization from his duty station the next morning. The agents also learned that only privately owned pool cues could be removed from the club premises, and that petitioner owned two cues — one of which had a bloodstain on it. The agents were told by various people that petitioner either had admitted committing the crime or had recounted details that clearly indicated his involvement in the killing.

On November 4, 1988, petitioner was interviewed at the NIS office. As required by military law, the agents advised petitioner that he was a suspect in the killing, that he was not required to make a statement, that any statement could be used against him at a trial by court-martial, and that he was entitled to speak with an attorney and have an attorney present during questioning. Petitioner waived his rights to remain silent and to counsel, both orally and in writing.

About an hour and a half into the interview, petitioner said, "Maybe I should talk to a lawyer." According to the uncontradicted testimony of one of the interviewing agents, the interview then proceeded as follows: "[We m]ade it very clear that we're not here to violate his rights, that if he wants a lawyer, then we will stop any kind of questioning with him, that we weren't going to pursue the matter unless we have it clarified is he asking for a lawyer or is he just making a comment about a lawyer, and he said, [']No, I'm not asking for a lawyer,' and then he continued on, and said, 'No, I don't want a lawyer.' "

After a short break, the agents reminded petitioner of his rights to remain silent and to counsel. The interview then continued for another hour, until petitioner said, "I think I want a lawyer before I say anything else." At that point, questioning ceased.

At his general court-martial, petitioner moved to suppress statements made during the November 4 interview. The Military Judge denied the motion, holding that "the mention of a lawyer by [petitioner] during the course of the interrogation [was] not in the form of a request for counsel and . . . the agents properly determined that [petitioner] was not indicating a desire for or invoking his right to counsel." Petitioner was convicted on one specification of unpremeditated murder. He was sentenced to confinement for life, a dishonorable discharge, forfeiture of all pay and allowances, and a reduction to the lowest pay grade. The convening authority approved the findings and sentence. The Navy-Marine Corps Court of Military Review affirmed.

II

The Sixth Amendment right to counsel attaches only at the initiation of adversary criminal proceedings and before proceedings are initiated a suspect in a criminal investigation has no constitutional right to the assistance of counsel. Nevertheless, we held in Miranda v. Arizona (1966), that a suspect subject to custodial interrogation has the right to consult with an attorney and to have counsel present during questioning, and that the police must explain this right to him before questioning begins. The right to counsel recognized in *Miranda* is sufficiently important to suspects in criminal investigations, we have held, that it "requir[es] the special protection of the knowing and intelligent waiver standard." Edwards v. Arizona. If the suspect effectively waives his right to counsel after receiving the *Miranda* warnings, law enforcement officers are free to question him. But if a suspect requests counsel at any time during the interview, he is not subject to further questioning until a lawyer has been made available or the suspect himself reinitiates conversation. This "second layer of prophylaxis for the *Miranda* right to counsel," is "designed to prevent police from badgering a defendant into waiving his previously asserted *Miranda* rights." To that end, we have held that a suspect who has invoked the right to counsel cannot be questioned regarding any offense unless an attorney is actually present.

The applicability of the " 'rigid' prophylactic rule" of *Edwards* requires courts to "determine whether the accused actually invoked his right to counsel." To avoid difficulties of proof and to provide guidance to officers conducting interrogations, this is an objective inquiry. Invocation of the *Miranda* right to counsel "requires, at a minimum, some statement that can reasonably be construed to be an expression of a desire for the assistance of an attorney." But if a suspect makes a reference to an attorney that is ambiguous or equivocal in that a reasonable officer in light of the circumstances would have understood only that the suspect might be invoking the right to counsel, our precedents do not require the cessation of questioning.

Rather, the suspect must unambiguously request counsel. As we have observed, "a statement either is such an assertion of the right to counsel or it is not." Although a suspect need not "speak with the discrimination of an Oxford don," he must articulate his desire to have counsel present sufficiently clearly that a reasonable police officer in the circumstances would understand the statement to be a request for an attorney. If the statement fails to meet the requisite level of clarity, *Edwards* does not require that the officers stop questioning the suspect.

We decline petitioner's invitation to extend *Edwards* and require law enforcement officers to cease questioning immediately upon the making of an ambiguous or equivocal reference to an attorney. The rationale underlying *Edwards* is that the police must respect a suspect's wishes regarding his right to have an attorney present during custodial interrogation. But when the officers conducting the questioning reasonably do not know whether or not the suspect wants a lawyer, a rule requiring the immediate cessation of questioning "would transform the *Miranda* safeguards into wholly irrational obstacles to legitimate police investigative activity," because it would needlessly prevent the police from questioning a suspect in the absence of counsel even if the suspect did not wish to have a lawyer present. Nothing in *Edwards* requires the provision of counsel to a suspect who consents to answer questions without the assistance of a lawyer. In *Miranda* itself, we expressly rejected the suggestion "that each police station must have a 'station house lawyer' present at all times to advise prisoners," and held instead that a suspect must be told of his right to have an attorney present and that he may not be questioned after invoking his right to counsel. We also noted that if a suspect is "indecisive in his request for counsel," the officers need not always cease questioning.

We recognize that requiring a clear assertion of the right to counsel might disadvantage some suspects who — because of fear, intimidation, lack of linguistic skills, or a variety of other reasons — will not clearly articulate their right to counsel although they actually want to have a lawyer present. But the primary protection afforded suspects subject to custodial interrogation is the *Miranda* warnings themselves. "[F]ull comprehension of the rights to remain silent and request an attorney [is] sufficient to dispel whatever coercion is inherent in the interrogation process." A suspect who knowingly and voluntarily waives his right to counsel after having that right explained to him has indicated his willingness to deal with the police unassisted. Although *Edwards* provides an additional protection — if a suspect subsequently requests an attorney, questioning must cease — it is one that must be affirmatively invoked by the suspect.

In considering how a suspect must invoke the right to counsel, we must consider the other side of the *Miranda* equation: the need for effective law enforcement. Although the courts ensure compliance with the *Miranda* requirements through the exclusionary rule, it is police officers who must actually decide whether or not they can question a suspect. The *Edwards* rule — questioning must cease if the suspect asks for a lawyer — provides a bright line that can be applied by officers in the real world of investigation and interrogation without unduly hampering the gathering of information. But if we were to require questioning to cease if a suspect makes a statement that might be a request for an attorney, this clarity and ease of application would be lost. Police officers would be forced to make difficult judgment calls about whether the suspect in fact wants a lawyer even though he has not said so, with the threat of suppression if they guess wrong. We therefore hold that, after a knowing and voluntary waiver of the *Miranda* rights, law enforcement officers may continue questioning until and unless the suspect clearly requests an attorney.

Of course, when a suspect makes an ambiguous or equivocal statement it will often be good police practice for the interviewing officers to clarify whether or not he actually wants an attorney. That was the procedure followed by the NIS agents in this case. Clarifying questions help protect the rights of the suspect by ensuring that he gets an attorney if he wants one, and will minimize the chance of a confession being suppressed due to subsequent judicial second-guessing as to the meaning of the suspect's statement regarding counsel. But we decline to adopt a rule requiring officers to ask clarifying questions. If the suspect's statement is not an unambiguous or unequivocal request for counsel, the officers have no obligation to stop questioning him.

To recapitulate: We held in *Miranda* that a suspect is entitled to the assistance of counsel during custodial interrogation even though the Constitution does not provide for such assistance. We held in *Edwards* that if the suspect invokes the right to counsel at any time, the police must immediately cease questioning him until an attorney is present. But we are unwilling to create a third layer of prophylaxis to prevent police questioning when the suspect might want a lawyer. Unless the suspect actually requests an attorney, questioning may continue.

Justice SOUTER, with whom Justice BLACKMUN, Justice STEVENS, and Justice GINSBURG join, concurring in the judgment.

In the midst of his questioning by naval investigators, petitioner said "Maybe I should talk to a lawyer." The investigators promptly stopped questioning Davis about the killing of Keith Shackleton and instead undertook to determine whether he meant to invoke his right to counsel. According to testimony accepted by the courts below, Davis answered the investigators' questions on that point by saying, "I'm not asking for a lawyer," and "No, I don't want to talk to a lawyer." Only then did the interrogation resume (stopping for good when petitioner said, "I think I want a lawyer before I say anything else").

I agree with the majority that the Constitution does not forbid law enforcement officers to pose questions (like those directed at Davis) aimed solely at clarifying whether a suspect's ambiguous reference to counsel was meant to assert his Fifth Amendment right. Accordingly I concur in the judgment affirming Davis's conviction, resting partly on evidence of statements given after agents ascertained that he did not wish to deal with them through counsel. I cannot, however, join in my colleagues' further conclusion that if the investigators here had been so inclined, they were at liberty to disregard Davis's reference to a lawyer entirely, in accordance with a general rule that interrogators have no legal obligation to discover what a custodial subject meant by an ambiguous statement that could reasonably be understood to express a desire to consult a lawyer. Our own precedent, the reasonable judgments of the majority of the many courts already to have addressed the issue before us, and the advocacy of a considerable body of law enforcement officials are to the contrary. All argue against the Court's approach today, which draws a sharp line between interrogated suspects who "clearly" assert their right to counsel and those who say something that may, but may not, express a desire for counsel's presence, the former suspects being assured that questioning will not resume without counsel present, the latter being left to fend for themselves. The concerns of fairness and practicality that have long anchored our *Miranda* case law point to a different response: when law enforcement officials "reasonably do not know whether or not the suspect wants a lawyer," they should stop their interrogation and ask him to make his choice clear.

C. THE SIXTH AMENDMENT RIGHT TO COUNSEL AND POLICE INTERROGATIONS

The right to counsel in interrogations required under Miranda v. Arizona discussed above is based on the Fifth Amendment's privilege against self-incrimination and is regarded as a key protector of that right. In addition, the Sixth Amendment provides that "in all criminal prosecutions, the accused shall enjoy the right . . . to have the Assistance of Counsel for his defense." Of course, one of the most important aspects of the Sixth Amendment is ensuring counsel at trial for those accused of crimes involving possible imprisonment. This is discussed in detail in Chapter 6.

Further, the Sixth Amendment right to counsel applies to police interrogations that occur after adversarial proceedings have begun; that is, the Court has said that the Sixth Amendment applies when judicial proceedings have been initiated against the accused "whether by way of formal charge, preliminary hearing, indictment, information, or arraignment."

There is obvious overlap between the Fifth Amendment and the Sixth Amendment rights to counsel: Both have been interpreted to require the provision of counsel to in-custodial interrogation of a criminal suspect after formal judicial proceedings have begun. But there are differences as well. The Fifth Amendment right to counsel under Miranda v. Arizona applies only to in-custodial interrogations; the Sixth Amendment right to counsel applies to all efforts by the police to deliberately elicit statements from a person after formal criminal proceedings have been initiated.

Subsection 1 looks at the origin of this rule in Massiah v. United States, Escobedo v. Illinois, and Brewer v. Williams. Subsection 2 focuses on the fact that this right is offense specific; the right only applies to those crimes where adversarial proceedings have begun and does not prevent questioning without counsel as to other crimes. Subsection 3 examines what is sufficient for a waiver of this right. Finally, Subsection 4 considers what is impermissible police eliciting of statements when someone is represented by counsel; specifically, does the use of undercover agents violate this right in that it involves communication through police agents without counsel after questioning without counsel is not allowed?

1.   The Sixth Amendment Right to Counsel During Interrogations

The initial key case in this area is Massiah v. United States. It continues to be the basis for the Sixth Amendment right to counsel during interrogations.

MASSIAH v. UNITED STATES
377 U.S. 201 (1964)

Justice STEWART delivered the opinion of the Court.

The petitioner was indicted for violating the federal narcotics laws. He retained a lawyer, pleaded not guilty, and was released on bail. While he was free on bail a federal agent succeeded by surreptitious means in listening to incriminating statements made by him. Evidence of these statements was introduced against the petitioner at his trial over his objection. He was convicted, and the Court of Appeals affirmed. We granted certiorari to consider whether, under the circumstances here presented, the prosecution's use at the trial of evidence of the petitioner's own incriminating statements deprived him of any right secured to him under the Federal Constitution.

The petitioner, a merchant seaman, was in 1958 a member of the crew of the S. S. Santa Maria. In April of that year federal customs officials in New York received information that he was going to transport a quantity of narcotics aboard that ship from South America to the United States. As a result of this and other information, the agents searched the Santa Maria upon its arrival in New York and found in the afterpeak of the vessel five packages containing about three and a half pounds of cocaine. They also learned of circumstances, not here relevant, tending to connect the petitioner with the cocaine. He was arrested, promptly arraigned, and subsequently indicted for possession of narcotics aboard a United States vessel. In July a superseding indictment was returned, charging the petitioner and a man named Colson with the same substantive offense, and in separate counts charging the petitioner, Colson, and others with having conspired to possess narcotics aboard a United States vessel, and to import, conceal, and facilitate the sale of narcotics. The petitioner, who had retained a lawyer, pleaded not guilty and was released on bail, along with Colson.

A few days later, and quite without the petitioner's knowledge, Colson decided to cooperate with the government agents in their continuing investigation of the nacotics activities in which the petitioner, Colson, and others had allegedly been engaged. Colson permitted an agent named Murphy to install a Schmidt radio transmitter under the front seat of Colson's automobile, by means of which Murphy, equipped with an appropriate receiving device, could overhear from some distance away conversations carried on in Colson's car.

On the evening of November 19, 1959, Colson and the petitioner held a lengthy conversation while sitting in Colson's automobile, parked on a New York street. By prearrangement with Colson, and totally unbeknown to the petitioner, the agent Murphy sat in a car parked out of sight down the street and listened over the radio to the entire conversation. The petitioner made several incriminating statements during the course of this conversation. At the petitioner's trial these incriminating statements were brought before the jury through Murphy's testimony, despite the insistent objection of defense counsel. The jury convicted the petitioner of several related narcotics offenses, and the convictions were affirmed by the Court of Appeals.

The petitioner argues that it was an error of constitutional dimensions to permit the agent Murphy at the trial to testify to the petitioner's incriminating statements which Murphy had overheard under the circumstances disclosed by this record. [I]t is said that the petitioner's Fifth and Sixth Amendment rights were violated by the use in evidence against him of incriminating statements which government agents had deliberately elicited from him after he had been indicted and in the absence of his retained counsel.

[A] constitutional principle established as long ago as Powell v. Alabama [1933], [is that] "during perhaps the most critical period of the proceedings . . . that is to say, from the time of their arraignment until the beginning of their trial, when consultation, thorough-going investigation and preparation [are] vitally important, the defendants . . . [are] as much entitled to such aid [of counsel] during that period as at the trial itself."

Here we deal not with a state court conviction, but with a federal case, where the specific guarantee of the Sixth Amendment directly applies. We hold that the petitioner was denied the basic protections of that guarantee when there was used against him at his trial evidence of his own incriminating words, which federal agents had deliberately elicited from him after he had been indicted and in the absence of his counsel.

The Solicitor General, in his brief and oral argument, has strenuously contended that the federal law enforcement agents had the right, if not indeed the duty, to continue their investigation of the petitioner and his alleged criminal associates even though the petitioner had been indicted. He points out that the Government was continuing its investigation in order to uncover not only the source of narcotics found on the S. S. Santa Maria, but also their intended buyer. He says that the quantity of narcotics involved was such as to suggest that the petitioner was part of a large and well-organized ring, and indeed that the continuing investigation confirmed this suspicion, since it resulted in criminal charges against many defendants. Under these circumstances the Solicitor General concludes that the Government agents were completely "justified in making use of Colson's cooperation by having Colson continue his normal associations and by surveilling them."

We do not question that in this case, as in many cases, it was entirely proper to continue an investigation of the suspected criminal activities of the defendant and his alleged confederates, even though the defendant had already been indicted. All that we hold is that the defendant's own incriminating statements, obtained by federal agents under the circumstances here disclosed, could not constitutionally be used by the prosecution as evidence against him at his trial.

Justice WHITE, with whom Justice CLARK and Justice HARLAN join, dissenting.

The current incidence of serious violations of the law represents not only an appalling waste of the potentially happy and useful lives of those who engage in such conduct but also an overhanging, dangerous threat to those unidentified and innocent people who will be the victims of crime today and tomorrow. This is a festering problem for which no adequate cures have yet been devised. At the very least there is much room for discontent with remedial measures so far undertaken. And admittedly there remains much to be settled concerning the disposition to be made of those who violate the law.

But dissatisfaction with preventive programs aimed at eliminating crime and profound dispute about whether we should punish, deter, rehabilitate or cure cannot excuse concealing one of our most menacing problems until the millennium has arrived. In my view, a civilized society must maintain its capacity to discover transgressions of the law and to identify those who flout it. This much is necessary even to know the scope of the problem, much less to formulate intelligent counter-measures. It will just not do to sweep these disagreeable matters under the rug or to pretend they are not there at all.

It is therefore a rather portentous occasion when a constitutional rule is established barring the use of evidence which is relevant, reliable and highly probative of the issue which the trial court has before it — whether the accused committed the act with which he is charged. Without the evidence, the quest for truth may be seriously impeded and in many cases the trial court, although aware of proof showing defendant's guilt, must nevertheless release him because the crucial evidence is deemed inadmissible. This result is entirely justified in some circumstances because exclusion serves other policies of overriding importance, as where evidence seized in an illegal search is excluded, not because of the quality of the proof, but to secure meaningful enforcement of the Fourth Amendment. But this only emphasizes that the soundest of reasons is necessary to warrant the exclusion of evidence otherwise admissible and the creation of another area of privileged testimony. With all due deference, I am not at all convinced that the additional barriers to the pursuit of truth which the Court today erects rest on anything like the solid foundations which decisions of this gravity should require.

The importance of the matter should not be underestimated, for today's rule promises to have wide application well beyond the facts of this case. The reason given for the result here — the admissions were obtained in the absence of counsel — would seem equally pertinent to statements obtained at any time after the right to counsel attaches, whether there has been an indictment or not; to admissions made prior to arraignment, at least where the defendant has counsel or asks for it; to the fruits of admissions improperly obtained under the new rule; to criminal proceedings in state courts; and to defendants long since convicted upon evidence including such admissions. The new rule will immediately do service in a great many cases.

Whatever the content or scope of the rule may prove to be, I am unable to see how this case presents an unconstitutional interference with Massiah's right to counsel. Massiah was not prevented from consulting with counsel as often as he wished. No meetings with counsel were disturbed or spied upon. Preparation for trial was in no way obstructed. It is only a sterile syllogism — an unsound one, besides — to say that because Massiah had a right to counsel's aid before and during the trial, his out-of-court conversations and admissions must be excluded if obtained without counsel's consent or presence. The right to counsel has never meant as much before, and its extension in this case requires some further explanation, so far unarticulated by the Court.

Since the new rule would exclude all admissions made to the police, no matter how voluntary and reliable, the requirement of counsel's presence or approval would seem to rest upon the probability that counsel would foreclose any admissions at all. This is nothing more than a thinly disguised constitutional policy of minimizing or entirely prohibiting the use in evidence of voluntary out-of-court admissions and confessions made by the accused. Carried as far as blind logic may compel some to go, the notion that statements from the mouth of the defendant should not be used in evidence would have a severe and unfortunate impact upon the great bulk of criminal cases.

Viewed in this light, the Court's newly fashioned exclusionary principle goes far beyond the constitutional privilege against self-incrimination, which neither requires nor suggests the barring of voluntary pretrial admissions. The Court presents no facts, no objective evidence, no reasons to warrant scrapping the voluntary-involuntary test for admissibility in this area. Without such evidence I would retain it in its present form.

Applying the new exclusionary rule is peculiarly inappropriate in this case. At the time of the conversation in question, petitioner was not in custody but free on bail. He was not questioned in what anyone could call an atmosphere of official coercion. What he said was said to his partner in crime who had also been indicted. There was no suggestion or any possibility of coercion.

Meanwhile, of course, the public will again be the loser and law enforcement will be presented with another serious dilemma. The general issue lurking in the background of the Court's opinion is the legitimacy of penetrating or obtaining confederates in criminal organizations. For the law enforcement agency, the answer for the time being can only be in the form of a prediction about the future application of today's new constitutional doctrine. More narrowly, and posed by the precise situation involved here, the question is this: when the police have arrested and released on bail one member of a criminal ring and another member, a confederate, is cooperating with the police, can the confederate be allowed to continue his association with the ring or must he somehow be withdrawn to avoid challenge to trial evidence on the ground that it was acquired after rather than before the arrest, after rather than before the indictment?

Massiah and those like him receive ample protection from the long line of precedents in this Court holding that confessions may not be introduced unless they are voluntary. In making these determinations the courts must consider the absence of counsel as one of several factors by which voluntariness is to be judged. This is a wiser rule than the automatic rule announced by the Court, which requires courts and juries to disregard voluntary admissions which they might well find to be the best possible evidence in discharging their responsibility for ascertaining truth.

The same year, in Escobedo v. Illinois, 378 U.S. 478 (1964), the Court extended the Sixth Amendment right to counsel to those who were questioned by the police but had not yet been formally charged. Escobedo had been arrested on suspicion of murder, but he had not been formally charged. During the police questioning, he several times requested a lawyer. Even though his mother had retained an attorney for him, the police refused to allow Escobedo to meet with the lawyer. The police obtained incriminating statements from Escobedo and the question was whether they had to be excluded.

The Supreme Court, in an opinion by Justice Goldberg, found that the police behavior violated the Sixth Amendment right to counsel. He stressed that the police had shifted from a "general investigation of an unsolved crime" to accusations directed at Escobedo. Although Escobedo had not been indicted, the Court found this distinction irrelevant. The Court said that *Massiah* was applicable because "no meaningful distinction can be drawn between interrogation of an accused before and after formal indictment."

Escobedo was very controversial at the time it was decided, but its holding has little lasting significance. Two years later, in Miranda v. Arizona, the Supreme Court found a right to counsel under the Fifth Amendment's privilege against self-incrimination for in-custodial police interrogation. This made it unnecessary to rely on the Sixth Amendment and *Escobedo* for police interrogations. Also, subsequent cases have made clear that the Sixth Amendment right to counsel applies only after the initiation of formal adversarial proceedings. For example, in Kirby v. Illinois, 406 U.S. 682 (1972), the Court held that the Sixth Amendment right to counsel at police identification procedures (such as lineups) applies only "at or after the initiation of adversary judicial criminal proceedings — whether by way of formal charge, preliminary hearing, indictment, information, or arraignment." (*Kirby* and the law concerning identification procedures are discussed in detail in Chapter 5.)

But *Massiah* remains an important case in holding that there is a Sixth Amendment right to counsel that applies whenever a person is questioned after adversarial proceedings have begun. Brewer v. Williams is a significant elaboration and application of this principle.

BREWER v. WILLIAMS
430 U.S. 387 (1977)

Justice STEWART delivered the opinion of the Court.

I

On the afternoon of December 24, 1968, a 10-year-old girl named Pamela Powers went with her family to the YMCA in Des Moines, Iowa, to watch a wrestling tournament in which her brother was participating. When she failed to return from a trip to the washroom, a search for her began. The search was unsuccessful.

Robert Williams, who had recently escaped from a mental hospital, was a resident of the YMCA. Soon after the girl's disappearance Williams was seen in the YMCA lobby carrying some clothing and a large bundle wrapped in a blanket. He obtained help from a 14-year-old boy in opening the street door of the YMCA and the door to his automobile parked outside. When Williams placed the bundle in the front seat of his car the boy "saw two legs in it and they were skinny and white." Before anyone could see what was in the bundle

Williams drove away. His abandoned car was found the following day in Daven-port, Iowa, roughly 160 miles east of Des Moines. A warrant was then issued in Des Moines for his arrest on a charge of abduction.

On the morning of December 26, a Des Moines lawyer named Henry McKnight went to the Des Moines police station and informed the officers present that he had just received a long-distance call from Williams, and that he had advised Williams to turn himself in to the Davenport police. Williams did surrender that morning to the police in Davenport, and they booked him on the charge specified in the arrest warrant and gave him the warnings required by Miranda v. Arizona. The Davenport police then telephoned their counterparts in Des Moines to inform them that Williams had surrendered. McKnight, the lawyer, was still at the Des Moines police headquarters, and Williams conversed with McKnight on the telephone. In the presence of the Des Moines chief of police and a police detective named Leaming, McKnight advised Williams that Des Moines police officers would be driving to Davenport to pick him up, that the officers would not interrogate him or mistreat him, and that Williams was not to talk to the officers about Pamela Powers until after consulting with McKnight upon his return to Des Moines. As a result of these conversations, it was agreed between McKnight and the Des Moines police officials that Detective Leaming and a fellow officer would drive to Davenport to pick up Williams, that they would bring him directly back to Des Moines, and that they would not question him during the trip.

In the meantime Williams was arraigned before a judge in Davenport on the outstanding arrest warrant. The judge advised him of his *Miranda* rights and committed him to jail. Before leaving the courtroom, Williams conferred with a lawyer named Kelly, who advised him not to make any statements until consulting with McKnight back in Des Moines.

Detective Leaming and his fellow officer arrived in Davenport about noon to pick up Williams and return him to Des Moines. Soon after their arrival they met with Williams and Kelly, who, they understood, was acting as Williams' lawyer. Detective Leaming repeated the *Miranda* warnings.

Williams then conferred again with *Kelly* alone, and after this conference Kelly reiterated to Detective Leaming that Williams was not to be questioned about the disappearance of Pamela Powers until after he had consulted with McKnight back in Des Moines. When Leaming expressed some reservations, Kelly firmly stated that the agreement with McKnight was to be carried out that there was to be no interrogation of Williams during the automobile journey to Des Moines. Kelly was denied permission to ride in the police car back to Des Moines with Williams and the two officers.

The two detectives, with Williams in their charge, then set out on the 160-mile drive. At no time during the trip did Williams express a willingness to be inter-rogated in the absence of an attorney. Instead, he stated several times that "[w]hen I get to Des Moines and see Mr. McKnight, I am going to tell you the whole story." Detective Leaming knew that Williams was a former mental patient, and knew also that he was deeply religious.

The detective and his prisoner soon embarked on a wide-ranging conversa-tion covering a variety of topics, including the subject of religion. Then, not long after leaving Davenport and reaching the interstate highway, Detective Leaming delivered what has been referred to in the briefs and oral arguments as the "Christian burial speech." Addressing Williams as "Reverend," the detective said: "I want to give you something to think about while we're traveling down the road. . . . Number one, I want you to observe the weather conditions, it's raining, it's sleeting, it's freezing, driving is very treacherous, visibility is poor, it's going to be dark early this evening. They are predicting several inches of snow for tonight, and I feel that you yourself are the only person that knows where this little girl's body is, that you yourself have only been there once, and if you get a snow on top of it you yourself may be unable to find it. And, since we will be going right past the area on the way into Des Moines, I feel that we could stop and locate the body, that the parents of this little girl should be entitled to a Christian burial for the little girl who was snatched away from them on Christmas [E]ve and murdered. And I feel we should stop and locate it on the way in rather than waiting until morning and trying to come back out after a snow storm and possibly not being able to find it at all."

Williams asked Detective Leaming why he thought their route to Des Moines would be taking them past the girl's body, and Leaming responded that he knew the body was in the area of Mitchellville [,] a town they would be passing on the way to Des Moines. Leaming then stated: "I do not want you to answer me. I don't want to discuss it any further. Just think about it as we're riding down the road."

As the car approached Grinnell, a town approximately 100 miles west of Davenport, Williams asked whether the police had found the victim's shoes. When Detective Leaming replied that he was unsure, Williams directed the officers to a service station where he said he had left the shoes; a search for them proved unsuccessful. As they continued towards Des Moines, Williams asked whether the police had found the blanket, and directed the officers to a rest area where he said he had disposed of the blanket. Nothing was found. The car continued towards Des Moines, and as it approached Mitchellville, Williams said that he would show the officers where the body was. He then directed the police to the body of Pamela Powers.

Williams was indicted for first-degree murder. Before trial, his counsel moved to suppress all evidence relating to or resulting from any statements Williams had made during the automobile ride from Davenport to Des Moines. The evidence in question was introduced over counsel's continuing objection at the subsequent trial. The jury found Williams guilty of murder, and the judgment of conviction was affirmed by the Iowa Supreme Court.

II

[T]here is no need to review in this case the doctrine of Miranda v. Arizona, a doctrine designed to secure the constitutional privilege against compulsory self-incrimination. For it is clear that the [conviction] in any event be [reversed] upon the ground that Williams was deprived of a different constitutional right: the right to the assistance of counsel.

This right, guaranteed by the Sixth and Fourteenth Amendments, is indispensable to the fair administration of our adversary system of criminal justice. Its vital need at the pretrial stage has perhaps nowhere been more succinctly explained than in Justice Sutherland's memorable words for the Court 44 years ago in Powell v. Alabama: "[D]uring perhaps the most critical period of the proceedings against these defendants, that is to say, from the time of their arraignment until the beginning of their trial, when consultation, thorough-going investigation and preparation were vitally important, the defendants did not have the aid of counsel in any real sense, although they were as much entitled to such aid during that period as at the trial itself."

There has occasionally been a difference of opinion within the Court as to the peripheral scope of this constitutional right. But its basic contours, which are identical in state and federal contexts, are too well established to require extensive elaboration here. Whatever else it may mean, the right to counsel granted by the Sixth and Fourteenth Amendments means at least that a person is entitled to the help of a lawyer at or after the time that judicial proceedings have been initiated against him "whether by way of formal charge, preliminary hearing, indictment, information, or arraignment."

There can be no doubt in the present case that judicial proceedings had been initiated against Williams before the start of the automobile ride from Davenport to Des Moines. A warrant had been issued for his arrest, he had been arraigned on that warrant before a judge in a Davenport courtroom, and he had been committed by the court to confinement in jail. The State does not contend otherwise.

There can be no serious doubt, either, that Detective Leaming deliberately and designedly set out to elicit information from Williams just as surely as and perhaps more effectively than if he had formally interrogated him. Detective Leaming was fully aware before departing for Des Moines that Williams was being represented in Davenport by Kelly and in Des Moines by McKnight. Yet he purposely sought during Williams' isolation from his lawyers to obtain as much incriminating information as possible. Indeed, Detective Leaming conceded as much when he testified at Williams' trial.

The state courts clearly proceeded upon the hypothesis that Detective Leaming's "Christian burial speech" had been tantamount to interrogation. Both courts recognized that Williams had been entitled to the assistance of counsel at the time he made the incriminating statements. Yet no such constitutional protection would have come into play if there had been no interrogation.

The circumstances of this case are thus constitutionally indistinguishable from those presented in Massiah v. United States. That the incriminating statements were elicited surreptitiously in the *Massiah* case, and otherwise here, is constitutionally irrelevant. Rather, the clear rule of *Massiah* is that once adversary proceedings have commenced against an individual, he has a right to legal representation when the government interrogates him. It thus requires no wooden or technical application of the *Massiah* doctrine to conclude that Williams was entitled to the assistance of counsel guaranteed to him by the Sixth and Fourteenth Amendments.

The District Court and the Court of Appeals were also correct in their understanding of the proper standard to be applied in determining the question of waiver as a matter of federal constitutional law — that it was incumbent upon the State to prove "an intentional relinquishment or abandonment of a known right or privilege." That standard has been reiterated in many cases. We have said that the right to counsel does not depend upon a request by the defendant and that courts indulge in every reasonable presumption against waiver. This strict standard applies equally to an alleged waiver of the right to counsel whether at trial or at a critical stage of pretrial proceedings.

Despite Williams' express and implicit assertions of his right to counsel, Detective Leaming proceeded to elicit incriminating statements from Williams.

Leaming did not preface this effort by telling Williams that he had a right to the presence of a lawyer, and made no effort at all to ascertain whether Williams wished to relinquish that right. The circumstances of record in this case thus provide no reasonable basis for finding that Williams waived his right to the assistance of counsel.

The crime of which Williams was convicted was senseless and brutal, calling for swift and energetic action by the police to apprehend the perpetrator and gather evidence with which he could be convicted. No mission of law enforcement officials is more important. Yet "[d]isinterested zeal for the public good does not assure either wisdom or right in the methods it pursues." Although we do not lightly affirm the issuance of a writ of habeas corpus in this case, so clear a violation of the Sixth and Fourteenth Amendments as here occurred cannot be condoned. The pressures on state executive and judicial officers charged with the administration of the criminal law are great, especially when the crime is murder and the victim a small child. But it is precisely the predictability of those pressures that makes imperative a resolute loyalty to the guarantees that the Constitution extends to us all.

Chief Justice BURGER, dissenting.

The result in this case ought to be intolerable in any society which purports to call itself an organized society. It continues the Court by the narrowest margin on the much criticized course of punishing the public for the mistakes and misdeeds of law enforcement officers, instead of punishing the officer directly, if in fact he is guilty of wrongdoing. It mechanically and blindly keeps reliable evidence from juries whether the claimed constitutional violation involves gross police misconduct or honest human error.

Williams is guilty of the savage murder of a small child; no member of the Court contends he is not. While in custody, and after no fewer than five warnings of his rights to silence and to counsel, he led police to the concealed body of his victim. The Court concedes Williams was not threatened or coerced and that he spoke and acted voluntarily and with full awareness of his constitutional rights. In the face of all this, the Court now holds that because Williams was prompted by the detective's statement — not interrogation but a statement — the jury must not be told how the police found the body.

Today's holding fulfills Judge (later Mr. Justice) Cardozo's grim prophecy that someday some court might carry the exclusionary rule to the absurd extent that its operative effect would exclude evidence relating to the body of a murder victim because of the means by which it was found. In so ruling the Court regresses to playing a grisly game of "hide and seek," once more exalting the sporting theory of criminal justice which has been experiencing a decline in our jurisprudence. I categorically reject the remarkable notion that the police in this case were guilty of unconstitutional misconduct, or any conduct justifying the bizarre result reached by the Court. Apart from a brief comment on the merits, however, I wish to focus on the irrationality of applying the increasingly discredited exclusionary rule to this case.

The evidence is uncontradicted that Williams had abundant knowledge of his right to have counsel present and of his right to silence. Since the Court does not question his mental competence, it boggles the mind to suggest that Williams could not understand that leading police to the child's body would have other than the most serious consequences. All of the elements necessary to make out a valid waiver are shown by the record and acknowledged by the Court; we thus are left to guess how the Court reached its holding.

Justice WHITE, with whom Justice BLACKMUN and Justice REHNQUIST join, dissenting.

The respondent in this case killed a 10-year-old child, holding that certain statements of unquestioned reliability were unconstitutionally obtained from him, and under the circumstances probably makes it impossible to retry him. Because there is nothing in the Constitution or in our previous cases which requires the Court's action, I dissent.

Respondent relinquished his right not to talk to the police about his crime when the car approached the place where he had hidden the victim's clothes. Men usually intend to do what they do, and there is nothing in the record to support the proposition that respondent's decision to talk was anything but an exercise of his own free will. Apparently, without any prodding from the officers, respondent—who had earlier said that he would tell the whole story when he arrived in Des Moines—spontaneously changed his mind about the timing of his disclosures when the car approached the places where he had hidden the evidence. However, even if his statements were influenced by Detective Leaming's above-quoted statement, respondent's decision to talk in the absence of counsel can hardly be viewed as the product of an overborne will. The statement by Leaming was not coercive; it was accompanied by a request that respondent not respond to it; and it was delivered hours before respondent decided to make any statement. Respondent's waiver was thus knowing and intentional.

The majority's contrary conclusion seems to rest on the fact that respondent "asserted" his right to counsel by retaining and consulting with one lawyer and by consulting with another. How this supports the conclusion that respondent's later relinquishment of his right not to talk in the absence of counsel was unintentional is a mystery. The fact that respondent consulted with counsel on the question whether he should talk to the police in counsel's absence makes his later decision to talk in counsel's absence better informed and, if anything, more intelligent.

The consequence of the majority's decision is, as the majority recognizes, extremely serious. A mentally disturbed killer whose guilt is not in question may be released. Why? Apparently the answer is that the majority believes that the law enforcement officers acted in a way which involves some risk of injury to society and that such conduct should be deterred. However, the officers' conduct did not, and was not likely to, jeopardize the fairness of respondent's trial or in any way risk the conviction of an innocent man[,] the risk against which the Sixth Amendment guarantee of assistance of counsel is designed to protect. The police did nothing "wrong," let alone anything "unconstitutional." To anyone not lost in the intricacies of the prophylactic rules of Miranda v. Arizona, the result in this case seems utterly senseless; the statements made by respondent were properly admitted. In light of these considerations, the majority's protest that the result in this case is justified by a "clear violation" of the Sixth and Fourteenth Amendments has a distressing hollow ring. I respectfully dissent.

Most recently, the Court applied *Massiah* and *Brewer* in Fellers v. United States, 540 U.S. 519 (2004). Fellers was indicted for conspiracy to distribute methamphetamines. Police came to his house to arrest him and Fellers made several incriminating statements. The Supreme Court held that the statements had to be excluded. Justice O'Connor, writing for the Court, said that "there is no question that the officers in this case 'deliberately elicited' information from petitioner. Indeed, the officers, upon arriving at petitioner's house, informed him that their purpose was to discuss his involvement in the distribution of methamphetamines and his association with certain charged co-conspirators." The Court concluded that "[b]ecause the ensuing discussion took place after petitioner had been indicted, outside the presence of counsel, and in the absence of any waiver of petitioner's Sixth Amendment rights" the statements made to the police had to be excluded.

2. The Sixth Amendment Right to Counsel Is Offense Specific

A key distinction between the Fifth Amendment right to counsel and the Sixth Amendment right to counsel is that the latter is offense specific. Under the Fifth Amendment right to counsel, police cannot initiate questioning as to any crime after a suspect has invoked the right to counsel. But under the Sixth Amendment the police are only limited in questioning the suspect about the specific crimes for which formal judicial proceedings have been initiated.

This was initially the holding in McNeil v. Wisconsin, 501 U.S. 171 (1981). McNeil was formally charged with armed robbery and asserted his right to counsel. Subsequently, police questioned McNeil about a murder and armed robbery in another part of the state. McNeil was given his *Miranda* warnings and confessed. The question was whether his earlier invocation of the right to counsel made the questioning about the other offenses impermissible.

In a 6-3 decision, the Court found no violation of the Sixth Amendment. In an opinion by Justice Scalia, the Court concluded that "just as the right is offense-specific," so is the effect of asserting the right to counsel "in police-initiated interviews offense-specific." The Court said that a contrary rule would interfere with effective law enforcement because then "most people in pretrial custody for serious offenses would be unapproachable by police officers suspecting them of involvement in other crimes, even though they have never expressed any unwillingness to be questioned."

The Court reaffirmed and clarified this in Texas v. Cobb.

TEXAS v. COBB
532 U.S. 162 (2001)

Chief Justice REHNQUIST delivered the opinion of the Court.

The Texas Court of Criminal Appeals held that a criminal defendant's Sixth Amendment right to counsel attaches not only to the offense with which he is charged, but to other offenses "closely related factually" to the charged offense. We hold that our decision in McNeil v. Wisconsin (1991), meant what it said, and that the Sixth Amendment right is "offense specific."

In December 1993, Lindsey Owings reported to the Walker County, Texas, Sheriff's Office that the home he shared with his wife, Margaret, and their 16-month-old daughter, Kori Rae, had been burglarized. He also informed police that his wife and daughter were missing. Respondent Raymond Levi Cobb lived across the street from the Owings. Acting on an anonymous tip that respondent was involved in the burglary, Walker County investigators questioned him about the events. He denied involvement. In July 1994, while under arrest for an unrelated offense, respondent was again questioned about the incident. Respondent then gave a written statement confessing to the burglary, but he denied knowledge relating to the disappearances. Respondent was subsequently indicted for the burglary, and Hal Ridley was appointed in August 1994 to represent respondent on that charge.

Shortly after Ridley's appointment, investigators asked and received his permission to question respondent about the disappearances. Respondent continued to deny involvement. Investigators repeated this process in September 1995, again with Ridley's permission and again with the same result.

In November 1995, respondent, free on bond in the burglary case, was living with his father in Odessa, Texas. At that time, respondent's father contacted the Walker County Sheriff's Office to report that respondent had confessed to him that he killed Margaret Owings in the course of the burglary. Walker County investigators directed respondent's father to the Odessa police station, where he gave a statement. Odessa police then faxed the statement to Walker County, where investigators secured a warrant for respondent's arrest and faxed it back to Odessa. Shortly thereafter, Odessa police took respondent into custody and administered warnings pursuant to Miranda v. Arizona. Respondent waived these rights.

After a short time, respondent confessed to murdering both Margaret and Kori Rae. Respondent explained that when Margaret confronted him as he was attempting to remove the Owings' stereo, he stabbed her in the stomach with a knife he was carrying. Respondent told police that he dragged her body to a wooded area a few hundred yards from the house. Respondent later led police to the location where he had buried the victims' bodies.

Respondent was convicted of capital murder for murdering more than one person in the course of a single criminal transaction. He was sentenced to death.

In McNeil v. Wisconsin (1991), we explained: "The Sixth Amendment right [to counsel] . . . is offense specific. It cannot be invoked once for all future prosecutions, for it does not attach until a prosecution is commenced, that is, at or after the initiation of adversary judicial criminal proceedings — whether by way of formal charge, preliminary hearing, indictment, information, or arraignment." Accordingly, we held that a defendant's statements regarding offenses for which he had not been charged were admissible notwithstanding the attachment of his Sixth Amendment right to counsel on other charged offenses.

Some state courts and Federal Courts of Appeals, however, have read into McNeil's offense-specific definition an exception for crimes that are "factually related" to a charged offense. We decline to do so.

Respondent predicts that the offense-specific rule will prove "disastrous" to suspects' constitutional rights and will "permit law enforcement officers almost complete and total license to conduct unwanted and uncounseled interrogations." Besides offering no evidence that such a parade of horribles has occurred in those jurisdictions that have not enlarged upon McNeil, he fails to appreciate the significance of two critical considerations. First, there can be no doubt that a suspect must be apprised of his rights against compulsory self-incrimination and to consult with an attorney before authorities may conduct custodial interrogation. In the present case, police scrupulously followed *Miranda*'s dictates when questioning respondent. Second, it is critical to recognize that the Constitution does not negate society's interest in the ability of police to talk to witnesses and suspects, even those who have been charged with other offenses.

It is also worth noting that, contrary to the dissent's suggestion, there is no "background principle" of our Sixth Amendment jurisprudence establishing that there may be no contact between a defendant and police without counsel present. The dissent would expand the Sixth Amendment right to the assistance of counsel in a criminal prosecution into a rule which "exists to prevent lawyers from taking advantage of uncounseled laypersons and to preserve the integrity of the lawyer-client relationship." The Sixth Amendment right to counsel is personal to the defendant and specific to the offense.

Although it is clear that the Sixth Amendment right to counsel attaches only to charged offenses, we have recognized in other contexts that the definition of an "offense" is not necessarily limited to the four corners of a charging instrument. In Blockburger v. United States (1932), we explained that "where the same act or transaction constitutes a violation of two distinct statutory provisions, the test to be applied to determine whether there are two offenses or only one, is whether each provision requires proof of a fact which the other does not." We have since applied the *Blockburger* test to delineate the scope of the Fifth Amendment's Double Jeopardy Clause, which prevents multiple or successive prosecutions for the "same offence." We see no constitutional difference between the meaning of the term "offense" in the contexts of double jeopardy and of the right to counsel. Accordingly, we hold that when the Sixth Amendment right to counsel attaches, it does encompass offenses that, even if not formally charged, would be considered the same offense under the *Blockburger* test.

It remains only to apply these principles to the facts at hand. At the time he confessed to Odessa police, respondent had been indicted for burglary of the Owings residence, but he had not been charged in the murders of Margaret and Kori Rae. As defined by Texas law, burglary and capital murder are not the same offense under *Blockburger*. Accordingly, the Sixth Amendment right to counsel did not bar police from interrogating respondent regarding the murders, and respondent's confession was therefore admissible.

Justice BREYER, with whom Justice STEVENS, Justice SOUTER, and Justice GINSBURG join, dissenting.

This case focuses upon the meaning of a single word, "offense," when it arises in the context of the Sixth Amendment. Several basic background principles define that context.

First, the Sixth Amendment right to counsel plays a central role in ensuring the fairness of criminal proceedings in our system of justice. Second, the right attaches when adversary proceedings, triggered by the government's formal accusation of a crime, begin. Third, once this right attaches, law enforcement officials are required, in most circumstances, to deal with the defendant through counsel rather than directly, even if the defendant has waived his Fifth Amendment rights.

Fourth, the particular aspect of the right here at issue — the rule that the police ordinarily must communicate with the defendant through counsel — has important limits. In particular, recognizing the need for law enforcement officials to investigate "new or additional crimes" not the subject of current proceedings, this Court has made clear that the right to counsel does not attach to any and every crime that an accused may commit or have committed. The right "cannot be invoked once for all future prosecutions," and it does not forbid "interrogation unrelated to the charge." In a word, as this Court previously noted, the right is "offense specific."

This case focuses upon the last-mentioned principle, in particular upon the meaning of the words "offense specific." These words appear in this Court's Sixth Amendment case law, not in the Sixth Amendment's text. The definition of these words is not self-evident. Sometimes the term "offense" may refer to words that are written in a criminal statute; sometimes it may refer generally to a course of conduct in the world, aspects of which constitute the elements of one or more crimes; and sometimes it may refer, narrowly and technically, just to the conceptually severable aspects of the latter. This case requires us to determine whether an "offense" — for Sixth Amendment purposes — includes factually related aspects of a single course of conduct other than those few acts that make up the essential elements of the crime charged.

We should answer this question in light of the Sixth Amendment's basic objectives as set forth in this Court's case law. At the very least, we should answer it in a way that does not undermine those objectives. But the Court today decides that "offense" means the crime set forth within "the four corners of a charging instrument," along with other crimes that "would be considered the same offense" under the test established by Blockburger v. United States (1932). In my view, this unnecessarily technical definition undermines Sixth Amendment protections while doing nothing to further effective law enforcement.

For one thing, the majority's rule, while leaving the Fifth Amendment's protections in place, threatens to diminish severely the additional protection that, under this Court's rulings, the Sixth Amendment provides when it grants the right to counsel to defendants who have been charged with a crime and insists that law enforcement officers thereafter communicate with them through that counsel.

For these reasons, the Sixth Amendment right at issue is independent of the Fifth Amendment's protections; and the importance of this Sixth Amendment right has been repeatedly recognized in our cases. The majority's rule permits law enforcement officials to question those charged with a crime without first approaching counsel, through the simple device of asking questions about any other related crime not actually charged in the indictment. Thus, the police could ask the individual charged with robbery about, say, the assault of the cashier not yet charged, or about any other uncharged offense (unless under Blockburger's definition it counts as the "same crime"), all without notifying counsel. Indeed, the majority's rule would permit law enforcement officials to question anyone charged with any crime in any one of the examples just given about his or her conduct on the single relevant occasion without notifying counsel unless the prosecutor has charged every possible crime arising out of that same brief course of conduct. What Sixth Amendment sense — what common sense — does such a rule make? What is left of the "communicate through counsel" rule? The majority's approach is inconsistent with any common understanding of the scope of counsel's representation. It will undermine the lawyer's role as " 'medium' " between the defendant and the government. And it will, on a random basis, remove a significant portion of the protection that this Court has found inherent in the Sixth Amendment.

[T]he simple-sounding *Blockburger* test has proved extraordinarily difficult to administer in practice. Judges, lawyers, and law professors often disagree about how to apply it. Yet the Court now asks, not the lawyers and judges who ordinarily work with double jeopardy law, but police officers in the field, to navigate *Blockburger* when they question suspects. Some will apply the test successfully; some will not. Legal challenges are inevitable. The result, I believe, will resemble not so much the Sargasso Sea as the criminal law equivalent of Milton's "Serbonian Bog . . . Where Armies whole have sunk."

There is, of course, an alternative. We can, and should, define "offense" in terms of the conduct that constitutes the crime that the offender committed on a particular occasion, including criminal acts that are "closely related to" or "inextricably intertwined with" the particular crime set forth in the charging instrument. This alternative is not perfect. The language used lacks the precision for which police officers may hope; and it requires lower courts to specify its meaning further as they apply it in individual cases. Yet virtually every lower court in the United States to consider the issue has defined "offense" in the Sixth Amendment context to encompass such closely related acts.

One cannot say in favor of this commonly followed approach that it is perfectly clear — only that, because it comports with common sense, it is far easier to apply than that of the majority. And, most importantly, the "closely related" test furthers, rather than undermines, the Sixth Amendment's "right to counsel," a right so necessary to the realization in practice of that most "noble ideal," a fair trial.

3. Waivers

The Sixth Amendment right to counsel, like the Fifth Amendment right to counsel under the privilege against self-incrimination, can be waived. Here, too, the Supreme Court has stressed that it must be a knowing and intelligent waiver. Moreover, the Supreme Court has held that once the Sixth Amendment right to counsel has been invoked, there is not a valid waiver if it was made in response to government-initiated interrogation.

MICHIGAN v. JACKSON
475 U.S. 625 (1986)

Justice STEVENS delivered the opinion of the Court.

In Edwards v. Arizona (1981), we held that an accused person in custody who has "expressed his desire to deal with the police only through counsel, is not subject to further interrogation by the authorities until counsel has been made available to him, unless the accused himself initiates further communication, exchanges, or conversations with the police."

The question presented by these two cases is whether the same rule applies to a defendant who has been formally charged with a crime and who has requested appointment of counsel at his arraignment. In both cases, the Michigan Supreme Court held that postarraignment confessions were improperly obtained — and the Sixth Amendment violated — because the defendants had "requested counsel during their arraignments, but were not afforded an opportunity to consult with counsel before the police initiated further interrogations." We agree with that holding.

I

The relevant facts may be briefly stated. Respondent Jackson was convicted of second-degree murder and conspiracy to commit second-degree murder. He was one of four participants in a wife's plan to have her husband killed on July 12, 1979. Arrested on an unrelated charge on July 30, 1979, he made a series of six statements in response to police questioning prior to his arraignment at 4:30 P.M. on August 1. During the arraignment, Jackson requested that counsel be appointed for him. The police involved in his investigation were present at the arraignment. On the following morning, before he had an opportunity to consult with counsel, two police officers obtained another statement from Jackson to "confirm" that he was the person who had shot the victim. As was true of the six prearraignment statements, the questioning was preceded by advice of his *Miranda* rights and Jackson's agreement to proceed without counsel being present.

The Michigan Court of Appeals held that the seventh statement was properly received in evidence. It distinguished *Edwards* on the ground that Jackson's request for an attorney had been made at his arraignment whereas Edwards' request had been made during a custodial interrogation by the police. Accordingly, it affirmed Jackson's conviction of murder, although it set aside the conspiracy conviction on unrelated grounds. The Michigan Supreme Court held that the postarraignment statements should have been suppressed, noting that the Sixth Amendment right to counsel attached at the time of the arraignments.

II

The question is not whether respondents had a right to counsel at their postarraignment, custodial interrogations. The existence of that right is clear. It has two sources. The Fifth Amendment protection against compelled self-incrimination provides the right to counsel at custodial interrogations. The Sixth Amendment guarantee of the assistance of counsel also provides the right to counsel at postarraignment interrogations. The arraignment signals "the initiation of adversary judicial proceedings" and thus the attachment of the Sixth Amendment[;] thereafter, government efforts to elicit information from the accused, including interrogation, represent "critical stages" at which the Sixth Amendment applies. The question in these cases is whether respondents validly waived their right to counsel at the postarraignment custodial interrogations.

In *Edwards*, the request for counsel was made to the police during custodial interrogation, and the basis for the Court's holding was the Fifth Amendment privilege against compelled self-incrimination. The Court noted the relevance of various Sixth Amendment precedents, but found it unnecessary to rely on the possible applicability of the Sixth Amendment. In these cases, the request for counsel was made to a judge during arraignment, and the basis for the Michigan Supreme Court opinion was the Sixth Amendment's guarantee of the assistance of counsel.

In our opinion, however, the reasons for prohibiting the interrogation of an uncounseled prisoner who has asked for the help of a lawyer are even stronger after he has been formally charged with an offense than before. The State's argument misapprehends the nature of the pretrial protections afforded by the Sixth Amendment. In United States v. Gouveia, we explained the significance of the formal accusation, and the corresponding attachment of the Sixth Amendment right to counsel: "[G]iven the plain language of the Amendment and its purpose of protecting the unaided layman at critical confrontations with his adversary, our conclusion that the right to counsel attaches at the initiation of adversary judicial criminal proceedings 'is far from a mere formalism.' It is only at that time 'that the government has committed itself to prosecute, and only then that the adverse positions of government and defendant have solidified. It is then that a defendant finds himself faced with the prosecutorial forces of organized society, and immersed in the intricacies of substantive and procedural criminal law.' "

As a result, the "Sixth Amendment guarantees the accused, at least after the initiation of formal charges, the right to rely on counsel as a 'medium' between him and the State." Thus, the Sixth Amendment right to counsel at a post-arraignment interrogation requires at least as much protection as the Fifth Amendment right to counsel at any custodial interrogation.

Indeed, after a formal accusation has been made — and a person who had previously been just a "suspect" has become an "accused" within the meaning of the Sixth Amendment — the constitutional right to the assistance of counsel is of such importance that the police may no longer employ techniques for eliciting information from an uncounseled defendant that might have been entirely proper at an earlier stage of their investigation. Far from undermining the *Edwards* rule, the difference between the legal basis for the rule applied in *Edwards* and the Sixth Amendment claim asserted in these cases actually provides additional support for the application of the rule in these circumstances.

The State points to another factual difference: the police may not know of the defendant's request for attorney at the arraignment. That claimed distinction is similarly unavailing. In the cases at bar, in which the officers in charge of the investigations of respondents were present at the arraignments, the argument is particularly unconvincing. More generally, however, Sixth Amendment principles require that we impute the State's knowledge from one state actor to another. For the Sixth Amendment concerns the confrontation between the State and the individual. One set of state actors (the police) may not claim ignorance of defendants' unequivocal request for counsel to another state actor (the court).

Finally, the State maintains that each of the respondents made a valid waiver of his Sixth Amendment rights by signing a postarraignment confession after again being advised of his constitutional rights. In *Edwards*, however, we rejected the notion that, after a suspect's request for counsel, advice of rights and acquiescence in police-initiated questioning could establish a valid waiver. We find no warrant for a different view under a Sixth Amendment analysis. Indeed, our rejection of the comparable argument in *Edwards* was based, in part, on our review of earlier Sixth Amendment cases. Just as written waivers are insufficient to justify police-initiated interrogations after the request for counsel in a Fifth Amendment analysis, so too they are insufficient to justify police-initiated interrogations after the request for counsel in a Sixth Amendment analysis.

III

Edwards is grounded in the understanding that "the assertion of the right to counsel [is] a significant event," and that "additional safeguards are necessary when the accused asks for counsel." We conclude that the assertion is no less significant, and the need for additional safeguards no less clear, when the request for counsel is made at an arraignment and when the basis for the claim is the Sixth Amendment. We thus hold that, if police initiate interrogation after a defendant's assertion, at an arraignment or similar proceeding, of his right to counsel, any waiver of the defendant's right to counsel for that police-initiated interrogation is invalid.

Although the *Edwards* decision itself rested on the Fifth Amendment and concerned a request for counsel made during custodial interrogation, the Michigan Supreme Court correctly perceived that the reasoning of that case applies with even greater force to these cases.

Justice REHNQUIST, with whom Justice POWELL and Justice O'CONNOR join, dissenting.

The Court's decision today rests on the following deceptively simple line of reasoning: Edwards v. Arizona (1981) created a bright-line rule to protect a defendant's Fifth Amendment rights; Sixth Amendment rights are even more important than Fifth Amendment rights; therefore, we must also apply the *Edwards* rule to the Sixth Amendment. The Court prefers this neat syllogism to an effort to discuss or answer the only relevant question: Does the *Edwards* rule make sense in the context of the Sixth Amendment? I think it does not, and I therefore dissent from the Court's unjustified extension of the *Edwards* rule to the Sixth Amendment.

My disagreement with the Court stems from our differing understandings of *Edwards*. In *Edwards*, this Court held that once a defendant has invoked his right under Miranda v. Arizona (1966), to have counsel present during custodial interrogation, "a valid waiver of that right cannot be established by showing only that he responded to further police-initiated custodial interrogation even if he has been advised of his rights."

What the Court today either forgets or chooses to ignore is that the "constitutional guarantee" is the Fifth Amendment's prohibition on compelled self-incrimination. This prohibition, of course, is also the constitutional underpinning for the set of prophylactic rules announced in *Miranda* itself. *Edwards*, like *Miranda*, imposes on the police a bright-line standard of conduct intended to help ensure that confessions obtained through custodial interrogation will not be "coerced" or "involuntary." Seen in this proper light, *Edwards* provides nothing more than a second layer of protection, in addition to those rights conferred by *Miranda*, for a defendant who might otherwise be compelled by the police to incriminate himself in violation of the Fifth Amendment.

The dispositive question in the instant cases, and the question the Court should address in its opinion, is whether the same kind of prophylactic rule is needed to protect a defendant's right to counsel under the Sixth Amendment. The answer to this question, it seems to me, is clearly "no." The Court does not even suggest that the police commonly deny defendants their Sixth Amendment right to counsel. Nor, I suspect, would such a claim likely be borne out by empirical evidence. Thus, the justification for the prophylactic rules this Court created in *Miranda* and *Edwards*, namely, the perceived widespread problem that the police were violating, and would probably continue to violate, the Fifth Amendment rights of defendants during the course of custodial inter- rogations, is conspicuously absent in the Sixth Amendment context. To put it simply, the prophylactic rule set forth in *Edwards* makes no sense at all except when linked to the Fifth Amendment's prohibition against compelled self- incrimination.

Not only does the Court today cut the *Edwards* rule loose from its analytical moorings, it does so in a manner that graphically reveals the illogic of the Court's position. The Court phrases the question presented in these cases as whether the *Edwards* rule applies "to a defendant who has been formally charged with a crime and who has requested appointment of counsel at his arraign- ment." And the Court ultimately limits its holding to those situations where the police "initiate interrogation after a defendant's assertion, at an arraign- ment or similar proceeding, of his right to counsel."

In other words, the Court most assuredly does not hold that the *Edwards* per se rule prohibiting all police-initiated interrogations applies from the moment the defendant's Sixth Amendment right to counsel attaches, with or without a request for counsel by the defendant. Such a holding would represent, after all, a shockingly dramatic restructuring of the balance this Court has tradition- ally struck between the rights of the defendant and those of the larger society.

This leaves the Court, however, in an analytical straitjacket. The problem with the limitation the Court places on the Sixth Amendment version of the *Edwards* rule is that, unlike a defendant's "right to counsel" under *Miranda*, which does not arise until affirmatively invoked by the defendant during custodial interro- gation, a defendant's Sixth Amendment right to counsel does not depend at all on whether the defendant has requested counsel.

The Court provides no satisfactory explanation for its decision to extend the *Edwards* rule to the Sixth Amendment, yet limit that rule to those defendants foresighted enough, or just plain lucky enough, to have made an explicit request for counsel which we have always understood to be completely unnecessary for Sixth Amendment purposes.

The truth is that there is no satisfactory explanation for the position the Court adopts in these cases. The glaring inconsistencies in the Court's opinion arise precisely because the Court lacks a coherent, analytically sound basis for its decision. The prophylactic rule of *Edwards*, designed from its inception to pro- tect a defendant's right under the Fifth Amendment not to be compelled to incriminate himself, simply does not meaningfully apply to the Sixth Amend- ment. I would hold that *Edwards* has no application outside the context of the Fifth Amendment.

By contrast, in Patterson v. Illinois, 487 U.S. 285 (1988), the Court held that *Massiah* does not apply to a defendant who is not represented by counsel and has never requested counsel. The Supreme Court expressly distinguished *Jackson* on the grounds that the defendant there had expressly invoked his right to counsel. The Court found that the defendant's waiver of his right to counsel under the Fifth Amendment pursuant to *Miranda* was also sufficient for a waiver of his Sixth Amendment right to counsel.

4.   What Is Impermissible Police Eliciting of Statements?

The Supreme Court has held that the Sixth Amendment and *Massiah* prevent the police from doing anything to elicit statements from an accused who has invoked the right to counsel once formal adversary proceedings have been initiated. The Court has said that once a person is represented by counsel, the "Sixth Amendment guarantees the accused, at least after the initiation of formal charges, the right to rely on counsel as a 'medium' between him and the State." Maine v. Moulton, 474 U.S. 159 (1985). In that case, the Court found a violation of the Sixth Amendment when the police put a wire on a co-defendant to record conversations with the accused. The Court held that the defendant's statements relating to the crimes for which he had been indicted were not admissible under the Sixth Amendment.

This raises a difficult question: When is there deliberate elicitation when police use informers to gain statements from an accused who is represented by counsel?. The Supreme Court has decided two major cases on this — United States v. Henry and Kuhlmann v. Wilson. In reading them, it is important to focus on whether they can be reconciled and when use of informers is allowed and when it is impermissible eliciting of statements.

UNITED STATES v. HENRY
447 U.S. 264 (1980)

Chief Justice BURGER delivered the opinion of the Court.

We granted certiorari to consider whether respondent's Sixth Amendment right to the assistance of counsel was violated by the admission at trial of incriminating statements made by respondent to his cellmate, an undisclosed Government informant, after indictment and while in custody.

I

The Janaf Branch of the United Virginia Bank/Seaboard National in Norfolk, Va., was robbed in August 1972. Witnesses saw two men wearing masks and carrying guns enter the bank while a third man waited in the car. No witnesses were able to identify respondent Henry as one of the participants. About an hour after the robbery, the getaway car was discovered. Inside was found a rent receipt signed by one "Allen R. Norris" and a lease, also signed by Norris, for a house in Norfolk. Two men, who were subsequently convicted of participating in the robbery, were arrested at the rented house. Discovered with them were the proceeds of the robbery and the guns and masks used by the gunman. Government agents traced the rent receipt to Henry; on the basis of this information,

Henry was arrested in Atlanta, Ga., in November 1972. Two weeks later he was indicted for armed robbery. He was held pending trial in the Norfolk city jail. Counsel was appointed on November 27.

On November 21, 1972, shortly after Henry was incarcerated, Government agents working on the Janaf robbery contacted one Nichols, an inmate at the Norfolk city jail, who for some time prior to this meeting had been engaged to provide confidential information to the Federal Bureau of Investigation as a paid informant. Nichols was then serving a sentence on local forgery charges. The record does not disclose whether the agent contacted Nichols specifically to acquire information about Henry or the Janaf robbery.

Nichols informed the agent that he was housed in the same cellblock with several federal prisoners awaiting trial, including Henry. The agent told him to be alert to any statements made by the federal prisoners, but not to initiate any conversation with or question Henry regarding the bank robbery. In early December, after Nichols had been released from jail, the agent again contacted Nichols, who reported that he and Henry had engaged in conversation and that Henry had told him about the robbery of the Janaf bank. Nichols was paid for furnishing the information.

When Henry was tried in March 1973, an agent of the Federal Bureau of Investigation testified concerning the events surrounding the discovery of the rental slip and the evidence uncovered at the rented house. Other witnesses also connected Henry to the rented house, including the rental agent who positively identified Henry as the "Allen R. Norris" who had rented the house and had taken the rental receipt described earlier. A neighbor testified that prior to the robbery she saw Henry at the rented house with John Luck, one of the two men who had by the time of Henry's trial been convicted for the robbery. In addition, palm prints found on the lease agreement matched those of Henry.

Nichols testified at trial that he had "an opportunity to have some conversations with Mr. Henry while he was in the jail," and that Henry told him that on several occasions he had gone to the Janaf Branch to see which employees opened the vault. Nichols also testified that Henry described to him the details of the robbery and stated that the only evidence connecting him to the robbery was the rental receipt. The jury was not informed that Nichols was a paid Government informant.

On the basis of this testimony, Henry was convicted of bank robbery and sentenced to a term of imprisonment of 25 years. On appeal he raised no Sixth Amendment claims.

On August 28, 1975, Henry moved to vacate his sentence pursuant to 28 U.S.C. § 2255. At this stage, he stated that he had just learned that Nichols was a paid Government informant and alleged that he had been intentionally placed in the same cell with Nichols so that Nichols could secure information about the robbery. Thus, Henry contended that the introduction of Nichols' testimony violated his Sixth Amendment right to the assistance of counsel. The District Court denied the motion without a hearing.

II

This Court has scrutinized postindictment confrontations between Government agents and the accused to determine whether they are "critical stages" of the prosecution at which the Sixth Amendment right to the assistance of counsel attaches. The present case involves incriminating statements made by the accused to an undisclosed and undercover Government informant while in custody and after indictment. The Government characterizes Henry's incriminating statements as voluntary and not the result of any affirmative conduct on the part of Government agents to elicit evidence. From this, the Government argues that Henry's rights were not violated, even assuming the Sixth Amendment applies to such surreptitious confrontations; in short, it is contended that the Government has not interfered with Henry's right to counsel.

The question here is whether under the facts of this case a Government agent "deliberately elicited" incriminating statements from Henry within the meaning of *Massiah*. Three factors are important. First, Nichols was acting under instructions as a paid informant for the Government; second, Nichols was ostensibly no more than a fellow inmate of Henry; and third, Henry was in custody and under indictment at the time he was engaged in conversation by Nichols.

The Court of Appeals viewed the record as showing that Nichols deliberately used his position to secure incriminating information from Henry when counsel was not present and held that conduct attributable to the Government. Nichols had been a paid Government informant for more than a year; moreover, the FBI agent was aware that Nichols had access to Henry and would be able to engage him in conversations without arousing Henry's suspicion. The arrangement between Nichols and the agent was on a contingent-fee basis; Nichols was to be paid only if he produced useful information. This combination of circumstances is sufficient to support the Court of Appeals' determination. Even if the agent's statement that he did not intend that Nichols would take affirmative steps to secure incriminating information is accepted, he must have known that such propinquity likely would lead to that result.

The Government argues that the federal agents instructed Nichols not to question Henry about the robbery. Yet according to his own testimony, Nichols was not a passive listener; rather, he had "some conversations with Mr. Henry" while he was in jail and Henry's incriminatory statements were "the product of this conversation." In *Massiah*, no inquiry was made as to whether Massiah or his codefendant first raised the subject of the crime under investigation.

It is quite a different matter when the Government uses undercover agents to obtain incriminating statements from persons not in custody but suspected of criminal activity prior to the time charges are filed. In Hoffa v. United States (1966), for example, this Court held that "no interest legitimately protected by the Fourth Amendment is involved" because "the Fourth Amendment [does not protect] a wrongdoer's misplaced belief that a person to whom he voluntarily confides his wrongdoing will not reveal it." Similarly, the Fifth Amendment has been held not to be implicated by the use of undercover Government agents before charges are filed because of the absence of the potential for compulsion. But the Fourth and Fifth Amendment claims made in those cases are not relevant to the inquiry under the Sixth Amendment here — whether the Government has interfered with the right to counsel of the accused by "deliberately eliciting" incriminating statements. Our holding today does not modify *White* or *Hoffa*.

When the accused is in the company of a fellow inmate who is acting by prearrangement as a Government agent, the same cannot be said. Conversation stimulated in such circumstances may elicit information that an accused would not intentionally reveal to persons known to be Government agents. Indeed, the *Massiah* Court noted that if the Sixth Amendment "is to have any efficacy it must apply to indirect and surreptitious interrogations as well as those conducted in the jailhouse."

Finally Henry's incarceration at the time he was engaged in conversation by Nichols is also a relevant factor. As a ground for imposing the prophylactic requirements in Miranda v. Arizona, this Court noted the powerful psychological inducements to reach for aid when a person is in confinement. While the concern in *Miranda* was limited to custodial police interrogation, the mere fact of custody imposes pressures on the accused; confinement may bring into play subtle influences that will make him particularly susceptible to the ploys of undercover Government agents. The Court of Appeals determined that on this record the incriminating conversations between Henry and Nichols were facilitated by Nichols' conduct and apparent status as a person sharing a common plight. That Nichols had managed to gain the confidence of Henry, as the Court of Appeals determined, is confirmed by Henry's request that Nichols assist him in his escape plans when Nichols was released from confinement.

Under the strictures of the Court's holdings on the exclusion of evidence, we conclude that the Court of Appeals did not err in holding that Henry's statements to Nichols should not have been admitted at trial. By intentionally creating a situation likely to induce Henry to make incriminating statements without the assistance of counsel, the Government violated Henry's Sixth Amendment right to counsel. This is not a case where, in Justice Cardozo's words, "the constable . . . blundered"; rather, it is one where the "constable" planned an impermissible interference with the right to the assistance of counsel.

Justice BLACKMUN, with whom Justice WHITE joins, dissenting.

In this case the Court, I fear, cuts loose from the moorings of Massiah v. United States and overlooks or misapplies significant facts to reach a result that is not required by the Sixth Amendment, by established precedent, or by sound policy.

Massiah mandates exclusion only if a federal agent "deliberately elicited" statements from the accused in the absence of counsel. The word "deliberately" denotes intent. *Massiah* ties this intent to the act of elicitation, that is, to conduct that draws forth a response. Thus *Massiah*, by its own terms, covers only action undertaken with the specific intent to evoke an inculpatory disclosure. Faced with Agent Coughlin's unequivocal expression of an intent not to elicit statements from respondent Henry, but merely passively to receive them, the Court, in its decision to affirm the judgment of the Court of Appeals, has no choice but to depart from the natural meaning of the *Massiah* formulation.

The Court deems it critical that informant Nichols had been a paid informant; that Agent Coughlin was aware that Nichols "had access" to Henry and "would be able to engage him in conversations without arousing Henry's suspicion"; and that payment to Nichols was on a contingent-fee basis. Thus, it is said, even if Coughlin's "statement is accepted . . . he must have known that such propinquity likely would lead to that result" (that is, that Nichols would take "affirmative steps to secure incriminating information"). Later, the Court goes even further, characterizing this as a case of "intentionally creating a situation likely to induce Henry to make incriminating statements." This deter-mination, coupled with the statement that Nichols "prompted" respondent Henry's remarks, leads the Court to find a *Massiah* violation.

Thus, while claiming to retain the "deliberately elicited" test, the Court really forges a new test that saps the word "deliberately" of all significance. The Court's extension of *Massiah* would cover even a "negligent" triggering of events result-ing in reception of disclosures. This approach, in my view, is unsupported and unwise.

KUHLMANN v. WILSON

477 U.S. 436 (1986)

Justice POWELL delivered the opinion of the Court.

This case requires us to define the circumstances under which federal courts should entertain a state prisoner's petition for writ of habeas corpus that raises claims rejected on a prior petition for the same relief.

In the early morning of July 4, 1970, respondent and two confederates robbed the Star Taxicab Garage in the Bronx, New York, and fatally shot the night dispatcher. Shortly before, employees of the garage had observed respondent, a former employee there, on the premises conversing with two other men. They also witnessed respondent fleeing after the robbery, carrying loose money in his arms. After eluding the police for four days, respondent turned himself in. Respondent admitted that he had been present when the crimes took place, claimed that he had witnessed the robbery, gave the police a description of the robbers, but denied knowing them. Respondent also denied any involvement in the robbery or murder, claiming that he had fled because he was afraid of being blamed for the crimes.

After his arraignment, respondent was confined in the Bronx House of Deten-tion, where he was placed in a cell with a prisoner named Benny Lee. Unknown to respondent, Lee had agreed to act as a police informant. Respondent made incriminating statements that Lee reported to the police. Prior to trial, respondent moved to suppress the statements on the ground that they were obtained in violation of his right to counsel. The trial court held an evidentiary hearing on the suppression motion, which revealed that the statements were made under the following circumstances.

Before respondent arrived in the jail, Lee had entered into an arrangement with Detective Cullen, according to which Lee agreed to listen to respondent's conversations and report his remarks to Cullen. Since the police had positive evidence of respondent's participation, the purpose of placing Lee in the cell was to determine the identities of respondent's confederates. Cullen instructed Lee not to ask respondent any questions, but simply to "keep his ears open" for the names of the other perpetrators. Respondent first spoke to Lee about the crimes after he looked out the cellblock window at the Star Taxicab Garage, where the crimes had occurred. Respondent said, "someone's messing with me," and began talking to Lee about the robbery, narrating the same story that he had given the police at the time of his arrest. Lee advised respondent that this explanation "didn't sound too good," but respondent did not alter his story. Over the next few days, however, respondent changed details of his original account. Respondent then received a visit from his brother, who mentioned that members of his family were upset because they believed that respondent had murdered the dispatcher. After the visit, respondent again described the crimes to Lee. Respondent now admitted that he and two other men, whom he never identified, had planned and carried out the robbery, and had murdered the dispatcher. Lee informed Cullen of respondent's statements and furnished Cullen with notes that he had written surreptitiously while sharing the cell with respondent.

After hearing the testimony of Cullen and Lee, the trial court found that Cullen had instructed Lee "to ask no questions of [respondent] about the crime but merely to listen as to what [respondent] might say in his presence." The court determined that Lee obeyed these instructions, that he "at no time asked any questions with respect to the crime," and that he "only listened to [respondent] and made notes regarding what [respondent] had to say." The trial court also found that respondent's statements to Lee were "spontaneous" and "unsolicited." Under state precedent, a defendant's volunteered statements to a police agent were admissible in evidence because the police were not required to prevent talkative defendants from making incriminating statements. The trial court accordingly denied the suppression motion. The jury convicted respondent of common-law murder and felonious possession of a weapon. On May 18, 1972, the trial court sentenced him to a term of 20 years to life on the murder count and to a concurrent term of up to 7 years on the weapons count.

Following this Court's decision in United States v. Henry (1980), which applied the *Massiah* test to suppress statements made to a paid jailhouse informant, respondent decided to relitigate his Sixth Amendment claim.

Even if the Court of Appeals had correctly decided to entertain this successive habeas petition, we conclude that it erred in holding that respondent was entitled to relief under United States v. Henry (1980). As the District Court observed, *Henry* left open the question whether the Sixth Amendment forbids admission in evidence of an accused's statements to a jailhouse informant who was "placed in close proximity but [made] no effort to stimulate conversations about the crime charged."

As our recent examination of the Sixth Amendment makes clear, the primary concern of the *Massiah* line of decisions is secret interrogation by investigatory techniques that are the equivalent of direct police interrogation. Since "the Sixth Amendment is not violated whenever — by luck or happenstance — the State obtains incriminating statements from the accused after the right to counsel has attached," a defendant does not make out a violation of that right simply by showing that an informant, either through prior arrangement or voluntarily, reported his incriminating statements to the police. Rather, the defendant must demonstrate that the police and their informant took some action, beyond merely listening, that was designed deliberately to elicit incriminating remarks.

It is thus apparent that the Court of Appeals erred in concluding that respondent's right to counsel was violated under the circumstances of this case. The state court found that Officer Cullen had instructed Lee only to listen to respondent for the purpose of determining the identities of the other participants in the robbery and murder. The police already had solid evidence of respondent's participation. The court further found that Lee followed those instructions, that he "at no time asked any questions" of respondent concerning the pending charges, and that he "only listened" to respondent's "spontane-ous" and "unsolicited" statements.

Chief Justice BURGER, concurring.

I agree fully with the Court's opinion and judgment. This case is clearly dis-tinguishable from United States v. Henry (1980). There is a vast difference between placing an "ear" in the suspect's cell and placing a voice in the cell to encourage conversation for the "ear" to record.

Furthermore, the abuse of the Great Writ needs to be curbed so as to limit, if not put a stop to, the "sporting contest" theory of criminal justice so widely practiced today.

Justice BRENNAN, with whom Justice MARSHALL joins, dissenting.

The Court holds that the Court of Appeals erred with respect to the merits of respondent's habeas petition. According to the Court, the Court of Appeals failed to accord § 2254(d)'s presumption of correctness to the state trial court's findings that respondent's cellmate, Lee, "at no time asked any questions" of respondent concerning the pending charges, and that Lee only listened to respondent's "spontaneous" and "unsolicited" statements, As a result, the Court concludes, the Court of Appeals failed to recognize that this case presents the question, reserved in *Henry*, whether the Sixth Amendment forbids the admission into evidence of an accused's statements to a jailhouse informant who was "placed in close proximity but [made] no effort to stimulate conversa-tions about the crime charged." I disagree with the Court's characterization of the Court of Appeals' treatment of the state court's findings and, consequently, I disagree with the Court that the instant case presents the "listening post" question.

The Sixth Amendment guarantees an accused, at least after the initiation of formal charges, the right to rely on counsel as the "medium" between himself and the State. Accordingly, the Sixth Amendment "imposes on the State an affirmative obligation to respect and preserve the accused's choice to seek [the assistance of counsel]," and therefore "[t]he determination whether particular action by state agents violates the accused's right to . . . counsel must be made in light of this obligation." To be sure, the Sixth Amendment is not violated whenever, "by luck or happenstance," the State obtains incrim-inating statements from the accused after the right to counsel has attached. It is violated, however, when "the State obtains incriminating statements by know-ingly circumventing the accused's right to have counsel present in a confronta-tion between the accused and a state agent." As we explained in *Henry*, where the accused has not waived his right to counsel, the government knowingly circum-vents the defendant's right to counsel where it "deliberately elicit[s]" inculpa-tory admissions, that is, "intentionally creat[es] a situation likely to induce [the accused] to make incriminating statements without the assistance of counsel."

In the instant case, as in *Henry*, the accused was incarcerated and therefore was "susceptible to the ploys of undercover Government agents." Like Nichols, Lee was a secret informant, usually received consideration for the services he ren-dered the police, and therefore had an incentive to produce the information which he knew the police hoped to obtain. Just as Nichols had done, Lee obeyed instructions not to question respondent and to report to the police any statements made by the respondent in Lee's presence about the crime in question. And, like Nichols, Lee encouraged respondent to talk about his crime by conversing with him on the subject over the course of several days and by telling respondent that his exculpatory story would not convince anyone without more work. However, unlike the situation in *Henry*, a disturbing visit from respondent's brother, rather than a conversation with the informant, seems to have been the immediate catalyst for respondent's confession to Lee. While it might appear from this sequence of events that Lee's comment regarding respondent's story and his general willingness to converse with respondent about the crime were not the immediate causes of respondent's admission, I think that the deliberate-elicitation standard requires consideration of the entire course of government behavior.

The State intentionally created a situation in which it was foreseeable that respondent would make incriminating statements without the assistance of counsel, — it assigned respondent to a cell overlooking the scene of the crime and designated a secret informant to be respondent's cellmate. The informant, while avoiding direct questions, nonetheless developed a relationship of cellmate camaraderie with respondent and encouraged him to talk about his crime. While the coup de grace was delivered by respondent's brother, the groundwork for respondent's confession was laid by the State. Clearly the State's actions had a sufficient nexus with respondent's admission of guilt to constitute deliberate elicitation within the meaning of *Henry*.

The use of prison informants is thus an area where the Fifth Amendment privilege against self-incrimination is different from the Sixth Amendment right to counsel. The former does not apply because there is not an interrogation. On the other hand, once formal adjudicatory proceedings have been initiated, the Sixth Amendment is violated by government-initiated communications to elicit statements from an individual represented by counsel.

D.   THE PRIVILEGE AGAINST SELF-INCRIMINATION IN OTHER CONTEXTS

Although the focus of this chapter has been on the privilege against self-incrimination in the interrogation context, obviously it is a privilege that applies through all of the stages of criminal proceedings. Indeed, a person has the right to refuse to incriminate him- or herself in giving testimony in civil or administrative proceedings as well.

In examining the privilege against self-incrimination in this broader context, there are three especially important questions: First, what are the requirements for the privilege against self-incrimination to apply? Second, does the privilege against self-incrimination apply to protect people from having to produce documents or other things? Third, can the government overcome the privilege against self-incrimination by according the individual immunity?

1. What Are the Requirements for the Privilege Against Self-Incrimination to Apply?

The Supreme Court has declared that "[t]o qualify for the Fifth Amendment privilege, a communication must be testimonial, incriminating, and compelled." Hiibel v. Sixth Judicial Dist. Court of Nevada, Humboldt County, 542 U.S. 177 (2004). For the privilege against self-incrimination to apply, it must be an individual, not an entity, that is asserting it; what is sought from the individual must be "testimonial"; there must be "compulsion"; and there must be the possibility of incrimination. Consider each of these requirements.

a. Only Individuals May Invoke the Privilege

Only individuals may invoke the privilege against self-incrimination. It has been long established that entities such as corporations or unions are not entitled to invoke this privilege. Hale v. Henkel, 201 U.S. 43 (1906). The Court has explained that, in part, this is because the privilege exists to protect the privacy and dignity of the individual. The Court has said that the privilege exists to protect that "private enclave where [a person] may lead a private life." Bellis v. United States, 417 U.S. 85 (1974). The Court has also explained that extending the privilege to entities would interfere with needed government regulation. The Court stated: "The greater portion of evidence of wrongdoing by an organization or its representatives is usually to be found in the official records and documents of that organization. Were the cloak of the privilege to be thrown around these impersonal records and documents, effective enforcement of many federal and state laws would be impossible."

b. The Privilege Applies Only to That Which Is Testimonial

Second, the privilege applies only if what is being sought is *testimonial.* A person cannot be required to give testimony that would be incriminating; but this does not prevent a person from giving physical evidence that would be incriminating. Schmerber v. California is a key case holding and illustrating this.

SCHMERBER v. CALIFORNIA
384 U.S. 757 (1966)

Justice BRENNAN delivered the opinion of the Court.

Petitioner was convicted in Los Angeles Municipal Court of the criminal offense of driving an automobile while under the influence of intoxicating liquor. He had been arrested at a hospital while receiving treatment for injuries suffered in an accident involving the automobile that he had apparently been driving. At the direction of a police officer, a blood sample was then withdrawn from petitioner's body by a physician at the hospital. The chemical analysis of this sample revealed a percent by weight of alcohol in his blood at the time of the offense which indicated intoxication, and the report of this analysis was admitted in evidence at the trial. Petitioner objected to receipt of this evidence of the analysis on the ground that the blood had been withdrawn despite his refusal, on the advice of his counsel, to consent to the test. He contended that in that circumstance the withdrawal of the blood and the admission of the analysis in evidence [violated his constitutional rights, including] his privilege against self-incrimination under the Fifth Amendment.

We hold that the privilege protects an accused only from being compelled to testify against himself, or otherwise provide the State with evidence of a testimonial or communicative nature, and that the withdrawal of blood and use of the analysis in question in this case did not involve compulsion to these ends.

It could not be denied that in requiring petitioner to submit to the withdrawal and chemical analysis of his blood the State compelled him to submit to an attempt to discover evidence that might be used to prosecute him for a criminal offense. He submitted only after the police officer rejected his objection and directed the physician to proceed. The officer's direction to the physician to administer the test over petitioner's objection constituted compulsion for the purposes of the privilege. The critical question, then, is whether petitioner was thus compelled "to be a witness against himself."

If the scope of the privilege coincided with the complex of values it helps to protect, we might be obliged to conclude that the privilege was violated. The withdrawal of blood necessarily involves puncturing the skin for extraction, and the percent by weight of alcohol in that blood, as established by chemical analysis, is evidence of criminal guilt. Compelled submission fails on one view to respect the "inviolability of the human personality." Moreover, since it enables the State to rely on evidence forced from the accused, the compulsion violates at least one meaning of the requirement that the State procure the evidence against an accused "by its own independent labors."

[H]owever, the privilege has never been given the full scope which the values it helps to protect suggest. History and a long line of authorities in lower courts have consistently limited its protection to situations in which the State seeks to submerge those values by obtaining the evidence against an accused through "the cruel, simple expedient of compelling it from his own mouth. In sum, the privilege is fulfilled only when the person is guaranteed the right 'to remain silent unless he chooses to speak in the unfettered exercise of his own will.'"

[B]oth federal and state courts have usually held that it offers no protection against compulsion to submit to fingerprinting, photographing, or measurements, to write or speak for identification, to appear in court, to stand, to assume a stance, to walk, or to make a particular gesture. The distinction which has emerged, often expressed in different ways, is that the privilege is a bar against compelling "communications" or "testimony," but that compulsion which makes a suspect or accused the source of "real or physical evidence" does not violate it.

Although we agree that this distinction is a helpful framework for analysis, we are not to be understood to agree with past applications in all instances. There will be many cases in which such a distinction is not readily drawn. Some tests seemingly directed to obtain "physical evidence," for example, lie detector tests measuring changes in body function during interrogation, may actually be directed to eliciting responses which are essentially testimonial. To compel a person to submit to testing in which an effort will be made to determine his guilt or innocence on the basis of physiological responses, whether willed or not, is to evoke the spirit and history of the Fifth Amendment. Such situations call to mind the principle that the protection of the privilege "is as broad as the mischief against which it seeks to guard."

In the present case, however, no such problem of application is presented. Not even a shadow of testimonial compulsion upon or enforced communication by the accused was involved either in the extraction or in the chemical analysis. Petitioner's testimonial capacities were in no way implicated; indeed, his participation, except as a donor, was irrelevant to the results of the test, which depend on chemical analysis and on that alone. Since the blood test evidence, although an incriminating product of compulsion, was neither petitioner's testimony nor evidence relating to some communicative act or writing by the petitioner, it was not inadmissible on privilege grounds.

[The Court also rejected other constitutional objections based on the Fourth Amendment, due process, and the right to counsel.]

Justice BLACK, with whom Justice DOUGLAS joins, dissenting.

I disagree with the Court's holding that California did not violate petitioner's constitutional right against self-incrimination when it compelled him, against his will, to allow a doctor to puncture his blood vessels in order to extract a sample of blood and analyze it for alcoholic content, and then used that analysis as evidence to convict petitioner of a crime.

The Court admits that "the State compelled [petitioner] to submit to an attempt to discover evidence (in his blood) that might be (and was) used to prosecute him for a criminal offense." To reach the conclusion that compelling a person to give his blood to help the State convict him is not equivalent to compelling him to be a witness against himself strikes me as quite an extraordinary feat. The Court, however, overcomes what had seemed to me to be an insuperable obstacle to its conclusion by holding that the privilege protects an accused only from being compelled to testify against himself, or otherwise provide the State with evidence of a testimonial or communicative nature, and that the withdrawal of blood and use of the analysis in question in this case did not involve compulsion to these ends.

I cannot agree that this distinction and reasoning of the Court justify denying petitioner his Bill of Rights' guarantee that he must not be compelled to be a witness against himself.

In the first place it seems to me that the compulsory extraction of petitioner's blood for analysis so that the person who analyzed it could give evidence to convict him had both a "testimonial" and a "communicative nature." The sole purpose of this project which proved to be successful was to obtain "testimony" from some person to prove that petitioner had alcohol in his blood at the time he was arrested. And the purpose of the project was certainly "communicative" in that the analysis of the blood was to supply information to enable a witness to communicate to the court and jury that petitioner was more or less drunk.

I think it unfortunate that the Court rests so heavily for its very restrictive reading of the Fifth Amendment's privilege against self-incrimination on the words "testimonial" and "communicative." These words are not models of clarity and precision as the Court's rather labored explication shows. Nor can the Court, so far as I know, find precedent in the former opinions of this Court for using these particular words to limit the scope of the Fifth Amendment's protection.

How can it reasonably be doubted that the blood test evidence was not in all respects the actual equivalent of "testimony" taken from petitioner when the result of the test was offered as testimony, was considered by the jury as testimony, and the jury's verdict of guilt rests in part on that testimony? The refined, subtle reasoning and balancing process used here to narrow the scope of the Bill of Rights' safeguard against self-incrimination provides a handy instrument for further narrowing of that constitutional protection, as well as others, in the future. Believing with the Framers that these constitutional safeguards broadly construed by independent tribunals of justice provide our best hope for keeping our people free from governmental oppression, I deeply regret the Court's holding.

The Supreme Court on many occasions has reaffirmed that the privilege against self-incrimination applies only to preventing a person from having to give testimony against him- or herself. For example, in United States v. Wade, 388 U.S. 218 (1967), the Supreme Court held that requiring a suspect to participate in a police lineup does not violate the privilege against self incrimination because it is not testimonial. The Court explained: "We have no doubt that compelling the accused merely to exhibit his person for observation by a prosecution witness prior to trial involves no compulsion of the accused to give evidence of testimonial significance. It is compulsion of the accused to exhibit his physical characteristics, not compulsion to disclose any knowledge he might have." (Issues concerning lineups and identification procedures are discussed in Chapter 5.)

Similarly, in Doe v. United States, 487 U.S. 201 (1988), the Court held that compelling a person's signature on a bank form was not testimonial. A court ordered an individual to sign a form authorizing a bank outside the United States to release records. It was stipulated that the person, by signing, was not admitting the existence of any account. The Court said that this was not testimonial because it did not "convey information or assert facts."

c. There Must Be Compulsion

The privilege against self-incrimination protects a person from being compelled to give testimony against him- or herself. Voluntary statements made to the police, of course, do not violate the privilege even if they are highly incriminating. Miranda v. Arizona, above, is based on the Court's judgment of the inherently coercive nature of in-custodial interrogation.

However, the Court has held that no adverse inference can be drawn by a jury in a criminal case from the defendant's invocation of the privilege against self-incrimination. In Griffin v. California, 380 U.S. 609 (1965), the Court explained that this would be "a penalty for exercising a constitutional privilege." Typically, juries are therefore instructed that they can draw no adverse inference from the failure of a criminal defendant to testify. In Mitchell v. United States, 526 U.S. 314 (1996), the Court likewise held that no adverse inference can be drawn in imposing punishment from a defendant's failure to testify during sentencing proceedings.

However, the fact that a person faces a hard choice has not been deemed sufficient to cross the line and constitute compulsion. For example, in Ohio Adult Parole Authority v. Woodward, 523 U.S. 272 (1998), the Court found that there was not a violation of the privilege against self-incrimination when a person applying for clemency had to answer questions that could include incriminating information. Chief Justice Rehnquist, writing for a unanimous Court, stated:

> It is difficult to see how a voluntary interview could "compel" respondent to speak. He merely faces a choice quite similar to the sorts of choices that a criminal defendant must make in the course of criminal proceedings, none of which has ever been held to violate the Fifth Amendment. Here respondent has the same choice of providing information to the Authority — at the risk of damaging his case for clemency or for postconviction relief — or of remaining silent. But this pressure to speak in the hope of improving his chance of being granted clemency does not make the interview compelled. We therefore hold that the Ohio clemency interview does not violate the Fifth Amendment privilege against compelled self-incrimination.

Similarly, in McKune v. Lile, 536 U.S. 24 (2002), the Court held that it did not violate the privilege against self-incrimination to require a prisoner seeking admission to a sex offender rehabilitation program to "admit having committed the crime for which he is being treated and other past offenses." Although the treatment program meant substantially more freedom for the inmate, the Court found that the pressure to admit to crimes that could lead to further criminal liability did not violate the Fifth Amendment. Justice Kennedy, writing for the Court in a 5-4 decision, said: "Determining what constitutes unconstitutional compulsion involves a question of judgment: Courts must determine whether the consequences of an inmate's choice to remain silent are closer to the physical torture against which the Constitution protects or the *de minimus* harms which it does not." The Court said that the prison had an important interest in the rehabilitation program, which required admission of past sex crimes.

d. There Must Be the Possibility of Incrimination

For the privilege against self-incrimination to apply, there must be the opportunity that the statements could lead to a person's criminal liability. In Ullman v. United States, 350 U.S. 422 (1956), the Supreme Court made clear that the fact that a statement could lead to civil liability and even social stigma was not enough to trigger the privilege unless there also was the possibility of criminal liability.

The Supreme Court recently confronted the question of whether a law requiring a person to identify him- or herself violated the privilege against self-incrimination. In Hiibel v. Sixth Judicial Dist. Court of Nevada, 542 U.S. 177 (2004), the police were investigating an anonymous tip of an assault. Hiibel fit the description of the assailant. The police stopped him and asked him to identify himself. Hiibel refused; 11 times the officer asked and 11 times Hiibel refused. He was convicted under a Nevada law that provides: "The officer may detain the person pursuant to this section only to ascertain his identity and the suspicious circumstances surrounding his presence abroad. Any person so detained shall identify himself, but may not be compelled to answer any other inquiry of any peace officer."

Hiibel was convicted of violating the law and challenged it as infringing both the Fourth and Fifth Amendments.[15] The Supreme Court, 5-4, ruled against him. As to the self-incrimination claim, Justice Kennedy, writing for the majority, stated:

> Respondents urge us to hold that the statements NRS § 171.123(3) requires are nontestimonial, and so outside the Clause's scope. We decline to resolve the case on that basis. "[T]o be testimonial, an accused's communication must itself, explicitly or implicitly, relate a factual assertion or disclose information." Doe v. United States (1988). Stating one's name may qualify as an assertion of fact relating to identity. Production of identity documents might meet the definition as well. Even if these required actions are testimonial, however, petitioner's challenge must fail because in this case disclosure of his name presented no reasonable danger of incrimination.
>
> The Fifth Amendment prohibits only compelled testimony that is incriminating. As we stated in Kastigar v. United States (1972), the Fifth Amendment privilege against compulsory self-incrimination "protects against any disclosures that the witness reasonably believes could be used in a criminal prosecution or could lead to other evidence that might be so used." Suspects who have been granted immunity from prosecution may, therefore, be compelled to answer; with the threat of prosecution removed, there can be no reasonable belief that the evidence will be used against them.
>
> In this case petitioner's refusal to disclose his name was not based on any articulated real and appreciable fear that his name would be used to incriminate him, or that it "would furnish a link in the chain of evidence needed to prosecute" him. As best we can tell, petitioner refused to identify himself only because he thought his name was none of the officer's business. Even today, petitioner does not explain how the disclosure of his name could have been used against him in a criminal case. While we recognize petitioner's strong belief that he should not have to disclose his identity, the Fifth Amendment does not override the Nevada Legislature's judgment to the contrary absent a reasonable belief that the disclosure would tend to incriminate him.
>
> The narrow scope of the disclosure requirement is also important. One's identity is, by definition, unique; yet it is, in another sense, a universal characteristic. Answering a request to disclose a name is likely to be so insignificant in the scheme of things as to be incriminating only in unusual circumstances. Even witnesses who plan to invoke the Fifth Amendment privilege answer when their names are called to take the stand. Still, a case may arise where there is a substantial allegation that furnishing identity at the time of a stop would have given the police a link in the chain of evidence needed to convict the individual of a separate offense. In that case, the court can then consider whether the privilege applies, and, if the Fifth Amendment has been violated, what remedy must follow. We need not resolve those questions here.

Justice Stevens, in a dissenting opinion, disagreed:

> "[T]here can be no doubt that the Fifth Amendment privilege is available outside of criminal court proceedings and serves to protect persons in all settings in which

---

15. Whether this violates the Fourth Amendment is discussed in Chapter 2. [Footnote by casebook authors.]

their freedom of action is curtailed in any significant way from being compelled to incriminate themselves." Miranda v. Arizona (1966). It is a "settled principle" that "the police have the right to request citizens to answer voluntarily questions concerning unsolved crimes," but "they have no right to compel them to answer." The protections of the Fifth Amendment are directed squarely toward those who are the focus of the government's investigative and prosecutorial powers. In a criminal trial, the indicted defendant has an unqualified right to refuse to testify and may not be punished for invoking that right. The unindicted target of a grand jury investigation enjoys the same constitutional protection even if he has been served with a subpoena. So does an arrested suspect during custodial interrogation in a police station.

There is no reason why the subject of police interrogation based on mere suspicion, rather than probable cause, should have any lesser protection. Indeed, we have said that the Fifth Amendment's protections apply with equal force in the context of *Terry* stops where an officer's inquiry "must be 'reasonably related in scope to the justification for [the stop's] initiation.'" "Typically, this means that the officer may ask the detainee a moderate number of questions to determine his identity and to try to obtain information confirming or dispelling the officer's suspicions. But the detainee is not obliged to respond." Given our statements to the effect that citizens are not required to respond to police officers' questions during a *Terry* stop, it is no surprise that petitioner assumed, as have we, that he had a right not to disclose his identity.

The Court correctly observes that a communication does not enjoy the Fifth Amendment privilege unless it is testimonial. Although the Court declines to resolve this question, I think it clear that this case concerns a testimonial communication. [T]he compelled statement at issue in this case is clearly testimonial. It is significant that the communication must be made in response to a question posed by a police officer. As we recently explained, albeit in the different context of the Sixth Amendment's Confrontation Clause, "[w]hatever else the term ['testimonial'] covers, it applies at a minimum . . . to police interrogations." Surely police questioning during a *Terry* stop qualifies as an interrogation, and it follows that responses to such questions are testimonial in nature.

Rather than determining whether the communication at issue is testimonial, the Court instead concludes that the State can compel the disclosure of one's identity because it is not "incriminating." But our cases have afforded Fifth Amendment protection to statements that are "incriminating" in a much broader sense than the Court suggests. It has "long been settled that [the Fifth Amendment's] protection encompasses compelled statements that lead to the discovery of incriminating evidence even though the statements themselves are not incriminating and are not introduced into evidence." By "incriminating" we have meant disclosures that "could be used in a criminal prosecution or could lead to other evidence that might be so used," — communications, in other words, that "would furnish a link in the chain of evidence needed to prosecute the claimant for a federal crime." Thus, "[c]ompelled testimony that communicates information that may 'lead to incriminating evidence' is privileged even if the information itself is not inculpatory."

Given a proper understanding of the category of "incriminating" communications that fall within the Fifth Amendment privilege, it is clear that the disclosure of petitioner's identity is protected. The Court reasons that we should not assume that the disclosure of petitioner's "name would be used to incriminate him, or that it would furnish a link in [a] chain of evidence needed to prosecute him." But why else would an officer ask for it? And why else would the Nevada Legislature require its disclosure only when circumstances "reasonably indicate that the person has committed, is committing or is about to commit a crime"? If the Court is correct, then petitioner's refusal to cooperate did not impede the police investigation. Indeed, if we accept the predicate for the Court's holding, the statute requires nothing more than a useless invasion of privacy. I think that, on the contrary, the Nevada Legislature intended to provide its police officers with a useful law enforcement tool, and that the very existence of the statute demonstrates the value of the information it demands.

A person's identity obviously bears informational and incriminating worth, "even if the [name] itself is not inculpatory." A name can provide the key to a broad array of information about the person, particularly in the hands of a police officer with access to a range of law enforcement databases. And that information, in turn, can be tremendously useful in a criminal prosecution. It is therefore quite wrong to suggest that a person's identity provides a link in the chain to incriminating evidence "only in unusual circumstances."

The officer in this case told petitioner, in the Court's words, that "he was conducting an investigation and needed to see some identification." As the target of that investigation, petitioner, in my view, acted well within his rights when he opted to stand mute.

2.   When May the Government Require the Production of Documents and Other Things?

The Supreme Court has held that a person can be forced to produce documents, even documents containing highly incriminating information, unless the very act of production would be incriminating. Required production of a preexisting document does not violate the privilege against self-incrimination because it is not demanding testimony from a person. Fisher v. United States is the key case here.

FISHER v. UNITED STATES
425 U.S. 391 (1976)

Justice WHITE delivered the opinion of the Court.

In these two cases we are called upon to decide whether a summons directing an attorney to produce documents delivered to him by his client in connection with the attorney-client relationship is enforceable over claims that the documents were constitutionally immune from summons in the hands of the client and retained that immunity in the hands of the attorney.

I

In each case, an Internal Revenue agent visited the taxpayer or taxpayers and interviewed them in connection with an investigation of possible civil or criminal liability under the federal income tax laws. Shortly after the interviews, the taxpayers obtained from their respective accountants certain documents relating to the preparation by the accountants of their tax returns. Shortly after obtaining the documents, the taxpayers transferred the documents to their lawyers respondent Kasmir and petitioner Fisher, respectively each of whom was retained to assist the taxpayer in connection with the investigation.

Upon learning of the whereabouts of the documents, the Internal Revenue Service served summonses on the attorneys directing them to produce documents listed therein. In each case the summons was ordered enforced by the District Court and its order was stayed pending appeal. [I]n our view the documents were not privileged either in the hands of the lawyers or of their clients.

II

All of the parties in these cases have concurred in the proposition that if the Fifth Amendment would have excused a Taxpayer from turning over the accountant's papers had he possessed them, the Attorney to whom they are delivered for the purpose of obtaining legal advice should also be immune from subpoena. Although we agree with this proposition, we are convinced that it is not the taxpayer's Fifth Amendment privilege that would excuse the Attorney from production.

The taxpayer's privilege under this Amendment is not violated by enforcement of the summonses involved in these cases because enforcement against a taxpayer's lawyer would not "compel" the taxpayer to do anything and certainly would not compel him to be a "witness" against himself. The Court has held repeatedly that the Fifth Amendment is limited to prohibiting the use of "physical or moral compulsion" exerted on the person asserting the privilege. In Couch v. United States [1973], we recently ruled that the Fifth Amendment rights of a taxpayer were not violated by the enforcement of a documentary summons directed to her accountant and requiring production of the taxpayer's own records in the possession of the accountant. We did so on the ground that in such a case "the ingredient of personal compulsion against an accused is lacking."

Here, the taxpayers are compelled to do no more than was the taxpayer in Couch. The taxpayers' Fifth Amendment privilege is therefore not violated by enforcement of the summonses directed toward their attorneys. This is true whether or not the Amendment would have barred a subpoena directing the taxpayer to produce the documents while they were in his hands.

The fact that the attorneys are agents of the taxpayers does not change this result. Couch held as much, since the accountant there was also the taxpayer's agent, and in this respect reflected a longstanding view.

Nor is this one of those situations where constructive possession is so clear or relinquishment of possession so temporary and insignificant as to leave the personal compulsion upon the taxpayer substantially intact.

[It is argued] that if the summons was enforced, the taxpayers' Fifth Amendment privilege would be, but should not be, lost solely because they gave their documents to their lawyers in order to obtain legal advice. But this misconceives the nature of the constitutional privilege. The Amendment protects a person from being compelled to be a witness against himself. Here, the taxpayers retained any privilege they ever had not to be compelled to testify against themselves and not to be compelled themselves to produce private papers in their possession. This personal privilege was in no way decreased by the transfer. It is simply that by reason of the transfer of the documents to the attorneys, those papers may be subpoenaed without compulsion on the taxpayer. The protection of the Fifth Amendment is therefore not available.

The proposition that the Fifth Amendment protects private information obtained without compelling self-incriminating testimony is contrary to the clear statements of this Court that under appropriate safeguards private incriminating statements of an accused may be overheard and used in evidence, if they are not compelled at the time they were uttered, and that disclosure of private information may be compelled if immunity removes the risk of incrimination. If the Fifth Amendment protected generally against the obtaining of private information from a man's mouth or pen or house, its protections would presumably not be lifted by probable cause and a warrant or by immunity. The privacy invasion is not mitigated by immunity; and the Fifth Amendment's strictures, unlike the Fourth's, are not removed by showing reasonableness. First Amendment values are also plainly not implicated in these cases.

Justice BRENNAN, concurring in the judgment.

I concur in the judgment. Given the prior access by accountants retained by the taxpayers to the papers involved in these cases and the wholly business rather than personal nature of the papers, I agree that the privilege against compelled self-incrimination did not in either of these cases protect the papers from production in response to the summonses. I do not join the Court's opinion, however, because of the portent of much of what is said of a serious crippling of the protection secured by the privilege against compelled production of one's private books and papers. Although as phrased in the Fifth Amendment "nor shall [any person] be compelled in any criminal case to be a witness against himself" the privilege makes no express reference, as does the Fourth Amendment, to "papers, and effects," private papers have long been held to have the protection of the privilege, designed as it is "to maintain inviolate large areas of personal privacy."

Expressions are legion in opinions of this Court that the protection of personal privacy is a central purpose of the privilege against compelled self-incrimination. "[I]t is the invasion of [a person's] indefeasible right of personal security, personal liberty and private property" that "constitutes the essence of the offence" that violates the privilege. The privilege reflects "our respect for the inviolability of the human personality and of the right of each individual 'to a private enclave where he may lead a private life.'" "It respects a private inner sanctum of individual feeling and thought and proscribes state intrusion to extract self-condemnation." "The Fifth Amendment in its Self-Incrimination Clause enables the citizen to create a zone of privacy which government may not force him to surrender to his detriment."

The Court pays lip service to this bedrock premise of privacy in the statement that "[w]ithin the limits imposed by the language of the Fifth Amendment, which we necessarily observe, the privilege truly serves privacy interests." But this only makes explicit what elsewhere highlights the opinion, namely, the view that protection of personal privacy is merely a by product and not, as our precedents and history teach, a factor controlling in part the determination of the scope of the privilege. This cart-before-the-horse approach is fundamentally at odds with the settled principle that the scope of the privilege is not constrained by the limits of the wording of the Fifth Amendment but has the reach necessary to protect the cherished value of privacy which it safeguards. The "Court has always construed provisions of the Constitution having regard to the principles upon which it was established. The direct operation or literal meaning of the words used do not measure the purpose or scope of its provisions. . . ."

That the privilege does not protect against the production of private information where there is no compulsion, or where immunity is granted, or where there is no threat of incrimination in nowise supports the Court's argument demeaning the privilege's protection of privacy. The unavailability of the privilege in those cases only evidences that, as is the case with the First and Fourth Amendments, the protection of privacy afforded by the privilege is not absolute. The critical question then is the definition of the scope of privacy that is sheltered by the privilege.

History and principle teach that the privacy protected by the Fifth Amendment extends not just to the individual's immediate declarations, oral or written, but also to his testimonial materials in the form of books and papers.

The common-law and constitutional extension of the privilege to testimonial materials, such as books and papers, was inevitable. An individual's books and papers are generally little more than an extension of his person. They reveal no less than he could reveal upon being questioned directly. Many of the matters within an individual's knowledge may as easily be retained within his head as set down on a scrap of paper. I perceive no principle which does not permit compelling one to disclose the contents of one's mind but does permit compelling the disclosure of the contents of that scrap of paper by compelling its production. Under a contrary view, the constitutional protection would turn on fortuity, and persons would, at their peril, record their thoughts and the events of their lives. The ability to think private thoughts, facilitated as it is by pen and paper, and the ability to preserve intimate memories would be curtailed through fear that those thoughts or events of those memories would become the subjects of criminal sanctions however invalidly imposed. Indeed, it was the very reality of those fears that helped provide the historical impetus for the privilege.

The Court's treatment of the privilege falls far short of giving it the scope required by history and our precedents. It is, of course, true "that the Fifth Amendment protects against 'compelled self-incrimination, not the disclosure of private information,'" but it is also true that governmental compulsion to produce private information that might incriminate violates the protection of the privilege. Similarly, although it is necessary that the papers "contain no testimonial declarations by [the taxpayer]" in order for the privilege not to operate as a bar to production, it does not follow that papers are not "testimonial" and thus producible because they contain no declarations. And while it may be that the unavailability of the privilege depends on a showing that "the preparation of all of the papers sought in these cases was wholly voluntary," again it does not follow that the protection is necessarily unavailable if the papers were prepared voluntarily, for it is the compelled production of testimonial evidence, not just the compelled creation of such evidence, against which the privilege protects.

Though recognizing that a subpoena served on a taxpayer involves substantial compulsion, the Court concludes that since the subpoena does not compel oral testimony or require the taxpayer to restate, repeat, or affirm the truth of the contents of the documents sought, compelled production of the documents by the taxpayer would not violate the privilege, even though the documents might incriminate the taxpayer. This analysis is patently incomplete: the threshold inquiry is whether the taxpayer is compelled to produce incriminating papers. That inquiry is not answered in favor of production merely because the subpoena requires neither oral testimony from nor affirmation of the papers' contents by the taxpayer. To be sure, the Court correctly observes that "[t]he taxpayer cannot avoid compliance with the subpoena merely by asserting that the item of evidence which he is required to produce contains incriminating writing, whether his own or that of someone else." For it is not enough that the production of a writing, or books and papers, is compelled. Unless those materials are such as to come within the zone of privacy recognized by the Amendment, the privilege against compulsory self-incrimination does not protect against their production.

We are not without guideposts for determining what books, papers, and writings come within the zone of privacy recognized by the Amendment. A precise cataloguing of private papers within the ambit of the privacy protected by the privilege is probably impossible. Some papers, however, do lend themselves to classification. Production of documentary materials created or authenticated by a State or the Federal Government, such as automobile registrations or property deeds, would seem ordinarily to fall outside the protection of the privilege. They hardly reflect an extension of the person.

Economic and business records may present difficulty in particular cases. The records of business entities generally fall without the scope of the privilege. But, as noted, the Court has recognized that the privilege extends to the business records of the sole proprietor or practitioner. Such records are at least an extension of an aspect of a person's activities, though concededly not the more intimate aspects of one's life. Where the privilege would have protected one's mental notes of his business affairs in a less complicated day and age, it would seem that that protection should not fall away because the complexities of another time compel one to keep business records. Nonbusiness economic records in the possession of an individual, such as canceled checks or tax records, would also seem to be protected. They may provide clear insights into a person's total lifestyle. They are, however, like business records and the papers involved in these cases, frequently, though not always, disclosed to other parties; and disclosure, in proper cases, may foreclose reliance upon the privilege. Personal letters constitute an integral aspect of a person's private enclave. And while letters, being necessarily interpersonal, are not wholly private, their peculiarly private nature and the generally narrow extent of their disclosure would seem to render them within the scope of the privilege. Papers in the nature of a personal diary are a fortiori protected under the privilege.

The Court's treatment in the instant cases of the question whether the evidence involved here is within the protection of the privilege is, with all respect, most inadequate. The gaping hole is in the omission of any reference to the taxpayer's privacy interests and to whether the subpoenas impermissibly invade those interests.

Fisher involved the question of whether the government may compel production of documents, but its rationale applies to anything that a person might be required to produce. For example, in Baltimore City Department of Social Services v. Bouknight, 493 U.S. 549 (1990), the Court held that a court could order a parent to produce a child over whom she had custody. A court gave the Department of Social Services custody over a child as being a "child in need of assistance." The child was returned to his mother with certain conditions. She did not comply with the conditions and the Court authorized the Department to remove the child. The mother did not relinquish the child and the Department was concerned that the child might no longer be alive. The court ordered the mother to produce the child and she invoked the Fifth Amendment privilege against self-incrimination.

The Court, in an opinion by Justice O'Connor, ruled against Bouknight. The Court stated: "The possibility that a production order will compel testimonial assertions that may prove incriminating does not, in all contexts, justify invoking the privilege to resist production. Even assuming that this limited testimonial assertion is sufficiently incriminating and 'sufficiently testimonial for purposes of the privilege,' Bouknight may not invoke the privilege to resist the production order because she has assumed custodial duties related to production and because production is required as part of a noncriminal regulatory scheme."

The Court concluded: "Finally, production in the vast majority of cases will embody no incriminating testimony, even if in particular cases the act of production may incriminate the custodian through an assertion of possession or the existence, or the identity, of the child. These orders to produce children cannot be characterized as efforts to gain some testimonial component of the act of production. In these circumstances, Bouknight cannot invoke the privilege to resist the order to produce Maurice."

3. May the Government Require Testimony If It Provides Immunity?

As explained above, the privilege against self-incrimination applies only if the statements could lead to a person's criminal liability. If a person is granted immunity and is promised that the statements will not be used for criminal prosecutions, there is no danger of self-incrimination.

There are two types of immunity. "Transactional immunity" promises the person that he or she will not be prosecuted for offenses related to the compelled testimony. "Use and derivative use immunity" promises the person that the government will not use the statements gained under immunity, or anything derived from those statements, in a criminal prosecution. Use and derivative use immunity is more common than transactional immunity and is specifically provided for by federal statute. 18 U.S.C. § 601, *et seq.* If a person makes statements after a promise of immunity, they can be used against the person only in a perjury prosecution.

Kastigar v. United States is an important case upholding the constitutionality of use immunity and clarifying the burden on prosecutors to prove that information gained was not the product of statements gained through immunity.

KASTIGAR v. UNITED STATES
406 U.S. 441 (1972)

Justice POWELL delivered the opinion of the Court.

This case presents the question whether the United States Government may compel testimony from an unwilling witness, who invokes the Fifth Amendment privilege against compulsory self-incrimination, by conferring on the witness immunity from use of the compelled testimony in subsequent criminal proceedings, as well as immunity from use of evidence derived from the testimony.

Petitioners were subpoenaed to appear before a United States grand jury in the Central District of California on February 4, 1971. The Government believed that petitioners were likely to assert their Fifth Amendment privilege. Prior to the scheduled appearances, the Government applied to the District Court for an order directing petitioners to answer questions and produce evidence before the grand jury under a grant of immunity conferred pursuant to 18 U.S.C. §§ 6002, 6003. Petitioners opposed issuance of the order, contending primarily that the scope of the immunity provided by the statute was not coextensive with the scope of the privilege against self-incrimination, and therefore was not sufficient to supplant the privilege and compel their testimony. The District Court rejected this contention, and ordered petitioners to appear before the grand jury and answer its questions under the grant of immunity.

Petitioners appeared but refused to answer questions, asserting their privilege against compulsory self-incrimination. They were brought before the District Court, and each persisted in his refusal to answer the grand jury's questions, notwithstanding the grant of immunity. The court found both in contempt, and committed them to the custody of the Attorney General until either they answered the grand jury's questions or the term of the grand jury expired. This Court granted certiorari to resolve the important question whether testimony may be compelled by granting immunity from the use of compelled testimony and evidence derived therefrom ("use and derivative use" immunity), or whether it is necessary to grant immunity from prosecution for offenses to which compelled testimony relates ("transactional" immunity).

I

The power of government to compel persons to testify in court or before grand juries and other governmental agencies is firmly established in Anglo-American jurisprudence. But the power to compel testimony is not absolute. There are a number of exemptions from the testimonial duty, the most important of which is the Fifth Amendment privilege against compulsory self-incrimination.

Immunity statutes, which have historical roots deep in Anglo-American jurisprudence, are not incompatible with these values. Rather, they seek a rational accommodation between the imperatives of the privilege and the legitimate demands of government to compel citizens to testify. The existence of these statutes reflects the importance of testimony, and the fact that many offenses are of such a character that the only persons capable of giving useful testimony are those implicated in the crime. Indeed, their origins were in the context of such offenses, and their primary use has been to investigate such offenses. Congress included immunity statutes in many of the regulatory measures adopted in the first half of this century. Indeed, prior to the enactment of the statute under consideration in this case, there were in force over 50 federal immunity statutes. In addition, every State in the Union, as well as the District of Columbia and Puerto Rico, has one or more such statutes. The commentators, and this Court on several occasions, have characterized immunity statutes as essential to the effective enforcement of various criminal statutes.

II

Petitioners contend, first, that the Fifth Amendment's privilege against compulsory self-incrimination, deprives Congress of power to enact laws that compel self-incrimination, even if complete immunity from prosecution is granted prior to the compulsion of the incriminatory testimony. In other words, petitioners assert that no immunity statute, however drawn, can afford a lawful basis for compelling incriminatory testimony. We find no merit to this contention.

III

Petitioners' second contention is that the scope of immunity provided by the federal witness immunity statute, 18 U.S.C. § 6002, is not coextensive with the scope of the Fifth Amendment privilege against compulsory self-incrimination, and therefore is not sufficient to supplant the privilege and compel testimony over a claim of the privilege. The statute provides that when a witness is compelled by district court order to testify over a claim of the privilege: "the witness may not refuse to comply with the order on the basis of his privilege against self-incrimination; but no testimony or other information compelled under the order (or any information directly or indirectly derived from such testimony or other information) may be used against the witness in any criminal case, except a prosecution for perjury, giving a false statement, or otherwise failing to comply with the order."

The constitutional inquiry, rooted in logic and history, as well as in the decisions of this Court, is whether the immunity granted under this statute is coextensive with the scope of the privilege. If so, petitioners' refusals to answer based on the privilege were unjustified, and the judgments of contempt were proper, for the grant of immunity has removed the dangers against which the privilege protects. If, on the other hand, the immunity granted is not as comprehensive as the protection afforded by the privilege, petitioners were justified in refusing to answer, and the judgments of contempt must be vacated.

Petitioners draw a distinction between statutes that provide transactional immunity and those that provide, as does the statute before us, immunity from use and derivative use. They contend that a statute must at a minimum grant full transactional immunity in order to be coextensive with the scope of the privilege.

The statute's explicit proscription of the use in any criminal case of "testimony or other information compelled under the order (or any information directly or indirectly derived from such testimony or other information)" is consonant with Fifth Amendment standards. We hold that such immunity from use and derivative use is coextensive with the scope of the privilege against self-incrimination, and therefore is sufficient to compel testimony over a claim of the privilege. While a grant of immunity must afford protection commensurate with that afforded by the privilege, it need not be broader. Transactional immunity, which accords full immunity from prosecution for the offense to which the compelled testimony relates, affords the witness considerably broader protection than does the Fifth Amendment privilege. The privilege has never been construed to mean that one who invokes it cannot subsequently be prosecuted. Its sole concern is to afford protection against being "forced to give testimony leading to the infliction of penalties affixed to . . . criminal acts." Immunity from the use of compelled testimony, as well as evidence derived directly and indirectly therefrom, affords this protection. It prohibits the prosecutorial authorities from using the compelled testimony in any respect, and it therefore insures that the testimony cannot lead to the infliction of criminal penalties on the witness.

Petitioners argue that use and derivative-use immunity will not adequately protect a witness from various possible incriminating uses of the compelled testimony: for example, the prosecutor or other law enforcement officials may obtain leads, names of witnesses, or other information not otherwise available that might result in a prosecution. It will be difficult and perhaps impossible, the argument goes, to identify, by testimony or cross-examination, the subtle ways in which the compelled testimony may disadvantage a witness, especially in the jurisdiction granting the immunity.

This argument presupposes that the statute's prohibition will prove impossible to enforce. The statute provides a sweeping proscription of any use, direct or indirect, of the compelled testimony and any information derived therefrom. A person accorded this immunity and subsequently prosecuted, is not dependent for the preservation of his rights upon the integrity and good faith of the prosecuting authorities.

This burden of proof, which we reaffirm as appropriate, is not limited to a negation of taint; rather, it imposes on the prosecution the affirmative duty to prove that the evidence it proposes to use is derived from a legitimate source wholly independent of the compelled testimony. This is very substantial protection, commensurate with that resulting from invoking the privilege itself. The privilege assures that a citizen is not compelled to incriminate himself by his own testimony. It usually operates to allow a citizen to remain silent when asked a question requiring an incriminatory answer. This statute, which operates after a witness has given incriminatory testimony, affords the same protection by assuring that the compelled testimony can in no way lead to the infliction of criminal penalties. The statute, like the Fifth Amendment, grants neither pardon nor amnesty. Both the statute and the Fifth Amendment allow the government to prosecute using evidence from legitimate independent sources.

There can be no justification in reason or policy for holding that the Constitution requires an amnesty grant where, acting pursuant to statute and accompanying safeguards, testimony is compelled in exchange for immunity from use and derivative use when no such amnesty is required where the government, acting without colorable right, coerces a defendant into incriminating himself.

We conclude that the immunity provided by 18 U.S.C. § 6002 leaves the witness and the prosecutorial authorities in substantially the same position as if the witness had claimed the Fifth Amendment privilege. The immunity therefore is coextensive with the privilege and suffices to supplant it.

Justice DOUGLAS, dissenting.

The Self-Incrimination Clause says: "No person . . . shall be compelled in any criminal case to be a witness against himself." I see no answer to the proposition that he is such a witness when only "use" immunity is granted. If, as some have thought, the Bill of Rights contained only "counsels of moderation" from which courts and legislatures could deviate according to their conscience or discretion, then today's contraction of the Self-Incrimination Clause of the Fifth Amendment would be understandable. But that has not been true, starting with Chief Justice Marshall's opinion in United States v. Burr, where he ruled that the reach of the Fifth Amendment was so broad as to make the privilege applicable when there was a mere possibility of a criminal charge being made.

When we allow the prosecution to offer only "use" immunity we allow it to grant far less than it has taken away. For while the precise testimony that is compelled may not be used, leads from that testimony may be pursued and used to convict the witness. My view is that the framers put it beyond the power of Congress to compel anyone to confess his crimes. The Self-Incrimination Clause creates, as I have said before, "the federally protected right of silence," making it unconstitutional to use a law "to pry open one's lips and make him a witness against himself." That is indeed one of the chief procedural guarantees in our accusatorial system. Government acts in an ignoble way when it stoops to the end which we authorize today.

It is also possible that use immunity might actually have an adverse impact on the administration of justice rather than promote law enforcement. A witness might believe, with good reason, that his "immunized" testimony will inevitably lead to a felony conviction. Under such circumstances, rather than testify and aid the investigation, the witness might decide he would be better off remaining silent even if he is jailed for contempt.

Justice MARSHALL, dissenting.

Today the Court holds that the United States may compel a witness to give incriminating testimony, and subsequently prosecute him for crimes to which that testimony relates. I cannot believe the Fifth Amendment permits that result. The Fifth Amendment gives a witness an absolute right to resist interrogation, if the testimony sought would tend to incriminate him. A grant of immunity may strip the witness of the right to refuse to testify, but only if it is broad enough to eliminate all possibility that the testimony will in fact operate to incriminate him. It must put him in precisely the same position, vis-à-vis the government that has compelled his testimony, as he would have been in had he remained silent in reliance on the privilege.

United States v. Hubbell is a recent Supreme Court case clarifying when production is incriminating and also what are the effects of a grant of immunity.

UNITED STATES v. HUBBELL

530 U.S. 27 (2000)

Justice STEVENS delivered the opinion of the Court.

The two questions presented concern the scope of a witness' protection against compelled self-incrimination: (1) whether the Fifth Amendment privilege protects a witness from being compelled to disclose the existence of incriminating documents that the Government is unable to describe with reasonable particularity; and (2) if the witness produces such documents pursuant to a grant of immunity, whether 18 U.S.C. § 6002 prevents the Government from using them to prepare criminal charges against him.

I

This proceeding arises out of the second prosecution of respondent, Webster Hubbell, commenced by the Independent Counsel appointed in August 1994 to investigate possible violations of federal law relating to the Whitewater Development Corporation. The first prosecution was terminated pursuant to a plea bargain. In December 1994, respondent pleaded guilty to charges of mail fraud and tax evasion arising out of his billing practices as a member of an Arkansas law firm from 1989 to 1992, and was sentenced to 21 months in prison. In the plea agreement, respondent promised to provide the Independent Counsel with "full, complete, accurate, and truthful information" about matters relating to the Whitewater investigation.

The second prosecution resulted from the Independent Counsel's attempt to determine whether respondent had violated that promise. In October 1996, while respondent was incarcerated, the Independent Counsel served him with a subpoena duces tecum calling for the production of 11 categories of documents before a grand jury sitting in Little Rock, Arkansas. On November 19, he appeared before the grand jury and invoked his Fifth Amendment privilege against self-incrimination. In response to questioning by the prosecutor, respondent initially refused "to state whether there are documents within my possession, custody, or control responsive to the Subpoena." Thereafter, the prosecutor produced an order, which had previously been obtained from the District Court pursuant to 18 U.S.C. § 6003(a), directing him to respond to the subpoena and granting him immunity "to the extent allowed by law." Respondent then produced 13,120 pages of documents and records and responded to a series of questions that established that those were all of the documents in his custody or control that were responsive to the commands in the subpoena, with the exception of a few documents he claimed were shielded by the attorney-client and attorney work-product privileges.

The contents of the documents produced by respondent provided the Independent Counsel with the information that led to this second prosecution. On April 30, 1998, a grand jury in the District of Columbia returned a 10-count indictment charging respondent with various tax-related crimes and mail and wire fraud. The District Court dismissed the indictment relying, in part, on the ground that the Independent Counsel's use of the subpoenaed documents violated § 6002 because all of the evidence he would offer against respondent at trial derived either directly or indirectly from the testimonial aspects of respondent's immunized act of producing those documents. The Court of Appeals vacated the judgment and remanded for further proceedings.

II

[It is a] settled proposition that a person may be required to produce specific documents even though they contain incriminating assertions of fact or belief because the creation of those documents was not "compelled" within the meaning of the privilege. On the other hand, we have also made it clear that the act of producing documents in response to a subpoena may have a compelled testimonial aspect. We have held that "the act of production" itself may implicitly communicate "statements of fact." By "producing documents in compliance with a subpoena, the witness would admit that the papers existed, were in his possession or control, and were authentic." Moreover, as was true in this case, when the custodian of documents responds to a subpoena, he may be compelled to take the witness stand and answer questions designed to determine whether he has produced everything demanded by the subpoena. The answers to those questions, as well as the act of production itself, may certainly communicate information about the existence, custody, and authenticity of the documents. Whether the constitutional privilege protects the answers to such questions, or protects the act of production itself, is a question that is distinct from the question whether the unprotected contents of the documents themselves are incriminating.

III

Acting pursuant to 18 U.S.C. § 6002, the District Court entered an order compelling respondent to produce "any and all documents" described in the grand jury subpoena and granting him "immunity to the extent allowed by law." The "compelled testimony" that is relevant in this case is not to be found in the contents of the documents produced in response to the subpoena. It is, rather, the testimony inherent in the act of producing those documents. The disagreement between the parties focuses entirely on the significance of that testimonial aspect.

IV

The Government correctly emphasizes that the testimonial aspect of a response to a subpoena duces tecum does nothing more than establish the existence, authenticity, and custody of items that are produced. We assume that the Government is also entirely correct in its submission that it would not have to advert to respondent's act of production in order to prove the existence, authenticity, or custody of any documents that it might offer in evidence at a criminal trial; indeed, the Government disclaims any need to introduce any of the documents produced by respondent into evidence in order to prove the charges against him. It follows, according to the Government, that it has no intention of making improper "use" of respondent's compelled testimony.

The question, however, is not whether the response to the subpoena may be introduced into evidence at his criminal trial. That would surely be a prohibited "use" of the immunized act of production. But the fact that the Government intends no such use of the act of production leaves open the separate question whether it has already made "derivative use" of the testimonial aspect of that act in obtaining the indictment against respondent and in preparing its case for trial. It clearly has.

It is apparent from the text of the subpoena itself that the prosecutor needed respondent's assistance both to identify potential sources of information and to produce those sources. Given the breadth of the description of the 11 categories of documents called for by the subpoena, the collection and production of the materials demanded was tantamount to answering a series of interrogatories asking a witness to disclose the existence and location of particular documents fitting certain broad descriptions. The assembly of literally hundreds of pages of material in response to a request for "any and all documents reflecting, referring, or relating to any direct or indirect sources of money or other things of value received by or provided to" an individual or members of his family during a 3-year period, is the functional equivalent of the preparation of an answer to either a detailed written interrogatory or a series of oral questions at a discovery deposition. Entirely apart from the contents of the 13,120 pages of materials that respondent produced in this case, it is undeniable that providing a catalog of existing documents fitting within any of the 11 broadly worded subpoena categories could provide a prosecutor with a "lead to incriminating evidence," or "a link in the chain of evidence needed to prosecute."

Indeed, the record makes it clear that that is what happened in this case. The documents were produced before a grand jury sitting in the Eastern District of Arkansas in aid of the Independent Counsel's attempt to determine whether respondent had violated a commitment in his first plea agreement. The use of those sources of information eventually led to the return of an indictment by a grand jury sitting in the District of Columbia for offenses that apparently are unrelated to that plea agreement. What the District Court characterized as a "fishing expedition" did produce a fish, but not the one that the Independent Counsel expected to hook. It is abundantly clear that the testimonial aspect of respondent's act of producing subpoenaed documents was the first step in a chain of evidence that led to this prosecution. The documents did not magically appear in the prosecutor's office like "manna from heaven." They arrived there only after respondent asserted his constitutional privilege, received a grant of immunity, and — under the compulsion of the District Court's order — took the mental and physical steps necessary to provide the prosecutor with an accurate inventory of the many sources of potentially incriminating evidence sought by the subpoena. It was only through respondent's truthful reply to the subpoena that the Government received the incriminating documents of which it made "substantial use . . . in the investigation that led to the indictment."

For these reasons, we cannot accept the Government's submission that respondent's immunity did not preclude its derivative use of the produced documents because its "possession of the documents [was] the fruit only of a simple physical act — the act of producing the documents." It was unquestionably necessary for respondent to make extensive use of "the contents of his own mind" in identifying the hundreds of documents responsive to the requests in the subpoena. The assembly of those documents was like telling an inquisitor the combination to a wall safe, not like being forced to surrender the key to a strongbox. The Government's anemic view of respondent's act of production as a mere physical act that is principally nontestimonial in character and can be entirely divorced from its "implicit" testimonial aspect so as to constitute a "legitimate, wholly independent source" (as required by *Kastigar*) for the documents produced simply fails to account for these realities.

In sum, we have no doubt that the constitutional privilege against self-incrimination protects the target of a grand jury investigation from being compelled to answer questions designed to elicit information about the existence of sources of potentially incriminating evidence. That constitutional privilege has the same application to the testimonial aspect of a response to a subpoena seeking discovery of those sources.

Given our conclusion that respondent's act of production had a testimonial aspect, at least with respect to the existence and location of the documents sought by the Government's subpoena, respondent could not be compelled to produce those documents without first receiving a grant of immunity under § 6003. As we construed § 6002 in *Kastigar*, such immunity is coextensive with the constitutional privilege. *Kastigar* requires that respondent's motion to dismiss the indictment on immunity grounds be granted unless the Government proves that the evidence it used in obtaining the indictment and proposed to use at trial was derived from legitimate sources "wholly independent" of the testimonial aspect of respondent's immunized conduct in assembling and producing the documents described in the subpoena. The Government, however, does not claim that it could make such a showing. Rather, it contends that its prosecution of respondent must be considered proper unless someone — presumably respondent — shows that "there is some substantial relation between the compelled testimonial communications implicit in the act of production (as opposed to the act of production standing alone) and some aspect of the information used in the investigation or the evidence presented at trial." We could not accept this submission without repudiating the basis for our conclusion in *Kastigar* that the statutory guarantee of use and derivative-use immunity is as broad as the constitutional privilege itself. This we are not prepared to do.

Accordingly, the indictment against respondent must be dismissed.

Justice THOMAS, with whom Justice SCALIA joins, concurring.

Our decision today involves the application of the act-of-production doctrine, which provides that persons compelled to turn over incriminating papers or other physical evidence pursuant to a subpoena duces tecum or a summons may invoke the Fifth Amendment privilege against self-incrimination as a bar to production only where the act of producing the evidence would contain "testimonial" features. I join the opinion of the Court because it properly applies this doctrine, but I write separately to note that this doctrine may be inconsistent with the original meaning of the Fifth Amendment's Self-Incrimination Clause. A substantial body of evidence suggests that the Fifth Amendment privilege protects against the compelled production not just of incriminating testimony, but of any incriminating evidence. In a future case, I would be willing to reconsider the scope and meaning of the Self-Incrimination Clause.

CHAPTER
5

IDENTIFICATION PROCEDURES

Eyewitness identification is enormously powerful evidence. A witness telling a jury that he or she saw the defendant commit the crime is often sufficient by itself to lead to a conviction. The problem is that there is a large body of social science research indicating that eyewitnesses are often mistaken.[1] Events happen so quickly and often under great stress; people tend to see what they expect; memories are faulty. Cross-racial identifications, where a person is identifying someone of a different race, are particularly inaccurate. There are many instances in which innocent individuals have been convicted of crimes, including capital crimes, based on flawed eyewitness testimony. The challenge for the law in this area is to preserve this often crucial type of evidence while increasing the likelihood of its accuracy.

There are two primary forms of identification procedures used during police investigations. First, lineups and showups occur when the police ask the witness, often the victim of the crime, to identify a particular person. In a lineup, police present a group of individuals and ask the witness if he or she can identify the person who committed the crime. In a showup, the witness is shown just one person, not a group, and asked if that is the person who committed the crime.

Second are photospreads, where police ask witnesses to look through a series of photographs and see if they can identify the person who they saw commit the crime. Sometimes this involves the witness being shown anywhere from five to ten photographs, essentially a photo lineup, and sometimes it involves the witness being given a book of photographs to examine.

A key danger with both of these investigative techniques is police suggestiveness. For example, police can construct lineups in a way that increases the likelihood that a particular person will be identified. If the witness says that the perpetrator is very tall, a suggestive lineup would include one tall person and four short ones. Also, police can make comments during identification procedures that make a witness more inclined to identify a particular suspect.

The Supreme Court has developed two constitutional protections in this area for suspects of crime. First, the Court has recognized a right to counsel in some identification situations, most notably for lineups that occur after indictments. The hope is that the presence of a lawyer for the suspect will reduce the likelihood of suggestiveness by the police. However, as discussed below, the Supreme

---

1. *See* Brian L. Cutler & Steven D. Penrod, *Mistaken Identification: The Eyewitness, Psychology and the Law* (1995); Elizabeth Loftus, *Eyewitness Testimony* (1979).

Court has not recognized a right to counsel for lineups before indictments or for photo identification procedures. Second, the Court has held that unnecessarily suggestive identification procedures violate due process.

Each of these lines of cases is discussed below. In reading these cases, it is important to consider whether the Court has done enough to protect suspects from false identifications and what other steps might be taken in this regard.

A. THE RIGHT TO COUNSEL

1. *The Right to Counsel in Lineups*

The right to counsel for criminal suspects during identification procedures comes largely from two Supreme Court cases decided the same day: United States v. Wade and Gilbert v. California.

UNITED STATES v. WADE
388 U.S. 218 (1967)

Justice BRENNAN delivered the opinion of the Court.

The question here is whether courtroom identifications of an accused at trial are to be excluded from evidence because the accused was exhibited to the witnesses before trial at a post-indictment lineup conducted for identification purposes without notice to and in the absence of the accused's appointed counsel.

The federally insured bank in Eustace, Texas, was robbed on September 21, 1964. A man with a small strip of tape on each side of his face entered the bank, pointed a pistol at the female cashier and the vice president, the only persons in the bank at the time, and forced them to fill a pillowcase with the bank's money. The man then drove away with an accomplice who had been waiting in a stolen car outside the bank. On March 23, 1965, an indictment was returned against respondent, Wade, and two others for conspiring to rob the bank, and against Wade and the accomplice for the robbery itself. Wade was arrested on April 2, and counsel was appointed to represent him on April 26. Fifteen days later an FBI agent, without notice to Wade's lawyer, arranged to have the two bank employees observe a lineup made up of Wade and five or six other prisoners and conducted in a courtroom of the local county courthouse. Each person in the line wore strips of tape such as allegedly worn by the robber and upon direction each said something like "put the money in the bag," the words allegedly uttered by the robber. Both bank employees identified Wade in the lineup as the bank robber.

At trial, the two employees, when asked on direct examination if the robber was in the courtroom, pointed to Wade. The prior lineup identification was then elicited from both employees on cross-examination. At the close of testimony, Wade's counsel moved for a judgment of acquittal or, alternatively, to strike the bank officials' courtroom identifications on the ground that conduct of the lineup, without notice to and in the absence of his appointed counsel, violated his Fifth Amendment privilege against self-incrimination and his

Sixth Amendment right to the assistance of counsel. The motion was denied, and Wade was convicted.

I.

Neither the lineup itself nor anything shown by this record that Wade was required to do in the lineup violated his privilege against self-incrimination. We have only recently reaffirmed that the pivilege "protects an accused only from being compelled to testify against himself, or otherwise provide the State with evidence of a testimonial or communicative nature."

We have no doubt that compelling the accused merely to exhibit his person for observation by a prosecution witness prior to trial involves no compulsion of the accused to give evidence having testimonial significance. It is compulsion of the accused to exhibit his physical characteristics, not compulsion to disclose any knowledge he might have. [C]ompelling Wade to speak within hearing distance of the witnesses, even to utter words purportedly uttered by the robber, was not compulsion to utter statements of a "testimonial" nature; he was required to use his voice as an identifying physical characteristic, not to speak his guilt.

II.

The fact that the lineup involved no violation of Wade's privilege against self-incrimination does not, however, dispose of his contention that the courtroom identifications should have been excluded because the lineup was conducted without notice to and in the absence of his counsel. [I]n this case it is urged that the assistance of counsel at the lineup was indispensable to protect Wade's most basic right as a criminal defendant—his right to a fair trial at which the witnesses against him might be meaningfully cross-examined.

The Framers of the Bill of Rights envisaged a broader role for counsel than under the practice then prevailing in England of merely advising his client in "matters of law," and eschewing any responsibility for "matters of fact." The constitutions in at least 11 of the 13 States expressly or impliedly abolished this distinction. This background is reflected in the scope given by our decisions to the Sixth Amendment's guarantee to an accused of the assistance of counsel for his defense. When the Bill of Rights was adopted, there were no organized police forces as we know them today. The accused confronted the prosecutor and the witnesses against him, and the evidence was marshalled, largely at the trial itself. In contrast, today's law enforcement machinery involves critical confrontations of the accused by the prosecution at pretrial proceedings where the results might well settle the accused's fate and reduce the trial itself to a mere formality. In recognition of these realities of modern criminal prosecution, our cases have construed the Sixth Amendment guarantee to apply to "critical" stages of the proceedings. The guarantee reads: "In all criminal prosecutions, the accused shall enjoy the right . . . to have the Assistance of Counsel for his defence." The plain wording of this guarantee thus encompasses counsel's assistance whenever necessary to assure a meaningful "defence."

It is central to that principle that in addition to counsel's presence at trial, the accused is guaranteed that he need not stand alone against the State at any stage of the prosecution, formal or informal, in court or out, where counsel's absence might derogate from the accused's right to a fair trial. The security of that right is as much the aim of the right to counsel as it is of the other guarantees of the Sixth Amendment—the right of the accused to a speedy and public trial by an impartial jury, his right to be informed of the nature and cause of the accusation, and his right to be confronted with the witnesses against him and to have compulsory process for obtaining witnesses in his favor. The presence of counsel at such critical confrontations, as at the trial itself, operates to assure that the accused's interests will be protected consistently with our adversary theory of criminal prosecution.

In sum, the principle of Powell v. Alabama (1932) and succeeding cases requires that we scrutinize any pretrial confrontation of the accused to determine whether the presence of his counsel is necessary to preserve the defendant's basic right to a fair trial as affected by his right meaningfully to cross-examine the witnesses against him and to have effective assistance of counsel at the trial itself. It calls upon us to analyze whether potential substantial prejudice to defendant's rights inheres in the particular confrontation and the ability of counsel to help avoid that prejudice.

III.

The Government characterizes the lineup as a mere preparatory step in the gathering of the prosecution's evidence, not different—for Sixth Amendment purposes—from various other preparatory steps, such as systematized or scientific analyzing of the accused's fingerprints, blood sample, clothing, hair, and the like. We think there are differences which preclude such stages being characterized as critical stages at which the accused has the right to the presence of his counsel. Knowledge of the techniques of science and technology is sufficiently available, and the variables in techniques few enough, that the accused has the opportunity for a meaningful confrontation of the Government's case at trial through the ordinary processes of cross-examination of the Government's expert witnesses and the presentation of the evidence of his own experts. The denial of a right to have his counsel present at such analyses does not therefore violate the Sixth Amendment; they are not critical stages since there is minimal risk that his counsel's absence at such stages might derogate from his right to a fair trial.

IV.

But the confrontation compelled by the State between the accused and the victim or witnesses to a crime to elicit identification evidence is peculiarly riddled with innumerable dangers and variable factors which might seriously, even crucially, derogate from a fair trial. The vagaries of eyewitness identification are well-known; the annals of criminal law are rife with instances of mistaken identification. Mr. Justice Frankfurter once said: "What is the worth of identification testimony even when uncontradicted? The identification of strangers is proverbially untrustworthy. The hazards of such testimony are established by a formidable number of instances in the records of English and American trials. These instances are recent — not due to the brutalities of ancient criminal procedure." The Case of Sacco and Vanzetti 30 (1927). A major factor contributing to the high incidence of miscarriage of justice from mistaken identification has been the degree of suggestion inherent in the manner in which the prosecution presents the suspect to witnesses for pretrial identification. A commentator has observed that "[t]he influence of improper suggestion upon identifying witnesses probably accounts for more miscarriages of justice than any other single factor — perhaps it is responsible for more such errors than all other factors combined." Wall, Eye-Witness Identification in Criminal Cases 26. Suggestion can be created intentionally or unintentionally in many subtle ways. And the dangers for the suspect are particularly grave when the witness' opportunity for observation was insubstantial, and thus his susceptibility to suggestion the greatest.

Moreover, it is a matter of common experience that, once a witness has picked out the accused at the lineup, he is not likely to go back on his word later on, so that in practice the issue of identity may (in the absence of other relevant evidence) for all practical purposes be determined there and then, before the trial.

The pretrial confrontation for purpose of identification may take the form of a lineup, also known as an "identification parade" or "showup," as in the present case, or presentation of the suspect alone to the witness, as in Stovall v. Denno (1967). It is obvious that risks of suggestion attend either form of confrontation and increase the dangers inhering in eyewitness identification. But as is the case with secret interrogations, there is serious difficulty in depicting what transpires at lineups and other forms of identification confrontations. "Privacy results in secrecy and this in turn results in a gap in our knowledge as to what in fact goes on." Miranda v. State of Arizona (1966). For the same reasons, the defense can seldom reconstruct the manner and mode of lineup identification for judge or jury at trial. Those participating in a lineup with the accused may often be police officers; in any event, the participants' names are rarely recorded or divulged at trial.

The impediments to an objective observation are increased when the victim is the witness. Lineups are prevalent in rape and robbery prosecutions and present a particular hazard that a victim's understandable outrage may excite vengeful or spiteful motives. In any event, neither witnesses nor lineup participants are apt to be alert for conditions prejudicial to the suspect. And if they were, it would likely be of scant benefit to the suspect since neither witnesses nor lineup participants are likely to be schooled in the detection of suggestive influences. Improper influences may go undetected by a suspect, guilty or not, who experiences the emotional tension which we might expect in one being confronted with potential accusers. Even when he does observe abuse, if he has a criminal record he may be reluctant to take the stand and open up the admission of prior convictions. Moreover any protestations by the suspect of the fairness of the lineup made at trial are likely to be in vain; the jury's choice is between the accused's unsupported version and that of the police officers present. In short, the accused's inability effectively to reconstruct at trial any unfairness that occurred at the lineup may deprive him of his only opportunity meaningfully to attack the credibility of the witness' courtroom identification.

The potential for improper influence is illustrated by the circumstances, insofar as they appear, surrounding the prior identifications in the three cases we decide today. In the present case, the testimony of the identifying witnesses elicited on cross-examination revealed that those witnesses were taken to the courthouse and seated in the courtroom to await assembly of the lineup. The courtroom faced on a hallway observable to the witnesses through an open door. The cashier testified that she saw Wade "standing in the hall" within sight of an FBI agent. Five or six other prisoners later appeared in the hall. The vice president testified that he saw a person in the hall in the custody of the agent who "resembled the person that we identified as the one that had entered the bank."

The lineup in *Gilbert* [v. California] was conducted in an auditorium in which some 100 witnesses to several alleged state and federal robberies charged to Gilbert made wholesale identifications of Gilbert as the robber in each other's presence, a procedure said to be fraught with dangers of suggestion. And the vice of suggestion created by the identification in *Stovall* [v. Denno] was the presentation to the witness of the suspect alone handcuffed to police officers. It is hard to imagine a situation more clearly conveying the suggestion to the witness that the one presented is believed guilty by the police. See Frankfurter, The Case of Sacco and Vanzetti 31-32.

The few cases that have surfaced therefore reveal the existence of a process attended with hazards of serious unfairness to the criminal accused and strongly suggest the plight of the more numerous defendants who are unable to ferret out suggestive influences in the secrecy of the confrontation. We do not assume that these risks are the result of police procedures intentionally designed to prejudice an accused. Rather we assume they derive from the dangers inherent in eyewitness identification and the suggestibility inherent in the context of the pretrial identification.

Insofar as the accused's conviction may rest on a courtroom identification in fact the fruit of a suspect pretrial identification which the accused is helpless to subject to effective scrutiny at trial, the accused is deprived of that right of cross-examination which is an essential safeguard to his right to confront the witnesses against him. And even though cross-examination is a precious safeguard to a fair trial, it cannot be viewed as an absolute assurance of accuracy and reliability. Thus in the present context, where so many variables and pitfalls exist, the first line of defense must be the prevention of unfairness and the lessening of the hazards of eyewitness identification at the lineup itself. The trial which might determine the accused's fate may well not be that in the courtroom but that at the pretrial confrontation, with the State aligned against the accused, the witness the sole jury, and the accused unprotected against the overreaching, intentional or unintentional, and with little or no effective appeal from the judgment there rendered by the witness — "that's the man."

Since it appears that there is grave potential for prejudice, intentional or not, in the pretrial lineup, which may not be capable of reconstruction at trial, and since presence of counsel itself can often avert prejudice and assure a meaningful confrontation at trial, there can be little doubt that for Wade the postindictment lineup was a critical stage of the prosecution at which he was "as much entitled to such aid (of counsel) as at the trial itself." Thus both Wade and his counsel should have been notified of the impending lineup, and counsel's presence should have been a requisite to conduct of the lineup, absent an "intelligent waiver."

No substantial countervailing policy considerations have been advanced against the requirement of the presence of counsel. Concern is expressed that the requirement will forestall prompt identifications and result in obstruction of the confrontations. As for the first, we note that in the two cases in which the right to counsel is today held to apply, counsel had already been appointed and no argument is made in either case that notice to counsel would have prejudicially delayed the confrontations. Moreover, we leave open the question whether the presence of substitute counsel might not suffice where notification and presence of the suspect's own counsel would result in prejudicial delay. And to refuse to recognize the right to counsel for fear that counsel will obstruct the course of justice is contrary to the basic assumptions upon which this Court has operated in Sixth Amendment cases. We rejected similar logic in Miranda v. State of Arizona, concerning presence of counsel during custodial interrogation.

In our view counsel can hardly impede legitimate law enforcement; on the contrary, for the reasons expressed, law enforcement may be assisted by preventing the infiltration of taint in the prosecution's indentification evidence. That result cannot help the guilty avoid conviction but can only help assure that the right man has been brought to justice.

V.

We come now to the question whether the denial of Wade's motion to strike the courtroom identification by the bank witnesses at trial because of the absence of his counsel at the lineup required, as the Court of Appeals held, the grant of a new trial at which such evidence is to be excluded. We do not think this disposition can be justified without first giving the Government the opportunity to establish by clear and convincing evidence that the in-court identifications were based upon observations of the suspect other than the lineup identification. Where, as here, the admissibility of evidence of the lineup identification itself is not involved, a per se rule of exclusion of courtroom identification would be unjustified. A rule limited solely to the exclusion of testimony concerning identification at the lineup itself, without regard to admissibility of the courtroom identification, would render the right to counsel an empty one. The lineup is most often used, as in the present case, to crystallize the witnesses' identification of the defendant for future reference. We have already noted that the lineup identification will have that effect. The State may then rest upon the witnesses' unequivocal courtroom identifications, and not mention the pretrial identification as part of the State's case at trial. Counsel is then in the predicament in which Wade's counsel found himself — realizing that possible unfairness at the lineup may be the sole means of attack upon the unequivocal courtroom identification, and having to probe in the dark in an attempt to discover and reveal unfairness, while bolstering the government witness' courtroom identification by bringing out and dwelling upon his prior identification. Since counsel's presence at the lineup would equip him to attack not only the lineup identification but the courtroom identification as well, limiting the impact of violation of the right to counsel to exclusion of evidence only of identification at the lineup itself disregards a critical element of that right.

We think it follows that the proper test to be applied in these situations is that quoted in Wong Sun v. United States [1963]: "[W]hether, granting establishment of the primary illegality, the evidence to which instant objection is made has been come at by exploitation of that illegality or instead by means sufficiently distinguishable to be purged of the primary taint." Application of this test in the present context requires consideration of various factors; for example, the prior opportunity to observe the alleged criminal act, the existence of any discrepancy between any pre-lineup description and the defendant's actual description, any identification prior to lineup of another person, the identification by picture of the defendant prior to the lineup, failure to identify the defendant on a prior occasion, and the lapse of time between the alleged act and the lineup identification. It is also relevant to consider those facts which, despite the absence of counsel, are disclosed concerning the conduct of the lineup.

On the record now before us we cannot make the determination whether the in-court identifications had an independent origin. This was not an issue at trial, although there is some evidence relevant to a determination. That inquiry is most properly made in the District Court. We therefore think the appropriate procedure to be followed is to vacate the conviction pending a hearing to determine whether the in-court identifications had an independent source, or whether, in any event, the introduction of the evidence was harmless error, and for the District Court to reinstate the conviction or order a new trial, as may be proper.

[Chief Justice WARREN and Justices DOUGLAS, BLACK, and FORTAS dissented from Part I of the Court's opinion, which found that there was not a violation of the Fifth Amendment privilege against self-incrimination. Justice BLACK also dissented from the remand of the case to the district court. He wrote: "[T]he Court remands the case to the District Court to consider whether the courtroom identification of Wade was the fruit of the illegal lineup, and, if it was, to grant him a new trial unless the court concludes that the courtroom identification was harmless error. I would reverse the Court of Appeals' reversal of Wade's conviction, but I would not remand for further proceedings since the prosecution not having used the out-of-court lineup identification against Wade at his trial, I believe the conviction should be affirmed."]

[Justice WHITE, joined by Justices HARLAN and STEWART, dissented from the portions of the Court's opinion requiring an attorney at post-indictment lineups.]

The Court has again propounded a broad constitutional rule barring the use of a wide spectrum of relevant and probative evidence, solely because a step in its ascertainment or discovery occurs outside the presence of defense counsel. This was the approach of the Court in Miranda v. State of Arizona (1966). I objected then to what I thought was an uncritical and doctrinaire approach without satisfactory factual foundation. I have much the same view of the present ruling and therefore dissent from the judgment and from Parts II, IV, and V of the Court's opinion.

The Court's opinion is far-reaching. It proceeds first by creating a new per se rule of constitutional law: a criminal suspect cannot be subjected to a pretrial identification process in the absence of his counsel without violating the Sixth Amendment. If he is, the State may buttress a later courtroom identification, of the witness by any reference to the previous identification. Furthermore, the courtroom identification is not admissible at all unless the State can establish by clear and convincing proof that the testimony is not the fruit of the earlier identification made in the absence of defendant's counsel—admittedly a heavy burden for the State and probably an impossible one. To all intents and purposes, courtroom identifications are barred if pretrial identifications have occurred without counsel being present.

The rule applies to any lineup, to any other techniques employed to produce an identification and a fortiori to a face-to-face encounter between the witness and the suspect alone, regardless of when the identification occurs, in time or place, and whether before or after indictment or information. It matters not how well the witness knows the suspect, whether the witness is the suspect's mother, brother, or long-time associate, and no matter how long or well the witness observed the perpetrator at the scene of the crime. The kidnap victim who has lived for days with his abductor is in the same category as the witness who has had only a fleeting glimpse of the criminal. Neither may identify the suspect without defendant's counsel being present. The same strictures apply regardless of the number of other witnesses who positively identify the defendant and regardless of the corroborative evidence showing that it was the defendant who had committed the crime.

The premise for the Court's rule is not the general unreliability of eyewitness identifications nor the difficulties inherent in observation, recall, and recognition. The Court assumes a narrower evil as the basis for its rule—improper police suggestion which contributes to erroneous identifications. The Court apparently believes that improper police procedures are so widespread that a broad prophylactic rule must be laid down, requiring the presence of counsel at all pretrial identifications, in order to detect recurring instances of police misconduct. I do not share this pervasive distrust of all official investigations. None of the materials the Court relies upon supports it. Certainly, I would bow to solid fact, but the Court quite obviously does not have before it any reliable, comprehensive survey of current police practices on which to base its new rule. Until it does, the Court should avoid excluding relevant evidence from state criminal trials.

The Court goes beyond assuming that a great majority of the country's police departments are following improper practices at pretrial identifications. To find the lineup a "critical" stage of the proceeding and to exclude identifications made in the absence of counsel, the Court must also assume that police "suggestion," if it occurs at all, leads to erroneous rather than accurate identifications and that reprehensible police conduct will have an unavoidable and largely undiscoverable impact on the trial. This in turn assumes that there is now no adequate source from which defense counsel can learn about the circumstances of the pretrial identification in order to place before the jury all of the considerations which should enter into an appraisal of courtroom identification evidence. But these are treacherous and unsupported assumptions resting as they do on the notion that the defendant will not be aware, that the police and the witnesses will forget or prevaricate, that defense counsel will be unable to bring out the truth and that neither jury, judge, nor appellate court is a sufficient safeguard against unacceptable police conduct occurring at a pretrial identification procedure. I am unable to share the Court's view of the willingness of the police and the ordinary citizenwitness to dissemble, either with respect to the identification of the defendant or with respect to the circumstances surrounding a pretrial identification.

There are several striking aspects to the Court's holding. First, the rule does not bar courtroom identifications where there have been no previous identifications in the presence of the police, although when identified in the courtroom, the defendant is known to be in custody and charged with the commission of a crime. Second, the Court seems to say that if suitable legislative standards were adopted for the conduct of pretrial identifications, thereby lessening the hazards in such confrontations, it would not insist on the presence of counsel. But if this is true, why does not the Court simply fashion what it deems to be constitutionally acceptable procedures for the authorities to follow? Certainly the Court is correct in suggesting that the new rule will be wholly inapplicable where police departments themselves have established suitable safeguards.

Third, courtroom identification may be barred, absent counsel at a prior identification, regardless of the extent of counsel's information concerning the circumstances of the previous confrontation between witness and defendant — apparently even if there were recordings or sound-movies of the events as they occurred. But if the rule is premised on the defendant's right to have his counsel know, there seems little basis for not accepting other means to inform. A disinterested observer, recordings, photographs — any one of them would seem adequate to furnish the basis for a meaningful cross-examination of the eyewitness who identifies the defendant in the courtroom.

I share the Court's view that the criminal trial, at the very least, should aim at truthful factfinding, including accurate eyewitness identifications. I doubt, however, on the basis of our present information, that the tragic mistakes which have occurred in criminal trials are as much the product of improper police conduct as they are the consequence of the difficulties inherent in eyewitness testimony and in resolving evidentiary conflicts by court or jury. I doubt that the Court's new rule will obviate these difficulties, or that the situation will be measurably improved by inserting defense counsel into the investigative processes of police departments everywhere.

But, it may be asked, what possible state interest militates against requiring the presence of defense counsel at lineups? After all, the argument goes, he may do some good, he may upgrade the quality of identification evidence in state courts and he can scarcely do any harm. Even if true, this is a feeble foundation for fastening an ironclad constitutional rule upon state criminal procedures. Absent some reliably established constitutional violation, the processes by which the States enforce their criminal laws are their own prerogative. The States do have an interest in conducting their own affairs, an interest which cannot be displaced simply by saying that there are no valid arguments with respect to the merits of a federal rule emanating from this Court.

Beyond this, however, requiring counsel at pretrial identifications as an invariable rule trenches on other valid state interests. One of them is its concern with the prompt and efficient enforcement of its criminal laws. Identifications frequently take place after arrest but before an indictment is returned or an information is filed. The police may have arrested a suspect on probable cause but may still have the wrong man. Both the suspect and the State have every interest in a prompt identification at that stage, the suspect in order to secure his immediate release and the State because prompt and early identification enhances accurate identification and because it must know whether it is on the right investigative track. Unavoidably, however, the absolute rule requiring the presence of counsel will cause significant delay and it may very well result in no pretrial identification at all. Counsel must be appointed and a time arranged convenient for him and the witnesses. Meanwhile, it may be necessary to file charges against the suspect who may then be released on bail, in the federal system very often on his own recognizance, with neither the State nor the defendant having the benefit of a properly conducted identification procedure.

Nor do I think the witnesses themselves can be ignored. They will now be required to be present at the convenience of counsel rather than their own. Many may be much less willing to participate if the identification stage is transformed into an adversary proceeding not under the control of a judge. Others may fear for their own safety if their identity is known at an early date, especially when there is no way of knowing until the lineup occurs whether or not the police really have the right man.

Finally, I think the Court's new rule is vulnerable in terms of its own unimpeachable purpose of increasing the reliability of identification testimony. I would not extend this system, at least as it presently operates, to police investigations and would not require counsel's presence at pretrial identification procedures. Counsel's interest is in not having his client placed at the scene of the crime, regardless of his whereabouts. Some counsel may advise their clients to refuse to make any movements or to speak any words in a lineup or even to appear in one. To that extent the impact on truthful factfinding is quite obvious. Others will not only observe what occurs and develop [the] possibility for later cross-examination, but will hover over witnesses and begin their cross-examination then, menacing truthful factfinding as thoroughly as the Court fears the police now do. Certainly there is an implicit invitation to counsel to suggest rules for the lineup and to manage and produce it as best he can. I therefore doubt that the Court's new rule, at least absent some clearly defined limits on counsel's role, will measurably contribute to more reliable pretrial identifications. My fears are that it will have precisely the opposite result. It may well produce fewer convictions, but that is hardly a proper measure of its long-run acceptability. In my view, the State is entitled to investigate and develop its case outside the presence of defense counsel. This includes the right to have private conversations with identification witnesses, just as defense counsel may have his own consultations with these and other witnesses without having the prosecutor present.

In *Wade*, the witness identified the defendant in court, but the prosecutor did not attempt to introduce the identification from the lineup as evidence. By contrast, in another case decided the same day, Gilbert v. California, 388 U.S. 263 (1967), the prosecutor had used the lineup identification as evidence at trial. Justice Brennan again wrote the opinion for the Court and stated:

The admission of the in-court identifications without first determining that they were not tainted by the illegal lineup but were of independent origin was constitutional error. We there held that a post-indictment pretrial lineup at which the accused is exhibited to identifying witnesses is a critical stage of the criminal prosecution; that police conduct of such a lineup without notice to and in the absence of his counsel denies the accused his Sixth Amendment right to counsel and calls in question the admissibility at trial of the in-court identifications of the accused by witnesses who attended the lineup. However, as in *Wade*, the record does not permit an informed judgment whether the in-court identifications at the two stages of the trial had an independent source. Gilbert is therefore entitled only to a vacation of his conviction pending the holding of such proceedings as the California Supreme Court may deem appropriate to afford the State the opportunity to establish that the in-court identifications had an independent source, or that their introduction in evidence was in any event harmless error.

Quite different considerations are involved as to the admission of the testimony of the manager of the apartment house at the guilt phase and of the eight witnesses at the penalty stage that they identified Gilbert at the lineup. That testimony is the direct result of the illegal lineup "come at by exploitation of [the primary] illegality." The State is therefore not entitled to an opportunity to show that that testimony had an independent source. Only a per se exclusionary rule as to such testimony can be an effective sanction to assure that law enforcement authorities will respect the accused's constitutional right to the presence of his counsel at the critical lineup. In the absence of legislative regulations adequate to avoid the hazards to a fair trial which inhere in lineups as presently conducted, the desirability of deterring the constitutionally objectionable practice must prevail over the undesirability of excluding relevant evidence. That conclusion is buttressed by the consideration that the witness' testimony of his lineup identification will enhance the impact of his in-court identification on the jury and seriously aggravate whatever derogation exists of the accused's right to a fair trial. Therefore, unless the California Supreme Court is "able to declare a belief that it was harmless beyond a reasonable doubt," Gilbert will be entitled on remand to a new trial or, if no prejudicial error is found on the guilt stage but only in the penalty stage, to whatever relief California law affords where the penalty stage must be set aside.

Justices White, Harlan, and Stewart dissented for the reasons they stated in United States v. Wade.

2.   *Limits on the Right to Counsel in Identification Procedures*

Within a few years of *Wade* and *Gilbert*, the Supreme Court imposed significant limits on the right to counsel in identification situations. First, in Kirby v. Illinois, the Court held that *Wade* applies only to post-indictment lineups; there is no right to counsel in lineups before indictments. Many lineups, of course, occur at this stage. Also, of course, if police want to avoid the presence of an attorney at the lineup, they can do so by holding the lineup before indictment. Second, in United States v. Ash, the Court held that defendants have no right to counsel at photographic identifications.

The key question in evaluating these cases is whether the distinctions they draw with *Wade* are desirable and whether this leaves adequate protection for suspects during identification procedures.

ILLINOIS v. KIRBY
406 U.S. 682 (1972)

Justice STEWART announced the judgment of the Court and an opinion in which Chief Justice [BURGER], Justice BLACKMUN, and Justice REHNQUIST join.

In United States v. Wade and Gilbert v. California, this Court held "that a post-indictment pretrial lineup at which the accused is exhibited to identifying witnesses is a critical stage of the criminal prosecution; that police conduct of such a lineup without notice to and in the absence of his counsel denies the accused his Sixth (and Fourteenth) Amendment right to counsel and calls in question the admissibility at trial of the in-court identifications of the accused by witnesses who attended the lineup." Those cases further held that no in-court identifications are admissible in evidence if their source is a lineup conducted in violation of this constitutional standard. "Only a per se exclusionary rule as to such testimony can be an effective sanction, the Court said, to assure that law enforcement authorities will respect the accused's constitutional right to the presence of his counsel at the critical lineup." In the present case we are asked to extend the *Wade-Gilbert* per se exclusionary rule to identification testimony based upon a police station showup that took place before the defendant had been indicted or otherwise formally charged with any criminal offense.

On February 21, 1968, a man named Willie Shard reported to the Chicago police that the previous day two men had robbed him on a Chicago street of a wallet containing, among other things, traveler's checks and a Social Security card. On February 22, two police officers stopped the petitioner and a companion, Ralph Bean, on West Madison Street in Chicago. When asked for identification, the petitioner produced a wallet that contained three traveler's checks and a Social Security card, all bearing the name of Willie Shard. Papers with Shard's name on them were also found in Bean's possession. When asked to explain his possession of Shard's property, the petitioner first said that the traveler's checks were "play money," and then told the officers that he had won them in a crap game. The officers then arrested the petitioner and Bean and took them to a police station.

Only after arriving at the police station, and checking the records there, did the arresting officers learn of the Shard robbery. A police car was then dispatched to Shard's place of employment, where it picked up Shard and brought him to the police station. Immediately upon entering the room in the police station where the petitioner and Bean were seated at a table, Shard positively identified them as the men who had robbed him two days earlier. No lawyer was present in the room, and neither the petitioner nor Bean had asked for legal assistance, or been advised of any right to the presence of counsel.

More than six weeks later, the petitioner and Bean were indicted for the robbery of Willie Shard. Upon arraignment, counsel was appointed to represent them, and they pleaded not guilty. A pretrial motion to suppress Shard's identification testimony was denied, and at the trial Shard testified as a witness for the prosecution. In his testimony he described his identification of the two men at the police station on February 22, and identified them again in the courtroom as the men who had robbed him on February 20. He was cross-examined at length regarding the circumstances of his identification of the two defendants. The jury found both defendants guilty, and the petitioner's conviction was affirmed on appeal.

In a line of constitutional cases in this Court stemming back to the Court's landmark opinion in Powell v. Alabama [1932], it has been firmly established that a person's Sixth and Fourteenth Amendment right to counsel attaches only at or after the time that adversary judicial proceedings have been initiated against him. This is not to say that a defendant in a criminal case has a constitutional right to counsel only at the trial itself. The *Powell* case makes clear that the right attaches at the time of arraignment, and the Court has recently held that it exists also at the time of a preliminary hearing. But the point is that, while members of the Court have differed as to existence of the right to counsel in the contexts of some of the above cases, all of those cases have involved points of time at or after the initiation of adversary judicial criminal proceedings — whether by way of formal charge, preliminary hearing, indictment, information, or arraignment.

The initiation of judicial criminal proceedings is far from a mere formalism. It is the starting point of our whole system of adversary criminal justice. For it is only then that the government has committed itself to prosecute, and only then that the adverse positions of government and defendant have solidified. It is then that a defendant finds himself faced with the prosecutorial forces of organized society, and immersed in the intricacies of substantive and procedural criminal law. It is this point, therefore, that marks the commencement of the "criminal prosecutions" to which alone the explicit guarantees of the Sixth Amendment are applicable.

In this case we are asked to import into a routine police investigation an absolute constitutional guarantee historically and rationally applicable only after the onset of formal prosecutorial proceedings. We decline to do so.

What has been said is not to suggest that there may not be occasions during the course of a criminal investigation when the police do abuse identification procedures. Such abuses are not beyond the reach of the Constitution. As the Court pointed out in *Wade* itself, it is always necessary to "scrutinize any pretrial confrontation." The Due Process Clause of the Fifth and Fourteenth Amendments forbids a lineup that is unnecessarily suggestive and conducive to irreparable mistaken identification. Stovall v. Denno (1967).

Justice POWELL, concurring in the result.

As I would not extend the *Wade-Gilbert* per se exclusionary rule, I concur in the result reached by the Court.[2]

Justice BRENNAN, with whom Justice DOUGLAS and Justice MARSHALL join, dissenting.

[T]he Court's formulation of the controlling principle for pretrial confrontations is that "the principle of Powell v. Alabama and succeeding cases requires that we scrutinize any pretrial confrontation of the accused to determine whether the presence of his counsel is necessary to preserve the defendant's basic right to a fair trial as affected by his right meaningfully to cross-examine the witnesses against him and to have effective assistance of counsel at the trial itself. It calls upon us to analyze whether potential substantial prejudice to defendant's rights inheres in the particular confrontation and the ability of counsel to help avoid that prejudice."

It was that constitutional principle that the Court applied in *Wade* to pretrial confrontations for identification purposes. The Court first met the Government's contention that a confrontation for identification is "a mere preparatory step in the gathering of the prosecution's evidence," much like the scientific

---

2. This is the entirety of Justice Powell's opinion. [Footnote by casebook authors.]

examination of fingerprints and blood samples. The Court responded that in the latter instances "the accused has the opportunity for a meaningful confrontation of the Government's case at trial through the ordinary processes of cross-examination of the Government's expert witnesses and the presentation of the evidence of his own experts." The accused thus has no right to have counsel present at such examinations: "they are not critical stages since there is minimal risk that his counsel's absence at such stages might derogate from his right to a fair trial."

In contrast, the Court said, "the confrontation compelled by the State between the accused and the victim or witnesses to a crime to elicit identification evidence is peculiarly riddled with innumerable dangers and variable factors which might seriously, even crucially, derogate from a fair trial." Most importantly, "the accused's inability effectively to reconstruct at trial any unfairness that occurred at the lineup may deprive him of his only opportunity meaningfully to attack the credibility of the witness' courtroom identification."

While it should go without saying, it appears necessary, in view of the plurality opinion today, to re-emphasize that *Wade* did not require the presence of counsel at pretrial confrontations for identification purposes simply on the basis of an abstract consideration of the words "criminal prosecutions" in the Sixth Amendment. Counsel is required at those confrontations because "the dangers inherent in eyewitness identification and the suggestibility inherent in the context of the pretrial identification," mean that protection must be afforded to the "most basic right [of] a criminal defendant—his right to a fair trial at which the witnesses against him might be meaningfully cross-examined."

In view of *Wade*, it is plain, and the plurality today does not attempt to dispute it, that there inhere in a confrontation for identification conducted after arrest the identical hazards to a fair trial that inhere in such a confrontation conducted "after the onset of formal prosecutional proceedings." The plurality apparently considers an arrest, which for present purposes we must assume to be based upon probable cause, to be nothing more than part of "a routine police investigation," and thus not "the starting point of our whole system of adversary criminal justice." An arrest, according to the plurality, does not face the accused "with the prosecutorial forces of organized society," nor immerse him "in the intricacies of substantive and procedural criminal law." Those consequences ensue, says the plurality, only with "[t]he initiation of judicial criminal proceedings," "[f]or it is only then that the government has committed itself to prosecute, and only then that the adverse positions of government and defendant have solidified."

If these propositions do not amount to "mere formalism," it is difficult to know how to characterize them. An arrest evidences the belief of the police that the perpetrator of a crime has been caught. A post-arrest confrontation for identification is not "a mere preparatory step in the gathering of the prosecution's evidence." A primary, and frequently sole, purpose of the confrontation for identification at that stage is to accumulate proof to buttress the conclusion of the police that they have the offender in hand. The plurality offers no reason, and I can think of none, for concluding that a post-arrest confrontation for identification, unlike a post-charge confrontation, is not among those "critical confrontations of the accused by the prosecution at pretrial proceedings where the results might well settle the accused's fate and reduce the trial itself to a mere formality."

The highly suggestive form of confrontation employed in this case under-scores the point. This showup was particularly fraught with the peril of mistaken identification. In the setting of a police station squad room where all present except petitioner and Bean were police officers, the danger was quite real that Shard's understandable resentment might lead him too readily to agree with the police that the pair under arrest, and the only persons exhibited to him, were indeed the robbers. It is hard to imagine a situation more clearly conveying the suggestion to the witness that the one presented is believed guilty by the police.

The State had no case without Shard's identification testimony, and safe-guards against that consequence were therefore of critical importance. Shard's testimony itself demonstrates the necessity for such safeguards. On direct exam-ination, Shard identified petitioner and Bean not as the alleged robbers on trial in the courtroom, but as the pair he saw at the police station. His testimony thus lends strong support to the observation, quoted by the Court in *Wade*, that "[i]t is a matter of common experience that, once a witness has picked out the accused at the line-up, he is not likely to go back on his word later on, so that in practice the issue of identity may (in the absence of other relevant evidence) for all practical purposes be determined there and then, before the trial."

The confrontation of a lineup cannot have a constitutional distinction based upon the lodging of a formal charge. Every reason set forth by the Supreme Court in *Wade* for the assistance of counsel post-indictment has equal or more impact when projected against a pre-indictment atmosphere.

Justice WHITE, dissenting.[3]
United States v. Wade (1967), and Gilbert v. California (1967), govern this case and compel reversal of the judgment below.

UNITED STATES v. ASH
413 U.S. 300 (1973)

Justice BLACKMUN delivered the opinion of the Court.
In this case the Court is called upon to decide whether the Sixth Amendment grants an accused the right to have counsel present whenever the Government conducts a post-indictment photographic display, containing a picture of the accused, for the purpose of allowing a witness to attempt an identification of the offender.

I

On the morning of August 26, 1965, a man with a stocking mask entered a bank in Washington, D.C., and began waving a pistol. He ordered an employee to hang up the telephone and instructed all others present not to move. Seconds later a second man, also wearing a stocking mask, entered the bank, scooped up money from tellers' drawers into a bag, and left. The gunman followed, and both men escaped through an alley. The robbery lasted three or four minutes.

---

3. This is the entirety of Justice White's dissent. [Footnote by casebook author.]

A Government informer, Clarence McFarland, told authorities that he had discussed the robbery with Charles J. Ash, Jr., the respondent here. Acting on this information, an FBI agent, in February 1966, showed five black-and-white mug shots of Negro males of generally the same age, height, and weight, one of which was of Ash, to four witnesses. All four made uncertain identifications of Ash's picture. At this time Ash was not in custody and had not been charged. On April 1, 1966, an indictment was returned charging Ash and a codefendant, John L. Bailey, in five counts related to this bank robbery.

Trial was finally set for May 1968, almost three years after the crime. In preparing for trial, the prosecutor decided to use a photographic display to determine whether the witnesses he planned to call would be able to make in-court identifications. Shortly before the trial, an FBI agent and the prosecutor showed five color photographs to the four witnesses who previously had tentatively identified the black-and-white photograph of Ash. Three of the witnesses selected the picture of Ash, but one was unable to make any selection. None of the witnesses selected the picture of Bailey which was in the group. This post-indictment identification provides the basis for respondent Ash's claim that he was denied the right to counsel at a "critical stage" of the prosecution.[4]

II

[T]he core purpose of the counsel guarantee was to assure "Assistance" at trial, when the accused was confronted with both the intricacies of the law and the advocacy of the public prosecutor. Later developments have led this Court to recognize that "Assistance" would be less than meaningful if it were limited to the formal trial itself.

This extension of the right to counsel to events before trial has resulted from changing patterns of criminal procedure and investigation that have tended to generate pretrial events that might appropriately be considered to be parts of the trial itself. At these newly emerging and significant events, the accused was confronted, just as at trial, by the procedural system, or by his expert adversary, or by both. In *Wade*, the Court explained the process of expanding the counsel guarantee to these confrontations: "When the Bill of Rights was adopted, there were no organized police forces as we know them today. The accused confronted the prosecutor and the witnesses against him, and the evidence was marshalled, largely at the trial itself. In contrast, today's law enforcement machinery involves critical confrontations of the accused by the prosecution at pretrial proceedings where the results might well settle the accused's fate and reduce the trial itself to a mere formality. In recognition of these realities of modern criminal prosecution, our cases have construed the Sixth Amendment guarantee to apply to 'critical' stages of the proceedings." The Court consistently has applied a historical interpretation of the guarantee, and has expanded the constitutional right to counsel only when new contexts appear presenting the same dangers that gave birth initially to the right itself.

---

4. Respondent Ash does not assert a right to counsel at the black-and-white photographic display in February 1966 because he recognizes that Kirby v. Illinois (1972), forecloses application of the Sixth Amendment to events before the initiation of adversary criminal proceedings. [Footnote by Justice Blackmun.]

Throughout this expansion of the counsel guarantee to trial-like confrontations, the function of the lawyer has remained essentially the same as his function at trial. In all cases considered by the Court, counsel has continued to act as a spokesman for, or advisor to, the accused. The accused's right to the "Assistance of Counsel" has meant just that, namely, the right of the accused to have counsel acting as his assistant.

The function of counsel in rendering "Assistance" continued at the lineup under consideration in *Wade* and its companion cases. Although the accused was not confronted there with legal questions, the lineup offered opportunities for prosecuting authorities to take advantage of the accused. Counsel was seen by the Court as being more sensitive to, and aware of, suggestive influences than the accused himself, and as better able to reconstruct the events at trial. Counsel present at lineup would be able to remove disabilities of the accused in precisely the same fashion that counsel compensated for the disabilities of the layman at trial. Thus, the Court mentioned that the accused's memory might be dimmed by "emotional tension," that the accused's credibility at trial would be diminished by his status as defendant, and that the accused might be unable to present his version effectively without giving up his privilege against compulsory self-incrimination. It was in order to compensate for these deficiencies that the Court found the need for the assistance of counsel.

This review of the history and expansion of the Sixth Amendment counsel guarantee demonstrates that the test utilized by the Court has called for examination of the event in order to determine whether the accused required aid in coping with legal problems or assistance in meeting his adversary.

III

We conclude that the dangers of mistaken identification, mentioned in *Wade*, [are not applicable in the context of photo identifications.] Although *Wade* did discuss possibilities for suggestion and the difficulty for reconstructing suggestivity, this discussion occurred only after the Court had concluded that the lineup constituted a trial-like confrontation, requiring the "Assistance of Counsel" to preserve the adversary process by compensating for advantages of the prosecuting authorities.

The structure of *Wade*, viewed in light of the careful limitation of the Court's language to "confrontations," makes it clear that lack of scientific precision and inability to reconstruct an event are not the tests for requiring counsel in the first instance. These are, instead, the tests to determine whether confrontation with counsel at trial can serve as a substitute for counsel at the pretrial confrontation. If accurate reconstruction is possible, the risks inherent in any confrontation still remain, but the opportunity to cure defects at trial causes the confrontation to cease to be "critical." The opinion of the Court even indicated that changes in procedure might cause a lineup to cease to be a "critical" confrontation.

IV

A substantial departure from the historical test would be necessary if the Sixth Amendment were interpreted to give Ash a right to counsel at the photographic identification in this case. Since the accused himself is not present at the time of the photographic display, and asserts no right to be present, no possibility arises that the accused might be misled by his lack of familiarity with the law or over-powered by his professional adversary. Similarly, the counsel guarantee would not be used to produce equality in a trial-like adversary confrontation. Rather, the guarantee was used by the Court of Appeals to produce confrontation at an event that previously was not analogous to an adversary trial.

Even if we were willing to view the counsel guarantee in broad terms as a generalized protection of the adversary process, we would be unwilling to go so far as to extend the right to a portion of the prosecutor's trial-preparation interviews with witnesses. Although photography is relatively new, the interview-ing of witnesses before trial is a procedure that predates the Sixth Amendment. In England in the 16th and 17th centuries counsel regularly interviewed wit-nesses before trial. The traditional counterbalance in the American adversary system for these interviews arises from the equal ability of defense counsel to seek and interview witnesses himself.

That adversary mechanism remains as effective for a photographic display as for other parts of pretrial interviews. No greater limitations are placed on defense counsel in constructing displays, seeking witnesses, and conducting photographic identifications than those applicable to the prosecution. Selection of the picture of a person other than the accused, or the inability of a witness to make any selection, will be useful to the defense in precisely the same manner that the selection of a picture of the defendant would be useful to the prosecution. Although we do not suggest that equality of access to photographs removes all potential for abuse, it does remove any inequality in the adversary process itself and thereby fully satisfies the historical spirit of the Sixth Amendment's counsel guarantee.

The argument has been advanced that requiring counsel might compel the police to observe more scientific procedures or might encourage them to utilize corporeal rather than photographic displays. This Court has recognized that improved procedures can minimize the dangers of suggestion. Commentators have also proposed more accurate techniques.

Pretrial photographic identifications, however, are hardly unique in offering possibilities for the actions of the prosecutor unfairly to prejudice the accused. Evidence favorable to the accused may be withheld; testimony of witnesses may be manipulated; the results of laboratory tests may be contrived. In many ways the prosecutor, by accident or by design, may improperly subvert the trial. The primary safeguard against abuses of this kind is the ethical responsibility of the prosecutor, who, as so often has been said, may "strike hard blows" but not "foul ones." If that safeguard fails, review remains available under due process stan-dards. These same safeguards apply to misuse of photographs.

We are not persuaded that the risks inherent in the use of photographic displays are so pernicious that an extraordinary system of safeguards is required. We hold, then, that the Sixth Amendment does not grant the right to counsel at photographic displays conducted by the Government for the purpose of allow-ing a witness to attempt an identification of the offender.

Justice STEWART, concurring in the judgment.

A photographic identification is quite different from a lineup, for there are substantially fewer possibilities of impermissible suggestion when photographs are used, and those unfair influences can be readily reconstructed at trial. It is true that the defendant's photograph may be markedly different from the others displayed, but this unfairness can be demonstrated at trial from an actual comparison of the photographs used or from the witness' description of the display. Similarly, it is possible that the photographs could be arranged in a suggestive manner, or that by comment or gesture the prosecuting authorities might single out the defendant's picture. But these are the kinds of overt influence that a witness can easily recount and that would serve to impeach the identification testimony. In short, there are few possibilities for unfair suggestiveness — and those rather blatant and easily reconstructed. Accordingly, an accused would not be foreclosed from an effective cross-examination of an identification witness simply because his counsel was not present at the photographic display. For this reason, a photographic display cannot fairly be considered a "critical stage" of the prosecution.

Justice BRENNAN, with whom Justice DOUGLAS and Justice MARSHALL join, dissenting.

The Court holds today that a pretrial display of photographs to the witnesses of a crime for the purpose of identifying the accused, unlike a lineup, does not constitute a "critical stage" of the prosecution at which the accused is constitutionally entitled to the presence of counsel. In my view, today's decision is wholly unsupportable in terms of such considerations as logic, consistency, and, indeed, fairness. As a result, I must reluctantly conclude that today's decision marks simply another step towards the complete evisceration of the fundamental constitutional principles established by this Court, only six years ago, in United States v. Wade (1967); Gilbert v. California (1967); and Stovall v. Denno (1967). I dissent.

In June 1967, this Court decided a trilogy of "lineup" cases which brought into sharp focus the problems of pretrial identification. In essence, those decisions held (1) that a pretrial lineup is a "critical stage" in the criminal process at which the accused is constitutionally entitled to the presence of counsel; (2) that evidence of an identification of the accused at such an uncounseled lineup is per se inadmissible; and (3) that evidence of a subsequent in-court identification of the accused is likewise inadmissible unless the Government can demonstrate by clear and convincing evidence that the in-court identification was based upon observations of the accused independent of the prior uncounseled lineup identification. The considerations relied upon by the Court in reaching these conclusions are clearly applicable to photographic as well as corporeal identifications.

As the Court of Appeals recognized, "the dangers of mistaken identification . . . set forth in *Wade* are applicable in large measure to photographic as well as corporeal identifications." To the extent that misidentification may be attributable to a witness' faulty memory or perception, or inadequate opportunity for detailed observation during the crime, the risks are obviously as great at a photographic display as at a lineup. Indeed, noting "the hazards of initial identification by photograph," we have expressly recognized that "a corporeal identification . . . is normally more accurate" than a photographic identification. Simmons v. United States (1968). Thus, in this sense at least, the dangers of misidentification are even greater at a photographic display than at a lineup.

Moreover, as in the lineup situation, the possibilities for impermissible suggestion in the context of a photographic display are manifold. Such suggestion, intentional or unintentional, may derive from three possible sources. First, the photographs themselves might tend to suggest which of the pictures is that of the suspect. For example, differences in age, pose, or other physical characteristics of the persons represented, and variations in the mounting, background, lighting, or markings of the photographs all might have the effect of singling out the accused.

Second, impermissible suggestion may inhere in the manner in which the photographs are displayed to the witness. The danger of misidentification is, of course, increased if the police display to the witness . . . the pictures of several persons among which the photograph of a single such individual recurs or is in some way emphasized. And, if the photographs are arranged in an asymmetrical pattern, or if they are displayed in a time sequence that tends to emphasize a particular photograph, any identification of the photograph which stands out from the rest is no more reliable than an identification of a single photograph, exhibited alone.

Third, gestures or comments of the prosecutor at the time of the display may lead an otherwise uncertain witness to select the "correct" photograph. For example, the prosecutor might "indicate to the witness that [he has] other evidence that one of the persons pictured committed the crime," and might even point to a particular photograph and ask whether the person pictured "looks familiar." More subtly, the prosecutor's inflection, facial expressions, physical motions, and myriad other almost imperceptible means of comm- unication might tend, intentionally or unintentionally, to compromise the witness' objectivity. Thus, as is the case with lineups, "[i]mproper photo- graphic identification procedures, . . . by exerting a suggestive influence upon the witnesses, can often lead to an erroneous identification. . . ." And "[r]egardless of how the initial misidentification comes about, the witness thereafter is apt to retain in his memory the image of the photograph rather than of the person actually seen . . . ." As a result, "the issue of identity may (in the absence of other relevant evidence) for all practical purposes be deter- mined there and then, before the trial."

Moreover, as with lineups, the defense can "seldom reconstruct" at trial the mode and manner of photographic identification. It is true, of course, that the photographs used at the pretrial display might be preserved for examination at trial. But it may also be said that a photograph can preserve the record of a lineup; yet this does not justify a lineup without counsel. Indeed, in reality, preservation of the photographs affords little protection to the unrepresented accused. For, although retention of the photographs may mitigate the dangers of misidentification due to the suggestiveness of the photographs themselves, it cannot in any sense reveal to defense counsel the more subtle, and therefore more dangerous, suggestiveness that might derive from the manner in which the photographs were displayed or any accompanying comments or gestures. Moreover, the accused cannot rely upon the witnesses themselves to expose these latter sources of suggestion, for the witnesses are not apt to be alert for conditions prejudicial to the suspect. And if they were, it would likely be of scant benefit to the suspect since the witnesses are hardly likely to be schooled in the detection of suggestive influences.

Finally, and unlike the lineup situation, the accused himself is not even present at the photographic identification, thereby reducing the likelihood that irregularities in the procedures will ever come to light.

Thus, the difficulties of reconstructing at trial an uncounseled photographic display are at least equal to, and possibly greater than, those involved in recon- structing an uncounseled lineup.

Ironically, the Court does not seriously challenge the proposition that presence of counsel at a pretrial photographic display is essential to preserve the accused's right to a fair trial on the issue of identification. Rather, in what I can only characterize a triumph of form over substance, the Court seeks to justify its result by engrafting a wholly unprecedented — and wholly unsupportable — limitation on the Sixth Amendment right of "the accused . . . to have the Assistance of Counsel for his defence." Although apparently conceding that the right to counsel attaches, not only at the trial itself, but at all "critical stages" of the prosecution, the Court holds today that, in order to be deemed "critical," the particular "stage of the prosecution" under consideration must, at the very least, involve the physical "presence of the accused," at a "trial-like confrontation" with the Government, at which the accused requires the "guiding hand of counsel." According to the Court a pretrial photographic identification does not, of course, meet these criteria.

But, contrary to the Court's assumption, this is merely one facet of the Sixth Amendment guarantee, and the decisions relied upon by the Court represent, not the boundaries of the right to counsel, but mere applications of a far broader and more reasoned understanding of the Sixth Amendment than that espoused today.

The fundamental premise underlying all of this Court's decisions holding the right to counsel applicable at "critical" pretrial proceedings, is that a "stage" of the prosecution must be deemed "critical" for the purposes of the Sixth Amendment if it is one at which the presence of counsel is necessary "to protect the fairness of the trial itself." This established conception of the Sixth Amendment guarantee is, of course, in no sense dependent upon the physical "presence of the accused," at a "trial-like confrontation" with the Government, at which the accused requires the "guiding hand of counsel."

There is something ironic about the Court's conclusion today that a pretrial lineup identification is a "critical stage" of the prosecution because counsel's presence can help to compensate for the accused's deficiencies as an observer, but that a pretrial photographic identification is not a "critical stage" of the prosecution because the accused is not able to observe at all. In my view, there simply is no meaningful difference, in terms of the need for attendance of counsel, between corporeal and photographic identifications. And applying established and well-reasoned Sixth Amendment principles, I can only conclude that a pretrial photographic display, like a pretrial lineup, is a "critical stage" of the prosecution at which the accused is constitutionally entitled to the presence of counsel.

B.   DUE PROCESS PROTECTION FOR IDENTIFICATION PROCEDURES

1.   Unnecessarily Suggestive Identification Procedures Violate Due Process

The other protection for criminal defendants with regard to identification is that the Supreme Court has held that unnecessarily suggestive identification procedures violate due process. This was initially the holding in Stovall v. Denno, 388 U.S. 293 (1967). It was the third case decided on the same day as

United States v. Wade (1967) and California v. Gilbert (1967). The specific issue in *Stovall* was whether *Wade* and *Gilbert* were to be applied retroactively to individuals who were convicted prior to these decisions. The Supreme Court held that *Wade* and *Gilbert* do not apply retroactively, that unnecessarily suggestive identification procedures violate due process, but that the identification procedure in this case was necessary under the circumstances.

Justice Brennan, writing for the Court, described the identification procedure:

> Dr. Paul Behrendt was stabbed to death in the kitchen of his home in Garden City, Long Island, about midnight August 23, 1961. Dr. Behrendt's wife, also a physician, had followed her husband to the kitchen and jumped at the assailant. He knocked her to the floor and stabbed her 11 times. The police found a shirt on the kitchen floor and keys in a pocket which they traced to petitioner. They arrested him on the afternoon of August 24. An arraignment was promptly held but was postponed until petitioner could retain counsel.
>
> Mrs. Behrendt was hospitalized for major surgery to save her life. The police, without affording petitioner time to retain counsel, arranged with her surgeon to permit them to bring petitioner to her hospital room about noon of August 25, the day after the surgery. Petitioner was handcuffed to one of five police officers who, with two members of the staff of the District Attorney, brought him to the hospital room. Petitioner was the only Negro in the room. Mrs. Behrendt identified him from her hospital bed after being asked by an officer whether he "was the man" and after petitioner repeated at the direction of an officer a "few words for voice identification." None of the witnesses could recall the words that were used. Mrs. Behrendt and the officers testified at the trial to her identification of the petitioner in the hospital room, and she also made an in-court identification of petitioner in the courtroom. Petitioner was convicted and sentenced to death.

Nonetheless, the Court affirmed the conviction and the sentence. The Court stated: "We hold that *Wade* and *Gilbert* affect only those cases and all future cases which involve confrontations for identification purposes conducted in the absence of counsel after this date. The rulings of *Wade* and *Gilbert* are therefore inapplicable in the present case. We think also that on the facts of this case petitioner was not deprived of due process of law in violation of the Fourteenth Amendment."

After holding that *Wade* and *Gilbert* do not apply retroactively, the Court said that apart from the right to counsel, unnecessarily suggestive identification procedures violate due process. The Court stated:

> We turn now to the question whether petitioner, although not entitled to the application of *Wade* and *Gilbert* to his case, is entitled to relief on his claim that in any event the confrontation conducted in this case was so unnecessarily suggestive and conducive to irreparable mistaken identification that he was denied due process of law. This is a recognized ground of attack upon a conviction independent of any right to counsel claim. The practice of showing suspects singly to persons for the purpose of identification, and not as part of a lineup, has been widely condemned. However, a claimed violation of due process of law in the conduct of a confrontation depends on the totality of the circumstances surrounding it, and the record in the present case reveals that the showing of Stovall to Mrs. Behrendt in an immediate hospital confrontation was imperative.
>
> Here was the only person in the world who could possibly exonerate Stovall. Her words, and only her words, "He is not the man" could have resulted in

freedom for Stovall. The hospital was not far distant from the courthouse and jail. No one knew how long Mrs. Behrendt might live. Faced with the responsibility of identifying the attacker, with the need for immediate action and with the knowledge that Mrs. Behrendt could not visit the jail, the police followed the only feasible procedure and took Stovall to the hospital room. Under these circumstances, the usual police station line-up, which Stovall now argues he should have had, was out of the question.[5]

Although the Court has said since *Stovall* that unnecessarily suggestive identifications violate due process, there is only one Supreme Court decision that has overturned a conviction on this basis.

FOSTER v. CALIFORNIA
394 U.S. 440 (1969)

Justice FORTAS delivered the opinion of the Court.

Petitioner was charged by information with the armed robbery of a Western Union office in violation of California Penal Code. The day after the robbery one of the robbers, Clay, surrendered to the police and implicated Foster and Grice. Allegedly, Foster and Clay had entered the office while Grice waited in a car. Foster and Grice were tried together. Grice was acquitted. Foster was convicted. We granted certiorari, limited to the question whether the conduct of the police lineup resulted in a violation of petitioner's constitutional rights.

Except for the robbers themselves, the only witness to the crime was Joseph David, the late-night manager of the Western Union office. After Foster had been arrested, David was called to the police station to view a lineup. There were three men in the lineup. One was petitioner. He is a tall man — close to six feet in height. The other two men were short — five feet, five or six inches. Petitioner wore a leather jacket which David said was similar to the one he had seen underneath the coveralls worn by the robber. After seeing this lineup, David could not positively identify petitioner as the robber. He "thought" he was the man, but he was not sure. David then asked to speak to petitioner, and petitioner was brought into an office and sat across from David at a table. Except for prosecuting officials there was no one else in the room. Even after this one-to-one confrontation David still was uncertain whether petitioner was one of the robbers: "truthfully — I was not sure," he testified at trial. A week or 10 days later, the police arranged for David to view a second lineup. There were five men

5. Justice Douglas dissented on the grounds that *Wade* and *Gilbert* should be applied retroactively. Justice Fortas dissented on the ground that the identification process violated due process. Justice Black dissented from the conclusion that unnecessarily suggestive identification procedures violate due process. He wrote:

> But even if the Due Process Clause could possibly be construed as giving such latitudinarian powers to the Court, I would still think the Court goes too far in holding that the courts can look at the particular circumstances or each identification lineup to determine at large whether they are too "suggestive and conducive to irreparable mistaken identification" to be constitutional. That result is to freeze as constitutional or as unconstitutional the circumstances of each case, giving the States and the Federal Government no permanent constitutional standards.

in that lineup. Petitioner was the only person in the second lineup who had appeared in the first lineup. This time David was "convinced" petitioner was the man.

At trial, David testified to his identification of petitioner in the lineups, as summarized above. He also repeated his identification of petitioner in the courtroom. The only other evidence against petitioner which concerned the particular robbery with which he was charged was the testimony of the alleged accomplice Clay.[6]

In United States v. Wade (1967), and Gilbert v. California (1967), this Court held that because of the possibility of unfairness to the accused in the way a lineup is conducted, a lineup is a "critical stage" in the prosecution, at which the accused must be given the opportunity to be represented by counsel. That holding does not, however, apply to petitioner's case, for the lineups in which he appeared occurred before June 12, 1967. Stovall v. Denno (1967). But in declaring the rule of *Wade* and *Gilbert* to be applicable only to lineups conducted after those cases were decided, we recognized that, judged by the "totality of the circumstances," the conduct of identification procedures may be "so unnecessarily suggestive and conducive to irreparable mistaken identification" as to be a denial of due process of law.

Judged by that standard, this case presents a compelling example of unfair lineup procedures. In the first lineup arranged by the police, petitioner stood out from the other two men by the contrast of his height and by the fact that he was wearing a leather jacket similar to that worn by the robber. When this did not lead to positive identification, the police permitted a one-to-one confrontation between petitioner and the witness. This Court pointed out in *Stovall* that "[t]he practice of showing suspects singly to persons for the purpose of identification, and not as part of a lineup, has been widely condemned." Even after this the witness' identification of petitioner was tentative. So some days later another lineup was arranged. Petitioner was the only person in this lineup who had also participated in the first lineup. This finally produced a definite identification.

The suggestive elements in this identification procedure made it all but inevitable that David would identify petitioner whether or not he was in fact "the man." In effect, the police repeatedly said to the witness, "This is the man." This procedure so undermined the reliability of the eyewitness identification as to violate due process.

Justice BLACK, dissenting.

[M]y objection [is] to the Court's basic holding that evidence can be ruled constitutionally inadmissible whenever it results from identification procedures that the Court considers to be "unnecessarily suggestive and conducive to irreparable mistaken identification." One of the proudest achievements of this country's Founders was that they had eternally guaranteed a trial by jury in criminal cases, at least until the Constitution they wrote had been amended in the manner they prescribed. Of course it is an incontestable fact in our judicial history that the jury is the sole tribunal to weigh and determine facts. That means that the jury must, if we keep faith with the Constitution, be allowed to hear

---

6. California law requires that an accomplice's testimony be corroborated. California Penal Code § 1111. There was also evidence that Foster had been convicted for a similar robbery committed six years before. [Footnote by Justice Fortas.]

eyewitnesses and decide for itself whether it can recognize the truth and whether they are telling the truth. It means that the jury must be allowed to decide for itself whether the darkness of the night, the weakness of a witness' eyesight, or any other factor impaired the witness' ability to make an accurate identification. To take that power away from the jury is to rob it of the responsibility to perform the precise functions the Founders most wanted it to perform. And certainly a Constitution written to preserve this indispensable, unerodible core of our system for trying criminal cases would not have included, hidden among its provisions, a slumbering sleeper granting the judges license to destroy trial by jury in whole or in part.

This brings me to the constitutional theory relied upon by the Court to justify its invading the constitutional right of jury trial. The Court here holds that: "[J]udged by the 'totality of the circumstances,' the conduct of identification procedures may be 'so unnecessarily suggestive and conducive to irreparable mistaken identification' as to be a denial of due process of law." The Constitution sets up its own standards of unfairness in criminal trials in the Fourth, Fifth, and Sixth Amendments, among other provisions of the Constitution. Many of these provisions relate to evidence and its use in criminal cases.

It has become fashionable to talk of the Court's power to hold governmental laws and practices unconstitutional whenever this Court believes them to be "unfair," contrary to basic standards of decency, implicit in ordered liberty, or offensive to "those canons of decency and fairness which express the notions of justice of English-speaking peoples." All of these different general and indefinable words or phrases are the fruit of the same, what I consider to be poisonous, tree, namely, the doctrine that this Court has power to make its own ideas of fairness, decency, and so forth, enforceable as though they were constitutional precepts.

2.   Limits on the Ability of Courts to Find That Identification Procedures Violate Due Process

As mentioned above, *Foster* is the only case in which the Supreme Court has found that an identification procedure violates due process. The Court has rejected due process challenges to identification procedures on three major grounds. First, the Court has found that highly suggestive procedures did not violate due process because they were necessary. In *Stovall*, above, the Court affirmed a conviction based on an identification where the suspect was brought to the victim in her hospital room and the suspect was handcuffed to a police officer and was the only African-American man in the room. The Court explained that the victim was critically injured and there was not time to arrange a lineup. Necessity also played a key role in Simmons v. United States, below.

Second, the Supreme Court has been willing to allow convictions based on suggestive identifications if the witness has an "independent source for the identification," such as other contacts with the suspect besides the police identification procedure. Neil v. Biggers, below, allowed a suggestive identification procedure on this basis.

Finally, and most importantly, the Court has rejected due process challenges to suggestive identification procedures if it concludes that there are sufficient indications of reliability. This is certainly expressed in Simmons v. United States and Neil v. Biggers, but it is most clearly expressed in the final case below, Manson v. Braithwaite.

In reading these three cases, it is important to see that these factors taken together make it difficult to challenge an identification on due process grounds. Again, the crucial question is whether this is appropriate deference to a necessary police procedure or whether it fails to provide adequate protection against a police procedure that often leads to the conviction of innocent people.

SIMMONS v. UNITED STATES
390 U.S. 377 (1968)

Justice HARLAN delivered the opinion of the Court.

This case presents issues arising out of the petitioners' trial and conviction in the United States District Court for the Northern District of Illinois for the armed robbery of a federally insured savings and loan association.

The evidence at trial showed that at about 1:45 P.M. on February 27, 1964, two men entered a Chicago savings and loan association. One of them pointed a gun at a teller and ordered her to put money into a sack which the gunman supplied. The men remained in the bank about five minutes. After they left, a bank employee rushed to the street and saw one of the men sitting on the passenger side of a departing white 1960 Thunderbird automobile with a large scrape on the right door. Within an hour police located in the vicinity a car matching this description. They discovered that it belonged to a Mrs. Rey, sister-in-law of petitioner Simmons. She told the police that she had loaned the car for the afternoon to her brother, William Andrews.

At about 5:15 P.M. the same day, two FBI agents came to the house of Mrs. Mahon, Andrews' mother, about half a block from the place where the car was then parked. The agents had no warrant, and at trial it was disputed whether Mrs. Mahon gave them permission to search the house. They did search, and in the basement they found two suitcases, of which Mrs. Mahon disclaimed any knowledge. One suitcase contained, among other items, a gun holster, a sack similar to the one used in the robbery, and several coin cards and bill wrappers from the bank which had been robbed.

The following morning the FBI obtained from another of Andrews' sisters some snapshots of Andrews and of petitioner Simmons, who was said by the sister to have been with Andrews the previous afternoon. These snapshots were shown to the five bank employees who had witnessed the robbery. Each witness identified pictures of Simmons as representing one of the robbers. A week or two later, three of these employees identified photographs of petitioner Garrett as depicting the other robber, the other two witnesses stating that they did not have a clear view of the second robber.

During the trial, all five bank employee witnesses identified Simmons as one of the robbers. Three of them identified Garrett as the second robber, the other two testifying that they did not get a good look at the second robber. The jury found Simmons and Garrett, as well as Andrews, guilty as charged.

The facts as to the identification claim are these. As has been noted previously, FBI agents on the day following the robbery obtained from Andrews' sister a number of snapshots of Andrews and Simmons. There seem to have been at least six of these pictures, consisting mostly of group photographs of Andrews,

Simmons, and others. Later the same day, these were shown to the five bank employees who had witnessed the robbery at their place of work, the photographs being exhibited to each employee separately. Each of the five employees identified Simmons from the photographs. At later dates, some of these witnesses were again interviewed by the FBI and shown indeterminate numbers of pictures. Again, all identified Simmons. At trial, the Government did not introduce any of the photographs, but relied upon in-court identification by the five eyewitnesses, each of whom swore that Simmons was one of the robbers.

Simmons, however, does not contend that he was entitled to counsel at the time the pictures were shown to the witnesses. Rather, he asserts simply that in the circumstances the identification procedure was so unduly prejudicial as fatally to taint his conviction. This is a claim which must be evaluated in light of the totality of surrounding circumstances. See Stovall v. Denno (1967). Viewed in that context, we find the claim untenable.

It must be recognized that improper employment of photographs by police may sometimes cause witnesses to err in identifying criminals. A witness may have obtained only a brief glimpse of a criminal, or may have seen him under poor conditions. Even if the police subsequently follow the most correct photographic identification procedures and show him the pictures of a number of individuals without indicating whom they suspect, there is some danger that the witness may make an incorrect identification. This danger will be increased if the police display to the witness only the picture of a single individual who generally resembles the person he saw, or if they show him the pictures of several persons among which the photograph of a single such individual recurs or is in some way emphasized. The chance of misidentification is also heightened if the police indicate to the witness that they have other evidence that one of the persons pictured committed the crime. Regardless of how the initial misidentification comes about, the witness thereafter is apt to retain in his memory the image of the photograph rather than of the person actually seen, reducing the trustworthiness of subsequent lineup or courtroom identification.

Despite the hazards of initial identification by photograph, this procedure has been used widely and effectively in criminal law enforcement, from the standpoint both of apprehending offenders and of sparing innocent suspects the ignominy of arrest by allowing eyewitnesses to exonerate them through scrutiny of photographs. The danger that use of the technique may result in convictions based on misidentification may be substantially lessened by a course of cross-examination at trial which exposes to the jury the method's potential for error. We are unwilling to prohibit its employment, either in the exercise of our supervisory power or, still less, as a matter of constitutional requirement. Instead, we hold that each case must be considered on its own facts, and that convictions based on eyewitness identification at trial following a pretrial identification by photograph will be set aside on that ground only if the photographic identification procedure was so impermissibly suggestive as to give rise to a very substantial likelihood of irreparable misidentification.

Applying the standard to this case, we conclude that petitioner Simmons' claim on this score must fail. In the first place, it is not suggested that it was unnecessary for the FBI to resort to photographic identification in this instance. A serious felony had been committed. The perpetrators were still at large. The inconclusive clues which law enforcement officials possessed led to Andrews and Simmons. It was essential for the FBI agents swiftly to determine whether they were on the right track, so that they could properly deploy their forces in Chicago and, if necessary, alert officials in other cities. The justification for this method of procedure was hardly less compelling than that which we found to justify the "one-man lineup" in Stovall v. Denno.

In the second place, there was in the circumstances of this case little chance that the procedure utilized led to misidentification of Simmons. The robbery took place in the afternoon in a well-lighted bank. The robbers wore no masks. Five bank employees had been able to see the robber later identified as Simmons for periods ranging up to five minutes. Those witnesses were shown the photographs only a day later, while their memories were still fresh. At least six photographs were displayed to each witness. Apparently, these consisted primarily of group photographs, with Simmons and Andrews each appearing several times in the series. Each witness was alone when he or she saw the photographs. There is no evidence to indicate that the witnesses were told anything about the progress of the investigation, or that the FBI agents in any other way suggested which persons in the pictures were under suspicion.

Under these conditions, all five eyewitnesses identified Simmons as one of the robbers. None identified Andrews, who apparently was as prominent in the photographs as Simmons. These initial identifications were confirmed by all five witnesses in subsequent viewings of photographs and at trial, where each witness identified Simmons in person. Notwithstanding cross-examination, none of the witnesses displayed any doubt about their respective identifications of Simmons. Taken together, these circumstances leave little room for doubt that the identification of Simmons was correct, even though the identification procedure employed may have in some respects fallen short of the ideal. We hold that in the factual surroundings of this case the identification procedure used was not such as to deny Simmons due process of law or to call for reversal under our supervisory authority.

NEIL v. BIGGERS
409 U.S. 188 (1972)

Justice POWELL delivered the opinion of the Court.

In 1965, after a jury trial in a Tennessee court, respondent was convicted of rape and was sentenced to 20 years' imprisonment. The State's evidence consisted in part of testimony concerning a station-house identification of respondent by the victim.

We proceed, then, to consider respondent's due process claim. As the claim turns upon the facts, we must first review the relevant testimony at the jury trial and at the habeas corpus hearing regarding the rape and the identification. The victim testified at trial that on the evening of January 22, 1965, a youth with a butcher knife grabbed her in the doorway to her kitchen:

A. [H]e grabbed me from behind, and grappled-twisted me on the floor. Threw me down on the floor.
Q. And there was no light in that kitchen?
A. Not in the kitchen.
Q. So you couldn't have seen him then?
A. Yes, I could see him, when I looked up in his face.

Q. In the dark?
A. He was right in the doorway—it was enough light from the bedroom shining
      through. Yes, I could see who he was.
Q. You could see? No light? And you could see him and know him then?
A. Yes.

When the victim screamed, her 12-year-old daughter came out of her bedroom and also began to scream. The assailant directed the victim to "tell her (the daughter) to shut up, or I'll kill you both." She did so, and was then walked at knifepoint about two blocks along a railroad track, taken into a woods, and raped there. She testified that "the moon was shining brightly, full moon." After the rape, the assailant ran off, and she returned home, the whole incident having taken between 15 minutes and half an hour.

She then gave the police what the Federal District Court characterized as "only a very general description," describing him as "being fat and flabby with smooth skin, bushy hair and a youthful voice." Additionally, though not mentioned by the District Court, she testified at the habeas corpus hearing that she had described her assailant as being between 16 and 18 years old and between five feet ten inches and six feet tall, as weighing between 180 and 200 pounds, and as having a dark brown complexion. This testimony was substantially corroborated by that of a police officer who was testifying from his notes.

On several occasions over the course of the next seven months, she viewed suspects in her home or at the police station, some in lineups and others in showups, and was shown between 30 and 40 photographs. She told the police that a man pictured in one of the photographs had features similar to those of her assailant, but identified none of the suspects. On August 17, the police called her to the station to view respondent, who was being detained on another charge. In an effort to construct a suitable lineup, the police checked the city jail and the city juvenile home. Finding no one at either place fitting respondent's unusual physical description, they conducted a showup instead.

The showup itself consisted of two detectives walking respondent past the victim. At the victim's request, the police directed respondent to say "shut up or I'll kill you." The testimony at trial was not altogether clear as to whether the victim first identified him and then asked that he repeat the words or made her identification after he had spoken. In any event, the victim testified that she had "no doubt" about her identification. At the habeas corpus hearing, she elaborated in response to questioning.

We must decide whether, as the courts below held, this identification and the circumstances surrounding it failed to comport with due process requirements. Some general guidelines emerge from [the prior] cases as to the relationship between suggestiveness and misidentification. It is, first of all, apparent that the primary evil to be avoided is "a very substantial likelihood of irreparable misidentification." While the phrase was coined as a standard for determining whether an in-court identification would be admissible in the wake of a suggestive out-of-court identification, with the deletion of "irreparable" it serves equally well as a standard for the admissibility of testimony concerning the out-of-court identification itself. It is the likelihood of misidentification which violates a defendant's right to due process, and it is this which was the basis of the exclusion of evidence in *Foster*. Suggestive confrontations are disapproved because they increase the likelihood of misidentification, and unnecessarily suggestive ones are condemned for the further reason that the increased chance of misidentification is gratuitous. But as *Stovall* makes clear, the admission of evidence of a showup without more does not violate due process.

We turn, then, to the central question, whether under the "totality of the circumstances" the identification was reliable even though the confrontation procedure was suggestive. As indicated by our cases, the factors to be considered in evaluating the likelihood of misidentification include the opportunity of the witness to view the criminal at the time of the crime, the witness' degree of attention, the accuracy of the witness' prior description of the criminal, the level of certainty demonstrated by the witness at the confrontation, and the length of time between the crime and the confrontation. Applying these factors, we disagree with the District Court's conclusion [overturning the conviction.]

In part, we think the District Court focused unduly on the relative reliability of a lineup as opposed to a showup, the issue on which expert testimony was taken at the evidentiary hearing. It must be kept in mind also that the trial was conducted before *Stovall* and that therefore the incentive was lacking for the parties to make a record at trial of facts corroborating or undermining the identification. The testimony was addressed to the jury, and the jury apparently found the identification reliable.

We find that the District Court's conclusions on the critical facts are unsupported by the record and clearly erroneous. The victim spent a considerable period of time with her assailant, up to half an hour. She was with him under adequate artificial light in her house and under a full moon outdoors, and at least twice, once in the house and later in the woods, faced him directly and intimately. She was no casual observer, but rather the victim of one of the most personally humiliating of all crimes. Her description to the police, which included the assailant's approximate age, height, weight, complexion, skin texture, build, and voice, might not have satisfied Proust but was more than ordinarily thorough. She had "no doubt" that respondent was the person who raped her. In the nature of the crime, there are rarely witnesses to a rape other than the victim, who often has a limited opportunity of observation. The victim here, a practical nurse by profession, had an unusual opportunity to observe and identify her assailant. She testified at the habeas corpus hearing that there was something about his face "I don't think I could ever forget."

There was, to be sure, a lapse of seven months between the rape and the confrontation. This would be a seriously negative factor in most cases. Here, however, the testimony is undisputed that the victim made no previous identification at any of the showups, lineups, or photographic showings. Her record for reliability was thus a good one, as she had previously resisted whatever suggestiveness inheres in a showup. Weighing all the factors, we find no substantial likelihood of misidentification. The evidence was properly allowed to go to the jury.

Justice BRENNAN, with whom Justice DOUGLAS and Justice STEWART join, dissenting in part.

Regrettably, the Court addresses the merits and delves into the factual background of the case to reverse the District Court's finding, upheld by the Court of Appeals, that under the "totality of the circumstances," the pre-*Stovall* showup was so impermissibly suggestive as to give rise to a substantial likelihood of misidentification. This is an unjustified departure from our long-established practice not to reverse findings of fact concurred in by two lower courts unless shown to be clearly erroneous.

As the Court recognizes, a pre-*Stovall* identification obtained as a result of an unnecessarily suggestive showup may still be introduced in evidence if, under the "totality of the circumstances," the identification retains strong indicia of reliability. After an extensive hearing and careful review of the state court record, however, the District Court found that, under the circumstances of this case, there existed an intolerable risk of misidentification. Moreover, in making this determination, the court specifically found that "the complaining witness did not get an opportunity to obtain a good view of the suspect during the commission of the crime," "the show-up confrontation was not conducted near the time of the alleged crime, but, rather, some seven months after its commission," and the complaining witness was unable to give "a good physical description of her assailant" to the police. The Court of Appeals, which conducted its own review of the record, upheld the District Court's findings in their entirety.

The Court argues further, however, that the rule is irrelevant here because, in its view, "the dispute between the parties is not so much over the elemental facts as over the constitutional significance to be attached to them." I cannot agree. Even a cursory examination of the Court's opinion reveals that its concern is not limited solely to the proper application of legal principles but, rather, extends to an essentially de novo inquiry into such "elemental facts" as the nature of the victim's opportunity to observe the assailant and the type of description the victim gave the police at the time of the crime. And although we might reasonably disagree with the lower courts' findings as to such matters, the "two-court" rule wisely inhibits us from cavalierly substituting our own view of the facts simply because we might adopt a different construction of the evidence or resolve the ambiguities differently. On the contrary, these findings are "final here in the absence of very exceptional showing of error." The record before us is simply not susceptible of such a showing and, indeed, the petitioner does not argue otherwise.

MANSON v. BRATHWAITE

432 U.S. 98 (1977)

Justice BLACKMUN delivered the opinion of the Court.

This case presents the issue as to whether the Due Process Clause of the Fourteenth Amendment compels the exclusion, in a state criminal trial, apart from any consideration of reliability, of pretrial identification evidence obtained by a police procedure that was both suggestive and unnecessary.

I

Jimmy D. Glover, a full-time trooper of the Connecticut State Police, in 1970 was assigned to the Narcotics Division in an undercover capacity. On May 5 of that year, about 7:45 P.M., e.d.t., and while there was still daylight, Glover and Henry Alton Brown, an informant, went to an apartment building at 201 Westland, in Hartford, for the purpose of purchasing narcotics from "Dickie Boy" Cicero, a known narcotics dealer. Cicero, it was thought, lived on the third floor of that apartment building. Glover and Brown entered the building, observed by back-up Officers D'Onofrio and Gaffey, and proceeded by stairs to the third floor. Glover knocked at the door of one of the two apartments served by the stairway. The area was illuminated by natural light from a window in the third floor hallway. The door was opened 12 to 18 inches in response to the knock. Glover observed a man standing at the door and, behind him, a woman. Brown identified himself. Glover then asked for "two things" of narcotics. The man at the door held out his hand, and Glover gave him two $10 bills. The door closed. Soon the man returned and handed Glover two glassine bags. While the door was open, Glover stood within two feet of the person from whom he made the purchase and observed his face. Five to seven minutes elapsed from the time the door first opened until it closed the second time.

Glover and Brown then left the building. This was about eight minutes after their arrival. Glover drove to headquarters where he described the seller to D'Onofrio and Gaffey. Glover at that time did not know the identity of the seller. He described him as being "a colored man, approximately five feet eleven inches tall, dark complexion, black hair, short Afro style, and having high cheekbones, and of heavy build. He was wearing at the time blue pants and a plaid shirt." D'Onofrio, suspecting from this description that respondent might be the seller, obtained a photograph of respondent from the Records Division of the Hartford Police Department. He left it at Glover's office. D'Onofrio was not acquainted with respondent personally but did know him by sight and had seen him "[s]everal times" prior to May 5. Glover, when alone, viewed the photograph for the first time upon his return to headquarters on May 7; he identified the person shown as the one from whom he had purchased the narcotics.

The toxicological report on the contents of the glassine bags revealed the presence of heroin. The report was dated July 16, 1970.

Respondent was arrested on July 27 while visiting at the apartment of a Mrs. Ramsey on the third floor of 201 Westland. This was the apartment at which the narcotics sale had taken place on May 5.

Respondent was charged, in a two-count information, with possession and sale of heroin, in violation of Conn.Gen.Stat. At his trial in January 1971, the photograph from which Glover had identified respondent was received in evidence without objection on the part of the defense. Glover also testified that, although he had not seen respondent in the eight months that had elapsed since the sale, "there [was] no doubt whatsoever" in his mind that the person shown on the photograph was respondent. Glover also made a positive in-court identification without objection. No explanation was offered by the prosecution for the failure to utilize a photographic array or to conduct a lineup.

The jury found respondent guilty on both counts of the information. He received a sentence of not less than six nor more than nine years.

[II]

In the present case the District Court observed that the "sole evidence tying Brathwaite to the possession and sale of the heroin consisted in his identifications by the police undercover agent, Jimmy Glover." On the constitutional issue, the court stated that the first inquiry was whether the police used an impermissibly suggestive procedure in obtaining the out-of-court identification. If so, the second inquiry is whether, under all the circumstances, that suggestive procedure gave rise to a substantial likelihood of irreparable misidentification.

Petitioner at the outset acknowledges that "the procedure in the instant case was suggestive (because only one photograph was used) and unnecessary" (because there was no emergency or exigent circumstance). The respondent, in agreement with the Court of Appeals, proposes a per se rule of exclusion that he claims is dictated by the demands of the Fourteenth Amendment's guarantee of due process. He rightly observes that this is the first case in which this Court has had occasion to rule upon strictly post-*Stovall* out-of-court identification evidence of the challenged kind.

There are, of course, several interests to be considered and taken into account. The driving force behind United States v. Wade (1967), Gilbert v. California (1967), and Stovall, all decided on the same day, was the Court's concern with the problems of eyewitness identification. Usually the witness must testify about an encounter with a total stranger under circumstances of emergency or emotional stress. The witness' recollection of the stranger can be distorted easily by the circumstances or by later actions of the police. Thus, *Wade* and its companion cases reflect the concern that the jury not hear eyewitness testimony unless that evidence has aspects of reliability. It must be observed that both approaches before us are responsive to this concern. The per se rule, however, goes too far since its application automatically and peremptorily, and without consideration of alleviating factors, keeps evidence from the jury that is reliable and relevant.

The second factor is deterrence. Although the per se approach has the more significant deterrent effect, the totality approach also has an influence on police behavior. The police will guard against unnecessarily suggestive procedures under the totality rule, as well as the per se one, for fear that their actions will lead to the exclusion of identifications as unreliable.

The third factor is the effect on the administration of justice. Here the per se approach suffers serious drawbacks. Since it denies the trier reliable evidence, it may result, on occasion, in the guilty going free. Also, because of its rigidity, the per se approach may make error by the trial judge more likely than the totality approach. And in those cases in which the admission of identification evidence is error under the per se approach but not under the totality approach — cases in which the identification is reliable despite an unnecessarily suggestive identification — procedure reversal is a Draconian sanction. Certainly, inflexible rules of exclusion that may frustrate rather than promote justice have not been viewed recently by this Court with unlimited enthusiasm.

The standard, after all, is that of fairness as required by the Due Process Clause of the Fourteenth Amendment. *Stovall*, with its reference to "the totality of the circumstances," and *Biggers*, with its continuing stress on the same totality, did not, singly or together, establish a strict exclusionary rule or new standard of due process.

We therefore conclude that reliability is the linchpin in determining the admissibility of identification testimony for both pre- and post-*Stovall* confrontations. The factors to be considered are set out in *Biggers*. These include the opportunity of the witness to view the criminal at the time of the crime, the witness' degree of attention, the accuracy of his prior description of the criminal, the level of certainty demonstrated at the confrontation, and the time between the crime and the confrontation. Against these factors is to be weighed the corrupting effect of the suggestive identification itself.

[III]

We turn, then, to the facts of this case and apply the analysis:

1. The opportunity to view. Glover testified that for two to three minutes he stood at the apartment door, within two feet of the respondent. The door opened twice, and each time the man stood at the door. The moments passed, the conversation took place, and payment was made. Glover looked directly at his vendor. It was near sunset, to be sure, but the sun had not yet set, so it was not dark or even dusk or twilight. Natural light from outside entered the hallway through a window. There was natural light, as well, from inside the apartment.

2. The degree of attention. Glover was not a casual or passing observer, as is so often the case with eyewitness identification. Trooper Glover was a trained police officer on duty and specialized and dangerous duty when he called at the third floor of 201 Westland in Hartford on May 5, 1970. Glover himself was a Negro and unlikely to perceive only general features of "hundreds of Hartford black males." It is true that Glover's duty was that of ferreting out narcotics offenders and that he would be expected in his work to produce results. But it is also true that, as a specially trained, assigned, and experienced officer, he could be expected to pay scrupulous attention to detail, for he knew that subsequently he would have to find and arrest his vendor. In addition, he knew that his claimed observations would be subject later to close scrutiny and examination at any trial.

3. The accuracy of the description. Glover's description was given to D'Onofrio within minutes after the transaction. It included the vendor's race, his height, his build, the color and style of his hair, and the high cheekbone facial feature. It also included clothing the vendor wore. No claim has been made that respondent did not possess the physical characteristics so described. D'Onofrio reacted positively at once. Two days later, when Glover was alone, he viewed the photograph D'Onofrio produced and identified its subject as the narcotics seller.

4. The witness' level of certainty. There is no dispute that the photograph in question was that of respondent. Glover, in response to a question whether the photograph was that of the person from whom he made the purchase, testified: "There is no question whatsoever." This positive assurance was repeated.

5. The time between the crime and the confrontation. Glover's description of his vendor was given to D'Onofrio within minutes of the crime. The photographic identification took place only two days later. We do not have here the passage of weeks or months between the crime and the viewing of the photograph.

These indicators of Glover's ability to make an accurate identification are hardly outweighed by the corrupting effect of the challenged identification itself. Although identifications arising from single-photograph displays may be viewed in general with suspicion, we find in the instant case little pressure on the witness to acquiesce in the suggestion that such a display entails. D'Onofrio had left the photograph at Glover's office and was not present when Glover first viewed it two days after the event. There thus was little urgency and Glover could view the photograph at his leisure. And since Glover examined the photograph alone, there was no coercive pressure to make an identification arising from the presence of another. The identification was made in circumstances allowing care and reflection.

Although it plays no part in our analysis, all this assurance as to the reliability of the identification is hardly undermined by the facts that respondent was arrested in the very apartment where the sale had taken place, and that he acknowledged his frequent visits to that apartment.

Surely, we cannot say that under all the circumstances of this case there is "a very substantial likelihood of irreparable misidentification." Short of that point, such evidence is for the jury to weigh. We are content to rely upon the good sense and judgment of American juries, for evidence with some element of untrustworthiness is customary grist for the jury mill. Juries are not so susceptible that they cannot measure intelligently the weight of identification testimony that has some questionable feature.

Of course, it would have been better had D'Onofrio presented Glover with a photographic array including "so far as practicable . . . a reasonable number of persons similar to any person then suspected whose likeness is included in the array." The use of that procedure would have enhanced the force of the identification at trial and would have avoided the risk that the evidence would be excluded as unreliable. But we are not disposed to view D'Onofrio's failure as one of constitutional dimension to be enforced by a rigorous and unbending exclusionary rule. The defect, if there be one, goes to weight and not to substance.

Justice MARSHALL, with whom Justice BRENNAN joins, dissenting.

Today's decision can come as no surprise to those who have been watching the Court dismantle the protections against mistaken eyewitness testimony erected a decade ago in United States v. Wade (1967); Gilbert v. California (1967); and Stovall v. Denno (1967). But it is still distressing to see the Court virtually ignore the teaching of experience embodied in those decisions and blindly uphold the conviction of a defendant who may well be innocent.

Apparently, the Court does not consider [Neil v.] *Biggers* controlling in this case. I entirely agree, since I believe that *Biggers* was wrongly decided. The Court, however, concludes that *Biggers* is distinguishable because it, like the identification decisions that preceded it, involved a pre-*Stovall* confrontation, and because a paragraph in *Biggers* itself seems to distinguish between pre- and post-*Stovall* confrontations. Accordingly, in determining the admissibility of the post-*Stovall* identification in this case, the Court considers two alternatives, a per se exclusionary rule and a totality-of-the-circumstances approach. The Court weighs three factors in deciding that the totality approach, which is essentially the test used in *Biggers*, should be applied. In my view, the Court wrongly evaluates the impact of these factors.

First, the Court acknowledges that one of the factors, deterrence of police use of unnecessarily suggestive identification procedures, favors the per se rule. Indeed, it does so heavily, for such a rule would make it unquestionably clear to the police they must never use a suggestive procedure when a fairer alternative is available. I have no doubt that conduct would quickly conform to the rule.

Second, the Court gives passing consideration to the dangers of eyewitness identification recognized in the *Wade* trilogy. It concludes, however, that the grave risk of error does not justify adoption of the per se approach because that would too often result in exclusion of relevant evidence. In my view, this conclusion totally ignores the lessons of *Wade*. The dangers of mistaken identification are simply too great to permit unnecessarily suggestive identifications.

Finally, the Court errs in its assessment of the relative impact of the two approaches on the administration of justice. The Court relies most heavily on this factor, finding that "reversal is a Draconian sanction" in cases where the identification is reliable despite an unnecessarily suggestive procedure used to obtain it. Relying on little more than a strong distaste for "inflexible rules of exclusion," the Court rejects the per se test. In so doing, the Court disregards two significant distinctions between the per se rule advocated in this case and the exclusionary remedies for certain other constitutional violations.

First, the per se rule here is not "inflexible." Where evidence is suppressed, for example, as the fruit of an unlawful search, it may well be forever lost to the prosecution. Identification evidence, however, can by its very nature be readily and effectively reproduced. The in-court identification, permitted under *Wade* and *Simmons* if it has a source independent of an uncounseled or suggestive procedure, is one example. Similarly, when a prosecuting attorney learns that there has been a suggestive confrontation, he can easily arrange another lineup conducted under scrupulously fair conditions. Since the same factors are evaluated in applying both the Court's totality test and the *Wade-Simmons* independent-source inquiry, any identification which is "reliable" under the Court's test will support admission of evidence concerning such a fairly conducted lineup. The evidence of an additional, properly conducted confrontation will be more persuasive to a jury, thereby increasing the chance of a justified conviction where a reliable identification was tainted by a suggestive confrontation. At the same time, however, the effect of an unnecessarily suggestive identification which has no value whatsoever in the law enforcement process will be completely eliminated.

Second, other exclusionary rules have been criticized for preventing jury consideration of relevant and usually reliable evidence in order to serve interest unrelated to guilt or innocence, such as discouraging illegal searches or denial of counsel. Suggestively obtained eyewitness testimony is excluded, in contrast, precisely because of its unreliability and concomitant irrelevance. Its exclusion both protects the integrity of the truth-seeking function of the trial and discourages police use of needlessly inaccurate and ineffective investigatory methods. Indeed, impermissibly suggestive identifications are not merely worthless law enforcement tools. They pose a grave threat to society at large in a more direct way than most governmental disobedience of the law. For if the police and the public erroneously conclude, on the basis of an unnecessarily suggestive confrontation, that the right man has been caught and convicted, the real outlaw must still remain at large. Law enforcement has failed in its primary function and has left society unprotected from the depredations of an active criminal.

For these reasons, I conclude that adoption of the per se rule would enhance, rather than detract from, the effective administration of justice. In my view, the Court's totality test will allow seriously unreliable and misleading evidence to be put before juries. Equally important, it will allow dangerous criminals to remain on the streets while citizens assume that police action has given them protection.

According to my calculus, all three of the factors upon which the Court relies point to acceptance of the per se approach.

Even more disturbing than the Court's reliance on the totality test, however, is the analysis it uses, which suggests a reinterpretation of the concept of due process of law in criminal cases. The decision suggests that due process violations in identification procedures may not be measured by whether the government employed procedures violating standards of fundamental fairness. By relying on the probable accuracy of a challenged identification, instead of the necessity for its use, the Court seems to be ascertaining whether the defendant was probably guilty. Until today, I had though that "equal justice under law" meant that the existence of constitutional violations did not depend on the race, sex, religion, nationality, or likely guilt of the accused. The Due Process Clause requires adherence to the same high standard of fundamental fairness in dealing with every criminal defendant, whatever his personal characteristics and irrespective of the strength of the State's case against him. Strong evidence that the defendant is guilty should be relevant only to the determination whether an error of constitutional magnitude was nevertheless harmless beyond a reasonable doubt. By importing the question of guilt into the initial determination of whether there was a constitutional violation, the apparent effect of the Court's decision is to undermine the protection afforded by the Due Process Clause. "It is therefore important to note that the state courts remain free, in interpreting state constitutions, to guard against the evil clearly identified by this case."

The use of a single picture (or the display of a single live suspect, for that matter) is a grave error, of course, because it dramatically suggests to the witness that the person shown must be the culprit. Why else would the police choose the person? And it is deeply ingrained in human nature to agree with the expressed opinions of others[,] particularly others who should be more knowledgeable when making a difficult decision. In this case, moreover, the pressure was not limited to that inherent in the display of a single photograph. Glover, the identifying witness, was a state police officer on special assignment. He knew that D'Onofrio, an experienced Hartford narcotics detective, presumably familiar with local drug operations, believed respondent to be the seller. There was at work, then, both loyalty to another police officer and deference to a better-informed colleague. Finally, of course, there was Glover's knowledge that without an identification and arrest, government funds used to buy heroin had been wasted.

The Court discounts this overwhelming evidence of suggestiveness, however. It reasons that because D'Onofrio was not present when Glover viewed the photograph, there was "little pressure on the witness to acquiesce in the suggestion." That conclusion blinks psychological reality. There is no doubt in my mind that even in D'Onofrio's absence, a clear and powerful message was telegraphed to Glover as he looked at respondent's photograph. He was emphatically told that "this is the man," and he responded by identifying respondent then and at trial "whether or not he was in fact 'the man.'"

I must conclude that this record presents compelling evidence that there was "a very substantial likelihood of misidentification" of respondent Brathwaite. The suggestive display of respondent's photograph to the witness Glover likely erased any independent memory that Glover had retained of the seller from his barely adequate opportunity to observe the criminal.

CHAPTER

6

RIGHT TO COUNSEL

A. INTRODUCTION

Of all the defendant's constitutional rights, none is more important than the defendant's right to counsel. With the assistance of counsel, a defendant can protect all of his other rights. From beginning to end, the defense lawyer serves as an advocate for the accused, ensuring that both law enforcement and prosecutors comply with the defendants' constitutional rights. Chapter 4 discusses the right to counsel during police interrogations and Chapter 5 discusses the right to counsel at post-charge identifications. This chapter focuses on the right to counsel at trial and pretrial proceedings.

Before examining the scope of the right to counsel, it is worth considering the practical challenges in providing quality counsel to the accused. Nationally, there is a shortage of funds to pay the fees for indigent counsel. As a result, in some areas of the country, defense lawyers are paid at little as $50 to handle a criminal case.[1] Not surprisingly, the low pay and demanding nature of the job make it difficult to recruit experienced and qualified lawyers to handle indigent criminal cases. While there are many dedicated public defenders who work countless hours of unpaid overtime, there continues to be a shortage of capable defense counsel.

As this chapter will discuss, the right to counsel is a crucial right, but it involves more than just the right to appointment of a lawyer. The Sixth Amendment provides for the right to the "effective" assistance of counsel. Section B discusses when that right is triggered. Section C reviews the genesis of the right to counsel. The right to counsel under the Sixth Amendment was not always recognized by the Supreme Court. Rather, it was considered an aspect of the right to due process. It was not until the landmark case of Gideon v. Wainwright, 372 U.S. 335 (1963), that the Supreme Court recognized an independent right to counsel under the Sixth Amendment. Section D discusses the standard to be used to measure whether the defendant has been afforded "effective" assistance of counsel. How good of a lawyer is a defendant

---

1. *See* Adam Gershowitz, *Raise the Proof: A Default Rule for Indigent Defense*, 40 Conn. L. Rev. 85 (2007). Defense lawyers are often outspent by a 3:1 margin.

entitled to under the Sixth Amendment? What resources should be available to a defense lawyer in representing his or her client? Does the right to counsel include the right to experts to assist counsel in his or her representation of the defendant?

Section E then addresses the right of self-representation. Although a defendant has the Sixth Amendment right to counsel, the defendant can waive the right and represent himself. Finally, Section F briefly addresses the situation of enemy combatants and the nature of the right to counsel.

B. WHEN THE RIGHT TO COUNSEL APPLIES

The Sixth Amendment provides that "[i]n all criminal prosecutions, the accused shall enjoy the right . . . to have the Assistance of Counsel for his defense." The right to counsel attaches at all "critical stages" of a criminal prosecution after the filing of formal charges. Kirby v. Illinois, 406 U.S. 682 (1972) (plurality opinion). Thus, the right attaches at all post-indictment pretrial lineups (United States v. Wade, 388 U.S. 218 (1967)), preliminary hearings (Coleman v. Alabama, 399 U.S. 1 (1970)), post-indictment interrogations (Massiah v. United States, 377 U.S. 201 (1964)), and arraignments (Hamilton v. Alabama, 368 U.S. 52 (1961)). The right to counsel before trial is critical given that most criminal defendants plead guilty and the assistance of counsel is most needed in investigating the case and negotiating a settlement with the prosecutor.

By contrast, the right does not attach at parole hearings or probation revocation hearings, Gagnon v. Scarpelli, 411 U.S. 778 (1973), or in civil matters such as habeas corpus proceedings, Pennsylvania v. Finley, 481 U.S. 551 (1987). By the terms of the Sixth Amendment, the right to assistance of counsel does not apply in civil cases, but only "[i]n all criminal prosecutions."

As for parole and probation revocation hearings, the Supreme Court refused to create a per se requirement for the appointment of counsel. Rather, using a due process case-by-case approach, the Court held that appointment of counsel was not automatically required by the Sixth Amendment. Justice Powell wrote:

> [T]he "purpose is to help individuals reintegrate into society as constructive individuals as soon as they are able . . .". The introduction of counsel into a revocation proceeding will alter significantly the nature of the proceeding. If counsel is provided for the probationer or parolee, the State in turn will normally provide its own counsel; lawyers, by training and disposition, are advocates and bound by professional duty to present all available evidence and arguments in support of their clients' positions and to contest with vigor all adverse evidence and views. The role of the hearing body itself, aptly described as being "predictive and discretionary" as well as factfinding, may become more akin to that of a judge at a trial, and less attuned to the rehabilitative needs of the individual probationer or parolee. In the greater self-consciousness of its quasi-judicial role, the hearing body may be less tolerant of marginal deviant behavior and feel more pressure to reincarcerate than to continue nonpunitive rehabilitation. Certainly, the decisionmaking process will be prolonged, and the financial cost to the State — for appointed counsel, counsel

for the State, a longer record, and the possibility of judicial review—will not be insubstantial.

In some cases, these modifications in the nature of the revocation hearing must be endured and the costs borne because the probationer's or parolee's version of a disputed issue can fairly be represented only by a trained advocate. But due process is not so rigid as to require that the significant interests in informality, flexibility, and economy must always be sacrificed.

In so concluding, we are of course aware that the case-by-case approach to the right to counsel in felony prosecutions adopted in Betts v. Brady (1942), was later rejected in favor of a per se rule in Gideon v. Wainwright (1963). *See also* Argersinger v. Hamlin (1972). We do not, however, draw from [these cases] the conclusion that a case-by-case approach to furnishing counsel is necessarily inadequate to protect constitutional rights: there are critical differences between criminal trials and probation or parole revocation hearings, and both society and the probationer or parolee have stakes in preserving these differences.

Gagnon v. Scarpelli, 411 U.S. at 783-791.

A defendant has a Sixth Amendment right to counsel in any felony case, or in a misdemeanor case if a sentence of incarceration is actually imposed. Argersinger v. Hamlin, 407 U.S. 25, 40 (1972). This includes cases in which the defendant received a suspended sentence, and was later incarcerated for a probation violation. Alabama v. Shelton, 535 U.S. 654, 674 (2002).

There is no right to a jury trial for petty offenses. *See* Blanton v. City of North Las Vegas, 489 U.S. 538, 541-542 (1989). By contrast, there is a right to counsel if the defendant is sentenced to jail. Why? Once again, the answer lies in the role defense counsel plays in a case.

ARGERSINGER v. HAMLIN

407 U.S. 25 (1972)

Justice DOUGLAS delivered the opinion of the Court.

Petitioner, an indigent, was charged in Florida with carrying a concealed weapon, an offense punishable by imprisonment up to six months, a $1,000 fine, or both. The trial was to a judge, and petitioner was unrepresented by counsel. He was sentenced to serve 90 days in jail, and brought this habeas corpus action alleging that being deprived of his right to counsel, he was unable as an indigent layman properly to raise and present to the trial court good and sufficient defenses to the charge for which he stands convicted.

"Originally, in England, a person charged with treason or felony was denied the aid of counsel, except in respect of legal questions which the accused himself might suggest. At the same time parties in civil cases and persons accused of misdemeanors were entitled to the full assistance of counsel. . . ."

The Sixth Amendment thus extended the right to counsel beyond its common-law dimensions. But there is nothing in the language of the Amendment, its history, or in the decisions of this Court, to indicate that it was intended to embody a retraction of the right in petty offenses wherein the common law previously did require that counsel be provided.

We reject, therefore, the premise that since prosecutions for crimes punishable by imprisonment for less than six months may be tried without a jury, they may also be tried without a lawyer.

The assistance of counsel is often a requisite to the very existence of a fair trial.[1] "In our adversary system of criminal justice, any person haled into court, who is too poor to hire a lawyer, cannot be assured a fair trial unless counsel is provided for him. This seems to us to be an obvious truth. Governments, both state and federal, quite properly spend vast sums of money to establish machinery to try defendants accused of crime. Lawyers to prosecute are everywhere deemed essential to protect the public's interest in an orderly society. Similarly, there are few defendants charged with crime, few indeed, who fail to hire the best lawyers they can get to prepare and present their defenses. That government hires lawyers to prosecute and defendants who have the money hire lawyers to defend are the strongest indications of the widespread belief that lawyers in criminal courts are necessities, not luxuries. The right of one charged with crime to counsel may not be deemed fundamental and essential to fair trials in some countries, but it is in ours."

The requirement of counsel may well be necessary for a fair trial even in a petty-offense prosecution. We are by no means convinced that legal and constitutional questions involved in a case that actually leads to imprisonment even for a brief period are any less complex than when a person can be sent off for six months or more. The trial of vagrancy cases is illustrative. While only brief sentences of imprisonment may be imposed, the cases often bristle with thorny constitutional questions.

Beyond the problem of trials and appeals is that of the guilty plea, a problem which looms large in misdemeanor as well as in felony cases. Counsel is needed so that the accused may know precisely what he is doing, so that he is fully aware of the prospect of going to jail or prison, and so that he is treated fairly by the prosecution.

In addition, the volume of misdemeanor cases, far greater in number than felony prosecutions, may create an obsession for speedy dispositions, regardless of the fairness of the result. An inevitable consequence of volume that large is the almost total preoccupation in such a court with the movement of cases. The calendar is long, speed often is substituted for care, and casually arranged out-of-court compromise too often is substituted for adjudication. Inadequate attention tends to be given to the individual defendant, whether in protecting his rights, sifting the facts at trial, deciding the social risk he presents, or determining how to deal with him after conviction. The frequent result is futility and failure. As Dean Edward Barrett recently observed:

> Wherever the visitor looks at the system, he finds great numbers of defendants being processed by harassed and overworked officials. Police have more cases than they can investigate. Prosecutors walk into courtrooms to try simple cases as they take their initial looks at the files. Defense lawyers appear having had no more than time for hasty conversations with their clients. Judges face long calendars with the certain knowledge that their calendars tomorrow and the next day will be, if anything, longer, and so there is no choice but to dispose of the cases.

1. [The Sixth Amendment] embodies a realistic recognition of the obvious truth that the average defendant does not have the professional legal skill to protect himself when brought before a tribunal with power to take his life or liberty, wherein the prosecution is represented by experienced and learned counsel. That which is simple, orderly and necessary to the lawyer, to the untrained layman may appear intricate, complex and mysterious.

Johnson v. Zerbst, 304 U.S. 458, 462-463 (1938). [Footnote by the Court.]

Suddenly it becomes clear that for most defendants in the criminal process, there is scant regard for them as individuals. They are numbers on dockets, faceless ones to be processed and sent on their way. The gap between the theory and the reality is enormous.

There is evidence of the prejudice which results to misdemeanor defendants from this "assembly-line justice." One study concluded that "misdemeanants represented by attorneys are five times as likely to emerge from police court with all charges dismissed as are defendants who face similar charges without counsel."

We must conclude, therefore, that the problems associated with misdemeanor and petty offenses often require the presence of counsel to insure the accused a fair trial.

We hold, therefore, that absent a knowing and intelligent waiver, no person may be imprisoned for any offense, whether classified as petty, misdemeanor, or felony, unless he was represented by counsel at his trial.

C. APPOINTMENT OF COUNSEL

The right to counsel is automatic; the defendant need not request counsel for the right to be triggered. *See* Brewer v. Williams, 430 U.S. 387, 404 (1977). Moreover, if a defendant cannot afford his own lawyer, the court must appoint counsel for him. This right was established by the Supreme Court in the landmark case of Gideon v. Wainwright.

Even prior to *Gideon*, most states were providing counsel to indigent defendants, but only in the most serious of cases, such as death penalty cases. In Powell v. Alabama, 287 U.S. 45, 64-65 (1932),[2] the Court recognized the importance of counsel. Powell and his co-defendants were young, black men accused of raping two white girls in Alabama. In what was to become the infamous "Scottsboro Boys" trial, no lawyer was designated to represent the defendants until the morning of trial. With no time to prepare, and facing an ignorant and hostile community, it was no surprise that the defendants were convicted. On appeal, the Supreme Court found that the defendants' due process rights were violated. Justice Sutherland wrote, "[W]e are of the opinion that, under the circumstances [of this case], the necessity of counsel was so vital and imperative that the failure of the trial court to make an effective appointment of counsel was . . . a denial of due process within the meaning of the Fourteenth Amendment."

The Court continued to decide on a case-by-case basis whether the lack of counsel denied the defendant due process at trial. In Betts v. Brady, 316 U.S. 455 (1942), the Court expressly refused to find that the Fourteenth Amendment incorporated the Sixth Amendment right to counsel to the states. Not surprisingly, this led to a flood of cases in which each defendant claimed that denial of counsel in his or her case denied the defendant due process. Courts were

---

2. This case is also discussed in Chapter 1 of this book.

inconsistent in their rulings and the time became ripe for the Court to reexamine the issue. It did so in Gideon v. Wainwright.

GIDEON v. WAINWRIGHT
372 U.S. 335 (1963)

Justice BLACK delivered the opinion of the Court.

Petitioner was charged in a Florida state court with having broken and entered a poolroom with intent to commit a misdemeanor. This offense is a felony under Florida law. Appearing in court without funds and without a lawyer, petitioner asked the court to appoint counsel for him, whereupon the following colloquy took place:

"The COURT: Mr. Gideon, I am sorry, but I cannot appoint Counsel to represent you in this case. Under the laws of the State of Florida, the only time the Court can appoint Counsel to represent a Defendant is when that person is charged with a capital offense. I am sorry, but I will have to deny your request to appoint Counsel to defend you in this case.

"The DEFENDANT: The United States Supreme Court says I am entitled to be represented by Counsel."

Put to trial before a jury, Gideon conducted his defense about as well as could be expected from a layman. He made an opening statement to the jury, cross-examined the State's witnesses, presented witnesses in his own defense, declined to testify himself, and made a short argument "emphasizing his innocence to the charge contained in the Information filed in this case." The jury returned a verdict of guilty, and petitioner was sentenced to serve five years in the state prison. Later, petitioner filed in the Florida Supreme Court this habeas corpus petition attacking his conviction and sentence on the ground that the trial court's refusal to appoint counsel for him denied him rights "guaranteed by the Constitution and the Bill of Rights by the United States Government."[3] Treating the petition for habeas corpus as properly before it, the State Supreme Court, "upon consideration thereof" but without an opinion, denied all relief. Since 1942, when Betts v. Brady was decided by a divided Court, [the rule has been that there is no automatic right to counsel unless counsel is needed to ensure due process to the defendant in his particular case]. [W]e appointed counsel to represent [Gideon] and requested both sides to discuss in their briefs and oral arguments the following: "Should this Court's holding in Betts v. Brady be reconsidered?"

The Sixth Amendment provides, "In all criminal prosecutions, the accused shall enjoy the right . . . to have the Assistance of Counsel for his defence." Betts argued that this right is extended to indigent defendants in state courts by the Fourteenth Amendment. On the basis of . . . historical data the Court concluded that "appointment of counsel is not a fundamental right, essential to a fair trial."

We accept Betts v. Brady's assumption, based as it was on our prior cases, that a provision of the Bill of Rights which is "fundamental and essential to a fair trial" is made obligatory upon the States by the Fourteenth Amendment. We think the

---

3. The Supreme Court accepted a handwritten petition Gideon wrote for himself. He stated, "I, Clarence Earl Gideon, claim that I was denied the rights of the 4th, 5th and 14th amendments of the Bill of Rights." See original opinion, fn.2. [Footnote by casebook authors.]

Court in *Betts* was wrong, however, in concluding that the Sixth Amendment's guarantee of counsel is not one of these fundamental rights.

"[The assistance of counsel] is one of the safeguards of the Sixth Amendment deemed necessary to insure fundamental human rights of life and liberty. . . . The Sixth Amendment stands as a constant admonition that if the constitutional safeguards it provides be lost, justice will not 'still be done.'" Johnson v. Zerbst (1938).

The fact is that in deciding as it did — that "appointment of counsel is not a fundamental right, essential to a fair trial" — the Court in Betts v. Brady made an abrupt break with its own well-considered precedents. In returning to these old precedents, sounder we believe than the new, we but restore constitutional principles established to achieve a fair system of justice. Not only these precedents but also reason and reflection require us to recognize that in our adversary system of criminal justice, any person haled into court, who is too poor to hire a lawyer, cannot be assured a fair trial unless counsel is provided for him. This seems to us to be an obvious truth. Governments, both state and federal, quite properly spend vast sums of money to establish machinery to try defendants accused of crime. Lawyers to prosecute are everywhere deemed essential to protect the public's interest in an orderly society. Similarly, there are few defendants charged with crime, few indeed, who fail to hire the best lawyers they can get to prepare and present their defenses. That government hires lawyers to prosecute and defendants who have the money hire lawyers to defend are the strongest indications of the widespread belief that lawyers in criminal courts are necessities, not luxuries. The right of one charged with crime to counsel may not be deemed fundamental and essential to fair trials in some countries, but it is in ours. From the very beginning, our state and national constitutions and laws have laid great emphasis on procedural and substantive safeguards designed to assure fair trials before impartial tribunals in which every defendant stands equal before the law. This noble ideal cannot be realized if the poor man charged with crime has to face his accusers without a lawyer to assist him. A defendant's need for a lawyer is nowhere better stated than in the moving words of Mr. Justice Sutherland in Powell v. Alabama:

"The right to be heard would be, in many cases, of little avail if it did not comprehend the right to be heard by counsel. Even the intelligent and educated layman has small and sometimes no skill in the science of law. If charged with crime, he is incapable, generally, of determining for himself whether the indictment is good or bad. He is unfamiliar with the rules of evidence. Left without the aid of counsel he may be put on trial without a proper charge, and convicted upon incompetent evidence, or evidence irrelevant to the issue or otherwise inadmissible. He lacks both the skill and knowledge adequately to prepare his defense, even though he have a perfect one. He requires the guiding hand of counsel at every step in the proceedings against him. Without it, though he be not guilty, he faces the danger of conviction because he does not know how to establish his innocence."

The Court in Betts v. Brady departed from the sound wisdom upon which the Court's holding in Powell v. Alabama rested. *Betts* was "an anachronism when handed down" and . . . it should now be overruled.

Gideon was afforded a new trial with counsel. Upon retrial, he was acquitted.

After *Gideon*, the Court extended the right to counsel to apply to a defendant's first appeal of right. *See* Evitts v. Lucey, 469 U.S. 387 (1985). Even if a defendant's appeal does not have merit, the defendant is entitled to appointed counsel who will examine the record carefully to identify any non-frivolous issues for the appellate court to review. Anders v. California, 386 U.S. 738 (1967).

D. STANDARD FOR "EFFECTIVE ASSISTANCE" OF COUNSEL

Following *Gideon*, the courts struggled with the issue of how competent counsel must be to satisfy Sixth Amendment standards. Is the defendant entitled to a lawyer who makes no mistakes? What if the lawyer makes mistakes but those mistakes were unlikely to affect the outcome of the defendant's trial? What does the Sixth Amendment mean when it guarantees the right to "effective" assistance of counsel? The Court settled upon its standard for effective assistance of counsel in Strickland v. Washington.

STRICKLAND v. WASHINGTON
466 U.S. 668 (1984)

Justice O'CONNOR delivered the opinion of the Court.

This case requires us to consider the proper standards for judging a criminal defendant's contention that the Constitution requires a conviction or death sentence to be set aside because counsel's assistance at the trial or sentencing was ineffective.

I

During a 10-day period in September 1976, respondent planned and committed three groups of crimes, which included three brutal stabbing murders, torture, kidnaping, severe assaults, attempted murders, attempted extortion, and theft. After his two accomplices were arrested, respondent surrendered to police and voluntarily gave a lengthy statement confessing to the third of the criminal episodes. The State of Florida indicted respondent for kidnaping and murder and appointed an experienced criminal lawyer to represent him.

Counsel actively pursued pretrial motions and discovery. He cut his efforts short, however, and he experienced a sense of hopelessness about the case, when he learned that, against his specific advice, respondent had also confessed to the first two murders. By the date set for trial, respondent was subject to indictment for three counts of first-degree murder and multiple counts of robbery, kidnaping for ransom, breaking and entering and assault, attempted murder, and conspiracy to commit robbery. Respondent waived his right to a jury trial, again acting against counsel's advice, and pleaded guilty to all charges, including the three capital murder charges.

In the plea colloquy, respondent told the trial judge that, although he had committed a string of burglaries, he had no significant prior criminal record and that at the time of his criminal spree he was under extreme stress caused by his inability to support his family. He also stated, however, that he accepted responsibility for the crimes. The trial judge told respondent that he had "a great deal of respect for people who are willing to step forward and admit their responsibility" but that he was making no statement at all about his likely sentencing decision.

Counsel advised respondent to invoke his right under Florida law to an advisory jury at his capital sentencing hearing. Respondent rejected the advice and waived the right. He chose instead to be sentenced by the trial judge without a jury recommendation.

In preparing for the sentencing hearing, counsel spoke with respondent about his background. He also spoke on the telephone with respondent's wife and mother, though he did not follow up on the one unsuccessful effort to meet with them. He did not otherwise seek out character witnesses for respondent. Nor did he request a psychiatric examination, since his conversations with his client gave no indication that respondent had psychological problems.

Counsel decided not to present and hence not to look further for evidence concerning respondent's character and emotional state. That decision reflected trial counsel's sense of hopelessness about overcoming the evidentiary effect of respondent's confessions to the gruesome crimes. It also reflected the judgment that it was advisable to rely on the plea colloquy for evidence about respondent's background and about his claim of emotional stress: the plea colloquy communicated sufficient information about these subjects, and by forgoing the opportunity to present new evidence on these subjects, counsel prevented the State from cross-examining respondent on his claim and from putting on psychiatric evidence of its own.

Counsel also excluded from the sentencing hearing other evidence he thought was potentially damaging. He successfully moved to exclude respondent's "rap sheet." Because he judged that a presentence report might prove more detrimental than helpful, as it would have included respondent's criminal history and thereby would have undermined the claim of no significant history of criminal activity, he did not request that one be prepared.

At the sentencing hearing, counsel's strategy was based primarily on the trial judge's remarks at the plea colloquy as well as on his reputation as a sentencing judge who thought it important for a convicted defendant to own up to his crime. Counsel argued that respondent's remorse and acceptance of responsibility justified sparing him from the death penalty. Counsel also argued that respondent had no history of criminal activity and that respondent committed the crimes under extreme mental or emotional disturbance, thus coming within the statutory list of mitigating circumstances. He further argued that respondent should be spared death because he had surrendered, confessed, and offered to testify against a codefendant and because respondent was fundamentally a good person who had briefly gone badly wrong in extremely stressful circumstances. The State put on evidence and witnesses largely for the purpose of describing the details of the crimes. Counsel did not cross-examine the medical experts who testified about the manner of death of respondent's victims.

The trial judge found several aggravating circumstances with respect to each of the three murders. He found that all three murders were especially heinous, atrocious, and cruel, all involving repeated stabbings. All three murders were committed in the course of at least one other dangerous and violent felony, and since all involved robbery, the murders were for pecuniary gain. All three murders were committed to avoid arrest for the accompanying crimes and to hinder law enforcement. In the course of one of the murders, respondent knowingly subjected numerous persons to a grave risk of death by deliberately stabbing and shooting the murder victim's sisters-in-law, who sustained severe — in one case, ultimately fatal — injuries.

With respect to mitigating circumstances, the trial judge made the same findings for all three capital murders. First, although there was no admitted evidence of prior convictions, respondent had stated that he had engaged in a course of stealing. In any case, even if respondent had no significant history of criminal activity, the aggravating circumstances "would still clearly far outweigh" that mitigating factor. Second, the judge found that, during all three crimes, respondent was not suffering from extreme mental or emotional disturbance and could appreciate the criminality of his acts. Third, none of the victims was a participant in, or consented to, respondent's conduct. Fourth, respondent's participation in the crimes was neither minor nor the result of duress or domination by an accomplice.

In short, the trial judge found numerous aggravating circumstances and no (or a single comparatively insignificant) mitigating circumstance. With respect to each of the three convictions for capital murder, the trial judge concluded: "A careful consideration of all matters presented to the court impels the conclusion that there are insufficient mitigating circumstances . . . to outweigh the aggravating circumstances." He therefore sentenced respondent to death on each of the three counts of murder and to prison terms for the other crimes.

Respondent subsequently sought collateral relief in state court on numerous grounds, among them that counsel had rendered ineffective assistance at the sentencing proceeding. Respondent challenged counsel's assistance in six respects. He asserted that counsel was ineffective because he failed to move for a continuance to prepare for sentencing, to request a psychiatric report, to investigate and present character witnesses, to seek a presentence investigation report, to present meaningful arguments to the sentencing judge, and to investigate the medical examiner's reports or cross-examine the medical experts. In support of the claim, respondent submitted 14 affidavits from friends, neighbors, and relatives stating that they would have testified if asked to do so. He also submitted one psychiatric report and one psychological report stating that respondent, though not under the influence of extreme mental or emotional disturbance, was "chronically frustrated and depressed because of his economic dilemma" at the time of his crimes.

The trial court denied relief.

In assessing attorney performance, all the Federal Courts of Appeals and all but a few state courts have now adopted the "reasonably effective assistance" standard in one formulation or another. Yet this Court has not had occasion squarely to decide whether that is the proper standard. [W]e granted certiorari to consider the standards by which to judge a contention that the Constitution requires that a criminal judgment be overturned because of the actual ineffective assistance of counsel.

II

In a long line of cases that includes . . . Gideon v. Wainwright (1963), this Court has recognized that the Sixth Amendment right to counsel exists, and is needed, in order to protect the fundamental right to a fair trial. The Constitution guarantees . . .

"In all criminal prosecutions, the accused shall enjoy the right to a speedy and public trial, by an impartial jury of the State and district wherein the crime shall have been committed, which district shall have been previously ascertained by law, and to be informed of the nature and cause of the accusation; to be confronted with the witnesses against him; to have compulsory process for obtaining witnesses in his favor, and to have the Assistance of Counsel for his defence."

Thus, a fair trial is one in which evidence subject to adversarial testing is presented to an impartial tribunal for resolution of issues defined in advance of the proceeding. The right to counsel plays a crucial role in the adversarial system embodied in the Sixth Amendment, since access to counsel's skill and knowledge is necessary to accord defendants the "ample opportunity to meet the case of the prosecution" to which they are entitled.

Because of the vital importance of counsel's assistance, this Court has held that, with certain exceptions, a person accused of a federal or state crime has the right to have counsel appointed if retained counsel cannot be obtained. See Argersinger v. Hamlin (1972). That a person who happens to be a lawyer is present at trial alongside the accused, however, is not enough to satisfy the constitutional command. The Sixth Amendment recognizes the right to the assistance of counsel because it envisions counsel's playing a role that is critical to the ability of the adversarial system to produce just results. An accused is entitled to be assisted by an attorney, whether retained or appointed, who plays the role necessary to ensure that the trial is fair.

For that reason, the Court has recognized that "the right to counsel is the right to the effective assistance of counsel." Government violates the right to effective assistance when it interferes in certain ways with the ability of counsel to make independent decisions about how to conduct the defense. See, e.g., Geders v. United States (1976) (bar on attorney-client consultation during overnight recess). Counsel, however, can also deprive a defendant of the right to effective assistance, simply by failing to render "adequate legal assistance," Cuyler v. Sullivan (actual conflict of interest adversely affecting lawyer's performance renders assistance ineffective).

The Court has not elaborated on the meaning of the constitutional requirement of effective assistance in the latter class of cases — that is, those presenting claims of "actual ineffectiveness." In giving meaning to the requirement, however, we must take its purpose — to ensure a fair trial — as the guide. The benchmark for judging any claim of ineffectiveness must be whether counsel's conduct so undermined the proper functioning of the adversarial process that the trial cannot be relied on as having produced a just result.

The same principle applies to a capital sentencing proceeding such as that provided by Florida law. We need not consider the role of counsel in an ordinary sentencing, which may involve informal proceedings and standardless discretion in the sentencer, and hence may require a different approach to the definition of constitutionally effective assistance. A capital sentencing proceeding like the one involved in this case, however, is sufficiently like a trial in its adversarial format and in the existence of standards for decision, that counsel's role in the proceeding is comparable to counsel's role at trial — to ensure that the adversarial testing process works to produce a just result under the standards governing decision. For purposes of describing counsel's duties, therefore, Florida's capital sentencing proceeding need not be distinguished from an ordinary trial.

III

A convicted defendant's claim that counsel's assistance was so defective as to require reversal of a conviction or death sentence has two components. First, the defendant must show that counsel's performance was deficient. This requires showing that counsel made errors so serious that counsel was not functioning as the "counsel" guaranteed the defendant by the Sixth Amendment. Second, the defendant must show that the deficient performance prejudiced the defense. This requires showing that counsel's errors were so serious as to deprive the defendant of a fair trial, a trial whose result is reliable. Unless a defendant makes both showings, it cannot be said that the conviction or death sentence resulted from a breakdown in the adversary process that renders the result unreliable.

A

As all the Federal Courts of Appeals have now held, the proper standard for attorney performance is that of reasonably effective assistance. . . . When a convicted defendant complains of the ineffectiveness of counsel's assistance, the defendant must show that counsel's representation fell below an objective standard of reasonableness.

More specific guidelines are not appropriate. The Sixth Amendment refers simply to "counsel," not specifying particular requirements of effective assistance. It relies instead on the legal profession's maintenance of standards sufficient to justify the law's presumption that counsel will fulfill the role in the adversary process that the Amendment envisions. The proper measure of attorney performance remains simply reasonableness under prevailing professional norms.

Representation of a criminal defendant entails certain basic duties. Counsel's function is to assist the defendant, and hence counsel owes the client a duty of loyalty, a duty to avoid conflicts of interest. From counsel's function as assistant to the defendant derive the overarching duty to advocate the defendant's cause and the more particular duties to consult with the defendant on important decisions and to keep the defendant informed of important developments in the course of the prosecution. Counsel also has a duty to bring to bear such skill and knowledge as will render the trial a reliable adversarial testing process.

These basic duties neither exhaustively define the obligations of counsel nor form a checklist for judicial evaluation of attorney performance. In any case presenting an ineffectiveness claim, the performance inquiry must be whether counsel's assistance was reasonable considering all the circumstances. Prevailing norms of practice as reflected in American Bar Association standards and the like are guides to determining what is reasonable, but they are only guides. No particular set of detailed rules for counsel's conduct can satisfactorily take account of the variety of circumstances faced by defense counsel or the range of legitimate decisions regarding how best to represent a criminal defendant. Any such set of rules would interfere with the constitutionally protected independence of counsel and restrict the wide latitude counsel must have in making tactical decisions.

Judicial scrutiny of counsel's performance must be highly deferential. It is all too tempting for a defendant to second-guess counsel's assistance after conviction or adverse sentence, and it is all too easy for a court, examining counsel's defense after it has proved unsuccessful, to conclude that a particular act or omission of counsel was unreasonable. A fair assessment of attorney performance requires that every effort be made to eliminate the distorting effects of hindsight, to reconstruct the circumstances of counsel's challenged conduct, and to evaluate the conduct from counsel's perspective at the time. Because of the difficulties inherent in making the evaluation, a court must indulge a strong presumption that counsel's conduct falls within the wide range of reasonable professional assistance; that is, the defendant must overcome the presumption that, under the circumstances, the challenged action "might be considered sound trial strategy." There are countless ways to provide effective assistance in any given case. Even the best criminal defense attorneys would not defend a particular client in the same way.

The availability of intrusive post-trial inquiry into attorney performance or of detailed guidelines for its evaluation would encourage the proliferation of ineffectiveness challenges. Criminal trials resolved unfavorably to the defendant would increasingly come to be followed by a second trial, this one of counsel's unsuccessful defense. Counsel's performance and even willingness to serve could be adversely affected. Intensive scrutiny of counsel and rigid requirements for acceptable assistance could dampen the ardor and impair the independence of defense counsel, discourage the acceptance of assigned cases, and undermine the trust between attorney and client.

Thus, a court deciding an actual ineffectiveness claim must judge the reasonableness of counsel's challenged conduct on the facts of the particular case, viewed as of the time of counsel's conduct. A convicted defendant making a claim of ineffective assistance must identify the acts or omissions of counsel that are alleged not to have been the result of reasonable professional judgment. The court must then determine whether, in light of all the circumstances, the identified acts or omissions were outside the wide range of professionally competent assistance. In making that determination, the court should keep in mind that counsel's function, as elaborated in prevailing professional norms, is to make the adversarial testing process work in the particular case. At the same time, the court should recognize that counsel is strongly presumed to have rendered adequate assistance and made all significant decisions in the exercise of reasonable professional judgment.

These standards require no special amplification in order to define counsel's duty to investigate, the duty at issue in this case. [C]ounsel has a duty to make reasonable investigations or to make a reasonable decision that makes particular investigations unnecessary.

The reasonableness of counsel's actions may be determined or substantially influenced by the defendant's own statements or actions. Counsel's actions are usually based, quite properly, on informed strategic choices made by the defendant and on information supplied by the defendant. In particular, what investigation decisions are reasonable depends critically on such information.

For example, when the facts that support a certain potential line of defense are generally known to counsel because of what the defendant has said, the need for further investigation may be considerably diminished or eliminated altogether. And when a defendant has given counsel reason to believe that pursuing certain investigations would be fruitless or even harmful, counsel's failure to pursue those investigations may not later be challenged as unreasonable. In short, inquiry into counsel's conversations with the defendant may be critical to a proper assessment of counsel's investigation decisions, just as it may be critical to a proper assessment of counsel's other litigation decisions.

B

An error by counsel, even if professionally unreasonable, does not warrant setting aside the judgment of a criminal proceeding if the error had no effect on the judgment. The purpose of the Sixth Amendment guarantee of counsel is to ensure that a defendant has the assistance necessary to justify reliance on the outcome of the proceeding. Accordingly, any deficiencies in counsel's performance must be prejudicial to the defense in order to constitute ineffective assistance under the Constitution.

In certain Sixth Amendment contexts, prejudice is presumed. Actual or constructive denial of the assistance of counsel altogether is legally presumed to result in prejudice. So are various kinds of state interference with counsel's assistance. Prejudice in these circumstances is so likely that case-by-case inquiry into prejudice is not worth the cost. Moreover, such circumstances involve impairments of the Sixth Amendment right that are easy to identify and, for that reason and because the prosecution is directly responsible, easy for the government to prevent.

One type of actual ineffectiveness claim warrants a similar, though more limited, presumption of prejudice. In Cuyler v. Sullivan, the Court held that prejudice is presumed when counsel is burdened by an actual conflict of interest. In those circumstances, counsel breaches the duty of loyalty, perhaps the most basic of counsel's duties. Moreover, it is difficult to measure the precise effect on the defense of representation corrupted by conflicting interests. Given the obligation of counsel to avoid conflicts of interest and the ability of trial courts to make early inquiry in certain situations likely to give rise to conflicts, *see, e.g.*, Fed. Rule Crim. Proc. 44(c), it is reasonable for the criminal justice system to maintain a fairly rigid rule of presumed prejudice for conflicts of interest.

Conflict of interest claims aside, actual ineffectiveness claims alleging a deficiency in attorney performance are subject to a general requirement that the defendant affirmatively prove prejudice. The government is not responsible for, and hence not able to prevent, attorney errors that will result in reversal of a conviction or sentence. Attorney errors come in an infinite variety and are as likely to be utterly harmless in a particular case as they are to be prejudicial. They cannot be classified according to likelihood of causing prejudice. Nor can they be defined with sufficient precision to inform defense attorneys correctly just what conduct to avoid. Representation is an art, and an act or omission that is unprofessional in one case may be sound or even brilliant in another. Even if a defendant shows that particular errors of counsel were unreasonable, therefore, the defendant must show that they actually had an adverse effect on the defense.

It is not enough for the defendant to show that the errors had some conceivable effect on the outcome of the proceeding. Virtually every act or omission of counsel would meet that test, and not every error that conceivably could have influenced the outcome undermines the reliability of the result of the proceeding. Respondent suggests requiring a showing that the errors "impaired the presentation of the defense." That standard, however, provides no workable principle. Since any error, if it is indeed an error, "impairs" the presentation of the defense, the proposed standard is inadequate because it provides no way of deciding what impairments are sufficiently serious to warrant setting aside the outcome of the proceeding.

On the other hand, we believe that a defendant need not show that counsel's deficient conduct more likely than not altered the outcome in the case. . . . The result of a proceeding can be rendered unreliable, and hence the proceeding itself unfair, even if the errors of counsel cannot be shown by a preponderance of the evidence to have determined the outcome.

Accordingly, the appropriate test for prejudice finds its roots in the test for materiality of exculpatory information not disclosed to the defense by the prosecution. The defendant must show that there is a reasonable probability that, but for counsel's unprofessional errors, the result of the proceeding would have been different. A reasonable probability is a probability sufficient to undermine confidence in the outcome.

When a defendant challenges a conviction, the question is whether there is a reasonable probability that, absent the errors, the factfinder would have had a reasonable doubt respecting guilt. When a defendant challenges a death sentence such as the one at issue in this case, the question is whether there is a reasonable probability that, absent the errors, the sentencer — including an appellate court, to the extent it independently reweighs the evidence — would have concluded that the balance of aggravating and mitigating circumstances did not warrant death.

In making this determination, a court hearing an ineffectiveness claim must consider the totality of the evidence before the judge or jury. Some of the factual findings will have been unaffected by the errors, and factual findings that were affected will have been affected in different ways. Some errors will have had a pervasive effect on the inferences to be drawn from the evidence, altering the entire evidentiary picture, and some will have had an isolated, trivial effect. Moreover, a verdict or conclusion only weakly supported by the record is more likely to have been affected by errors than one with overwhelming record support. Taking the unaffected findings as a given, and taking due account of the effect of the errors on the remaining findings, a court making the prejudice inquiry must ask if the defendant has met the burden of showing that the decision reached would reasonably likely have been different absent the errors.

IV

A number of practical considerations are important for the application of the standards we have outlined. Most important, in adjudicating a claim of actual ineffectiveness of counsel, a court should keep in mind that the principles we have stated do not establish mechanical rules. Although those principles should guide the process of decision, the ultimate focus of inquiry must be on the fundamental fairness of the proceeding whose result is being challenged. In every case the court should be concerned with whether, despite the strong presumption of reliability, the result of the particular proceeding is unreliable because of a breakdown in the adversarial process that our system counts on to produce just results.

Although we have discussed the performance component of an ineffectiveness claim prior to the prejudice component, there is no reason for a court deciding an ineffective assistance claim to approach the inquiry in the same order or even to address both components of the inquiry if the defendant makes an insufficient showing on one. In particular, a court need not determine whether counsel's performance was deficient before examining the prejudice suffered by the defendant as a result of the alleged deficiencies. The object of an ineffectiveness claim is not to grade counsel's performance. If it is easier to dispose of an ineffectiveness claim on the ground of lack of sufficient prejudice, which we expect will often be so, that course should be followed. Courts should strive to ensure that ineffectiveness claims not become so burdensome to defense counsel that the entire criminal justice system suffers as a result.

V

Application of the governing principles is not difficult in this case. The facts as described make clear that the conduct of respondent's counsel at and before respondent's sentencing proceeding cannot be found unreasonable. They also make clear that, even assuming the challenged conduct of counsel was unreasonable, respondent suffered insufficient prejudice to warrant setting aside his death sentence.

With respect to the performance component, the record shows that respondent's counsel made a strategic choice to argue for the extreme emotional distress mitigating circumstance and to rely as fully as possible on respondent's acceptance of responsibility for his crimes. Although counsel understandably felt hopeless about respondent's prospects, that counsel's sense of hopelessness distorted his professional judgment. Counsel's strategy choice was well within the range of professionally reasonable judgments, and the decision not to seek more character or psychological evidence than was already in hand was likewise reasonable.

The trial judge's views on the importance of owning up to one's crimes were well known to counsel. The aggravating circumstances were utterly overwhelming. Trial counsel could reasonably surmise from his conversations with respondent that character and psychological evidence would be of little help. Respondent had already been able to mention at the plea colloquy the substance of what there was to know about his financial and emotional troubles. Restricting testimony on respondent's character to what had come in at the plea colloquy ensured that contrary character and psychological evidence and respondent's criminal history, which counsel had successfully moved to exclude, would not come in. On these facts, there can be little question, even without application of the presumption of adequate performance, that trial counsel's defense, though unsuccessful, was the result of reasonable professional judgment.

With respect to the prejudice component, the lack of merit of respondent's claim is even more stark. The evidence that respondent says his trial counsel should have offered at the sentencing hearing would barely have altered the sentencing profile presented to the sentencing judge. As the state courts and District Court found, at most this evidence shows that numerous people who knew respondent thought he was generally a good person and that a psychiatrist and a psychologist believed he was under considerable emotional stress that did not rise to the level of extreme disturbance. Given the overwhelming aggravating factors, there is no reasonable probability that the omitted evidence would have changed the conclusion that the aggravating circumstances outweighed the mitigating circumstances and, hence, the sentence imposed. Indeed, admission of the evidence respondent now offers might even have been harmful to his case: his "rap sheet" would probably have been admitted into evidence, and the psychological reports would have directly contradicted respondent's claim that the mitigating circumstance of extreme emotional disturbance applied to his case.

Failure to make the required showing of either deficient performance or sufficient prejudice defeats the ineffectiveness claim. Here there is a double failure. More generally, respondent has made no showing that the justice of his sentence was rendered unreliable by a breakdown in the adversary process caused by deficiencies in counsel's assistance. Respondent's sentencing proceeding was not fundamentally unfair.

We conclude, therefore, that the District Court properly declined to issue a writ of habeas corpus.

Justice MARSHALL, dissenting.

The Sixth and Fourteenth Amendments guarantee a person accused of a crime the right to the aid of a lawyer in preparing and presenting his defense. It has long been settled that "the right to counsel is the right to the effective assistance of counsel."

My objection to the performance standard adopted by the Court is that it is so malleable that, in practice, it will either have no grip at all or will yield excessive variation in the manner in which the Sixth Amendment is interpreted and applied by different courts. To tell lawyers and the lower courts that counsel for a criminal defendant must behave "reasonably" and must act like "a reasonably competent attorney," is to tell them almost nothing. In essence, the majority has instructed judges called upon to assess claims of ineffective assistance of counsel to advert to their own intuitions regarding what constitutes "professional" representation, and has discouraged them from trying to develop more detailed standards governing the performance of defense counsel. In my view, the Court has thereby not only abdicated its own responsibility to interpret the Constitution, but also impaired the ability of the lower courts to exercise theirs.

I object to the prejudice standard adopted by the Court for two independent reasons. First, it is often very difficult to tell whether a defendant convicted after a trial in which he was ineffectively represented would have fared better if his lawyer had been competent. Seemingly impregnable cases can sometimes be dismantled by good defense counsel. On the basis of a cold record, it may be impossible for a reviewing court confidently to ascertain how the government's evidence and arguments would have stood up against rebuttal and cross-examination by a shrewd, well-prepared lawyer. The difficulties of estimating prejudice after the fact are exacerbated by the possibility that evidence of injury to the defendant may be missing from the record precisely because of the incompetence of defense counsel. In view of all these impediments to a fair evaluation of the probability that the outcome of a trial was affected by ineffectiveness of counsel, it seems to me senseless to impose on a defendant whose lawyer has been shown to have been incompetent the burden of demonstrating prejudice.

Second and more fundamentally, the assumption on which the Court's holding rests is that the only purpose of the constitutional guarantee of effective assistance of counsel is to reduce the chance that innocent persons will be convicted. In my view, the guarantee also functions to ensure that convictions are obtained only through fundamentally fair procedures. The majority contends that the Sixth Amendment is not violated when a manifestly guilty defendant is convicted after a trial in which he was represented by a manifestly ineffective attorney. I cannot agree. Every defendant is entitled to a trial in which his interests are vigorously and conscientiously advocated by an able lawyer. A proceeding in which the defendant does not receive meaningful assistance in meeting the forces of the State does not, in my opinion, constitute due process.

The same day that the Court issued its decision in *Strickland,* it punctuated its decision by deciding Cronic v. United States, 466 U.S. 648 (1984). In *Cronic,* a young real estate lawyer had less than 30 days to prepare for his first criminal case (a mail fraud check kiting scheme) after the government had taken four-and-a-half years to prepare its prosecution. The defendant argued that his lawyer's lack of preparation time and inexperience gave rise to a presumption of prejudice. Writing for the Court, Justice Stevens rejected Cronic's argument:

> Neither the period of time that the Government spent investigating the case, nor the number of documents that its agents reviewed during that investigation, is necessarily relevant to the question whether a competent lawyer could prepare to defend the case in 25 days. The Government's task of finding and assembling admissible evidence that will carry its burden of proving guilt beyond a reasonable doubt is entirely different from the defendant's task in preparing to deny or rebut a criminal charge.
>
> * * *
>
> That conclusion is not undermined by the fact that respondent's lawyer was young, that his principal practice was in real estate, or that this was his first jury trial. Every experienced criminal defense attorney once tried his first criminal case. Moreover, a lawyer's experience with real estate transactions might be more useful in preparing to try a criminal case involving financial transactions than would prior experience in handling, for example, armed robbery prosecutions.
>
> * * * *
>
> This case is not one in which the surrounding circumstances make it unlikely that the defendant could have received the effective assistance of counsel. . . . [On remand, respondent] can therefore make out a claim of ineffective assistance only by pointing to specific errors made by trial counsel.

In *Cronic,* the Court identified three circumstances under which prejudice may be presumed: (1) if there has been a complete denial of counsel; (2) "if counsel entirely fails to subject the prosecution's case to meaningful adversarial testing"; or (3) when there is an actual conflict of interest for counsel.

Thus, in Holloway v. Arkansas, 435 U.S. 475 (1978), the Supreme Court held that it violates a defendant's Sixth Amendment rights to force defense counsel to represent codefendants over counsel's timely objection. When there is a potential conflict of interest, the trial court should inquire regarding it and whether the defendant will still be able to receive effective assistance of counsel. However, in Cuyler v. Sullivan, 446 U.S. 335 (1980), the Supreme Court ruled that a defendant can demonstrate a Sixth Amendment violation only by showing: (1) defense counsel was actively representing conflicting interests; and (2) the conflict adversely affected counsel's performance for the defendant.

Accordingly, there is generally no per se rule of reversal when defense counsel has an actual or potential conflict of interest. Rather, the burden is on the defendant to demonstrate that defense counsel's conflicting interests negatively impacted counsel's performance at trial. For example, in Mickens v. Taylor, 535 U.S. 162 (2002), the Court held that there was no automatic claim of ineffective assistance of counsel even though defense counsel in that capital murder case had previously represented the murder victim.

When there is a conflict of interest, the defendants may waive the right to conflict-free assistance of counsel if the waiver is knowing and intelligent. Holloway v. Arkansas, 435 U.S. at 483 n.5. However, the trial judge is not obliged to accept this waiver. The court still carries the responsibility of deciding whether the conflicted counsel can adequately represent the defendant's interests. See Wheat v. United States, 486 U.S. 153 (1988); see also Federal Rule of Criminal Procedure 44.

Defense counsel has broad leeway in deciding on trial strategy. In *Strickland*, the Supreme Court cautioned against second-guessing defense counsel's decision. Generally, it is very difficult for a defendant to succeed on a claim of ineffective assistance of counsel because an attorney's poor performance is excused if the evidence is otherwise strong in the case and the defendant, therefore, cannot satisfy the prejudice prong of *Strickland*'s ineffective assistance of counsel test. Courts have said that there is no per se rule of reversal even if defense counsel sleeps through portions of the trial. *See* Tippins v. Walker, 77 F.3d 682 (2d Cir. 1996) (in some cases, defense counsel's appearance of sleeping can be a tactical maneuver; however, in this case daily sleeping by counsel met *Cronic* standard of ineffective assistance of counsel).

However, are there any limits on the trial strategy a defense lawyer may choose without violating the Sixth Amendment? For example, what if defense counsel in a death penalty case concedes a defendant's guilt? Does that still meet *Strickland*'s standard for effective assistance of counsel?

FLORIDA v. NIXON
543 U.S. 175 (2004)

Justice GINSBURG delivered the opinion of the Court.

This capital case concerns defense counsel's strategic decision to concede, at the guilt phase of the trial, the defendant's commission of murder, and to concentrate the defense on establishing, at the penalty phase, cause for sparing the defendant's life. Any concession of that order, the Florida Supreme Court held, made without the defendant's express consent — however gruesome the crime and despite the strength of the evidence of guilt — automatically ranks as prejudicial ineffective assistance of counsel necessitating a new trial. We reverse the Florida Supreme Court's judgment.

Defense counsel undoubtedly has a duty to discuss potential strategies with the defendant. *See* Strickland v. Washington (1984). But when a defendant, informed by counsel, neither consents nor objects to the course counsel describes as the most promising means to avert a sentence of death, counsel is not automatically barred from pursuing that course. The reasonableness of counsel's performance, after consultation with the defendant yields no response, must be judged in accord with the inquiry generally applicable to ineffective-assistance-of-counsel claims: Did counsel's representation "f[a]ll below an objective standard of reasonableness"? The Florida Supreme Court erred in applying, instead, a presumption of deficient performance, as well as a presumption of prejudice; that latter presumption, we have instructed, is reserved for cases in which counsel fails meaningfully to oppose the prosecution's case. United States v. Cronic (1984). A presumption of prejudice is not in order based solely on a defendant's failure to provide express consent to a tenable strategy counsel has adequately disclosed to and discussed with the defendant.

I

On Monday, August 13, 1984, near a dirt road in the environs of Tallahassee, Florida, a passing motorist discovered Jeanne Bickner's charred body. Bickner had been tied to a tree and set on fire while still alive. Her left leg and arm, and most of her hair and skin, had been burned away. The next day, police found Bickner's car, abandoned on a Tallahassee street corner, on fire. Police arrested 23-year-old Joe Elton Nixon later that morning, after Nixon's brother informed the sheriff's office that Nixon had confessed to the murder.

Questioned by the police, Nixon described in graphic detail how he had kidnaped Bickner, then killed her. . . . The State gathered overwhelming evidence establishing that Nixon had committed the murder in the manner he described.

Nixon was indicted in Leon County, Florida, for first-degree murder, kidnaping, robbery, and arson. Assistant public defender Michael Corin, assigned to represent Nixon, filed a plea of not guilty, and deposed all of the State's potential witnesses. Corin concluded, given the strength of the evidence, that Nixon's guilt was not "subject to any reasonable dispute."[4] Corin thereupon commenced plea negotiations, hoping to persuade the prosecution to drop the death penalty in exchange for Nixon's guilty pleas to all charges. Negotiations broke down when the prosecutors indicated their unwillingness to recommend a sentence other than death.

Faced with the inevitability of going to trial on a capital charge, Corin turned his attention to the penalty phase, believing that the only way to save Nixon's life would be to present extensive mitigation evidence centering on Nixon's mental

---

4. Every court to consider this case, including the judge who presided over Nixon's trial, agreed with Corin's assessment of the evidence. [Footnote by the Court.]

instability. Experienced in capital defense, . . . Corin concluded that the best strategy would be to concede guilt, thereby preserving his credibility in urging leniency during the penalty phase.

Corin attempted to explain this strategy to Nixon at least three times. Nixon was generally unresponsive during their discussions. He never verbally approved or protested Corin's proposed strategy. Overall, Nixon gave Corin very little, if any, assistance or direction in preparing the case. Corin eventually exercised his professional judgment to pursue the concession strategy.

When Nixon's trial began on July 15, 1985, his unresponsiveness deepened into disruptive and violent behavior. On the second day of jury selection, Nixon pulled off his clothing, demanded a black judge and lawyer, refused to be escorted into the courtroom, and threatened to force the guards to shoot him. When the judge examined Nixon on the record in a holding cell, Nixon stated he had no interest in the trial and threatened to misbehave if forced to attend. The judge ruled that Nixon had intelligently and voluntarily waived his right to be present at trial.

The guilt phase of the trial thus began in Nixon's absence. In his opening statement, Corin acknowledged Nixon's guilt and urged the jury to focus on the penalty phase:

"In this case, there won't be any question, none whatsoever, that my client, Joe Elton Nixon, caused Jeannie Bickner's death. . . . [T]hat fact will be proved to your satisfaction beyond any doubt.

"This case is about the death of Joe Elton Nixon and whether it should occur within the next few years by electrocution or maybe its natural expiration after a lifetime of confinement. . . .

"Now, in arriving at your verdict, in your penalty recommendation, for we will get that far, you are going to learn many facts . . . about Joe Elton Nixon. Some of those facts are going to be good. That may not seem clear to you at this time. But, and sadly, most of the things you learn of Joe Elton Nixon are not going to be good. But, I'm suggesting to you that when you have seen all the testimony, heard all the testimony and the evidence that has been shown, there are going to be reasons why you should recommend that his life be spared."

At the start of the penalty phase, Corin argued to the jury that "Joe Elton Nixon is not normal organically, intellectually, emotionally or educationally or in any other way." Corin presented the testimony of eight witnesses. Relatives and friends described Nixon's childhood emotional troubles and his erratic behavior in the days preceding the murder. A psychiatrist and a psychologist addressed Nixon's antisocial personality, his history of emotional instability and psychiatric care, his low IQ, and the possibility that at some point he suffered brain damage.

In his closing argument, Corin emphasized Nixon's youth, the psychiatric evidence, and the jury's discretion to consider any mitigating circumstances. Corin urged that, if not sentenced to death, "Joe Elton Nixon would [n]ever be released from confinement." The death penalty, Corin maintained, was appropriate only for "intact human being[s]," and "Joe Elton Nixon is not one of those. He's never been one of those. He never will be one of those." Corin concluded: "You know, we're not around here all that long. And it's rare when we have the opportunity to give or take life. And you have that opportunity to give life. And I'm going to ask you to do that. Thank you." After deliberating for approximately three hours, the jury recommended that Nixon be sentenced to death.

We granted certiorari to resolve an important question of constitutional law, i.e., whether counsel's failure to obtain the defendant's express consent to a strategy of conceding guilt in a capital trial automatically renders counsel's performance deficient, and whether counsel's effectiveness should be evaluated under *Cronic* or *Strickland.*

II

An attorney undoubtedly has a duty to consult with the client regarding "important decisions," including questions of overarching defense strategy. That obligation, however, does not require counsel to obtain the defendant's consent to "every tactical decision." But certain decisions regarding the exercise or waiver of basic trial rights are of such moment that they cannot be made for the defendant by a surrogate. A defendant, this Court affirmed, has "the ultimate authority" to determine "whether to plead guilty, waive a jury, testify in his or her own behalf, or take an appeal." Concerning those decisions, an attorney must both consult with the defendant and obtain consent to the recommended course of action.

The Florida Supreme Court required Nixon's "affirmative, explicit acceptance" of Corin's strategy because it deemed Corin's statements to the jury "the functional equivalent of a guilty plea." We disagree with that assessment.

Corin was obliged to, and in fact several times did, explain his proposed trial strategy to Nixon. Given Nixon's constant resistance to answering inquiries put to him by counsel and court, Corin was not additionally required to gain express consent before conceding Nixon's guilt. The two evidentiary hearings conducted by the Florida trial court demonstrate beyond doubt that Corin fulfilled his duty of consultation by informing Nixon of counsel's proposed strategy and its potential benefits. Nixon's characteristic silence each time information was conveyed to him, in sum, did not suffice to render unreasonable Corin's decision to concede guilt and to home in, instead, on the life or death penalty issue.

On the record thus far developed, Corin's concession of Nixon's guilt does not rank as a "fail[ure] to function in any meaningful sense as the Government's adversary." Although such a concession in a run-of-the-mine trial might present a closer question, the gravity of the potential sentence in a capital trial and the proceeding's two-phase structure vitally affect counsel's strategic calculus. Attorneys representing capital defendants face daunting challenges in developing trial strategies, not least because the defendant's guilt is often clear. Prosecutors are more likely to seek the death penalty, and to refuse to accept a plea to a life sentence, when the evidence is overwhelming and the crime heinous. In such cases, "avoiding execution [may be] the best and only realistic result possible."

Renowned advocate Clarence Darrow, we note, famously employed a similar strategy as counsel for the youthful, cold-blooded killers Richard Loeb and Nathan Leopold. Imploring the judge to spare the boys' lives, Darrow declared: "I do not know how much salvage there is in these two boys. . . . I will be honest with this court as I have tried to be from the beginning. I know that these boys are not fit to be at large."

To summarize, in a capital case, counsel must consider in conjunction both the guilt and penalty phases in determining how best to proceed. When counsel informs the defendant of the strategy counsel believes to be in the defendant's best interest and the defendant is unresponsive, counsel's strategic choice is not impeded by any blanket rule demanding the defendant's explicit consent. Instead, if counsel's strategy, given the evidence bearing on the defendant's guilt, satisfies the *Strickland* standard, that is the end of the matter; no tenable claim of ineffective assistance would remain.

The Court has held firm to its decision not to require lawyers to follow specific guidelines in trying cases. However, in her opinion in Wiggins v. Smith, 539 U.S. 510 (2003), Justice O'Connor suggested that compliance with ABA Standards for Criminal Justice   especially those setting forth a lawyer's responsibility in investigating a case — may provide defense lawyers a safe harbor against claims of ineffective assistance of counsel. Kevin Wiggins was convicted of murder and sentenced to death. He argued that his Sixth Amendment right to counsel was violated because his lawyer failed to investigate his personal background, which would have provided mitigating evidence for his capital sentencing proceedings. If his lawyer had made the effort, he would have found that Wiggins had lived a nightmare as a child. He was abandoned by his mother, ended up in foster care where he was repeatedly raped and tortured, and ended up homeless with diminished mental capacities. In these extreme circumstances, the Supreme Court held that there was a reasonable probability that the sentencing jury would have returned a different verdict had it known of these facts.

More recently, in Rompilla v. Beard, 545 U.S. 374 (2005), the Supreme Court also found that it was ineffective assistance of counsel in a capital case for defense counsel not to request defendant's file from prior cases that would have shown that he too suffered from mental health issues and childhood deprivations that could have been presented to the jury in mitigation of his sentence. Together with *Wiggins*, these cases emphasize that pretrial investigation is a critical aspect of defense counsel's responsibilities, especially in capital cases.

Yet, the right to counsel does not include the right to have counsel present any evidence the defendant wishes to admit. The right to counsel does not include the right to have counsel engage in dishonest or unethical behavior for the defendant. In Nix v. Whiteside, 475 U.S. 157 (1986), the Court held that the defendant was not denied his right to counsel because he told the defendant that he would seek to withdraw if his client perjured himself on the witness stand.

The right to counsel also does not entitle an indigent defendant to select his or her counsel. *See, e.g.,* United States v. Allen, 789 F.2d 90 (1st Cir. 1986). However, if the defendant retains his own counsel, it is a per se error for the court to deny the defendant his counsel of choice if the lawyer has not violated any of the court's rules. United States v. Gonzales-Lopez, 126 S. Ct. 2557 (2006).[5]

---

5. Moreover, it is a Sixth Amendment violation for the government to intrude on the attorney-client relationship. *See* Weatherford v. Bursey, 429 U.S. 545 (1977). The court considers four factors in determining whether the government has interfered with the right to counsel: (1) whether the government purposely intruded into the attorney-client relationship; (2) whether the government obtained any evidence it used at trial from the intrusion, (3) whether the prosecutor obtained any details about the defense's trial strategy from the intrusion, and (4) whether the information obtained was used in any other way to the substantial detriment of the defendant.

In addition to the right to counsel, the defendant enjoys a limited due process right to the use of experts who will assist in the presentation of the defense. In Ake v. Oklahoma, 470 U.S. 68 (1985), the Supreme Court recognized an indigent defendant's right to a psychiatrist to assist with the defendant's insanity defense in a capital murder case. Justice Marshall wrote:

> This Court has long recognized that when a State brings its judicial power to bear on an indigent defendant in a criminal proceeding, it must take steps to assure that the defendant had a fair opportunity to present his defense. This elementary principle, grounded in significant part on the Fourteenth Amendment's due process guarantee of fundamental fairness, derives from the belief that justice cannot be equal where, simply as a result of his poverty, a defendant is denied the opportunity to participate meaningfully in a judicial proceeding in which his liberty is at stake.
>
> [A] criminal trial is fundamentally unfair if the State proceeds against an individual defendant without making certain that he has access to the raw materials integral to the building of an effective defense. Thus, while the Court has not held that a State must purchase for the indigent defendant all the assistance that his wealthier counterpart might buy, it has often reaffirmed that fundamental fairness entitles indigent defendants to "an equal opportunity to present their claims within the adversary system."
>
> Without the assistance of a psychiatrist . . . to help determine whether the insanity defense is viable . . . , the risk of an inaccurate resolution of sanity issues is extremely high. With such assistance, the defendant is fairly able to present at least enough information to the jury, in a meaningful manner, as to permit it to make a sensible determination.

Ake does not put defendants on equal footing with the prosecution, but it does provide a basis for requesting those "basic tools" necessary to present an effective defense, including access to investigators and expert witnesses. Although linked to a defendant's Sixth Amendment right to counsel, it is a right that actually derives (like the right to counsel once did) from the Due Process clause.

E. RIGHT OF SELF-REPRESENTATION

Instead of being represented by counsel, can a defendant represent himself? The Sixth Amendment refers to the right to "assistance of counsel." Does that encompass the right of self-representation?

FARETTA v. CALIFORNIA
422 U.S. 806 (1975)

Justice STEWART delivered the opinion of the Court.

The Sixth and Fourteenth Amendments of our Constitution guarantee that a person brought to trial in any state or federal court must be afforded the right to the assistance of counsel before he can be validly convicted and punished by imprisonment. The question before us now is whether a defendant in a state criminal trial has a constitutional right to proceed without counsel when he voluntarily and intelligently elects to do so. Stated another way, the question is whether a State may constitutionally hale a person into its criminal courts and there force a lawyer upon him, even when he insists that he wants to conduct his own defense. It is not an easy question, but we have concluded that a State may not constitutionally do so.

I

Anthony Faretta was charged with grand theft. At the arraignment, the Superior Court Judge assigned to preside at the trial appointed the public defender to represent Faretta. Well before the date of trial, however, Faretta requested that he be permitted to represent himself. Questioning by the judge revealed that Faretta had once represented himself in a criminal prosecution, that he had a high school education, and that he did not want to be represented by the public defender because he believed that that office was "very loaded down with . . . a heavy case load." The judge responded that he believed Faretta was "making a mistake" and emphasized that in further proceedings Faretta would receive no special favors. Nevertheless, after establishing that Faretta wanted to represent himself and did not want a lawyer, the judge, in a "preliminary ruling," accepted Faretta's waiver of the assistance of counsel. The judge indicated, however, that he might reverse this ruling if it later appeared that Faretta was unable adequately to represent himself.

Several weeks thereafter, but still prior to trial, the judge sua sponte held a hearing to inquire into Faretta's ability to conduct his own defense, and questioned him specifically about both the hearsay rule and the state law governing the challenge of potential jurors.[6]

---

6. The colloquy was as follows:

THE COURT: In the Faretta matter, I brought you back down here to do some reconsideration as to whether or not you should continue to represent yourself.
   "How have you been getting along on your research?
THE DEFENDANT: Not bad, your Honor.
   Last night I put in the mail a 995 motion and it should be with the Clerk within the next day or two.
THE COURT: Have you been preparing yourself for the intricacies of the trial of the matter?
THE DEFENDANT: Well, your Honor, I was hoping that the case could possibly be disposed of on the 995.
   Mrs. Ayers informed me yesterday that it was the Court's policy to hear the pretrial motions at the time of trial. If possible, your Honor, I would like a date set as soon as the Court deems adequate after they receive the motion, sometime before trial.
THE COURT: Let's see how you have been doing on your research.
   How many exceptions are there to the hearsay rule?
THE DEFENDANT: Well, the hearsay rule would, I guess, be called the best evidence rule, your Honor. And there are several exceptions in case law, but in actual statutory law, I don't feel there is none.
THE COURT: What are the challenges to the jury for cause?
THE DEFENDANT: Well, there is twelve peremptory challenges.
THE COURT: And how many for cause?
THE DEFENDANT: Well, as many as the Court deems valid.
THE COURT: And what are they? What are the grounds for challenging a juror for cause?
THE DEFENDANT: Well, numerous grounds to challenge a witness — I mean, a juror, your Honor, one being the juror is perhaps suffered, was a victim of the same type of offense, might be prejudiced toward the defendant. Any substantial ground that might make the juror prejudice[d] toward the defendant.
THE COURT: Anything else?
THE DEFENDANT: Well, a relative perhaps of the victim.
THE COURT: Have you taken a look at that code section to see what it is?
THE DEFENDANT: Challenge a juror?
THE COURT: Yes.

The California Court of Appeal affirmed the trial judge's ruling that Faretta had no federal or state constitutional right to represent himself and the California Supreme Court denied review. We granted certiorari.

II

In the federal courts, the right of self-representation has been protected by statute since the beginnings of our Nation. . . . With few exceptions, each of the several States also accords a defendant the right to represent himself in any criminal case.

III

This consensus is soundly premised. The right of self-representation finds support in the structure of the Sixth Amendment, as well as in the English and colonial jurisprudence from which the Amendment emerged.

The Sixth Amendment includes a compact statement of the rights necessary to a full defense:

> In all criminal prosecutions, the accused shall enjoy the right . . . to be informed of the nature and cause of the accusation; to be confronted with the witnesses against him; to have compulsory process for obtaining witnesses in his favor, and to have the Assistance of Counsel for his defence.

Because these rights are basic to our adversary system of criminal justice, they are part of the "due process of law" that is guaranteed by the Fourteenth Amendment to defendants in the criminal courts of the States.

THE DEFENDANT: Yes, your Honor. I have done —
THE COURT: What is the code section?
THE DEFENDANT: On voir diring a jury, your Honor?
THE COURT: Yes.
THE DEFENDANT: I am not aware of the section right offhand.
THE COURT: What code is it in?
THE DEFENDANT: Well, the research I have done on challenging would be in Witkins Jurisprudence.
THE COURT: Have you looked at any of the codes to see where these various things are taken up?
THE DEFENDANT: No, your Honor, I haven't.
THE COURT: Have you looked in any of the California Codes with reference to trial procedure?
THE DEFENDANT: Yes, your Honor.
THE COURT: What codes?
THE DEFENDANT: I have done extensive research in the Penal Code, your Honor, and the Civil Code.
THE COURT: If you have done extensive research into it, then tell me about it.
THE DEFENDANT: On empaneling a jury, your Honor?
THE COURT: Yes.
THE DEFENDANT: Well, the District Attorney and the defendant, defense counsel, has both the right to 12 peremptory challenges of a jury. These 12 challenges are undisputable. Any reason that the defense or prosecution should feel that a juror would be inadequate to try the case or to rule on a case, they may then discharge that juror.
  But if there is a valid challenge due to grounds of prejudice or some other grounds, then these aren't considered in the 12 peremptory challenges. There are numerous and the defendant, the defense and the prosecution both have the right to make any inquiry to the jury as to their feelings toward the case.

[Footnote by the Court.]

The Sixth Amendment does not provide merely that a defense shall be made for the accused; it grants to the accused personally the right to make his defense. It is the accused, not counsel, who must be "informed of the nature and cause of the accusation," who must be "confronted with the witnesses against him," and who must be accorded "compulsory process for obtaining witnesses in his favor." Although not stated in the Amendment in so many words, the right to self-representation — to make one's own defense personally — is thus necessarily implied by the structure of the Amendment. The right to defend is given directly to the accused; for it is he who suffers the consequences if the defense fails.

The counsel provision supplements this design. It speaks of the "assistance" of counsel, and an assistant, however expert, is still an assistant. The language and spirit of the Sixth Amendment contemplate that counsel, like the other defense tools guaranteed by the Amendment, shall be an aid to a willing defendant — not an organ of the State interposed between an unwilling defendant and his right to defend himself personally. To thrust counsel upon the accused, against his considered wish, thus violates the logic of the Amendment. In such a case, counsel is not an assistant, but a master; and the right to make a defense is stripped of the personal character upon which the Amendment insists. . . . An unwanted counsel "represents" the defendant only through a tenuous and unacceptable legal fiction. Unless the accused has acquiesced in such representation, the defense presented is not the defense guaranteed him by the Constitution, for, in a very real sense, it is not his defense.

In the American Colonies the insistence upon a right of self-representation was, if anything, more fervent than in England.

The colonists brought with them an appreciation of the virtues of self-reliance and a traditional distrust of lawyers. When the Colonies were first settled, "the lawyer was synonymous with the cringing Attorneys-General and Solicitors-General of the Crown and the arbitrary Justices of the King's Court, all bent on the conviction of those who opposed the King's prerogatives, and twisting the law to secure convictions." This prejudice gained strength in the Colonies where "distrust of lawyers became an institution."

The right of self-representation was guaranteed in many colonial charters and declarations of rights. These early documents establish that the "right to counsel" meant to the colonists a right to choose between pleading through a lawyer and representing oneself.

[T]here is no evidence that the colonists and the Framers ever doubted the right of self-representation, or imagined that this right might be considered inferior to the right of assistance of counsel. To the contrary, the colonists and the Framers, as well as their English ancestors, always conceived of the right to counsel as an "assistance" for the accused, to be used at his option, in defending himself. The Framers selected in the Sixth Amendment a form of words that necessarily implies the right of self-representation. That conclusion is supported by centuries of consistent history.

IV

There can be no blinking the fact that the right of an accused to conduct his own defense seems to cut against the grain of this Court's decisions holding that the

Constitution requires that no accused can be convicted and imprisoned unless he has been accorded the right to the assistance of counsel.

But it is one thing to hold that every defendant, rich or poor, has the right to the assistance of counsel, and quite another to say that a State may compel a defendant to accept a lawyer he does not want. The value of state-appointed counsel was not unappreciated by the Founders, yet the notion of compulsory counsel was utterly foreign to them. And whatever else may be said of those who wrote the Bill of Rights, surely there can be no doubt that they understood the inestimable worth of free choice.

It is undeniable that in most criminal prosecutions defendants could better defend with counsel's guidance than by their own unskilled efforts. But where the defendant will not voluntarily accept representation by counsel, the potential advantage of a lawyer's training and experience can be realized, if at all, only imperfectly. To force a lawyer on a defendant can only lead him to believe that the law contrives against him. Moreover, it is not inconceivable that in some rare instances, the defendant might in fact present his case more effectively by conducting his own defense. Personal liberties are not rooted in the law of averages. The right to defend is personal. The defendant, and not his lawyer or the State, will bear the personal consequences of a conviction. It is the defendant, therefore, who must be free personally to decide whether in his particular case counsel is to his advantage. And although he may conduct his own defense ultimately to his own detriment, his choice must be honored out of "that respect for the individual which is the lifeblood of the law."

V

When an accused manages his own defense, he relinquishes, as a purely factual matter, many of the traditional benefits associated with the right to counsel. For this reason, in order to represent himself, the accused must "knowingly and intelligently" forgo those relinquished benefits. Although a defendant need not himself have the skill and experience of a lawyer in order competently and intelligently to choose self-representation, he should be made aware of the dangers and disadvantages of self-representation, so that the record will establish that "he knows what he is doing and his choice is made with eyes open."

Here, weeks before trial, Faretta clearly and unequivocally declared to the trial judge that he wanted to represent himself and did not want counsel. The record affirmatively shows that Faretta was literate, competent, and understanding, and that he was voluntarily exercising his informed free will. The trial judge had warned Faretta that he thought it was a mistake not to accept the assistance of counsel, and that Faretta would be required to follow all the "ground rules" of trial procedure. We need make no assessment of how well or poorly Faretta had mastered the intricacies of the hearsay rule and the California code provisions that govern challenges of potential jurors on voir dire. For his technical legal knowledge, as such, was not relevant to an assessment of his knowing exercise of the right to defend himself.

In forcing Faretta, under these circumstances, to accept against his will a state-appointed public defender, the California courts deprived him of his constitutional right to conduct his own defense.

Chief Justice BURGER, with whom Justices BLACKMUN and REHNQUIST join, dissenting.

This case is another example of the judicial tendency to constitutionalize what is thought "good." That effort fails on its own terms here, because there is nothing desirable or useful in permitting every accused person, even the most uneducated and inexperienced, to insist upon conducting his own defense to criminal charges. Moreover, there is no constitutional basis for the Court's holding, and it can only add to the problems of an already malfunctioning criminal justice system. I therefore dissent.

I

The most striking feature of the Court's opinion is that it devotes so little discussion to the matter which it concedes is the core of the decision, that is, discerning an independent basis in the Constitution for the supposed right to represent oneself in a criminal trial. Its ultimate assertion that such a right is tucked between the lines of the Sixth Amendment is contradicted by the Amendment's language and its consistent judicial interpretation.

[T]his Court's decisions have consistently included the right to counsel as an integral part of the bundle making up the larger "right to a defense as we know it."

[It is not] accurate to suggest, as the Court seems to later in its opinion, that the quality of his representation at trial is a matter with which only the accused is legitimately concerned. Although we have adopted an adversary system of criminal justice, the prosecution is more than an ordinary litigant, and the trial judge is not simply an automaton who insures that technical rules are adhered to. Both are charged with the duty of insuring that justice, in the broadest sense of that term, is achieved in every criminal trial. That goal is ill-served, and the integrity of and public confidence in the system are undermined, when an easy conviction is obtained due to the defendant's ill-advised decision to waive counsel. . . . The system of criminal justice should not be available as an instrument of self-destruction.

In short, both the "spirit and the logic" of the Sixth Amendment are that every person accused of crime shall receive the fullest possible defense; in the vast majority of cases this command can be honored only by means of the expressly guaranteed right to counsel, and the trial judge is in the best position to determine whether the accused is capable of conducting his defense. True freedom of choice and society's interest in seeing that justice is achieved can be vindicated only if the trial court retains discretion to reject any attempted waiver of counsel and insist that the accused be tried according to the Constitution.

There is no way to reconcile the idea that the Sixth Amendment impliedly guaranteed the right of an accused to conduct his own defense with the contemporaneous action of the Congress in passing a statute explicitly giving that right. If the Sixth Amendment created a right to self-representation it was unnecessary for Congress to enact any statute on the subject at all.

IV

Society has the right to expect that, when courts find new rights implied in the Constitution, their potential effect upon the resources of our criminal justice system will be considered. However, such considerations are conspicuously absent from the Court's opinion in this case.

It hardly needs repeating that courts at all levels are already handicapped by the unsupplied demand for competent advocates, with the result that it often takes far longer to complete a given case than experienced counsel would require.

Justice BLACKMUN, with whom Chief Justice BURGER and Justice REHNQUIST join, dissenting.

Today the Court holds that the Sixth Amendment guarantees to every defendant in a state criminal trial the right to proceed without counsel whenever he elects to do so. I find no textual support for this conclusion in the language of the Sixth Amendment. I find the historical evidence relied upon by the Court to be unpersuasive, especially in light of the recent history of criminal procedure. Finally, I fear that the right to self-representation constitutionalized today frequently will cause procedural confusion without advancing any significant strategic interest of the defendant. I therefore dissent.

I

The starting point, of course, is the language of the Sixth Amendment:

"In all criminal prosecutions, the accused shall enjoy the right to a speedy and public trial, by an impartial jury of the State and district wherein the crime shall have been committed, which district shall have been previously ascertained by law, and to be informed of the nature and cause of the accusation; to be confronted with the witnesses against him; to have compulsory process for obtaining witnesses in his favor, and to have the Assistance of Counsel for his defence."

It is self-evident that the Amendment makes no direct reference to self-representation. Indeed, the Court concedes that the right to self-representation is "not stated in the Amendment in so many words."

Where then in the Sixth Amendment does one find this right to self-representation? According to the Court, it is "necessarily implied by the structure of the Amendment." Stated somewhat more succinctly, the Court reasons that because the accused has a personal right to "a defense as we know it," he necessarily has a right to make that defense personally. I disagree. Although I believe the specific guarantees of the Sixth Amendment are personal to the accused, I do not agree that the Sixth Amendment guarantees any particular procedural method of asserting those rights. If an accused has enjoyed a speedy trial by an impartial jury in which he was informed of the nature of the accusation, confronted with the witnesses against him, afforded the power of compulsory process, and represented effectively by competent counsel, I do not see that the Sixth Amendment requires more.

The Court seems to suggest that so long as the accused is willing to pay the consequences of his folly, there is no reason for not allowing a defendant the right to self-representation. That view ignores the established principle that the interest of the State in a criminal prosecution "is not that it shall win a case, but that justice shall be done." For my part, I do not believe that any amount of pro se pleading can cure the injury to society of an unjust result, but I do believe that a just result should prove to be an effective balm for almost any frustrated pro se defendant.

III

In conclusion, I note briefly the procedural problems that, I suspect, today's decision will visit upon trial courts in the future. Although the Court indicates that a pro se defendant necessarily waives any claim he might otherwise make of ineffective assistance of counsel, the opinion leaves open a host of other procedural questions. Must every defendant be advised of his right to proceed pro se? If so, when must that notice be given? Since the right to assistance of counsel and the right to self-representation are mutually exclusive, how is the waiver of each right to be measured? If a defendant has elected to exercise his right to proceed pro se, does he still have a constitutional right to assistance of standby counsel? How soon in the criminal proceeding must a defendant decide between proceeding by counsel or pro se? Must he be allowed to switch in midtrial? May a violation of the right to self-representation ever be harmless error? Must the trial court treat the pro se defendant differently than it would professional counsel? I assume that many of these questions will be answered with finality in due course. Many of them, however, such as the standards of waiver and the treatment of the pro se defendant, will haunt the trial of every defendant who elects to exercise his right to self-representation. The procedural problems spawned by an absolute right to self-representation will far outweigh whatever tactical advantage the defendant may feel he has gained by electing to represent himself.

If there is any truth to the old proverb that "one who is his own lawyer has a fool for a client," the Court by its opinion today now bestows a constitutional right on one to make a fool of himself.

In *Faretta*, the Court suggested that a court could appoint standby counsel over the defendant's objection. The Supreme Court upheld the appointment of standby counsel in McKaskle v. Wiggins, 465 U.S. 168 (1984), even though standby counsel openly argued with the defendant during trial. Most of their arguments took place outside of the presence of the jury. Ultimately, the Supreme Court upheld the appointment of standby counsel but warned that standby counsel cannot act in a manner that will "destroy the jury's perception that the defendant is representing himself." The Court further noted that there is no constitutional right to "hybrid counsel"; i.e., appointment of counsel that allows the defendant to perform some of the "core functions" of the lawyer. Courts can insist that the defendant decide whether he wants to represent himself or have counsel appointed to represent him. Moreover, the defendant also does not have a right to be represented by a non-lawyer. *See* United States v. Turnbull, 888 F.2d 636 (9th Cir. 1989).

There is a right to self-representation at trial, but a defendant does not have the right to represent himself on appeal. In Martinez v. Court of Appeal, 528 U.S. 152 (2000), the Court found that "the overriding state interest in the fair and efficient administration of justice" outweighed whatever interest in personal autonomy a defendant has after conviction.

F.   RIGHT OF COUNSEL FOR ENEMY COMBATANTS

Since September 11, 2001, the issue has arisen as to whether detainees designated as "enemy combatants" are entitled to the right to counsel. The Executive Branch has taken the position that enemy combatants have no such right. However, in Hamdi v. Rumsfeld, 542 U.S. 507 (2004), the Court held that "due process demands that a citizen held in the United States as an enemy combatant be given a meaningful opportunity to test the factual basis for that detention before a neutral decisionmaker." In her opinion, Justice O'Connor noted the integral role of counsel in whatever proceedings are formulated for enemy combatants, stating that Hamdi "unquestionably had the right to access to counsel in connection with the proceedings on remand."

TABLE OF CASES

Adamson v. California, 332 U.S. 46 (1947), 20 & nn.16, 19, 20
Aguilar v. Texas, 378 U.S. 108 (1964), 82
Ake v. Oklahoma, 470 U.S. 68 (1985), 576
Alabama v. Shelton, 535 U.S. 654 (2002), 555
Alabama v. White, 496 U.S. 325 (1990), *264*
Allen; United States v., 789 F.2d 90 (1st Cir. 1986), 575
American Civil Liberties Union v. National Sec. Agency, 438 F. Supp. 2d 754 (E.D. Mich. 2006), *rev'd*, 493 F.3d 644 (6th Cir. 2007), 289
Anders v. California, 386 U.S. 738 (1967), 560
Andresen v. Maryland, 427 U.S. 463 (1976), *98*
Apodaca v. Oregon, 406 U.S. 404 (1972), 25
Argersinger v. Hamlin, 407 U.S. 25 (1972), *555*
Arizona v. Fulminante, 499 U.S. 279 (1991), *361*
Arizona v. Hicks, 480 U.S. 321 (1987), 82, 135
Arizona v. Mauro, 481 U.S. 520 (1987), 412
Arnold v. Cleveland, 616 N.E.2d 163 (Ohio 1993), 24 n.23
Arvizu; United States v., 534 U.S. 266 (2002), *260*
Ash; United States v., 413 U.S. 300 (1973), 526, *530*
Ashcraft v. Tennessee, 322 U.S. 143 (1944), 361
Atwater v. City of Lago Vista, 532 U.S. 318 (2001), *239*

Baltimore City Dept. of Soc. Servs. v. Bouknight, 493 U.S. 549 (1990), 505
Banks; United States v., 540 U.S. 31 (2004), 115
Barron v. Mayor & City of Baltimore, 32 U.S. (7 Pet.) 243 (1833), 18, 24
Beckwith v. United States, 425 U.S. 341 (1976), 398
Bellis v. United States, 417 U.S. 85 (1974), 494
Berger v. United States, 388 U.S. 41 (1967), 279, 280
Berkemer v. McCarty, 468 U.S. 420 (1984), *403*
Blanton v. City of N. Las Vegas, 489 U.S. 538 (1989), 555
Board of Educ. of Indep. Sch. Dist. No. 92 of Pottawatomie County v. Earls, 536 U.S. 822 (2002), 200, *208*
Bram v. United States, 168 U.S. 532 (1897), 358
Brendlin v. California, 127 S. Ct. 2400 (2007), 235, 310, *314*
Brewer v. Williams, 430 U.S. 387 (1977), 466, *471*, 477
Brigham City, Utah v. Stuart, 126 S. Ct. 1943 (2006), *222*
Brinegar v. United States, 338 U.S. 160 (1949), 82
Brown v. Illinois, 422 U.S. 590 (1975), *330*

Brown v. Mississippi, 297 U.S. 278 (1936), 358, *359*, 360, 361
Browning-Ferris Indus. of Vt., Inc. v. Kelco Disposal, Inc., 492 U.S. 257 (1989), 24 n.27
Burch v. Louisiana, 441 U.S. 130 (1979), 25 n.32

Calandra; United States v., 428 U.S. 465 (1976), 291
Calandra; United States v., 414 U.S. 338 (1974), 292
California v. Acevedo, 500 U.S. 565 (1991), *142*
California v. Carney, 471 U.S. 386 (1985), *139*
California v. Ciraolo, 476 U.S. 207 (1986), *46*, 49, 65
California v. Greenwood, 486 U.S. 35 (1988), *61*
California v. Hodari D., 499 U.S. 621 (1991), *235*
California v. Prysock, 453 U.S. 355 (1981), *417*
California Bankers Assn. v. Schultz, 416 U.S. 21 (1974), 74
Camara v. Municipal Court of City & County of S.F., 387 U.S. 523 (1967), *191*, 195
Carroll v. United States, 267 U.S. 132 (1925), 82, 138, 139
Chadwick; United States v., 433 U.S. 1 (1977), 142
Chambers v. Maroney, 399 U.S. 42 (1970), 141
Chandler v. Miller, 520 U.S. 305 (1997), 200
Chavez v. Martinez, 538 U.S. 760 (2003), 392
Chicago, Burlington & Quincy R.R. Co. v. City of Chicago, 166 U.S. 226 (1897), 18
Chimel v. California, 395 U.S. 752 (1969), *122*
Citizens for a Safer Cmty. v. City of Rochester, 627 N.Y.S.2d 193 (Sup. Ct. 1994), 24 n.23
Coleman v. Alabama, 399 U.S. 1 (1970), 554
Colorado v. Connelly, 479 U.S. 157 (1986), *368*, 452
Coolidge v. New Hampshire, 403 U.S. 443 (1971), 97, 98, *131*, 135
Crane v. Kentucky, 476 U.S. 683 (1986), 361
Crawford v. Washington, 541 U.S. 36 (2004), 26 n.33
Cronic v. United States, 466 U.S. 648 (1984), 570, 571
Crooker v. California, 357 U.S. 433 (1958), 368
Culombe v. Connecticut, 367 U.S. 568 (1961), 368
Cuyler v. Sullivan, 446 U.S. 335 (1980), 571

Davis v. Mississippi, 394 U.S. 21 (1969), 256
Davis v. United States, 512 U.S. 452 (1994), *462*
Defore; People v., 242 N.Y. 13, 150 N.E. 585 (1926), 292
Devenpeck v. Alford, 543 U.S. 146 (2004), 95
Di Re; United States v., 332 U.S. 581 (1948), 146

Dickerson v. United States, 530 U.S. 428 (2000), 388, *389,* 392, 394

Doe v. United States, 487 U.S. 201 (1988), 497

Dow Chem. v. United States, 476 U.S. 227 (1986), 49

Drayton; United States v., 536 U.S. 194 (2002), 181, 235

Duckworth v. Eagan, 492 U.S. 195 (1989), 417, *420*

Dunaway v. New York, 442 U.S. 200 (1979), 255

Duncan v. Louisiana, 391 U.S. 145 (1968), *21,* 24 n.28

Dunn; United States v., 480 U.S. 294 (1987), *42*

Edwards v. Arizona, 451 U.S. 477 (1981), *455,* 458

Englbom v. Carey, 677 F.2d 957 (2d Cir. 1982), 24 n.24

Escobedo v. Illinois, 378 U.S. 478 (1964), 466, 470, 471

Evitts v. Lucey, 469 U.S. 387 (1985), 560

Fare v. Michael C., 442 U.S. 707 (1979), 394, 451

Faretta v. California, 422 U.S. 806 (1975), *576,* 583

Fellers v. United States, 540 U.S. 519 (2004), 477

Ferguson v. City of Charleston, 532 U.S. 67 (2001), 191, *215*

Fisher v. United States, 425 U.S. 391 (1976), *501,* 505

Fiske v. Kansas, 274 U.S. 380 (1927), 19

Flores-Montano; United States v., 541 U.S. 149 (2004), *159*

Florida v. Bostick, 501 U.S. 429 (1991), 234

Florida v. J.L., 529 U.S. 266 (2000), 264, *266*

Florida v. Nixon, 543 U.S. 175 (2004), *571*

Florida v. Riley, 488 U.S. 445 (1989), *49,* 55

Florida v. Royer, 460 U.S. 491 (1983), 255

Foster v. California, 394 U.S. 440 (1969), *538,* 540

Franks v. Delaware, 438 U.S. 154 (1978), 355

Frazier v. Cupp, 394 U.S. 731 (1969), 368

Fresno Rifle & Pistol Club, Inc. v. Van de Kamp, 965 F.2d 723 (9th Cir. 1992), 24 n.23

Gagnon v. Scarpelli, 411 U.S. 778 (1973), 554, 555

Georgia v. Randolph, 547 U.S. 103 (2006), *182*

Gerstein v. Pugh, 420 U.S. 103 (1975), 6

Gideon v. Wainwright, 372 U.S. 335 (1963), 27, 553, 557, *558,* 560

Gilbert v. California, 388 U.S. 263 (1967), 516, 525, 526, 537

Gitlow v. New York, 268 U.S. 652 (1925), 19

Goldman v. United States, 316 U.S. 129 (1942), 279

Gonzales-Lopez; United States v., 126 S. Ct. 2557 (2006), 575

Griffin v. California, 380 U.S. 609 (1965), 19, 20 n.20, 497

Groh v. Ramirez, 540 U.S. 551 (2004), 97, *101,* 122, 353 n.8

Grubbs; United States v., 547 U.S. 90 (2006), 105

Hale v. Henkel, 201 U.S. 43 (1906), 494

Hamdi v. Rumsfeld, 542 U.S. 507 (2004), 584

Hamilton v. Alabama, 368 U.S. 52 (1961), 554

Harris v. New York, 401 U.S. 222 (1971), 439, *440*

Hayes v. Florida, 470 U.S. 811 (1985), 256

Henry; United States v., 447 U.S. 264 (1980), *486*

Hester v. United States, 265 U.S. 57 (1924), 36

Hiibel v. Sixth Judicial Dist. Court of Nev., 542 U.S. 177 (2004), *257,* 494, 498

Holloway v. Arkansas, 435 U.S. 475 (1978), 571

Hopt v. People of Territory of Utah, 110 U.S. 574 (1884), 358

Horton v. California, 496 U.S. 128 (1990), *133,* 135

Hubbell; United States v., 530 U.S. 27 (2000), *510*

Hudson v. Michigan, 126 S. Ct. 2159 (2006), 115, 116, *292,* 295, 353, 355

Hurtardo v. California, 110 U.S. 516 (1884), 24 n.25

Illinois v. Caballes, 543 U.S. 405 (2005), *79*

Illinois v. Gates, 462 U.S. 213 (1983), 82, *83,* 90, 263

Illinois v. Lafayette, 462 U.S. 640 (1983), 156, *157*

Illinois v. Lidster, 540 U.S. 419 (2004), 174

Illinois v. McArthur, 531 U.S. 326 (2001), 29

Illinois v. Perkins, 496 U.S. 292 (1990), *413*

Illinois v. Wardlow, 528 U.S. 119 (2000), *269*

Indianapolis, City of, v. Edmond, 531 U.S. 32 (2000), *171,* 175

Jackson v. Denno, 378 U.S. 368 (1964), 361

Johnson v. Louisiana, 406 U.S. 356 (1972), 25

Jones v. United States, 362 U.S. 257 (1960), 304

Karo; United States v., 468 U.S. 705 (1984), 67, *68*

Kastigar v. United States, 406 U.S. 441 (1972), *506*

Katz v. United States, 389 U.S. 347 (1967), *30,* 35, 36, 65, 280

Kirby v. Illinois, 406 U.S. 682 (1972), 471, *526,* 554

Knights; United States v., 534 U.S. 112 (2001), *186*

Knotts; United States v., 460 U.S. 276 (1983), *65,* 67

Knowles v. Iowa, 525 U.S. 113 (1998), 125, *126*

Kuhlmann v. Wilson, 477 U.S. 436 (1986), 486, *490*

Kyllo v. United States, 533 U.S. 27 (2001), *55*

Lawrence v. Texas, 539 U.S. 558 (2003), 26

Leon; United States v., 468 U.S. 897 (1984), *336,* 353

Leyra v. Dennis, 347 U.S. 556 (1954), 367-368

Lo-Ji Sales, Inc. v. New York, 442 U.S. 319 (1979), 98

Los Angeles County, Cal. v. Rettele, 127 S. Ct. 1989 (2007), *119*

Love v. Pepersack, 47 F.3d 120 (4th Cir. 1995), 24 n.23

Lynumn v. Illinois, 372 U.S. 528 (1963), 367

Maine v. Moulton, 474 U.S. 159 (1985), 486

Malloy v. Hogan, 378 U.S. 1 (1964), 25 nn.30, 31

Manson v. Brathwaite, 432 U.S. 98 (1977), 541, *546*

Mapp v. Ohio, 367 U.S. 643 (1961), 295 n.3, 298, *299*

Martinez v. Court of Appeal, 528 U.S. 152 (2000), 583
Martinez-Fuerte; United States v., 428 U.S. 543 (1976), 161
Maryland v. Garrison, 480 U.S. 79 (1987), *116*
Maryland v. Pringle, 540 U.S. 366 (2003), *90*
Maryland v. Wilson, 519 U.S. 408 (1997), 147
Massachusetts v. Sheppard, 468 U.S. 961 (1984), 353
Massiah v. United States, 377 U.S. 201 (1964), 466, *467,* 471, 477, 485, 486, 554
Matlock; United States v., 415 U.S. 164 (1974), 182, 356
McKaskle v. Wiggins, 465 U.S. 168 (1984), 583
McKune v. Lile, 536 U.S. 24 (2002), 498
McNeil v. Wisconsin, 501 U.S. 171 (1981), 477
Mendenhall; United States v., 446 U.S. 544 (1980), *229, 234,* 235
Michigan v. Buie, 494 U.S. 325 (1990), 256
Michigan v. Jackson, 475 U.S. 625 (1986), 458, *481,* 486
Michigan v. Long, 463 U.S. 1032 (1983), 246, 256
Michigan v. Mosley, 423 U.S. 96 (1975), *452*
Michigan v. Summers, 452 U.S. 692 (1981), 107
Michigan v. Tucker, 417 U.S. 433 (1974), 423
Michigan Dept. of State Police v. Sitz, 496 U.S. 444 (1990), *169,* 171
Mickens v. Taylor, 535 U.S. 162 (2002), 571
Mincey v. Arizona, 437 U.S. 385 (1978), 222
Minneapolis & St. Louis R.R. Co. v. Bombolis, 241 U.S. 211 (1916), 24 n.26
Minnesota v. Carter, 525 U.S. 83 (1998), 310, *311*
Minnesota v. Dickerson, 508 U.S. 366 (1993), *136,* 256
Minnesota v. Murphy, 465 U.S. 420 (1984), 398
Minnick v. Mississippi, 498 U.S. 146 (1990), *458*
Miranda v. Arizona, 384 U.S. 436 (1966), 357, 360, 373, *374,* 388, 389, 392, 393-396, 398, 403, 407, 413, 417, 423, 424, 429, 430, 439, 440 & n.12, 442, 449, 450, 452, 466, 471, 477, 486, 497
Missouri v. Seibert, 542 U.S. 600 (2004), 429, *430*
Mitchell v. United States, 526 U.S. 314 (1996), 497
Montoya de Hernandez; United States v., 473 U.S. 531 (1985), 159, *164*
Moran v. Burbine, 475 U.S. 412 (1986), 452
Muehler v. Mena, 544 U.S. 93 (2005), *107*
Murray v. United States, 487 U.S. 533 (1988), *318*

National Treasury Employees Union v. Von Raab, 489 U.S. 656 (1989), 200
Neil v. Biggers, 409 U.S. 188 (1972), 540, 541, *543*
New Hampshire v. Sanne, 364 A.2d 630 (N.H. 1976), 24 n.23
New Jersey v. T.L.O., 469 U.S. 325 (1985), 82, 200, 260
New York v. Belton, 453 U.S. 454 (1981), *147,* 149, 150, 246
New York v. Burger, 482 U.S. 691 (1987), *196*
New York v. Harris, 495 U.S. 14 (1990), 336
New York v. Quarles, 467 U.S. 649 (1984), *442*
Nix v. Whiteside, 475 U.S. 157 (1986), 575
Nix v. Williams, 467 U.S. 431 (1984), *323*
North Carolina v. Butler, 441 U.S. 369 (1979), *450*

Ohio v. Robinette, 519 U.S. 33 (1996), 181
Ohio Adult Parole Auth. v. Woodward, 523 U.S. 272 (1998), 498
Oliver v. United States, 466 U.S. 170 (1984), *36,* 42
Olmstead v. United States, 277 U.S. 438 (1928), 30, 278, 279, 280
Oregon v. Elstad, 470 U.S. 298 (1985), *424,* 430
Oregon v. Mathiason, 429 U.S. 492 (1977), *396*
Orozco v. Texas, 394 U.S. 324 (1969), 395

Palko v. Connecticut, 302 U.S. 319 (1937), 20 & nn.17, 18
Patane; United States v., 542 U.S. 630 (2004), 429, 430, *436*
Patterson v. Former Chicago Police Lt. Burge, 328 F. Supp. 2d 878 (N.D. Ill. 2004), *14,* 16
Patterson v. Illinois, 487 U.S. 285 (1988), 485
Payne v. Arkansas, 356 U.S. 560 (1958), 361, 368
Payton v. New York, 445 U.S. 573 (1980), *128*
Pennsylvania v. Finley, 481 U.S. 551 (1987), 554
Pennsylvania v. Mimms, 434 U.S. 106 (1977), 147
Pennsylvania v. Muniz, 496 U.S. 582 (1990), 449
People v. See name of defendant
Place; United States v., 462 U.S. 696 (1983), 78, 79, 256
Powell v. Alabama, 287 U.S. 45 (1932), *11,* 14, 19, 557
Presser v. Illinois, 116 U.S. 252 (1886), 24 n.22

Quilici v. Village of Morton Grove, 695 F.2d 261 (7th Cir. 1982), *cert. denied,* 464 U.S. 863 (1983), 24 n.23

Rakas v. Illinois, 439 U.S. 128 (1978), *304,* 310
Ramsey; United States v., 431 U.S. 606 (1977), *162*
Rawlings v. Kentucky, 448 U.S. 98 (1980), 310, 336
Rhode Island v. Innis, 446 U.S. 291 (1980), *407,* 412
Richards v. Wisconsin, 520 U.S. 385 (1997), *112*
Riverside, County of, v. McLaughlin, 500 U.S. 44 (1991), 6
Robinson; United States v., 414 U.S. 218 (1973), 125
Rompilla v. Beard, 545 U.S. 374 (2005), 575

Samson v. California, 126 S. Ct. 2193 (2006), *188*
Schmerber v. California, 384 U.S. 757 (1966), *494*
Schneckloth v. Bustamonte, 412 U.S. 218 (1973), *176,* 181
See v. City of Seattle, 387 U.S. 541 (1967), 195
Segura v. United States, 468 U.S. 796 (1984), 318
Shadwick v. City of Tampa, 407 U.S. 345 (1972), 98
Sharpe; United States v., 470 U.S. 675 (1985), 256
Silverman v. United States, 365 U.S. 505 (1961), 279

Simmons v. United States, 390 U.S. 377 (1968), 540, *541*

Skinner v. Railway Executives' Assn., 489 U.S. 602 (1989), 199, 200

Smith v. Maryland, 442 U.S. 735 (1979), *74*

Sokolow; United States v., 490 U.S. 1 (1989), *273*

South Dakota v. Opperman, 428 U.S. 364 (1976), *153,* 156

Spano v. New York, 360 U.S. 315 (1959), *364,* 368, 373

Spinelli v. United States, 393 U.S. 410 (1969), 82

Spring v. Colorado, 479 U.S. 564 (1987), 452

Stansbury v. California, 511 U.S. 318 (1994), 398

State v. *See* name of defendant

Stovall v. Denno, 388 U.S. 293 (1967), 536, 537, 538, 540

Strickland v. Washington, 466 U.S. 668 (1984), *560,* 570, 571

Terry v. Ohio, 392 U.S. 1 (1968), 246, *247,* 255, 256, 260, 273

Texas v. Cobb, 532 U.S. 162 (2001), *477*

Thornton v. United States, 541 U.S. 615 (2004), 149, *150*

Tippens v. Walker, 77 F.3d 682 (2d Cir. 1996), 571

Turnbull; United States v., 888 F.2d 636 (9th Cir. 1989), 583

Twining v. New Jersey, 211 U.S. 78 (1908), 19

Ullman v. United States, 350 U.S. 422 (1956), 498

United States v. *See* name of defendant.

United States Dist. Court for the E. Dist. of Mich.; United States v., 407 U.S. 297 (1972), *283*

Verdugo-Urquidez; United States v., 494 U.S. 259 (1990), 30

Vernonia Sch. Dist. 47J v. Acton, 515 U.S. 646 (1995), 82, 200, *201*

Wade; United States v., 388 U.S. 218 (1967), 497, *516,* 525, 526, 537, 554

Wallace v. Jaffree, 472 U.S. 38 (1985), 25 n.29

Warden, Md. Penitentiary v. Hayden, 387 U.S. 294 (1967), *127*

Watson; United States v., 423 U.S. 411 (1976), *224*

Weatherford v. Bursey, 429 U.S. 545 (1977), 575 n.5

Weeks v. United States, 232 U.S. 383 (1914), *296,* 298

Welsh v. Wisconsin, 466 U.S. 740 (1984), 219, *220*

Wheat v. United States, 486 U.S. 153 (1988), 571

White; United States v., 401 U.S. 745 (1971), 73

Whorton v. Bockting, 127 S. Ct. 1173 (2007), 26 & n.33

Whren v. United States, 517 U.S. 806 (1996), *92,* 95

Wiggins v. Smith, 539 U.S. 510 (2003), 575

Williams v. Florida, 399 U.S. 78 (1970), 25

Wilson v. Arkansas, 514 U.S. 927 (1995), *110,* 112

Wolf v. Colorado, 338 U.S. 25 (1949), 298

Wong Sun v. United States, 371 U.S. 471 (1963), 329

Wyoming v. Houghton, 526 U.S. 295 (1999), 146

Yarborough v. Alvarado, 541 U.S. 652 (2004), *398*

Ybarra v. Illinois, 444 U.S. 85 (1979), 107

Zurcher v. Stanford Daily, 436 U.S. 547 (1978), 106

INDEX

Accusatory criminal procedure, 1
Administrative searches, 191-199
Aerial surveillance, 45-54
Appeals, 10-11
Arraignment
　on complaint, 7
　on indictment, 8
　on information, 8
　initial, 7
　preliminary, 7
Arrest, 5-6
　constitutional provision, 17
　crimes for which arrest may be made, 239-246
　fingerprinting and, 256
　minor criminal offenses, 239-246
　probable cause for, 224
　search incident to, 229
　　warrant requirement, exception to, 122-127
　stops versus, 255-256
　warrantless, 224-229
ATF. See Bureau of Alcohol, Tobacco and
　　Firearms (ATF)
Attorney, right to. See Counsel, right to
Automobile exception to warrant requirement,
　　138-153
　arrest, searches incident to, 147-153
　containers in automobiles, 142-147
　inventory search of car, 153-156
　occupants, packages of, 146
　rationale for, 138-142

Bail, excessive, 1
Bank records, inspection of, 74
Bank Secrecy Act of 1970, 74
Beepers, planting of, 67-75
Bill of Rights
　content of incorporated rights, 24-26
　current law as to what is incorporated, 21-24
　incorporation, debate over, 19-21. See also
　　　Incorporation of Bill of Rights
　key provisions, 17-18
　states, application to, 18-28
Binding case over, 7
Border crossing
　intrusive searches, 164-168
　searches at, 159-169
　warrantless searches at, 159-168
Bureau of Alcohol, Tobacco and Firearms
　　(ATF), 3
Bureau of Customs and Borders Prosecution
　　(CBP), 3

CBP. See Bureau of Customs and Borders
　　Prosecution (CBP)
Charging mechanisms
　grand jury. See Grand jury
　preliminary hearing. See Preliminary hearing
Checkpoints
　constitutionality of, 169-176
　sobriety checkpoints, 169-176
　warrantless searches at, 159-168
Coercive questioning, 373-374
Complaint, filing of, 6
Confessions
　age of suspect, 368
　bodily needs, deprivation of, 361
　coercive questioning, 373-374
　deception, use of, 367-368
　deprivation of basic bodily needs, 361
　educational level of suspect, 368
　false, 357
　force, use of, 361-364
　length of interrogation, 361
　mental condition of suspect, 368-373
　psychological pressure tactics, use of, 364-367
　threats of force, use of, 361-364
　torture, use of, 373-374
　voluntariness of, 292, 358-373
　　advantage of voluntariness test, 373
Confrontation, right of
　constitutional provision, 17
Constitution
　key provisions, 17-26
Contraband
　dogs, drug-sniffing, use of, 78-81
Corrections officials, role of, 4
Counsel, right to, 1, 553
　after adversarial proceedings begin, 471-477
　on appeal, 560, 583
　appointment of counsel, 557-560
　automatic, 557
　conflict of interest, 571
　constitutional provision, 17
　effective assistance of counsel, 10, 553, 560-576
　elicitation of statements, impermissible,
　　486-493
　for enemy combatants, 584
　in felony case, 555
　under Fifth Amendment. See Interrogation,
　　in-custodial; Miranda
　at identification procedures, 471, 515,
　　516-536
　impermissible eliciting of statements,
　　486-493

Counsel, right to (*contd.*)
  in in-custodial interrogations. *See* Interrogation,
      in-custodial; *Miranda*
  for indigent clients, 553
  ineffective assistance of counsel, habeas corpus
      relief for, 10
  informants, use of, to elicit statements from
      accused represented by counsel,
      486-493
  during interrogations, 467-477
  limits on right in identification procedures,
      526-536
  at lineups, 471, 515, 516-536
  Miranda rights and, 455-466
  petty offenses, 555
  prejudice, presumption of, 570-571
  self-representation, right of, 554, 576-583
  under Sixth Amendment, 466-493
      limit on questioning is offense specific,
          477-481
      offense-specific right, 477-481
      waiver of right, 481-486
  trial strategy, leeway given counsel, 571-575
  waiver of right, 481-486
  when right attaches, 554-557
Cross-examination of witnesses, 8. *See also*
      Confrontation, right of
Cross-racial identification, 515
Cruel and unusual punishment
  constitutional provision, 18
Curtilage, searches of, 36-45
Custodial interrogation. *See* Interrogation, in-
      custodial

DEA. *See* Drug Enforcement Administration
      (DEA)
Defendants, role of, 2
Defense counsel, role of, 2
Depositions. *See also* Discovery; Evidence
  limited use in criminal cases, 617
Digital Telephony Act of 1994, 280
Discovery, 8. *See also* Evidence
Dogs, drug-sniffing, 78-81
Double jeopardy, 1
  constitutional provision, 17
Drug Enforcement Administration (DEA), 3
Drug testing
  in employment context, 199-200
  in hospitals, 215-219
  in schools, 200-215
  warrantless, 199-219
Due process right, 1
  constitutional provision, 17
  voluntariness of confessions. *See* Confessions

Eavesdropping. *See* Electronic eavesdropping
Effective assistance of counsel. *See* Counsel,
      right to
Electronic communications, interception of. *See*
      Electronic eavesdropping; Electronic
      surveillance; Pen registers
Electronic Communications Privacy Act of 1964,
      280
Electronic eavesdropping, 29, 30-35

domestic security and, 282-289
foreign threats to national security, 282-290
as search, 278-290
warrantless, 282-290
Electronic surveillance, 277-290
  interception, defined, 280-281
  minimization, 281
  privacy right and, 278-280
  statutory requirements, 280-282
Enemy combatants
  counsel right for, 584
Evidence
  discovery of. *See* Discovery
Excessive bail, 1
Exclusionary rule, 29, 291-356
  arguments against, 292-296
  attenuation of taint, 329-336
  criticism of, 292-295
  exceptions to, 317-355
  federal government, application to, 296-298
  fruit of poisonous tree, 329
  good faith exception, 336-353
  inadequate causal connection, 329-336
  independent source exception, 318-323
  inevitable discovery exception, 323-329
  knock and announce requirement, violations
      of, 115-116, 353-355
  origins of, 296-304
  passenger in car, raising of rule by, 314-317
  standing to challenge search or seizure,
      304-310
  states, application to, 298-304
  suppression hearings, 355-356
  taint, attenuation of, 329-336
  violation of Fourth Amendment rights,
      presence of, 304-317
  visitor in home, raising of rule by, 311-314
  who may raise rule, 304-317
Exigent circumstances
  warrantless searches, 219-224
Experts, right to use of, 576
Eyewitness identification, 515

Federal Bureau of Investigation (FBI), 3
First appearance, 7
Foreign Intelligence Surveillance Act, 282
Frisking. *See* Stop and frisk

Gerstein review, 6
Grand jury, 4, 7
  indictments. *See* Indictments
Guilty pleas, 8-9

Habeas corpus proceedings, 10-11
Hospitals
  drug testing in, 215-219
Hot pursuit, searches made in
  warrant requirement, exception to, 127-131

ICE. *See* Immigration and Customs Enforcement
      (ICE)
Identification procedures, 515-552

counsel, right to, 471, 515, 516-536
cross-racial identifications, 515
due process challenges, limits on, 540-552
due process protections for, 536-552
eyewitness identification, 515
lineups, 515
photospreads, 515
suggestiveness of, 536-552
unnecessarily suggestive procedures, 536-540
Immigration and Customs Enforcement (ICE), 3
Immunity
derivative use, 506
self-incrimination privilege and, 506-514
transactional, 506
use, 506
Incorporation of Bill of Rights
content of incorporated rights, 24
current law, 21-24
debate over, 19-21
defined, 18-19
selective incorporation, 20
total incorporation, 20
Incrimination. *See* Self-incrimination, privilege
against
In-custodial interrogation. *See* Interrogation,
in-custodial; *Miranda*
Indictment
arraignment on, 8
constitutional provision, 17
Informants, use of, 82-90
Aguilar-Spinelli test, 82-90
reasonable suspicion based on tip, 263-268
Information
arraignment on, 8
Interception of communication, defined, 280
Interrogation, in-custodial, 255
"in custody," determining when person is,
395-407
interrogation, defined, 407-417
limits on, 374-466. *See also Miranda*
roadside questioning of motorist, 403-407
Inventory searches, 153-159
of automobile, 153-156
of person's possessions, 156-159
Investigation, pre-arrest, 5

Joinder. *See* Severance and joinder
Judges, role of, 3-4
Jury
challenges for cause, 9-10
grand. *See* Grand jury
peremptory challenges, 9-10
public jury trial
constitutional provision, 17
role of jury, 4
selection of jury, 9-10

Knock and announce requirement
exclusionary rule exception, 115-116, 353-355
warrants and, 110-116

Law enforcement officers, role of, 3
Lineups, 515

counsel, right to, 471, 515, 516-536
pre- versus post-indictment lineups,
526-536
suggestive, 292, 515

Magistrates, role of, 3-4
Mail inspection at border
warrantless searches, 161-164
Media, role of, 4-5
Military Commission Act of 2006, 374
Miranda
application of, 374-466
booking exception, 449
counsel, right to, 455-466
criticism of, 393-394
defense of, 394
emergency situations, 442-449
equivocal request for counsel, 462-466
exceptions to, 439-466
fruits of violation, admissibility of,
424-439
impeachment exception, 439-442
implied waiver of rights, 450-451
"in custody," determining when person is,
395-407
interrogation, defined, 407-417
police, requirements of, 417-423
requirements for application of, 395-423
unclear request for counsel, 462-466
violation of, consequences of, 423-439
waiver of rights, 360, 450-466
after assertion of rights, 452-462
counsel, invocation of right to, 455-466
Mobile home, search of, 139-141
Motions
in limine, 8
pretrial, 8

Nolo contendere plea, 8-9

Omnibus Crime Control and Safe Streets Act
of 1968, 280
Open fields doctrine, 36-45

Parolees
searches of, warrantless, 186-191
Pen registers, use of, 74-78
Peremptory challenges, 9-10
Photospreads, 515
Plain smell, 136
Plain touch, 136-138
Plain view exception
inadvertence, 133
warrant requirement and, 131-138
Plea bargaining, 8-9
Pleas
nolo contendere, 8-9
Police officers, role of, 3
Pre-arrest investigation, 5
Preliminary hearing, 7-8
Preponderance of evidence, 90
Pretrial motions, 8

Privacy interests, 30-81, 278
  reasonable expectation of privacy, 35, 61, 279
Privacy Protection Act of 1990, 106
Privilege against self-incrimination. *See*
      Self-incrimination, privilege against
Probable cause, 29
  Gerstein review, 6
  for initial charges, 6
  objective standard, 92-96
  requirement of, 82-96
  standard for, 82-96
  subjective standard, 92-96
  what is sufficient belief, 82-92
Probationers
  searches of, warrantless, 186-191
Procedural rules
  importance of, 14
  purpose of, 11-16
  retroactivity of, 26-27
Production of documents and other things
  self-incrimination, privilege against, 501-506,
      510-514
Profiling
  racial, 255
  reasonable suspicion based on profiles, 273-277
  in stops, 273-277
Prosecutors
  discretion in exercise of duties, 2
  role of, 2-3, 4
Public behavior
  observation/monitoring of, 65-78
Public, role of, 4

Racial profiling, 255
Reasonable expectation of privacy. *See* Privacy
      interests; Searches
Retroactivity
  of criminal procedure rule, 26-27
  "watershed" rules of criminal procedure, 26-27

Schools
  drug testing in, 200-215
  searches in
    purses, students', 82
    student athletes, 82
Scottsboro trial, 11
Screening of cases. *See* Grand jury; Preliminary
      hearing
Searches
  administrative, 191-199
  aerial, 45-54
  arrest, incident to, 147-153
    warrant requirement, exception to, 122-127
  automobiles, warrantless searches of, 138-153
  bank records, inspection of, 74
  beepers, planting of, 67-75
  at border crossing, 159-169
    intrusive searches, 164-168
    warrantless searches at, 159-168
  business premises, 195-199
  calls, monitoring of, 74-78
  at checkpoint
    warrantless searches at, 159-168
  commercial property, 195-199

  consent to, 176-185
    voluntariness of, 176-185
  constitutional provision, 17
  containers in automobiles, 142-147
  of curtilage, 42, 45
  defined, 30-81
  dogs, drug-sniffing, use of, 78-81
  of dwelling, 110-116
  electronic surveillance as, 277-290
  exclusionary rule. *See* Exclusionary rule
  in hot pursuit
    warrant requirement, exception to,
        127-131
  inventory, 153-159
  knock and announce requirement, 110-116
  of mobile home, 139-141
  of newsrooms, 106
  open fields. *See* Open fields doctrine
  of parolees, warrantless, 186-191
  pen registers, use of, 74-78
  phone numbers dialed or received, 74
  of probationers, warrantless, 186-191
  public-behavior monitoring, 65-78
  special needs, presence of, 191-219
  thermal imagine of homes, 55-61
  tracking devices, planting of, 67-75
  of trash, 61-65
  unreasonable searches and seizures, 29
  warrant requirement. *See* Warrant requirement
Secret Service, 3
Securities and Exchange Commission, 3
Seizure of person
  chasing of person, 235-239
  defined, 229-239
  exclusionary rule. *See* Exclusionary rule
  reasonable person test, 235
  stop and frisk and, 229
  unreasonable searches and seizures, 29
Self-incrimination, privilege against, 357
  in administrative proceedings, 493
  adverse inferences
    from invocation of privilege, 497
  in civil proceedings, 493
  compulsion, requirement of, 497-498
  constitutional provision, 17
  entities, inapplicability to, 494
  false confessions, 357
  immunity granted to person, effect of, 506-514
  incrimination must be a possibility, 498-501,
        506-514
  in-custodial interrogation. *See* Interrogation,
        in-custodial; *Miranda*
  individuals, applicability to, 494
  involuntary confession and, 358
  nontestimonial, slurred speech as, 449
  physical characteristics, observation of, 449
  physical evidence and, 449
  production of documents, 501-506
  requirements for application, 494-501
  testimony, requirement of, 494-497
  voluntary statements and, 497
Self-representation, right of, 554, 576-583
Sentencing, 10
Showups, 515
Sobriety checkpoints
  constitutionality of, 169-176

Speedy trial right, 1, 8
  constitutional provision, 17
Stop and frisk, 29
  authority for, 246-255
  plain feel, 256-257
  plain touch, 256-257
  race as factor in stop, 255
  seizure of person and, 229
Stops
  arrests versus, 255-256
  avoidance of officer, effect of, 268-273
  duration of detention, 256
  frisks during. *See* Stop and frisk
  identify self, refusal to, 257-260
  informant's tip, sufficiency of, 263-268
  profiles, use of, 273-277
  racial disparities in, 255
  reasonable suspicion for, 260-277
    avoidance of officer, effect of, 268-273
    informant's tip, sufficiency of, 263-268
    person's trying to avoid officer, 268-273
    profiles, use of, 273-277
    refusal to identify self, 257-260
  what police may do during, 256-260
Suppression hearings, 355-356
Surveillance
  aerial, 45-54
  electronic, 277-290

Terrorism, war on, 373-374
  coercive questioning, 373-374
  torture, 373-374
Thermal imaging of homes, 55-61
Torture, use of, 373-374
Tracking devices, planting of, 67-75
"Trap" and "trace" equipment. *See* Pen registers
Trash, searches of, 61-65
Trial
  bench, 9
  court, 9
  jury. *See* Jury

USA Patriot Act, 78, 282

Venire, 9. *See also* Jury
Victims, role of, 3

Warrant requirement, 29, 96-224. *See also* Searches
  affidavit supporting request, 97
  anticipatory warrant, 105

application for warrant, 97-98
arrest, searches incident to, 122-127, 224-229
automobile exception, 122, 138-153
border crossing
  intrusive searches at border, 164-168
  warrantless searches at, 122, 159-168
checkpoints, 122, 169-176
consent to search, 122, 176-185
  voluntariness of, standard for, 176-185
  who may give consent, 182-185
drug testing and, 199-219
  in employment context, 199-200
  in hospitals, 215-219
  in schools, 200-215
  warrantless, 199-219
eavesdropping, warrantless, 282-290
exceptions to, 122-224
execution of warrants, requirements in, 106-122
exigent circumstances, 110, 112, 122, 219-224
form warrant must take, 98-106
hot pursuit, searches made in, 127-131
information to include in application, 97-98
intrusive searches at border, 164-168
inventory searches, 122, 153-159
knock and announce requirement, 110-116
mail inspection at border, 161-164
mistakes in execution of warrant, 116-122
neutral and detached magistrate, 97
parolees, warrantless searches of, 122, 186-191
particularity, requirement for, 101-105
persons present when warrant executed, treatment of, 107-110
plain smell, 136
plain touch, 136-138
plain view exception, 122, 131-138
  inadvertence and, 133-135
presence when warrant executed, effect of, 107-110
probationers, warrantless searches of, 122, 186-191
residence, entry into, 110-116
searches incident to arrest, 122-127, 147-153
sneak and peek warrants, 282
sobriety checkpoints, 169-176
special needs, presence of, 122, 191-210
time period for execution, 97
treatment of those present when warrant executed, 107-110
unforeseen circumstances while executing warrant, 116-122
Watershed rule, 26
Wiretapping. *See* Electronic eavesdropping